# Triumph Bonneville
# water-cooled twins
# Service and Repair Manual

## by Matthew Coombs

**Models covered**

(6401-320-8AR1)

| | | |
|---|---|---|
| Street Twin | 900cc | 2016 to 2017 |
| Street Cup | 900cc | 2017 |
| Street Scrambler | 900cc | 2017 |
| Bonneville T100 | 900cc | 2017 |
| Bonneville T120 | 1200cc | 2016 to 2017 |
| Bobber | 1200cc | 2017 |
| Thruxton | 1200cc | 2016 to 2017 |
| Thruxton R | 1200cc | 2016 to 2017 |

*Includes Special Edition models*

© Haynes Publishing 2018

ABCDE
FGHIJ
KLMNO
PQR

**A book in the Haynes Service and Repair Manual Series**

ISBN: **978 1 78521 401 1**

**Library of Congress Control Number 2017949633**

Printed in the UK

**Haynes Publishing**
Sparkford, Yeovil, Somerset BA22 7JJ, England

**Haynes North America, Inc**
859 Lawrence Drive, Newbury Park, California 91320, USA

# Contents

## LIVING WITH YOUR TRIUMPH

## MAINTENANCE

# Contents

# A Pheonix from the ashes

Where is the most modern motorcycle factory in the World? Tokyo? Berlin? Turin, maybe? No, it's in Hinckley, Leicestershire. Improbable as it may seem, the Triumph factory in the Midlands of England is a more advanced production facility than anything the mighty Japanese industry, German efficiency or Italian flair can boast. Still more amazingly, the first motorcycle rolled off the brand new production line in July 1991, nine years after the last of the old Triumphs had trickled out of the old Meriden factory.

It's important to realise that the new Triumph company has very little to do with the company that was a giant on the world stage in the post-war years when British motorcycle makers dominated the global markets. It is true that new owner John Bloor bought the patents, manufacturing rights and, most importantly, trademarks when the old factory's assets were sold in 1983, but the products of the old and new companies bear no relation at all to one another. Apart, of course, from the name on the tanks. Bloor's research-and-development team started work in Collier Street, Coventry and in 1985 work started on the ten-acre green-field factory site which was occupied for the first time the following year.

The R & D team soon dispensed with the old Meriden factory's project for a modern DOHC, eight-valve twin known within the factory as the Diana project (after Princess Di) but shown at the NEC International Bike Show in 1982 as the Phoenix. The world got to see the new Triumphs for the first time at the Cologne Show in late 1990. The company was obviously anxious to distance itself from the old, leaky, unreliable image of the traditional British motorcycle, but it was equally anxious not to engage in a head-on technology war with the big four Japanese factories. The new motto was 'proven technology', the new engines were in-line threes and fours with double overhead camshafts and four valves per cylinder. They were all housed in a universal steel chassis with a large-diameter tubular backbone, and interestingly the new bikes would all carry famous model names from Triumph's past.

If you were looking to compare the technology level with an established machine, you'd have to point to the Kawasaki GPZ900R launched back in '84. Do not take this as a suggestion, current in '91, that the new Triumphs were in some way Kawasakis in disguise because the cam chain was sited on the right-hand side of the motor rather than between the middle cylinders. Yes, of course Triumph had looked at the technology and manufacturing of the Japanese companies and naturally found that an in-line multi-cylinder motor was the most economical way to go. It's just the same in the car world, the straight four is cheaper than the V6 because it uses fewer, simpler parts. In fact the layout of the new motor would seem to indicate that designers from the car world had been brought in by John Bloor. If anyone still harbours the belief that Triumph copied or co-operated with Kawasaki, try and find a contemporary Kawasaki that uses wet liners (cylinder liners in direct contact with coolant as opposed to sleeves fitted into the barrels).

But if Triumph's technology wasn't exactly path-breaking it was certainly very clever. The key concept was the modular design of the motor based around long and short-throw crankshafts in three and four-cylinder configurations. Every engine used the common 76 mm bore with either 55 or 65 mm throw cranks so that the short-stroke engine would be 750 cc in three-cylinder form and 1000 cc as a four. Put the long-stroke crank in and you get a 900 cc triple and a 1200 cc four. The first bike to hit the shops was the 1200 Trophy, a four-cylinder sports tourer which was immediately competitive in a very strong class. There was also a 900 cc, three-cylinder Trophy. The 750 and 1000 Daytonas used the short-stroke motor in three and four-cylinder forms in what were intended to be the sportsters of the range. The other two models, 750 and 900 cc three-cylinder Tridents, cashed in on the early-'90s fad for naked retro bikes that followed the world-wide success of the Kawasaki Zephyr.

The reborn Triumphs were received with acclaim from the motorcycle press – tinged with not a little surprise. They really were very good motorcycles, the big Trophy was a match for the Japanese opposition in a class full of very accomplished machinery. The fact it could live with a modern day classic like the Yamaha FJ1200 straight off the drawing board was a tribute to John Bloor's designers and production engineers. The bike was big, fast, heavy and quite high, but it worked and worked well. And it didn't leak oil or break down, it was obvious that whatever else people were going to say about Triumphs they weren't going to able to resurrect the old jokes about British bangers leaving puddles of lubricant under them. As the rest of the range arrived and tests of them got into print, the star

**The 1200 Trophy, the first of the modular design models from the new Triumph company**

of the show emerged; it was the long-stroke, three-cylinder, 900 cc motor. It didn't matter how it was dressed up, the big triple had that indefinable quality – character. It was the motor the Japanese would never have made, very torquey but with a hint of vibration that endears rather than annoys. Somewhere among the modern, water-cooled, multi-valve technology, the 900-triple had the genes of the old air-cooled OHV Triumph Tridents that appeared in 1969 and stayed in production until '75.

The range stayed basically unchanged for two years, until the Cologne Show of '92. Looking back at the first range it is now easy to see – hindsight again – that the identity of all the models was far too close. The sports tourer Trophy models were reckoned to be a little too sporting, the basic Tridents still had the handlebar and footrest positions of faired bikes. Triumph management later agreed that the first range evinced a certain lack of confidence, that was certainly not the case with the revamped 1993 range.

Visitors to the Cologne Show in September '92 agreed that the Triumphs were the stars, any lack of confidence there may have been two years earlier was completely gone. Any shyness the management may have felt about the Triumph name's past was shaken off as the new Tridents went retro style. Overall, the identities of the original bikes became more individual and more obviously separated; the Trophy models became more touring oriented, the Daytona more sporty looking and the Trident models more traditional. The factory even had the confidence to put small Union Flag emblems on the side panels of each model, no more apologising for the imagined shortcomings of British engineering. Despite this spreading of the range's appeal, all these bikes were still built on the original modular concept.

There was, however, an exception to this rule of uniformity in the shape of a brand new bike, the Tiger 900. This model was in the enduro/desert-racer style much favoured on Continental Europe but not at all popular in the UK. Here was a Triumph with a 19-inch front tyre, wire wheels and a lower power output than the other 900s. Judging their market as cleverly as ever, the factory held back another new model for the International Bike Show at the Birmingham NEC. This was the Daytona 1200, an out and out speed machine with a hidden political agenda. Its high-compression, 147 PS engine gave it brutal straight-line performance in much the same way as the big Kawasakis of the mid-'80s, and like them it wasn't too clever in the corners because of its weight and length. The bike was built as much to show that Triumph could do it as to sell in big numbers, it also had the secondary function of thumbing the corporate nose at the UK importers' gentlemen's agreement not to bring in bikes of over 125 PS.

Next year's NEC show saw two more new Triumphs, both reworkings of what was now

**The legendary Bonneville reappeared in 2001 with a 790cc air-cooled parallel twin engine**

regarded as a modern classic, the 900 triple. The Speed Triple was a clever reincarnation of the British cafe racer style, complete with clip-on handlebars and rear-set footrests. The other newcomer was a more radical project, the Daytona Super III. Externally the motor looked like the usual 900 cc three with 115 PS as opposed to the standard 900 Daytona's 98 PS.

Triumph's next big step was into the US market, where the old company was so strong in the post-war years when the only competition was Harley-Davidson and where there is considerable affection for the marque. The name Triumph chose to spearhead this new challenge was Thunderbird, a trademark sourced in Native American mythology. This

time the famous name adorned yet another version of the 900 triple but this time heavily restyled and in a retro package. Dummy cooling fins give it the look of an air-cooled motor, the logo was cast into the clutch cover, and there were soft edges and large expanses of polished alloy. Inside those restyled cases, the motor was retuned even more than the Tiger's for a very user-friendly dose of low-down punch and mid-range power. The cycle parts were given an equally radical redesign, although the retro style stopped short of giving the Thunderbird twin rear shock absorbers. But everything else, the shape of the tank, the chrome headlight and countless other details, harks back to the

**The Bonneville T100 with 900cc water-cooled engine**

**The 1200cc T120 with styling reminisant of the iconic 1959 Bonnie**

original Thunderbird and nothing does so as shamelessly as the 'mouth-organ' tank badge, a classic icon if ever there was one.

The first Thunderbird derivative, the Adventurer, appeared for 1996 with a different rear subframe and rear-end styling including a sissy bar and single seat. That same year, the short-stroke 750 cc motor bowed out of the range, but it went with a bang not a whimper not in a final batch of Tridents but in a limited-edition run of 750 Speed Triples. The bigger Speed Triple's motor was inserted in the Sprint and the result called the Sprint Sport. The reason for using up all those motors was the advent of the new range of fuel-injected and heavily revised three-cylinder engines that first powered the T509 Speed Triple and T595 Daytona of 1997.

The first fuel-injected Triumph, the Daytona T595, was a major milestone for the Factory. It represented a change of policy, the first time Triumph would venture to confront their opposition on the cutting edge of technology. In early 1997, the Honda FireBlade and Ducati 916 ruled. The T595 was able to play in the same ball park. Only on a race track could the Japanese and Italian machines be shown to be better. In the real world the T595 was at least as good a bike. The old long stroke of 65 mm was retained but everything else was new, it was a radical departure from the modular concept that had dominated production until now. You could see how the new motor was a lightened version of the old triple, but fuel injection was new and the

frame was a radical departure from previous practice. Serpentine tubing ran from steering head to swingarm pivot and it was aluminium. Bodywork looked tasty too. Despite what Triumph had said about not taking on the Japanese back in 1991, the T595 came out of comparative tests with the 'Blade and 916 on equal terms. The new bike was also given the Speed Triple treatment and adorned with bug-eyed twin headlights in the fashionable 'streetfighter' style. You liked it or loathed it, but you couldn't ignore it.

The trouble with the Supersports end of the market is that the goal posts keep moving, so Triumph hedged their bets by softening the 955i's nominal 128 PS to 108, housing it in a simpler twin-beam frame and calling the result the Sprint ST. This continuation of the original Sprint concept was one of the hits of 1999. As a sports tourer, the fuel-injected Sprint ST was right up there with Honda's class leader, the VFR. Some magazines even preferred the British bike. High praise. The Tiger got the fuel-injected 855 cc motor in '99.

**The Street series base model, the 900cc Street Twin...**

**... is joined by the cafe racer styled Street Cup...**

**... and the Street Scrambler**

Not that development of the carburetted bikes was neglected. Triumph got a Thunderbird derivative right in 1998 with the Thunderbird Sport. The Legend TT is the same bike with a different exhaust system and graphics.

Up to 1999 Triumph concentrated on big bikes but then they took another giant step towards the big time by taking on the Japanese in the most competitive market sector of them all, Supersports 600, with the TT600.

From a standing start in 1991, the Hinckley factory was competing in all the major motorcycle market sectors. Much bigger production volumes meant the original modular concept was no longer a necessity. By the dawn of the 21 st Century Triumph had sold over 100,000 motorcycles. Then the factory was struck by one of the biggest fires ever at a British industrial site. In March 2002 the production line, moulding shop and stores were destroyed and many other parts of the plant severely damaged. Just six months later the rebuilt factory was running at full capacity. The first new product out of the doors was the Daytona 600, a replacement for the TT600. Where the first Supersports 600 Triumph had failed to compete with the Japanese this one was good enough to win an Isle of Man TT.

With an eye on America Triumph then unleashed their most audacious bike yet: the Rocket III. (Whisper it, but Rocket III was actually a BSA model name back in the 1970s.) They call it a cruiser but behemoth would be a better description, it's the first production bike to boast a capacity of over two litres and the only thing on the roads that can make a Harley V-Rod look shy and retiring.

It took Hinckley ten years to work up the courage to use the most iconic name in their back-catalogue: Bonneville. The original 1959 Bonneville was a twin-carburettor version of the 650cc T100 parallel twin, marketed to take advantage of a land-speed record set using a much-modified T100 engine on, of course, the Bonneville Salt Flats. The Bonneville went on to become the archetypal twin-cylinder

**The 1200cc Thruxton...**

**... and higher spec Thruxton R**

**The factory custom 1200cc Bobber**

motorcycle of the Golden Era of the British industry and probably the best-known model name of any motorcycle. The question for Hinckley was how best to tap into the goodwill and nostalgia that name generated.

The answer was to wait until 2001 when the factory launched its first parallel twin, the layout that not just Triumph but all of the big names of the British industry used for their flagship models from the post-War period right up until the Honda CB750 appeared and beyond. The first of the new Bonnies used an air- and oil-cooled 790cc parallel-twin motor packaged to look more than slightly reminiscent of the original bike. The first

Bonneville was a top-of-the-range sportster, the new one an entry-level bike but it really didn't matter. It didn't even seem like a risk to use the name. Triumph was now a major manufacturer again and the new model was predictably popular in a market grown tired of sports bikes.

Counter to previous practice the T100 designation was used for the top-specification version of the Bonneville, the first to get the 865cc motor. The T120 designation used on the very first Meriden-made Bonnevilles wasn't brought out of retirement until the all-new water-cooled bike was launched in 2016. Originally, the 120 had referred to the

650cc Bonneville's notional top speed. This time it referenced the liquid-cooled, 1200cc motor, a single-overhead cam design with 270-degree crankshaft phasing. If anything, the new bigger bike looked even more like the original article than its predecessor. Any reticence the modern Triumph factory had about trading on its heritage had long since disappeared and the new Bonneville range was marketed under the banner "Modern Classics." Triumph caught the zeitgeist better than anyone, even Harley-Davidson.

The newest Bonneville range, there are so many variations it's easiest to think of them that way, presses all the current trend buttons. The enthusiasm for all things retro, the return of customising as a mainstream motorcycling interest, and all the other trends that emerged following the decline of interest in sports bikes are represented in the range. The T120 and T100 echo the looks of the best of the original Bonnies, the pre-oil-in-frame 650cc unit engine models of the late 1960s. The Scrambler takes its cues from the US-export high-pipe originals, the Bobber is an out-and-out factory custom, and the Thruxton and Street Cup are throwbacks to the cafe racer styling beloved of the rockers of the '60s.

All of them have that undefinable cool that confers credibility on its rider. You wouldn't be surprised to learn that the design team had a test for their bikes, and that was "Would Steve McQueen have ridden this?" It is fair to say that in the case of the new Bonnevilles the answer would undoubtedly be yes.

## Acknowledgements

Our thanks are due to Fowlers of Bristol who supplied the machines featured in the illustrations throughout this manual. We would also like to thank NGK Spark Plugs (UK) Ltd for supplying the colour spark plug condition photographs, the Avon Rubber Company for supplying information on tyre fitting and Draper Tools Ltd for some of the workshop tools shown.

Thanks are also due to Julian Ryder who wrote the introduction 'A Phoenix from the Ashes' and to Triumph Motorcycles, Hinckley, for permission to use model pictures of the Triumph models. Triumph Motorcycles Limited bears no responsibility for the content of this book, having had no part in its origination or preparation.

## About this Manual

The aim of this manual is to help you get the best value from your motorcycle. It can do so in several ways. It can help you decide what work must be done, even if you choose to have it done by a dealer; it provides information and procedures for routine maintenance and servicing; and it offers diagnostic and repair procedures to follow when trouble occurs.

We hope you use the manual to tackle the work yourself. For many simpler jobs, doing it yourself may be quicker than arranging an appointment to get the motorcycle into a dealer and making the trips to leave it and pick it up. More importantly, a lot of money can be saved by avoiding the expense the shop must pass on to you to cover its labour and overhead costs. An added benefit is the sense of satisfaction and accomplishment that you feel after doing the job yourself.

References to the left or right side of the motorcycle assume you are sitting on the seat, facing forward.

We take great pride in the accuracy of information given in this manual, but motorcycle manufacturers make alterations and design changes during the production run of a particular motorcycle of which they do not inform us. No liability can be accepted by the authors or publishers for loss, damage or injury caused by any errors in, or omissions from, the information given.

## Illegal copying

## Frame and engine numbers

The VIN, or frame serial number, is stamped into the right-hand side of the steering head. The engine number is stamped into the top of the crankcase on the right-hand side. These numbers should be recorded and kept in a safe place so they can be given to the police in the event of a theft.

It is helpful to record the frame and engine numbers and keep them in a handy place (such as with your driver's licence) so that they are always available when ordering parts for your bike.

## Buying spare parts

for reference when buying parts. Since the manufacturers change specifications, parts and vendors (companies that manufacture various components on the machine), providing the ID numbers is the only way to be reasonably sure that you are buying the correct parts.

Whenever possible, take the worn part to the dealer so direct comparison with the new component can be made. Along the trail from the manufacturer to the parts shelf, there are numerous places that the part can end up with the wrong number or be listed incorrectly.

The two places to purchase new parts for

your motorcycle – the accessory store and the franchised dealer – differ in the type of parts they carry. While dealers can obtain virtually every part for your motorcycle, the accessory dealer is usually limited to normal high wear items such as spark plugs, chains, sprockets, brake pads, etc.

Used parts can be obtained for roughly half the price of new ones, but you can't always be sure of what you're getting. Once again, take your worn part to the breaker's yard for direct comparison.

Whether buying new, used or rebuilt parts, the best course is to deal directly with someone who specialises in parts for your particular make.

The engine number is on the top of the crankcase on the right-hand side

The **VIN** or frame number is stamped into the right-hand side of the steering head

Professional mechanics are trained in safe working procedures. However enthusiastic you may be about getting on with the job at hand, take the time to ensure that your safety is not put at risk. A moment's lack of attention can result in an accident, as can failure to observe simple precautions.

There will always be new ways of having accidents, and the following is not a comprehensive list of all dangers; it is intended rather to make you aware of the risks and to encourage a safe approach to all work you carry out on your bike.

## Asbestos

● Certain friction, insulating, sealing and other products - such as brake pads, clutch linings, gaskets, etc. - contain asbestos. Extreme care must be taken to avoid inhalation of dust from such products since it is hazardous to health. If in doubt, assume that they do contain asbestos.

## Fire

● Remember at all times that petrol is highly flammable. Never smoke or have any kind of naked flame around, when working on the vehicle. But the risk does not end there - a spark caused by an electrical short-circuit, by two metal surfaces contacting each other, by careless use of tools, or even by static electricity built up in your body under certain conditions, can ignite petrol vapour, which in a confined space is highly explosive. Never use petrol as a cleaning solvent. Use an approved safety solvent.

● Always disconnect the battery earth terminal before working on any part of the fuel or electrical system, and never risk spilling fuel on to a hot engine or exhaust.

● It is recommended that a fire extinguisher of a type suitable for fuel and electrical fires is kept handy in the garage or workplace at all times. Never try to extinguish a fuel or electrical fire with water.

## Fumes

● Certain fumes are highly toxic and can quickly cause unconsciousness and even death if inhaled to any extent. Petrol vapour comes into this category, as do the vapours from certain solvents such as trichloro-ethylene. Any draining or pouring of such volatile fluids should be done in a well ventilated area.

● When using cleaning fluids and solvents, read the instructions carefully. Never use materials from unmarked containers - they may give off poisonous vapours.

● Never run the engine of a motor vehicle in an enclosed space such as a garage. Exhaust fumes contain carbon monoxide which is extremely poisonous; if you need to run the engine, always do so in the open air or at least have the rear of the vehicle outside the workplace.

## The battery

● Never cause a spark, or allow a naked light near the vehicle's battery. It will normally be giving off a certain amount of hydrogen gas, which is highly explosive.

● Always disconnect the battery ground (earth) terminal before working on the fuel or electrical systems (except where noted).

● If possible, loosen the filler plugs or cover when charging the battery from an external source. Do not charge at an excessive rate or the battery may burst.

● Take care when topping up, cleaning or carrying the battery. The acid electrolyte, evenwhen diluted, is very corrosive and should not be allowed to contact the eyes or skin. Always wear rubber gloves and goggles or a face shield. If you ever need to prepare electrolyte yourself, always add the acid slowly to the water; never add the water to the acid.

## Electricity

● When using an electric power tool, inspection light etc., always ensure that the appliance is correctly connected to its plug and that, where necessary, it is properly grounded (earthed). Do not use such appliances in damp conditions and, again, beware of creating a spark or applying excessive heat in the vicinity of fuel or fuel vapour. Also ensure that the appliances meet national safety standards.

● A severe electric shock can result from touching certain parts of the electrical system, such as the spark plug wires (HT leads), when the engine is running or being cranked, particularly if components are damp or the insulation is defective. Where an electronic ignition system is used, the secondary (HT) voltage is much higher and could prove fatal.

## Remember...

✗ **Don't** start the engine without first ascer-taining that the transmission is in neutral.

✗ **Don't** suddenly remove the pressure cap from a hot cooling system - cover it with a cloth and release the pressure gradually first, or you may get scalded by escaping coolant.

✗ **Don't** attempt to drain oil until you are sure it has cooled sufficiently to avoid scalding you.

✗ **Don't** grasp any part of the engine or exhaust system without first ascertaining that it is cool enough not to burn you.

✗ **Don't** allow brake fluid or antifreeze to contact the machine's paintwork or plastic components.

✗ **Don't** siphon toxic liquids such as fuel, hydraulic fluid or antifreeze by mouth, or allow them to remain on your skin.

✗ **Don't** inhale dust - it may be injurious to health (see Asbestos heading).

✗ **Don't** allow any spilled oil or grease to remain on the floor - wipe it up right away, before someone slips on it.

✗ **Don't** use ill-fitting spanners or other tools which may slip and cause injury.

✗ **Don't** lift a heavy component which may be beyond your capability - get assistance.

✗ **Don't** rush to finish a job or take unverified short cuts.

✗ **Don't** allow children or animals in or around an unattended vehicle.

✗ **Don't** inflate a tyre above the recommended pressure. Apart from overstressing the carcass, in extreme cases the tyre may blow off forcibly.

✔ **Do** ensure that the machine is supported securely at all times. This is especially important when the machine is blocked up to aid wheel or fork removal.

✔ **Do** take care when attempting to loosen a stubborn nut or bolt. It is generally better to pull on a spanner, rather than push, so that if you slip, you fall away from the machine rather than onto it.

✔ **Do** wear eye protection when using power tools such as drill, sander, bench grinder etc.

✔ **Do** use a barrier cream on your hands prior to undertaking dirty jobs - it will protect your skin from infection as well as making the dirt easier to remove afterwards; but make sure your hands aren't left slippery. Note that long-term contact with used engine oil can be a health hazard.

✔ **Do** keep loose clothing (cuffs, ties etc. and long hair) well out of the way of moving mechanical parts.

✔ **Do** remove rings, wristwatch etc., before working on the vehicle - especially the electrical system.

✔ **Do** keep your work area tidy - it is only too easy to fall over articles left lying around.

✔ **Do** exercise caution when compressing springs for removal or installation. Ensure that the tension is applied and released in a controlled manner, using suitable tools which preclude the possibility of the spring escaping violently.

✔ **Do** ensure that any lifting tackle used has a safe working load rating adequate for the job.

✔ **Do** get someone to check periodically that all is well, when working alone on the vehicle.

✔ **Do** carry out work in a logical sequence and check that everything is correctly assembled and tightened afterwards.

✔ **Do** remember that your vehicle's safety affects that of yourself and others. If in doubt on any point, get professional advice.

● If in spite of following these precautions, you are unfortunate enough to injure yourself, seek medical attention as soon as possible.

# Engine oil level

## Before you start:
✔ Support the motorcycle upright on level ground.
✔ Start the engine and let it idle for several minutes until it reaches normal operating temperature, then stop the engine.
*Caution: Do not run the engine in an enclosed space such as a garage or workshop.*
✔ Leave the motorcycle undisturbed for a few minutes to allow the oil level to stabilise.

## Bike care:
● If you have to add oil frequently, check whether there are any oil leaks. If there is no sign of oil leakage from the joints and gaskets the engine could be burning oil (see *Fault Finding*).

## The correct oil:
● Modern engines place great demands on their oil. It is very important that the correct oil for your bike is used – do not use car engine oils.

● Always top up with a good quality motorcycle oil of the specified type and viscosity and do not overfill the engine.

| | |
|---|---|
| Oil type | Fully synthetic API grade SH or higher, JASO grade MA, is recommended, though a semi-synthetic of the same grade can be used if necessary |
| Oil viscosity | SAE 10W40 is recommended, but in ambient temperatures above 40°C use a 10W50 |

**1** The oil level window is in the right-hand side of the crankcase, between the alternator cover and the front sprocket cover. The oil must lie between the upper and lower lines (arrowed)

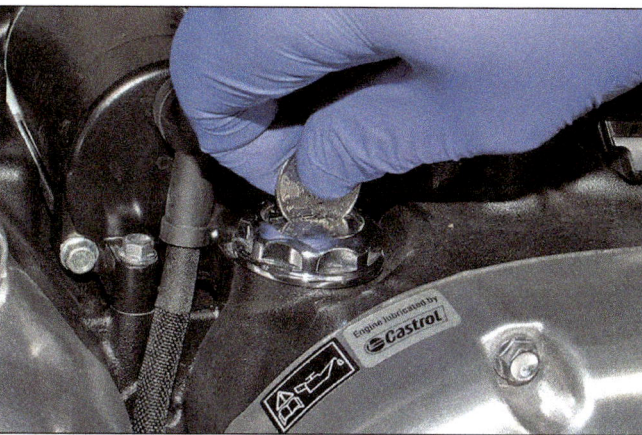

**2** If the level is below the lower level line unscrew the filler cap, using a coin or tool if necessary

**3** Add the recommended grade and type of oil to bring the level almost up to the upper level line. Do not overfill

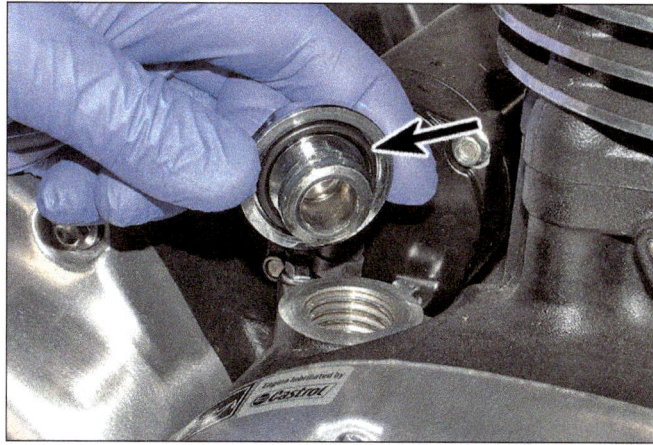

**4** Make sure the filler cap O-ring (arrowed) is correctly seated, then fit the cap

# Suspension, steering and drive chain

## Suspension and Steering:
● Check that the front and rear suspension operates smoothly without binding.
● Check that the rear suspension is adjusted as required, where possible.
● Check that the steering moves smoothly from lock-to-lock.

## Drive chain:
● Check that the drive chain slack isn't excessive, and adjust it if necessary (see Chapter 1).
● If the chain looks dry, lubricate it (see Chapter 1).

# Coolant level

## Before you start:

✔ Check the coolant level when the engine is cold.
✔ Support the motorcycle upright on level ground.

## Bike care:

● Use only the specified coolant type – Triumph HD4X Hybrid OAT (organic acid technology). This ready-mixed coolant contains the correct proportion of anti-freeze. Do not top up using only water, as the system will become too diluted.

> ⚠ **Warning: DO NOT remove the radiator pressure cap to add coolant. Topping up is done via the coolant reservoir tank filler. DO NOT leave open containers of coolant about, as it is poisonous.**

● Do not overfill the reservoir. If the coolant is significantly above the MAX level line at any time, siphon or drain the surplus to prevent the possibility of it being expelled out of the overflow hose.

● If the coolant level falls steadily, check the system for leaks (see Chapter 1). If no leaks are found and the level continues to fall, fit a new pressure cap. If this does not solve the problem take the bike to a Triumph dealer for a pressure test.

### T100, T120, Street Twin, Street Cup, Scrambler

**1** The reservoir is mounted at the back of the engine on the left-hand side. The coolant level must be between the MAX and MIN level lines (arrowed) marked on the reservoir cover

**2** If the coolant level is near, on or below the MIN level line, open the reservoir filler cap

**3** Top up to the MAX level line with the recommended coolant, then fit the cap

### Bobber

**1** The reservoir is behind the front sprocket cover on the right-hand side of the engine. The coolant level must be between the MAX and MIN level lines (arrowed) marked on the rear end of the reservoir

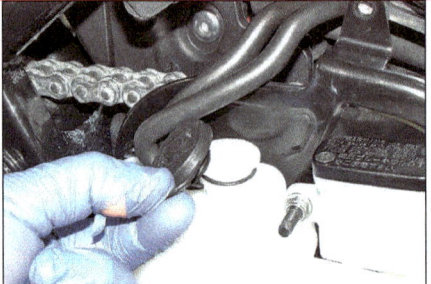

**2** If the coolant level is near, on or below the MIN level line, remove the front sprocket cover (see Chapter 6), then open the reservoir filler cap

**3** Top up to the MAX level line with the recommended coolant, then fit the cap and the front sprocket cover

### Thruxton and Thruxton R

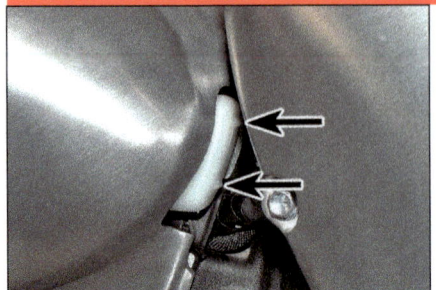

**1** The reservoir is behind the front sprocket cover on the right-hand side of the engine. The coolant level must be between the MAX and MIN level lines (arrowed) marked on the front end of the reservoir

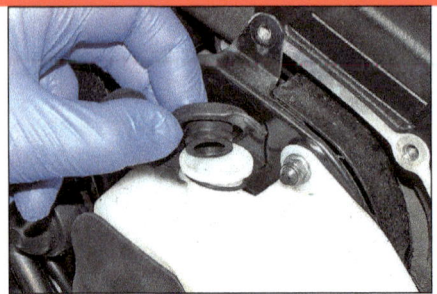

**2** If the coolant level is near, on or below the MIN level line, remove the front sprocket cover (see Chapter 6), then open the reservoir filler cap

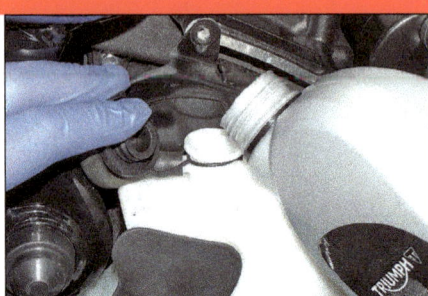

**3** Top up to the MAX level line with the recommended coolant, then fit the cap and the front sprocket cover

# Tyres

### Tyre tread depth:

● At the time of writing UK law requires that the tread depth must be at least 1 mm over the entire tread breadth all the way around the tyre, with no bald patches. Many riders, however, consider 2 mm tread depth minimum to be a safer limit.

● Tyres incorporate wear indicators in the tread. Identify the triangular pointer or TWI mark on the tyre sidewall to locate the indicator bar and fit a new tyre if the tread has worn down to the bar.

### The correct pressures:

● The tyre pressures must be checked when cold, not immediately after riding. Note that excessively low or high tyre pressures will cause abnormal tread wear and unsafe handling.

| Model | Front | Rear |
|---|---|---|
| T100, T120, Street Twin and Cup | 32 psi (2.2 Bar) | 36 psi (2.5 Bar) |
| Bobber | 32 psi (2.2 Bar) | 42 psi (2.9 Bar) |
| Scrambler | 30 psi (2.1 Bar) | 36 psi (2.5 Bar) |
| Thruxton and Thruxton R | 36 psi (2.5 Bar) | 36 psi (2.5 Bar) |

● Use an accurate pressure gauge. If you buy your own, spend as much as you can justify on a quality gauge.

● Correct air pressure will increase tyre life and provide maximum stability, handling capability and ride comfort. Tyre pressures are printed on a label stuck to the swingarm or chainguard.

### Tyre care:

● Check the tyres carefully for cuts, tears, embedded nails or other sharp objects and excessive wear. Operation of the motorcycle with excessively worn tyres is extremely hazardous, as traction and handling are directly affected.

● Check the condition of the tyre valve and make sure a dust cap is fitted.

● Pick out any stones or nails which may have become embedded in the tyre tread. If left, they will eventually penetrate through the casing and cause a puncture.

● If tyre damage is apparent, or unexplained loss of pressure is experienced, seek the advice of a tyre fitting specialist without delay.

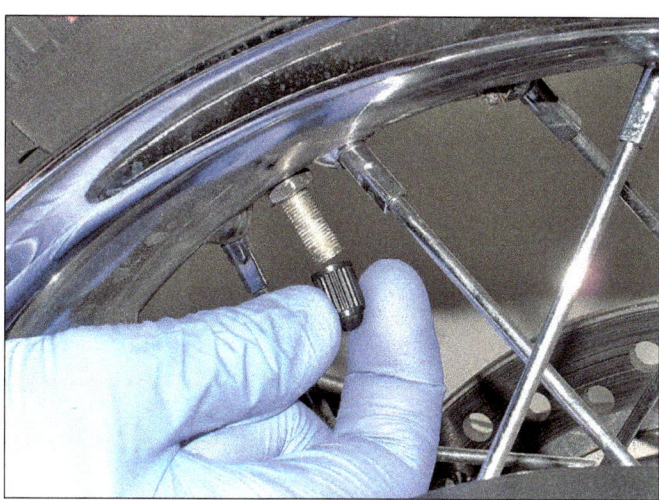

**1** Remove the cap from the valve – if it's missing, fit a new one.

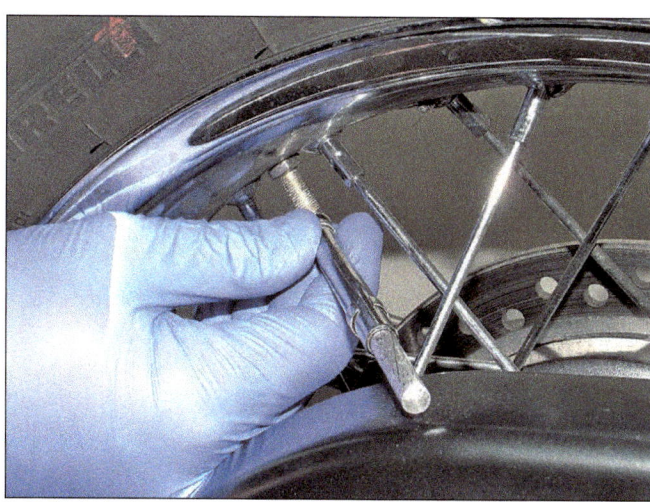

**2** Check the tyre pressures when the tyres are cold and keep them properly inflated. Fit the cap on completion.

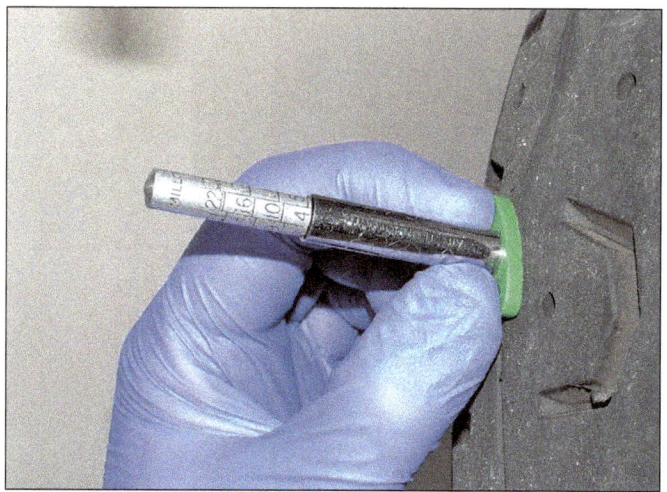

**3** Measure tread depth at the centre of the tyre using a tread depth gauge.

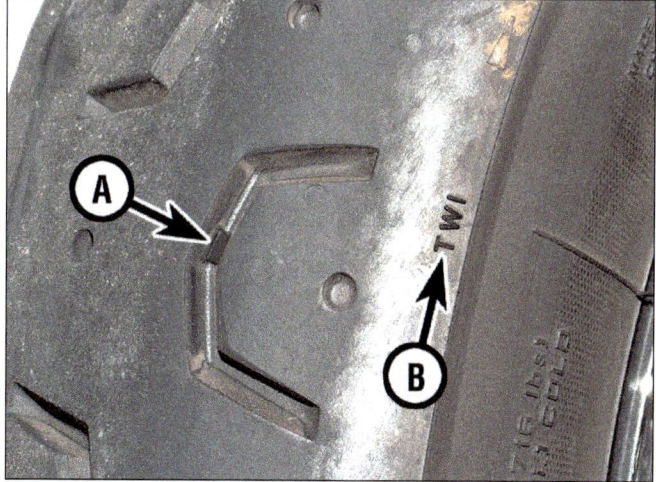

**4** Tyre tread wear indicator bar (A) and its location marking (B) (usually either an arrow, a triangle or the letters TWI) on the sidewall.

# Brake fluid levels

> ⚠️ **Warning: Brake hydraulic fluid can harm your eyes and damage painted surfaces, so use extreme caution when handling and pouring it and cover surrounding surfaces with rag. Do not use fluid that has been standing open for some time, as it absorbs moisture from the air which can cause a dangerous loss of braking effectiveness.**

## Before you start:

✔ The front brake fluid reservoir is on the right-hand handlebar. The rear brake fluid reservoir is behind the right-hand side panel on the T100, T120, Street Twin, Cup and Scrambler, and Thruxton models, and behind the front sprocket cover on the Bobber.
✔ Make sure you have a supply of DOT 4 hydraulic fluid.
✔ Wrap a rag around the reservoir being worked on to ensure that any spillage does not come into contact with painted surfaces.
✔ Support the bike upright on level ground.

## Bike care:

● The fluid in the front and rear brake master cylinder reservoirs will drop very gradually as the brake pads wear down. When the level is low check the brake pads for wear (see Chapter 1).
● If either fluid reservoir requires repeated topping-up there could be a leak somewhere in the system, which must be investigated immediately.
● Check the operation of both brakes before taking the machine on the road; if there is evidence of air in the system (spongy feel to lever or pedal), it must be bled (see Chapter 6).

### FRONT BRAKE – T100, T120, Bobber and Thruxton

**1** The front brake fluid level is visible through the window in the reservoir body – it must be above the LOWER level line (arrowed)

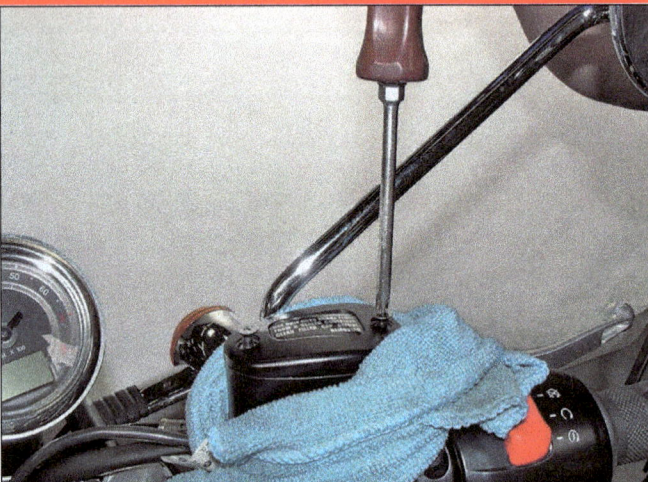

**2** If the level is low undo the reservoir cover screws and remove the cover, diaphragm plate and diaphragm

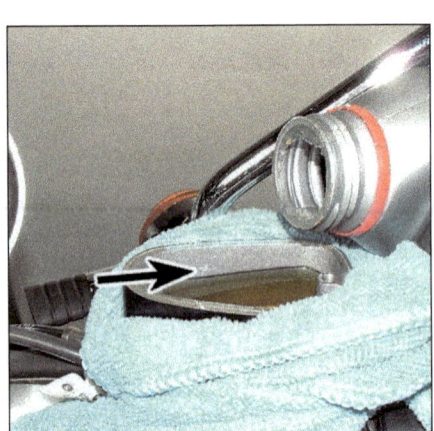

**3** Top-up with new DOT 4 hydraulic fluid until the level is at the top of the level indicator (arrowed) cast on the inside of the reservoir. Take care to avoid spills (see Warning) and do not overfill

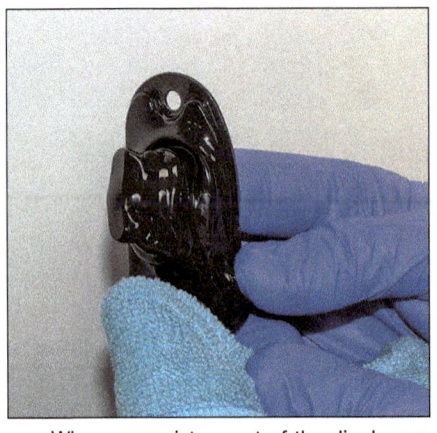

**4** Wipe any moisture out of the diaphragm using a clean lint-free cloth

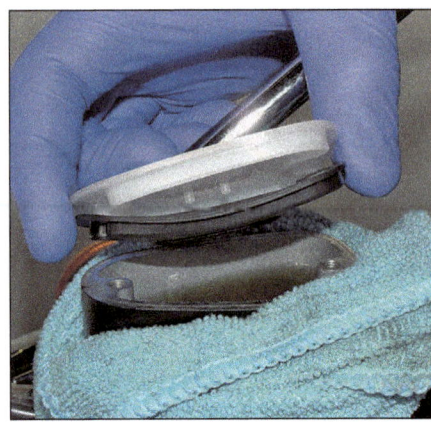

**5** Make sure the diaphragm and plate are correctly seated before fitting the cover

**REAR BRAKE**

**1** On all models except the Bobber remove the right-hand side panel (see Chapter 7). The rear brake fluid level is visible through the reservoir body – it must be between the UPPER and LOWER level lines (arrowed).

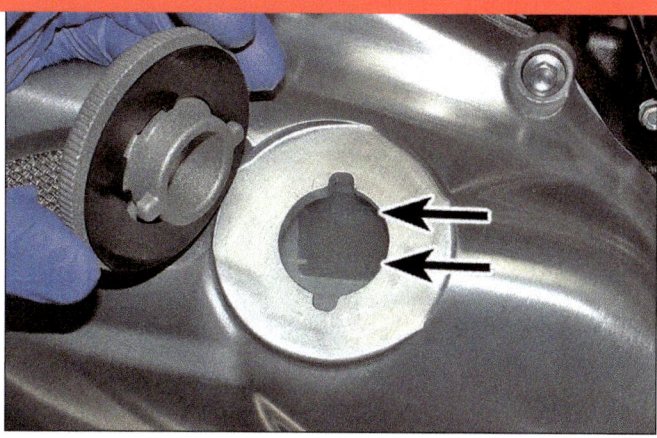

**2** On the Bobber remove the reservoir inspection cap from the front sprocket cover by turning it anti-clockwise – there is a tool supplied with the bike for doing this if required (it is attached to the fusebox, which is behind the left-hand side panel). The rear brake fluid level is visible through the reservoir body and must lie between the UPPER and LOWER level lines (arrowed)

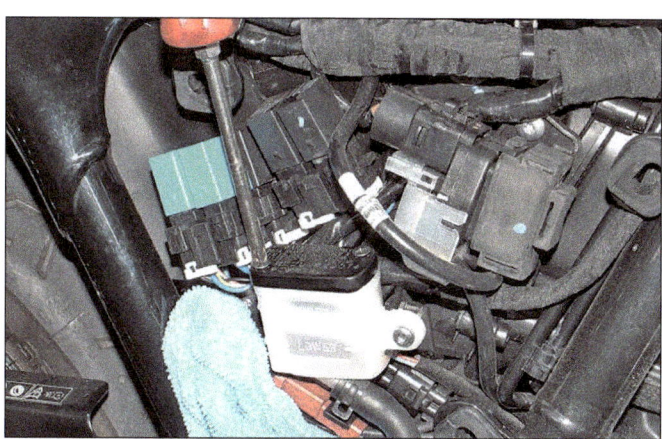

**3** On the T100, T120, Bobber, Street Twin, Street Cup, Thruxton and Thruxton R, undo the reservoir cover screws and remove the cover, diaphragm plate and diaphragm, and on the Scrambler unscrew the cap and remove the diaphragm

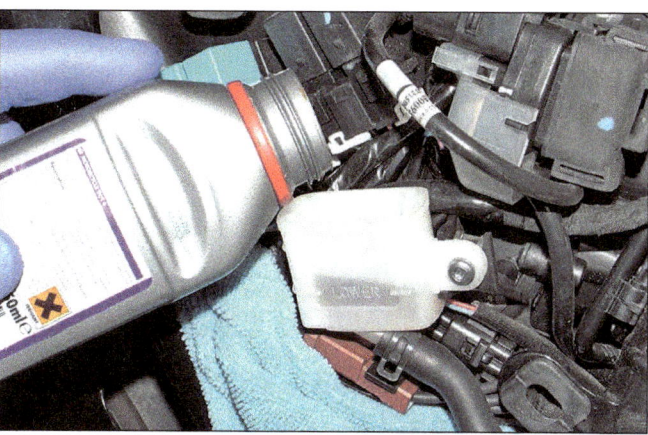

**4** Top-up with new DOT 4 hydraulic fluid until the level is up to the UPPER level line. Take care to avoid spills (see Warning) and do not overfill

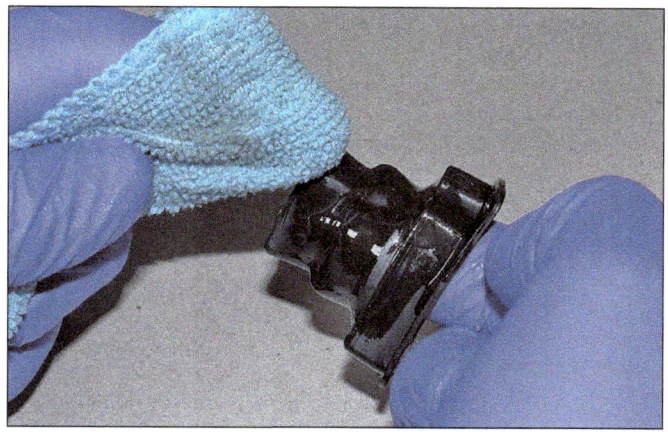

**5** Wipe any moisture out of the diaphragm using a clean lint-free cloth

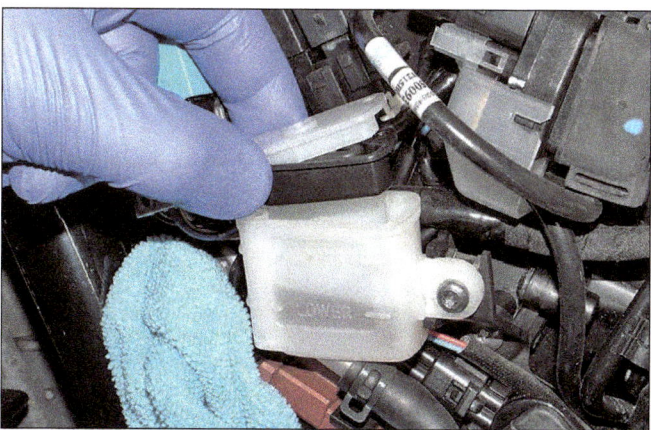

**6** Make sure the diaphragm is correctly seated before fitting the plate and cover or cap

**FRONT BRAKE – Street Twin, Street Cup, Scrambler, Thruxton R**

**1** The front brake fluid level is visible through the reservoir body – it must be between the UPPER and LOWER or MAX and MIN level lines (arrowed)

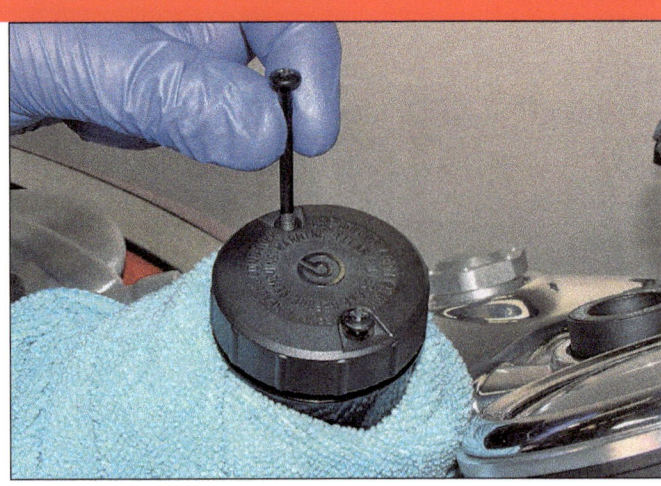

**2** If the level is low, either undo the cap clamp screw then unscrew the cap, or undo the cap screws and remove the cap, according to the type fitted, then on all types remove the diaphragm

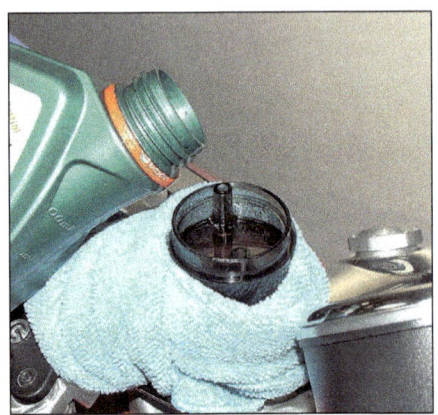

**3** Top-up with new DOT 4 hydraulic fluid until the level is up to the UPPER level line. Take care to avoid spills (see Warning) and do not overfill

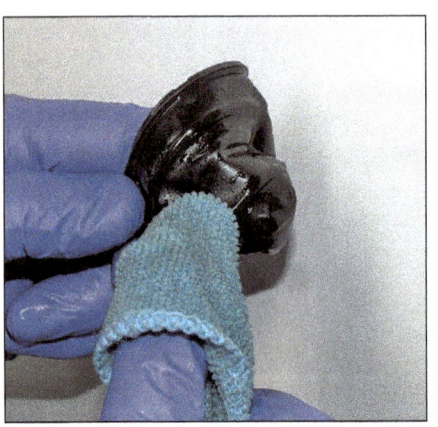

**4** Wipe any moisture out of the diaphragm using a clean lint-free cloth

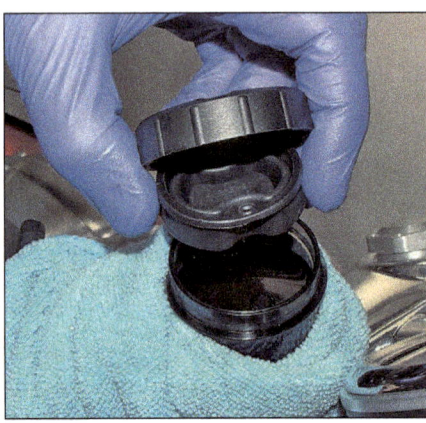

**5** Make sure the diaphragm is correctly seated before fitting the cap

# Legal and safety

### Lighting and signalling:
● Take a minute to check that the headlight, tail light, brake light, instrument lights and turn signals all work correctly.
● Check that the horn sounds when the switch is operated.
● A working speedometer graduated in mph is a statutory requirement in the UK.

### Safety:
● Check that the steering moves freely from lock-to-lock.
● Check that the brake lever and pedal, clutch lever and gearchange lever operate smoothly. Lubricate them at the specified intervals or when necessary (see Chapter 1).
● Check that the engine shuts off when the kill switch is operated.
● Check that the stand return springs hold the stand(s) up securely when retracted.

### Fuel:
● This may seem obvious, but check that you have enough fuel to complete your journey. If you notice signs of fuel leakage rectify the cause immediately.
● Make sure you use the correct grade fuel – see Chapter 4.

## The engines

Two new liquid-cooled parallel twin engines are used, one of 900cc and one of 1200cc. The 900 engine is in the new T100 Bonneville, and is used across the Street range, incorporating the Street Twin, the Street Cup and the Scrambler. The 1200 engine is in the new T120 Bonneville, the Bonneville Bobber, and in the Thruxton and Thruxton R.

Both engines have a 270° degree crank and twin balancer shafts, with a chain-driven single overhead camshaft (SOHC) acting on four valves per cylinder via rocker arms. Power is routed via a wet multi-plate clutch through a five speed gearbox on 900 engines, and a six-speed box on 1200 engines. Drive to the rear wheel is by chain and sprockets.

The crankcase divides horizontally, and the lubrication system stores the oil in a wet sump. A single pump unit, driven by chain off the back of the clutch housing, circulates both the oil and the coolant.

All engines are fed by a fully electronic 'fly-by-wire' fuel injection system, with a single throttle body and intake manifold on 900 engines and a twin throttle body on 1200's. Both engines have a single fuel rail with a fuel injector for each cylinder. All models have a two-into-two exhaust system incorporating a catalytic converter and closed loop oxygen sensors.

The engine sits in a tubular steel twin-cradle frame, with removable cradles.

## The new Bonnevilles

There are three models in the new Bonneville range, the T100, launched in 2017, the T120, launched in 2016, and the Bobber, launched in 2017. The T100 has the 900cc engine, and the T120 and Bobber have the 1200cc engine.

On the T100, front suspension is by KYB conventional 41 mm oil-damped telescopic forks. Rear suspension is by tubular steel swingarm pivoting through the frame and acting on twin KYB shock absorbers with adjustable spring pre-load. The front brake has a Nissin twin-piston sliding caliper acting on a single 310 mm disc, and the rear brake has a Nissin twin-piston sliding caliper acting on a 255 mm disc, with ABS as standard. The wheels are steel-spoked and have tubed tyres.

On the T120, front suspension is also by KYB 41 mm oil-damped telescopic forks, but with cartridge damping in the right-hand fork and conventional damping in the left-hand fork. Rear suspension is by tubular steel swingarm pivoting through the frame and acting on twin KYB shock absorbers with adjustable spring pre-load. The front brake has two Nissin twin-piston sliding calipers acting on 310 mm discs, and the rear brake has a Nissin twin-piston sliding caliper acting on a 255 mm disc, with ABS as standard. The wheels are steel-spoked and have tubed tyres.

On the Bobber, front suspension is by KYB conventional 41 mm oil-damped telescopic forks. Rear suspension is by tubular steel swingarm pivoting through the frame and acting on a single KYB shock absorber via a rising rate linkage. The front brake has a Nissin twin-piston sliding caliper acting on a single 310 mm disc, and the rear brake has a Nissin twin-piston sliding caliper acting on a 255 mm disc, with ABS as standard. The wheels are steel-spoked and have tubed tyres.

## The Street range

There are three models in the Street range, the Street Twin, launched in 2016, the Street Cup, launched in 2017, and the Street Scrambler, launched in 2017. All three use the 900cc engine.

On all models front suspension is by KYB conventional 41 mm oil-damped telescopic forks. Rear suspension is by tubular steel swingarm pivoting through the frame and acting on twin KYB shock absorbers with adjustable spring pre-load. The front brake has a Nissin twin-piston sliding caliper acting on a single 310 mm disc, and the rear brake has a Nissin twin-piston sliding caliper acting on a 255 mm disc, with ABS as standard. The wheels are cast alloy with tubeless tyres on the Street Twin and Street Cup, and steel-spoked with tubed tyres on the Scrambler.

## Thruxton and Thruxton R

The Thruxton and Thruxton R were launched in 2016, and both use the 1200cc engine.

On the Thruxton, front suspension is by KYB 41 mm oil-damped telescopic forks, with cartridge dampers in both forks. Rear suspension is by tubular steel swingarm pivoting through the frame and acting on twin KYB shock absorbers with adjustable spring pre-load. The front brake has two Nissin twin-piston sliding calipers acting on 310 mm discs, and the rear brake has a Nissin twin-piston sliding caliper acting on a 220 mm disc, with ABS as standard. The wheels are steel-spoked and have tubed tyres.

On the Thruxton R, front suspension is by Showa 43 mm 'big piston' oil-damped USD telescopic forks with adjustable spring pre-load and compression and rebound damping. Rear suspension is by tubular steel swingarm pivoting through the frame and acting on twin Ohlins shock absorbers with adjustable spring pre-load and compression and rebound damping. The front brake has two Brembo four-piston radial monobloc calipers acting on 310 mm discs, and the rear brake has a Nissin twin-piston sliding caliper acting on a 220 mm disc, with ABS as standard. The wheels are steel-spoked and have tubed tyres.

## Seat height and weight

Seat height
| | |
|---|---|
| T100 | 790 mm |
| T120 | 785 mm |
| Bobber | 690 mm |
| Street Twin | 750 mm |
| Street Cup | 780 mm |
| Scrambler | 792 mm |
| Thruxton | 805 mm |
| Thruxton R | 810 mm |

Dry weight
| | |
|---|---|
| T100 | 213 kg |
| T120 | 224 kg |
| Bobber | not available |
| Thruxton | 206 kg |
| Thruxton R | 203 kg |

Max. load (weight of rider/passenger/luggage and accessories)
| | |
|---|---|
| T100, T120, Street Twin, Street Cup, Scrambler, Thruxton and Thruxton R | 210 kg |
| Bobber | 125 kg |

# Engine

| | |
|---|---|
| Type | Four-stroke 8-valve parallel twin |
| Capacity | 900 or 1200 cc |
| Bore | |
| 900 engine | 84.6 mm |
| 1200 engine | 97.6 mm |
| Stroke | 80.0 mm |
| Compression ratio | |
| 900 engine | 10.55 to 1 |
| 1200 engine | |
| T120 and Bobber | 10.0 to 1 |
| Thruxton and Thruxton R | 11.0 to 1 |
| Cooling system | Liquid cooled |
| Clutch | Wet multi-plate, torque-assisted |
| Transmission | |
| 900 engine | Five-speed constant mesh |
| 1200 engine | Six-speed constant mesh |
| Final drive | Chain and sprockets |
| Camshaft | SOHC, chain-driven |
| Engine management | Multi-point sequential fuel injection |

## Chassis

| | |
|---|---|
| Frame type . . . . . . . . . . . . . . . . . . . . . . . . . . . . . . . . . . . . . . . . . . . . . | Tubular steel, cradle |
| Fuel tank capacity (including reserve) | |
|    T100, T120 . . . . . . . . . . . . . . . . . . . . . . . . . . . . . . . . . . . . . . | 14.5 litres |
|    Thruxton, Thruxton R . . . . . . . . . . . . . . . . . . . . . . . . . . . . . . . | 14.0 litres |
|    Street Twin, Street Cup, Scrambler . . . . . . . . . . . . . . . . . . . . . | 12.0 litres |
|    Bobber . . . . . . . . . . . . . . . . . . . . . . . . . . . . . . . . . . . . . . . . . . | 9.1 litres |
| Fuel tank reserve capacity (when low fuel warning light comes on) | |
|    T100, T120, Street Twin, Street Cup, Scrambler, Thruxton and | |
|    Thruxton R . . . . . . . . . . . . . . . . . . . . . . . . . . . . . . . . . . . . . . . | 3.5 litres |
|    Bobber . . . . . . . . . . . . . . . . . . . . . . . . . . . . . . . . . . . . . . . . . . | 2.5 litres |
| Front suspension . . . . . . . . . . . . . . . . . . . . . . . . . . . . . . . . . . . . . . . | |
|   Type | |
|     T100, T120, Bobber, Street Twin, Street Cup, Scrambler, Thruxton . . | 41 mm oil-damped telescopic forks |
|     Thruxton R . . . . . . . . . . . . . . . . . . . . . . . . . . . . . . . . . . . . . | 43 mm Showa big piston USD forks |
|   Travel | |
|     T100, T120, Street Twin, Street Cup, Scrambler, Thruxton, | |
|     Thruxton R . . . . . . . . . . . . . . . . . . . . . . . . . . . . . . . . . . . . | 120 mm |
|     Bobber . . . . . . . . . . . . . . . . . . . . . . . . . . . . . . . . . . . . . . | 90 mm |
|   Adjustment . . . . . . . . . . . . . . . . . . . . . . . . . . . . . . . . . . . . . . | |
|     T100, T120, Bobber, Street Twin, Street Cup, Scrambler, Thruxton . . | None |
|     Thruxton R . . . . . . . . . . . . . . . . . . . . . . . . . . . . . . . . . . . . . | Spring pre-load, rebound and compression damping |
| Rear suspension | |
|   Type | |
|     T100, T120, Street Twin, Street Cup, Scrambler, Thruxton, | |
|     Thruxton R . . . . . . . . . . . . . . . . . . . . . . . . . . . . . . . . . . . . | Twin shock absorbers |
|     Bobber . . . . . . . . . . . . . . . . . . . . . . . . . . . . . . . . . . . . . . | Monoshock with rising rate linkage |
|   Travel | |
|     T100, T120, Street Twin, Street Cup, Scrambler, Thruxton, | |
|     Thruxton R . . . . . . . . . . . . . . . . . . . . . . . . . . . . . . . . . . . . | 120 mm at wheel |
|     Bobber . . . . . . . . . . . . . . . . . . . . . . . . . . . . . . . . . . . . . . | 77 mm at wheel |
|   Adjustment . . . . . . . . . . . . . . . . . . . . . . . . . . . . . . . . . . . . . . | |
|     T100, T120, Street Twin, Street Cup, Scrambler, Thruxton . . . . . . | Spring pre-load |
|     Thruxton R . . . . . . . . . . . . . . . . . . . . . . . . . . . . . . . . . . . . | Spring pre-load, rebound and compression damping |
|     Bobber . . . . . . . . . . . . . . . . . . . . . . . . . . . . . . . . . . . . . . | none |
| Wheels | |
|   T100, T120 . . . . . . . . . . . . . . . . . . . . . . . . . . . . . . . . . . . . . . | Steel spoke, 18 x 2.75 inch front, 17 x 4.25 inch rear |
|   Bobber . . . . . . . . . . . . . . . . . . . . . . . . . . . . . . . . . . . . . . . . . | Steel spoke, 19 x 2.5 inch front, 16 x 3.5 inch rear |
|   Street Twin, Street Cup . . . . . . . . . . . . . . . . . . . . . . . . . . . . . . | 10-spoke alloys, 18 x 2.75 inch front, 17 x 4.25 inch rear |
|   Scrambler . . . . . . . . . . . . . . . . . . . . . . . . . . . . . . . . . . . . . . | Steel spoke, 19 x 2.5 inch front, 17 x 4.25 inch rear |
|   Thruxton, Thruxton R . . . . . . . . . . . . . . . . . . . . . . . . . . . . . . . | Steel spoke, 17 x 3.5 inch front, 17 x 5.0 inch rear |
| Tyres | |
|   T100, T120 | |
|     Front . . . . . . . . . . . . . . . . . . . . . . . . . . . . . . . . . . . . . . . . . | 100/90-18 56H tubed |
|     Rear . . . . . . . . . . . . . . . . . . . . . . . . . . . . . . . . . . . . . . . . . | 150/70R17 69H tubed |
|   Bobber | |
|     Front . . . . . . . . . . . . . . . . . . . . . . . . . . . . . . . . . . . . . . . . . | 100/90-19 tubed |
|     Rear . . . . . . . . . . . . . . . . . . . . . . . . . . . . . . . . . . . . . . . . . | 150/80R16 tubed |
|   Street Twin, Street Cup | |
|     Front . . . . . . . . . . . . . . . . . . . . . . . . . . . . . . . . . . . . . . . . . | 100/90-18 56H tubeless |
|     Rear . . . . . . . . . . . . . . . . . . . . . . . . . . . . . . . . . . . . . . . . . | 150/70R17 69H tubeless |
|   Scrambler | |
|     Front . . . . . . . . . . . . . . . . . . . . . . . . . . . . . . . . . . . . . . . . . | 100/90-19 tubed |
|     Rear . . . . . . . . . . . . . . . . . . . . . . . . . . . . . . . . . . . . . . . . . | 150/70R17 tubed |
|   Thruxton, Thruxton R | |
|     Front . . . . . . . . . . . . . . . . . . . . . . . . . . . . . . . . . . . . . . . . . | 120/70ZR17 58W tubed |
|     Rear . . . . . . . . . . . . . . . . . . . . . . . . . . . . . . . . . . . . . . . . . | 160/60ZR17 69W tubed |
| Front brake . . . . . . . . . . . . . . . . . . . . . . . . . . . . . . . . . . . . . . . . . . . . | |
|   T100, Bobber, Street Twin, Street Cup, Scrambler . . . . . . . . . . . . | Single 310 mm disc with a two-piston sliding caliper |
|   T120, Thruxton . . . . . . . . . . . . . . . . . . . . . . . . . . . . . . . . . . . . | Twin 310 mm discs with two-piston sliding calipers |
|   Thruxton R . . . . . . . . . . . . . . . . . . . . . . . . . . . . . . . . . . . . . . | Twin 310 mm discs with four-piston opposed calipers |
| Rear brake . . . . . . . . . . . . . . . . . . . . . . . . . . . . . . . . . . . . . . . . . . . . . | |
|   T100, T120, Bobber, Street Twin, Street Cup, Scrambler . . . . . . . . | Single 255 mm disc with a two-piston sliding caliper |
|   Thruxton, Thruxton R . . . . . . . . . . . . . . . . . . . . . . . . . . . . . . . | Single 220 mm disc with a two-piston sliding caliper |

# Chapter 1
## Routine maintenance and servicing

## Contents

## Degrees of difficulty

| **Easy,** suitable for novice with little experience | **Fairly easy,** suitable for beginner with some experience | **Fairly difficult,** suitable for competent DIY mechanic | **Difficult,** suitable for experienced DIY mechanic | **Very difficult,** suitable for expert DIY or professional |
|---|---|---|---|---|

## Engine

Spark plugs
Type . . . . . . . . . . . . . . . . . . . . . . . . . . . . . . . . . . . . . . . . . NGK LMAR8A-9
Electrode gap . . . . . . . . . . . . . . . . . . . . . . . . . . . . . . . . . . . 0.8 to 0.9 mm
Cylinder identification. . . . . . . . . . . . . . . . . . . . . . . . . . . . . . . No. 1 – left, No. 2 – right
Valve clearances (COLD engine)
Intake valves. . . . . . . . . . . . . . . . . . . . . . . . . . . . . . . . . . . . . 0.05 to 0.13 mm
Exhaust valves . . . . . . . . . . . . . . . . . . . . . . . . . . . . . . . . . . . 0.08 to 0.18 mm

## Cycle parts

Drive chain slack – see text
T100, T120, Street Twin, Street Cup, Scrambler, Thruxton, Thruxton R . . 20 to 30 mm
Bobber . . . . . . . . . . . . . . . . . . . . . . . . . . . . . . . . . . . . . . . . . 26 to 33 mm
Clutch cable freeplay . . . . . . . . . . . . . . . . . . . . . . . . . . . . . . 2 to 3 mm
Tyre pressures (cold). . . . . . . . . . . . . . . . . . . . . . . . . . . . . . see *Pre-ride checks*

## Lubricants and fluids

Fuel . . . . . . . . . . . . . . . . . . . . . . . . . . . . . . . . . . . . . . . . . . . . . see Chapter 4
Engine oil type . . . . . . . . . . . . . . . . . . . . . . . . . . . . . . . . . . . Fully synthetic API grade SH or higher, JASO grade MA, SAE 10W40
(or 10W50 above 40ºC). Semi-synthetic can also be used

Engine oil capacity
Oil change. . . . . . . . . . . . . . . . . . . . . . . . . . . . . . . . . . . . . . . 3.2 litres
Oil and filter change . . . . . . . . . . . . . . . . . . . . . . . . . . . . . . . 3.4 litres
Following engine overhaul – dry engine, new filter. . . . . . . . . . . . 3.8 litres
Coolant type. . . . . . . . . . . . . . . . . . . . . . . . . . . . . . . . . . . . . Triumph HD4X Hybrid OAT (organic acid technology) ready-mixed
coolant

Coolant capacity
T100, Street Twin, Street Cup, Scrambler . . . . . . . . . . . . . . . . . 1.52 litres
T120, Bobber, Thruxton, Thruxton R . . . . . . . . . . . . . . . . . . . . . 1.56 litres
Brake fluid . . . . . . . . . . . . . . . . . . . . . . . . . . . . . . . . . . . . . . . DOT 4
Drive chain . . . . . . . . . . . . . . . . . . . . . . . . . . . . . . . . . . . . . . Aerosol chain lubricant suitable for O-ring chains
Rear suspension bearings and pivots, wheel bearing seals,
clutch lever pivot, brake pedal pivot . . . . . . . . . . . . . . . . . . . . . Lithium-based multi-purpose grease to NLGI 2 spec
Steering head bearings . . . . . . . . . . . . . . . . . . . . . . . . . . . . . . Heavy duty lithium-based grease (Castrol LCX222)
Stand pivot(s) . . . . . . . . . . . . . . . . . . . . . . . . . . . . . . . . . . . . Castrol high temperature grease
Front brake lever pivot and tip . . . . . . . . . . . . . . . . . . . . . . . . . Silicone grease

## Torque wrench settings

Fork clamp bolts (top yoke)
T100, T120, Bobber, Street Twin, Street Cup and Scrambler . . . . . . 24 Nm
Thruxton and Thruxton R . . . . . . . . . . . . . . . . . . . . . . . . . . . . . 20 Nm
Oil drain plug . . . . . . . . . . . . . . . . . . . . . . . . . . . . . . . . . . . . . 25 Nm
Oil filter . . . . . . . . . . . . . . . . . . . . . . . . . . . . . . . . . . . . . . . . . 10 Nm
Rear axle nut . . . . . . . . . . . . . . . . . . . . . . . . . . . . . . . . . . . . . 110 Nm
Rocker shaft bolts . . . . . . . . . . . . . . . . . . . . . . . . . . . . . . . . . 10 Nm
Spark plugs . . . . . . . . . . . . . . . . . . . . . . . . . . . . . . . . . . . . . . 12 Nm
Steering head bearing adjuster nut – using peg spanner tool
Initial setting. . . . . . . . . . . . . . . . . . . . . . . . . . . . . . . . . . . . . 40 Nm
Final setting . . . . . . . . . . . . . . . . . . . . . . . . . . . . . . . . . . . . . 15 Nm
Steering head bearing adjuster locknut . . . . . . . . . . . . . . . . . . . 40 Nm
Steering stem nut. . . . . . . . . . . . . . . . . . . . . . . . . . . . . . . . . . 90 Nm

## 1 Maintenance schedule

### Pre-ride
☐ See *Pre-ride checks* at the beginning of this manual.

### After the initial 500 miles (800 km)
**Note:** *This check is performed by a Triumph dealer after the first 500 miles (800 km) from new. Thereafter, maintenance is carried out according to the following intervals of the schedule.*

### Every 200 miles (300 km)
☐ Check, adjust, clean and lubricate the drive chain (Section 3)

### Every 500 miles (800 km)
☐ Check the drive chain for wear and stretch and the sprockets for wear (Section 3)

### Every 10,000 miles (16,000 km) or 12 months
☐ Change the engine oil and fit a new filter (Section 4)
☐ Check and adjust the spark plugs (Section 5)
☐ Fit a new air filter (Section 6)
☐ Check the fuel system and EVAP system (Section 7)
☐ Check and adjust throttle body synchronisation (1200 engines only) (Section 8)
☐ Check the engine management system (Section 9)
☐ Check and adjust the clutch cable (Section 10)
☐ Lubricate the clutch/gearchange/brake lever/brake pedal/stand pivots and clutch cable (Section 11)
☐ Check the cooling system (Section 12)
☐ Check the brake system (Section 13)

### Every 10,000 miles (16,000 km) or 12 months (continued)
☐ Check the condition of the wheels, wheel bearings and tyres (Section 14)
☐ Check the front and rear suspension (Section 15)
☐ Check and adjust the steering head bearings (Section 16)
☐ Check the sidestand and starter safety circuit (Section 17)
☐ Check the tightness of all nuts, bolts and fasteners (Section 18)
☐ Check the battery (Section 19)

### Every 20,000 miles (32,000 km)
☐ Check and adjust the valve clearances (Section 20)
☐ Fit new spark plugs (see Section 5)
☐ Fit a new fuel filter (Section 7)
☐ Re-grease the steering head bearings (Chapter 5)

### Every 40,000 miles (64,000 km)
☐ Change the fork oil (Chapter 5)

### Every two years
☐ Change the brake fluid (Chapter 6)

### Every three years
☐ Change the coolant (Section 12)

### Every four years
☐ Fit new fuel and EVAP system hoses (Section 7)

## Component locations – T100, T120, Street Twin, Cup and Scrambler right side

1 Rear brake fluid reservoir
2 Main fuse
3 Engine number
4 Spark plug

5 Cooling system pressure cap
6 Front brake fluid reservoir
7 Frame number
8 Coolant hose (for draining)

9 Engine oil filler cap
10 Engine oil level window
11 Drive chain adjuster

## Component locations – T100, T120, Street Twin, Cup and Scrambler left side

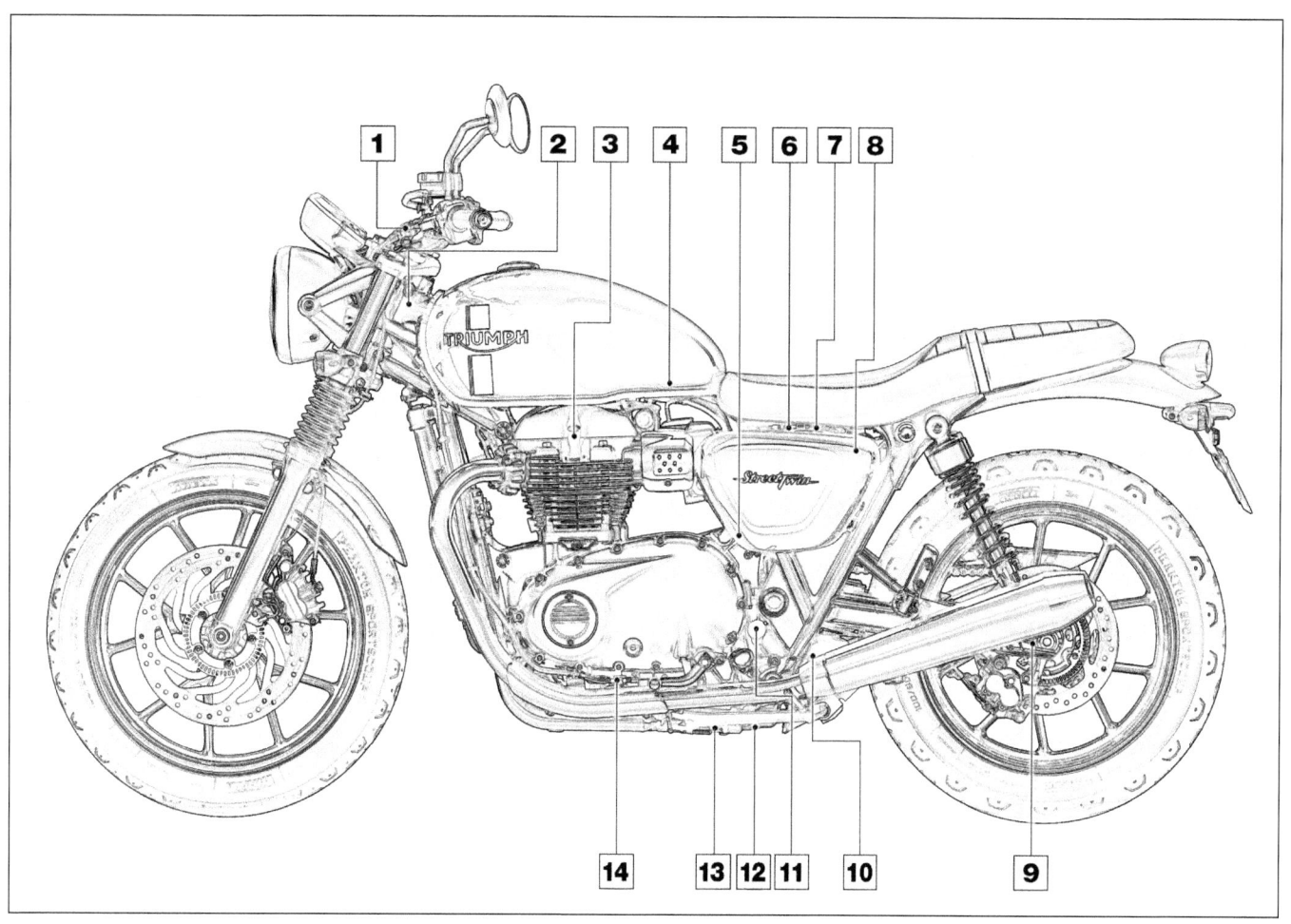

1 Clutch cable adjuster at lever
2 Steering head bearing adjuster
3 Spark plug
4 Fuel filter/strainer
5 Air filter
6 Fusebox
7 OBD2 diagnostic socket
8 Battery
9 Drive chain adjuster
10 Coolant level marks
11 Coolant tank filler
12 Engine oil filter
13 Engine oil drain plug
14 Clutch cable lower adjuster

## Component locations – Thruxton and Thruxton R right side

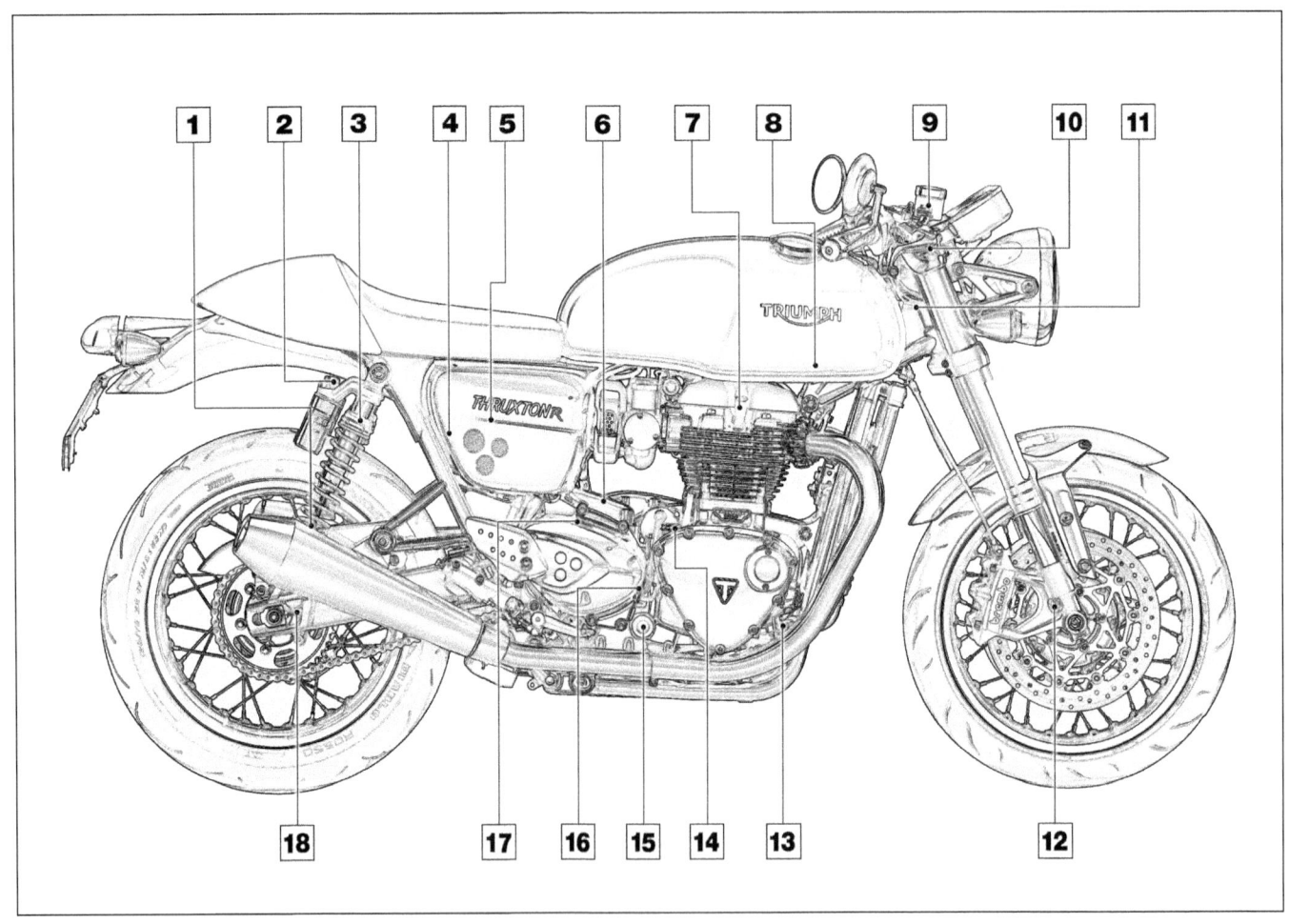

1 Shock rebound damping
  adjuster (R)
2 Shock compression damping
  adjuster (R)
3 Shock pre-load adjuster (R)
4 Rear brake fluid reservoir
5 Main fuse

6 Engine number
7 Spark plug
8 Cooling system pressure cap
9 Front brake fluid reservoir
10 Fork damping adjusters (R)
11 Frame number
12 Fork pre-load adjuster (R)

13 Coolant hose for draining
14 Engine oil filler cap
15 Engine oil level window
16 Coolant level marks
17 Coolant filler cap
18 Drive chain adjuster

## Component locations – Thruxton and Thruxton R left side

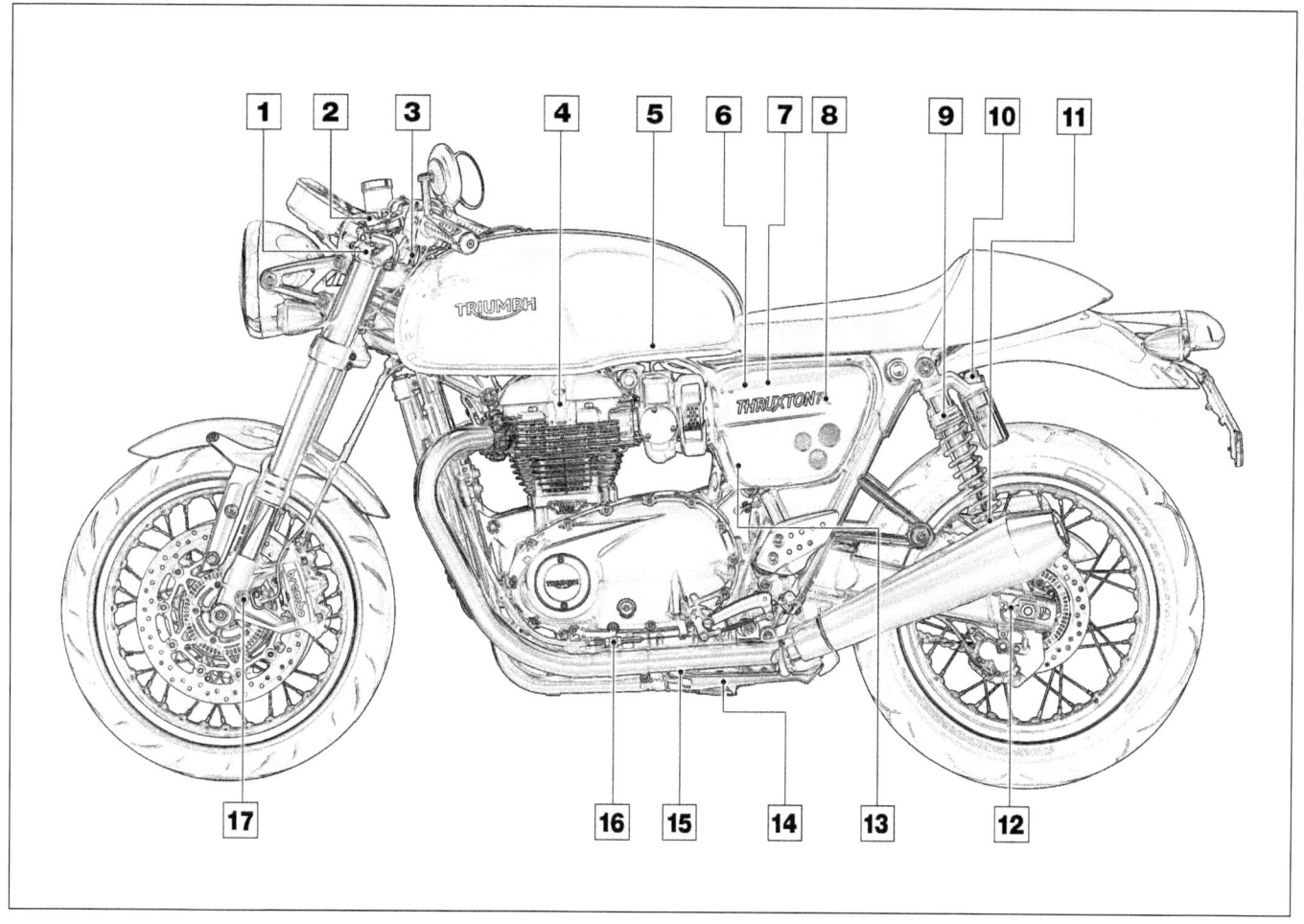

1 Fork damping adjusters (R)
2 Clutch cable adjuster at lever
3 Steering head bearing
  adjuster
4 Spark plug
5 Fuel filter/strainer
6 Fusebox

7 OBD2 diagnostic socket
8 Battery
9 Shock pre-load adjuster (R)
10 Shock compression damping
  adjuster (R)
11 Shock rebound damping
  adjuster (R)

12 Drive chain adjuster
13 Air filter
14 Engine oil filter
15 Engine oil drain plug
16 Clutch cable lower adjuster
17 Fork pre-load adjuster (R)

## Component locations – Bobber right side

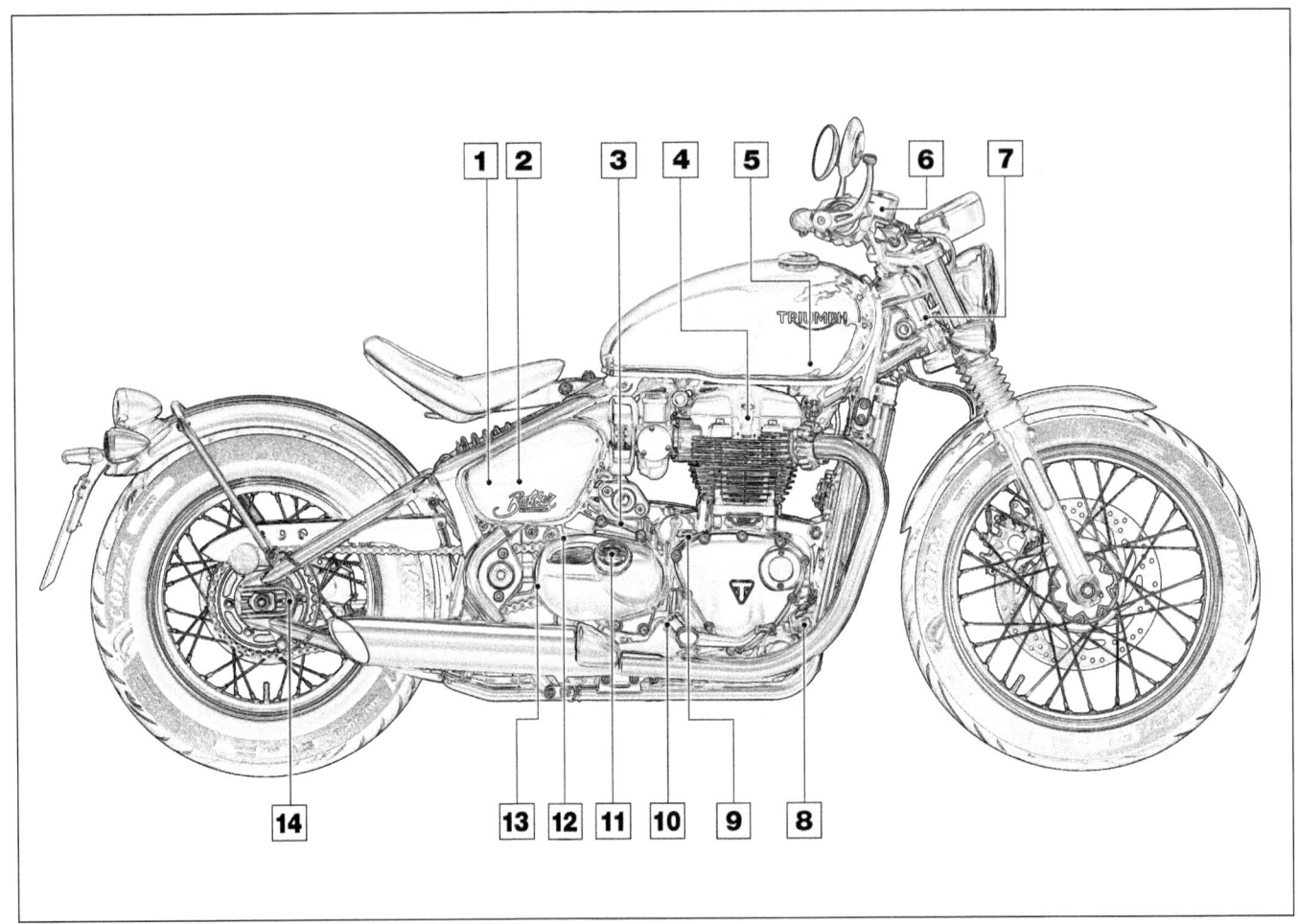

1 OBD2 diagnostic socket
2 Air filter
3 Engine number
4 Spark plug
5 Cooling system pressure cap

6 Front brake fluid reservoir
7 Frame number
8 Coolant hose for draining
9 Engine oil filler cap
10 Engine oil level window

11 Rear brake fluid reservoir
12 Coolant filler cap
13 Coolant level marks
14 Drive chain adjuster

## Component locations – Bobber left side

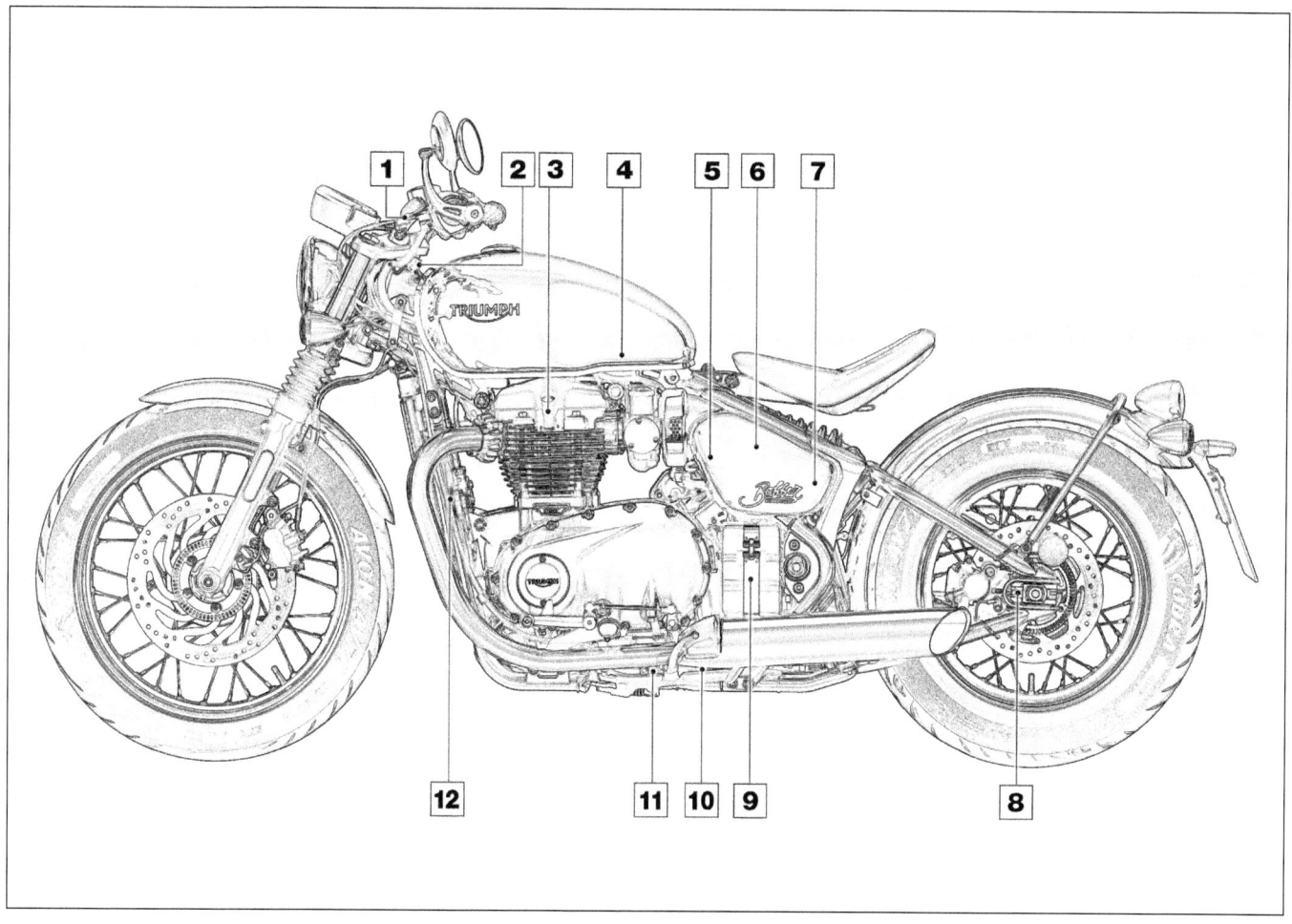

1 Clutch cable adjuster at lever
2 Steering head bearing adjuster
3 Spark plug
4 Fuel filter/strainer

5 Main fuse
6 Air filter
7 Fusebox
8 Drive chain adjuster

9 Battery
10 Engine oil filter
11 Engine oil drain plug
12 Clutch cable in-line adjuster

## 2  General information

**1** This Chapter is designed to help the home mechanic maintain his/her motorcycle for safety, economy, long life and peak performance.

**2** Deciding where to start or plug into the routine maintenance schedule depends on several factors. If the warranty period on your motorcycle has just expired, and if it has been maintained according to the warranty standards, you may want to pick up routine maintenance as it coincides with the next mileage interval. If you have owned the machine for some time but have never performed any maintenance on it, then you may want to start at the beginning and include all frequent procedures to ensure that nothing important is overlooked. If you have just had a major engine overhaul, then you should start the engine maintenance routines from the beginning. If you have a used machine and have no knowledge of its history or maintenance record, you should combine all the checks into one large initial service and then settle into the maintenance schedule prescribed.

**3** The motorcycle has a service indicator

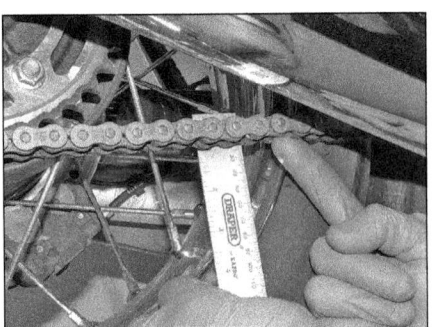

**3.4 Measuring chain slack**

spanner (wrench) symbol in the instruments. When the ignition is first switched on the symbol and remaining distance if under 500 miles (800 km) from the next service will be displayed. The symbol will remain on once zero miles (km) is reached and display distance as a negative number. Resetting of the service indicator is a Triumph dealer operation, but can also be done with the TuneECU android phone app and an OBD2 code reader.

**4** Before beginning any maintenance or repair, the machine should be cleaned thoroughly, especially around the oil filter, oil drain plug and chain area. Cleaning will help ensure that dirt does not contaminate the engine and will allow you to detect wear and damage that could otherwise easily go unnoticed.

**5** Certain maintenance information is sometimes printed on decals attached to the motorcycle. If any information on the decals differs from that included here, use the information on the decal.

 *Warning: Read the Safety first! section of this manual carefully before starting work.*

## 3  Drive chain and sprockets

### Check

**1** A neglected drive chain won't last long and can quickly damage the sprockets. Routine chain adjustment and lubrication isn't difficult and will ensure maximum chain and sprocket life.

*Caution: Riding the bike with excess slack in the chain could lead to damage.*

**2** Check chain slack with the bike held upright if possible, or on the sidestand if not. There should be no weight on the bike.

**3** Make sure that the transmission is in neutral.

**4** Hold a ruler against the bottom run of the chain mid-way between the sprockets, then push the chain up and measure the amount of slack **(see illustration)**

**5** Compare the result with the range given in the Specifications.

**6** Since the chain will rarely wear evenly, roll the bike forward so that another section of chain can be checked; do this several times to check the entire length of chain, and mark the tightest spot.

**7** In some cases where lubrication has been neglected, corrosion and dirt may cause the links to bind and kink, which effectively shortens the chain's length and makes it tight **(see illustration)**. Thoroughly clean and work free any such links, then highlight them with a marker pen or paint. Take the bike for a short ride, then repeat the measurement for slack in the highlighted area.

**8** If the chain has kinked again and is still tight, fit a new one (see Chapter 6). A rusty, kinked or worn chain will damage the sprockets and can damage transmission bearings. If in any doubt as to the condition of a chain, it is far better to fit a new one than risk damage to other components and possibly yourself.

**9** Check the entire length of the chain for worn or damaged rollers and sideplates, loose links and pins, and missing O-rings and fit a new one if necessary.

*Caution: Never fit a new chain onto old sprockets, and never use the old chain if you fit new sprockets – replace the chain and sprockets as a set – see Chapter 6.*

### Adjustment

**10** If the amount of slack at the tightest point exceeds the upper limit of the specified range it must be adjusted. Rotate the rear wheel until the chain is positioned with the tightest spot at the centre of its bottom run.

**11** Loosen the rear wheel axle nut **(see illustration)**.

**12** Loosen the locknut on the adjuster bolt

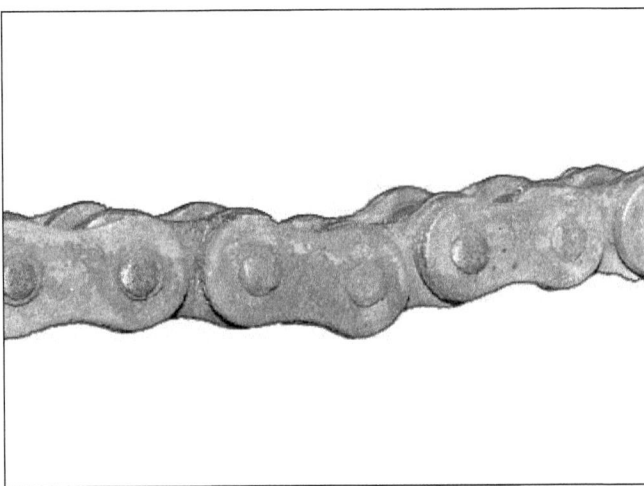

**3.7 Neglect has caused the links in this chain to kink**

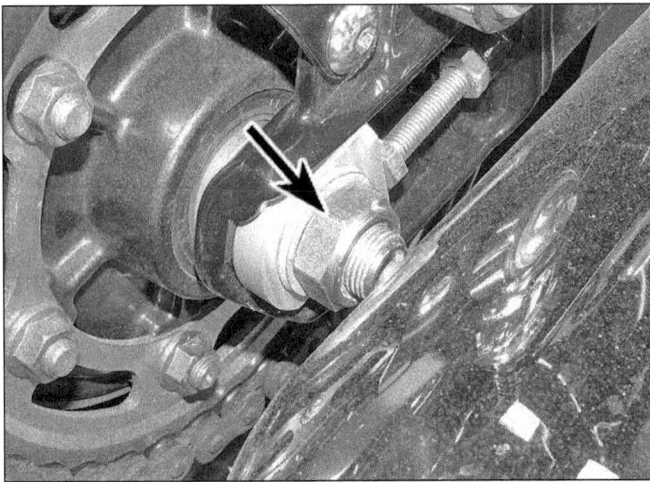

**3.11 Rear axle nut (arrowed)**

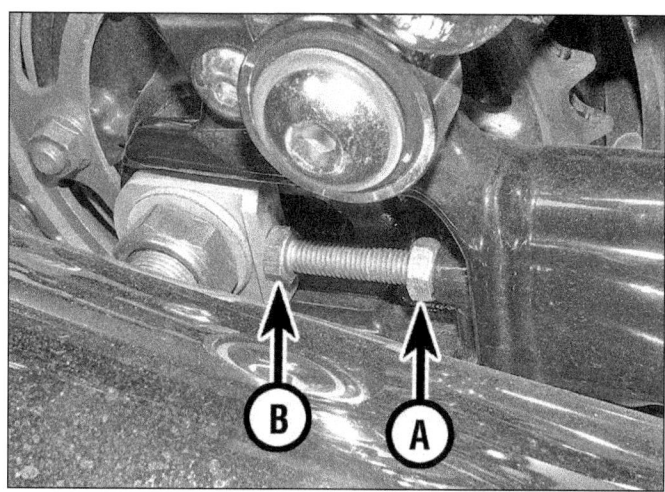

3.12a Slacken the locknut (A) on each side and turn the adjuster bolt (B) as required

3.12b On the T100, T120, Bobber, Street Twin, Street Cup and Scrambler make sure the front of the adjuster plate relative to the index marks (arrowed) on the swingarm is the same on each side

3.12c On the Thruxton and Thruxton R make sure the rear of the adjuster plate relative to the index marks (arrowed) on the swingarm is the same on each side

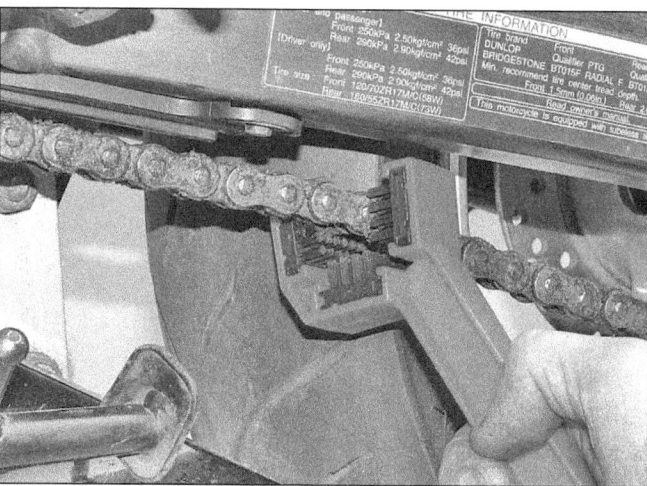

3.18 Specially shaped chain cleaning brushes are available from good suppliers

on each side of the swingarm, then turn the adjuster bolts evenly and a small amount at a time, anti-clockwise to reduce slack and clockwise to increase it, keeping some forward pressure on the wheel to make sure the adjuster plates remain butted against the bolt heads, until the amount of slack is within the specified range (see illustration). Now, on all models except the Thruxton and Thruxton R check that the front of each adjuster plate is equally aligned relative to the index marks on each side of the swingarm, and on the Thruxton and Thruxton R check that the rear of each adjuster plate is equally aligned relative to the index marks on each side of the swingarm (see illustrations) – if not, the rear wheel will be out of alignment with the front.

**13** If there is a discrepancy in the position of the alignment marks, correct it with the adjusters and then check the chain tension again as described above.

**14** Push the wheel forwards to make sure the adjuster plates butt against the adjuster bolt heads, then tighten the axle nut to 110 Nm.

**15** Counter-hold the adjuster bolts and tighten the locknuts (see illustration 3.12a). Recheck the adjustment.

**16** At the prescribed interval, or if the chain is difficult to adjust satisfactorily, or if it is close to the end of available adjustment, check the chain stretch as described below.

### Cleaning and lubrication

**Note:** *If using a Scottoiler or equivalent automatic chain lubrication system you do not need to manually apply any other lubricant.*

**17** The best time to lubricate the chain is after the motorcycle has been ridden. When the chain is warm, the lubricant will penetrate

the joints between the sideplates better than when cold.

**18** If required, wash the chain using a dedicated aerosol cleaner or paraffin (kerosene), then wipe it off and allow it to dry, using compressed air if available (see illustration).

*Caution: Don't use petrol (gasoline), solvent or other cleaning fluids which might damage the internal sealing properties of the chain. Don't use high-pressure water. The entire process shouldn't take longer than five to six minutes – if it does, the O-rings in the chain rollers could be damaged.*

**19** Use an aerosol chain lube that is specifically for O-ring chains. Engine oil can be used but it will not stick to the chain as well as dedicated chain lube and therefore not provide long lasting lubrication. Apply

**3.19 Apply the lubricant to the overlap between the sideplates**

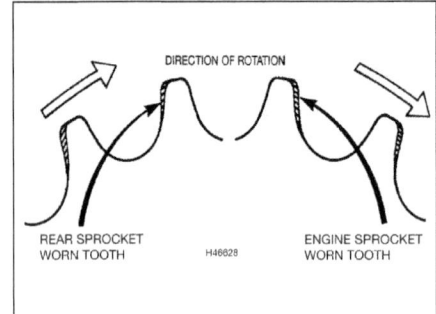

**3.23 Check the sprockets in the areas indicated to see if they are worn excessively**

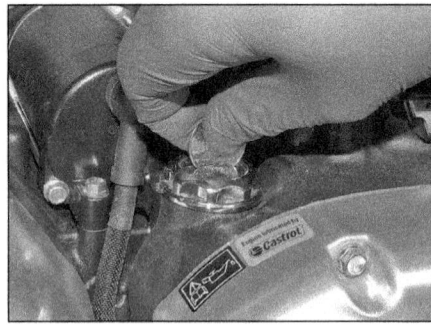

**4.3 Unscrew the oil filler cap**

the lubricant to the area where the sideplates overlap – not the middle of the rollers. Protect the tyre from overspray with a rag or piece of cardboard **(see illustration)**.

> ⚠️ *Warning: Take care not to get any lubricant on the tyre or brake system components. If any of the lubricant inadvertently contacts them, clean it off thoroughly using a suitable solvent or dedicated brake cleaner before riding the machine.*

### Chain stretch check

**20** Chain condition can be determined by the amount it has stretched between a specified number of links. To assess the chain accurately, clean it (see above) and make sure it is free of any kinks – binding links must be loosened-up before the check is made.
**21** To check the amount of chain wear (stretch), hang a 10 to 20 kg (20 to 40 lb) weight from the middle of the bottom run of the chain. Measure along the top run the length of 20 links (from the centre of the 1st pin to the centre of the 21st pin) and note the reading. Rotate the wheel so that several sections of the chain are measured, then calculate the average. If the

measurement exceeds 319 mm fit a new one (see Chapter 6).

### Sprocket wear check

**22** If the drive chain is worn or damaged, it is likely that the sprockets will also be worn.
**23** Remove the front sprocket cover (see Chapter 6). Check the teeth on the front and rear sprockets for wear **(see illustration)**. If the sprocket teeth are worn excessively, follow the procedure in Chapter 6 and replace the chain and both sprockets with a new set.
**24** Check the front and rear sprocket nuts are tight (refer to Chapter 6 for torque settings).
**25** Inspect the drive chain slider on the front of the swingarm for excessive wear and damage and fit a new one if necessary (see Chapter 5).

### 4 Engine oil and oil filter

> ⚠️ *Warning: Be careful when draining the oil, as the exhaust pipes, the engine, and the oil itself can cause severe burns.*

**Special tool:** *A filter removing tool is necessary for this job (see illustration 4.5a).*
**1** Regular oil changes are the single most important maintenance procedure you can perform on a motorcycle. The oil not only lubricates the internal parts of the engine, transmission and clutch, but it also acts as a coolant, a cleaner, a sealant, and a protector. Because of these demands, the oil takes a terrific amount of abuse and must be changed at the specified intervals with new oil of the recommended grade and type and marked as suitable for motorcycles. Saving a little money on the difference in cost between a good oil and a cheap oil won't pay off if the engine is damaged. The oil filter should be changed with every oil change.
**2** Before changing the oil, warm up the engine so the oil will drain easily.
**3** Place a clean drain tray under the oil drain plug. Unscrew the oil filler cap to vent the engine unit and to act as a reminder that there is no oil in the engine **(see illustration)**.
**4** Unscrew the oil drain plug and allow the oil to flow into the drain tray **(see illustrations)**. Remove the sealing washer from the plug – a new one must be used.

**4.4a Unscrew the oil drain plug...**

**4.4b ...and allow the oil to drain**

4.5a Unscrew the filter...

4.5b ... and drain the oil from it

4.6 Always use a new sealing washer

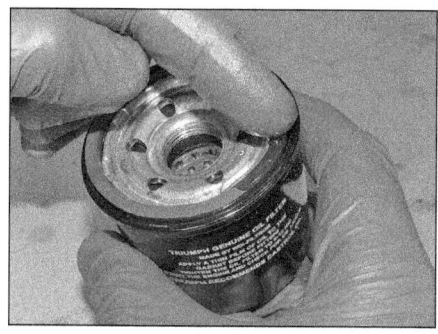

4.7a Lubricate the seal if necessary...

4.7b ... and thread it onto the boss

**5** Unscrew the filter using a filter removal tool **(see illustration)** – the type that can be used with a socket wrench is the best as it allows the new filter to be tightened to the correct torque, but make sure you have the correct size to fit the filter cartridge as many sizes are available (part No. for the Triumph tool is T3880313). Tip any residual oil into the drain tray **(see illustration)**.

**6** When the oil has completely drained, clean around the drain plug seat, then fit the plug with its new washer and tighten it to 25 Nm **(see illustration)**. Avoid overtightening, as you will damage the sump.

**7** Clean the filter mating surface on the crankcase carefully with a suitable solvent. Remove any protective packaging from the new filter. If the filter seal is not pre-greased smear clean engine oil onto it **(see illustration)**. Screw the filter on until the seal just seats **(see illustration)**. If a suitable oil filter tool is being used, tighten the filter to

10 Nm. Otherwise, tighten the filter as tight as possible by hand, or by the number of turns specified on the filter or its packaging. Do not use a strap or chain wrench to tighten the filter as you will damage it.

**8** Refill the engine using the type and amount of oil given in the Specifications so the level lies between the upper and lower level lines on the window with the bike upright **(see illustrations)**. Make sure the filler cap O-ring

4.8a Pour the oil in

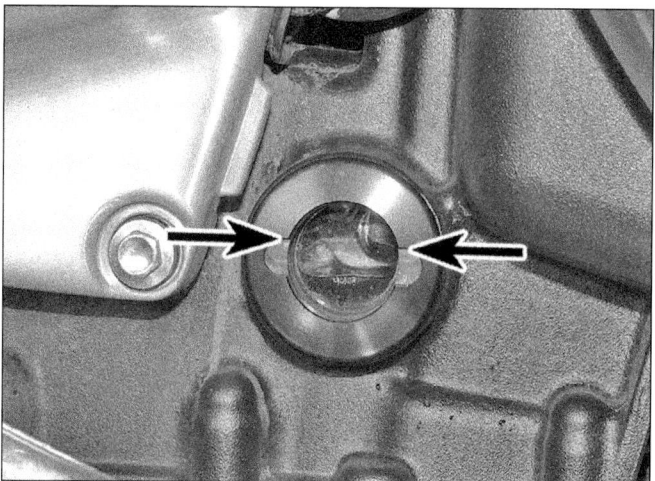

4.8b Do not fill beyond the upper level lines (arrowed)

**4.8c Check the O-ring (arrowed) then fit the cap**

is in place then fit the cap **(see illustration)**. Start the engine and let it run for two or three minutes – make sure the oil pressure warning light goes out soon after starting the engine. Stop the engine, wait a few minutes, then check the oil level. If necessary, add more oil until the level is correct. Check that there are no leaks around the drain plug and filter.

**9** The old oil drained from the engine cannot be re-used and must be disposed of properly. Check with your local refuse disposal company, disposal facility or environmental

**Note: It is illegal and anti-social to dump oil down the drain. To find the location of your local oil recycling bank in the UK, call 03708 506 506 or visit www.oilbankline.org.uk.**
**In the US note that any oil supplier must accept used oil for recycling.**

agency to see whether they will accept the used oil for recycling – most will. Don't pour used oil into drains or onto the ground.

**5 Spark plugs**

**1** To remove the spark plugs you need a 14mm spark plug socket.
**2** Pull the cap off each plug **(see illustration)**.
**3** Clean around the base of each plug to get rid of any dirt that may otherwise fall into the cylinders when the plugs are removed.
**4** Using the plug socket, unscrew the plugs and lift them out of the cylinder head **(see**

illustration). Lay each plug out in relation to its cylinder so that if either plug shows up a problem it is easy to identify the troublesome cylinder.
**5** Inspect the electrodes for wear. Both the centre and side electrodes should have square edges and the side electrode should be of uniform thickness. Look for excessive deposits and evidence of a cracked or chipped insulator around the centre electrode.
**6** Compare your spark plugs to the accompanying firing end examples on the inside rear cover. Check the threads, the washer and the ceramic insulator body for cracks and other damage.
**7** If the electrodes are not excessively worn, and if the deposits can be easily removed with a wire brush, and there are no cracks or chips visible in the insulator, the plugs can be re-gapped and re-used. If in doubt concerning the condition of the plugs, replace them with new ones, as the expense is minimal. Note that new spark plugs should be fitted at every second service interval.
**8** Before installing the plugs, refer to the Specifications and make sure they are the correct type and heat range and check the gap between the side (earth) electrode and the centre electrode **(see illustrations)**.

**5.2 Pull the caps off the plugs**

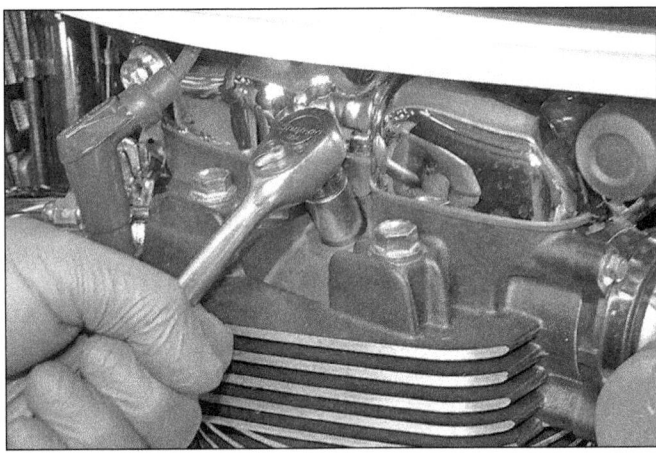

**5.4 Unscrew and remove each plug**

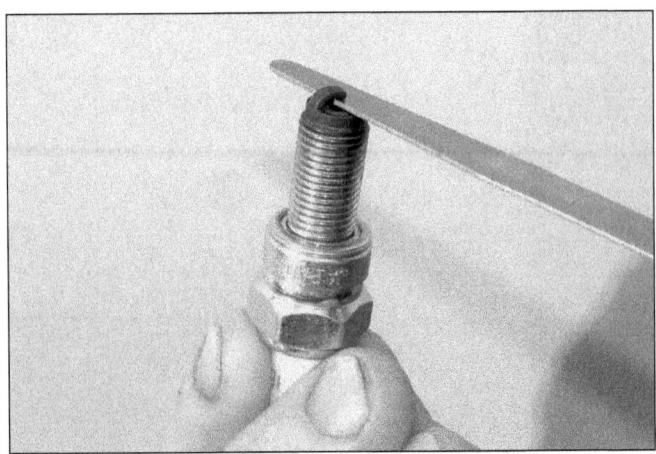

**5.8a Using a feeler gauge to measure the spark plug electrode gap**

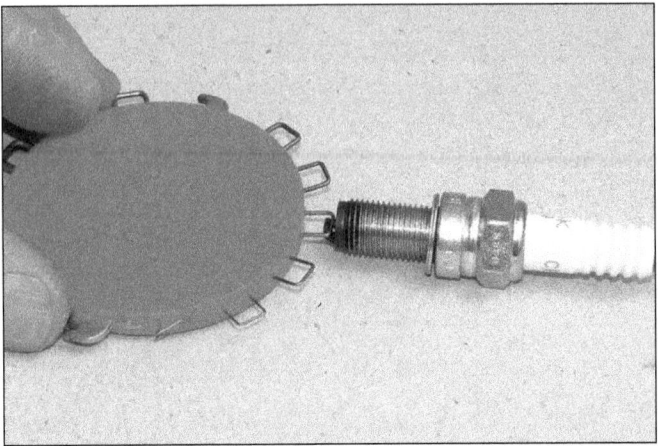

**5.8b Using a wire type gauge to measure the spark plug electrode gap**

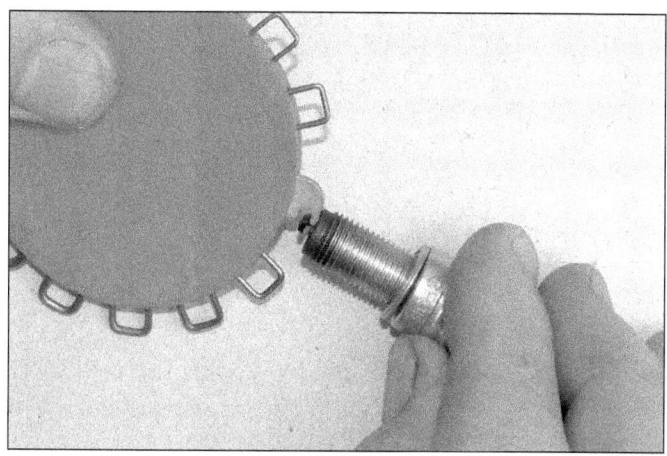

**5.8c Adjust the electrode gap by bending the side electrode only**

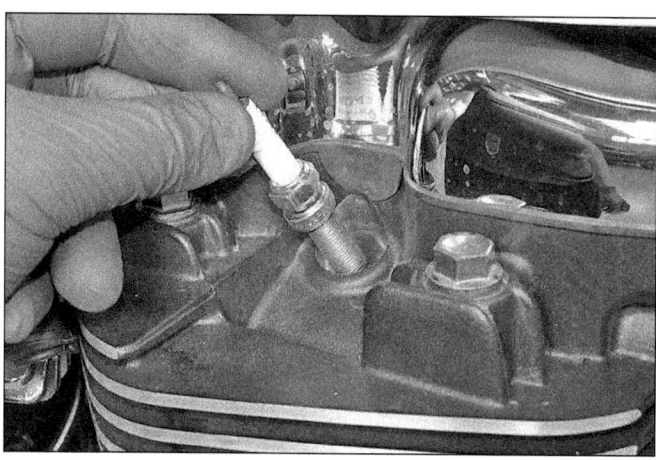

**5.9 Take care when threading the plugs in**

Adjust the gap as necessary by bending the side electrode, but be very careful not to chip or crack the insulator nose **(see illustration)**. Make sure the sealing washer is in place on the plug before installing it.

**9** Carefully thread the plugs into the head by hand initially, making sure they do not cross-thread **(see illustration)** – if they become prematurely tight remove them and start again,

do not force them or you will damage the threads in the cylinder head. Once the plugs are finger-tight, the job can be finished with the tool handle or a socket wrench. If a torque wrench is available, tighten the spark plugs to 12 Nm. Otherwise tighten them by 1/4 to 1/2 turn after they have been fully hand tightened and have seated. Do not over-tighten them.

**10** Push the plug caps firmly onto the plugs.

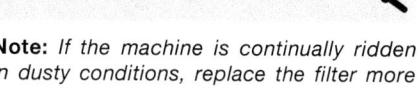

## 6  Air filter(s)

**Note:** *If the machine is continually ridden in dusty conditions, replace the filter more frequently than specified.*

**Note:** *All models are fitted with a disposable oil-impregnated paper element that cannot be cleaned. Replace the filter with a new one at the specified service interval.*

**1** Remove the side panels (see Chapter 7).

**2** On all models except the Bobber remove the crankcase breather hose **(see illustration)**. On 900cc models undo the breather separator bracket screw and detach the separator from the air filter cover.

**3** On all models except the Bobber undo the air filter cover screws and remove the cover **(see illustration)**. Withdraw the filter from the housing, then remove the filter from its holder **(see illustrations)**. Check the condition of the cover seal and fit a new one if necessary.

**4** On the Bobber there is a filter housing on

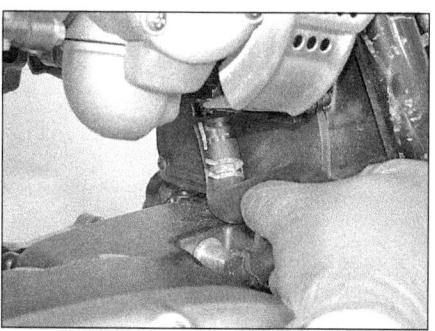

**6.2 Release the clamps and pull the hose off each end**

**6.3a Undo the four screws and remove the cover**

**6.3b Slide the filter and its holder out...**

**6.3c ... then lift the filter from the holder**

**6.4a Undo the screws...**

**6.4b ... and slide the filter out**

**6.5 Air filter housing drain tube (arrowed)**

each side – undo the two screws and withdraw the filter from each side **(see illustrations)**. Check the condition of the filter seals and fit new ones with the new filters if necessary.

**5** Clean out any dirt and residue from the filter housing, and on all models except the Bobber clean the cover, and squeeze the drain tube so that any residue is expelled into the housing and can be wiped up **(see illustration)**.

**6** Fit the new filter(s) into the housing(s) in a reverse of the removal procedure.

**7** Check the crankcase breather hose(s) for cracks and deterioration.

**8** Install all remaining components.

## 7 Fuel system and EVAP system

**Warning: Petrol (gasoline) is extremely flammable, so take extra precautions when you work on any part of the fuel system. Don't smoke or allow open flames or bare light bulbs near the work area, and don't work in a garage where a natural gas-type appliance is present. If you spill any fuel on your skin, rinse it off immediately with soap and water. When you perform any kind of work on the fuel system, wear safety glasses and have a fire extinguisher suitable for a Class B type fire (flammable liquids) on hand.**

### General checks

**1** For best visual access raise the back of the fuel tank (see Chapter 4). Check for signs of fuel leakage from each end of the fuel hose, the fuel rail and injectors, and from the fuel pump assembly base on the underside of the fuel tank **(see illustrations)**.

**2** If there is evidence of leakage from top of the fuel hose make sure the banjo bolt is tight,

and if it is remove the tank, then remove the hose from the pump base and fit new sealing washers. If there is evidence of leakage from the bottom of the hose make sure it is fully pushed onto the fuel rail and cannot be pulled off. If necessary, and every four years regardless of mileage, fit a new hose.

**3** If there is evidence of leakage from between the fuel and the injectors, or the injectors and the intakes, refer to Chapter and fit new injector seals.

**4** If the tank has been leaking from the fuel pump base, tightening the mounting plate bolts may help – remove the tank (see Chapter 4), then rest it upside down on some rag to do this. Slacken the bolts a little at first, then refer to Chapter 4, Section 3 for the tightening sequence and torque setting to ensure the plate is evenly seated. If leaks persist, remove the pump assembly and fit a new seal.

**5** Check all the breather hoses between the tank, roll-over valve, the EVAP system canister, the purge valve and the throttle body(ies) for loose connections, cracks and deterioration, and fit new ones if necessary, and every four years regardless of mileage. Refer to Chapter for more information on the EVAP system.

**7.1a Fuel hose connector to fuel rail**

**7.1b Fuel pump seal (arrowed)**

## Idle speed

6 Engine idle speed is controlled electronically and cannot be adjusted manually. If the idle speed is not steady and correct when the engine is at normal temperature, check the air filter is clean (Section 6), the spark plugs are clean and their gaps are correct (Section 5), the valve clearances are correct (Section 20), and on 1200 engines the throttle bodies are synchronised (balanced). Also check for loose bolts and leaking seals between the throttle body, the intake manifold and the cylinder head on 900 engines, and for loose clamps or bolts between the throttle bodies, the intake ducts and the cylinder head on 1200 engines – any extra air getting in will affect the idle speed. If all is good so far check cylinder compression (see Chapter 2).

7 If no problem can be found take the bike to a Triumph dealer for assessment of the idle speed control system and the throttle system using the diagnostic tester.

## Fuel strainer and filter

8 A fuel filter is incorporated in the fuel pump assembly inside the tank. A new filter should be fitted every 20,000 miles (32,000 km) – refer to Chapter 4 to remove the fuel pump assembly and fit a new filter.

## 8 Throttle body synchronisation – 1200 engines

1 Throttle body synchronisation is the process of adjusting the throttle bodies so they pass the same amount of air to each cylinder. Throttle bodies that are out of synchronisation could result in uneven tickover, decreased fuel mileage, increased engine temperature, less than ideal throttle response and higher vibration levels.

2 The throttle bodies cannot be synchronised in the normal way by measuring the vacuum present in each throttle body using a set of vacuum gauges or a manometer. They can only be synchronised using the Triumph engine management system diagnostic tool. Take the bike to a Triumph dealer.

## 9 Engine management system check

1 The engine management system should be checked for any stored diagnostic fault codes. To do this, either the Triumph diagnostic tool or an EOBD (OBD2) fault code reader is essential – both of these plug into the socket under the seat on all models except the Bobber, and behind the right-hand side panel on the Bobber. If you don't have access to an after-market reader take the bike to a dealer and have them check the system – it should not take them long. Note that an after-market reader will only be able to read any stored fault codes, while the Triumph tool is able to diagnose faults in more detail and adjust operating parameters for fine-tuning. The Triumph tool is however only available to dealers.

2 If any problems with the system occur during use, the malfunction indicator light (MIL) in the instrument cluster will illuminate. If this happens, the management system may switch itself into 'limp home' mode, in which case you should not be left stranded. Depending on the problem, it is possible that you will notice no difference in the running of the motorcycle. In order to diagnose the fault and to turn the MIL off, the diagnostic tool is essential, so again the machine must be taken to a Triumph dealer. If however the fault clears itself the MIL will turn itself off after a pre-determined number of no-fault engine warm-up cycles.

3 Further information on the system, including all tests and checks that can be performed is contained in Chapter 4.

## 10 Clutch

1 Check that the clutch lever operates smoothly and easily.

2 If the lever action is heavy or stiff, disconnect the cable (see Chapter 2) and lubricate it (Section 11). If the inner cable still does not run smoothly in the outer cable, replace the cable with a new one. With the cable disconnected check the action of the lever, and if it is stiff see Step 3. Install the lubricated or new cable (see Chapter 2).

3 If the lever is stiff, remove it (see Chapter 5) and check for damage or distortion, or any other cause, and remedy as necessary. Clean and lubricate the pivot and contact areas (Section 11).

4 If the lever and cable are good, refer to Chapter 2 and check the release mechanism in the clutch cover and the clutch itself.

5 With the clutch operating smoothly, check that the cable is correctly adjusted. Periodic adjustment is necessary to compensate for wear in the clutch plates and stretch of the cable. Check that the amount of freeplay in the clutch lever before the cable moves, measured in terms of the gap between the inner end of the lever and the lever bracket at the front as shown, is within the range given in the Specifications at the beginning of the Chapter **(see illustration)**.

6 If adjustment is required, slacken the adjuster lock-ring, then turn the adjuster in or out of the lever bracket on the handlebar until the required amount of freeplay is obtained **(see illustration)**. To increase freeplay, turn the adjuster clockwise (into the lever bracket). To reduce freeplay, turn the adjuster anti-clockwise (out of the lever bracket). Make sure the cable removal slots in the adjuster and lock-ring do not align with the slot in the lever bracket.

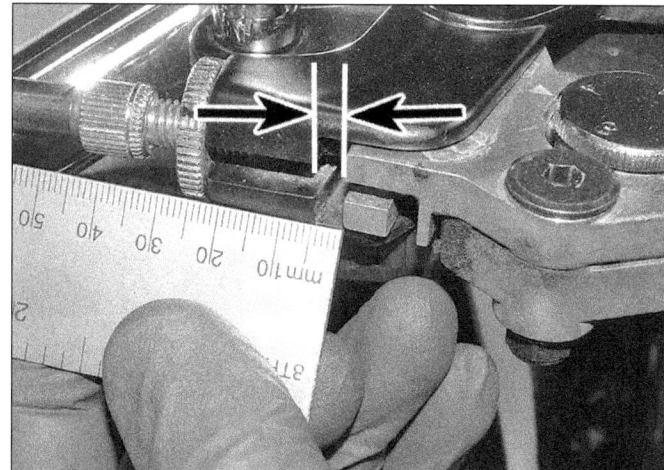

**10.5 Clutch cable freeplay is measured in terms of the gap between lever and bracket before the cable is actuated**

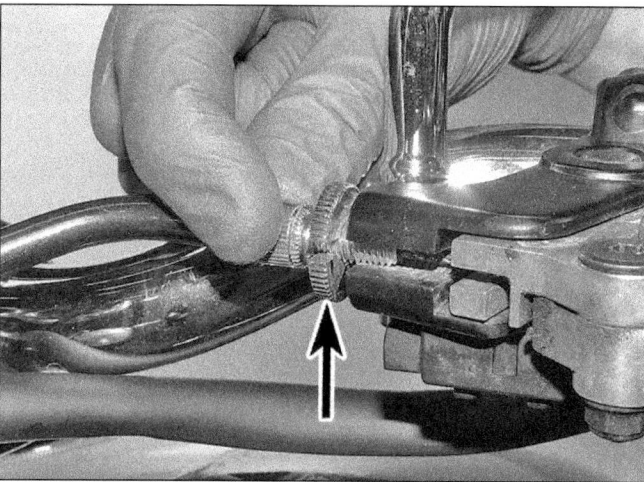

**10.6 Slacken the lockring (arrowed) then turn the adjuster to set the correct freeplay**

10.8 Slacken then reposition the nuts (arrowed) as required

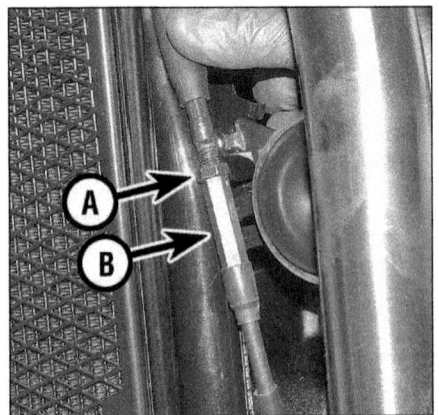

10.9 Clutch cable adjuster locknut (A) and adjuster (B)

10.10 Align the required setting number with the triangle mark (arrowed)

**7** If all the adjustment has been taken up at the lever end, reset the adjuster to give the maximum amount of freeplay, then set the correct amount of freeplay using the adjuster at the lower end of the cable just ahead of the gearchange lever on all models except the Bobber (Step 8), and in the middle of the cable next to the left-hand side of the radiator on the Bobber (Step 9).

**8** On all models except the Bobber, slacken the nuts securing the threaded section of the cable in the bracket, then thread the nuts up or down the cable as required to obtain the correct freeplay **(see illustration)** – thread them down the cable to decrease freeplay and up the cable to increase it. When the correct amount of freeplay has been achieved seat the nuts againstthe bracket and tighten them. Any minor adjustments can now be made at the handlebar end as described above.

**9** On the Bobber slide the rubber boot up off the adjuster, then slacken the adjuster locknut and turn the adjuster as required to obtain the correct freeplay **(see illustration)** – turn it anti-clockwise away from the locknut to decrease freeplay and clockwise towards the locknut to increase it. When the correct amount of freeplay has been achieved tighten the locknut against the adjuster. Any minor adjustments can now

be made at the handlebar end as described above.

**10** The lever has a span adjuster that alters the distance of the lever from the handlebar. Each setting is identified by a number on the adjuster, which must align with the triangle mark on the lever **(see illustration)**. Pull the lever away from the handlebar and turn the adjuster until the setting that best suits the rider is obtained. There are four settings – setting 1 gives the largest span, and setting 4 the smallest. Make sure the selected setting number aligns exactly with the mark to ensure correct engagement of the adjuster setting.

## 11 Stand pivot, lever pivots and cable lubrication

**1** Since the controls, clutch cable and various other components of a motorcycle are exposed to the elements, they should be checked and lubricated periodically to ensure safe and trouble-free operation.

### Pivot points

**2** The clutch and brake lever pivots, footrest pivots, brake pedal pivot, on Bobber and Thruxton models the gearchange lever pivot and linkage, and stand pivot(s) should be lubricated

frequently. In order for the lubricant to be applied where it will do the most good, the component should be removed and cleaned before applying fresh lubricant (see Chapter 5).

**3** Many types of lubricant are available, from a general purpose lithium-based grease to aerosol sprays to dry film lubricants, and there are dedicated cable lubricants. Read the label before purchase to check suitability for the required application. The lubricants recommended by Triumph are listed in the Specifications at the beginning of the Chapter.

**4** If grease is used, apply it sparingly as it may attract dirt (which could cause the controls to bind or wear at an accelerated rate). If an aerosol lubricant is being used, it can be applied to the pivot joint gaps and will usually work its way into the areas where friction occurs, so less disassembly of the component is needed (however it is always better to do so and clean off all corrosion, dirt and old lubricant first). A dry-film lubricant may need to be applied more frequently.

### Clutch cable

**Special tool:** *A cable lubricating adapter is necessary for this procedure.*

**5** To lubricate the cable, disconnect it at its upper end (see Chapter 2), then lubricate it with a pressure adapter and aerosol cable lubricant **(see illustrations)**.

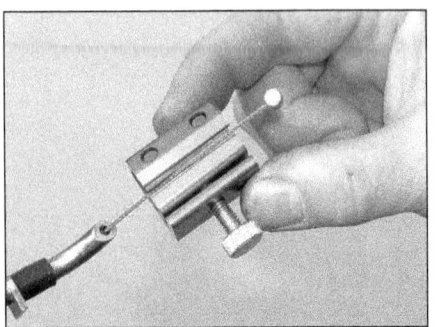

11.5a Fit the cable into the adapter...

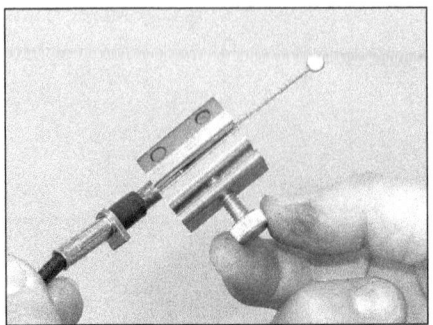

11.5b...and tighten the screw to seal it in...

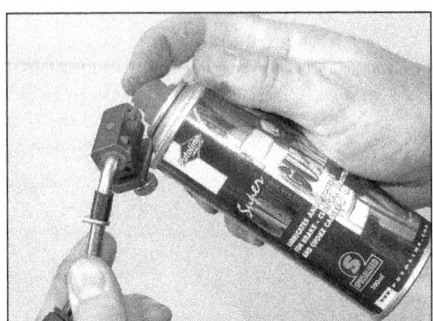

11.5c...then apply the lubricant using the nozzle provided inserted in the hole in the adapter

12.3a Cooling system top (outlet) hose (arrowed)

12.3b Cooling system bottom (inlet) hose (arrowed)

## 12 Cooling system

### Check

 **Warning: The engine must be cool before beginning this procedure.**

1 Check the coolant level in the reservoir (see *Pre-ride checks*).

2 Check the entire cooling system for evidence of leaks.

3 Check each coolant hose for cracks, splits, abrasions and other signs of damage or deterioration **(see illustrations)**. Squeeze each hose at various points. They should feel firm, yet pliable, and return to their original shape when released. If they are cracked or hard, replace them with new ones (see Chapter 3). Check the hose clamps are tight.

4 Check the water pump drain tube exit on the underside of the sump for evidence of

leakage **(see illustration)**. If there is coolant leaking, remove the oil/water pump assembly and replace it with a new one (see Chapter 2) – the pump comes as an assembly and individual parts are not available.

5 Check the thermostat cover and ECT (engine coolant temperature) sensor on the front of the cylinder head for signs of leakage **(see illustration)**. If coolant is leaking from the cover check that the cover bolts are tight, and if there is leakage from around the sensor check it is tight. If they are, fit a new thermostat seal or sensor sealing washer (see Chapter 3). Similarly check the coolant union on the front of the crankcase **(see illustration 12.3b)** – it has an O-ring between it and the engine.

6 Check the radiator for leaks and other damage. Leaks in the radiator leave tell-tale scale deposits or coolant stains on the outside of the core below the leak. If leaks are noted, remove the radiator (see Chapter 3) and have it repaired by a specialist, or fit a new one.

***Caution: Do not use a liquid leak stopping compound to try to repair leaks.***

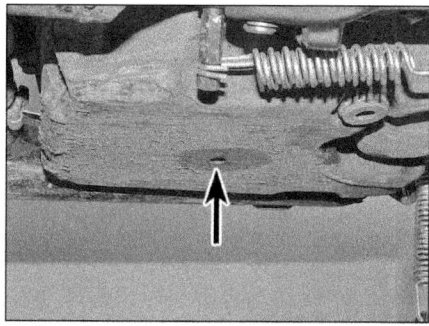

12.4 Water pump drain hole (arrowed)

7 Check the radiator fins for mud, dirt and insects, which may impede the flow of air through the radiator. If the fins are dirty, remove the radiator (see Chapter 3) and clean it, using water or low pressure compressed air directed through the fins from the back. If the fins are bent or distorted, straighten them carefully with a screwdriver **(see illustration)**.

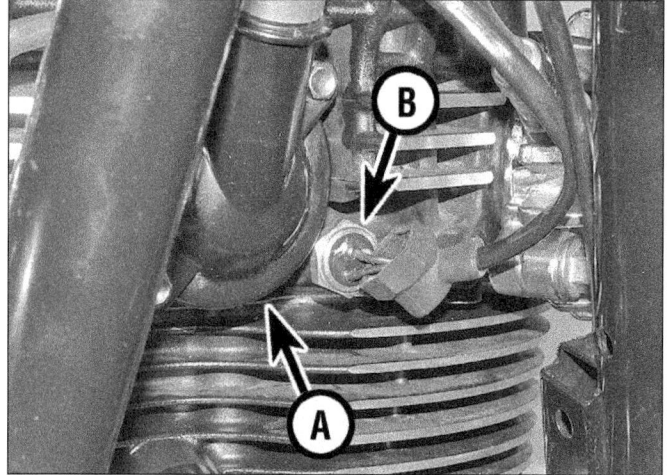

12.5 Thermostat cover (A), ECT sensor (B)

12.7 Check the radiator fins for blockages and carefully straighten any bent ones

12.8 Remove the pressure cap as described

12.9 Using an anti-freeze tester

12.16a Release the clamp using suitable pliers or grips...

12.16b ...or a dedicated clamp tool

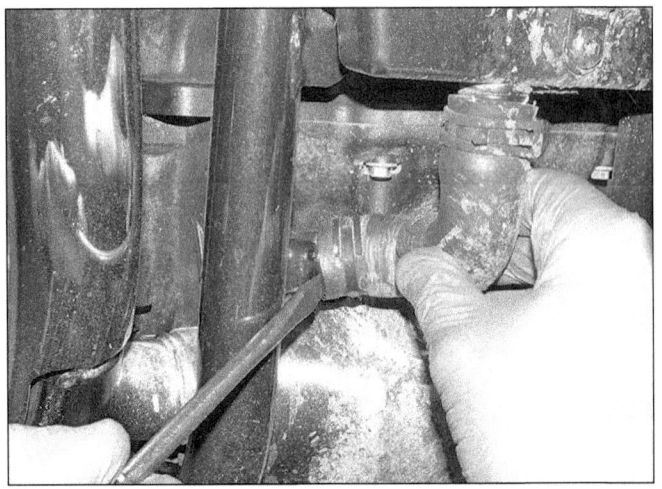

12.16c Ease the hose off the union...

12.16d ...and allow the coolant to drain

Bent or damaged fins will restrict the airflow and impair the efficiency of the radiator causing the engine to overheat. Where there is substantial damage to the radiator's surface area, replace the radiator with a new one.

8 Remove the fuel tank for access to the pressure cap and filler neck (see Chapter 4). Remove the pressure cap from the filler neck by turning it anti-clockwise until it reaches a stop **(see illustration)**. If you hear a hissing sound (indicating that there is still pressure in the system), wait until it stops. Now press down on the cap and continue turning until it can be removed.

9 Check the condition of the coolant in the system. If it is rust-coloured or if accumulations of scale are visible, drain and flush the system and refill with new coolant (see below). Check the antifreeze content of the coolant with an antifreeze tester if available **(see illustration)** – a 50% content should give a reading of 1.084 at 5°C to 1.074 at 25°C, varying accordingly in between. The system must contain the correct coolant mixture (see Specifications) – if the coolant is too weak (i.e. too little anti-freeze giving a low reading – anything below 1.07 when cold and 1.06 when hot) there will not be adequate protection against freezing and corrosion, and if it is too strong the ability to cool the engine is reduced. If the hydrometer indicates an incorrect mixture, drain and refill the system (see below).

10 The function of the pressure cap is crucial to the correct running of the cooling system. Check the cap seal for cracks and other damage. If the coolant level consistently drops and/or the bike overheats, and no evidence of leaks can be found, have the cap pressure checked by a Triumph dealer, or just fit a new filler neck – the cap is not available separately.

11 Fit the cap by turning it clockwise until it reaches the first stop then push down on the cap and continue turning until it will turn no further **(see illustration 12.8)**.

12 Start the engine and let it reach normal operating temperature, then check for leaks again. As the coolant temperature increases beyond normal, the fan should come on automatically and the temperature should begin to drop. If it does not, refer to Chapter 3 and check the fan circuit.

13 If the coolant level is consistently low, and no evidence of leaks can be found, and you have fitted a new filler neck/pressure cap, have the entire system pressure-checked by a Triumph dealer.

## Changing the coolant

⚠️ **Warning: Allow the engine to cool completely before performing this maintenance operation. Coolant contains anti-freeze – don't allow it to come into contact with your skin or the painted surfaces of the motorcycle. Rinse off spills immediately with plenty of water. Antifreeze is highly toxic if ingested.**

*Never leave coolant lying around in an open container or in puddles on the floor; children and pets are attracted by its sweet smell and may drink it. Check with local authorities (councils) about disposing of used coolant – many communities have collection centres where it can be disposed of safely. The antifreeze content of coolant is also combustible, so don't store it near open flames.*

### Draining

14 Refer to *Pre-ride checks* for access and suck out the contents of the reservoir using a large syringe or pump into a suitable container.

15 Remove the radiator pressure cap (see Step 8).

16 Position a suitable container beneath the coolant inlet hose on the front of the crankcase. Release the hose clamp and slide it along the hose, then disconnect the hose and allow the coolant to drain **(see illustrations)**.

### Flushing

17 Flush the system with clean tap water by inserting a garden hose in the radiator filler neck. Allow the water to run through the system until it is clear when it flows out. If there is a lot of rust in the water, remove the radiator (see Chapter 3) and have it professionally cleaned.

### Refilling

18 Fit the hose onto the inlet union and secure it with the clamp **(see illustration 12.16a or b)**.

19 To fill the system it is best to raise the rear wheel off the ground so the filler neck is higher than the top of the radiator – on the T120 use the centrestand, and on other models use a rear paddock stand, or roll the rear wheel onto a block of wood and place a similar block under the sidestand. Fill the system via the filler neck with the specified coolant

**12.19 Fill the system as described**

(see Specifications) **(see illustration)** – pour the coolant in slowly to minimise the amount of air entering the system. When the system appears full, move the bike off its stand then squeeze the hoses and shake the bike slightly to dislodge any air bubbles and dissipate the coolant, then place the bike back on the stand and top the system up.

20 When the system is full (all the way up to the top of the filler neck), fit the pressure cap (see Step 11). Now fill the coolant reservoir to the UPPER level line mark and fit the cap (see *Pre-ride checks*).

21 Install the fuel tank (see Chapter 4). Start the engine and allow it to run for several minutes. Flick the throttle open 3 or 4 times, so that the engine speed rises to approximately 4000 – 5000 rpm, then stop the engine. Any air trapped in the system should bleed back to the top of the radiator, and the level will drop.

22 Wait a few minutes for the coolant to settle, then remove the pressure cap as described in Step 8 and check the coolant level in both the filler neck and the coolant reservoir. If necessary, top up to the base of the filler neck, then fit the pressure cap. Also top up the coolant reservoir to the UPPER level line if necessary.

23 Check the system for leaks.

24 Do not dispose of the old coolant by pouring it down the drain. Instead pour it into a heavy plastic container, cap it tightly and take it into an authorised disposal site or garage.

## 13 Brake system

### Brake system check

1 A routine check of the brake system will ensure that any problems are discovered and remedied before the rider's safety is jeopardised.

2 Check the brake lever and pedal for looseness, rough action, excessive play, bends, and other damage. Replace any damaged parts with new ones (see Chapter 5). Clean and lubricate the lever and pedal pivots if their action is stiff or rough (Section 11).

3 Make sure all brake component fasteners are tight – refer to the torque settings in Chapter 6. Check the fluid level in the reservoirs (see *Pre-ride checks*). Inspect the brake pads for wear (see Steps 9 and 10).

4 If the lever or pedal action is spongy, bleed the brakes (see Chapter 6). Change the brake fluid at the specified service interval.

5 Look for leaks at the brake hose connections to the master cylinders, calipers and modulator, and where the hoses join the banjo fittings, and check for cracks in the hoses and pipes and for corrosion and cracks

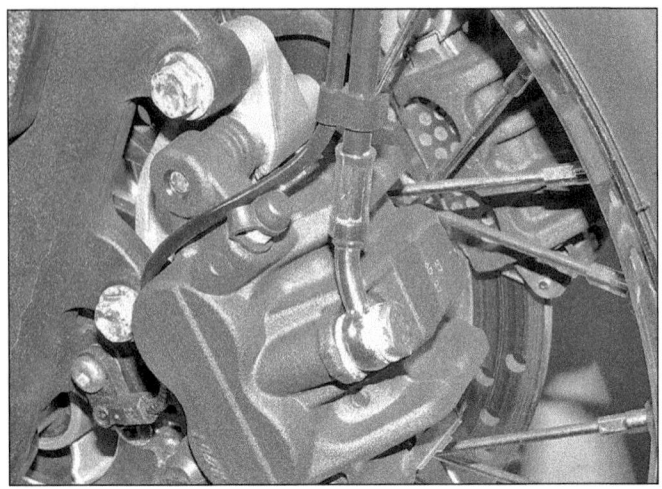

13.5 Check the hoses as described

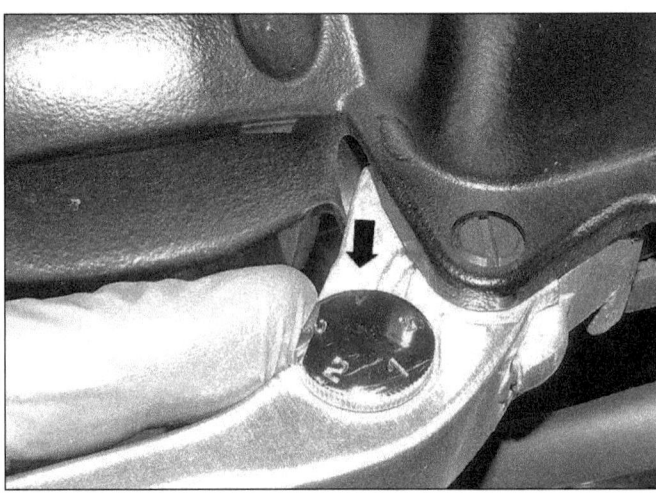

13.8a Adjusting brake lever span on all models except Thruxton R

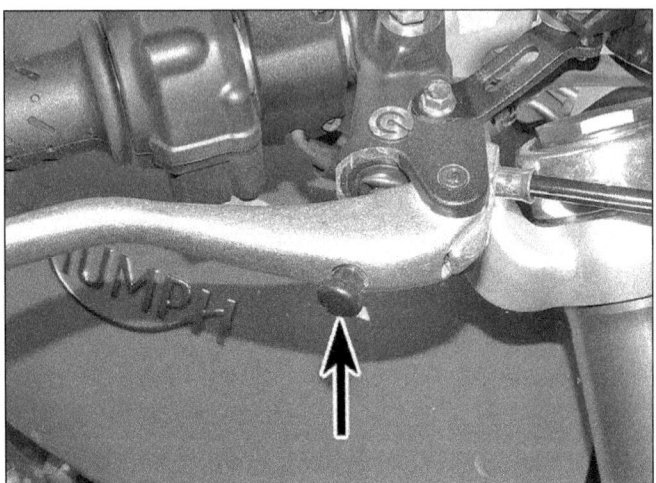

13.8b Front brake lever span adjuster (arrowed) – Thruxton R

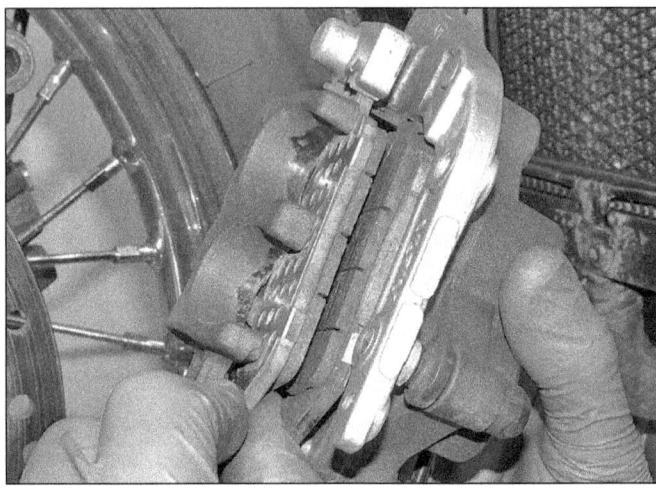

13.9 The brake pads have grooves that act as the wear indicators – caliper shown displaced for clarity

in the banjo unions **(see illustration)**. If there is leakage at a banjo union check that the bolt is tightened to 25 Nm, and if it is disconnect the hose and fit new sealing washers, and check for any cracks in the union or bolt (see Chapter 6). If any hose or pipe shows signs of deterioration or damage replace it with a new one (see Chapter 6). After any work on the brake hoses/pipes the system must be bled (see Chapter 6).

**6** Check the brake master cylinder and caliper seals for signs of leaking fluid (see Step 12).

**7** Make sure the brake light operates when the front brake lever and rear brake pedal are applied. If it fails to operate properly, check the circuit (see Chapter 8).

**8** The front brake lever has a span adjuster that alters the distance of the lever from the handlebar. On all models except the Thruxton R each setting is identified by a number on the adjuster, which must align with the arrowhead on the lever **(see illustration)**. Pull the lever away from the handlebar and turn

the adjuster until the setting that best suits the rider is obtained. There are five settings – setting 1 gives the largest span, and setting 5 the smallest. Make sure the selected setting number aligns exactly with the mark to ensure correct engagement of the adjuster setting. On the Thruxton R there is a span adjuster knob on the front of the lever **(see illustration)** – pull the lever away from the handlebar and turn the knob clockwise to increase span and anti-clockwise to reduce it.

### Brake pad wear check

⚠️ **Warning: The dust created by the brake system is harmful to your health. Never blow it out with compressed air and don't inhale any of it. An approved filtering mask should be worn when working on the brakes.**

**9** The pads fitted as original equipment have grooves in the friction material **(see illustration)**. When the friction material has worn to the bottom of the grooves the pads

must be replaced with new ones (see Chapter 6). If you are in doubt as to the amount of friction material remaining, or to clean the pads, remove them from the caliper (see Chapter 6).

**Note:** *Normal road dirt can be cleaned from the pad friction material, but it is not possible to effectively remove oil or grease – if necessary fit a new set of pads.*

**10** Some after-market pads may use different wear indicators. If so a minimum thickness of 1.5 mm is specified for the friction material – if required remove the pads and measure the amount of friction material remaining.

### Brake fluid change

**11** The brake fluid should be changed every two years, or whenever a master cylinder or caliper overhaul is carried out. Refer to Chapter 6 for details. Make sure that all the old fluid is pumped from the system. Check the levels in the fluid reservoirs and test the brakes before riding the motorcycle.

## Brake caliper and master cylinder seals

**12** Brake system seals will deteriorate over a period of time and lose their effectiveness. Old master cylinder seals will cause sticky operation of the brake lever or pedal or fluid leakage; old caliper seals will cause the pistons to stick or fluid leakage. The seals should be replaced with new ones if defects are evident (see Chapter 6).

## 14 Wheels, wheel bearings and tyres

### Wheels

#### Cast alloy wheels

**1** Cast alloy wheels are virtually maintenance free, but they should be kept clean and checked periodically for cracks and other damage. Never attempt to repair cast wheels – if damaged they must be replaced with new ones. Also check wheel run-out and alignment (see Chapter 6). Check that the wheel balance weights are fixed firmly to the wheel rim. If you suspect that a weight has fallen off, have the wheel rebalanced by a motorcycle tyre specialist.

#### Steel spoked wheels

**2** Visually check the spokes for damage and corrosion. A broken or bent spoke must be replaced with a new one immediately because the load taken by it will be transferred to adjacent spokes which may in turn fail. Check the tension in each spoke by tapping each one lightly with a screwdriver and noting the sound produced – each should make the same sound of the correct pitch – properly tensioned spokes will make a sharp pinging sound, loose ones will produce a lower pitch dull sound, and tight ones will be higher pitched. If a spoke needs adjustment turn the adjuster at the rim using a spoke adjustment tool or a 6 mm open-ended spanner **(see illustration)**.

**3** Unevenly tensioned spokes will promote rim/hub misalignment and excessive runout – refer to information on wheel runout in Chapter 6 and seek the advice of a Triumph dealer or wheel building specialist if the wheel needs realigning, which it may well do if many spokes are unevenly tensioned. Check that any wheel balance weights are fixed firmly to the wheel rim. If you suspect that a weight has fallen off, have the wheel rebalanced by a motorcycle tyre specialist.

### Wheel bearings

**Note:** *Avoid using a high pressure cleaner around the wheel hubs. Water may penetrate the wheel bearing seals and wash out the grease, leading to corrosion and premature bearing failure.*

**4** Wheel bearings will wear over a period of time and result in handling problems.

**5** Support the motorcycle so the wheel being checked is off the ground. Check for any play in the bearings by pushing and pulling each wheel against the hub **(see illustration)**. Also rotate the wheels and check that they spin smoothly and quietly, but do not mistake brake pad-to-disc noise for noisy bearings.

**6** If any play is detected in the hub, or if the wheel does not rotate smoothly (and this is not due to brake or chain drag), the wheel must be removed for thorough inspection of the bearings (see Chapter 6).

### Tyres

**7** Check the tyre condition and tread depth thoroughly (see *Pre-ride checks*).

**8** Check that the valve cap is in place and tight **(see illustration)**. On the Street Twin and Street Cup (both have cast alloy wheels)

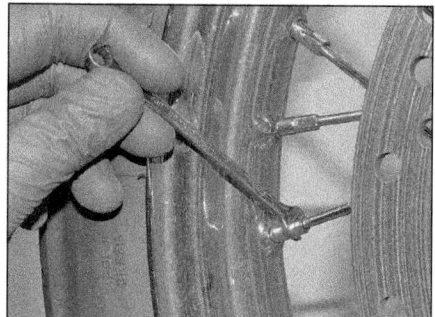

**14.2 Adjusting the tension of a spoke**

check the tyre valve rubber seal for signs of damage or deterioration and have it replaced with a new one if necessary. Check the valve itself for signs of damage. If tyre deflation occurs and it is not due to a slow puncture the valve core may be loose or it could be leaking past the seal – remove the cap and make sure the core is tight using a core removal tool (sometimes incorporated in the valve cap). If it is tight then it could be leaking – unscrew the core from the valve housing and thread a new one in its place. A valve core tool can be made quite easily by cutting a slot into the threaded end of a bolt using a hacksaw – the bolt must fit inside the valve housing and the slot must be the correct thickness to fit over the top of the core so it seats around the flats.

## 15 Suspension

**1** The suspension components must be maintained in top operating condition to ensure rider safety. Loose, worn or damaged suspension parts decrease the motorcycle's stability and control.

**14.5 Checking for play in the wheel bearings**

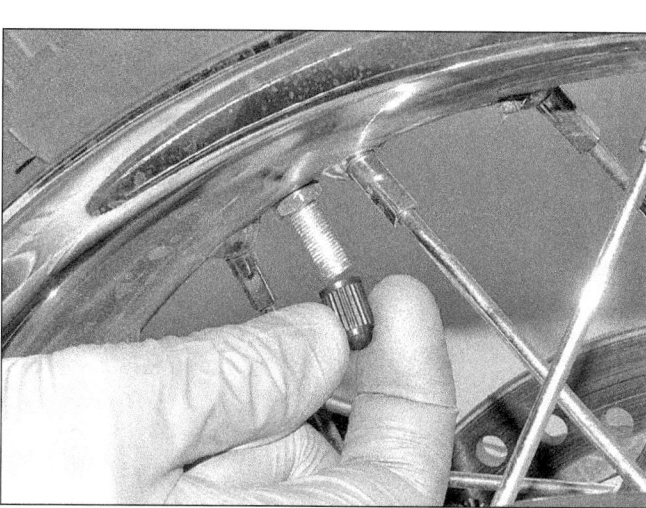

**14.8 Make sure a valve cap is fitted**

**15.3 Pump the forks to check their action**

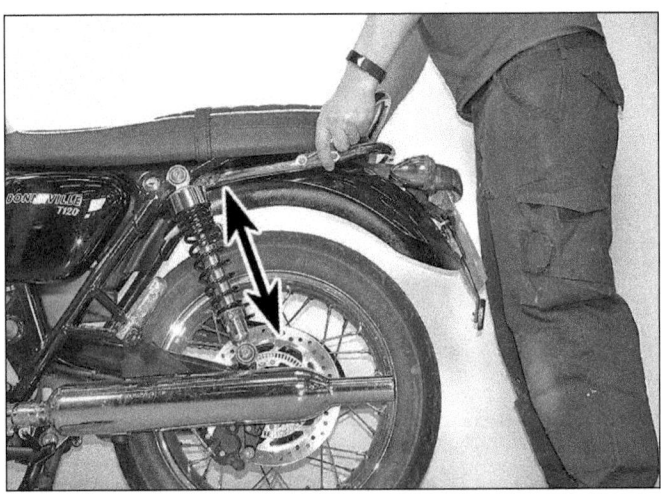

**15.6 Pump the rear suspension to check its action**

**2** Check the tightness of all suspension nuts and bolts to be sure none have worked loose, referring to the torque settings given in Chapter 5.

### Front suspension check

**3** While standing alongside the motorcycle, apply the front brake and push on the handlebars to compress the forks several times **(see illustration)**. Check that they move up and down smoothly without binding. If binding is felt, the forks should be disassembled and inspected (see Chapter 5).
**4** On all models except the Thruxton R and Street Cup lift the bottom of the fork gaiter. Inspect the fork inner tubes for signs of scratches, corrosion and pitting, and oil leaks. Carefully lever the dust seal from the top of each fork outer tube on all models except Thruxton R, and from the bottom on Thruxton R, using a flat-bladed screwdriver and inspect the area around the fork seals. Any scratches, corrosion and pitting will cause premature seal failure. If the damage is excessive, new tubes

should be installed. If there is oil leakage new seals must be fitted – seals can leak even if the tube itself is in perfect condition. If there is evidence of corrosion between the seal retaining ring and its groove in the fork outer tube fit new dust seals as it means water is getting past them. Refer to Chapter 5 for all procedures on the forks.

### Rear suspension check

**Note:** *Avoid using a high pressure cleaner around the swingarm pivots and the suspension linkage and shock absorber pivots. Water may penetrate the bearing seals and wash out the grease, leading to corrosion and premature bearing failure.*
**5** Inspect the rear shock(s) for fluid leaks and loose mountings. If a shock is leaking, generally a new one should be fitted and on twin shock models both shocks should be renewed at the same time (see Chapter 5). Note that on the Thruxton R which has Ohlins shocks, seek advice from a suspension specialist about having them rebuilt.

**6** With the aid of an assistant to support the bike, compress the rear suspension several times **(see illustration)**. It should move up and down freely without binding. If any binding is felt, the worn or faulty component must be identified and checked. The problem could be due to either the shock absorber(s), the suspension linkage components on the Bobber, or the swingarm components (see Chapter 5).
**7** Support the motorcycle so that the rear wheel is off the ground. Grasp the swingarm and rock it from side to side – there should be no discernible movement at the ends of the swingarm **(see illustration)**. If there is a little movement or a slight clicking can be heard, inspect the tightness of all the rear suspension mounting bolts and nuts, referring to the torque settings specified at the beginning of Chapter 5, and re-check for movement.
**8** Next, grasp the top of the rear wheel and pull it upwards – there should be no discernible freeplay before the shock absorber(s) begins to compress **(see illustration)**. Any freeplay

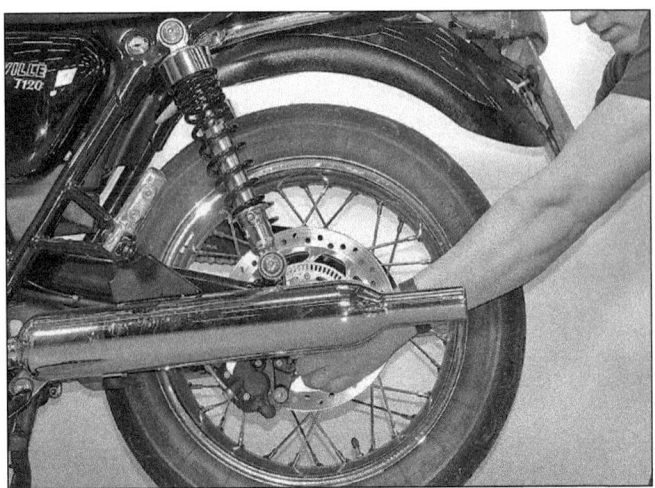

**15.7 Checking for play in the swingarm bearings**

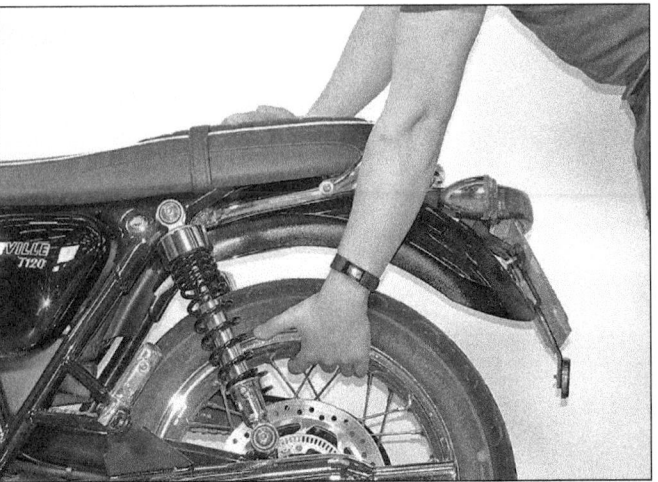

**15.8 Checking for play in the suspension bearings and shock mounts**

**16.4 Checking for play in the steering head bearings**

**16.6a Rest the handlebars as shown**

felt in either check indicates worn bearings in the swingarm, or the suspenion linkage on the Bobber, or worn shock absorber mountings. The worn components must be identified and checked (see Chapter 5).

### Front fork oil change

**9** The fork oil will degrade over a period of time and lose its damping qualities, and should be changed at the specified service interval. Refer to Chapter 5 for details of front fork removal, oil draining and refilling. The forks do not need to be completely disassembled to change the oil.

### Rear suspension bearing lubrication

**10** Over a period of time the grease in the swingarm bearings (including the suspension linkage arm bearings on the Bobber) will be washed out if pressure washers are used or will harden allowing the ingress of dirt and water. Regreasing requires the removal of the components (see Chapter 5).

## 16 Steering head bearings

**1** Steering head bearings can become dented, rough or loose during normal use of the machine – wear or damage will be noticeable in the way the bike handles. In extreme cases, worn or loose steering head bearings can cause steering wobble – a condition that is potentially dangerous. Check the bearings and adjust them if necessary as described below.

### Check

**2** Support the motorcycle in an upright position using the centrestand where fitted, or an auxiliary stand, and raise the front wheel

off the ground by placing a support under the engine.

**3** Point the front wheel straight-ahead and slowly move the handlebars from side-to-side. Any dents or roughness in the bearing races will be felt and the bars will not move smoothly and freely. Again point the wheel straight-ahead, and tap the front of the wheel to one side. The wheel should 'fall' under its own weight to the limit of its lock, indicating that the bearings are not too tight (take into account the restriction that the cables, brake hose and wiring have). Check for similar movement to the other side.

**4** Next, grasp the forks and try to pull and push them forward and backward **(see illustration)**. Any looseness in the steering head bearings will be felt as front-to-rear movement of the forks. If play is felt in the bearings, adjust the steering head as follows.

> **HAYNES HINT** *Make sure you are not mistaking any movement between the bike and stand, or between the stand and the ground, for freeplay in the bearings. Do not pull and push the forks too hard – a gentle movement is all that is needed. Freeplay between the fork tubes due to worn bushes can also be misinterpreted as steering head bearing play – do not confuse the two.*

### Adjustment

**Special tool:** *Either the Triumph peg spanner, Part No. T3880023, or its equivalent bought commercially, is useful, but not essential, for slackening and tightening the adjuster nut and its locknut. The advantage of using a peg spanner is that the correct torque settings can be applied. If you are not using the peg spanner you need a C-spanner of the*

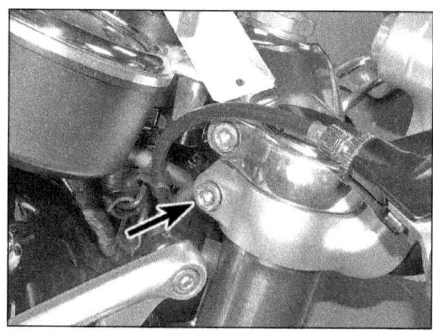

**16.6b Slacken the handlebar clamp bolt (arrowed) on each side**

*correct size, or an adjustable one, and the bearings must be adjusted by feel. You also need a 37mm socket or spanner to loosen and tighten the steering stem nut – this is not a common size, but they are available from good tool suppliers, or you can use a large adjustable spanner as shown* **(see illustration 16.8)**. *The socket is preferable as the nut can then be tightened to the correct torque.*

**Caution: Take great care not to apply excessive pressure when adjusting the bearings because this will cause premature bearing failure.**

**5** Remove the fuel tank to avoid the possibility of damage should a tool slip (see Chapter 4).

**6** On all models except the Thruxton and Thruxton R displace the handlebars from the top yoke (see Chapter 5), and rest them on some rag **(see illustration)**. If you are using a spanner to slacken and tighten the steering stem nut, on the T100, T120, Street Twin, Street Cup and Scrambler you may also need to remove the handlebar holders and the top rubber dampers for clearance, depending on the type of spanner being used (see Chapter 5). On Thruxton and Thruxton R models slacken the handlebar clamp bolts **(see illustration)**.

**16.7 Slacken the clamp bolt (arrowed) on each side**

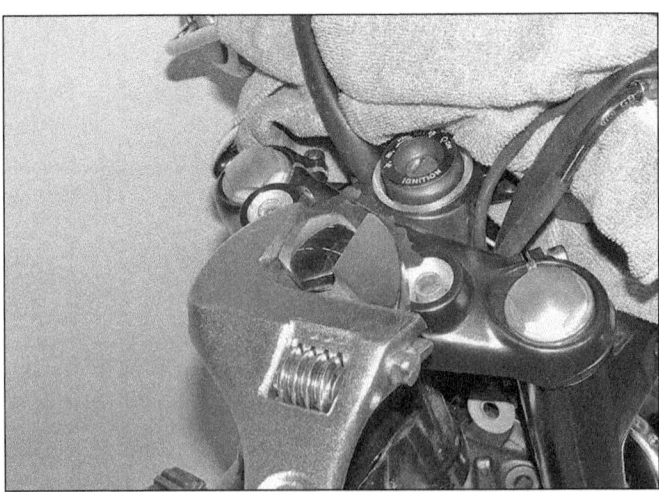

**16.8 Use an adjustable spanner to unscrew the steering stem nut if you don't have a 37mm socket or spanner**

**16.9 Lift the top yoke up**

**7** Slacken the fork clamp bolts in the top yoke **(see illustration)**.

**8** Stick some masking tape onto the top yoke and around the steering stem nut to protect its finish. Unscrew the nut, and on the Bobber remove the washer **(see illustration)**.

**9** Ease the top yoke up **(see illustration)**-

if you are using the Triumph peg spanner or equivalent to apply the correct torque settings to the adjuster nut then you need to displace the yoke completely off the stem and forks and lay it aside, but if you are using a C-spanner to adjust the bearings by feel then you only need raise the yoke up to the top of the stem and forks, not off them, just to give enough clearance. The instrument bracket is bolted to the underside of the yoke and so movement of the yoke is restricted by this, but if required you can release the bracket from the yoke. On the Street Twin, Street Cup, Scrambler, Thruxton and Thruxton R the headlight brackets locate in the underside of the yoke, and once the yoke is clear there may be some movement in the headlight assembly.

**10** Using either a peg spanner or a C-spanner, unscrew the locknut, then lift off the tabbed washer **(see illustration)**- remove them if the yoke has been displaced, or just hold them clear of the adjuster nut if not.

**11** If using a peg spanner, slacken the

adjuster nut slightly, then with the tool fitted to a torque wrench, apply a torque of 40 Nm to the adjuster nut – this will preload the bearings. Now slacken the nut and tighten it to the final torque setting of 15 Nm.

**12** If using a C-spanner slacken the adjuster nut slightly until pressure is just released, then tighten it until all freeplay is removed, then tighten it a little more **(see illustration)**. This pre-loads the bearings. Now slacken the nut, then tighten it again, setting it so that all freeplay is just removed yet the steering is able to move freely from side to side. To do this tighten the nut only a little at a time, and after each tightening repeat the checks outlined above (see Steps 3 and 4) until the bearings are correctly set. The object is to set the adjuster nut so that the bearings are under a very light loading, just enough to remove any freeplay.

**13** If removed fit the tabbed washer, locating the tab in the slot, and thread the locknut on, and if not seat the washer against the

**16.10 Unscrew the locknut using a C-spanner**

**16.12 Using a C-spanner to adjust the steering head bearings**

16.14a Where applicable make sure the rubber on the top of each bracket locates in the hole in the underside of the top yoke (arrow – Thruxton R shown)

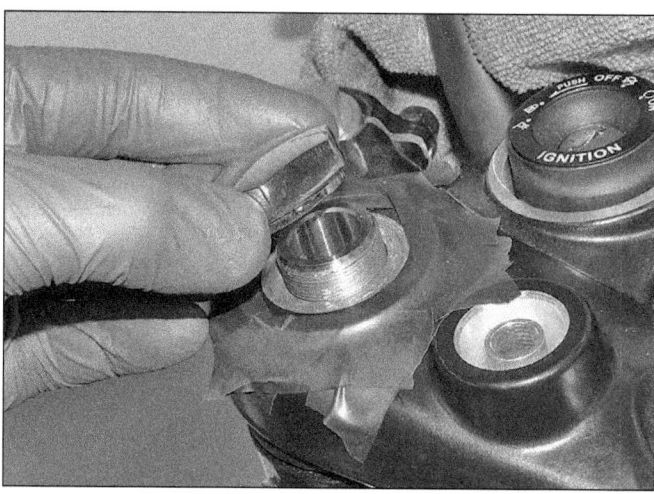

16.14b Fit the steering stem nut and tighten to the specified torque

adjuster nut and thread the locknut down **(see illustration 16.10)**. Tighten the locknut to 40 Nm if the tool is available, or using a C-spanner if not – the tabbed lockwasher is there to prevent the adjuster nut turning with it.

**14** Seat the top yoke **(see illustration 16.9)**, making sure the instrument bracket has been fitted if it was displaced, and the headlight bracket tops seat correctly on the Street Twin, Street Cup, Scrambler, Thruxton and Thruxton R **(see illustration)**. Fit the steering stem nut, along with the washer on the Bobber, and tighten it to 90 Nm **(see illustration)**. Now tighten the fork clamp bolts to 24 Nm on all models except the Thruxton and Thruxton R, and to 20 Nm on the Thruxton and Thruxton R **(see illustration 16.7)**.

**15** Fit the handlebar holder rubbers, washers and holders if removed, then relocate the handlebars, following the procedure and applying the torque settings for your model in Chapter 5.

**16** Install the fuel tank (see Chapter 4).

## *Lubrication*

**17** Triumph specify that the steering head bearings must be re-greased at every

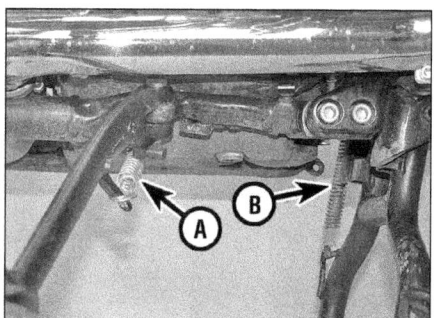

17.1 Sidestand springs (A) and centrestand springs (B)

second check and adjustment service interval. Re-greasing involves removing the steering stem – follow the procedure in Chapter 5 to remove and install the stem and adjust the bearings as described above on reassembly.

## 17 Sidestand and starter safety circuit

**1** The sidestand return springs, and on the T120 the centrestand return springs, must be capable of retracting the stand(s) fully, and holding them retracted when the motorcycle is in use **(see illustration)**. If a spring has sagged or broken it must be replaced with a new one.

**2** Lubricate the stand pivot regularly (Section 11).

**3** The sidestand switch prevents the motorcycle being started if it is in gear and the stand is down, and cuts the engine if the stand is put down while it is running and in gear. Check its operation by shifting the transmission into neutral, retracting the stand, pulling the clutch lever in and starting the engine. Pull in the clutch lever again and select a gear. Extend the sidestand. The engine should stop as the sidestand is extended. If the sidestand switch does not operate as described, check its circuit (see Chapter 8).

**4** The neutral and clutch switches are also part of the same circuit – to check them, make sure the engine can be started with the sidestand in either position, as long as the transmission is in neutral and the clutch is pulled in, and cannot be started with transmission in gear, even with the stand up and the clutch pulled in. If any of the situations are not as stated, check the circuit (see Chapter 8).

## 18 Nuts, bolts and fasteners

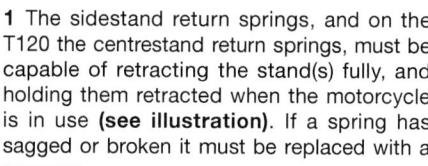

**1** Since vibration of the machine tends to loosen fasteners, all nuts, bolts, screws, etc. should be periodically checked for tightness.

**2** Pay particular attention to the following:
- Brake caliper and master cylinder mounting bolts
- Brake hose banjo bolts and caliper bleed valves
- Brake disc bolts
- Exhaust system bolts/nuts
- Engine oil drain plug
- Engine mounting bolts/nuts
- Lever and pedal bolts
- Handlebar clamp bolts
- Footrest bracket and sidestand pivot and bracket bolts
- Shock absorber and suspension linkage mounting bolts/nuts
- Swingarm pivot bolt nut
- Front fork clamp bolts (top and bottom yoke) and fork top bolts
- Steering stem nut
- Front axle and axle clamp bolt(s)
- Rear axle nut
- Front and rear sprocket nuts
- Chain adjuster locknuts

**3** If a torque wrench is available, use it along with the torque settings given in the Specifications at the beginning of this and other Chapters.

## 19 Battery check

**1** A sealed maintenance-free battery is fitted on all models.

**20.5 This shows both camshaft lobes pointing away from the rollers on the rockers so there is no contact between them, so all four valve clearances for that cylinder can be checked at the same time**

**20.6 Measure the valve clearance using a feeler gauge**

*Caution: Do not attempt to open the battery as resulting damage will mean it will be unfit for further use.*

**2** All that should be done is to check that the terminals are clean and tight and that the casing is not damaged or leaking. See Chapter 8 for further details.

**3** If the machine is not in regular use, disconnect the battery and give it a refresher charge every month to six weeks (see Chapter 8, Section 4).

## 20 Valve clearances

**1** The engine must be cold for this maintenance procedure.

**2** Remove the spark plugs (Section 5).

**3** Remove the valve cover (see Chapter 2).

**4** The cylinders are numbered 1 – left, 2 – right, viewed as normally seated on the bike. Each cylinder has four valves, two on the intake side and two on the exhaust. Each pair of valves is actuated by one rocker. Make a chart or sketch of all valve positions so that a note of each clearance can be made against the relevant valve.

**5** To check the valve clearances the engine must be turned so that the valves being checked are closed. The valves are closed when the camshaft lobe acting on the rocker that actuates the two valves being checked is pointing down away from the roller on the rocker, so there is no contact between them **(see illustration)**. At this point there is a clearance between the rocker arms and the shims on the tops of the valves. When the piston is at TDC on its compression stroke both the intake and exhaust valves are closed, so all four valves for that cylinder can be checked at the same time. The engine is turned by selecting a high gear and turning the rear wheel in its normal direction of rotation – this can be done by rolling the bike forwards, or by supporting the bike on a paddock stand, or the centrestand on the T120, and turning the wheel by hand.

**6** Check the clearances on each pair of valves in turn. Insert a feeler gauge of the same thickness as the correct valve clearance (see Specifications) between the rocker arm and the shim of each valve and check that it is a firm sliding fit **(see illustration)** – you should feel a slight drag when you pull the gauge out. If not, use the feeler gauges to measure

the exact clearance. Record the measured clearance on your chart.

**7** When all clearances have been measured and recorded, identify whether the clearance on any valve falls outside that specified. If it does, the shim must be replaced with one of a thickness that will restore the correct clearance.

**8** Shim replacement requires removal of the rocker that actuates the relevant valve – before removing a rocker make sure the engine is turned so that the cam lobe that actuates that rocker is pointing down as for the clearance check. Only remove one rocker at at time, and complete the shim replacement procedure for the shims relevant to that rocker and refit the rocker before changing any other shim(s). Place rags over the spark plug holes and the cam chain tunnel to prevent a shim accidentally dropping into the engine on removal.

**9** To remove a rocker unscrew the two bolts and lift the shaft and rocker off **(see illustrations)**.

**10** Remove the shim from the top of the valve using either a magnet, a small screwdriver with a dab of grease on it (the shim will stick to the grease), or a screwdriver and a pair of pliers **(see illustration)**. Do not allow the shim to fall into the engine.

**20.9a Unscrew the bolts...**

**20.9b ... and remove the rocker assembly**

**20.10 Removing the shim using a magnet**

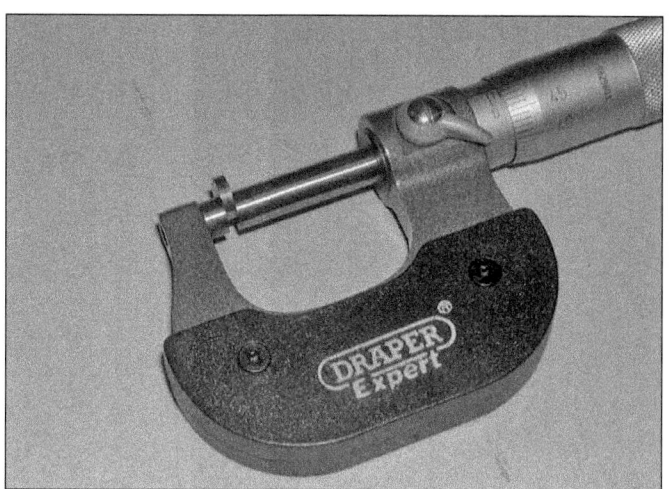

20.11 Measure the shim using a micrometer to confirm its size

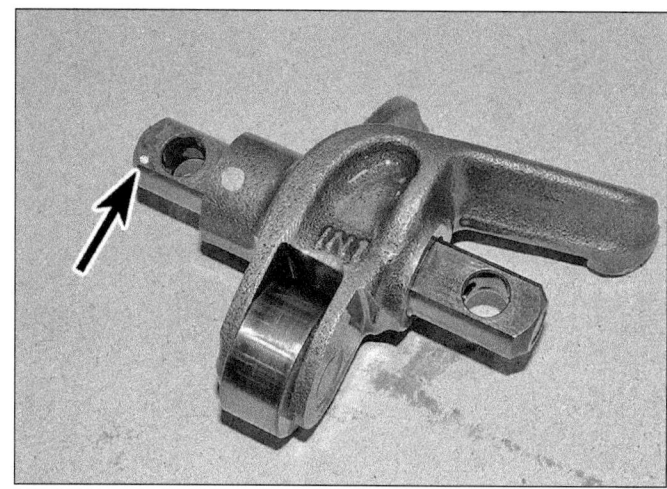

20.14 Align the shaft in the rocker so the punch mark (arrowed) faces up and is on the inner side

**11** Measure the thickness of the shim using a micrometer **(see illustration)**. A size should be marked on the lower face of the shim (though it could have rubbed off) – a shim marked 275 is 2.75 mm thick, but the shim must be measured anyway to allow for wear.

**12** If the measured clearance is greater than the upper limit of the range given, you need a thicker shim, and if it is less than the lower limit of the range you need a thinner shim. Calculate by how much thicker or thinner than the existing shim the replacement shim needs to be to bring the clearance to the middle of the specified range, noting that shims are available in 0.025 mm increments from 1.725 mm to 3.100 mm. For example, if the measured clearance on an intake valve is 0.19 mm, this is 0.1 mm greater than the middle of the range (which is 0.09 mm). So add 0.1 mm to the the size of the current shim to get the size of the required replacement shim. If the required replacement size does not correspond exactly to an available size, round it up or down to the next size that is nearest to bring it closest to the middle of the range.

**13** Obtain the replacement shim, then lubricate it with molybdenum disulphide oil (a 50/50 mix of molybdenum disulphide grease and engine oil) and fit it into its recess in the top of the valve, with the size marking facing down **(see illustration 20.10)**. Check that the shim is correctly seated.

**14** Align the shaft in the rocker so the punch mark faces up and is on the inner side of the rocker so when installed it will face toward the cam chain sprocket **(see illustration)**. Position the rocker and the shaft, double-checking the punch mark on the shaft faces up and toward the sprocket **(see illustration 20.9b)**. Fit the bolts and tighten to 10 Nm, tightening the inner bolt first **(see illustration 20.9a)**.

**15** Repeat the process for any other valves until all the clearances are correct.

**16** Rotate the rear wheel several turns to seat the new shim(s), then check the clearances again.

**17** Install the valve cover (see Chapter 2) and the spark plugs (Section 5).

# Chapter 2
## Engine, clutch and transmission

## Contents

## Degrees of difficulty

| **Easy,** suitable for novice with little experience 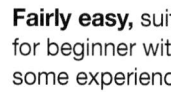 | **Fairly easy,** suitable for beginner with some experience | **Fairly difficult,** suitable for competent DIY mechanic | **Difficult,** suitable for experienced DIY mechanic | **Very difficult,** suitable for expert DIY or professional  |
|---|---|---|---|---|

## Specifications

### General

| | |
|---|---|
| Type | Four-stroke 8-valve parallel twin |
| Capacity | 900 or 1200 cc |
| Bore | |
| 900 engine | 84.6 mm |
| 1200 engine | 97.6 mm |
| Stroke | 80.0 mm |
| Compression ratio | |
| 900 engine | 10.55 to 1 |
| 1200 engine | |
| T120 and Bobber | 10.0 to 1 |
| Thruxton and Thruxton R | 11.0 to 1 |
| Cylinder numbering | No. 1 – left, No. 2 – right |
| Cooling system | Liquid cooled |
| Clutch | Wet multi-plate |
| Transmission | |
| 900 engine | Five-speed constant mesh |
| 1200 engine | Six-speed constant mesh |
| Final drive | Chain and sprockets |
| Camshaft | SOHC, chain-driven |

## Camshaft

| | |
|---|---|
| Journal diameter | 22.930 to 22.960 mm |
| Holder diameter | 23.000 to 23.021 mm |
| Journal oil clearance | |
|   Standard | 0.040 to 0.091 mm |
|   Service limit | 0.130 mm |
| Runout (max) | 0.015 mm |
| End-float | 0.05 to 0.20 mm |

## Cylinder head

| | |
|---|---|
| Warpage (max) | 0.03 mm |

## Valves, guides and springs

| | Standard | Service limit |
|---|---|---|
| Valve clearances | see Chapter 1 | |
| Intake valve | | |
|   Stem diameter | 4.975 to 4.990 mm | 4.965 mm |
|   Guide bore diameter | 5.000 to 5.015 mm | 5.043 mm |
|   Stem-to-guide clearance | 0.010 to 0.040 mm | 0.078 mm |
|   Seat width on head | 1.000 to 1.100 mm | 1.500 mm |
|   Seat width on valve | 1.50 to 1.85 mm | |
| Exhaust valve | | |
|   Stem diameter | 4.970 to 4.980 mm | 4.960 mm |
|   Guide bore diameter | 5.000 to 5.015 mm | 5.043 mm |
|   Stem-to-guide clearance | | |
|     900 engine | 0.030 to 0.060 mm | 0.098 mm |
|     1200 engine | 0.020 to 0.045 mm | 0.083 mm |
|   Seat width on head | 1.200 to 1.300 mm | 1.700 mm |
|   Seat width on valve | 1.50 to 1.85 mm | |
| Valve spring free length | 49.9 mm | |
| Valve spring load at length | 204 to 224 N at 39.5 mm | |

## Clutch

| | |
|---|---|
| Friction plates | |
|   Quantity | 8 |
|   Thickness | |
|     Standard | 2.90 to 3.10 mm |
|     Service limit | 2.80 mm |
|   Warpage (max) | 0.20 mm |
| Plain plates | |
|   Quantity | 7 |
|   Warpage (max) | 0.15 mm |
| Clutch plate pack height | 37.34 to 38.34 mm |

## Lubrication system

| | Standard | Service limit |
|---|---|---|
| Engine oil pressure (engine warm) | 43.5 to 52.2 psi (3.0 to 3.6 Bar) @ 3500 rpm | |
| Oil pump | | |
|   Inner rotor tip-to-outer rotor clearance | 0.15 mm | 0.20 mm |
|   Outer rotor-to-housing clearance | 0.15 to 0.239 mm | 0.369 mm |
|   Rotor end-float | 0.04 to 0.09 mm | 0.12 mm |

## Cylinder bores

**900 engine**

| Diameter | Standard | Service limit |
|---|---|---|
|   10 mm from top | 84.585 to 84.597 mm | 84.647 mm |
|   97 mm from top | 84.600 to 84.615 mm | 84.665 mm |

**1200 engine**

| Diameter | Standard | Service limit |
|---|---|---|
|   10 mm from top | 97.585 to 97.601 mm | not available |
|   97 mm from top | 97.600 to 97.615 mm | not available |

## Pistons

| | Standard | Service limit |
|---|---|---|
| Piston diameter (10 mm up from skirt, at 90° to piston pin axis) | | |
|   900 engine | 84.570 to 84.580 mm | 84.530 mm |
|   1200 engine | 97.570 to 97.580 mm | 97.830 mm |
| Piston pin diameter | 20.995 to 21.000 mm | 20.985 mm |
| Piston pin bore diameter in piston | 21.004 to 21.012 mm | 21.040 mm |

## Piston rings

### 900 engine

| Ring end gap (installed) | Standard | Service limit |
|---|---|---|
| Top ring | 0.093 to 0.281 mm | 0.401 mm |
| Second ring | 0.253 to 0.441 mm | 0.561 mm |
| Oil ring side rail | 0.053 to 0.341 mm | 0.481 mm |

Ring groove width
| | | |
|---|---|---|
| Top and second rings | 1.01 to 1.03 mm | |
| Oil ring | 2.01 to 2.03 mm | |
| Piston ring-to-groove clearance – top and second rings | 0.02 to 0.06 mm | 0.075 mm |

### 1200 engine

| Ring end gap (installed) | Standard | Service limit |
|---|---|---|
| Top ring | 0.183 to 0.383 mm | 0.503 mm |
| Second ring | 0.353 to 0.553 mm | 0.673 mm |
| Oil ring side rail | 0.153 to 0.703 mm | 0.843 mm |

Ring groove width
| | |
|---|---|
| Top ring | 1.21 to 1.24 mm |
| Second ring | 1.01 to 1.03 mm |
| Oil ring | 2.51 to 2.53 mm |

| Piston ring-to-groove clearance | Standard | Service limit |
|---|---|---|
| Top ring | 0.02 to 0.07 mm | 0.085 mm |
| Second ring | 0.02 to 0.06 mm | 0.075 mm |

## Crankshaft and main bearings

| | Standard | Service limit |
|---|---|---|
| Main bearing oil clearance | 0.018 to 0.042 mm | 0.10 mm |
| Main bearing journal diameter | 43.108 mm | 43.052 mm |
| Crankpin journal diameter | 37.984 to 38.000 mm | 37.947 mm |
| Crankshaft end-float | 0.05 to 0.20 mm | 0.50 mm |
| Crankshaft run-out | 0.02 mm | 0.035 mm |

## Connecting rods and bearings

| | Standard | Service limit |
|---|---|---|
| Small-end diameter | 21.016 to 21.029 mm | 21.039 mm |
| Big-end side clearance | 0.15 to 0.30 mm | 0.50 mm |
| Big-end bearing oil clearance | 0.036 to 0.061 mm | 0.100 mm |

## Transmission

Gear ratios (no. of teeth)
| | |
|---|---|
| Primary reduction | 1.26 to 1 (93/74) |

Final reduction
| | |
|---|---|
| T100, Street Twin, Street Cup, Scrambler | 2.41 to 1 (41/17) |
| T120, Bobber | 2.18 to 1 (37/17) |
| Thruxton, Thruxton R | 2.63 to 1 (42/16) |
| 1st gear | 3.50 to 1 (49/14) |
| 2nd gear | 2.50 to 1 (45/18) |
| 3rd gear | 1.85 to 1 (37/20) |
| 4th gear | 1.48 to 1 (37/25) |
| 5th gear | 1.30 to 1 (35/27) |
| 6th gear (1200 engine only) | 1.17 to 1 (34/29) |

## Selector drum and forks

| | Standard | Service limit |
|---|---|---|
| Selector fork end thickness | 5.9 to 6.0 mm | 5.8 mm |
| Selector fork groove width in gears | 6.1 to 6.2 mm | 6.3 mm |
| Selector fork-to-groove clearance | 0.1 to 0.3 mm | 0.5 mm |

## Torque wrench settings

| | |
|---|---|
| Balancer deadshaft clamp bolts | 10 Nm |
| Balancer deadshaft clamp positioning bolts | 10 Nm |
| Balancer rear deadshaft retaining plate screw | 12 Nm |
| Cam chain tensioner blade bolts | 10 Nm |
| Cam chain tensioner | 16 Nm |
| Camshaft holder bolts | 10 Nm |
| Camshaft sprocket bolts | 22 Nm |
| Clutch cover bolts | 10 Nm |
| Clutch nut | 98 Nm |
| Clutch spring bolts | 10 Nm |

Connecting rod cap bolts
| | |
|---|---|
| Initial setting | 14 Nm |
| Final setting (see Section 24) | + 210° |

## Torque wrench settings (continued)

| | |
|---|---|
| Crankcase bolts . . . . . . . . . . . . . . . . . . . . . . . . . . . . . . . . . . . . . . . . . | see Section 20 |
| Crankshaft end cap . . . . . . . . . . . . . . . . . . . . . . . . . . . . . . . . . . . . . | 10 Nm |
| Cylinder head bolts . . . . . . . . . . . . . . . . . . . . . . . . . . . . . . . . . . . . | see Section 10 |
| Engine mounting bolts/nuts . . . . . . . . . . . . . . . . . . . . . . . . . . . . . | see Section 4 |
| Footrest bracket assembly bolts . . . . . . . . . . . . . . . . . . . . . . . . | 24 Nm |
| Intermediate gear bolt . . . . . . . . . . . . . . . . . . . . . . . . . . . . . . . . . | 10 Nm |
| Oil pump cover bolts . . . . . . . . . . . . . . . . . . . . . . . . . . . . . . . . . . | 11 Nm |
| Oil pump sprocket bolt . . . . . . . . . . . . . . . . . . . . . . . . . . . . . . . . . | 12 Nm |
| Oil pump mounting bolts . . . . . . . . . . . . . . . . . . . . . . . . . . . . . . . | 10 Nm |
| Oil sump bolts . . . . . . . . . . . . . . . . . . . . . . . . . . . . . . . . . . . . . . . . | 10 Nm |
| Selector drum detent wheel bolt . . . . . . . . . . . . . . . . . . . . . . . . | 12 Nm |
| Selector drum retainer plate screw . . . . . . . . . . . . . . . . . . . . . . | 12 Nm |
| Selector fork shaft plug . . . . . . . . . . . . . . . . . . . . . . . . . . . . . . . | 22 Nm |
| Selector fork shaft retaining plate screw . . . . . . . . . . . . . . . . . | 12 Nm |
| Starter clutch bolts . . . . . . . . . . . . . . . . . . . . . . . . . . . . . . . . . . . | 16 Nm |
| Starter clutch plate bolts . . . . . . . . . . . . . . . . . . . . . . . . . . . . . . | 12 Nm |
| Stopper arm bolt . . . . . . . . . . . . . . . . . . . . . . . . . . . . . . . . . . . . . | 12 Nm |
| Valve cover bolts . . . . . . . . . . . . . . . . . . . . . . . . . . . . . . . . . . . . | 14 Nm |

## 1  General Information

1 The engine is a liquid-cooled parallel twin, with four valves per cylinder. The valves are opened by rocker arms that are actuated by a single overhead camshaft that is chain driven off the intermediate gear, which in turn is driven by a gear in the middle of the crankshaft. The camshaft on the 1200 engine incorporates a decompression mechanism that acts on the exhaust valves for easier starting. The engine assembly is constructed from aluminium alloy. The crankcase divides horizontally.

2 The crankcase incorporates a wet sump, pressure-fed lubrication system that has a dual-rotor oil pump, an oil filter, a relief valve and an oil pressure switch. The pump unit incorporates the water pump, and is driven by chain off the back of the clutch housing.

3 The alternator is on the right-hand end of the crankshaft, and the starter clutch is on the left-hand end.

4 Power from the crankshaft is routed to the transmission via the clutch. The clutch is a wet multi-plate type and is gear-driven off the crankshaft. The transmission is a five speed constant-mesh unit on the 900 engine, and six speed on the 1200. Final drive to the rear wheel is by chain and sprockets.

5 Read the *Safety First!* section of this manual carefully before starting work.

## 2  Component access

### *Operations possible with the engine in the frame*

1 The components and assemblies listed below can be removed without having to remove the engine assembly from the frame. If however, a number of areas require attention at the same time, removal of the engine is recommended.

● Valve cover
● Rockers and camshaft
● Cam chain tensioner and blade
● Clutch
● Gearchange mechanism
● Alternator
● Starter motor
● Starter clutch
● Oil sump and oil strainer
● Oil/water pump and pressure relief valve
● Operations requiring engine removal

2 It is necessary to remove the engine from the frame to gain access to the following components.

● Cylinder head
● Cylinder block and pistons
● Crankshaft and bearings
● Balancer shafts
● Connecting rods and bearings
● Transmission shafts
● Selector drum and forks

## 3  Engine wear assessment

1 Poor engine performance may be caused by leaking valves, incorrect valve clearances, a leaking head gasket, or worn pistons, piston rings or cylinders. A cylinder compression check will highlight these conditions and can also indicate the presence of excessive carbon deposits in the cylinder head, and a leakdown test (for which special equipment is needed – consult a Triumph dealer) will pinpoint the actual cause(s) of the problem.

### *Cylinder compression check*

**Special tool:** *A compression gauge is needed – use one with a threaded hose and adaptor to fit the spark plug holes. Depending on the* outcome of the initial test, a squirt-type oil can may also be needed.

**Note:** *A cylinder compression test is normally done with the throttle held fully open, but a safety measure built into the electronic throttle system means that the engine will not turn over on the starter if it is. The starter will only operate with the throttle held up to about a quarter open. Having a dealer use the Triumph diagnostic tool will override this. If you want to do the test yourself then the readings obtained will be lower than with the throttle fully open – the readings we obtained from a very low mileage engine are given in the text.*

2 Make sure the valve clearances are correctly set (see Chapter 1).

3 Run the engine until it is at normal operating temperature.

4 Remove the fuel tank (see Chapter 4). Disconnect the primary wiring connectors from the ignition coils **(see illustration)**. Note that the wiring that connects to the right-hand side of the front coil has red tape around it, and that the terminals on each coil are different sizes so the wiring cannot be wrongly connected.

5 Remove the spark plugs (see Chapter 1).

6 Select the adapter that matches the spark

**3.4 Disconnect the wiring from each coil – note that the wiring to the front coil has red tape around it**

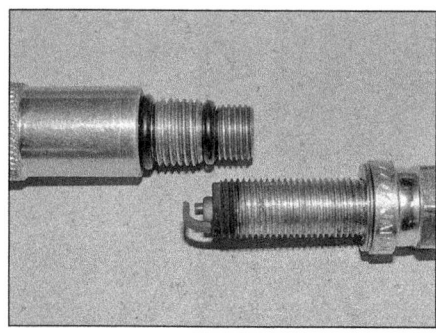

3.6a Make sure the adapter matches the plug...

3.6b ...then thread it into the plug hole

3.7 Checking cylinder compression

plug threads and fit it onto the gauge **(see illustration)**. Fit the gauge into the left-hand cylinder spark plug hole **(see illustration)**.

7 With the ignition switch ON, the kill switch set to RUN, the clutch lever pulled in and the throttle closed, turn the engine over on the starter motor until the gauge reading has built up and stabilised **(see illustration)**. Note the reading on the gauge. Perform the test again with the throttle about a quarter open, and again note the reading.

8 Repeat for the other cylinder.

9 Triumph give no specification for cylinder compression, but generally a range of 150 to 180 psi (10 to 12.5 Bar) is normal with the throttle fully open. We obtained readings of 100 psi with the throttle closed and 110 psi with it a quarter open. Readings much above or below these can be considered high or low and should be investigated. Also, there should be no more than about 25 psi (1.7 Bar) difference between the cylinders, even if the figures for both cylinders are within the general limits.

10 If a reading is low, it could be due to a worn cylinder bore, piston or rings, failure of the head gasket, or worn valve seats. To determine which is the cause, pour a small quantity of engine oil into the spark plug hole to seal the rings, then repeat the compression test. If the figures are noticeably higher the cause is worn cylinder, piston or rings. If there is no change the cause is a leaking head gasket or worn valve seats.

11 If a reading is high there could be a build-up of carbon deposits in the combustion chamber. Remove the cylinder head and scrape all deposits off the piston and the cylinder head.

### Leak-down (cylinder leakage) test

12 A leak down or 'cylinder leakage' test is similar to a compression test in that it tells you how well a cylinder is sealing, but it does so by testing how much pressure is lost through leakage, as opposed to how much pressure is created through compression. Many professionals prefer a leak test to a compression test as it more accurately pin-points the cause of the problem before

any disassembly is done, as it is easy to tell where the leakage is occurring. Generally however the required equipment is more expensive than for a compression test and a source of compressed air is essential. If you think a test is needed take the bike to a suitably equipped dealer or workshop. If you decide to purchase your own equipment follow the manufacturer's instructions.

13 A leakage test can also be used in conjunction with a compression test to diagnose other kinds of problems, such as a faulty valve train component, incorrect valve timing, faulty ignition or fuel delivery problems.

### Oil pressure check

**Special tool:** *An oil pressure gauge and adapter that screws into the oil pressure switch are needed. Triumph do not list an adapter as a spare part, but it is worth checking with a dealer as to availability. Otherwise, remove the pressure switch (see Chapter 8), and take it to an accessory dealer to match it up – if you are buying a pressure gauge, it may well come with a range of adapters.*

14 Warm the engine up to normal operating temperature then stop it.

15 Remove the oil pressure switch (see Chapter 8). Select the adapter that matches the switch threads and fit it onto the gauge. Screw the gauge adapter into the switch hole. Connect the gauge to the adapter.

16 Start the engine and increase the engine speed to 3500 rpm whilst watching the gauge reading. The oil pressure should be similar to that given in the Specifications at the start of this Chapter.

17 If the pressure is significantly lower than the standard, either the relief valve is stuck open, the oil pump is faulty, the oil pump pick-up strainer is blocked or there is other engine damage. Begin diagnosis by checking the oil pump pick-up strainer, then the oil pump. If those items check out okay, chances are the bearing oil clearances are excessive and the engine needs to be overhauled.

18 If the pressure is too high, the relief valve is stuck closed.

19 Stop the engine. Unscrew the gauge and adapter from the crankcase. Install the oil pressure switch.

## 4 Engine removal and installation

*Caution: The engine is very heavy. Engine removal and installation should be carried out with the aid of at least one assistant, but two is best. Personal injury or damage could occur if the engine falls or is dropped. An hydraulic or mechanical floor jack should be used to support and lower or raise the engine, if possible. It is best to remove as many components as possible (particularly the ones with easy access, such as the clutch, alternator and starter motor) to reduce the weight of the engine before removing it.*

**Note:** *The nuts used on the engine mounting bolts and swingarm pivot bolt are locknuts that Triumph specify should only be used once, so new ones should be used when installing the engine.*

### Removal

**Note:** *If you intend to remove the alternator or clutch with the engine removed from the frame, it is best to slacken the rotor bolt and clutch nut while the engine is still in the frame – they are tight and the engine needs to be held securely while they are undone. Refer to Chapter 8 for the alternator, and Section 15 for the clutch.*

1 On the Thruxton, Thruxton R and Bobber remove the regulator/rectifier (see Chapter 8).

2 Support the motorcycle securely in an upright position using the centrestand where fitted, or an auxiliary stand or stands that support the bike through the rear of the frame, but not through the cradle sections as they must be removed, or the swingarm or rear wheel as the swingarm pivot has to be removed. Tie the front brake lever on so the bike can't move. Work can be made easier by raising the machine to a suitable working height on an hydraulic ramp or a suitable platform. Make sure the motorcycle is secure and will not topple over. When disconnecting any wiring, cables and hoses, it is advisable to mark or tag them as a reminder of where

4.9 ECT sensor wiring connector

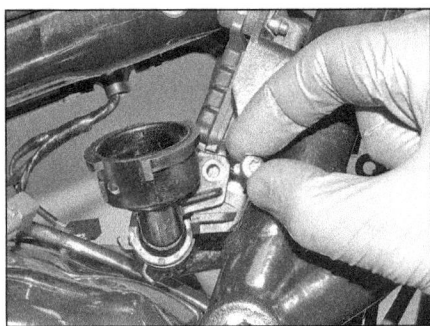

4.11a Disconnect the hose...


4.11b ... and undo the screw

they connect, and make a note of any ties and guides that secure them and how they are routed.

**3** Remove the seat and the side panels, and on the Scrambler remove the belly-pan and its bracket (see Chapter 7).

**4** Disconnect the battery (see Chapter 8).

**5** If the engine is dirty, particularly around its mountings, wash it thoroughly before starting any major dismantling work. This will make work much easier and rule out the possibility of dirt falling inside.

4.12 Undo the screws and displace the control unit

**6** Drain the engine oil and the coolant (see Chapter 1).

**7** Remove the fuel tank (see Chapter 4). On the Bobber remove the air filter housings (see Chapter 4). Remove the throttle body, and on the 900 engine remove the intake manifold (see Chapter 4). Plug the intake ports with clean rag.

**8** Remove the fuel injectors (see Chapter 4).

**9** Remove the ignition coil assembly (see Chapter 4). Disconnect the ECT sensor wiring connector **(see illustration)**.

4.13a Release the clamp...

**10** Remove the entire exhaust system (see Chapter 4) – on all models except the Scrambler this involves removing the engine cradles from the frame. On the Scrambler, after removing the exhaust system follow the procedure in the exhaust collector box sub-section for the T100, T120 and Street models to remove the frame cradles.

**11** Remove the radiator (see Chapter 3). Disconnect the overflow hose from the filler neck **(see illustration)**. Undo the radiator filler neck screw **(see illustration)**.

**12** On all models except the Bobber undo the immobiliser control unit holder screws **(see illustration)**, displace the control unit assembly and hang it over the right-hand side of the frame.

**13** Release the coolant hose from the thermostat cover and remove the filler neck hose assembly **(see illustrations)**.

**14** On the T100, T120, Street Twin, Street Cup and Scrambler, remove the rider's left-hand footrest bracket assembly **(see illustration)**. On the Thruxton and Thruxton R, remove the rider's left-hand heel guard, then remove the left-hand footrest bracket assembly.

**15** Detach the clutch cable from the release mechanism arm (Section 14).

4.13b ... and remove the hose assembly

4.14 Unscrew the footrest bracket bolts and remove the footrest assembly

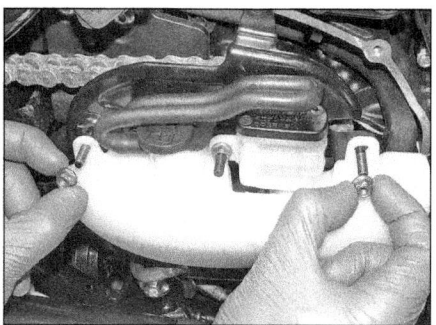

4.17a Unscrew the nuts and displace the coolant reservoir...

4.17b ... then unscrew the nut and displace the brake fluid reservoir

4.17c Unscrew the bolts...

**16** Remove the front sprocket cover (see Chapter 6).

**17** On the Bobber displace and support the coolant reservoir and the rear brake fluid reservoir **(see illustrations)**- keep them upright and wrap them in rag. Unscrew the reservoir mounting plate bolts, release the hoses from the guide and remove the plate **(see illustrations)**.

**18** On the Thruxton and Thruxton R displace and support the rear brake fluid reservoir **(see illustration 4.21a)** – keep it upright and wrap it in rag. Displace and support the coolant reservoir **(see illustration)** – keep it upright and wrap it in rag. Unscrew the coolant reservoir mounting plate bolts, release the wiring from the guide and remove the plate **(see illustrations)**.

**19** Detach the engine earth lead **(see illustration)**.

**20** Peel back the boot on the starter motor terminal, then unscrew the nut and detach the lead **(see illustration)**. Secure the lead clear of the engine. Remove the starter motor if required (see Chapter 8). If you don't remove it, on the Bobber undo the ignition switch bracket bolts and support the switch assembly clear **(see illustration)**.

**21** On the T100, T120, Street Twin, Street Cup and Scrambler, undo the rear brake fluid reservoir screw, the brake hose guide bolt and the rider's footrest/brake pedal/

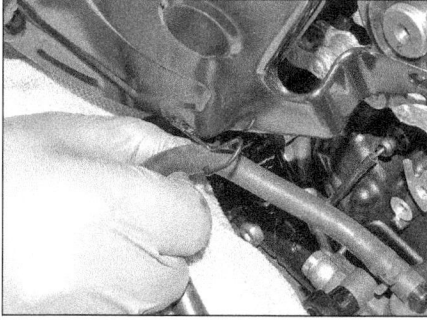

4.17d ...release the hoses and remove the plate

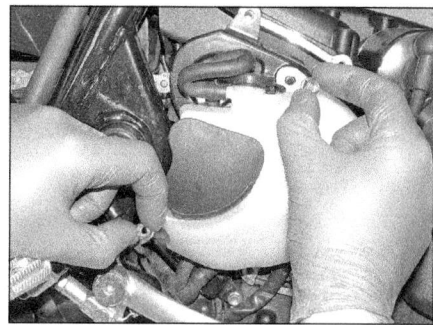

4.18a Unscrew the nuts and displace the coolant reservoir

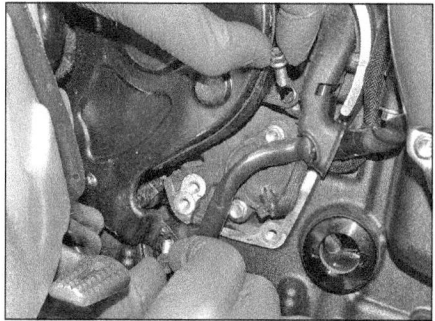

4.18b Unscrew the bolts...

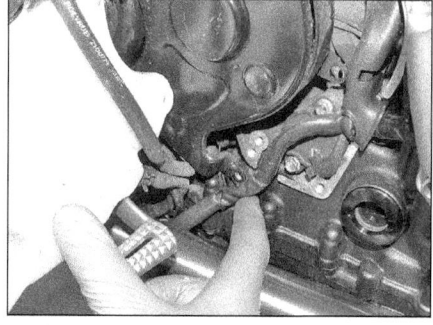

4.18c ...release the wiring and remove the plate

4.19 Unscrew the bolt (arrowed) securing the engine earth lead

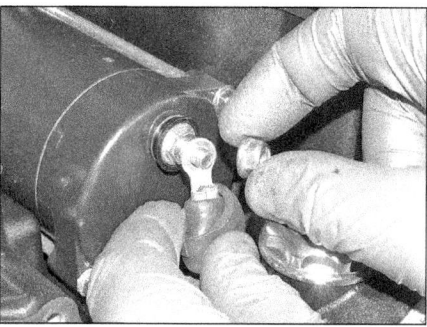

4.20a Unscrew the nut (arrowed) and detach the starter lead

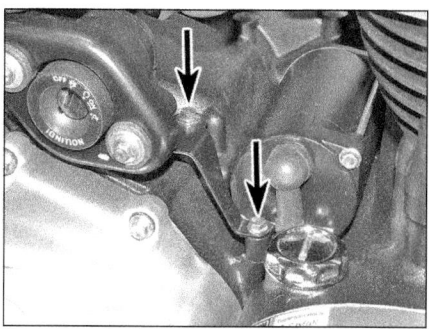

4.20b Ignition switch bracket bolts (arrowed)

4.21a Displace the reservoir...

4.21b ... and release the hose guide...

4.21c ... then unscrew the bracket bolts and displace the assembly

4.22 Disengage the chain and lay it over the swingarm

4.23a Release and disconnect the three connectors (arrowed)

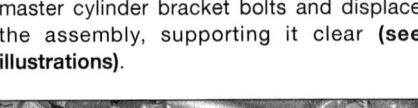

4.23b Wiring guide bolts (arrowed)

master cylinder bracket bolts and displace the assembly, supporting it clear **(see illustrations)**.

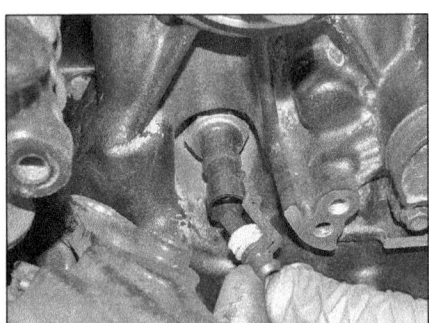

4.23c Draw the wiring out and release it from the guide

4.24 Lift the clip and pull the connector off

**22** If required remove the front sprocket (see Chapter 6), then leave the chain dangling over the front of the swingarm so it is clear of

the transmission output shaft. If you are not removing the front sprocket, create enough slack in the chain (see Chapter 1) to slip the chain off the sprocket **(see illustration)**.

**23** On all models except the Bobber release and disconnect the gear position sensor, CKP sensor and alternator wiring connectors **(see illustration)**. Undo the wiring guide bolts, displace the guide and draw the wiring out, noting its routing **(see illustrations)**.

**24** Disconnect the oil pressure switch wiring connector and secure the lead clear of the engine, noting its routing **(see illustration)**.

**25** On the Bobber remove the inner cover **(see illustrations)**. Remove the wiring guide, noting the routing of the wiring in it, then unscrew the starter relay bracket bolts and

4.25a Undo the screws (arrowed)...

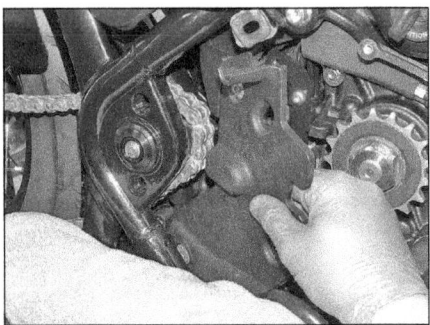

4.25b ...release the hose...

4.25c ...and remove the cover

**4.25d Wiring guide bolt and relay bracket screws (arrowed)**

**4.25e Disconnect the connectors (arrowed)**

**4.26a Remove the cover**

displace the relay assembly (see illustration). Disconnect the GP sensor and CKP sensor wiring connectors (see illustration). Release the wiring from any clips or ties on the frame and feed the GP sensor wire to the sensor and the CKP sensor and alternator wire to the alternator cover, noting its routing.

26 On all models except the Bobber place a support under the front of the swingarm. Remove the swingarm pivot cover from the left-hand side of the frame (see illustration). On the right-hand side unscrew the swingarm pivot bolt nut and remove the washer (see illustration). Withdraw the swingarm pivot with its washer from the left-hand side, then slide it part-way into the right-hand side so it keeps the swingarm in position but does not go all the way through the adjuster sleeve in the left-hand side of the frame (see illustrations). Unscrew the adjuster sleeve a few turns using either the Triumph tool (T3880104) or an equivalent tool that engages the slots in the rim (see illustration). Now push the pivot bolt all the way through.

27 On the Bobber slacken each swingarm pivot cover screw until the covers can be removed (see illustration). On the left-hand side unscrew the swingarm pivot bolt nut and remove the washer (see illustration). Push the swingarm pivot bolt in so the end is clear of the adjuster sleeve in the frame (see illustration). Unscrew the adjuster sleeve a few turns using either the Triumph tool (T3880104) or an equivalent tool that engages the slots in the rim (see illustration).

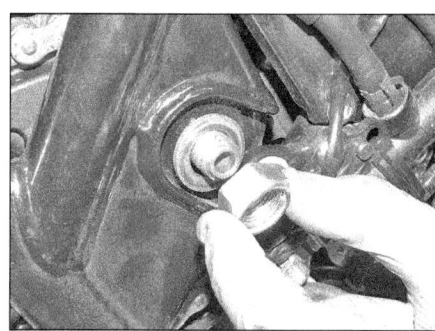

**4.26b Unscrew the nut and remove the washer**

**4.26c Withdraw the pivot from the left...**

**4.26d ...and reinsert it from the right**

**4.26e Slacken the adjuster sleeve a few turns**

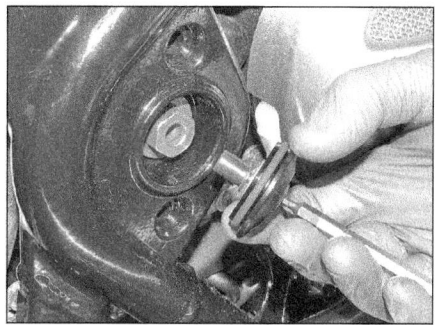

**4.27a Remove the cover from each side**

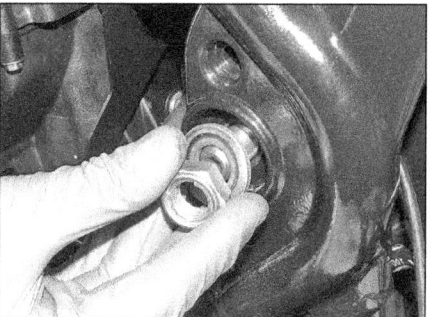

**4.27b Unscrew the nut and remove the washer**

**4.27c Push the pivot bolt in then slacken the adjuster sleeve a few turns**

4.28 This is how we supported the engine

4.30 Release the brake hoses (arrowed) from the guide plate as described – T120 shown from behind with swingarm and EVAP canister removed for clarity

**28** At this point, position an hydraulic or mechanical jack under the engine, using a block or blocks of wood as required according to the type of jack used **(see illustration)**. Make sure the jack is centrally positioned so the engine will not topple in any direction when the last mounting bolt is removed and the engine is supported only by the jack. Take the weight of the engine on the jack, but make sure the bike is not being lifted.

**29** Check around the engine and frame to make sure that all the necessary wiring, cables and hoses have been disconnected, and that any that remain connected to the engine are not retained by any clips, guides or brackets on the frame, and that any staying behind are not held to the engine.

**30** There are two brake hoses clipped onto a guide plate that is screwed to the back of the engine, and the hoses must be released from the plate **(see illustration)**. To do this use a long screwdriver inserted from the right-hand side to carefully lever them out of the clips. If you are not sure whether they have completely released then check as you begin to remove the engine when they are more visible, but do not move the engine too far in case they catch, as the hoses are joined to sections of solid pipe that could distort.

**31** On all models except the Bobber unscrew the nut and remove the washer where fitted from each engine mounting bolt **(see illustrations)**. Remove the left-hand front mounting bolt with its washer **(see illustration)**. Unscrew each adjuster sleeve on the left-hand side a few turns (until the inner flanged end just contacts the frame) using either the Triumph tool (T3880377) or an equivalent tool that engages the slots in the rim, pushing the middle and rear bolts in just enough to fit the tool **(see illustrations)**. Remove the right-hand front mounting bolt **(see illustration)**. Make sure the engine is properly supported on the jack, and have an assistant support it as well. Remove the middle bolt, then unscrew the middle

mounting bracket bolts and remove the bracket **(see illustrations)**. Remove the upper rear bolt **(see illustration)**. Remove the lower rear bolt and collect the spacer from between the engine and frame on the right-hand side, then manoeuvre the engine out, taking care not to snag the brake pipes at the back of the crankcase **(see illustrations)**.

**32** On the Bobber unscrew the nut and remove the washer where fitted from each engine mounting bolt **(see illustrations 4.31a, c and d)**. Remove the left-hand front mounting bolt with its washer **(see illustration 4.31e)**. Unscrew each adjuster sleeve on the left-hand side a few turns (until the inner flanged end just contacts the frame) using either the Triumph tool (T3880377) or an equivalent tool that engages the slots in the rim, pushing the rear bolts in just enough to fit the tool **(see illustrations 4.31f, g, h and j)**. Remove the right-hand front mounting bolt **(see illustration 4.31k)**. Make sure the engine is properly supported on the jack, and have an assistant support it as well. Remove the upper rear bolt **(see illustration 4.31n)**. Remove the lower rear bolt **(see illustration 4.31o)** and

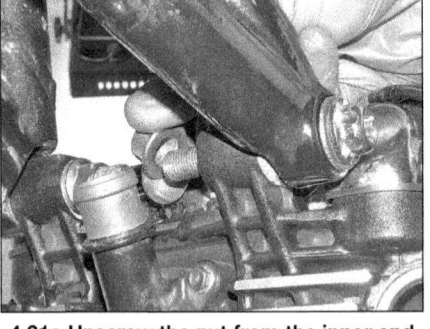

4.31a Unscrew the nut from the inner end of the front mounting bolt on each side

4.31b Unscrew the nut and remove the washer from the middle mounting bolt...

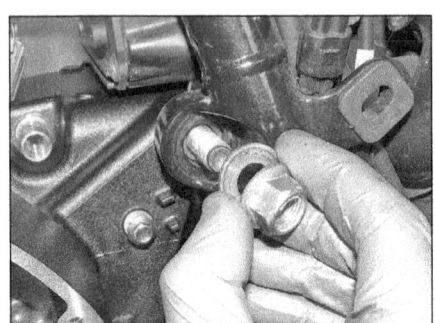

4.31c ...the upper rear mounting bolt...

4.31d ... and the lower rear mounting bolt

4.31e Remove the front left bolt and washer

4.31f Push the lower rear bolt in...

4.31g ...then slacken the adjuster a few turns...

4.31h ...and do the same for the upper rear bolt and adjuster...

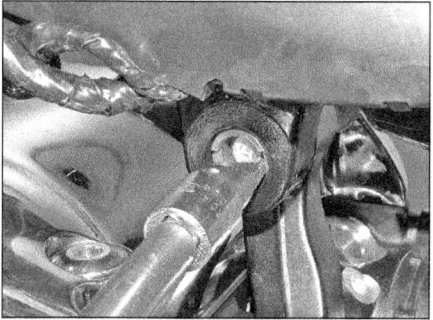

4.31i ...and the middle bolt and adjuster...

4.31j ...then slacken the front adjuster

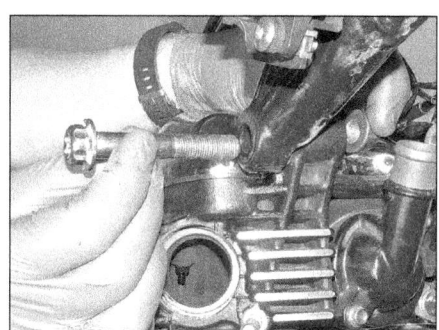

4.31k Remove the front right bolt

4.31l Remove the middle bolt...

4.31m ...then unscrew the bolts and remove the bracket

4.31n Withdraw the upper rear bolt

4.31o Withdraw the lower rear bolt...

4.31p ...and remove the spacer

**4.32 Left-hand spacer (arrowed) for the lower rear engine mount**

**4.33 Make sure the brake pipe is correctly seated in its clip(s) – T120 shown**

collect the spacer from between the engine and frame on each side **(see illustration and 4.31p)**, then manoeuvre the engine out, taking care not to snag the brake pipes at the back of the crankcase.

### Installation

**33** Before fitting the engine, make sure the brake pipe from the rear master cylinder to the ABS modulator is correctly seated in the clip(s) on the front of the ABS modulator bracket **(see illustration)**.

**34** With the aid of an assistant, place the engine unit onto the jack and block of wood and carefully raise it into position so that the mounting bolt holes align. Make sure no wires, cables or hoses become trapped between the engine and the frame. Secure the brake pipes in the holder on the back of the crankcase **(see illustration 4.30)**.

**35** Fit and tighten the engine mounting bolts in the following order:

● Fit the left-hand front mounting bolt with its washer **(see illustration 4.31e)**. Fit the right-hand front mounting bolt, then fit the new nut and tighten it finger-tight **(see illustration 4.31k)**.

● On all models except the Bobber position the spacer for the lower rear mount between the engine and frame on the right-hand side, then insert the lower rear mounting bolt from the right, leaving it loose **(see illustrations 4.31p and o)**. Insert the upper rear mounting bolt from the right-hand side, leaving it loose **(see illustration 4.31n)**. Fit the middle mounting bracket and tighten the bolts to 24 Nm **(see illustration 4.31m)**. Fit the middle mounting bolt from the right-hand side, leaving it loose **(see illustration 4.31l)**.

● On the Bobber position the long spacer for the lower rear mount between the engine and frame on the right-hand side, then insert the lower rear mounting bolt from the right, pushing it in part way, then fit the short spacer between the engine and frame on the left and push the bolt all the way through, leaving it loose **(see illustrations 4.31p and o and 4.32)**. Insert the upper rear mounting bolt from the right-hand side, leaving it loose **(see illustration 4.31n)**.

● Using either the Triumph tool (T3880377) or equivalent tighten the adjuster sleeve in the left-hand side of the lower rear mount to 5 Nm, pushing the bolt in just enough to fit the tool **(see illustrations 4.31f and g)**. Repeat for the upper rear mount **(see illustration 4.31h)**. Push the bolts all the way back in, then fit the washer and a new nut onto each and tighten them finger-tight **(see illustrations 4.31d and c)**.

● Counter-hold the nut on the front mounting bolt on the right-hand side and tighten the bolt to 24 Nm.

● Remove the left-hand front mounting bolt **(see illustration 4.31e)**. Using either the Triumph tool (T3880377) or equivalent tighten the adjuster sleeve in the left-hand front mount to 5 Nm **(see illustration 4.31j)**. Push the bolt all the way back in, then fit the washer and a new nut and tighten it finger-tight **(see illustration 4.31a)**.

● On all models except the Bobber, using either the Triumph tool (T3880377) or equivalent tighten the adjuster sleeve in the middle mount to 5 Nm, pushing the bolt in just enough to fit the tool **(see illustration 4.31i)**. Push the bolt all the way back in, then fit the washer and a new nut and tighten it finger-tight **(see illustration 4.31b)**.

● Counter-hold the head of the lower rear mounting bolt and tighten the nut to 80 Nm. Repeat for the upper rear mounting bolt.

● Counter-hold the nut on the front mounting bolt on the right-hand side and tighten the bolt to 105 Nm. Repeat for the front mounting bolt on the left-hand side.

● On all models except the Bobber counter-hold the nut on the middle mounting bolt and tighten the bolt to 105 Nm.

● On all models except the Bobber, using either the Triumph tool (T3880104) or equivalent tighten the swingarm pivot adjuster sleeve in the left-hand side of the frame to 6 Nm, pushing the bolt in just enough to fit the tool **(see illustration 4.26e)**. Make sure the support is under the swingarm, then withdraw the pivot bolt with its washer from the right-hand side and slide it all the way though from the left-hand side **(see illustrations 4.26d and c)**. Fit the washer and a new nut onto the right-hand end,

counter-hold the bolt head and tighten the nut to 110 Nm **(see illustration 4.26b)**. Fit the pivot cover **(see illustration 4.26a)**.

● On the Bobber, using either the Triumph tool (T3880104) or equivalent tighten the swingarm pivot adjuster sleeve in the left-hand side of the frame to 6 Nm, pushing the bolt in just enough to fit the tool **(see illustration 4.27c)**. Push the bolt all the way in from the right-hand side. Fit the washer and a new nut onto the left-hand end, counter-hold the bolt head and tighten the nut to 110 Nm **(see illustration 4.27b)**. Fit the pivot covers and tighten the screws until the covers are secure **(see illustration 4.27a)**.

**36** The remainder of installation is the reverse of removal, noting the following points:

● Tighten the footrest bracket assembly bolts to 24 Nm.

● Make sure all wires, cables and hoses are correctly routed and connected, and secured by any clips or ties.

● Refill the engine with oil and coolant to the correct levels (see Chapter 1).

● Check the clutch cable freeplay (see Chapter 1).

● Adjust the drive chain tension (see Chapter 1).

● Start the engine and check that there are no oil or coolant leaks.

## 5 Engine overhaul general information

**1** Before beginning the engine overhaul, read through the related procedures to familiarise yourself with the scope and requirements of the job. Overhauling an engine is not all that difficult, but it is time consuming. Check on the availability of parts and make sure that any necessary special tools are obtained in advance.

**2** Most work can be done with a decent set of typical workshop hand tools, although a number of precision measuring tools are required for inspecting parts to determine if they are worn.

**3** To ensure maximum life and minimum trouble from a rebuilt engine, everything must be assembled with care in a spotlessly clean environment, using the correct lubricant where directed.

### Disassembly

**4** Before disassembling the engine, thoroughly clean and degrease its external surfaces. This will prevent contamination of the engine internals, and will also make the job a lot easier and cleaner. A high flash-point solvent, such as paraffin (kerosene) can be used, or better still, a proprietary engine degreaser such as Gunk. Use old paintbrushes and toothbrushes to work the solvent into the various recesses of the casings. Take care to exclude solvent or water from the electrical components and intake and exhaust ports.

**Warning: The use of petrol (gasoline) as a cleaning agent should be avoided because of the risk of fire.**

**5** When clean and dry, position the engine on the workbench, leaving a suitable clear area for working. Gather a selection of small containers, plastic bags and some labels so that parts can be grouped together in an easily identifiable manner. Also get some paper and a pen so that notes can be taken. You will also need a supply of clean rag, which should be as absorbent as possible.

**6** Before commencing work, read through the appropriate section so that some idea of the necessary procedure can be gained. When removing components note that great force is seldom required, unless specified (checking the specified torque setting of the particular bolt being removed will indicate how tight it is, and therefore how much force should be needed). In many cases, a component's reluctance to be removed is indicative of an incorrect approach or removal method; if in any doubt, re-check with the text.

**7** When disassembling the engine, keep 'mated' parts together (including gears, pistons, connecting rods, valve assemblies, etc, that have been in contact with each other during engine operation). These ' mated' parts must be reused or replaced as an assembly.

**8** A complete engine disassembly should be done in the following general order with reference to the appropriate Sections (or Chapters, where indicated).
● Remove the valve cover
● Remove the cam chain tensioner
● Remove the rocker arms and camshaft
● Remove the cylinder head
● Remove the cylinder block and pistons
● Remove the clutch
● Remove the gearchange mechanism
● Remove the alternator rotor
● Remove the starter clutch
● Remove the starter motor (see Chapter 8)
● Remove the sump and oil strainer and the oil/water pump
● Separate the crankcase halves
● Remove the transmission shafts
● Remove the connecting rods and crankshaft
● Remove the balancer shafts
● Remove the selector drum and forks

### Reassembly

**9** Reassembly is accomplished by reversing the general disassembly sequence.

## 6  Valve cover

### Removal

**1** Remove the fuel tank and the ignition coil assembly (see Chapter 4).

**2** Remove the spark plugs (see Chapter 1).
**3** Undo the cooling system filler neck screw **(see illustration)**.
**4** On all models except the Bobber undo the immobiliser control unit holder screws **(see illustration)**, displace the control unit assembly and hang it over the right-hand side of the frame.
**5** Unscrew and remove the valve cover bolts **(see illustration)**. Lift the cover off the cylinder head and remove it from the right-hand side **(see illustration)**. If it is stuck, break the gasket seal by tapping gently around the edge with a soft-faced hammer or block of wood. Do not lever the cover off as this will damage the sealing surface.

### Installation

**6** Examine the valve cover gasket for signs of damage or deterioration and fit a new one if necessary, making sure it seats correctly **(see illustration)**. Similarly check the cover bolt sealing washers for cracks, hardening and deterioration and use new ones if necessary **(see illustration 6.8)**.
**7** Clean the mating surface of the cylinder head with a suitable solvent.
**8** Position the valve cover on the cylinder head, making sure it is the correct way round and the gasket stays in place **(see illustration 6.5b)**. Apply a smear of clean oil to the sealing washers, then fit the bolts and tighten them to 14 Nm **(see illustration)**.
**9** Install the remaining components in the reverse order of removal.

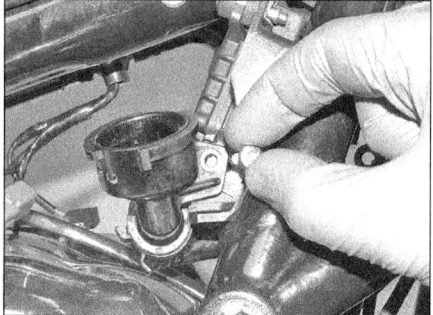
6.3 Undo the screw

6.4 Undo the screws and displace the control unit

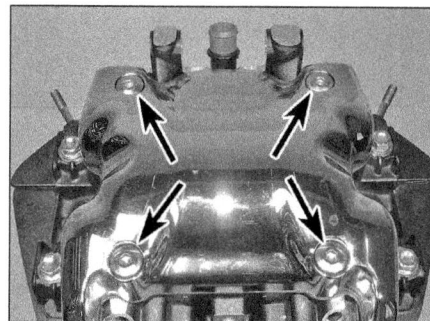
6.5a Valve cover bolts (arrowed)

6.5b Remove the valve cover out to the right

6.6 Check the gasket

6.8 Use new sealing washers if necessary

## 7 Cam chain tensioner

**Note:** *If you are just removing the tensioner and are not removing the rockers or camshaft then it is essential to fit the locking tool to the camshaft as described in Step 3. If the rockers are being removed by themselves, i.e. you are not removing the camshaft, the tensioner does not need to be removed. If the camshaft is being removed then you will need the tool described in Step 4, not so much for the removal procedure (as it does not really matter if the cam chain jumps the sprocket at that stage), but definitely for installation, so it is best to obtain and use it for removal so you can see how it all fits and aligns correctly before the camshaft is removed which will make installation easier.*

### Removal

1 Remove the valve cover (Section 6).
2 Remove the alternator cover (see Chapter 8).
3 Remove the spark plugs (see Chapter 1).
4 Turn the crankshaft clockwise using the alternator rotor bolt, until the hole in the rotor is aligned with the hole in the crankcase, and the offset slots in the right-hand end of the camshaft are above and parallel with the top of the cylinder head **(see illustrations)**. If the slots in the camshaft are below the cylinder head surface when the holes align, turn the crankshaft clockwise one full turn so that the holes again align – the slots in the camshaft end will now be above the head. Fit either the Triumph locking pin, part No. T3880601 and not expensive, or a suitable equivalent, such as a 6 mm bolt or pin, through the holes in the rotor, crankcase and crankshaft web to lock the crankshaft in position **(see illustrations)**. The offset slots on the right-hand end of the camshaft must also be used for locking the camshaft in the exact correct position to set the timing as otherwise the camshaft is likely to move from the pressure of the rocker from open valves on the camshaft lobe and the chain is likely to jump a tooth on the sprocket – to lock the camshaft, use either the Triumph tool, part No. T3880650, or a piece of steel bar of the correct thickness and shape as shown to fit in the slot and lay across it and on the cylinder head surface **(see illustration)**. Fit the tool or bar into the slot, and if the Triumph tool is being used bolt it in place using two M6 x 12 mm bolts, and if a bar is being used hold it in place, so the camshaft is locked in the correct position **(see illustration)**. Note that if you are using the Triumph tool there are two ends to it (A and B), and if end A does not fit in the slot use end B. Do not attempt to turn the crankshaft with the locking pin and tool or bar fitted.
5 Unscrew and withdraw the tensioner, noting that the plunger will be pushed out under spring pressure **(see illustration 7.10)**. Remove the O-rings – new ones must be used **(see illustration 7.9)**. Do not remove the crankshaft and camshaft locking tools unless the camshaft is being removed.

### Inspection

6 Examine the tensioner for signs of wear or damage **(see illustration 7.9)**.
7 Hold the ends of the resister ring together

7.4a Turn the engine clockwise until the holes (arrowed) align...

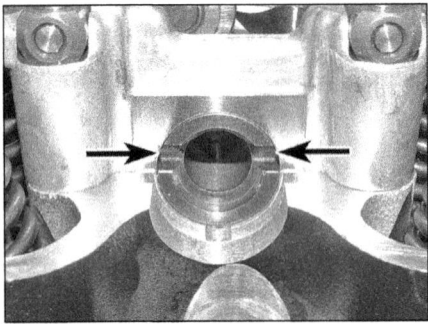

7.4b ...and the offset slot (arrowed) is parallel with and above the top of the cylinder head

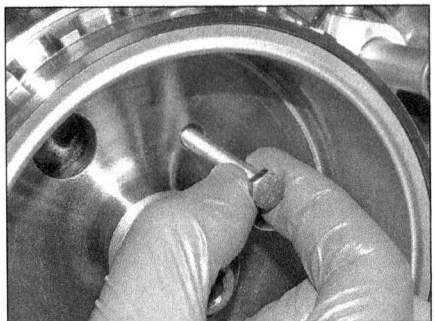

7.4c We used a 6 mm bolt as a locking pin

7.4d Make sure the bolt or pin is fully inserted so the crankshaft is locked

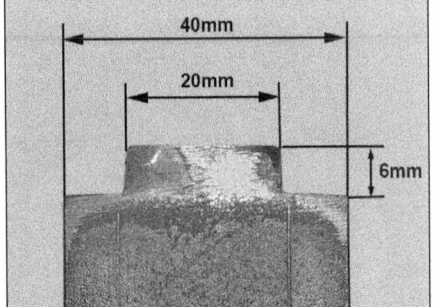

7.4e We cut a piece of steel bar to the dimensions shown to use as a locking tool for the camshaft

7.4f The ends of the tool need to be chamfered slightly to match the curve of the camshaft end

7.4g Camshaft locking tool fitted into the offset slot and seated against the head

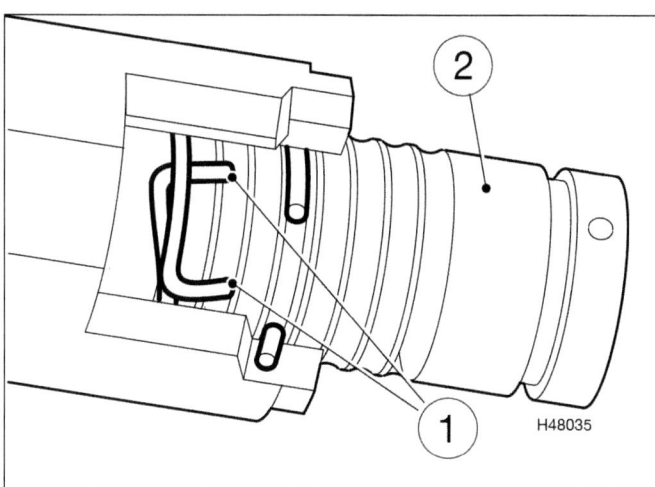

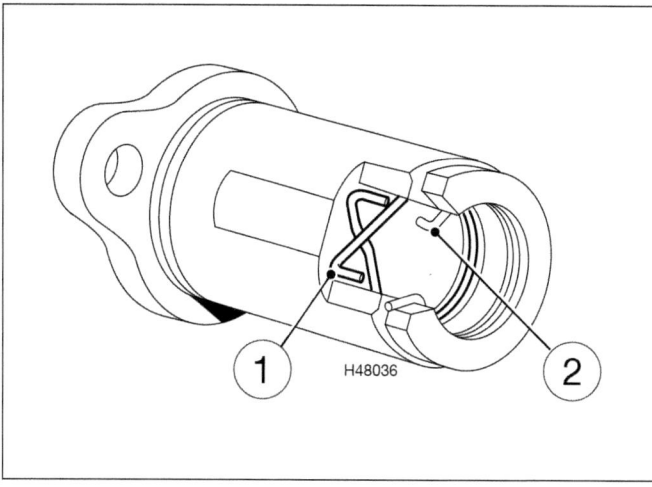

**7.7a Hold the resister ring ends (1) together and withdraw the plunger (2) and spring**

**7.7b Make sure the resister ring (1) and snap ring (2) are correctly located**

and withdraw the plunger and spring **(see illustration)**. Drain the oil out of the body. Clean all components. Check the spring for distortion and the outer end of the plunger for wear. Make sure the resister ring and snap ring are correctly located in their grooves **(see illustration)**. Fit the spring back into the tensioner. Hold the ends of the resister ring together to expand it and push the plunger through it and all the way in **(see illustration 7.7a)** – when the snap ring aligns with the outer groove in the plunger keep it held there, release the resister ring, then move one end of the snap ring into the groove and hold it there, then slowly release the plunger so the snap ring holds it in the retracted position **(see illustration)**.

## Installation

**Note:** *If a new tensioner is being fitted it will come with the plunger compressed into the body ready for installation – do not release the plunger before fitting.*

**8** If the original tensioner is being refitted, and if not already done, refer to Step 7 and drain and clean the tensioner, then reset the plunger in the retracted position as described.
**9** Fit new O-rings on the tensioner body **(see illustration)**.
**10** Push the top of the tensioner blade forwards so the lower half of the blade is pushed against the chain to tension it, and keep it held there until the tensioner plunger is released in Step 13 – this is particularly important when the rockers are in place to prevent camshaft movement and subsequent jumping of the chain round the sprocket when the locking tools are removed, and it is best to have an assistant hold it so maximum pressure is maintained. With the blade pushed forwards insert the tensioner and tighten it to 16 Nm **(see illustration)**.
**11** If the rockers and camshaft holders have been removed temporarily fit the No. 2 cylinder holder and rocker shafts, but

not the rockers, and tighten the holder bolts hand-tight so the camshaft is held in place.
**12** Remove the crankshaft locking pin, then remove the camshaft locking tool or bar, making sure the camshaft does not move and the chain is not seen, felt or heard to jump on the sprocket – if it does you must remove the tensioner again, refer to Section 8 and remove the rockers and holders, then reposition the camshaft and chain.
**13** The tensioner plunger is released by turning the engine in the opposite direction to normal so the slack side of the chain is tensioned and the tensioner blade is pushed against the end of the plunger, which releases the snap ring allowing the plunger to extend. Turn the engine anti-clockwise two full turns, making sure the plunger is heard and seen to release, then turn it clockwise until the timing marks align as in Step 4 and the locking tools can be fitted. Check that the tensioner plunger is correctly located and centred against the tensioner blade when viewed from above, and that the chain is tensioned. Remove the locking tools and rotate the crankshaft clockwise through four full turns, then reset it in position as described in Step 4. Check again that the tensioner plunger is correctly located against the tensioner blade when viewed from above, and that the chain

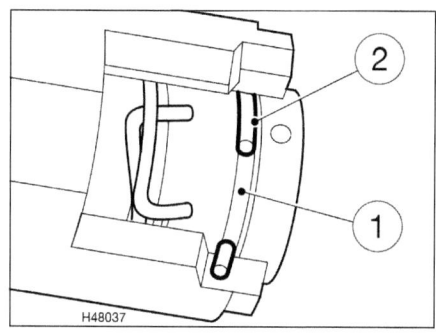

**7.7c Locate the snap ring (2) in the groove (1) then release the plunger, which should lock in place**

is tensioned, and that the timing marks align correctly.
**14** Install the rocker arms and holders now if removed, fitting the No. 1 cylinder components before removing the No. 2 holder temporarily fitted to hold the camshaft in place (Section 8).
**15** Install the alternator cover (see Chapter 8), spark plugs (see Chapter 1), and valve cover (Section 6).
**16** Note that when the engine is first started the cam chain and tensioner blade will be noisy until full oil pressure is present in the tensioner – this can take up to five seconds.

**7.9 Tensioner O-rings (arrowed)**

**7.10 Push forward on the top of the tensioner blade as you fit the tensioner**

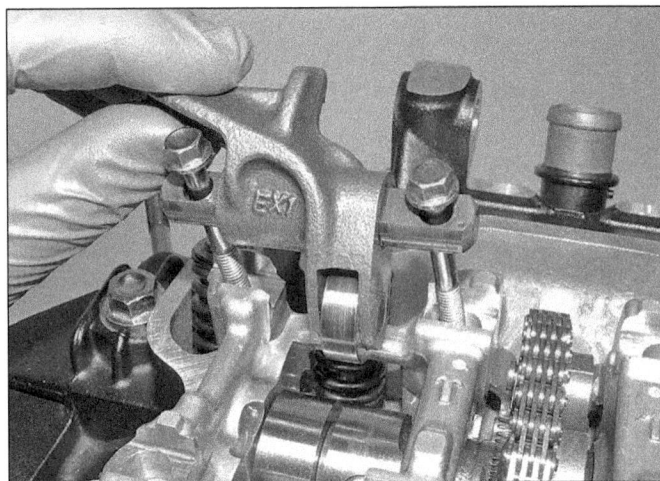

8.2a Camshaft rocker and holder layout

8.2b Unscrew the bolts as described and remove the rockers

## 8 Rockers and camshaft

**Note:** *The rockers can be removed without disturbing the camshaft holders and camshaft, and the camshaft holders can be removed without disturbing the camshaft. The tensioner does not need to be removed to remove the rockers and holders – only remove the tensioner if removing the camshaft.*

### Removal

**1** Refer to Section 7, Steps 1 to 4, and position the crankshaft and camshaft as described and fit the crankshaft locking pin and camshaft locking tool or bar.
**2** Before removing the rockers, note they are marked IN 1, EX 1, IN 2, EX 2 **(see illustration)** – these marks identify the location of each rocker (i.e intake rocker for No.1 (left) cylinder) to ensure they cannot be wrongly fitted on reassembly. Unscrew the rocker shaft/camshaft holder bolts evenly and a little at a time until loose, then lift off the rockers and shafts **(see illustration)**. Keep each rocker on its shaft so mated parts stay together.
**3** Before removing the camshaft holders, note

there is an arrow on the top of the inner bridge section on each camshaft holder that points to the front of the engine **(see illustration)** – these marks ensure the holders cannot be wrongly fitted on reassembly. Lift off the holders **(see illustration)** – retrieve the dowels from either the holder or the cylinder head if they are loose. *Caution: If the bolts for the No. 2 cylinder exhaust (EX2) rocker/holder are loosened carelessly and the rocker shaft does not come away from the holder squarely under the pressure of the open valves, the shaft could break.*

**4** Remove the cam chain tensioner (Section 7).
**5** Remove the camshaft locking tool.
**6** Unscrew the cam chain tensioner blade bolts, then lift the camshaft and draw the blade out **(see illustrations)**.
**7** Disengage the chain from the camshaft sprocket and slide the camshaft out to the right of the head **(see illustration 8.24a)**. Secure the cam chain to prevent it dropping down the tunnel, and avoid rotating the crankshaft in case the chain jams between the drive sprocket and the case **(see illustration)**.

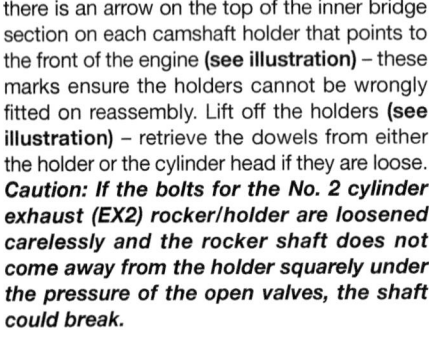
8.3a Note the forward pointing arrows adjacent to the sprocket

8.3b Lift the holders off the head

8.6a Unscrew the bolts...

8.6b ...then lift the camshaft slightly for clearance to draw the blade out

8.7 Support the cam chain to prevent it dropping

**8** If the shims are being removed from the cylinder head, obtain a container that is divided into eight compartments, and label each compartment with the location of its corresponding valve in the cylinder head. If a container is not available, use labelled plastic bags (egg cartons also work very well). Remove the shim from the top of each valve using either a magnet, a small screwdriver with a dab of grease on it (the shim will stick to the grease), or a screwdriver and a pair of pliers **(see illustration)**. Do not allow a shim to fall into the engine.

### Inspection

**9** Inspect the bearing surfaces on the camshafts and in the cylinder head and camshaft holder. Look for score marks, deep scratches and evidence of spalling (a pitted appearance). Check the camshaft lobes for heat discoloration (blue appearance), score marks, chipped areas, flat spots and spalling.
**10** Next, check the camshaft bearing oil clearances, using a product called Plastigauge – it is available from Triumph under part No. 3880150-T0301, as well as from other sources.
**11** Clean the camshaft journals, the bearing surfaces in the cylinder head and each camshaft holder with a clean, lint-free cloth, then lay the camshaft in place in the cylinder head – there is no need to engage the chain on the sprocket. Apply a thin smear of grease to each journal and silicone release agent to each bearing surface in the holder.
**12** Cut strips of Plastigauge and lay one piece on each camshaft journal, parallel with the camshaft centreline. Note that throughout this procedure it is important that the camshaft does not turn once the holders have been fitted – if it does the Plastiguage will be smeared and a false clearance reading will result. Fit the dowels if removed, then fit the camshaft holders with the arrows pointing to the front of the engine and next to the camshaft sprocket, making sure each holder is seated over the dowels and against the head **(see illustrations 8.3b and a)**. Withdraw each shaft from its rocker and seat it in its correct location on its holder according to rocker position **(see illustration 8.2a)**, making sure the punch mark on each shaft faces up and in **(see illustration 8.29)**. Clean and lightly oil the camshaft holder bolt threads. Fit the bolts and tighten them finger-tight. Making sure the camshaft does not rotate, tighten the bolts evenly and a little at a time to 10 Nm.
**13** Now unscrew the bolts evenly and a little at a time and carefully lift off the holders, again making sure the camshaft does not turn.
**14** To determine the oil clearance, compare the crushed Plastigauge (at its widest point) on each journal to the scale printed on the Plastigauge container. Compare the results to that given in the Specifications at the beginning of the Chapter. If the oil clearance is greater than specified, measure the diameter of the camshaft journal with a micrometer. If the journal diameter is less than the minimum

8.8 Lift out the shims using a magnet if available

specified, replace the camshaft with a new one and recheck the clearance. If the clearance is still too great, or if the camshaft journal is within its range, replace the cylinder head and holders as a set with new ones – individual components are not available. Note that if specialist measuring tools are available, the camshaft journal bore diameter can be measured (with the holders bolted onto the head without the camshaft in place) and compared with the specification.
**15** Check the amount of camshaft runout by supporting each end of the camshaft on V-blocks, and measuring any runout using a dial gauge. If the runout exceeds the specified limit the camshaft must be replaced with a new one.

> **HAYNES HiNT** *Refer to Tools and WorkshopTips (Section 3) in the Reference section for details of how to read a micrometer and dial gauge.*

**Note:** *Do not loosen the camshaft sprocket bolts or remove the sprocket from the camshaft unless either a new sprocket or a new camshaft is being fitted – this is because the alignment of the sprocket on the camshaft is adjustable, and if disturbed the position must be accurately set, preferably using an array of expensive special tools only available from Triumph, but if necessary using the alternatives and method described in the installation procedure.*
**16** Inspect the camshaft sprocket. If it shows signs of wear, cracks or other damage, unscrew the two bolts and remove it from the

8.18a With the arm (A) at rest the pin (B) should be as shown...

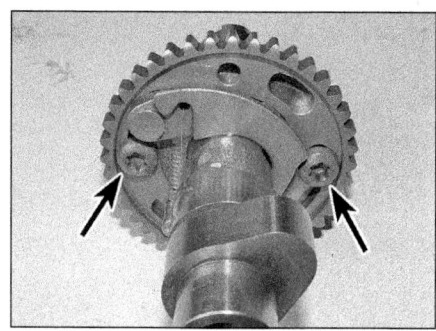

8.16 Camshaft sprocket bolts (arrowed) – 1200 shown

camshaft **(see illustration)** – note that the bolts fit into the elongated slots that allow adjustment of the sprocket position. Clean the threads of the bolts. Note that Triumph specify to use new bolts because they are pre-encapsulated with threadlock, but if necessary you can apply fresh threadlock to the original bolts. Position the new sprocket and fit the bolts, at this stage using the old cleaned bolts (the new or threadlocked bolts will be fitted later after the position of the sprocket has been adjusted), and aligning the sprocket so the bolts are central in the slots, but only tighten them lightly at this stage, enough to prevent the sprocket moving by itself but loose enough so the sprocket can be turned by hand. During the camshaft installation procedure make sure you follow all the Steps that begin 'If the sprocket bolts were loosened...'
**17** If the camshaft sprocket is worn, it is likely the cam chain and the drive sprocket on the driven gear assembly will be worn as well. Refer to Section 9 for details of how to remove the cam chain and check it for wear. Make a visual check of the drive sprocket.
**18** On the 1200 engine check the action of the decompression mechanism – with the weight on the outside of the sprocket at rest the decompression pin should protrude slightly from the bottom of the adjacent lobe, and when the weight is moved outwards the pin should retract, with everything moving smoothly **(see illustrations)**.
**19** Check each rocker shaft and the bore of its rocker for evidence of scoring, wear or other damage.

8.18b ...and with the arm lifted the pin should retract

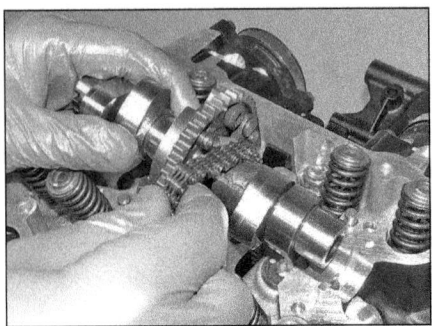

**8.24a Keeping the rear run of the chain taut, fit the camshaft as described...**

### Installation

**Note:** *It is important that the shims are returned to their original valves otherwise the valve clearances will be inaccurate.*

**20** If removed, lubricate each shim with molybdenum disulphide oil (a 50/50 mix of molybdenum disulphide grease and engine oil) and fit it into its recess in the top of the valve with the size marking facing down **(see illustration 8.8)**. Check that the shims are correctly seated.

**21** Make sure the bearing surfaces in the cylinder head, on the camshafts and in the holder are clean, then apply molybdenum disulphide oil (a 50/50 mixture of molybdenum disulphide grease and engine oil) to each of them and to the camshaft lobes.

**22** Check that the crankshaft is positioned as described in Section 7, Step 4, and the locking pin is fitted.

**23** If the sprocket bolts were loosened check the sprocket is positioned so the bolts are central in their slots, and that the bolts are tight enough to hold it in that position, but not so tight that the sprocket can't be moved by hand.

**24** Lift the cam chain, and make sure that it is engaged around the drive sprocket. Keeping the rear run of the chain taut, pass the camshaft through the chain and lay it in position so that the offset slot on its right-hand end is uppermost and is parallel with the top mating surface of the cylinder head, then engage the chain on the sprocket teeth, keeping the rear run taut so that the slack lies in the front run where it will be taken up by the tensioner **(see illustrations)**.

**8.29 Align the shaft in the rocker so the punch mark (arrowed) faces up and is on the inner side**

**8.24b ...aligning the offset slot as shown**

**25** Clean the threads of the tensioner blade bolts and apply some threadlock. Lift the camshaft and fit the tensioner blade, and tighten the bolts to 10 Nm **(see illustrations 8.6b and a)**.

**26** Make sure the camshaft is correctly seated and the offset slot is exactly aligned, then fit the locking tool or bar as described in Section 7, Step 4.

**27** If the sprocket bolts were loosened, the position of the sprocket can now be set. To do this you need the Triumph special tools, part Nos. T3880651 and T3880609, so the chain is accurately tensioned to a determined amount. Temporarily fit the No. 2 cylinder holder and rocker shafts, but not the rockers, and tighten the holder bolts hand-tight so the camshaft is held in place. Fit tool T3880651 in the place of the cam chain tensioner and tighten to 16 Nm. Now tighten its centre stud using tool T3880609, which sets the chain at exactly the correct tension by tightening the stud to 0.6 Nm so the sprocket is in exactly the right position. With the chain tensioned remove the exposed camshaft sprocket bolt from the sprocket and either replace it with one of the new encapsulated bolts or apply some thread locking compound, then fit the bolt and tighten to 22 Nm. Remove the camshaft locking tool or bar and the crankshaft locking pin, and turn the crankshaft clockwise one full turn as before until the other sprocket bolt is exposed, then refit the crankshaft locking pin. Remove the sprocket bolt and fit the other new one or apply some thread locking compound, then fit the bolt and tighten to

**8.30 Fit the No. 2 cylinder holder and rockers**

22 Nm. Remove the locking pin, and turn the crankshaft clockwise one full turn as before until the timing marks align, then refit the crankshaft locking pin and the camshaft tool or bar. Remove the tensioning tool.

**28** Install the cam chain tensioner (Section 7).

**29** Now fit the camshaft holders and rockers in their correct location (see Step 2), fitting the No. 1 cylinder components before removing the No. 2 holder temporarily fitted to hold the camshaft in place while installing the tensioner. Fit the holder dowels into the holder or cylinder head if removed. Fit the holder over the camshaft and onto the head with the arrow next to the sprocket and pointing to the front of the engine **(see illustrations 8.3b and a)** – make sure the dowels locate correctly and the holder is fully seated on the head all round. Lubricate each rocker bore and shaft with clean oil. Insert each shaft into its rocker, making sure the punch mark on each shaft faces up and is on the inner end of the rocker **(see illustration)**. Position the rockers and shafts on the holder with the roller above the camshaft and the rocker arms above the valves, and the punch mark facing up and in **(see illustration 8.2b)**. Clean and lightly oil the camshaft holder bolt threads. Fit the bolts and tighten them finger-tight **(see illustration 8.2a)**. Tighten the rocker shaft/holder bolts evenly and a little at a time to 10 Nm, particularly making sure when fitting the No. 2 holder and rockers that the EX2 shaft is tightened down square as it opens the valves **(see illustration)**.

**30** Now remove the temporarily fitted No. 2 holder, and install it and the No. 2 rockers as described above for the No. 1 components **(see illustration)**. When all are fitted double check that the rocker marked IN1 is fitted to the rear side of the left-hand holder, EX1 is fitted to the front of the left-hand holder, IN2 is fitted to the rear of the right-hand holder, and EX2 to the front, and that all punch marks are correctly positioned, facing up and in **(see illustration 8.2a)**.

**31** With all bolts tightened down, check again that the timing marks all align (see Section 7, Step 4).

**32** Check the valve clearances (see Chapter 1).

### 9  Cam chain and intermediate gear assembly

### Removal

**1** Remove the cylinder block (Section 12).

**2** Make sure the crankshaft is correctly aligned as it was when removing the cam chain tensioner and the locking pin is fitted (Section 7).

**3** Mark the right-hand side of the cam chain with a paint mark so it can be refitted the same way round on installation.

**4** Unscrew the intermediate gear bolt, then withdraw the gear shaft and lift the cam chain and gear out **(see illustrations 9.13e, d and a)**. Triumph specify to use a new bolt as it

9.7 Check the gear and sprocket teeth and the bearings

9.9 6 mm punch with insulating tape positioned to make it a snug fit in the holes

9.12 Engage the chain around the sprocket

is pre-encapsulated with threadlock, but if necessary you can clean the threads of the old bolt and apply new threadlock on installation.

### Inspection

**5** Check the cam chain for binding, loose pins and worn or damaged plates and replace it with a new one if necessary.

**6** If the chain appears to be in good condition, check it for stretch as follows. Hang the chain from a hook and attach a 13 kg (28 lb) weight to its lower end. Measure the length of 24 pins (from the outer edge of the 1st pin to the outer edge of the 24th pin). If the section measured is longer than 147.5 mm it is worn and must be replaced with a new one.

**7** Inspect the intermediate gear teeth, the drive gear on the crankshaft, and the cam chain sprocket for worn, chipped or missing teeth **(see illustration)**. Check the bearings in the gear and the surface of the shaft.

**8** Check the sliding surfaces of the cam chain blades for excessive wear, deep grooves, cracking and other obvious damage.

### Installation

**9** The intermediate gear must be positioned and locked with a pin so it is correctly timed to the crankshaft when it is installed. The intermediate gear locking pin can only be fitted with the alternator rotor removed, so do this if not already done (see Chapter 8), then refit the crankshaft locking pin. The intermediate gear locking pin fits through two holes in the crankcase and into a hole in the intermediate gear – each of these holes is a different

diameter, and for the gear to be locked accurately in position you need a pin that is sized to match each hole. Triumph can supply a locking pin, part No. T3880039 and not too expensive, or alternatively you can use a 6 mm punch, which is the size of the hole in the gear, with insulating tape wrapped around the shaft and the handle as shown so it is a snug fit in the holes in the crankcase **(see illustration)**.

**10** Make sure the crankshaft is correctly aligned and the locking pin is fitted (Section 7).

**11** The intermediate gear is spring-loaded, and the teeth of the sprung gear must be aligned with those on the main gear when fitting the gear assembly and inserting the intermediate gear locking pin – this can be done by fitting a large flat-bladed screwdriver between the teeth and twisting it as you seat the gear on the drive gear and insert the pin.

**12** Seat the cam chain around the sprocket with the paint mark made earlier facing the gear

9.13a Position the gear and align the locking pin and holes...

so it will face the right-hand side of the engine **(see illustration)** – if you are fitting a new chain it does not matter which way round it fits.

**13** If not using a new intermediate gear bolt clean the threads of the original bolt and apply fresh threadlock. Lubricate the shaft and bearings with oil, then locate the gear assembly in the crankcase, aligning the locking pin hole with that in the crankcase, and insert the locking pin part-way so it enters the hole in the sprung gear, then twist the screwdriver to align the sprung teeth so the gears engage with the gear on the crankshaft, and slide the locking pin all the way in **(see illustrations)**. Insert the gear shaft and thread the bolt in, then hold the end of the shaft using a hex key and tighten the bolt to 10 Nm **(see illustrations)**. Remove the locking pin.

**14** Install the cylinder block and all other removed parts.

9.13b ...then insert the end of the pin in the hole in the gear...

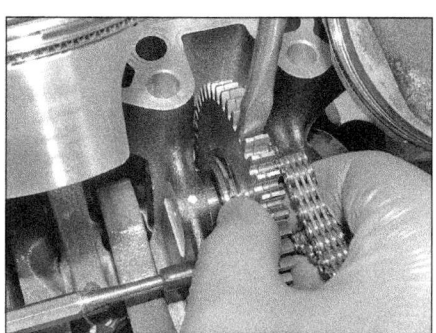

9.13c ...and twist the gear teeth so they align and engage with the crankshaft gear

9.13d Fit the shaft and thread the bolt in...

9.13e ...then counter-hold the shaft while tightening the bolt

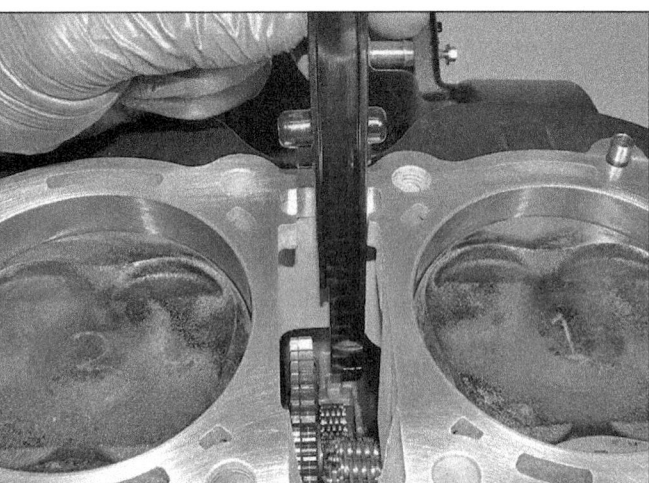

**10.4 Lift and remove the head**

**10.12 Make sure the blade seats correctly as described**

## 10 Cylinder head removal and installation

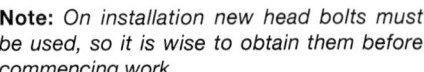

**Note:** *On installation new head bolts must be used, so it is wise to obtain them before commencing work.*

### Removal

**1** Remove the engine (Section 4).

**2** Remove the rockers, camshaft and shims (Section 8).

**3** The cylinder head is secured by eight bolts. Unscrew the bolts evenly and a little at a time in the sequence shown **(see illustration 10.15b)**. When all the bolts are loose, remove them with their washers. New bolts must be used, but the washers can be reused.

**4** Pull the cylinder head up off the cylinder block and remove it, passing the cam chain down the tunnel and laying it over the front of the block **(see illustration)**. If the head is stuck, hold the block and tap around the joint faces of the head with a soft-faced hammer or block of wood to free it. Do not attempt to free the head by inserting a lever between it and the cylinder block or you might damage the sealing surfaces.

**5** Remove the cylinder head gasket, and the dowels if loose **(see illustration 10.13)**. A new gasket must be used.

**6** If required lift the cam chain guide blade out, noting how the lugs seat in the slots **(see illustration 10.12)**.

**7** Check the cylinder head gasket and the mating surfaces on the cylinder head and block for signs of leaks from the cylinders, or the oil or coolant passages, which could indicate that the head is warped. Refer to Section 11, Step 14, for a warpage check.

**8** Lay a clean cloth over the cylinders while the head is off to prevent any dirt getting in.

**9** If required remove the thermostat (see Chapter 3).

### Installation

**10** Clean all traces of old gasket material from the cylinder head and block. If you need to use a scraper, take care not to scratch or gouge the soft aluminium. Be careful not to let any of the gasket material fall into the crankcase, the cylinder bores or the oil or coolant passages.

**11** Fit the thermostat if removed (see Chapter 3).

**12** If removed fit the cam chain guide blade, making sure the bottom of the blade sits in its seat and the lugs near its top locate in the cut-outs in the cylinder block **(see illustration)**.

**13** Fit the dowels if removed, then lay the new head gasket over the dowels with the lettering uppermost and at the back **(see illustration)**.

**14** Carefully position the cylinder head on the cylinder block, passing the cam chain up through the tunnel, and making sure it locates onto the dowels **(see illustration 10.4)**.

**15** Fit the washers onto the new bolts **(see illustration)**. Lubricate the threads, washers and under the heads of the bolts with clean engine oil. Fit the bolts and tighten them finger-tight. Now tighten the bolts in the sequence shown first to 20 Nm, and then to

**10.13 Fit the dowels (arrowed) then lay the new gasket on the block**

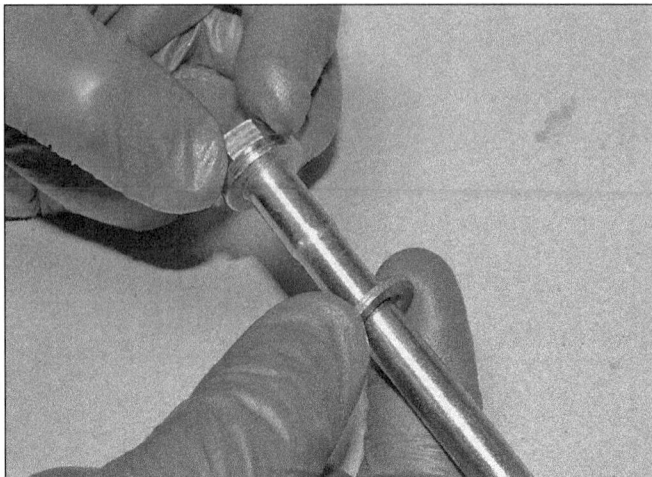

**10.15a Use new bolts fitted with the old washers, and lubricate as described**

**10.15b Cylinder head bolt tightening sequence**

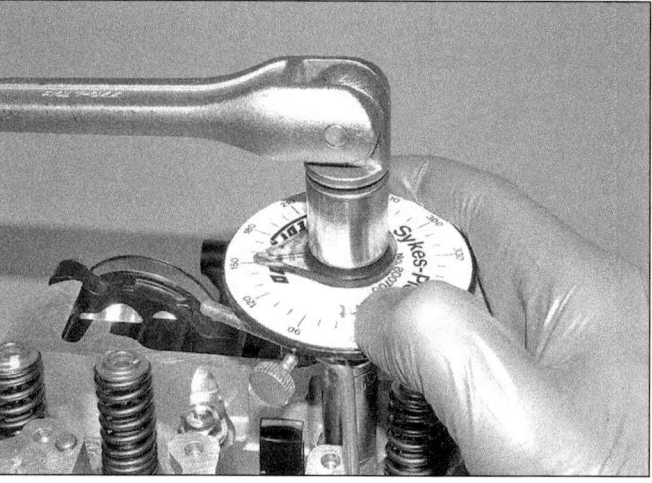

**10.15c Use a degree disc for the final tightening**

30 Nm **(see illustration)**. Working in the same sequence and using a degree disc, now tighten the bolts through 150° **(see illustration)**. Mark the top of each bolt with a marker pen once you have completed its angle tightening to ensure none get omitted or done twice.

**16** Install the remaining components in the reverse order of removal, referring to the relevant Sections and Chapters as directed.

### 11 Cylinder head and valve overhaul

**1** Because of the complex nature of this job and the special tools and equipment required, most owners leave servicing of the valves, valve seats and valve guides to a professional. However, you can make an initial assessment of whether the valves are seating correctly, and therefore sealing, by pouring a small amount of solvent into each of the valve ports. If the solvent leaks past any valve into the combustion chamber area the valve is not seating correctly and sealing.

**2** With the correct tools (a valve spring compressor is essential – make sure it is suitable for motorcycle work), you can also remove the valves and associated components from the cylinder head, clean

them and check them for wear to assess the extent of the work needed, and, unless seat cutting or guide replacement is required, reassemble them in the head.

**3** A dealer service department or engine specialist can replace the guides and re-cut the valve seats.

**4** After the valve service has been performed, be sure to clean it very thoroughly before installation on the engine to remove any metal particles or abrasive grit that may still be present from the valve service operations. Use compressed air, if available, to blow out all the holes and passages.

### Disassembly

**5** Before proceeding, arrange to label and store the valves along with their related components in such a way that they can be returned to their original locations without getting mixed up **(see illustration)**. Either use the same container as the valve shims are stored in (see Section 8), or obtain a separate container which is divided into eight compartments, and label each compartment with the identity of the valve which will be stored in it. Alternatively, labelled plastic bags will do just as well.

**6** Compress the valve spring on the first valve with a spring compressor, making sure it is correctly located onto each end of the valve assembly **(see illustration)**. On the top of the

valve the adaptor needs to be about the same size as the spring retainer **(see illustration)**. On the underside of the head make sure the plate (where present) on the compressor only contacts the valve and not the soft aluminium of the head **(see illustration)** – if the plate is

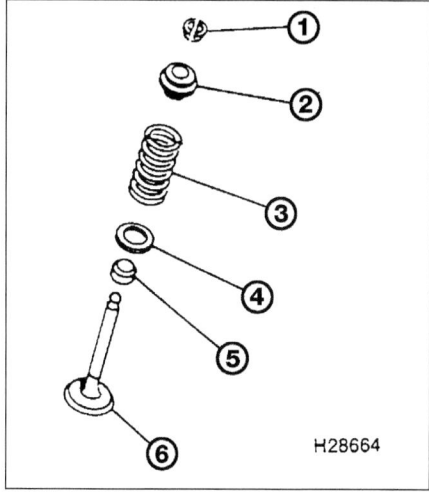

**11.5 Valve components**

| | |
|---|---|
| 1 Collets | 4 Spring seat |
| 2 Spring retainer | 5 Valve stem oil seal |
| 3 Valve spring | 6 Valve |

**11.6a Compressing the valve springs using a valve spring compressor**

**11.6b Make sure the compressor is a good fit both on the top...**

**11.6c ...and the bottom of the valve assembly**

11.7a Remove the collets with needle-nose pliers, tweezers, a magnet or a screwdriver with a dab of grease on it

11.7b Remove the spring retainer and the spring...

11.7c...then push the valve down and draw it out

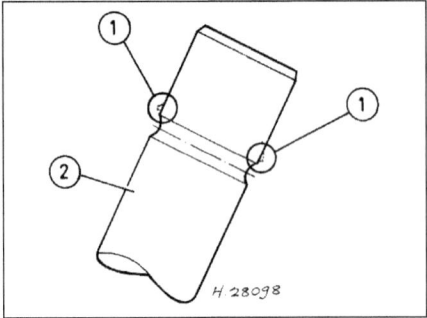

11.7d If the valve stem (2) won't pull through the guide, deburr the area above the collet groove (1)

11.8a Pull the seal off the top of the guide...

11.8b...then remove the spring seat

too big for the valve, use a spacer between them. Do not compress the spring any more than is absolutely necessary.

**7** Remove the collets using needle-nose pliers, tweezers, a magnet or a screwdriver with a dab of grease on it **(see illustration)**. Carefully release the valve spring compressor and remove the spring retainer, noting which way up it fits, the spring and the valve **(see illustrations)**. If the valve binds in the guide (won't pull through), push it back into the head and deburr the area around the collet groove with a very fine file or whetstone **(see illustration)**.

**8** Pull the valve stem seal off the top of the valve guide with pliers and discard it (the old seals cannot be reused) **(see illustration)**.

Remove the spring seat, noting which way up it fits – using a magnet is the easiest way to lift the seat off the head **(see illustration)**.

**9** Repeat the procedure for the remaining valves. Remember to keep the parts for each valve together and labelled so they can be reinstalled in the correct location.

**10** Clean the cylinder head with solvent and dry it thoroughly. Compressed air will speed the drying process and ensure that all holes and recessed areas are clean.Do not use a wire brush mounted in a drill motor to clean the combustion chambers as the head material is soft and may be scratched or eroded away by the wire brush.

**11** Clean the valve components with solvent and dry them thoroughly – clean the parts

from one valve at a time so they don't get mixed up.

**12** Scrape off any deposits that may have formed on the valves, using a motorised wire brush if available and necessary. Again, make sure the valves do not get mixed up.

### Inspection

**13** Inspect the head very carefully for cracks and other damage. If cracks are found, a new head is required. Check the camshaft bearing surfaces for wear and evidence of seizure. Check the camshafts and holders for wear as well (Section 8).

**14** Using a precision straight-edge and a feeler gauge, check the head gasket mating surface for warpage. Refer to *Tools and Workshop Tips* in the Reference section for details of how to use the straight-edge. If the head is warped beyond the limit specified at the beginning of this Chapter, consult your Triumph dealer or take it to an engineer for correction.

**15** Examine the valve seats in the combustion chamber and on the valve. If they are pitted, cracked or burned, the head will require work beyond the scope of the home mechanic. Measure the valve seat width and compare it to that given in the Specifications **(see illustration)**. If it is outside of the range, or if it varies around its circumference seek the advice of a Triumph dealer or engineer.

**16** Examine each valve face for cracks, pits and burned spots **(see illustration)**.

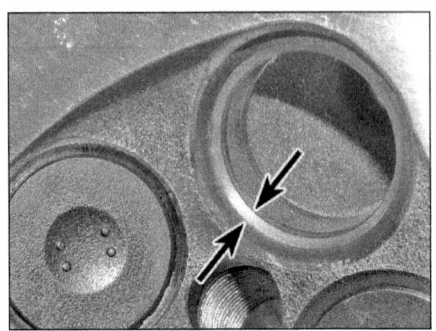

11.15 Measure the valve seat width with a ruler (or for greater precision use a Vernier caliper)

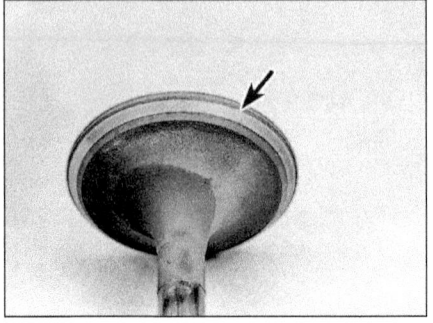

11.16 Check the valve face (arrowed) for wear and damage

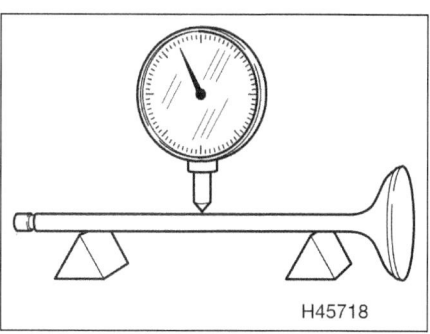

11.17 Measure valve stem runout with V-blocks and a dial gauge

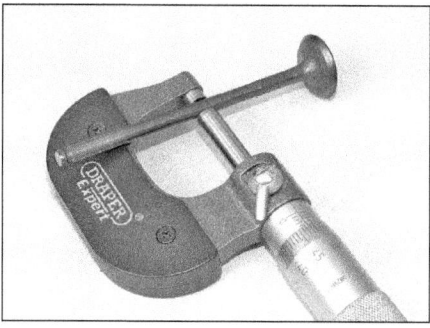

11.18a Measure the valve stem diameter with a micrometer...

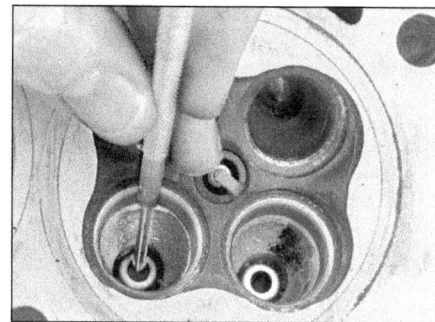

11.18b ...and the guide bore width with a bore gauge

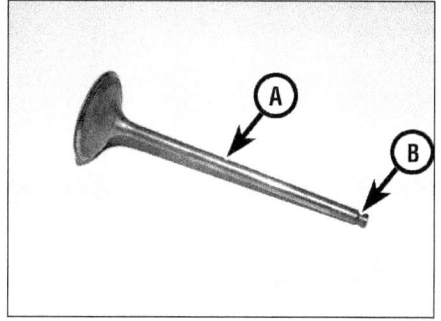

11.19 Check the stem (A) and collet groove (B)

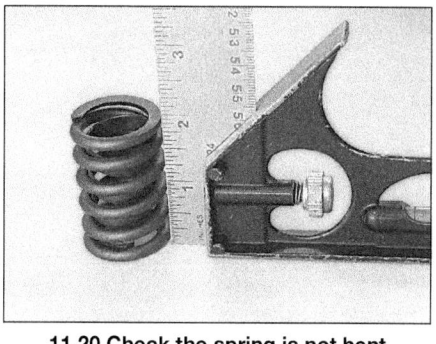

11.20 Check the spring is not bent

11.23 Fit the seat over the guide

**17** Rotate the valve and check for any obvious indication that it is bent. Using V-blocks and a dial gauge if available, check for valve stem runout **(see illustration)**. A slightly bent valve stem will prevent the valve from seating properly in the head.

**18** Measure the valve stem diameter **(see illustration)**. Clean the valve guides to remove any carbon build-up, then measure the inside diameters of the guides (at both ends and the centre of the guide) with a small hole gauge and micrometer (see *Tools and Workshop Tips* in the Reference section) **(see illustration)**. Measure the guides at the ends and at the centre to determine if they are worn in a bell-mouth pattern (more wear at the ends). Subtract the stem diameter from the valve guide diameter to obtain the valve stem-to-guide clearance. If the stem-to-guide clearance is greater than given in the Specifications, replace whichever components are worn beyond their specified limits with new ones. If the valve guide is within specifications, but is worn unevenly, fit a new one.

**Note:** *It is good practice to fit a new valve guide whenever a new valve is fitted.*

**19** Inspect the valve stem and collet groove area for scuffing and cracks **(see illustration)**. Check the end of the stem for pitting and wear.

**20** Measure the spring length with the specified load on it (see Specifications) and compare it to that listed. If any spring

compresses further than specified it has sagged and must be replaced with a new one – it is a good policy to replace the springs on all valves at the same time. Also place the spring upright on a flat surface and check it for bend by placing a ruler against it. If the bend in any spring is excessive, it must be replaced with a new one.

**21** Check the spring retainers and collets for obvious wear and cracks.

**22** If the inspection indicates that no overhaul work is required, the valve components can be reinstalled in the head. Any questionable parts should not be reused, as extensive damage will occur in the event of failure during engine operation.

## Reassembly

**23** Working on one valve at a time, lay the spring seat in place in the cylinder head so that its shouldered side faces upwards **(see illustration)**.

**24** Fit a new valve stem seal onto the guide and use your fingers, an appropriate size deep socket or a small screwdriver as shown to press the seal over the end of the valve guide until it is felt to clip into place **(see illustrations)**. Don't twist or cock the seal, or it will not seal properly against the valve stem. Also, don't remove it again or it will be damaged.

**25** Coat the valve stem with molybdenum disulphide oil (a 50/50 mixture of molybdenum

11.24a Fit the valve stem seal – you can use the shaft of a screwdriver as a guide to locate the seal...

11.24b ... and the handle to push it on

11.25a Fit the spring...

11.25b ... then fit the retainer

11.26a A small dab of grease will help to keep the collets in place on the valve while the spring is released

11.26b Seat the rib on the inner side of each collet into the groove in the valve stem

disulphide grease and engine oil), then slide it into its guide, rotating it slowly to avoid damaging the seal **(see illustration 11.7c)**. Check that the valve moves up and down freely in the guide. Next, fit the spring, with the closer-wound coils facing down into the cylinder head, then fit the spring retainer, with its shouldered side facing down so that it fits into the top of the spring **(see illustrations)**.

**26** Apply a small amount of grease to the inside of the collets to help stick them in place when fitting them on the valve stem **(see illustration)**. Compress the spring with the

valve spring compressor **(see illustrations 11.6a, b and c)** – when compressing the spring, do so only as far as is necessary to slip the collets into place. Fit the collets with the thick end at the top and seat the ribs in the groove **(see illustration)**. Make certain that the collets are securely located in the groove, then release the spring compressor.

**27** Repeat the procedure for the remaining valves. Remember to keep the parts for each valve together and separate from the other valves so they can be reinstalled in their original locations.

**28** Support the cylinder head on blocks so the valves can't contact the workbench top, then very gently tap the top of each valve stem to seat the collets in the groove.

**29** After the shims, camshaft and rockers have been installed, check the valve clearances (see Chapter 1).

## 12 Cylinder block

### Removal

**1** Remove the cylinder head (Section 10).

**2** If not already done lift the cam chain guide blade out, noting how the lugs seat in the slots **(see illustration 10.12)**.

**3** Pull the cylinder block up off the crankcase, supporting the pistons so the connecting rods do not knock against the crankcase, and feeding the cam chain down and laying it over the front **(see illustration)**. If the block is stuck, tap around the joint faces with a soft-faced mallet. Do not attempt to free it by inserting a screwdriver between the block and crankcase mating surfaces – you'll damage them.

**4** Remove the base gasket – a new one must be used. If they are loose, remove the dowels from the crankcase or the underside of the cylinder block **(see illustration)**.

**5** Stuff some clean rag into the crankcase and around the connecting rods and pistons to protect and support them and to prevent anything falling into the engine.

**6** Clean all traces of old gasket material from the cylinder block and crankcase. If a scraper is used, take care not to scratch or gouge the soft aluminium. Be careful not to let any of the gasket material fall into the engine.

### Inspection

**7** Check the cylinder walls carefully for scratches and score marks. The bores'

12.3 Carefully lift the block up off the crankcase

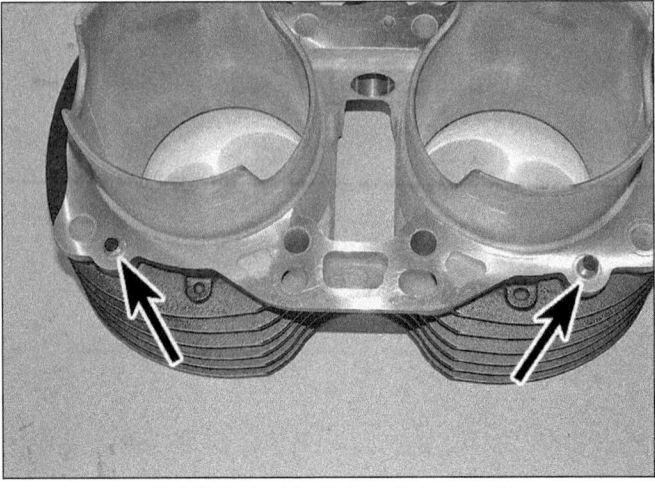

12.4 Cylinder block dowels (arrowed)

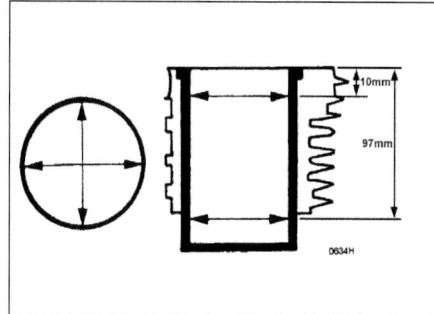

**12.8 Measure the cylinder bore in the directions shown using a telescoping gauge, then measure the gauge with a micrometer**

hard plated surface should last the life of the motorcycle under normal operating conditions.

8 Using a telescoping bore gauge and a micrometer, check the dimensions of the cylinder to assess the amount of wear, taper and ovality – measure 10 mm from the top

and 97 mm from the top of the bore, both parallel to and across the crankshaft axis **(see illustrations)**. Compare the results to the Specifications at the beginning of the Chapter. If a cylinder is worn, oval or tapered beyond the service limit the block must be replaced with a new one and new pistons and rings fitted. Reboring is not possible.

9 If the precision measuring tools are not available, take the cylinder block to a Triumph dealer or specialist motorcycle repair shop for assessment and advice.

### Installation

10 Check that the mating surfaces of the cylinder block and crankcase are free from oil or pieces of old gasket.

11 If removed, fit the dowels into the crankcase and push them firmly home.

12 Remove the rag from around the pistons, taking care not to let the connecting rods fall against the rim of the crankcase. Lay the new base gasket in place, locating it over the dowels **(see illustration)**. The gasket can only fit one way, so if all the holes do not line

up properly it is the wrong way round. Never re-use the old gasket.

13 Check the piston ring end gaps are positioned correctly before fitting the cylinder block (see Section 13) **(see illustration 13.23)**. If possible, have an assistant to support the cylinder block while the piston rings are fed into the bore.

14 Lubricate the cylinder bores, pistons and piston rings with clean engine oil. Carefully lower the block onto the pistons until the crowns fit into the bores **(see illustration)**.

15 Carefully compress and feed each ring into the bores as the block is lowered – the lower rim of each bore is chamfered to ease entry and there are cut-outs in the sides of the skirts to help compress the rings, so excess downward force on the block should not be necessary. If the block appears stuck, which could be due to a ring not being seated correctly in its groove, lift the block to check rather than trying to force it down as rings are easily broken **(see illustrations)**. If necessary, use your hand to gently tap the cylinder down, but do not use force.

**12.12 Lay the new gasket onto the crankcase**

**12.14 Carefully fit the piston into the bore and feed each ring in as you lower the block**

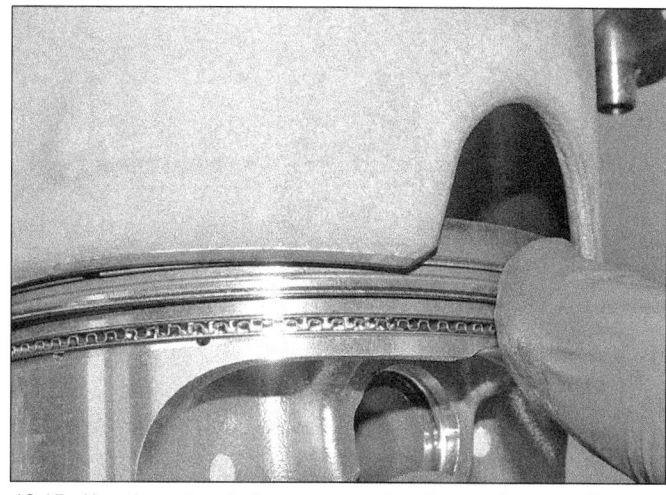

**12.15a Use the cut-outs to compress the rings using your finger...**

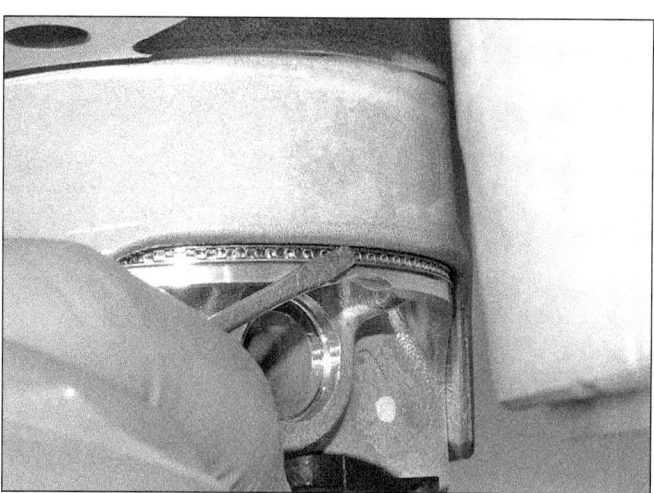

**12.15b ...or a small screwdriver**

**12.16a Push the block down onto the crankcase...**

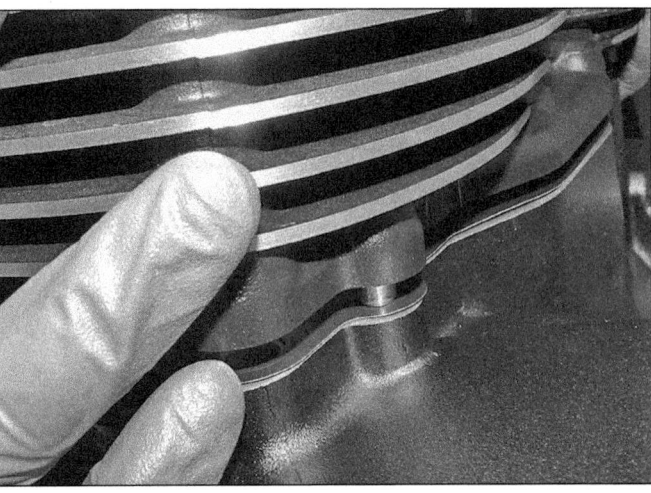

**12.16b ...making sure the dowels locate**

**16** When the pistons and rings are correctly located in the bore, feed the cam chain up through the tunnel and lay it over the front of the block, then press the cylinder block down onto the base gasket, making sure the dowels locate **(see illustrations)**.

**17** Fit the cam chain guide blade, making sure the bottom of the blade sits in its seat and the lugs near its top locate in the cut-outs in the cylinder block **(see illustration 10.12)**.

**18** Install the cylinder head (Section 10).

## 13 Pistons and piston rings

### Removal

**1** Remove the cylinder block (Section 12).

**2** Before removing the pistons, mark the cylinder number (left-hand cylinder No. 1, right-hand No. 2) on the crown **(see illustration)**. Also note the triangular mark on each crown which points to the front of the engine – if the mark is not visible, make your own as the piston must be installed the correct way round.

**3** Carefully prise out the circlip on the outer side of the piston using needle-nose pliers or

a small flat-bladed screwdriver inserted into the notch **(see illustration)**. Push the piston pin out from the other side to free the piston from the connecting rod **(see illustration)**. Remove the other circlip and discard them as new ones must be used. When the piston has been removed, fit its pin back into its bore so that related parts do not get mixed up. Remember the importance of the rag in preventing dropped circlips from falling into the crankcase.

> **HAYNES HINT**
> *To prevent the circlip from pinging away, pass a rod or screwdriver, which has a diameter greater than the gap between the circlip ends, through the piston pin. This will trap the circlip if it springs out.*

> **HAYNES HINT**
> *If a piston pin is a difficult to remove, check to see if there is a burr on the circlip groove rim that is stopping it coming out, and if so clean it up using a file. If not use a heat gun to expand the alloy piston sufficiently to release its grip of the pin.*

**4** If you are removing the rings from the pistons, carefully ease each one out of its groove, noting that they are brittle and easily broken if bent or over-expanded **(see illustrations 13.22, 13.21a, 13.19c, b and a)**. Do not nick or gouge the pistons in the process. Carefully note which way up each ring fits and in which groove as they must be installed in their original positions and the same way up if being re-used. The upper surface of the top and second rings should be marked 1T and 2T respectively – if the mark on each ring is different, note which mark is for the top ring and which is for the second. The rings can also be distinguished by their different profiles.

### Inspection

#### Pistons

**5** Scrape all traces of carbon from the tops of the pistons. A hand-held soft wire brush or a piece of scouring pad or fine emery cloth can be used once most of the deposits have been scraped away. Do not, under any circumstances, use a wire brush mounted in a drill motor to remove deposits from the pistons; the piston material is soft and will be eroded away by the wire brush.

**6** Use a piston ring groove cleaning tool to

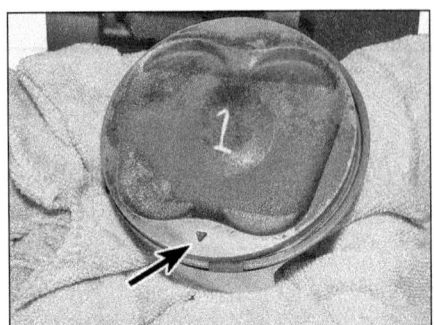

**13.2 Mark each piston with its cylinder number, and note the triangular mark (arrowed)**

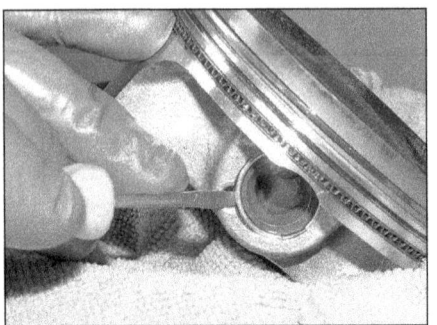

**13.3a Use a small screwdriver or pointed instrument inserted in the notch to lever out the circlip**

**13.3b Withdraw the pin and remove the piston**

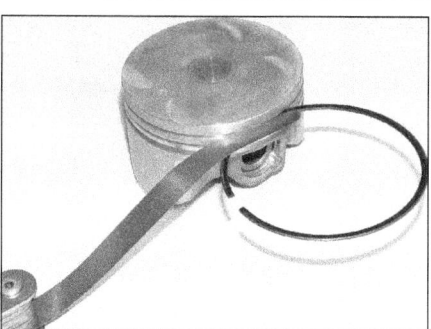

13.10 Measure the piston ring-to-groove
clearance with a feeler gauge

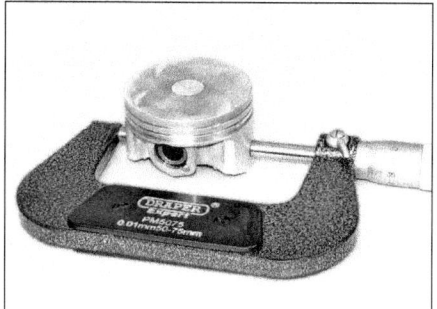

13.11 Measure the piston diameter with a
micrometer at the specified distance from
the bottom of the skirt

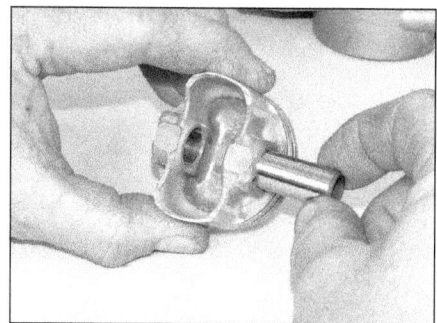

13.12a Measure the internal diameter of
the small-end bore, the external diameter
of the pin...

remove any carbon deposits from the ring
grooves. If a tool is not available, a piece
broken off an old ring will do the job. Be very
careful to remove only the carbon deposits.
Do not remove any metal and do not nick or
gouge the sides of the ring grooves.

**7** Once the deposits have been removed,
clean the pistons with solvent and dry them
thoroughly. Make sure the oil return holes
below the oil ring groove are clear.

**8** Carefully inspect each piston for cracks
around the skirt, at the pin bosses and at the
ring lands. Normal piston wear appears as
even, vertical wear on the thrust surfaces of
the piston and slight looseness of the top ring
in its groove. If the skirt is scored or scuffed,
the engine may have been suffering from
overheating and/or abnormal combustion,
which caused excessively high operating
temperatures. The oil pump and cooling
systems should be checked thoroughly.

**9** A hole in the piston crown, an extreme
to be sure, is an indication that abnormal
combustion (pre-ignition) was occurring.
Burned areas at the edge of the piston
crown are usually evidence of spark knock
(detonation). If any of the above problems
exist, the causes must be corrected or the
damage will occur again.

**10** Measure the piston ring-to-groove
clearance by laying the ring in its groove
and slipping a feeler blade in beside it **(see
illustration)**. Make sure you have the correct
ring for the groove – the two compression

rings can be identified by their markings (see
Step 4). Check the clearance at three or four
locations around the groove. If the clearance
is greater than that given in the Specifications,
replace the pistons and rings as a set.

**11** Measure the piston diameter 10 mm up
from the bottom of the skirt and at 90° to the
piston pin axis **(see illustration)**. If outside
of the figure given in the Specifications, the
piston is worn – fit new pistons and rings.

**12** Apply clean engine oil to the piston
pin, insert it part way into the piston and
check for any freeplay between the two **(see
illustration)**. If the necessary measuring
equipment is available, measure the piston pin
diameter at each end and the corresponding
inside diameter of the pin bores in the piston
**(see illustration)**. Replace any component
that has worn beyond the limits given in the
Specifications with a new one.

### Piston rings

**13** It is good practice to use new piston rings
when an engine is being overhauled. Before
fitting the piston rings, the ring end gaps must
be checked.

**14** Lay out the pistons and the ring sets so the
rings will be matched with their same piston
and cylinder during the end gap measurement
procedure and engine assembly.

**15** Fit the top ring into the top of its bore
and square it up with the cylinder walls by
pushing it in with the top of the piston until
the third groove in the piston is level with and

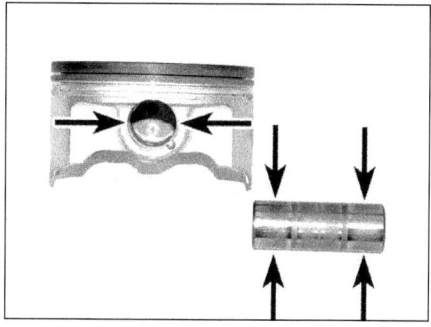

13.12b ...and the internal diameter of the
bore in the piston

parallel all the way round to the top of the
liner **(see illustrations)**. To measure the end
gap, slip a feeler blade between the ends of
the ring and compare the measurement to the
Specifications **(see illustration)**.

**16** If the gap is too small, check the bore for
distortion (Section 12). If the bore is good,
and new rings are being measured, get
another set of rings from your dealer, who
should exchange them if you explain the
circumstances, as they should fit correctly.
If you are measuring the end gaps of the old
rings, fit new ones.

**17** If the end gap exceeds the service limit
specified with the old rings, fit new rings and
check again. If it is still excessive check the
bore for wear (Section 12).

**18** Repeat the procedure for each ring

13.15a Ease the ring into the cylinder...

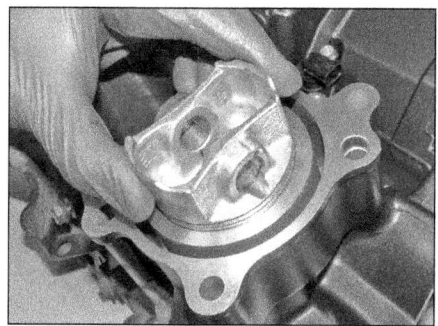

13.15b ...pushing it down to the depth of
the third groove in the piston, and making
sure it is square

13.15c Measuring piston ring installed end
gap

13.19a Fit the oil ring expander in its groove...

13.19b ...then fit the lower side rail...

13.19c ...and the upper side rail each side of it

13.21a Fit the second ring into the middle groove

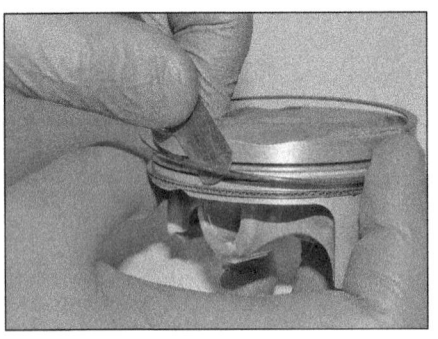

13.21b A feeler gauge blade can be used to guide the ring over the piston

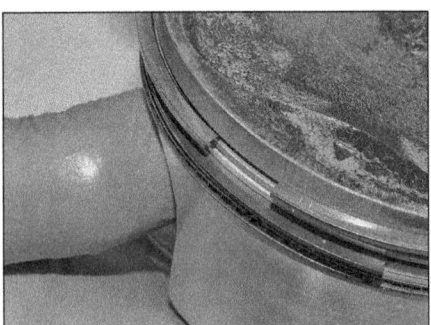

13.22 Fit the top ring into the top groove

(except the oil control ring expander) that will be installed in the first cylinder and for each ring in the other cylinder. Remember to keep the rings, pistons and cylinders matched up.

### Installation

19 The oil control ring (lowest on the piston) is installed first. It is composed of three separate components, the expander and the upper and lower side rails. First slip the expander into the groove, making sure the ends butt against each other and do not

overlap. Next fit the lower side rail, then the upper (see illustrations). New side rails can be fitted either way up, but if the removed ones are being reused they must be installed the same way up as they were removed. Do not use a piston ring installation tool on the side rails as they may be damaged. Instead, place one end of the side rail into the groove between the expander and the ring land. Hold it firmly in place and slide a finger around the piston while pushing the rail into the groove.

20 After the three oil ring components have

been installed, check to make sure that both the upper and lower side rails can be turned smoothly in the ring groove.

21 Fit the second (middle) ring next – it should be marked 2T at one end, and this mark must face up. If no mark is visible the second ring and top rings can be distinguished by their different profiles, the top ring having a chamfered inner top edge – make sure you have the correct ring. Fit the ring into the middle groove on the piston (see illustration)- do not over-expand the ends or twist or bend the ring out of flat when fitting it over the piston; if required you can slip a feeler gauge blade between the ring and piston to guide it into its groove (see illustration).

*Caution: Do not expand the ring any more than is necessary to slide it into place – the ring material is brittle and is easily broken if overstressed.*

22 Finally, fit the top ring into the top groove in the same manner – make sure the 1T mark near the end gap is facing up (see illustration).

23 Position the ring end gaps around the piston as shown (see illustration).

24 Stuff clean rag into the crankcase mouth to prevent any dropped circlips falling in. Fit a new circlip into the groove in the inner side of the piston.

25 Lubricate the piston pin and the connecting rod small-end bore with engine oil. Locate the piston on its rod (No. 1 piston on the left-hand rod) with the triangular mark on its crown pointing to the front of the engine, then push the piston pin fully into the piston

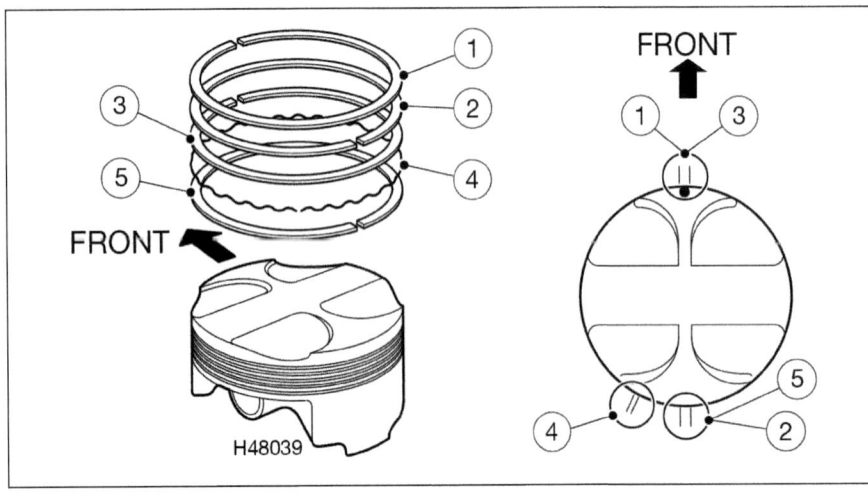

13.23 Stagger the ring end gaps as shown

1 Top ring end gap
2 Second (middle) ring end gap
3 Top oil ring side rail end gap
4 Oil ring expander ends
5 Bottom oil ring side rail end gap

and secure with a second new circlip – make sure the circlip is fully seated in its groove **(see illustrations)**.

**26** Fit the other piston in the same way.

**27** Check that the piston rings are still correctly positioned in relation to the front of the engine **(see illustration 13.23)**.

**28** Install the cylinder block (Section 12).

## 14 Clutch cable

### *All models except the Bobber*

**1** Remove the cable guide from the left-hand side of the steering head **(see illustration)**. Release the cable clips by pushing one side in using a small screwdriver and pulling the clip out **(see illustrations)**.

**2** At the handlebar end release the lockring and thread the cable adjuster into the lever bracket **(see illustration)**. Align the slots in the adjuster and lockring with the slot in the bracket.

**3** Slide the rubber cap off the lower end of the outer cable **(see illustration)**. Slacken the nuts securing the cable in the bracket on the clutch cover, and thread the front nut up as far as it will go and thread the rear nut off **(see illustrations)**.

**4** Slide the cable into the bracket and slip the cable end out of the retainer on the release arm, noting how it fits **(see illustration)**.

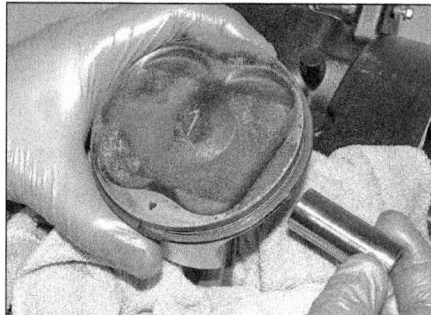

13.25a Slide the pin through the piston and rod...

13.25b ...and secure it with a new circlip

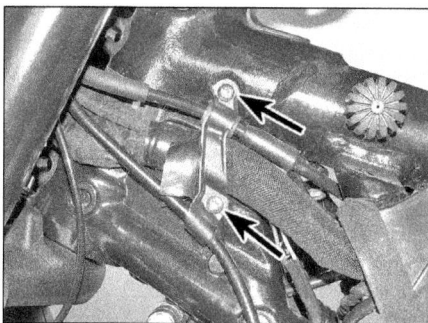

14.1a Undo the screws (arrowed) and remove the guide

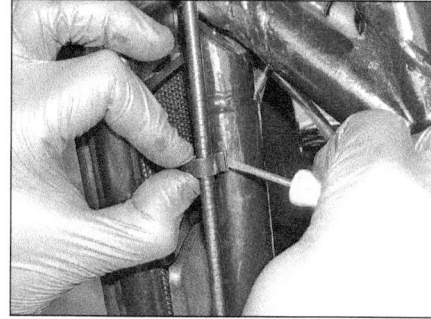

14.1b Release the cable clips from the frame...

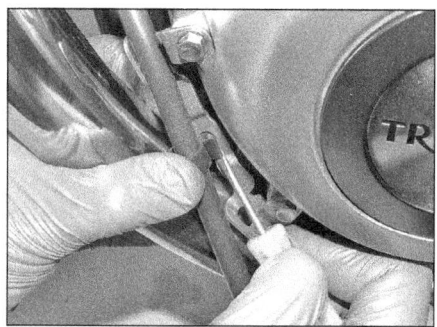

14.1c ...and the bracket

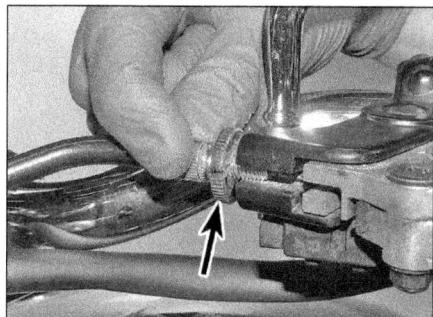

14.2 Slacken the lockring (arrowed) and turn the adjuster into the bracket

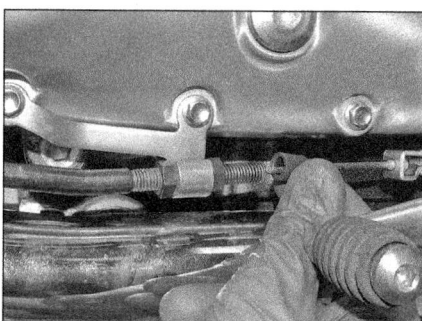

14.3a Slide the cap off

14.3b Slacken the nuts...

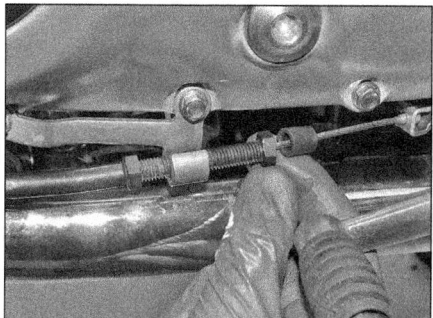

14.3c ... and thread the front nut up and the rear nut off

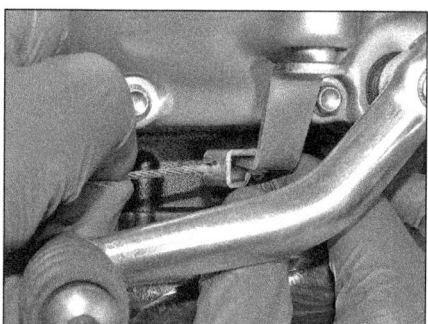

14.4a Detach the cable end...

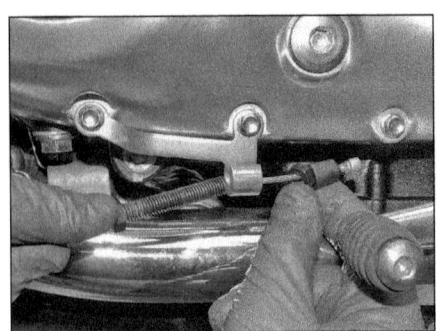

**14.4b ...and draw the cable out of the bracket**

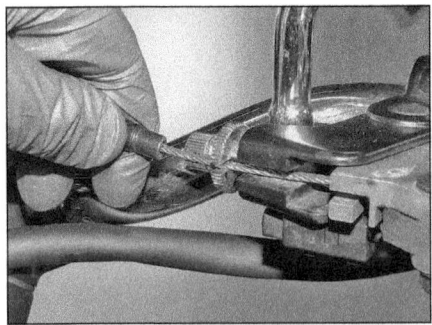

**14.5a Draw the outer cable end from the adjuster and slip the inner cable out via the slots...**

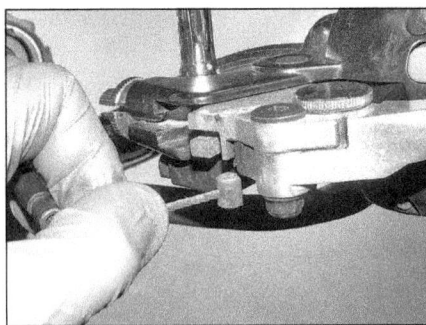

**14.5b ...then detach the inner cable end from the lever**

Draw the cable out of the bracket **(see illustration)**.

**5** Pull the upper end of the outer cable end from the socket in the adjuster and release the inner cable from the lever **(see illustrations)**. Remove the cable from the machine, noting its routing.

**6** Unless a new cable is being fitted check the cable ends for security of the nipples and any loose strands and fraying. Make sure the inner cable slides smoothly and freely in the outer cable. If required lubricate the cable using a pressure adapter (see Chapter 1).

**7** Turn the clutch release mechanism arm to check for smooth operation of the shaft in the cover and any signs of wear or damage.

Remove it for inspection if required (Section 15).

**8** Installation is the reverse of removal. Apply grease to the cable ends. Make sure the cable is correctly routed. Make sure the cable lower end is properly located in the retainer on the release mechanism arm. Fit the cable clips and guide.

**9** Adjust the clutch lever freeplay (see Chapter 1).

### Bobber

**10** Remove the cable guide from the left-hand side of the steering head **(see illustration)**. Release the cable clip by pushing one side in

using a small screwdriver and pulling the clip out **(see illustration and 14.1b)**.

**11** Note the alignment of the punch marks on the gearchange linkage arm and shaft, then unscrew the pinch bolt and slide the arm off **(see illustration)**. Unscrew the footrest/lever assembly bracket bolts and remove the assembly **(see illustrations)**.

**12** Slide the rubber boot up off the cable adjuster next to the radiator, then fully slacken the locknut and turn the adjuster fully in to create maximum freeplay **(see illustration)**. At the handlebar end release the lockring and thread the cable adjuster into the lever bracket **(see illustration 14.2)**. Align the slots in the adjuster and lockring with the slot in the bracket.

**14.10a Undo the screws (arrowed) and remove the guide**

**14.10b Release the cable clip (arrowed) from the frame**

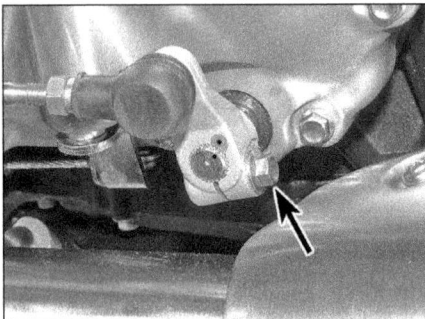

**14.11a Note the alignment, then unscrew the bolt (arrowed) to release the arm**

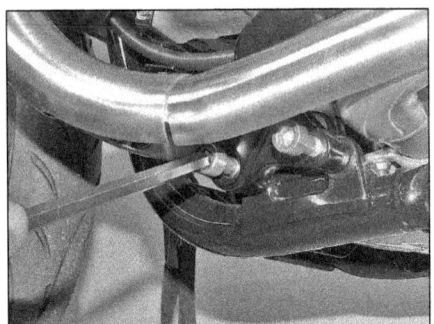

**14.11b Unscrew the bracket bolts using a ball-end hex key to give some angle**

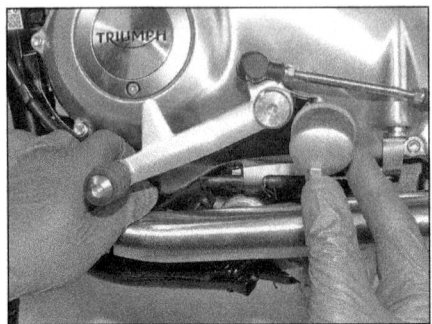

**14.11c Lift the footrest/gearchange lever assembly out**

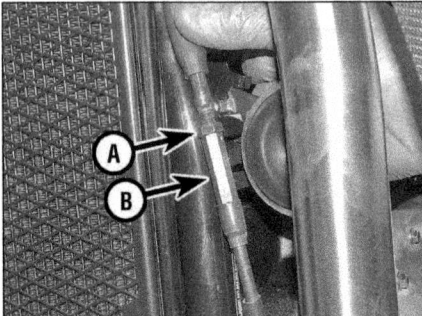

**14.12 Thread the locknut (A) all the way up then turn the adjuster (B) all the way in**

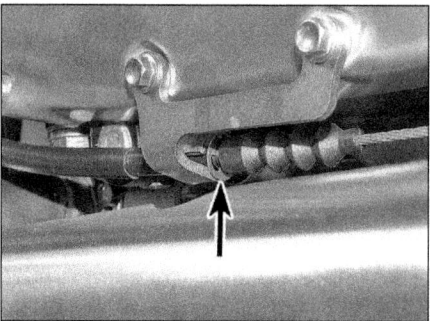

**14.13 Unscrew the bolt (arrowed) to release the bracket**

**14.14a Slide the boot off then release the E-clip (arrowed)**

**14.14b Release the cable end from the retainer (arrowed)**

**13** Unscrew the clutch cover bolt that secures the cable bracket **(see illustration)**.

**14** Pull the rubber boot off the lower end of the outer cable, then ease the E-clip off the cable using a small screwdriver **(see illustration)**. Slip the cable end out of the retainer on the release arm, noting how it fits **(see illustration)**. Draw the outer cable forwards out of the bracket and slip the inner cable through the gap.

**15** At the handlebar end pull the outer cable end from the socket in the adjuster and release the inner cable from the lever **(see illustrations 14.5a and b)**. Remove the cable from the machine, noting its routing.

**16** Unless a new cable is being fitted check the cable ends for security of the nipples and any loose strands and fraying. Make sure the inner cable slides smoothly and freely in the outer cable. If required lubricate the cable using a pressure adapter (see Chapter 1).

**17** Turn the clutch release mechanism arm to check for smooth operation of the shaft in the cover and any signs of wear or damage. Remove it for inspection if required (Section 15).

**18** Installation is the reverse of removal. Apply grease to the cable ends. Make sure the cable is correctly routed. Make sure the cable lower end is properly located in the retainer on the release mechanism arm. Tighten the clutch cover bolt to 10 Nm.

**19** Adjust the clutch lever freeplay (see Chapter 1).

## 15 Clutch

**Special tool:** *A clutch centre holding tool is useful, although not essential – see Step 11.*

### Removal

**1** Drain the engine oil (see Chapter 1).

**2** Refer to Chapter 5 and remove the gearchange lever or displace the linkage arm from the shaft, according to model.

**3** Disconnect the clutch cable from the release arm and release the cable from the clutch cover (Section 14).

**4** Working evenly in a criss-cross pattern, unscrew the clutch cover bolts, noting the positions of the clutch cable brackets and which bolts fit where as there are different lengths. Remove the cover, being prepared to catch any residual oil **(see illustration)**. If the cover will not lift away easily, break the gasket seal by tapping gently around the edge with a soft-faced hammer or block of wood. There is a washer on the end of the gearchange shaft **(see illustration 15.39b)** – make sure it has not stuck to the cover. Check the condition of the balancer shaft O-rings and fit new ones on installation if necessary **(see illustration 15.39c)**.

**5** Remove the cover gasket **(see illustration 15.39a)** – a new one must be fitted.

**15.4 Remove the cover**

Note the position of the four locating pins and remove them if they are loose – they should be tight in the crankcase, but if loose they could be in the cover.

**6** Withdraw the No. 2 starter idle gear shaft and remove the gear **(see illustration)**.

**7** Working in a criss-cross pattern, gradually slacken the clutch spring plate bolts until spring pressure is released, counter-holding the clutch using a rag, and when loose remove the bolts, plate and springs **(see illustrations)**.

**8** Remove the pressure plate, bringing the outermost friction and plain plates with it, noting how the tabs of the outer friction plate locate in the shallow slots in the housing,

**15.6 Withdraw the shaft and remove the gear**

**15.7a Unscrew the bolts and remove the plate...**

**15.7b ...and springs**

**15.9 You can remove most of the plates in one go by pushing them out via the tab slots, then hook the rest out**

**15.10 Unstake the rim of the nut**

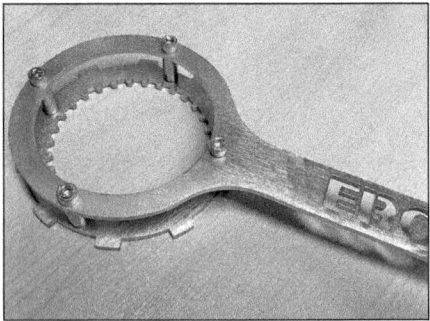

**15.11 This aftermarket EBC tool is ideal for holding the clutch centre**

**15.14 Ease the bearing sleeve and bearing out and remove the bearing...**

**15.15 ...then remove the clutch housing**

offset from the rest **(see illustration 15.36b)**. Remove the pull-rod from the pressure plate bearing or from the transmission shaft **(see illustration 15.36a)**.

**9** Remove the clutch plates **(see illustration)** – unless the plates are being replaced with new ones, keep them in their original order. Remove the anti-judder spring and spring seat **(see illustrations 15.32b and a)**.

**10** Use a small pointed tool to unstake the rim of the clutch nut from the indent in the end of the shaft **(see illustration)**.

**11** To unscrew the clutch nut, the transmission input shaft must be locked. This can be done by selecting top gear and having an assistant hold the brakes on hard with the rear tyre in firm contact with the ground. Alternatively, the Triumph service tool Pt. No. T3880307, or a similar commercially available

tool, can be used to hold the clutch centre while the nut is loosened **(see illustration)**. With the clutch held, unscrew the nut and remove the spring washer and plain washer **(see illustrations 15.31c and b)**. A new nut and spring washer should be used on reassembly.

**12** Slide the clutch centre and the thrust washer off the input shaft **(see illustrations 15.31a and 15.30)**.

**13** Note how the primary driven gear on the clutch housing engages with the primary drive gear on the crankshaft. Note also that the oil pump drive chain runs behind the clutch housing – the chain loops round a sprocket that engages with the back of the housing.

**14** Ease out the bearing sleeve and needle bearing from between the clutch housing and the input shaft using a pair of pliers and by

sliding the housing on the shaft to help push them along, and remove the bearing, leaving the sleeve in place **(see illustration)**.

**15** Remove the clutch housing **(see illustration)**.

### Inspection

**16** After an extended period of service the clutch friction plates will wear and promote clutch slip. Measure the thickness of each friction plate using a Vernier caliper **(see illustration)**. If any plate has worn to or beyond the service limit given in the Specifications, the friction plates must be replaced with a new set. Also, if any of the plates smell burnt or are glazed, they must be replaced as a set.

**17** If the plates are good, but the clutch has been slipping, it could be that the springs have sagged. As no specification is available for the spring free length, the only way to check them is to compare them with new ones. If the springs have sagged or tilt, fit a new set.

**18** The plain plates should not show any signs of excess heating (bluing). Check for warpage using a flat surface and feeler gauges **(see illustration)**. If any plate exceeds the maximum amount of warpage given in the Specifications, or shows signs of bluing, all the plain plates must be replaced with a new set.

**19** Check the spring plate for cracks and the spring seats for distortion **(see illustration)** – you can remove the seats by squeezing their sides until their open ends are clear of the groove.

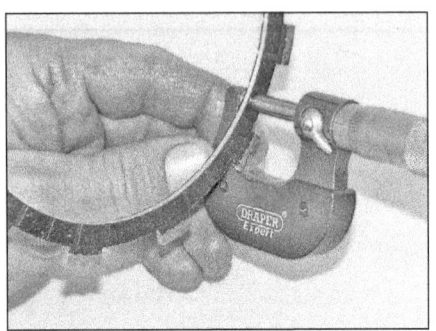

**15.16 Measuring clutch friction plate thickness**

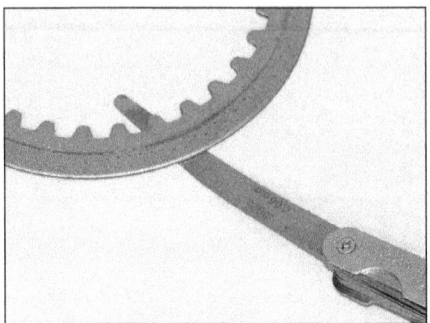

**15.18 Checking the plain plates for warpage**

**15.19 Check each spring seat (arrowed)**

15.20a Check for wear of the friction plate tabs and the clutch housing slots...

15.20b...and of the plain plate tongues and clutch centre slots

15.21 Check for wear on the sliding surfaces

15.22 Inspect the needle bearing, the bearing centre and the bearing surface in the housing

15.24a Check the pressure plate and bearing

15.24b Check the pull-rod and shaft

20  Inspect the friction plate tabs and the clutch housing slots for burrs and indentations **(see illustration)**. Similarly check for wear between the inner teeth of the plain plates and the slots in the clutch centre **(see illustration)**. Wear of this nature will cause clutch drag and slow disengagement during gear changes as the plates will snag when the pressure plate is lifted. With care a small amount of wear can be corrected by dressing with a fine file, but if this is excessive the worn components should be replaced with new ones.
21  Check the slipper mechanism drive and driven cams on the clutch centre and the back of the pressure plate for wear and damage **(see illustration)**.
22  Inspect the needle roller bearing, the

internal bearing surface of the clutch housing and the external surface of the bearing sleeve **(see illustration)**. If there are any signs of wear, pitting or other damage the affected parts must be replaced with new ones.
23  Check the teeth of the primary driven gear on the clutch housing and the corresponding teeth of the primary drive gear on the crankshaft. Replace the clutch housing with a new one if any teeth are worn or chipped. The primary drive gear is an integral part of the crankshaft (see Section 23 for removal of the crankshaft).
24  Check the pressure plate and its bearing for signs of wear or damage and roughness **(see illustration)**. Check the pull-rod head for signs of wear or damage, and check engaging

piece on the release shaft in the cover **(see illustration)**. Replace any parts, as necessary, with new ones, referring to the next Step for the shaft. To remove the pressure plate bearing push or drive it out from the outside using a socket. Push or drive the new bearing in from the inside using a socket that bears on the outer race until it seats.
25  Check the clutch release mechanism shaft turns smoothly in its housing in the cover. If it is rough, draw the shaft out of the cover and remove the return spring, noting how the spring ends locate **(see illustration)**. Remove the oil seal (a new one will be required), and clean and check the bearings **(see illustrations)**. Replace the bearings with new ones if necessary, referring to *Tools and*

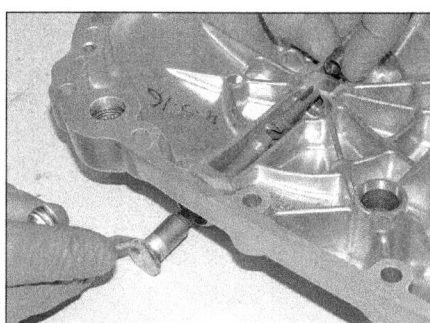

15.25a Withdraw the shaft and remove the spring from the bottom

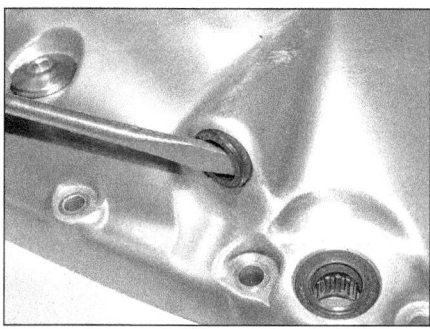

15.25b Lever the seal out...

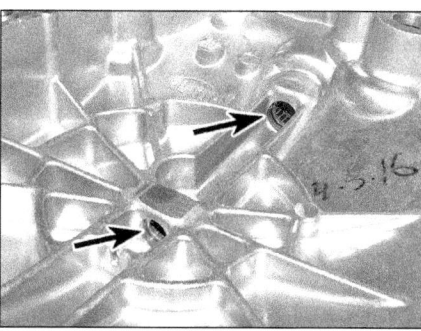

15.25c...and check the bearings (arrowed)

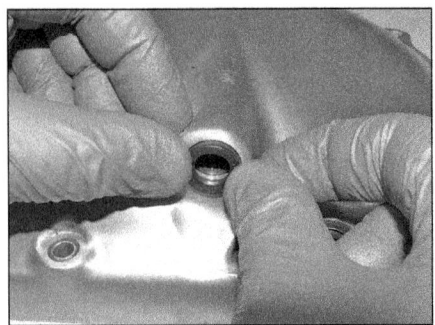

**15.25d Push the seal in, setting it flush**

**15.25e Make sure the spring seats over the end of the shaft and the ends are located as shown**

*Workshop Tips*. On reassembly lubricate the bearings with engine oil. Fit a new oil seal with its marked side facing out, and lubricate its lip with grease **(see illustration)**. Slide the shaft in and fit the spring, making sure the ends locate correctly **(see illustration)**. Refer to Section 17, Step 1 and fit a new gearchange shaft seal, and check and lubricate the shaft bearing in the cover.

### Installation

26 Remove all traces of old gasket from the crankcase and clutch cover surfaces.

27 Make sure the No. 1 starter idle gear is in place **(see illustration 16.9)**.

28 Make sure the oil pump chain is correctly engaged around the oil pump sprockets. Align the holes in the back of the clutch housing with the drive pins on the sprocket and slide the housing onto the shaft, engaging the primary drive and driven gear teeth, and making sure the pump sprocket pins locate in the holes **(see illustration)**.

29 Lubricate the needle roller bearing with clean engine oil. Support the clutch housing and slide the bearing into the housing **(see illustration)**. If correctly fitted the sleeve, bearing and clutch housing rims should all be flush – if the housing is sitting proud of the sleeve and bearing the pump sprocket drive pins have not located in the holes, and the housing must be turned until they do.

30 Lubricate the thrust washer with clean engine oil and slide it onto the shaft **(see illustration)**.

31 Slide the clutch centre onto the shaft splines **(see illustration)**. Fit the thrust washer

**15.28 Align the three holes with the pins and slide the shaft on**

**15.29 Centre the housing and insert the bearing**

**15.30 Fit the thrust washer**

**15.31a Fit the clutch centre...**

**15.31b ... the washers ...**

**15.31c ... and a new clutch nut**

**15.31d Tighten the nut to the specified torque then stake the rim into the indent**

and the new spring washer with the OUT mark facing out **(see illustration)**. Fit the new clutch centre nut and fit it with the thin rim facing out, then lock the input shaft as before (see Step 11) and tighten the nut to 98 Nm **(see illustration)**. Check that the clutch centre rotates freely after tightening the nut. Stake the rim of the nut into the

indents in the end of the shaft **(see illustration)**.
**32** Fit the anti-judder spring seat, then fit the spring so its outer rim is raised off the seat **(see illustrations)**.
**33** There are eight friction plates and seven plain plates. Of the eight friction plates there are two different types, 1 and 2. First identify the

three Type 1 friction plates with the wider internal diameter **(see illustration)** – these plates fit first and last (one innermost and two outermost). Of the seven plain friction plates there are two different types, A and B. First identify the single Type A plain plate with the wider internal diameter – this plate fits outermost, between the two outer Type 1 friction plates.

**15.32a Fit the seat...**

**15.32b ...and the spring...**

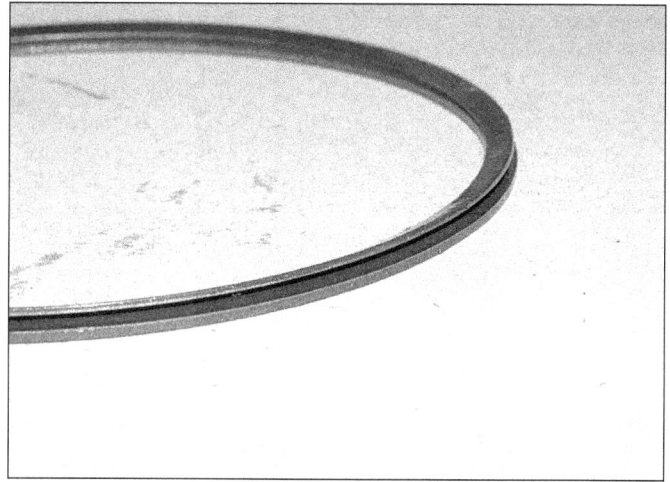

**15.32c ...so the outer rim of the spring is raised off the seat**

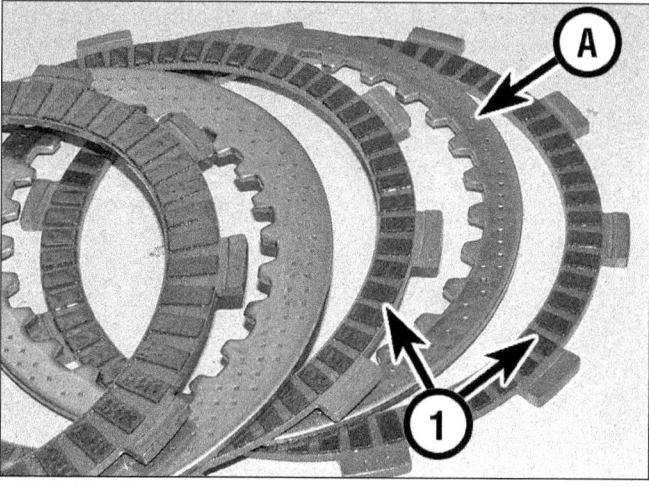

**15.33 Identify the type 1 friction plates and type A plain plate by their wider ID, or narrower rim**

15.35a Fit a Type 1 friction plate ...

15.35b ...then a Type B plain plate...

15.35c ... then a Type 2 friction plate, and so on as described until all Type 2 and B plates are fitted...

15.35d ...then fit the second of the Type 1 friction plates

15.35e Fit the outermost Type 1 friction plate and the Type A plain plate onto the back of the pressure plate

15.36a Insert the pull-rod

**34** If new clutch plates are being fitted the clutch plate pack thickness must be checked – assemble them all (8 friction plates and 7 plain plates) as a pack on the bench and measure the total thickness of all the plates – it should be within the range given in the Specifications. If the thickness is outside the range you need to replace the outer Type B plain plate with a thicker or thinner one as required to restore the thickness within the range. The Type B plain plates are 2mm thick as standard, with alternatives of 1.6 mm and 2.3 mm available.

**35** Lay the clutch plates out in order as described in Step 33. Coat each plate with clean engine oil prior to installation. Build up the plates, starting with a Type 1 friction plate and aligning its tabs with the deep slots, and seating it around the anti-judder spring and seat, then fit a Type B plain plate, then alternate Type 2 friction plates and B plain plates until all are fitted, with the thicker or thinner Type B plain plate fitted last if being used, then fit the second Type 1 friction plate **(see illustrations)**. Fit the outermost Type 1 friction plate and the Type A plain plate onto the pressure plate **(see illustrations)**.

**36** Make sure the bearing and spring seats are correctly seated in the pressure plate and lubricate the bearing with clean engine oil. Fit the pull-rod into the shaft **(see illustration)**. Fit the pressure plate, aligning the outermost friction plate tabs with the shallow slots in the housing so they are offset from the rest **(see illustration)**.

**37** Fit the clutch springs, the plate with the OUT mark facing out, and the bolts, then hold the clutch housing and tighten the bolts evenly and a little at a time in a criss-cross sequence to 10 Nm **(see illustrations 15.7b and a)**.

**38** Lubricate the No. 2 starter idle gear with clean oil, position the gear and insert the shaft **(see illustration 15.6)**.

**39** Before fitting the cover, if not already done refer to Step 25 and check the release mechanism components and gearchange shaft oil seal. If removed, fit the four cover locating pins into the crankcase. Fit the new gasket onto the pins **(see illustration)**.

15.36b Seat the friction plate tabs into the offset slots

15.39a Fit a new gasket onto the pins (arrowed)

15.39b Check the washer is fitted

15.39c Check and lubricate the O-rings (arrowed)

Make sure the washer is on the gearchange shaft **(see illustration)**. Fit the balancer shaft O-rings if removed, using new ones if necessary, and smear them with grease **(see illustration)**. Smear some grease onto the gearchange shaft oil seal lips, and lubricate the shaft bearing in the cover with oil.

**40** Pull the pull-rod as far out as it will come so it seats against the bearing in the pressure plate. Set the release shaft arm so that it points back, then fit the cover **(see illustration 15.4)**. Check that the cover is located on the dowels and is seated all round, then push the release arm in so it is at right-angles to the cover **(see illustration)** – if it doesn't

move in it is not engaging around the pull rod head, in which case push the shaft up or draw it down and out slightly until it does engage.

**41** Clean the threads of the two shortest clutch cover bolts that fit on either side of the gearchange shaft, and apply some threadlock **(see illustration)**. The four longest bolts fit around the front in the holes that sit further out than the rest, and do not forget to fit the cable brackets **(see illustrations for all models except the Bobber, and see illustrations 14.13 and 14.14b for the Bobber)**. Tighten the cover bolts evenly in a criss-cross sequence to 10 Nm, then go clockwise

round the bolts once again to ensure all are tightened to 10 Nm.
**42** Connect the clutch cable, then adjust it (see Chapter 1).
**43** Refer to Chapter 5 and fit the gearchange lever or the linkage arm onto the shaft, according to model.
**44** Refill the engine with the correct type and amount of oil (see Chapter 1).

## 16 Starter clutch and gears

### *Check*

**1** The operation of the starter clutch can be checked while it is in place – remove the clutch cover (Section 15). Withdraw the No. 2 starter idle gear shaft and remove the gear **(see illustration 15.6)**, then check that the starter driven gear is able to rotate freely clockwise as you look at it from the left-hand side of the bike, but locks when rotated anti-clockwise **(see illustration)**. If not, the starter clutch is faulty and should be removed for inspection.

### *Removal*

**2** Remove the clutch cover (Section 15).
**3** Withdraw the No. 2 starter idle gear shaft and remove the gear **(see illustration 15.6)**.

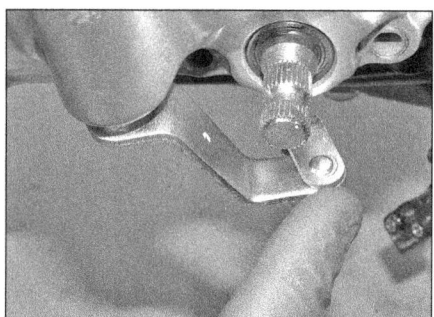

15.40 Push the arm in – it should move 90°
from the position shown

15.41a Threadlock the two short bolts and
fit them as shown

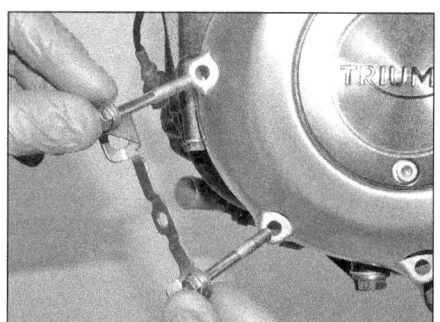

15.41b On all models except the Bobber fit
the clutch cable brackets...

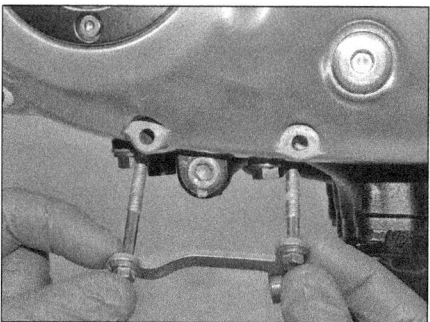

15.41c ...as shown

16.1 Check the gear rotates clockwise and
locks anti-clockwise

16.4a Remove the plate...

16.4b ...and the driven gear

16.5a Hold the rotor to unscrew the bolts...

16.5b ...then remove the clutch

16.6 Check the gear rotates clockwise and locks anti-clockwise

**4** Unscrew the starter clutch plate bolts and remove the plate **(see illustration)**. Remove the starter driven gear from the clutch, turning it clockwise as you do **(see illustration)**.
**5** Hold the flywheel using a rotor strap, then unscrew the starter clutch bolts and remove the clutch **(see illustrations)**.

### Inspection

**6** Fit the driven gear into the clutch, turning it clockwise. Check that the gear rotates smoothly and freely when turned clockwise and locks solid against the clutch when turned anti-clockwise **(see illustration)**.
**7** Remove the driven gear from the clutch. Inspect the condition of the sprags in the clutch and the outer surface of the driven gear hub **(see illustration)**. If there is wear or damage or it does not operate as described in Step 6, remove the sprag assembly from the housing and fit a new one, making sure it seats correctly **(see illustration)**.
**8** Inspect the inner surface of the driven gear hub and the bearing on the end of the crankshaft **(see illustration)**. If the bearing is worn use a puller to remove it from the end of the crankshaft, and a press to fit the new one – do not drive the new bearing on.
**9** Inspect the teeth on the starter motor shaft, the idle/reduction gears and the starter driven gear for wear and damage. Check the idle gear shafts and the bores they run in. Fit new parts if required – to remove the No. 1 starter idle gear first remove the clutch (Section 15), then remove the gear **(see illustration)**.

### Installation

**10** If removed lubricate the No. 1 starter idle gear with clean oil, position the gear and insert the shaft **(see illustration 16.9)**. Install the clutch (Section 15).
**11** Make sure the sprag assembly is seated in the clutch housing **(see illustration 16.7b)**. Lubricate the needle bearing on the crankshaft with clean oil **(see illustration 16.8)**.
**12** Clean the starter clutch bolt threads and apply threadlock. Fit the clutch onto the flywheel, aligning the bolt holes **(see illustration 16.5b)**. Fit the bolts, hold the rotor as before and tighten the bolts in a criss-cross

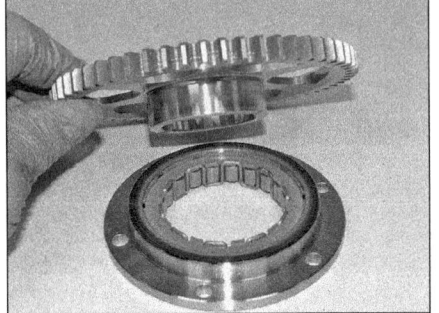

16.7a Check the sprags in the clutch and the driven gear hub

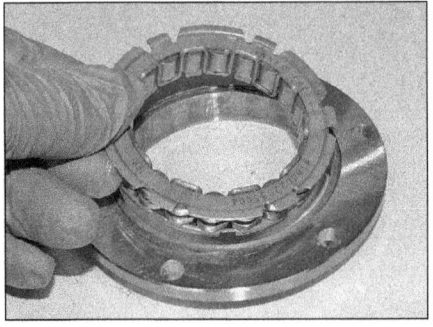

16.7b The sprag assembly can be removed from the housing if required

16.8 Check the bearing

16.9 Remove the No. 1 idle gear and its shaft

pattern to 16 Nm **(see illustration and 16.5a)**. Go clockwise round the bolts once again to ensure all are tightened to 16 Nm.

**13** Lubricate the starter driven gear hub with clean engine oil, then fit it into the starter clutch, rotating it clockwise to spread the sprags and allow the hub to enter **(see illustration 16.4b)**. Check the operation of the starter clutch as described in Step 1.

**14** Clean and threadlock the starter clutch plate bolts, fit the plate and tighten the bolts to 12 Nm **(see illustration 16.4a)**.

**15** Lubricate the No. 2 starter idle gear with clean oil, position the gear and insert the shaft.**(see illustration 15.6)**.

**16** Install the clutch cover (Section 15).

## 17 Gearchange mechanism

### *Gearchange shaft oil seal*

**1** If there is oil leakage from the left-hand end of the gearchage shaft a new seal can be fitted after removing the clutch cover (Section 15). Lever out the old seal with a small flat-bladed screwdriver **(see illustration)**. With the seal removed check the bearing **(see illustration)**. Refer to *Tools and workshop tips* if a new bearing is needed. Grease the lips of the new seal, then push it squarely into place, with its marked side facing out, using your fingers or a blunt drift, until it seats **(see illustration)**.

### *Removal*

**2** Remove the clutch (Section 15). If a gear was selected to unscrew the clutch nut, shift the transmission back to neutral.

**3** Remove the oil pump drive sprocket and chain and the chain guide (Section 19, Step 2).

**4** Withdraw the centralising spring pin, noting how the spring ends locate against it **(see illustration)**.

**5** Note how the pawls on the selector arm locate onto the pins on the end of the selector drum, then withdraw the gearchange shaft assembly **(see illustration)**.

**6** Note how the stopper arm spring locates, and how the roller on the stopper arm locates in the neutral detent on the selector drum **(see illustration)**. Unhook and remove the spring **(see illustration 17.13b)**. Unscrew the stopper arm bolt, noting the washer, and remove the arm **(see illustration 17.13a)**. The arm sits on a shouldered dowel, which should be tight, but remove it if loose **(see illustration)**.

### *Inspection*

**7** Inspect the splines on the end of the gearchange shaft; if they are worn or damaged, or if the shaft is bent, fit a new one.

**8** Check the shaft selector arm for cracks, distortion and wear of its pawls, and check for any corresponding wear on the selector

**16.12 Clean the bolts and apply threadlock**

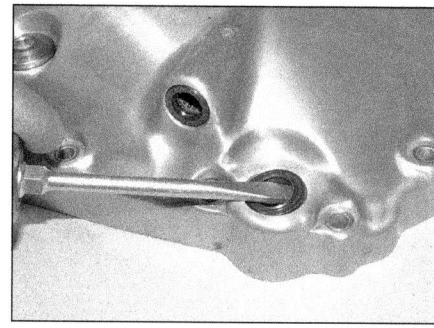

**17.1a Lever out the old seal...**

**17.1b Check the bearing**

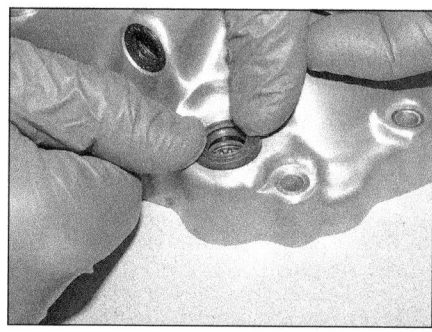

**17.1c Push the new seal in**

**17.4 Withdraw the pin**

**17.5 Pull the shaft assembly out, noting how it locates**

**17.6a Note how everything is positioned, then unhook the spring, undo the screw (arrowed) and remove the arm**

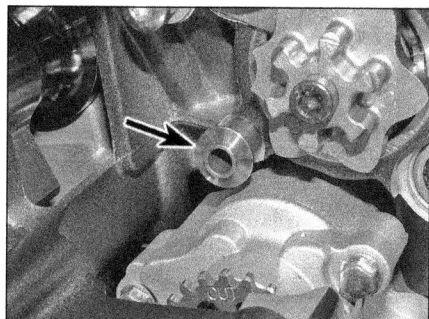

**17.6b Check the dowel (arrowed) is tight**

17.8 Check the pawls and pins for wear

17.9 Check the roller and the detents

pins on the selector drum detent wheel **(see illustration)**.

**9** Check the stopper arm roller and the detents in the selector drum detent wheel for any wear or damage, and make sure the roller turns freely **(see illustration)**. Check the spring for distortion and make sure the spring post in the crankcase is tight.

**10** If the detent wheel is worn or damaged, hold the wheel and unscrew its bolt. Remove the wheel – note that there is a locating pin in the end of the selector drum, which

should be tight, but take care as it could drop out. Fit the detent wheel seating the cut-out over the pin. Clean the threads of the bolt, then apply a suitable non-permanent thread locking compound and tighten it to 12 Nm.

**11** Inspect the centralising spring and the pawl plate spring for fatigue, wear or damage **(see illustrations)**. New springs can be fitted by releasing the circlips and removing the washers from each end of the shaft, noting their correct fitted order. Note how the ends of

the centralising spring locate each side of the pin on the arm.

**12** Refer to Step 1 to fit a new gearchange shaft oil seal and to check the bearing in the clutch cover, and also check the bearing in the crankcase **(see illustration)**.

### Installation

**13** Make sure the stopper arm dowel is in place **(see illustration 17.6b)**. Clean the threads of the stopper arm bolt. Fit the washer onto the bolt then apply some threadlock. Seat the arm over the dowel, fit the bolt and tighten to 12 Nm **(see illustration)**. Hook the spring over the post and onto the cut-out in the arm, seating the roller in the neutral detent in the wheel **(see illustration)**. Check everything is correctly positioned **(see illustration 17.6a)**.

**14** Lubricate the gearchange shaft bearing in the crankcase with engine oil. If removed, slide the outer washer onto the shaft.

**15** Slide the gearchange shaft assembly into the crankcase, locating the selector arm pawls over the pins on the selector drum detent wheel **(see illustration 17.5)**.

**16** Insert the centralising spring pin

17.11a Check the centralising spring...

17.11b ...and the pawl plate spring

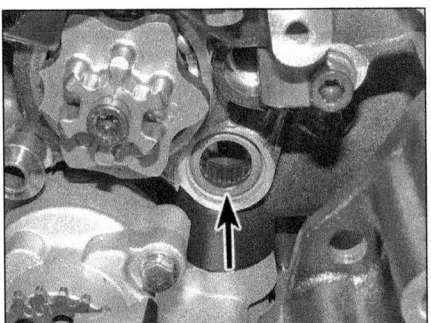

17.12 Check the bearing (arrowed)

17.13a Seat the arm and secure it with the bolt

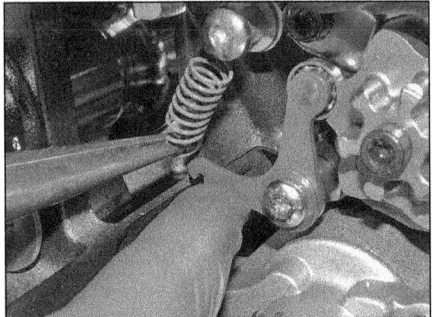

17.13b Make sure the spring ends locate correctly

17.16 Check that everything is correctly in place

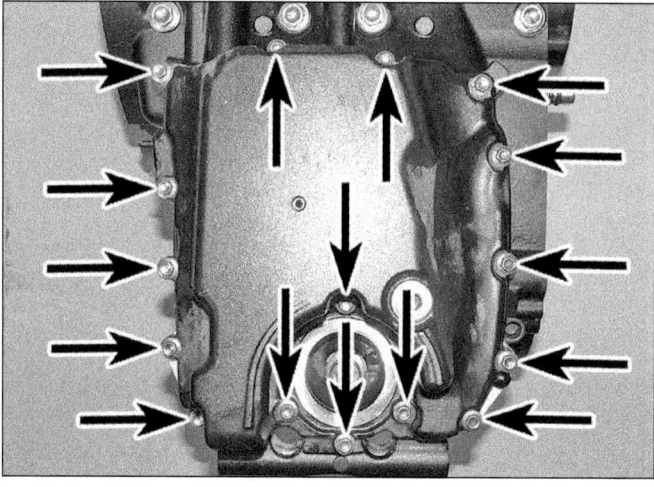

18.2 Sump bolts (arrowed)

between the spring ends and into its bore (see illustration 17.4). Check that everything is correctly positioned (see illustration).

**17** Install the oil pump drive chain guide, chain and sprocket (Section 19, Steps 18 and 19).

**18** Install the clutch (Section 15).

**19** Check the gearchange mechanism by raising the rear wheel off the ground, and spinning it forwards by hand while selecting each gear in turn, then back to neutral.

## 18 Oil sump and oil strainer

### *Removal*

**1** Drain the engine oil and remove the filter (see Chapter 1). Remove the exhaust system and the collector box bracket (see Chapter 4).

**2** Unscrew the sump bolts, slackening them evenly in a criss-cross sequence, and remove the sump **(see illustration)**. If necessary, break the gasket seal by tapping gently around the edge of the sump with a soft-faced hammer or block of wood – do not lever the sump off as this will damage the sealing surface. Remove the gasket – a new one must be used. Remove the sump locating pins if loose.

**3** Remove the water pump drain pipe from either the sump or the crankcase **(see illustration)** – new O-rings should be used, there are two on each end.

**4** Remove the strainer, noting how it locates **(see illustration)**. Remove the strainer seal **(see illustration 18.9)** – a new one should be used.

**5** If required remove the lower breather drain

18.3 Remove the drain pipe with its four O-rings

pipe **(see illustration)** – a new O-ring should be used.

### *Inspection*

**6** Remove all traces of gasket from the sump and crankcase mating surfaces, and clean the inside of the sump with a suitable solvent.

**7** Clean the strainer in solvent, flushing it through from the inside, and remove any debris caught in the mesh **(see**

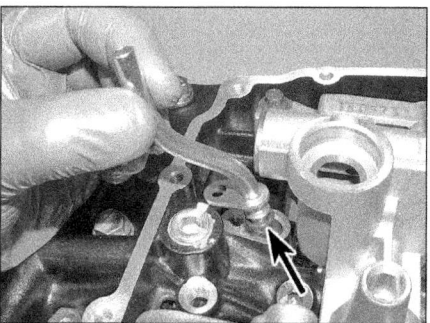

18.5 Unscrew the bolt and remove the pipe with its O-ring (arrowed)

18.4 Remove the strainer

illustration). Check the mesh for any signs of wear or damage and fit a new strainer if necessary.

### *Installation*

**8** Lubricate the new O-ring for the lower breather drain pipe with petroleum jelly and fit it onto the pipe **(see illustration 18.5)**. Clean the threads of the pipe bolt and apply some fresh threadlock. Fit the pipe and tighten the bolt to 9 Nm.

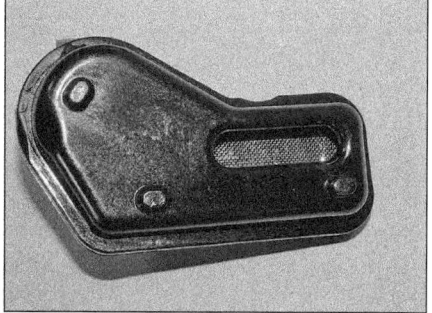

18.7 Clean and check the strainer mesh

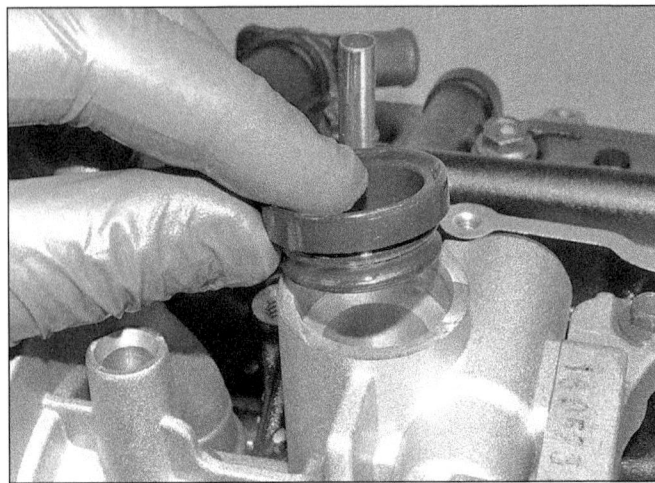

18.9 Lubricate the new seal and fit it into the pump

18.11 Use a new gasket, seating it over the locating pins (arrowed)

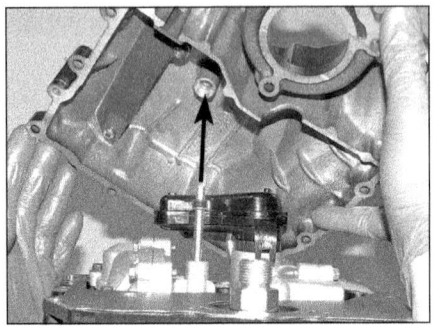

18.12 Keep the sump aligned and square so the pipe locates in the hole (arrowed)

19.2a Remove the sleeve...

19.2b ...and the bearing...

19.2c ...disengage the chain from the pump...

19.2d ...slide the sprocket and chain off...

19.2e ...and remove the thrust washer

9 Lubricate the new seal for the oil strainer with oil and fit it into the oil pump passage (see illustration). Push the strainer into the seal and seat the cutout over the rib (see illustration 18.4).

10 Lubricate the new O-rings for the water pump drain pipe with petroleum jelly and fit them onto the pipe (see illustration 18.3). Push the pipe into the crankcase until it seats.

11 Fit the sump locating pins if removed, into the sump if the engine is in the frame or into the crankcase if the engine has been removed and is upside down. Lay a new gasket onto the sump if the engine is in the frame or onto the crankcase if the engine has been removed, seating it over the pins (see illustration).

12 Position the sump on the crankcase, making sure the water pump drain tube enters the hole (see illustration). Check the sump is seated all round then fit and finger-tighten all bolts (see illustration 18.2). Tighten the bolts evenly and a little at a time in a criss-cross pattern to 10 Nm. Go clockwise round the bolts once again to ensure all are tightened to 10 Nm.

13 Install the exhaust system (see Chapter 4).

14 Fit a new oil filter and fill the engine with the correct type and quantity of oil (see Chapter 1).

15 Start the engine and check that there are no leaks around the sump before taking the bike on the road.

## 19 Oil/water pump

### Removal

1 Drain the coolant (see Chapter 1). Remove the sump and oil strainer (Section 18). Remove the clutch (Section 15).

2 Withdraw the sleeve and bearing from between the pump drive sprocket and the shaft (see illustrations). Disengage the chain and remove the sprocket and chain (see illustrations). Slide the thrust washer off the shaft (see illustration).

**19.4a Unscrew the bolts...**

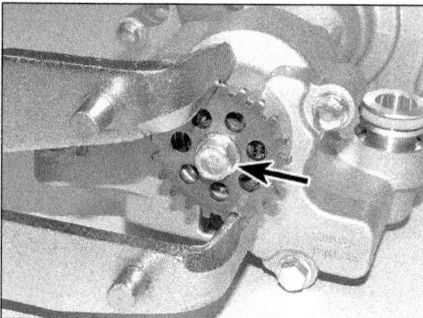

**19.4b ...and remove the pump**

**19.5 Hold the sprocket to unscrew the bolt (arrowed)**

**19.6 Unscrew the bolts and remove the cover**

**19.8 Measure the outer rotor to housing clearance as shown**

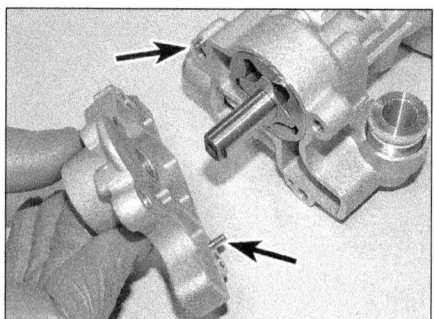

**19.9 Measure the inner rotor tip to outer rotor clearance as shown**

**3** If required unscrew the chain guide bolts and remove the guide **(see illustrations 19.18b and a)**.

**4** Unscrew the pump mounting bolts and remove the pump **(see illustrations)**. Remove the pipes from the pump or crankcase, then remove the O-rings from the pipes **(see illustrations 19.15c and b)**. Also remove the coolant passage O-ring from the crankcase **(see illustration 19.15a)**.

### Inspection

#### Oil pump

**5** Hold the sprocket and unscrew the bolt, then remove the sprocket and the washer **(see illustration)**.

**6** Unscrew the oil pump cover bolts and

remove the cover from the rotor housing **(see illustration)**. Remove the locating pins if loose.

**7** Inspect the rotors and pump housing for scoring and wear. If any damage, scoring or uneven or excessive wear is evident, replace the pump with a new one – individual components are not available.

**8** Measure the clearance between the outer rotor and housing with a feeler gauge and compare it to the maximum clearance listed in the Specifications **(see illustration)**. If the clearance measured exceeds the service limit, fit a new pump.

**9** Position the inner rotor as shown and measure the clearance between the inner rotor tip and the outer rotor with a feeler gauge and compare it to the maximum clearance given in the Specifications **(see illustration)**. If the

clearance measured exceeds the service limit, fit a new pump.

**10** Check the pump sprockets and the chain for wear or damage.

**11** Fit the locating pins if removed, then fit the cover **(see illustration)**. Clean the cover bolts and apply threadlock, and tighten the bolts to 11 Nm **(see illustration 19.6)**.

**12** Fit the washer onto the shaft **(see illustration)**. Clean the sprocket bolt threads and apply threadlock, then fit the sprocket with the OUT mark facing out, aligning the flats on the sprocket with those on the shaft **(see illustration)**. Hold the sprocket and tighten the bolt to 12 Nm **(see illustration 19.5)**.

**13** Unscrew the pressure relief valve cap, then withdraw the valve using a hooked tool **(see illustrations)**. Push on the plunger and

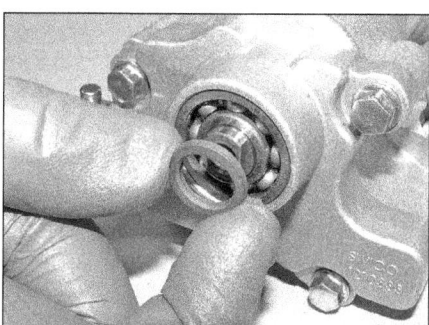

**19.11 Check the locating pins (arrowed) are in place before fitting the cover**

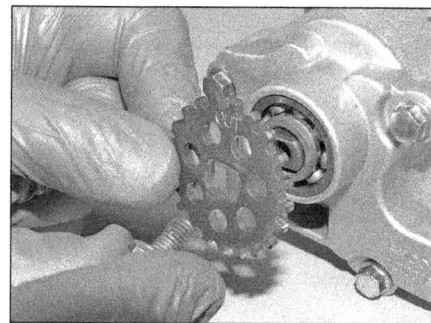

**19.12a Fit the washer...**

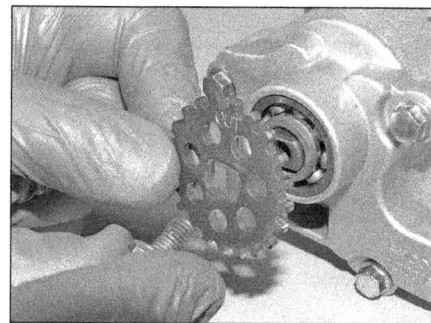

**19.12b ... and the sprocket**

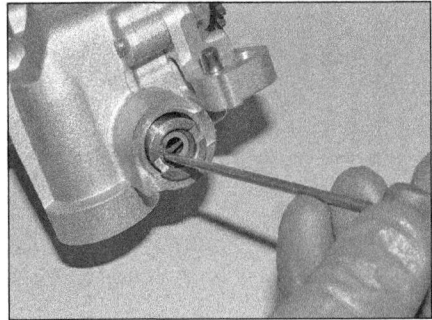

**19.13a Unscrew the cap...**

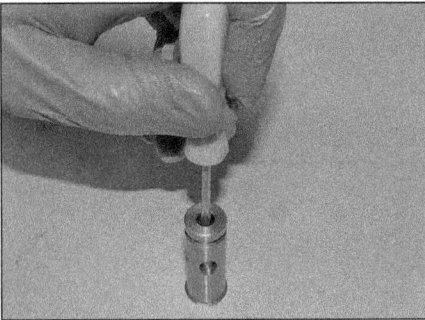

**19.13b ... and hook the valve out**

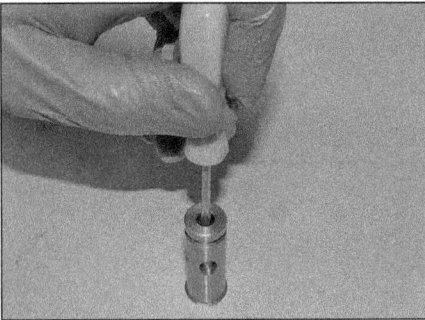

**19.13c Check the plunger**

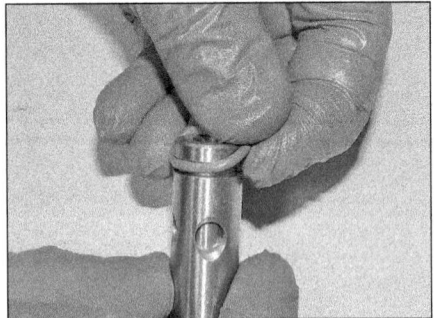

**19.13d Fit a new O-ring...**

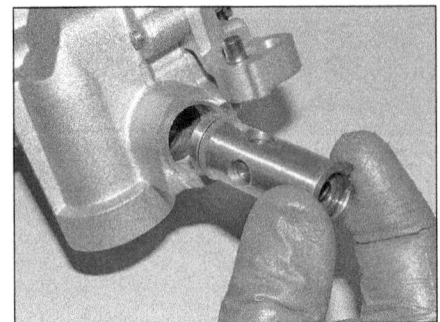

**19.13e ...insert the valve...**

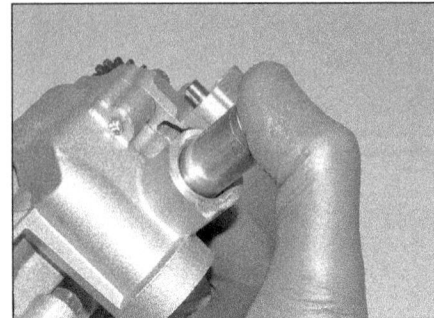

**19.13f ...and push it all the way in**

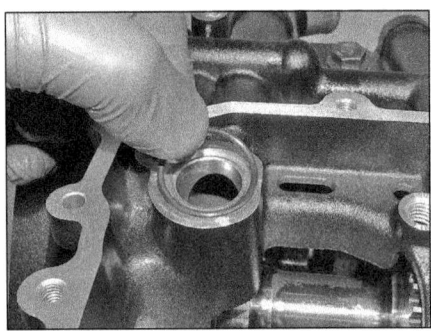

**19.15a Fit new O-ring onto the passage...**

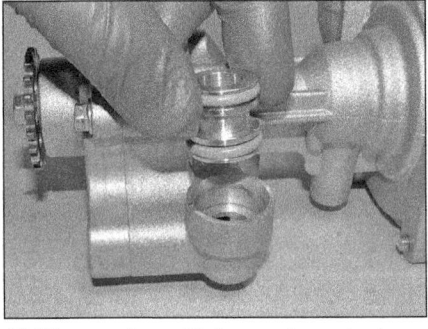

**19.15b ... and new O-rings onto each pipe...**

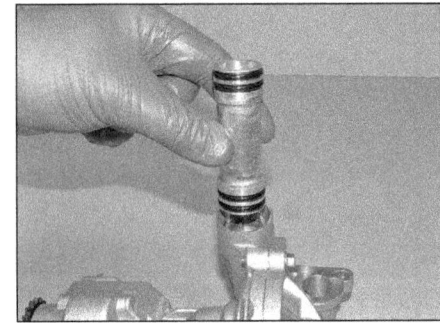

**19.15c ... before fitting them into the pump**

check that it moves smoothly and returns under spring pressure **(see illustration)**. Fit the valve using a new O-ring and push it all the way in using a socket until it seats, then fit the cap and tighten to 10 Nm **(see illustrations)**.

**Water pump**

**14** If there has been leakage from the pump drain pipe that exits on the underside of the sump fit a new oil/water pump assembly – the seals are not available separately.

### *Installation*

**15** Fit a new O-ring into the groove around the coolant passage in the crankcase **(see illustration)**. Fit new O-rings onto the oil and coolant pipes and smear them with petroleum jelly, then fit the pipes into the pump **(see illustrations)**.

**16** Before fitting the pump, prime it with clean engine oil, turning the sprocket as you do to ensure all internal surfaces are coated.

**17** Clean the threads of the pump bolts and

apply some threadlock. Fit the pump, making sure the pipes enter their bores and the pump seats all round, and tighten the pump bolts to 10 Nm, then go round them again as sometimes the first bolt tightened will loosen slightly as the others are tightened **(see illustrations 19.4b and a)**.

**18** If removed clean the pump chain guide

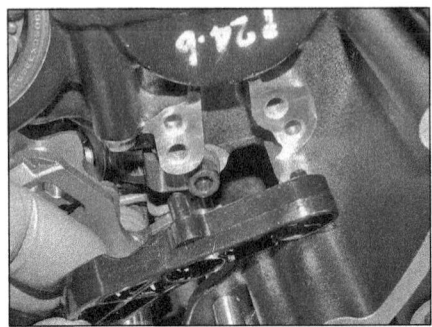

**19.18a Fit the pegs into the unthreaded holes...**

bolts and apply threadlock, then fit the guide, locating the pegs in the holes, and tighten the bolts to 9 Nm **(see illustrations)**.

**19** Slide the thrust washer onto the shaft **(see illustration 19.2e)**. Engage the chain around the sprockets and slide the sprocket onto the shaft, then insert the bearing and the sleeve **(see illustrations 19.2d, c, b and a)**.

**19.18b ...and threadlock the bolts**

**20** Install the clutch (Section 15). Install the sump and oil strainer (Section 18).
**21** Fill the engine with the specified quantity and type of engine oil (see Chapter 1).

## 20 Crankcase separation and reassembly

### Separation

**1** To gain access to the connecting rods, crankshaft, balancer shafts, transmission shafts, selector drum and forks, and all related bearings, the crankcase must be split into two parts.
**2** Remove the engine from the frame (Section 4).
**3** Before the separating the crankcases for a full engine strip remove all the components listed below. If you separating the crankcases just to remove to the crankshaft, balancer shafts, transmission shafts or selector drum and forks, the cylinder head can stay in place, but if you are removing the connecting rods the head, block and pistons must be removed. In all cases the valve cover, clutch, alternator rotor, sump, oil strainer and oil/water pump and pipes must be removed.

● Camshaft (Section 8)
● Cylinder head (Section 10)
● Cylinder block (Section 12)
● Pistons (Section 13)
● Alternator rotor (Chapter 8)
● Starter motor (Chapter 8)
● Cam chain and intermediate gear (Section 9)
● Clutch (Section 15)
● Starter clutch and gears (Section 16)
● Gearchange mechanism (Section 17)
● Oil filter (see Chapter 1)
● Oil sump, strainer and drain pipes (Section 18)
● Oil/water pump and pipes (Section 19)

**4** Turn the engine upside down. The crankcases are joined by eight M10 (10mm thread diameter) bolts with washers (Nos. 1 to 8), five M8 (8mm thread diameter) bolts (Nos. 9 to 13), and eleven M6 (6mm thread diameter) bolts (Nos. 14 to 24) **(see illustration)**. First

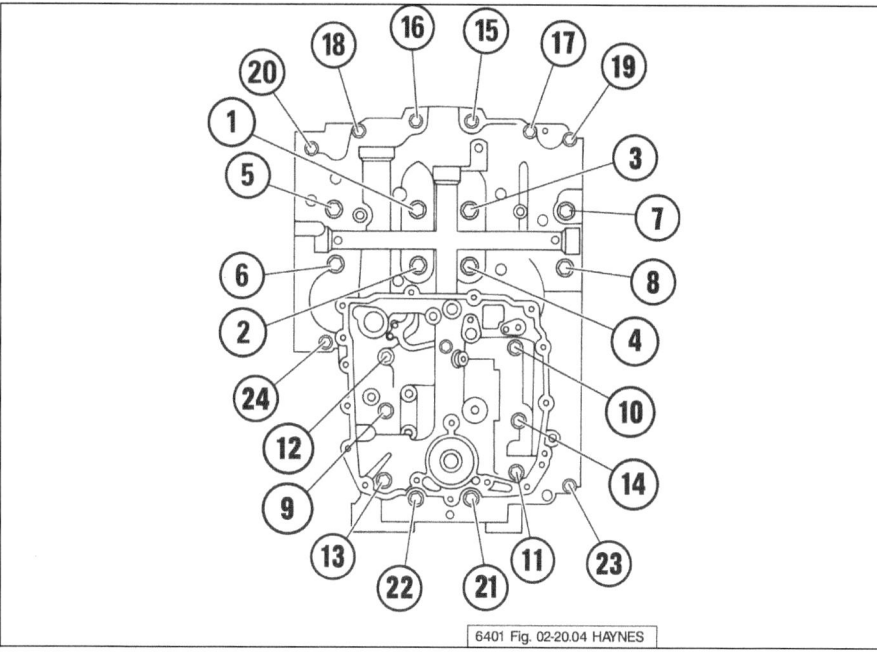

**20.4 Crankcase bolt numbering**

unscrew the M6 bolts (14 to 24) a quarter turn at a time in any order. Next unscrew the M8 bolts a quarter turn at a time in a reverse of the bolt numbering sequence (i.e. from 13 to 9). Finally unscrew the M10 bolts a quarter turn at a time in a reverse of the bolt numbering sequence (i.e. from 8 to 1), then remove them with their washers.
**5** Carefully lift the lower crankcase half off the upper half, using a soft-faced hammer or block of wood to tap around the joint to initially separate the halves, if necessary **(see illustration)**. If the halves do not separate easily, make sure all fasteners have been removed. Do not try and separate the halves by levering between the sealing surfaces as they are easily damaged and will leak oil on reassembly.
**6** Remove the three locating dowels from the crankcase (they could be in either half) **(see**

illustration 20.13a)**. Remove the O-ring from the upper breather drain pipe – a new one must be used **(see illustration 20.13b)**.
**7** Refer to Sections 21 to 28 for the removal and installation of the components housed within the crankcases.

### Reassembly

**8** Remove all traces of old sealant from the crankcase mating surfaces.
**9** Check that all components and their bearings are in place in the upper and lower crankcase halves. If the transmission shafts have not been removed, remove the oil seal from the right-hand end of the output shaft and fit a new one – apply some grease to its lip **(see illustration 26.5b)**. Check that the selector drum is in the neutral position **(see illustration)**.

**20.5 Lift the lower half of the crankcase off the upper half**

**20.9 Align the neutral detent (arrowed) as shown**

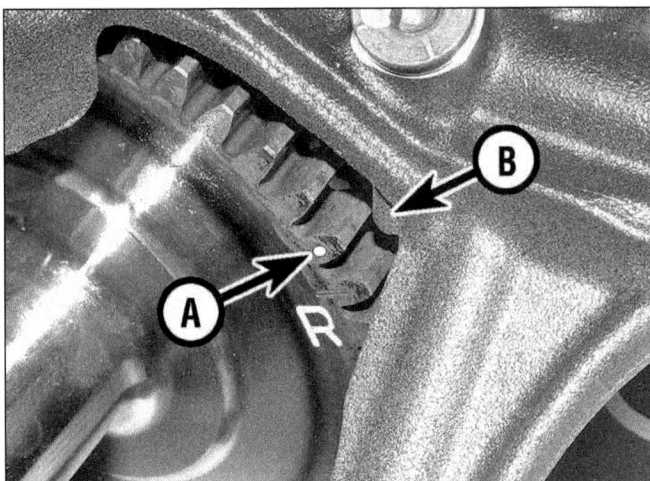

20.12a Align the punch mark (A) with the projection (B)...

20.12b ...then use a screwdriver to keep the gear in that position

10 Check that the crankshaft and front balancer shaft are correctly timed, and that the crankshaft locking pin is fitted, and if the intermediate gear has not been removed make sure it is correctly timed to the crankshaft and the locking pin is fitted (Section 23).

11 Generously lubricate the crankshaft, transmission shafts and selector drum and forks, particularly around the bearings, with clean engine oil, then use a rag soaked in high flash-point solvent to wipe over the mating surfaces of both crankcase halves to remove all traces of oil.

12 The rear balancer shaft must be positioned and locked so that when the lower crankcase is fitted it is correctly timed to the crankshaft. With the lower crankcase upside down, turn the balancer shaft until the punch mark on the gear tooth above the R line aligns with the projection on the crankcase, then fit a stubby flat-bladed screwdriver in the hole in the crankcase above the gear so the screwdriver tip sits in between two gear teeth and so holds it in position (see illustrations).

13 If removed, fit the three locating dowels into the upper crankcase (see illustration). Fit a new O-ring smeared with grease onto the upper breather pipe (see illustration). Check again that all components are in position, particularly that the bearing shells are located in their seats in the lower crankcase half.

14 Apply a small amount of suitable sealant (such as ThreeBond 1216E) to the mating surface of the lower crankcase half as shown (see illustrations).

Caution: Do not apply an excessive amount of sealant as it will ooze out when the case halves are assembled and may obstruct oil passages.

15 There are four things to note as you fit the lower crankcase down onto the upper: first that the selector forks must engage correctly in their grooves in the transmission shafts (see illustration 20.16a); second that the rear balancer shaft will try to turn as its gear teeth engage with those on the crankshaft, and so you need to wiggle the screwdriver so that the punch mark sits slightly above the projection

on the crankcase just before the teeth engage, and that they do engage correctly (it is possible that the teeth ends may butt each other, preventing engagement, in which case the screwdriver must be wiggled to align them correctly), and that as they engage and the balancer shaft turns slightly the punch mark and projection come into exact alignment (see Step 12) (see illustrations 20.12a and b); third that the breather pipe enters its passage centrally and the O-ring does not get squashed out to one side over the pipe rib (see illustration 20.16b); and fourth that the dowels locate correctly (see illustration 20.13a).

16 Fit the lower crankcase half onto the upper crankcase half (see illustration 20.5), making sure the selector forks, crankshaft/rear balancer shaft gear teeth, breather pipe O-ring and dowels all engage and locate correctly (see illustrations).

17 Check that the lower crankcase half is seated all the way round. The crankcase halves should fit together without being

20.13a Fit the dowels (arrowed) if removed

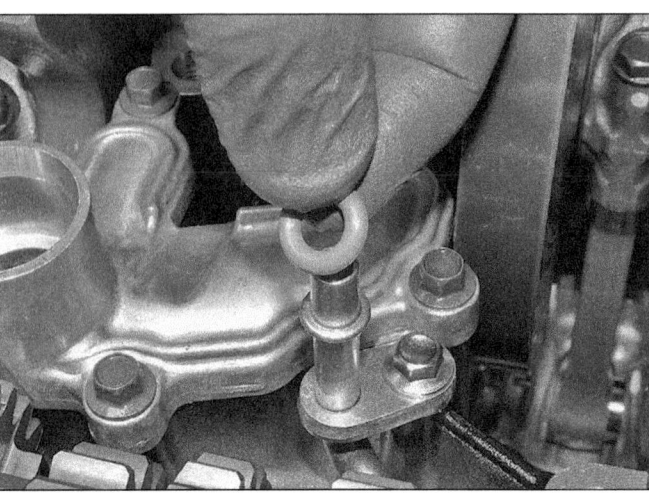

20.13b Fit a new O-ring onto the pipe

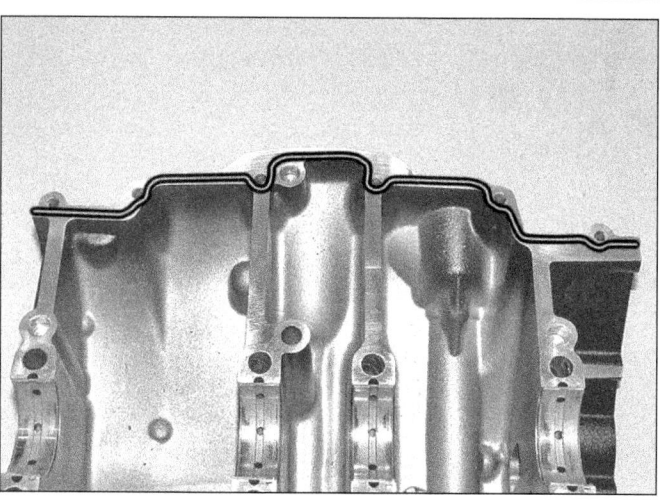

20.14a Apply the sealant across the front...

20.14b ...the back...

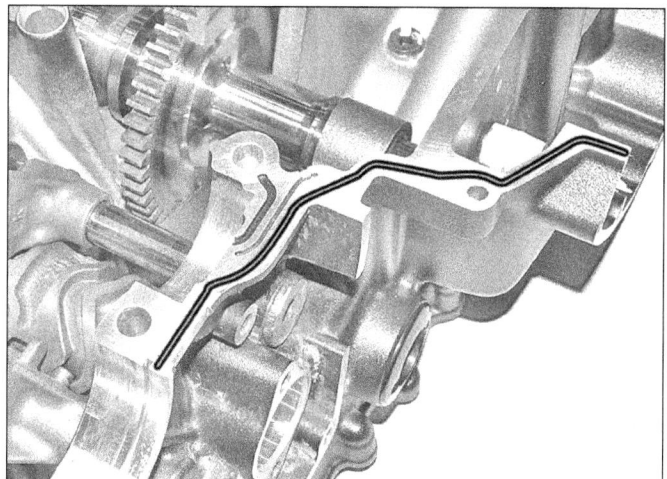

20.14c ... and the side of the crankcase as shown

20.16a Check the selector forks seat in their grooves

forced. If the casings are not correctly seated, remove the lower crankcase half and investigate the problem. Do not attempt to pull them together using the crankcase bolts as the casing could crack and be ruined.

**18** Make sure the threads of the crankcase bolts are clean before fitting them. Make sure the washers are fitted with the M10 bolts 1 to 8 **(see illustration)**.

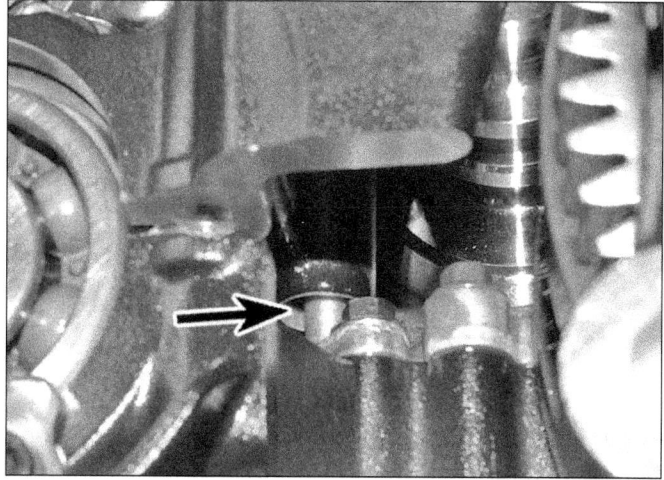

20.16b Make sure the pipe (arrowed) enters centrally and square and the O-ring does not get squashed out

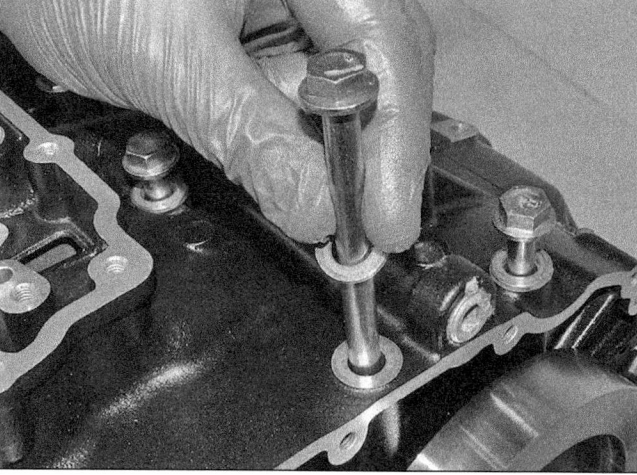

20.18 Bolts 1 to 8 have washers

**19** Fit the bolts in their correct locations as follows (see illustration 20.4):
● M10 bolts – fit the eight bolts with washers in positions 1 to 8.
● M8 bolts – fit the 50mm bolt in position 10, the 85mm bolts in positions 11 and 12, and the 100mm bolts in positions 9 and 13.
● M6 bolts – fit the 55mm bolt in position 14, the 30mm bolts in positions 15 to 24.
**20** First tighten all bolts in numerical sequence 1 to 24 to 10 Nm. Next loosen bolts 1 to 8 in sequence, turning them 140°. Next tighten bolts 1 to 8 in sequence to 10 Nm. Using a degree disc, tighten bolts 1 to 8 in sequence through 75°. Mark the top of each bolt with a marker pen once you have completed its final stage tightening to ensure none get omitted or done twice.
**21** Now tighten the M8 bolts 9 to 13 in sequence to 32 Nm. Next tighten the M6 bolts 14 to 24 in sequence to 12 Nm.
**22** With all crankcase bolts tightened, check that the crankshaft, balancer shafts and transmission shafts rotate smoothly and easily, and check that everything is correctly timed. Check that all gears can be selected and that the shafts rotate freely in every gear. If there are any signs of undue stiffness, rough spots, or of any other problem, the fault must be rectified before proceeding further.
**23** Install all the removed components in the reverse order of removal.

## 21 Crankcases

**1** After the crankcases have been separated, remove the crankshaft, connecting rods and main bearing shells, the balancer shafts, transmission shafts and selector drum and forks, and any other components (such as the oil pressure switch) or assemblies not already removed, referring to the relevant Sections of this and other Chapters (see Step 3 of Section 20), and Chapter 8 for the oil pressure switch.
**2** Remove the piston oil jets from the upper crankcase (see illustration). Remove their O-rings – new ones must be used.
**3** Remove the coolant distribution chamber cover, its O-ring, and the dowels if loose (see

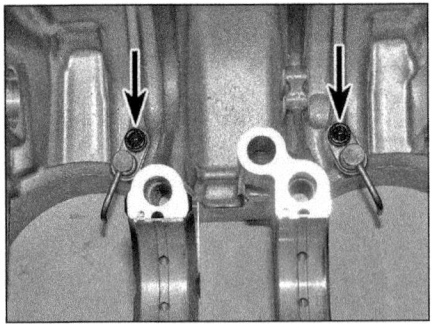

**21.2 Piston oil jet bolts (arrowed)**

illustration) – a new O-ring must be used. Remove the upper breather drain pipe (see illustration) – a new O-ring must be used. Remove the breather chamber cover (see illustration) – a new gasket must be used.
**4** Clean the crankcases thoroughly with solvent and dry them with compressed air. Blow out all oil passages and pipes with compressed air.
**5** Remove all traces of old gasket sealant from the mating surfaces. Minor damage to the surfaces can be cleaned up with careful use of a fine sharpening stone.
*Caution: Be very careful not to nick or gouge the crankcase mating surfaces, or oil leaks will result. Check both crankcase halves very carefully for cracks and other damage.*
**6** Inspect the bearing seats for signs of damage, especially if an engine or transmission bearing has overheated or seized and spun. If bearing shells or a ball bearing cage are not a precise fit in their seats, ask your Triumph dealer for a suitable bearing locking compound which will overcome small amounts of wear. Otherwise the crankcase halves will have to be replaced with a new set.
**7** Small cracks or holes in aluminium castings can be repaired with an epoxy resin adhesive as a temporary measure. Permanent repairs can only be effected by argon-arc welding, and only a specialist in this process is in a position to advise on the economy or practical aspect of such a repair. Note that low temperature aluminium welding kits are available for minor repairs. If any damage

is found that can't be repaired, replace the crankcase halves with a new set.
**8** Damaged threads can be economically reclaimed by using a diamond section wire insert which is easily fitted after drilling and re-tapping the affected thread.
**9** Sheared studs or screws can usually be removed with stud or screw extractors; if you are in any doubt consult a Triumph dealer or specialist motorcycle engineer.
**10** Fit the coolant distribution chamber cover dowels if removed, and fit the cover using a new O-ring (see illustration 21.3a). Fit the upper breather drain pipe using a new O-ring (see illustration 21.3b). Fit the breather chamber cover using a new gasket (see illustration 21.3c).
**11** Lightly grease the new O-rings for the piston oil jets, then fit them into the grooves on the jets. Clean the threads of the jet bolts and apply threadlock, then fit the jets into the upper crankcase (see illustration 21.2).
**12** Install the remaining components in the reverse order of removal.

## 22 Main and big-end bearing information

**1** Even though main and connecting rod bearings are generally replaced with new ones during an engine overhaul, the old bearings should be carefully examined as they can reveal valuable information about the condition of the engine.
**2** Bearing failure occurs mainly because of lack of lubrication, the presence of dirt or other foreign particles, overloading the engine and/or corrosion. Regardless of the cause of bearing failure, it must be corrected before the engine is reassembled to prevent it from happening again.
**3** When examining the bearings, match them with their corresponding journal on the crankshaft to help identify the cause of any problem.
**4** Dirt and other foreign particles get into the engine in a variety of ways. They may be left in the engine during assembly or they may pass through filters or breathers, then get into the oil and from there into the bearings.

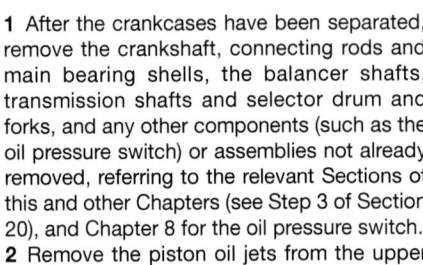

**21.3a Coolant distribution chamber cover (arrowed)**

**21.3b Upper breather drain pipe bolt (arrowed)**

**21.3c Breather chamber cover (arrowed)**

Metal chips from machining operations and normal engine wear are often present. Abrasives are sometimes left in engine components after reconditioning operations, especially when parts are not thoroughly cleaned using the proper cleaning methods. Whatever the source, foreign objects often end up imbedded in the soft bearing material and are easily recognised. Large particles will not imbed in the bearing and will score or gouge the bearing and journal. The best prevention for this type of bearing failure is to clean all parts thoroughly and keep everything spotlessly clean during engine reassembly. Regular oil and filter changes are also essential.

5 Lack of lubrication or lubrication breakdown have a number of interrelated causes. Excessive heat (which thins the oil), overloading (which squeezes the oil from the bearing face) and oil throw-off (from excessive bearing clearances, a worn oil pump or high engine speeds) all contribute to a breakdown of the protective lubricating film. Blocked oil passages will starve a bearing of lubrication and destroy it. When lack of lubrication is the cause of bearing failure, the bearing material is wiped or extruded from the steel backing of the bearing. Temperatures may increase to the point where the steel backing and the journal turn blue from overheating.

6 Riding habits can have a definite effect on bearing life. Full throttle, low speed operation, or labouring the engine, puts very high loads on bearings, which tend to squeeze out the oil film. These loads cause the bearings to flex, which produces fine cracks in the bearing face (fatigue failure). Eventually the bearing material will loosen in pieces and tear away from the steel backing. Short trip riding leads to corrosion of bearings, as insufficient engine heat is produced to drive off the condensed water and corrosive gases produced. These products collect in the engine oil, forming acid and sludge. As the oil is carried to the engine bearings, the acid attacks and corrodes the bearing material.

7 Incorrect bearing installation during engine assembly will lead to bearing failure as well. Tight fitting bearings which leave insufficient bearing oil clearances result in oil starvation. Dirt or foreign particles trapped behind a bearing shell result in high spots on the bearing which lead to failure.

8 To avoid bearing problems, clean all parts thoroughly before reassembly, double check all bearing clearance measurements and lubricate the new bearings with clean engine oil during installation.

## 23 Crankshaft and main bearings

### *Removal*

1 Remove the alternator rotor (see Chapter 8). Remove the engine from the frame (Section 4). Remove the spark plugs (see Chapter 1). Separate the crankcase halves (Section 21).

2 If the crankshaft is being removed with the intermediate gear still in place, the intermediate gear must be positioned and locked with a pin so it will be correctly timed to the crankshaft when it is installed. The locking pin can only be fitted with the alternator rotor removed. The locking pin fits through two holes in the crankcase and into a hole in the intermediate gear – each of these holes is a different diameter, and for the gear to be locked accurately in position you need a pin that is sized to match each hole. Triumph can supply a locking pin, part No. T3880039 and not too expensive, or alternatively you can use a 6 mm punch, which is the size of the hole in the gear, with insulating tape wrapped around the shaft and the handle as shown so it is a snug fit in the holes in the crankcase **(see illustration 9.9)**. There is also a hole in the crankcase and the crankshaft web so the crankshaft can be locked in its correct position for timing the engine, and Triumph can supply the pin for the crankshaft, part No. T3880601 and not expensive, or alternatively use a 6 mm bolt or pin **(see illustration 7.4c)**. Turn the engine using the flywheel on the left-hand end of the crankshaft until the holes in both the crankcase and the crankshaft align and the holes in the crankcase and intermediate gear

align simultaneously, then fit both the pins – note that due to the different sizes of the drive gear on the crankshaft and the intermediate gear it could take up to seven turns of the crankshaft before the locking pin holes in both the crankshaft and the intermediate gear align simultaneously **(see illustrations)**.

3 Refer to Section 24 and, if the cylinder block has been removed, remove the connecting rods, with or without the pistons attached as required, or if the cylinder block has not been removed, detach the connecting rods from the crankshaft and push them and the pistons up to the tops of the bores so that the big-ends are clear of the crankshaft. Note that if the pistons have been removed, the rods can remain attached to the crankshaft, and removed later if required.

4 Remove the crankshaft locking pin – do not remove the intermediate gear locking pin. Lift the crankshaft out of the upper crankcase half **(see illustration 23.25a)**.

5 If required, remove the main bearing shells from the crankcase halves **(see illustration)**. Keep the shells in order so that they can be returned to their original locations for the oil clearance check and if being reused.

6 If required and not already done remove the connecting rods (Section 24).

### *Inspection*

7 Clean the crankshaft with solvent, squirting it through all oil passages. If available, blow it through and dry with compressed air. Check the primary and balancer shaft drive gear teeth for wear and damage, and also check the driven gears on the back of the clutch housing and the balancer shafts.

8 Refer to Section 22 and examine the main bearing shells. If they are scored, badly scuffed or appear to have been seized, new shells must be installed. Always renew the main bearings as a set. If they are badly damaged, check the corresponding crankshaft journals. Evidence of extreme heat, such as discoloration, indicates that lubrication failure has occurred. Be sure to thoroughly check the oil pump and pressure relief valve as well as all oil holes and passages before reassembling the engine.

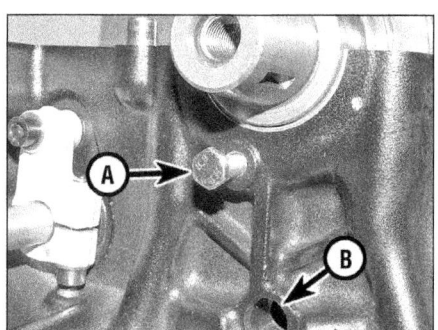

23.2a Crankshaft locking pin (6mm bolt) (A), and hole for intermediate gear locking pin (B)...

23.2b ...this shows the intermediate gear locking pin fitted, but with the engine the correct way up and the cylinder block removed

23.5 Remove the main bearing shells from their housings

**23.13 Lay a strip (arrowed) on each journal**

**23.16 Check the squashed strip against the scale provided**

**9** Inspect the crankshaft journals, paying particular attention where damaged bearing shells have been discovered. If the journals are scored or pitted in any way a new crankshaft will be required. Note that oversize shells are not available, precluding the option of re-grinding the crankshaft.

### Oil clearance check

**10** Whether new bearing shells are being fitted or the original ones are being re-used, the main bearing oil clearance should be checked prior to reassembly. To do this remove the balancer shafts from the crankcases to prevent crankshaft rotation as the cases are joined, which will disturb the Plastigauge Section 25.

**11** If not already done, remove the bearing shells from the crankcase halves by pushing their centres to the side, then lifting them out (see illustration 25.5). Keep the shells in order. Clean the backs of the shells and their locations in both the crankcase halves.

**12** Press the bearing shells back into their locations, making sure that the tab on each shell engages in the notch. Make sure the shells are fitted in the correct locations and take care not to touch any shell's bearing surface with your fingers. Apply a smear of grease to each journal and a smear of silicone release agent to each bearing shell.

**13** Lay the crankshaft in position in the upper crankcase (see illustration 23.25a). Cut several lengths of the appropriate size Plastigauge (they should be slightly shorter than the width of the crankshaft journal). Place a strand of Plastigauge on each crankshaft journal (see illustration).

**14** Refer to Section 20 and fit the lower crankcase half onto the upper half. Fit the M10 crankshaft journal bolts 1 to 8 with their washers in their original locations and tighten them in sequence in the stages and to the torque settings and angle as described in Section 20. Make sure that the crankshaft does not rotate as the bolts are tightened.

**15** Slacken and remove the bolts, working in reverse sequence from 8 to 1, then carefully lift off the lower crankcase half, making sure the Plastigauge is not disturbed.

**16** Compare the width of the crushed Plastigauge on each crankshaft journal to the scale printed on the Plastigauge envelope to obtain the main bearing oil clearance (see illustration).

**17** If the clearance is within the range listed in the Specifications and the bearing shells are in perfect condition, they can be reused. If the clearance is beyond the specified service limit, first measure the diameter of the crankshaft journals with a micrometer and compare the results with the Specifications. If the journal diameters are larger than the service limit, new bearing shells can be fitted (see Steps 19 and 20). If the journal diameters are smaller than the service limit, the crankshaft must be replaced with a new one.

**18** On completion carefully scrape away all traces of the Plastigauge material from the journals and bearing shells using a fingernail or other object which will not score the bearing surfaces.

### Bearing shell selection

**19** The main bearing oil clearance is controlled in production by selecting one of three grades of bearing shell. The grades are indicated by a colour-coding marked on the edge of each shell (see illustration)- if the colour is visible on each shell replace each shell with one of the same colour. If the colour is not visible on some of the shells, or you are not sure, select new shells with reference to the following chart, having first measured the crankshaft journal diameter and the crankcase bore diameter as described in the next Step.

**20** Measure the diameter of each crankshaft journal with a micrometer and record the results (see illustration 23.13). Next, assemble the crankcase halves with the bearing shells and crankshaft removed, and tighten the M10 mm crankshaft journal bolts 1 to 8 in sequence and in the stages and to the torque settings and angle as described in Section 20. Measure each crankshaft journal bore diameter using a bore gauge and micrometer and record the results. Refer to *Tools and Workshop Tips* in the Reference Section for details on how to use the measuring equipment.

| Crankcase bore diameter | Crankshaft journal diameter | Shell colour |
|---|---|---|
| 46.105 to 46.097 mm | 43.099 to 43.092 mm | Red |
| 46.114 to 46.106 mm | 43.108 to 43.100 mm | Red |
| 46.114 to 46.106 mm | 43.099 to 43.092 mm | Blue |
| 46.123 to 46.115 mm | 43.108 to 43.100 mm | Blue |
| 46.123 to 46.115 mm | 43.099 to 43.092 mm | Green |

### *Installation*

**21** Make sure the backs of the bearing shells, the bearing seats in both crankcase halves, and the main bearing journals on the crankshaft are clean. If new shells are being fitted clean any protective grease off using paraffin (kerosene). Wipe the shells and crankcase halves dry with a lint-free cloth. Make sure all the oil passages and holes are clear, and blow them through with compressed air if it is available.

**22** Press the bearing shells into their seats, locating the tab on each shell in the notch in the crankcase (see illustration). Unless you are fitting new shells make sure they are fitted in their original locations. Lubricate the shells with clean engine oil.

**23** The front balancer shaft must be positioned and locked so that when the crankshaft is fitted they are correctly timed. Turn the balancer shaft until the punch mark on the gear tooth next to the F mark is 60 mm from the front of the crankcase wall

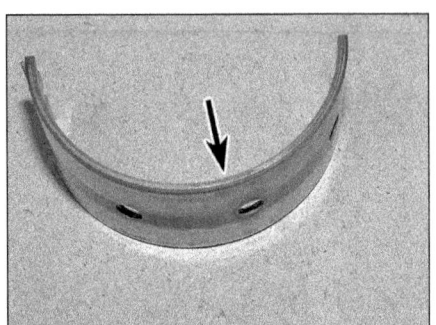

**23.19 Bearing shell colour code (arrowed) is on the edge, but may have rubbed off**

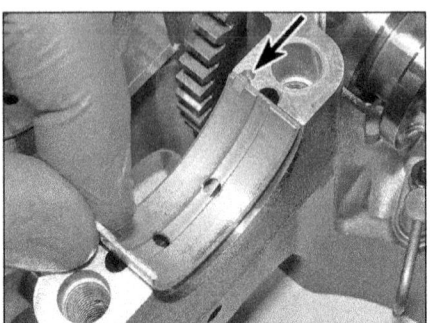

**23.22 Press each shell into place, locating the tab in the notch (arrowed)**

**23.23 Measure and set the distance of the punch mark from the front of the crankcase as shown and described**

**23.25a Fit the crankcase with the indent (arrowed) level with the crankcase surface**

measured as shown **(see illustration)** – this is the position it must be in once the crankshaft is fitted, however the balancer shaft will turn as its gear teeth engage with those on the crankshaft, and so you need to set the punch mark so it is 55 mm from the front edge before fitting the crankshaft so that it will end up at 60 mm once it is fitted. When positioned at 55 mm stuff some rag between the gear and the crankcase to prevent the shaft turning due to the balancer weight.

**24** Unless the intermediate gear has been removed, make sure the gear is correctly positioned with the locking pin fitted (Step 2) – if the gear is in place but the pin has been removed from the gear since the crankshaft was removed you will need to align the sprung gear teeth with the main gear teeth using a screwdriver as shown **(see illustration 9.13c)** before the pin can be fitted through both gears.

**25** Align the crankshaft so the circular indent in the outside of the right-hand web is parallel with the crankcase mating surface, then lower it into position in the upper crankcase, engaging its gear teeth with those of the balancer shaft **(see illustration)**. When the crankshaft is seated check that the balancer shaft mark is now 60 mm from the front edge, and the crankshaft indent is level with the crankcase surface **(see illustration)** – if not lift the crankshaft and reposition either it or the balancer shaft as required until the alignment is correct. As a double check make sure the locking pin can be fitted into the crankshaft, confirming its correct alignment, and that the mark on the balancer shaft weight is visible through the hole for the shaft clamp positioning bolt (remove the bolt to do this). Remove the intermediate gear and crankshaft locking pins

**26** Refer to Section 24 and fit the connecting rods onto the crankshaft using new bolts.
**27** Reassemble the crankcase halves (Section 20).

## 24 Connecting rods and bearings

**Note:** *On installation new connecting rod bolts must be used, so it is wise to obtain them before commencing work.*

### Removal

**1** Remove the engine from the frame (Section 4).
**2** Remove the cylinder block (Section 12), and the pistons if required (Section 13).
**3** Turn the engine over and raise the front on a block so the pistons (if not removed) or rods are clear of the bench and have sufficient room to be removed. Separate the crankcase halves (Section 20).
**4** Using paint or a marker pen, mark the cylinder identity on the top of each piston (if not removed), and across the front of each connecting rod and cap. Cylinders are numbered 1 – left, 2 – right. Note that the number across the back of the rod and cap is the part number, that there is a letter on the front of the bottom of the rod, and that the projection on the cap faces the left side of the engine **(see illustration 24.5a).**

**23.25b Check the distance is 60mm and the indent is level**

**5** Unscrew the connecting rod cap bolts and remove the caps, complete with the lower bearing shells, from the crankpins **(see illustrations)**. If a cap appears stuck, thread the bolts part-way in, then push them or tap them lightly and evenly to push the rod down slightly. Note that new bolts must be fitted.

**24.5a Connecting rod cap bolts (A). Note the projection (B) facing the left-hand side of the engine (shown upside down)**

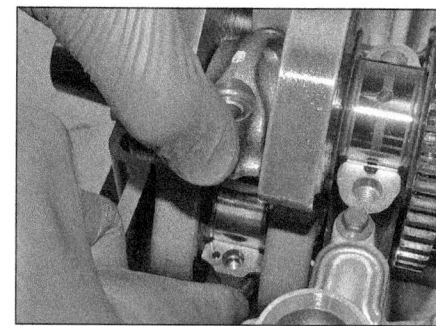

**24.5b Remove the bolts and pull the cap off the connecting rod**

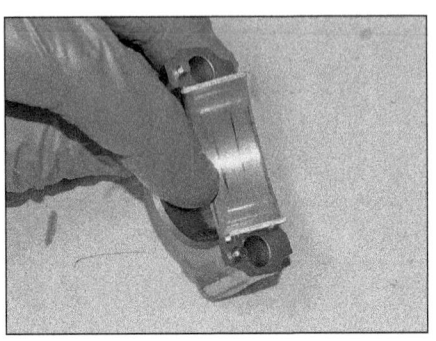

**24.6 Push each rod down off its crankpin**

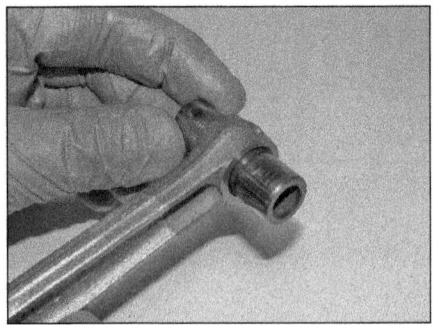

**24.10 Check for freeplay between the pin and the small-end**

**6** Detach the connecting rods from the crankpins and remove them from the top of the crankcase **(see illustration)**.

**7** Fit the related bearing shells (if removed), bearing cap, and bolts on each piston/connecting rod assembly so that they are all kept together as a matched set.New bolts must be used on final assembly, but use the old bolts for the oil clearance check.

**8** If required and not already done remove the pistons from the connecting rods (Section 13).

## Inspection

**9** Check the connecting rods for cracks and other obvious damage.

**10** Apply clean engine oil to the No. 1 piston pin, insert it into its connecting rod small-end and check for any freeplay between the two **(see illustration)**. If freeplay is excessive, measure the external diameter at the centre of the pin. Compare the result to the figure given in the Specifications. Replace the pin with a new one if it is worn beyond its specified limits. If the pin diameter is within specifications, replace the connecting rod with a new one. Repeat the measurements for the No. 2 pin and rod.

**11** Refer to Section 22 and examine the connecting rod bearing shells. If they are scored, badly scuffed or appear to have seized, new shells must be fitted. Always replace the shells in the connecting rods as a set. If they are badly damaged, check the corresponding crankpin. Evidence of extreme heat, such as bluing, indicates that lubrication

failure has occurred. Be sure to thoroughly check the oil pump and pressure relief valve as well as all oil holes and passages before reassembling the engine.

**12** Have the rods checked by a Triumph dealer if you think they may be twisted or bent.

## Oil clearance check

**13** Whether new bearing shells are being fitted or the original ones are being re-used, the connecting rod big-end bearing oil clearance should be checked prior to reassembly. Bearing oil clearance is measured with a product known as Plastigauge.

**Note:** *It is essential that, throughout this procedure, the connecting rod does not rotate on the crankshaft. If the procedure is being carried out on a bench find some way of clamping the crankshaft so it cannot move, and also the connecting rod once it has been fitted onto its journal. The best way is with the crankshaft in the crankcase and with the pistons and block fitted to keep the connecting rods held steady.*

**14** Remove the bearing shells from the rods and caps, keeping them in order **(see illustration)**. Clean the backs of the shells, the bearing housings in both the connecting rod and cap, and the crankpin journal with a suitable solvent.

**15** Press the bearing shells into their locations, locating the tab on each shell in the notch in the connecting rod or cap **(see illustration)**. Make sure the shells are fitted in the correct locations and take care not to

touch any shell's bearing surface with your fingers.

**16** Work on one rod at a time. Cut an appropriate size length of Plastigauge (it should be slightly shorter than the width of the crankpin) and place it on the crankpin journal to be checked **(see illustration 23.13)**. Do not place Plastigauge over the oil holes in the journal.

**17** Apply molybdenum disulphide grease to the threads and under the heads of the bolts. Fit the connecting rod and cap onto the crankpin – make sure they are fitted the correct way around so the previously made markings align (see Step 4). Fit the old bolts and tighten them finger-tight. It is essential throughout this procedure that the connecting rod does not rotate on the crankshaft.

**18** Tighten the bolts to 14 Nm with a torque wrench. Now tighten each bolt in turn and in one continuous movement through 210° using a degree disc (torque angle gauge) **(see illustration 24.29)**.

**19** Slacken the bolts and remove the cap and rod from the crankshaft.

**20** Compare the width of the crushed Plastigauge on the crankpin to the scale printed on the Plastigauge envelope to obtain the connecting rod bearing oil clearance **(see illustration 23.16)**. Compare the reading to that given in the Specifications. If the clearance is within the range specified and the bearings are in perfect condition, they can be reused.

**21** If the clearance is beyond the specified service limit, first measure the diameter of the crankpin journals with a micrometer and compare the results with the Specifications. If the journal diameters are larger than the service limit, new bearing shells can be fitted (see Steps 24 to 26). If the journal diameters are smaller than the service limit, the crankshaft must be replaced with a new one.

**22** Carefully clean away all traces of the Plastigauge from the crankpin journal and bearing shells using a fingernail or other object which will not score the bearing surfaces.

**23** Repeat the procedure for the other connecting rod, then discard the old big-end bolts.

### Bearing shell selection

**24** The connecting rod big-end bearing oil clearance is controlled in production by selecting one of two grades of bearing shell. The grades are indicated by a colour-coding marked on the edge of each shell **(see illustration 23.19)**. New bearing shells are selected as follows according to the crankpin journal diameter.

**25** Measure the crankpin journal diameter using a micrometer and record the result.

**26** Match the measured journal diameter to the required bearing shells using the following table.

| Crankpin journal diameter | Shell colour |
| --- | --- |
| 37.993 to 38.000 mm | White |
| 37.984 to 37.992 mm | Red |

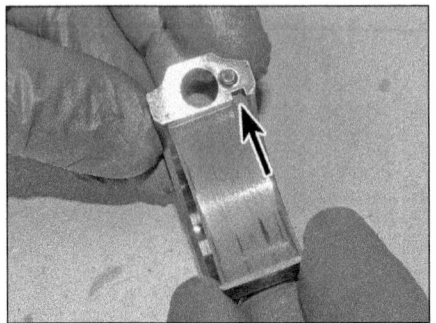

**24.14 Remove the shells from the rods and caps**

**24.15 Locate the tab (arrowed) in the notch**

## Installation

**Note:** *New big-end bolts must be used on final assembly.*

27 Make sure that the backs of the bearing shells, the bearing seats in the caps and rods and the crankpin journals are clean. If new shells are being fitted, remove any protective grease using paraffin (kerosene). Dry the shells, caps, rods and journals with a clean, lint-free cloth. Fit the shells, locating the tab on each shell in the notch in the cap or rod, and making sure the end of each shell is flush with the cap or rod **(see illustration 24.15)**. If the original bearing shells are to be fitted, make sure that they are in their correct locations. Take care not to touch any bearing surfaces with your fingers.

28 Apply molybdenum disulphide grease to the threads and under the heads of the bolts. Fit the connecting rod and cap onto the crankpin **(see illustrations 24.5b)** – make sure they are fitted the correct way around so the previously made markings align (see Step 4). Fit new bolts and tighten them finger-tight **(see illustration)**.

29 Tighten the bolts to 14 Nm with a torque wrench. Now tighten each bolt in turn and in one continuous movement through 210° using a degree disc (torque angle gauge) **(see illustration)**.

30 Turn the crankshaft and check the rods move smoothly and freely. If there are any signs of roughness or tightness, detach the rods and recheck the assembly. Sometimes tapping the bottom of the connecting rod cap will relieve tightness.

31 Reassemble the crankcase halves (Section 20) and the rest of the engine.

## 25 Balancer shafts

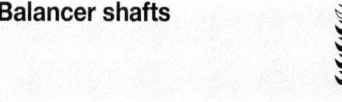

1 The balancer shafts have eccentric deadshafts running through them that provide a small amount of adjustment of the engagement depth (or backlash) between the teeth on the driven gear and those of the drive gear on the crankshaft – when the shafts are correctly adjusted and the teeth are perfectly meshed they should run silently. If they mesh too deep there will be a whining noise, and if they mesh too shallow there will be a clatter. If either noise is heard when the engine is running perform the dynamic adjustment procedure given below before going to the extent of removing the shafts for inspection. If the shafts run fine and are being removed for other reasons, mark the alignment of the punch mark on the deadshaft with the crankcase as described in the removal procedure so the shaft can be reset in the same position on installation. If new parts are being fitted, or if you prefer to check the setting on installation of the original parts,

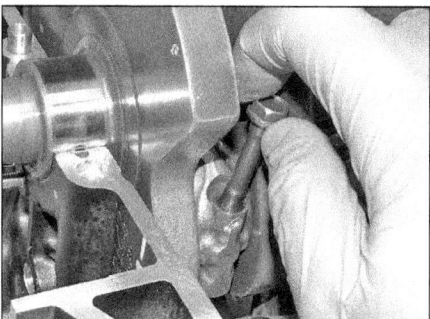

**24.28 Use new bolts**

the punch mark on the deadshaft can be aligned with the index mark already on the crankcase on installation, and this is the mid-way point in the adjustment range. When the engine has been rebuilt final adjustment can be made with the engine running as described in the dynamic adjustment procedure.

## Removal

2 Remove the engine from the frame (Section 4) and separate the crankcase halves (Section 20) – the front balancer shaft stays in the upper crankcase and the rear balancer shaft comes away in the lower crankcase.

### Front balancer shaft

3 Remove the crankshaft (Section 23).

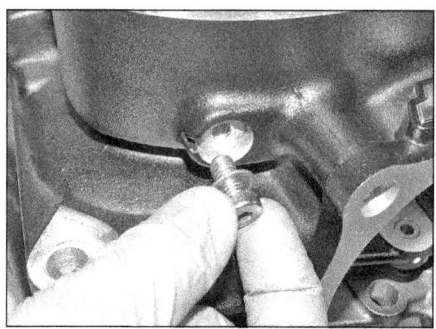

**25.4a Remove the blanking screw...**

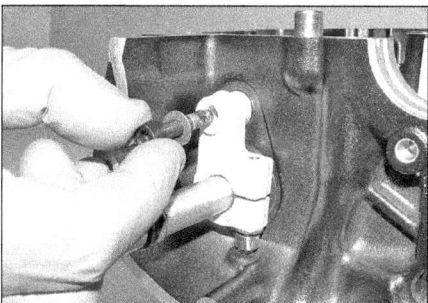

**25.4c ...and unscrew the positioning bolt**

**24.29 Use a degree disc for the final tightening of the bolts**

4 Undo the deadshaft clamp bolt blanking screw from the crankcase, noting the sealing washer **(see illustration)** – a new one should be used. Slacken the clamp bolt using a hex key through the blanking screw hole **(see illustration)**. Unscrew the clamp positioning bolt, noting the washer **(see illustration)**. Slide the clamp along the shaft up to the two outer O-rings.

5 Identify the punch mark on the deadshaft and make an alignment mark next to it on the crankcase **(see illustration)**. Also identify the manufacturer's index mark already on the crankcase.

6 Hold the balancer shaft, then withdraw the deadshaft, using a lever against the inner end to help push it out if required to overcome the

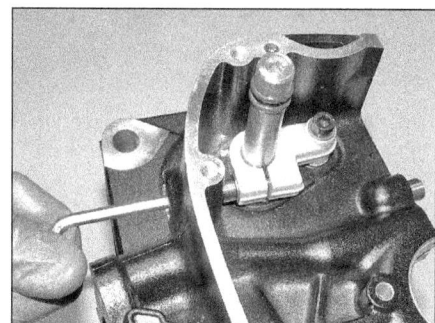

**25.4b ...then slacken the clamp bolt...**

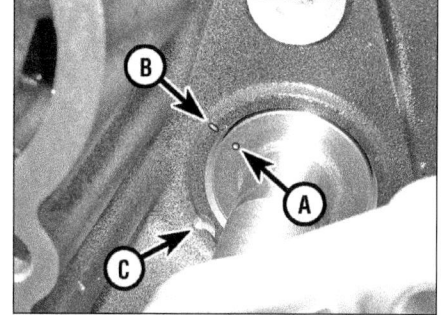

**25.5 Deadshaft punch mark (A) and alignment mark (B), manufacturer's index mark (C)**

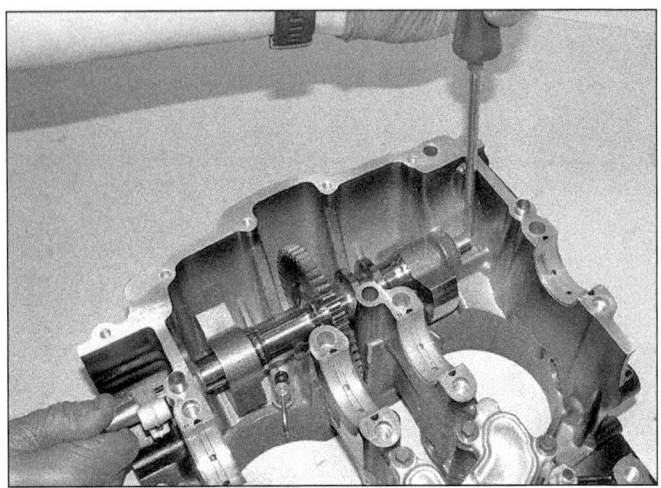

25.6a Use a screwdriver as shown to initially push the shaft...

25.6b ...then withdraw it and lift the balancer out

25.7 Remove the retainer plate

25.8 Slacken the clamp bolt (arrowed) and remove the positioning bolt

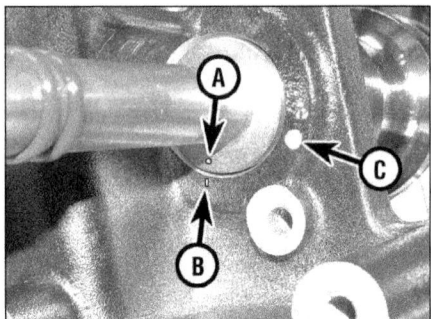

25.9 Deadshaft punch mark (A) and alignment mark (B), manufacturer's index mark (C)

inner O-rings, and remove the balancer **(see illustrations)**.

### Rear balancer shaft

**7** Undo the deadshaft retainer plate screw and remove the plate **(see illustration)**.

**8** Slacken the deadshaft clamp bolt, then unscrew the clamp positioning bolt, noting the washer **(see illustration)**.
**9** Identify the punch mark on the deadshaft and make an alignment mark next to it on the crankcase **(see illustration)**. Also identify

the manufacturer's index mark already on the crankcase.
**10** Hold the clamp and withdraw the deadshaft until the clamp is free to be removed, then hold the balancer shaft, fully withdraw the deadshaft and remove the balancer **(see illustration)**.

25.10a Partially withdraw the shaft and remove the clamp...

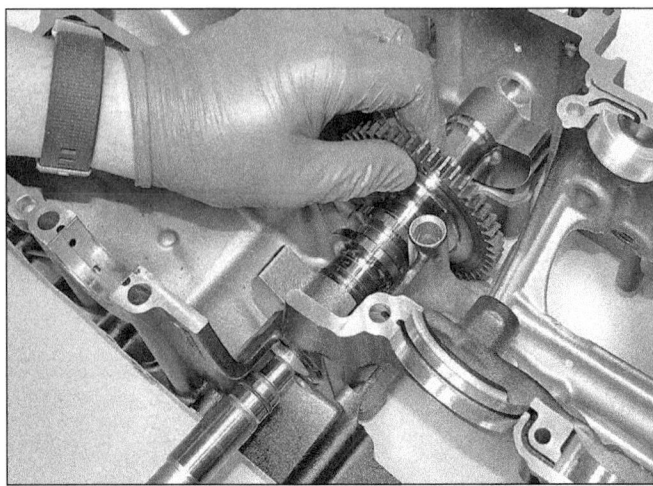

25.10b ...then fully withdraw the shaft and lift the balancer out

## Inspection

**11** Clean the balancer shaft with a suitable solvent. Check the gear teeth for wear or damage. If any of the teeth are excessively worn, chipped or broken, the balancer shaft must be replaced with a new one. Check the drive gear on the crankshaft for corresponding wear or damage.

**12** Check the needle bearing in each end of the balancer, and check the bearing surfaces on the deadshaft **(see illustration)**. The bearings are not available separately from the balancer shafts, so if they are worn or damaged a new balancer shaft must be fitted. The deadshafts are available separately.

## Installation

**13** Remove the O-rings from each deadshaft and fit new ones **(see illustration)** – if the front deadshaft clamp is removed from the shaft fit it onto the shaft before fitting the small outer O-rings, and make sure the F mark on the clamp is facing out, towards the small O-rings, and slide the clamp next to the O-rings so you can see the alignment marks.

### Front balancer shaft

**14** Lubricate the balancer shaft bearings and the deadshaft inner O-rings with clean oil. Position the balancer in the crankcase, making sure the two ribs between the gear and the left-hand weight are in the left-hand side of the crankcase (remember the crankcase is upside down so as you look down on it from the back the ribs will actually be to your right), and insert the shaft, pushing it in all the way until the O-rings and shaft seat **(see illustration)**.

**15** Using a hex key in the right-hand end of the deadshaft, turn it to align the punch mark on the shaft with either the alignment mark you made on removal, or the manufacturer's index mark, according to whether you will be using the original adjustment setting, or carrying out the dynamic adjustment later **(see illustration and 25.5)** – see the information in Step 1 if required.

**16** Slide the clamp up against the crankcase

**25.12 Check the bearing in each end of the balancer**

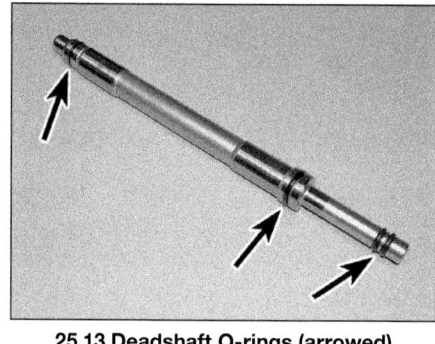

**25.13 Deadshaft O-rings (arrowed)**

**25.14 Position the weight and insert the shaft**

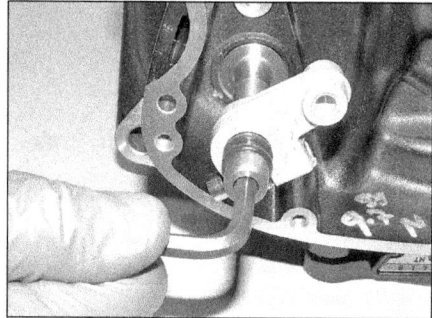

**25.15 Use a hex key to align the shaft as required**

and align the bolt holes, making sure the deadshaft does not turn. Clean the threads of the clamp positioning bolt and apply some threadlock, then fit the bolt with its washer and tighten to 10 Nm **(see illustration 25.4c)**. Tighten the clamp bolt to 10 Nm **(see illustration 25.4b)**. Fit a new sealing washer onto the clamp bolt blanking screw **(see illustration 25.4a)** – if you have set the balancer shaft adjustment to its original setting and are not carrying out the adjustment procedure tighten the screw to 10 Nm, and if you are carrying out the adjustment procedure tighten the screw finger-tight only at this stage.

**17** Install the crankshaft (Section 23).

### Rear balancer shaft

**18** Lubricate the balancer shaft bearings and the deadshaft inner O-rings with clean oil. Position the balancer in the crankcase, making sure the two ribs between the gear and the left-hand weight are in the left-hand side of the crankcase (as you look down on it from the back), and insert the shaft, pushing it in until the right-hand end is flush with the outer wall of the crankcase, then position the clamp with the R mark facing out and push the shaft through the clamp until the O-rings and shaft seat **(see illustrations)**.

**19** Using a hex key in the left-hand end of the deadshaft, turn it to align the punch mark on

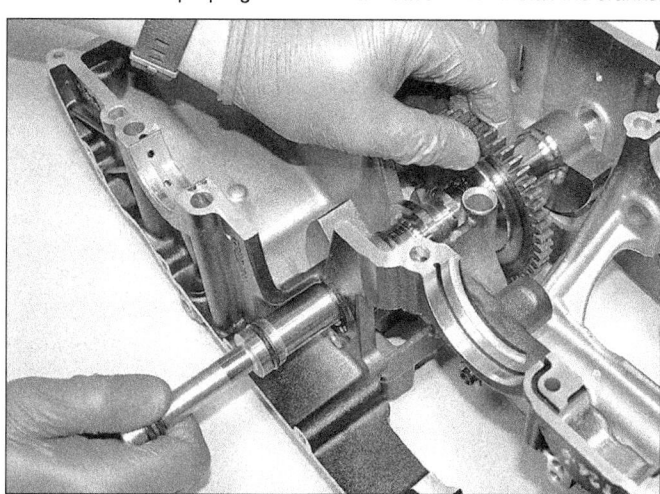

**25.18a Position the weight and insert the shaft...**

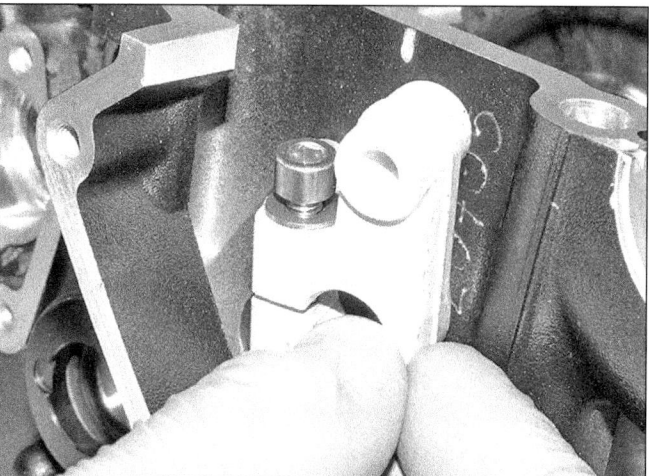

**25.18b ...fitting the clamp before it is all the way through**

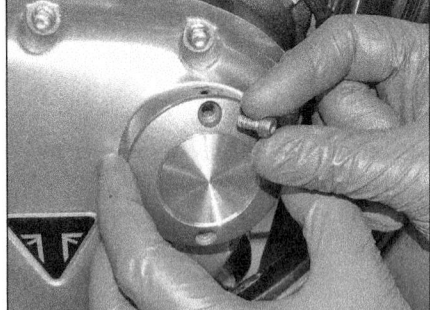

25.23a Remove the access cap...

25.23b ...and the blanking screw...

the shaft with either the alignment mark you made on removal, or the manufacturer's index mark, according to whether you will be using the original adjustment setting, or carrying out the dynamic adjustment later **(see illustration and 25.9)** – see the information in Step 1 if required.

**20** Clean the threads of the clamp positioning bolt and apply some threadlock, then fit the bolt with its washer and tighten to 10 Nm **(see illustration 25.8).** Tighten the clamp bolt to 10 Nm. Clean the threads of the deadshaft retainer plate screw and apply some threadlock, fit the plate and tighten the screw to 12 Nm **(see illustration 25.7).**

**21** Install the crankshaft (Section 23).

### Dynamic adjustment

**Note:** *Adjustment is provided so that the gears mesh at their optimum point for quiet running with minimal wear. If the amount of mesh is too small (too much backlash), the gears run loose and will clatter. If the amount of mesh is too great (not enough backlash) the gears run tight and will whine, and wear very quickly. At the optimum point the gears will run very quietly – it is easy to tell the difference with the engine running. Adjustment is possible due to the offset in the deadshaft which allows eccentric movement of the balancer shaft gear in relation to its drive gear on the crankshaft when the deadshaft is turned.*

**Note:** *This procedure must be carried out when the engine is warm. Always carry out the adjustment to both shafts.*

**22** Start the engine and allow it to warm up to the point when the cooling fan cuts in, then stop it.

**23** To adjust the front balancer shaft, remove the access cap from the alternator cover on the right-hand side of the engine, then undo the deadshaft clamp bolt blanking screw from the top of the crankcase **(see illustrations)** – unless already fitted during the shaft installation procedure above, a new sealing washer is needed for the screw. Slacken the

deadshaft clamp bolt no more than two turns using a hex key inserted in the blanking screw hole **(see illustration)**. Refit the blanking screw loosely to prevent oil splash.

**24** To adjust the rear balancer shaft, unscrew the blanking plug from the clutch cover on the left-hand side of the engine, then remove the oil filler cap from the alternator cover on the right-hand side **(see illustrations)**. Slacken the deadshaft clamp bolt no more than two turns using a hex key inserted in the oil filler hole **(see illustration)**. Refit the oil filler cap to prevent oil splash.

**25** Start the engine and allow it to idle. Turn the deadshaft slowly clockwise using a hex key inserted via the access cap hole in the alternator cover for the front balancer shaft and the blanking plug hole in the clutch cover for the rear balancer shaft to find the point at which the gears start to whine, then turn it anti-clockwise until they run at their quietest **(see illustrations)** – if you go too far anti-clockwise and you start to hear a clatter, go

25.23c ...then slacken the clamp bolt

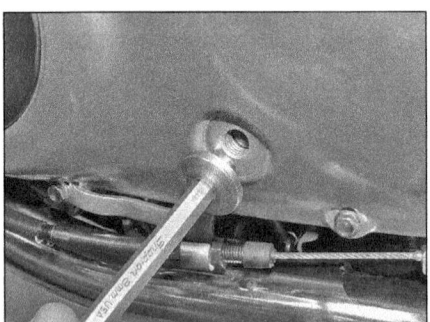

25.24a Remove the blanking plug...

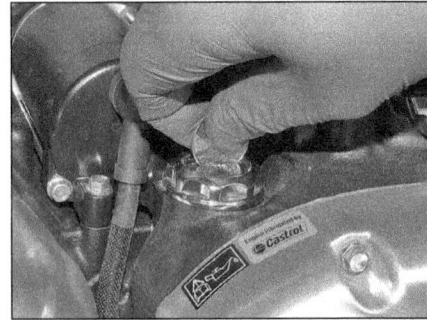

25.24b ...and the oil filler cap...

25.24c ...then slacken the clamp bolt

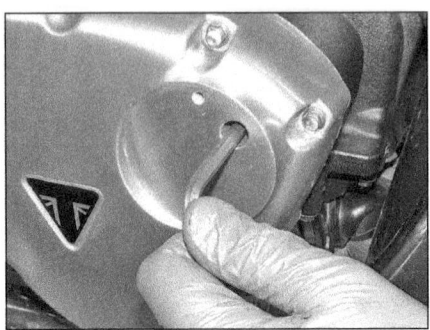

25.25a Adjusting the front balancer shaft

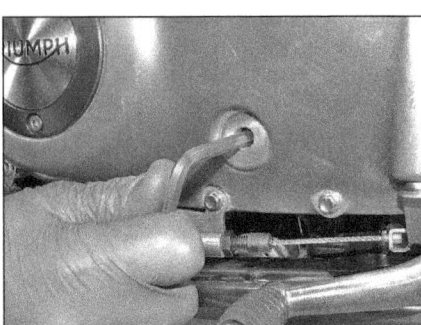

25.25b Adjusting the rear balancer shaft

26.2 Remove the output shaft...

26.3 ...then the input shaft

26.4 Seat the bearing pin in the cut-out

clockwise again, until you reach the quietest point. Rev the engine and check that there is no unwanted noise at varying speeds.

26 On completion, remove the blanking screw and oil filler cap and tighten the deadshaft clamp bolts to 10 Nm, then fit the blanking screw with its new sealing washer into the crankcase and the oil filler cap and access cap onto the alternator cover, and the blanking cap into the clutch cover.

## 26 Transmission shaft removal and installation

### Removal

1 Remove the engine from the frame (Section 4), then separate the crankcase halves (Section 20).

2 Lift the output shaft out of the crankcase (see illustration) – note how the retaining ring between the oil seal and the bearing on the right-hand end locates in the groove, and the pin in the left-hand bearing locates in the hole (see illustration 26.6a and b). A new oil seal must be used on installation (see illustration 26.5b).

3 Lift the input shaft out of the crankcase, noting that there is a washer on the right-hand end that can easily drop off – note how the pin in the right-hand bearing locates in the cut-out (see illustration and 26.4).

### Installation

4 Make sure the washer is fitted on the right-hand end of the input shaft (see illustration 27.3). Seat the shaft in the crankcase (see illustration 26.3), locating the pin in the right-hand bearing in the cut-out in the crankcase (see illustration).

5 Smear the lip of the new output shaft seal with grease. Make sure the retaining ring is in place, then slide the seal onto the right-hand end of the shaft (see illustrations).

6 Seat the output shaft in the upper crankcase (see illustration 26.2), locating the pin in the left-hand bearing in the hole and the retaining ring on the right-hand end in the groove (see illustrations).

26.5a Make sure the retaining ring is fitted

*Caution: If the locating pins and retaining ring are not correctly seated, the crankcase halves will not join correctly.*

7 Position the gears in the neutral position and check the shafts are free to rotate easily and independently (i.e. the input shaft can turn whilst the output shaft is held stationary) before proceeding further.

8 Reassemble the crankcase halves (Section 20).

## 27 Transmission shaft overhaul

1 Remove the transmission shafts from the crankcase (Section 26).

26.6a Fit the pin into the hole...

26.5b Use a new oil seal

 **HAYNES HiNT** *When disassembling a transmission shaft, as you remove each component place it on a long rod or thread a wire through to keep them in order and the correct way round.*

### Input shaft

#### Disassembly and reassembly

2 The only parts available for the input shaft are the bearings – the shaft and all the gears are only available as an assembly. A needle bearing is fitted on the right-hand end of the shaft and a ball bearing on the left – if the ball bearing is removed a new one must be fitted.

3 Remove the washer from the right-hand

26.6b ...and the ring in the groove (arrowed)

**27.3 Note the washer fitted on the outside of the bearing**

end of the shaft and slide the bearing off **(see illustration)**. Lubricate the bearing before fitting it.

**4** To remove the ball bearing from the left-hand end of the shaft you need a puller set up as shown, with the flat sides, not the dished sides, of the puller jaws against the bearing, and a spacer between the puller bolt and the end of the shaft to protect the shaft **(see illustration)**. Alternatively set the puller jaws up as shown, place them on the support bars of a hydraulic press and push the shaft out of the bearing, making sure you do not allow the shaft to drop onto the floor. To fit a new bearing either drive it on until it seats using a tubular drift that is long enough and that locates on the inner race of the bearing, not the outer, or place the bearing onto the support bars of a press so the inner race is supported and press the shaft through the bearing until the bearing is seated.

### Inspection

**5** Check the gear teeth for cracking, chipping, pitting and other obvious wear or damage.
**6** Inspect the dogs and the dog holes in the gears for cracks, chips, and excessive wear especially in the form of rounded edges. Make sure mating gears engage properly.
**7** Check for signs of scoring or bluing on the pinions. This could be caused by overheating due to inadequate lubrication. Replace any worn or damaged parts with new ones.
**8** Check that each gear moves freely around or along the shaft or its bush but without undue freeplay.
**9** If there is any damage or wear evident fit a complete new input shaft – a new ball bearing will come fitted on the shaft, but you will need to buy and fit a new needle bearing (Step 3).

### *Output shaft*

#### Disassembly

**10** Slide the bearing outer race off the left-hand end of the shaft, then release the circlip and slide the bearing off **(see illustrations 27.34c, b and a)**.
**11** Slide the thrust washer off the shaft, followed by the 1st gear pinion and its bearing **(see illustrations 27.33c, b and a)**.
**12** Slide the 5th gear pinion off the shaft **(see illustration 27.32)**.

**27.4 Puller set-up for removing the left-hand bearing**

**13** Remove the circlip securing the 4th gear pinion, then slide the splined washer, the pinion and its bush off the shaft **(see illustrations 27.31d, c, b and a)**. A new circlip must be fitted on reassembly.
**14** To remove the 2nd, 6th and 3rd gear pinions from the right-hand end of the shaft you must first remove the bearing and spacer using a puller set up as shown, with the dished sides, not the flat sides, of the puller jaws against the bearing **(see illustration)**. Alternatively set the puller jaws up as shown, place them on the support bars of a hydraulic press and push the shaft out of the bearing, making sure you do not allow the shaft to drop onto the floor. A new bearing must be fitted when the shaft is reassembled.
**15** Slide the thrust washer, the 2nd gear pinion and its bush, followed by the thrust washer, off the shaft **(see illustration 27.27)**.
**16** On models with a five speed transmission slide the gear selector off the shaft, and models with a six speed transmission slide the 6th gear pinion off the shaft **(see illustration 27.27)**.
**17** Remove the circlip securing the 3rd gear pinion, then slide the splined washer, the pinion and its bush off the shaft **(see illustration 27.27)**.

### Inspection

**18** Clean all parts in solvent.
**19** Check the gear teeth for cracking, chipping, pitting and other obvious wear or damage.
**20** Inspect the dogs and the dog holes in the gears for cracks, chips, and excessive wear especially in the form of rounded edges. Make sure mating gears engage properly. Replace mating gears as a set if necessary.

**27.14 Puller set-up for removing the right-hand bearing**

**21** Check for signs of scoring or bluing on the pinions, bushes and shaft. This could be caused by overheating due to inadequate lubrication. Check that all the oil holes and passages are clear. Replace any worn or damaged parts with new ones.
**22** Check that each pinion moves freely on the shaft or its bush but without undue freeplay. Check that each bush moves freely on the shaft but without undue freeplay.
**23** The shaft is unlikely to sustain damage unless the engine has seized, placing an unusually high loading on the transmission, or the machine has covered a very high mileage. Check the plain surfaces of the shaft, especially where a pinion turns on it, and check the splines on the shaft and in the relevant pinions, and replace the shaft with a new one if it has scored or picked up, or if there are any cracks.
**24** Check the washers and replace any that are bent or worn with new ones.
**25** Check the bearings referring to *Tools and Workshop Tips* in the Reference section. The input shaft left-hand bearing is housed in the crankcase, and is available, but if the right-hand bearing is worn a new shaft must be fitted. The output shaft bearings are available.

### Reassembly

**26** During reassembly, apply engine oil or molybdenum disulphide oil (a 50/50 mixture of molybdenum disulphide grease and engine oil) to the mating surfaces of the shaft, pinions and bushes. When fitting the new circlips, do not expand their ends any further than is necessary to slide them along the shaft. Fit chamfered circlips with the chamfered side facing the pinion it secures so the flat side takes the thrust (see Correct fitting of a stamped circlip illustration in *Tools and Workshop Tips* in the Reference section).
**27** Slide the 3rd gear pinion bush onto the right-hand end of the shaft, offsetting the oil holes, then slide on the 3rd gear pinion with its dog holes facing out, followed by the splined washer **(see illustration)**. Fit the new circlip, making sure it is locates correctly in its groove on the shaft.
**28** On models with a five speed transmission slide the gear selector onto the shaft, and models with a six speed transmission slide the 6th gear pinion onto the shaft, in each

**27.27 3rd gear pinion (C), gear selector or 6th gear pinion (B), 2nd gear pinion (A)**

27.30 Bearing and spacer in fitted position on right-hand end of shaft

27.31a Fit the 4th gear pinion bush...

27.31b ...then slide on the 4th gear pinion...

case with the selector fork groove facing the 3rd gear pinion (see illustration 27.27).

29  Slide the thrust washer and the 2nd gear pinion bush onto the shaft, making sure the oil hole in the bush is offset from the hole in the shaft, then fit the 2nd gear pinion with its flat side facing out, and fit the thrust washer (see illustration 27.27).

30  To fit a new bearing either drive it on until it seats using a tubular drift that is long enough and that locates on the inner race of the bearing, not the outer, or place the bearing onto the support bars of a press so the inner race is supported and press the shaft through the bearing until the bearing is seated. (see illustration). When the bearing is seated fit the spacer in the same way, with its chamfered end facing out, so its seats against the bearing inner race.

31  Slide the 4th gear pinion bush onto the left-hand end of the shaft, making sure the oil hole in the bush is offset from the hole in the shaft, then fit the 4th gear pinion with its dog holes facing out, and the splined washer (see illustrations). Fit the new circlip, making sure it locates correctly in its groove in the shaft (see illustrations).

32  Slide the 5th gear pinion onto the shaft with its selector fork groove facing the 4th gear pinion (see illustration).

33  Slide the 1st gear pinion bearing onto the shaft, followed by the 1st gear pinion with its dog holes facing the 5th gear pinion, and the thrust washer (see illustrations).

27.31c...and the splined washer...

27.31d...and secure them with the circlip...

27.31e ...making sure it locates correctly

27.32 Slide the 5th gear pinion onto the shaft

27.33a Fit the 1st gear pinion bearing...

27.33b...then slide the 1st gear pinion...

27.33c ...and the thrust washer onto the shaft

**27.34a Fit the bearing...**

**27.34b ...the circlip...**

**27.34c ...and the outer race**

**27.35 The assembled transmission output shaft**

**34** Fit the bearing onto the end of the shaft and secure it with a new circlip, then fit the bearing outer race **(see illustrations)**.

**35** Check that all components have been correctly installed. The assembled shaft should look as shown **(see illustration)**.

identification. On the engine photographed the input shaft fork has the letter K facing the right-hand side of the engine, and the output shaft left-hand fork has N, and the right-hand fork O, facing the left-hand side. Letters may vary across the range, but the side they face should be the same.

**3** On the right-hand side of the crankcase unscrew the input shaft fork shaft plug, then withdraw the shaft and remove the fork **(see illustrations)**.

**4** On the left-hand side of the crankcase unscrew the output shaft fork shaft retainer plate screw and remove the plate, then

## 28 Selector drum and forks

### Removal

**1** Remove the engine from the frame (Section 4), then separate the crankcase halves (Section 20). The selector drum and forks are in the lower crankcase half. If not already done remove the gear position sensor (see Chapter 8).

**2** Note that each selector fork is lettered for

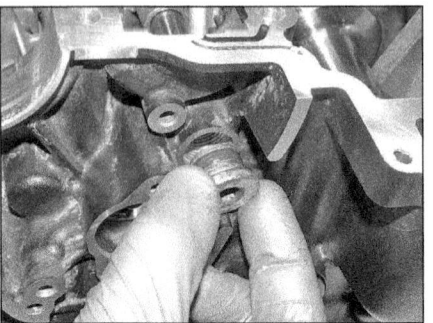

**28.3a Unscrew the plug**

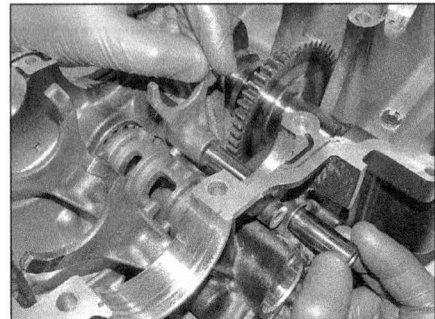

**28.3b Slide the shaft out and remove the fork**

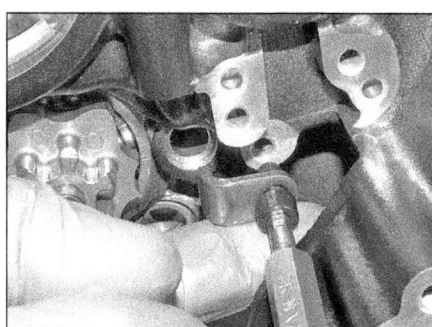

**28.4a Undo the screw and remove the retainer plate**

**28.4b Slide the shaft out and remove the right-hand fork...**

**28.4c ...and the left-hand fork**

withdraw the shaft and remove the forks **(see illustration)**.

**5** Undo the selector drum retainer plate screw and remove the plate, then slide the selector drum out **(see illustrations)**.

### Inspection

**6** Inspect the selector forks for any signs of wear or damage, especially around the fork ends where they engage with the grooves in the pinions **(see illustration)** – measure the thickness of the fork ends and compare with the figure given in the Specifications to check whether they're worn. Check that each fork fits correctly in its pinion groove. Check closely to see if the forks are bent. If the forks are in any way damaged fit new ones.

**7** Check that the forks fit correctly on their shaft **(see illustration)**. They should move freely with a light fit but no appreciable freeplay. Check that the fork shaft holes in the casing are not worn or damaged.

**8** Check the selector fork shafts for runout using V-blocks and a dial gauge – a bent shaft will cause difficulty in selecting gears and make the gearchange action heavy.

**9** Inspect the selector drum tracks and selector fork guide pins for signs of wear or damage **(see illustration)**.

**10** Check the selector drum bearings referring to *Tools and Workshop Tips* in the Reference section **(see illustration)**. If the bearing on the drum is worn hold the drum as shown, unscrew the detent wheel bolt, remove the wheel and slide the bearing off **(see illustration)**. Fit the new bearing. Fit the

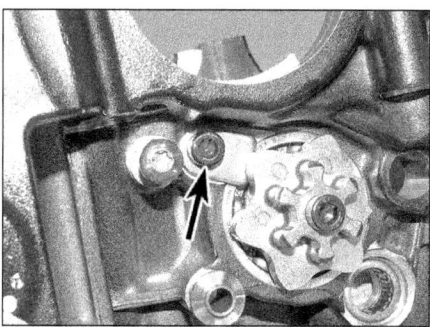

**28.5a Undo the screw (arrowed) and remove the plate...**

**28.5b ...and slide the drum out**

**28.6 Check the fork ends and their pinion grooves**

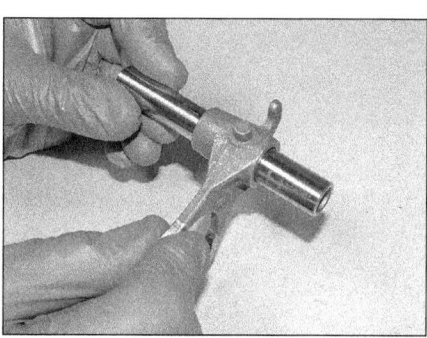

**28.7 Check the fit of each fork on its shaft**

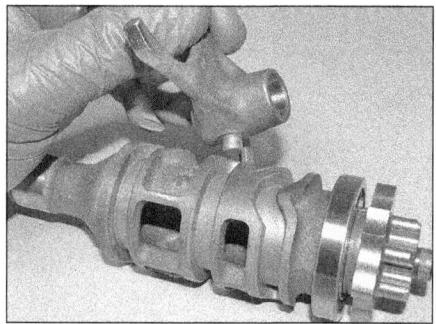

**28.9 Check the tracks and guide pins for wear and damage**

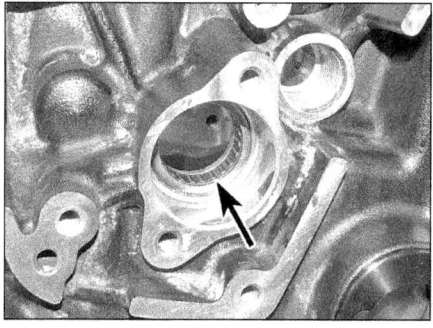

**28.10a There is a ball bearing on the drum and a needle bearing (arrowed) in the crankcase**

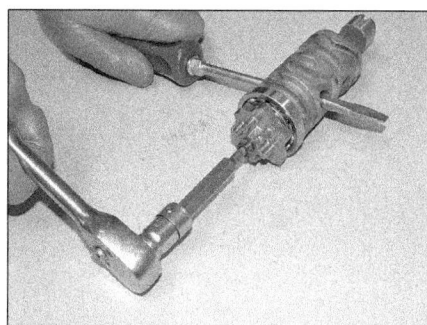

**28.10b Hold the drum to unscrew the detent wheel bolt**

detent wheel seating the cut-out over the pin **(see illustration)**. Clean the threads of the bolt, then apply a suitable non-permanent thread locking compound and tighten it to 12 Nm. Also check that the gear position sensor contact plunger is not damaged or worn away. If required, replace the plunger and spring with new ones.

### Installation

**11** Installation is the reverse of removal. Lubricate the moving surfaces of all components with engine oil before fitting them. Align the neutral detent in the selector drum wheel as shown **(see illustration 20.9)**. Make sure the forks are fitted the correct way round as described in Step 2, and seat the guide pins in the tracks in the drum **(see illustrations 28.4c and b and 28.3b)**. Clean the threads of the retainer plate screws and the shaft plug and apply threadlock. Tighten the screws to 12 Nm and the plug to 22 Nm.

### 29 Running-in procedure

**1** Make sure the engine oil and coolant levels are correct (see *Pre-ride checks*).
**2** Make sure there is fuel in the tank.
**3** Turn the ignition 'ON' and check that the warning lights for engine trouble, coolant temperature and immobiliser (where fitted) come on for a few seconds and then go off. The oil pressure warning light should also come on and stay on until the engine is started. Make sure that the transmission is in neutral and that the neutral light is on.

**28.10c Align the cut-out with the pin (arrowed)**

**4** Start the engine, then allow it to run at a moderately fast idle until it reaches normal operating temperature. Make sure the oil pressure light goes out after starting the engine.
**5** If a lubrication failure is suspected, stop the engine immediately and try to find the cause. If an engine is run without oil, even for a short period of time, severe damage will occur. After running the rebuilt engine for 600 miles (1000 km), change the engine oil and filter (see Chapter 1).
**6** Check carefully that there are no oil or coolant leaks and make sure the transmission and controls, especially the brakes and clutch, work properly before road testing the machine.
**7** Treat the machine gently for the first few miles to allow the oil to circulate throughout the engine and any new parts installed to seat.
**8** Great care is necessary if the engine has been extensively overhauled – the bike will

have to be run in as when new. This means more use of the transmission and a restraining hand on the throttle until at least 1000 miles (1600 km) have been covered. There is no point in keeping to any set road speed, the main idea is to keep from labouring the engine and to gradually increase performance up to the 1000 mile (1600 km) mark. These recommendations apply less when only a partial overhaul has been done, though it does depend to an extent on the nature of the work carried out and which components have been renewed. Experience is the best guide, since it is easy to tell when an engine is running freely. If in any doubt, consult a Triumph dealer. The following maximum engine speed limitations, which Triumph provides for new motorcycles, can be used as a guide.

| Up to 500 miles (800 km) | Do not use full throttle or high revs. Vary engine speed but do not exceed 3/4 throttle |
| --- | --- |
| 500 to 1000 miles (800 to 1600 km) | Vary throttle position/ speed. Engine speed can be increased to the rev limit for short periods |
| Over 1000 miles (1600 km) | Normal riding. Do not over rev the engine when cold. Prevent the engine labouring by changing down a gear |

**9** Upon completion of the road test, and after the engine has cooled down completely, recheck the valve clearances (see Chapter 1) and check the engine oil and coolant levels (see *Pre-ride checks*).

# Chapter 3
# Cooling system

## Contents

## Degrees of difficulty

| **Easy,** suitable for novice with little experience  | **Fairly easy,** suitable for beginner with some experience | **Fairly difficult,** suitable for competent DIY mechanic | **Difficult,** suitable for experienced DIY mechanic | **Very difficult,** suitable for expert DIY or professional  |
|---|---|---|---|---|

## Specifications

### Coolant

| | |
|---|---|
| Coolant type. . . . . . . . . . . . . . . . . . . . . . . . . . . . . . . . . . . . . | Triumph HD4X Hybrid OAT (organic acid technology) ready-mix coolant |

Coolant capacity
| | |
|---|---|
| T100, Street Twin, Street Cup, Scrambler . . . . . . . . . . . . . . . . . . | 1.52 litres |
| T120, Bobber, Thruxton, Thruxton R . . . . . . . . . . . . . . . . . . . . | 1.56 litres |

### Radiator

| | |
|---|---|
| Cap valve opening pressure. . . . . . . . . . . . . . . . . . . . . . . . . . . | 17.5 psi (1.2 Bar) |

### Cooling fan

| | |
|---|---|
| Cooling fan cut-in temperature . . . . . . . . . . . . . . . . . . . . . . . . | 103°C |

### Thermostat

| | |
|---|---|
| Opening temperature. . . . . . . . . . . . . . . . . . . . . . . . . . . . . . . | 88°C |

### Torque wrench settings

| | |
|---|---|
| Coolant inlet union bolt . . . . . . . . . . . . . . . . . . . . . . . . . . . . . | 9 Nm |
| Thermostat cover bolts . . . . . . . . . . . . . . . . . . . . . . . . . . . . . | 9 Nm |

## 1 General Information

**1** The cooling system uses a water/antifreeze mixture to carry excess heat away from the engine. The cylinders are surrounded by a water jacket, through which the coolant is circulated by a water pump. The water pump is housed with the oil pump in a pump assembly that is driven chain driven off the back of the clutch.

**2** Heated coolant from the engine flows through the radiator, where it is cooled by the airflow across it. A thermostat fitted in the front of the cylinder head is closed when the engine is cold to prevent the coolant flowing, therefore accelerating the speed at which the engine reaches normal operating temperature, and opens as the engine warms up, allowing the coolant to flow.

**3** A coolant temperature (ECT) sensor is fitted into the front of the cylinder head, and provides signals for the coolant temperature warning light on the instrument panel and for the ECM as part of the engine management system.

**4** A relay-controlled cooling fan is fitted behind the radiator, to aid cooling in extreme conditions. The relay is controlled by a signal from the ECM.

**5** The complete cooling system is partially sealed and pressurised, the pressure being controlled by a spring-loaded valve contained in the pressure cap. By pressurising the coolant the boiling point is raised, preventing premature boiling in adverse conditions. The overflow hose from the system is connected to a reservoir into which excess coolant is expelled under pressure. The discharged coolant automatically returns to the radiator when the engine cools.

**6** If the engine is over-heating the temperature warning light will come on – turn the engine OFF immediately. When the engine has cooled, check the cooling system as described in Chapter 1.

 *Warning: Do not remove the pressure cap from the filler neck when the engine is hot. Scalding hot coolant and steam may be blown out under pressure and could cause serious injury. When the engine has cooled,*

*place a thick rag such as a towel over the pressure cap; slowly rotate the cap anti-clockwise to the first stop. This procedure allows any residual pressure to escape. When the pressure has stopped escaping, press down on the cap while turning it anti-clockwise, and remove it.*

⚠️ **Warning: Do not allow coolant to come into contact with your skin, or painted surfaces of the motorcycle. Rinse off any spills immediately with plenty of water. The antifreeze content of coolant is highly toxic if ingested. Never leave antifreeze lying around in an open container or in puddles on the floor; children and pets are attracted by its sweet smell and may drink it. Check with the local authorities about disposing of used coolant – many communities will have collection centres which will see that it is disposed of safely.**

7 Read the *Safety first!* section of this manual carefully before starting work.

## 2 Radiator

### Removal

⚠️ **Warning: The engine must be completely cool before carrying out this procedure.**

1 Drain the cooling system (see Chapter 1).
2 On the Bobber undo the wiring connector

holder screw on the right-hand side of the frame **(see illustration)**.
3 Disconnect the loom side of the cooling fan wiring connector, then release the fan side of the connector from the holder and feed the wiring to the radiator, noting its routing **(see illustrations)**. Release the wiring guides from the inner side of the left-hand frame cradle by pushing one side in using a small screwdriver and pulling the clip out **(see illustration)**.
4 Unscrew the radiator mounting bolt, noting the collar **(see illustration)**. Pull the top of the radiator forwards, then release the hose clamp and pull the radiator out of the hose **(see illustration)**. Lift the radiator to release the grommets from the lugs **(see illustration)**.
5 If required remove the cooling fan (Section 3).
6 Check the radiator for signs of damage and clear any dirt or debris that might obstruct airflow and inhibit cooling. Radiator fins can be straightened carefully with a flat-bladed screwdriver, but if the fins are badly damaged or broken the radiator must be replaced with a new one. Check the condition of the three mounting grommets – fit new ones if necessary.

### Installation

7 Installation is the reverse of removal, noting the following.
● Make sure the coolant hoses are in good condition.

**2.2 Undo the screw (arrowed)**

● Make sure the collar for the mounting bolt is in the grommet or fitted with the bolt **(see illustration 2.4a)**.
● Make sure the coolant hoses are securely retained by their clamps – use new clamps if necessary.
● Make sure that the wiring is correctly routed and the connector is secure.
● Refill the cooling system as described in Chapter 1.

### Radiator pressure cap

8 If problems such as overheating or loss of coolant occur, check the entire system as described in Chapter 1. The radiator cap opening pressure should be checked by a Triumph dealer with the special tester required for the job. If the cap is defective, fit a new one.

**2.3a Disconnect the connector...**

**2.3b ...then release it from the holder**

**2.3c Release the clips from the frame using a small screwdriver**

**2.4a Unscrew the bolt and remove the collar**

**2.4b Release the clamp and pull the radiator forwards out of the hose**

**2.4c Lift the radiator off the bottom lugs**

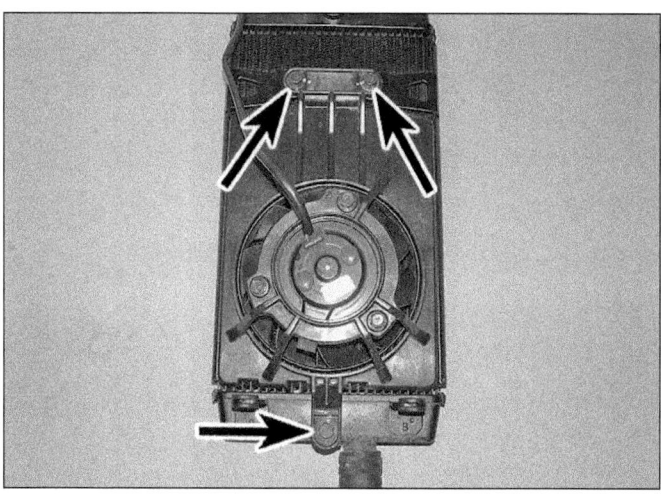

3.5 Cooling fan screws (arrowed)

4.3a Unscrew the bolts and displace the cover

4.3b Remove the thermostat

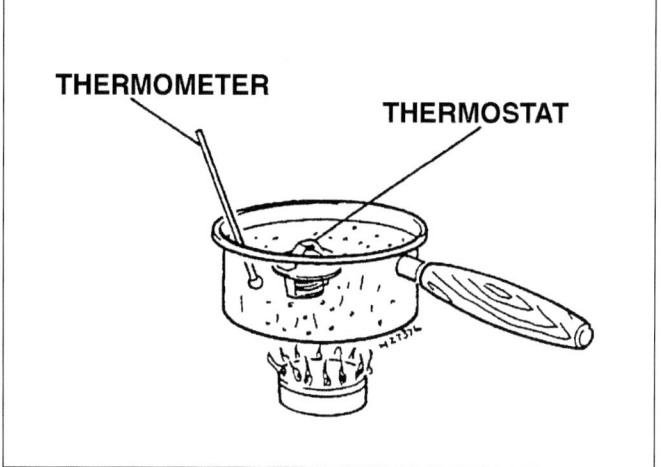

4.5 Thermostat testing set-up

## 3  Cooling fan

### Check

1  If the engine is overheating and the coolant temperature warning light comes on, yet the cooling fan isn't cutting in, first check the fan fuse in the fusebox (see Chapter 8).
2  If the fuse is good, remove the fuel tank (see Chapter). On the Bobber undo the wiring connector holder screw on the right-hand side of the frame **(see illustration 2.2)**. Disconnect the fan wiring connector **(see illustration 2.3a)**. Using a 12 volt battery and two jumper wires, connect the positive (+) battery lead to the brown/pink wire terminal in the fan side of the wiring connector and the negative (–) lead to the black wire terminal. Once connected, the fan should operate. If it does not, and the wiring between the connector and the fan is good, then the fan is faulty.

3  If the fan motor works check the fan relay (see Chapter 8), then the ECT sensor (see Chapter 4). If they work check the wiring and connectors in the cooling fan circuit, referring to Chapter 8, Section 2 and to the wiring diagram for your model at the end of Chapter 8.

### Removal and installation

⚠ Warning: The engine must be completely cool before carrying out this procedure.
4  Remove the radiator (Section 2).
5  Undo the fan screws and remove the fan **(see illustration)**.
6  Installation is the reverse of removal.

## 4  Thermostat

⚠ Warning: The engine must be completely cool before carrying out this procedure.
1  The thermostat is automatic in operation and

should give many years service without requiring attention. In the event of a failure, if the valve stays open the engine will take much longer than normal to warm up, and if the valve stays shut the coolant will be unable to circulate and the engine will overheat. Neither condition is acceptable, and the fault must be investigated promptly.

### Removal

2  Drain the cooling system (see Chapter 1).
3  Unscrew the thermostat cover bolts, displace the cover and remove the thermostat **(see illustrations)**.

### Check

4  Examine the thermostat visually before carrying out the test. If it remains in the open position at room temperature, it is faulty.
5  Suspend the thermostat by a piece of wire in a container of cold water. Suspend a thermometer capable of reading temperatures up to 110°C in the water so that the bulb is close to the thermostat **(see illustration)**. Make sure neither the thermostat nor

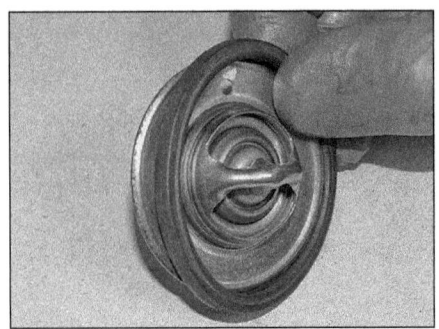

**4.8 Seal must be in good condition**

**6.5 Coolant inlet union bolts to front of crankcase**

thermometer touches the container. Heat the water and check the thermostat opens at around 88°C. Also check the amount the valve opens after it has been heated for a few minutes – Triumph do not specify how much, but generally it should open at least 8 mm.

**6** In the event of thermostat failure, if the thermostat is permanently closed, as an emergency measure only it can be removed and the machine used without it (this is better than leaving it in as the engine will overheat). If it is permanently open you are better to leave it in. In both cases take care when starting the engine from cold as it will take much longer than usual to warm up. Ensure that a new unit is installed as soon as possible.

**7** Check the condition of the seal and fit a new one if it is damaged or deformed – it is available separately.

### Installation

**8** Make sure the seal is correctly seated around the rim of the thermostat **(see illustration)**.

**9** Fit the thermostat with the breather hole at the top **(see illustration 4.3b)**. Fit the cover and tighten the bolts to 9 Nm **(see illustration 4.3a)**.

**10** Fill the cooling system (see Chapter 1).

## 5  Water pump

**1** The water pump is an integral part of the oil/water pump assembly, and is covered in Chapter 2, Section 19. No parts are available for the water pump so if there is a fault or the pump is leaking from the drain tube exit on the underside of the sump a complete new pump assembly must be fitted.

## 6  Coolant hoses, pipes and unions

### Removal

**Note:** *Automotive type hose clamps are used on the large bore coolant hoses. To release the clamps squeeze the ends together using large pliers, or use a dedicated automotive clamp tool, available from good tool suppliers.*

**1** There are two main large bore hoses – a short one between the bottom of the radiator and the engine, and a T-shaped one between the top of the radiator, the thermostat housing on the front of the engine, and the filler neck under the right-hand side of the fuel tank. There is a small bore hose running from the filler neck to the coolant reservoir.

**2** Before removing a hose or union, drain the coolant (see Chapter 1) – this involves detaching the bottom hose from the inlet union on the engine.

**3** Release the hose clamps, then slide them back along the hose.

**Caution: The radiator unions are fragile. Do not use excessive force when attempting to remove the hoses.**

**4** Release the hose by rotating it on its union before working it off, or slip a plastic tool between the hose and the union. If all else fails, carefully cut the hose with a sharp knife – obviously this means fitting a new hose.

**5** Remove the coolant inlet union on the engine by unscrewing the bolt **(see illustration)**. Remove the O-ring – a new one must be used. See Section 4 for removal of the thermostat cover.

### Installation

**6** If the inlet union has been removed, clean the threads of the bolt and apply threadlock, then fit a new O-ring and tighten the bolt to 9 Nm. See Section 4 for installation of the thermostat cover.

**7** Slide the clamps onto the hose and then work the hose onto its unions, making sure it is correctly orientated so the hose aligns correctly at each end.

**HAYNES HINT** *If the hose is difficult to push on its union, it can be softened by soaking it in very hot water, or alternatively a little soapy water can be used as a lubricant.*

**8** Slide the clamps into place. Make sure there is 3 to 7 mm of hose exposed between the clamp and the end of the hose.

# Chapter 4
# Engine management system (fuel and ignition)

## Contents

## Degrees of difficulty

| **Easy,** suitable for novice with little experience | **Fairly easy,** suitable for beginner with some experience | **Fairly difficult,** suitable for competent DIY mechanic | **Difficult,** suitable for experienced DIY mechanic | **Very difficult,** suitable for expert DIY or professional |
|---|---|---|---|---|

## Specifications

### Fuel

| | |
|---|---|
| Grade | Unleaded, minimum 91 RON (Europe Research Octane Number), or minimum 87 (R+M)/2 (US CLC or AKI Octane rating) |

Fuel tank capacity
| | |
|---|---|
| T100, T120 | 14.5 litres |
| Bobber | 9.1 litres |
| Street Twin, Street Cup, Scrambler | 12 litres |
| Thruxton, Thruxton R | 14 litres |

Fuel quantity remaining when low level warning light comes on
| | |
|---|---|
| T100, T120, Street Twin, Street Cup, Scrambler, Thruxton, Thruxton R | 3.5 litres |
| Bobber | 2.5 litres |

### Fuel injection system

| | |
|---|---|
| Pump operating pressure (nominal) | 50 psi (3.5 Bar) |
| Fuel injector resistance | 11.4 to 13.0 ohms |
| EVAP system purge valve resistance | 22 to 30 ohms |

### Engine management system

| | |
|---|---|
| Type | Electronic |
| Control sensors | Atmospheric pressure, engine coolant temperature, crankshaft position, gear position, manifold absolute pressure, intake air temperature, throttle position, twist grip position, oxygen content (lambda), speed (road), tip-over |

ECT (Engine Coolant Temperature) sensor resistance
| | |
|---|---|
| Warm engine | 100 to 400 ohms |

Cold engine
| | |
|---|---|
| 20°C ambient | 2.22 to 2.71 K-ohms |
| -10°C ambient | 8.5 to 10.25 K-ohms |

IAT (Intake Air Temperature) sensor resistance
| | |
|---|---|
| 80°C ambient | 200 to 400 ohms |
| 20°C ambient | 2.35 to 2.65 K-ohms |
| -10°C ambient | 8.5 to 10.25 K-ohms |

## Ignition system

| | |
|---|---|
| Type . . . . . . . . . . . . . . . . . . . . . . . . . . . . . . . . . . . . . . . . . . . . . . . . . . . . . | Digital inductive |
| Cylinder identification. . . . . . . . . . . . . . . . . . . . . . . . . . . . . . . . . . . . . . . . | 1 – left, 2 – right |
| Spark plugs . . . . . . . . . . . . . . . . . . . . . . . . . . . . . . . . . . . . . . . . . . . . . . . . . | see Chapter 1 |
| Ignition coil resistance | |
|     Primary. . . . . . . . . . . . . . . . . . . . . . . . . . . . . . . . . . . . . . . . . . . . . . . . . . | 3.0 to 4.2 ohms |
|     Secondary . . . . . . . . . . . . . . . . . . . . . . . . . . . . . . . . . . . . . . . . . . . . . . . | approx. 18.5 K-ohms (see Section 10) |
| Rev limiter cut-in . . . . . . . . . . . . . . . . . . . . . . . . . . . . . . . . . . . . . . . . . . . | 7000 rpm |

## Torque settings

| | |
|---|---|
| Engine coolant temperature (ECT) sensor . . . . . . . . . . . . . . . . . . . . . . | 18 Nm |
| Exhaust header pipe flange nuts . . . . . . . . . . . . . . . . . . . . . . . . . . . . . | 19 Nm |
| Footrest/brake pedal/gearchange/lever bracket bolts. . . . . . . . . . . . . | 24 Nm |
| Frame cradle bolts | |
|     Top and rear bolts. . . . . . . . . . . . . . . . . . . . . . . . . . . . . . . . . . . . . . . | 40 Nm |
|     Middle bolt . . . . . . . . . . . . . . . . . . . . . . . . . . . . . . . . . . . . . . . . . . . . . | 105 Nm |
| Fuel pump mounting plate bolts . . . . . . . . . . . . . . . . . . . . . . . . . . . . | 5 Nm |
| Fuel rail bolts . . . . . . . . . . . . . . . . . . . . . . . . . . . . . . . . . . . . . . . . . . . . . | 6 Nm |
| Fuel tank nut/bolts | |
|     All models except the Bobber . . . . . . . . . . . . . . . . . . . . . . . . . . . . | 8 Nm |
|     Bobber . . . . . . . . . . . . . . . . . . . . . . . . . . . . . . . . . . . . . . . . . . . . . . . . | 30 Nm |
| Gear position sensor bolts. . . . . . . . . . . . . . . . . . . . . . . . . . . . . . . . . . | 5 Nm |
| Intake piece bolts to cylinder head (1200 engines) . . . . . . . . . . . . . . | 9 Nm |
| Oxygen sensors . . . . . . . . . . . . . . . . . . . . . . . . . . . . . . . . . . . . . . . . . . | 25 Nm |
| Throttle body and intake manifold bolts (900 engines) . . . . . . . . . . . | 9 Nm |
| Tip-over sensor bolts. . . . . . . . . . . . . . . . . . . . . . . . . . . . . . . . . . . . . . . | 3 Nm |

---

## 1  General information and precautions

### General information

**1** All models have an adaptive electronic engine management system that controls both the fuel and ignition system functions. The system is controlled by an electronic control module, or ECM. The ECM receives information from various sensors around the motorcycle, which it uses to determine the optimum fuel requirements for the fuel injection system and the optimum timing for the ignition system for all engine speeds and loads.

**2** The sensors used are for atmospheric pressure, crankshaft position, engine coolant temperature, manifold absolute pressure, intake air temperature, oxygen (lambda), road speed, throttle position, twistgrip position, gear position, and tip-over. Information on the function of these sensors is in Section 13.

**3** The fuel system consists of the fuel tank, the fuel pump and filter, pressure regulator and level sensor, the fuel hose, fuel rail and injectors, a single throttle body on 900 engines and two throttle bodies on 1200 engines, an electronic throttle control system, and the air intake system. The fuel pump, filter, and level sensor are housed inside the tank. There is an injector for each cylinder, mounted directly on the cylinder head. Cold starting and idle speed is controlled by the ECM which reacts to the information sent by the intake air temperature sensor and the coolant temperature sensor.

**4** The exhaust system is a two-into-two design via an underslung box containing a catalytic converter.

**5** The ignition system type is digital inductive, which due to its lack of mechanical parts is totally maintenance free. There is a conventional type coil for each spark plug. The system incorporates an electronic advance system controlled by the ECM, which reacts to the information sent to it from the various sensors to provide the spark at the optimum time. A rev limiter prevents the engine exceeding its maximum rpm. The system incorporates a starter safety circuit that will cut the ignition if the sidestand is put down whilst the engine is running and in gear, or if a gear is selected whilst the engine is running and the sidestand is down. The tip-over sensor will cut the ignition if it detects that the machine has fallen over.

**6** The engine management system has an in-built two-stage diagnostic function. The initial stage is fault detection, whereupon the system notes the fault and counts the occurrences, looking for repetition. If the fault was a temporary glitch that does not reoccur, no DTC (diagnostic trouble code, or fault code) is registered. If the fault continues a DTC is registered, and the ECM records and stores all engine and system data at that moment, and the malfunction indicator lamp (MIL) in the instrument cluster illuminates. Recorded faults can then be checked using a diagnostic tool, which reads the data and lists a code to indicate the exact fault. If this happens, the management system in most cases switches itself into 'limp home' mode, so that in theory you should not be left stranded, or in some cases switches itself off depending on the severity of the fault – with minor faults it is possible that you will notice no difference in the running of the motorcycle. If after the DTC has been logged and the MIL comes on the fault clears itself, the MIL will remain on until the engine has been through three of engine warm-up and system power-down cycles without the fault recurring, and the DTC will self-erase after forty such cycles. If the fault does not clear itself but is repaired the DTC can be erased using a diagnostic tool and the MIL will turn itself off.

**7** All UK models are fitted with an immobiliser that will only allow the engine to be started if the signal sent from a transponder in the ignition key is recognised by the ECM. The signal from the transponder is picked up and transmitted by a receiver fitted around the top of the ignition switch to the immobiliser control unit, which in turn corresponds with the ECM. The system has its own self-diagnostic function. The immobiliser system components must be paired with the ECM and this can only be done using the Triumph diagnostic tool.

**8** Because of their nature, the individual system components can be checked but not repaired. If system troubles occur, and the faulty component can be isolated, the only cure for the problem is to replace the part with a new one. Keep in mind that most electrical parts, once purchased, cannot be returned. To avoid unnecessary expense, make very sure the faulty component has been positively identified before buying a new part.

### Precautions

 *Warning: Petrol (gasoline) is extremely flammable, so take extra precautions when you work on any part of the fuel system.*

*Don't smoke or allow open flames or bare light bulbs near the work area, and don't work in a garage where a natural gas-type appliance is present. If you spill any fuel on your skin, rinse it off immediately with soap and water. When you perform any kind of work on the fuel system, wear safety glasses and have a fire extinguisher suitable for a class B type fire (flammable liquids) on hand.*

**9** Always perform fuel-related procedures in a well-ventilated area to prevent a build-up of fumes.

**10** Never work in a building containing a gas appliance with a pilot light, or any other form of naked flame. Ensure that there are no naked light bulbs or any sources of flame or sparks nearby.

**11** Do not smoke (or allow anyone else to smoke) while in the vicinity of petrol (gasoline) or of components containing it. Remember the possible presence of vapour from these sources and move well clear before smoking.

**12** Check all electrical equipment belonging to the house, garage or workshop where work is being undertaken (see the *Safety first!* section of this manual). Remember that certain electrical appliances such as drills, cutters etc. create sparks in the normal course of operation and must not be used near petrol (gasoline) or any component containing it. Again, remember the possible presence of fumes before using electrical equipment.

**13** Always mop up any spilt fuel and safely dispose of the rag used.

**14** Any stored fuel that is drained off during servicing work must be kept in sealed containers that are suitable for holding petrol (gasoline), and clearly marked as such; the containers themselves should be kept in a safe place. Note that this last point applies equally to the fuel tank if it is removed from the machine; also remember to keep its filler cap closed at all times.

**15** Read the *Safety first!* section of this manual carefully before starting work.

**16** Owners of machines used in the US, particularly California, should note that their machines must comply at all times with Federal or State legislation governing the

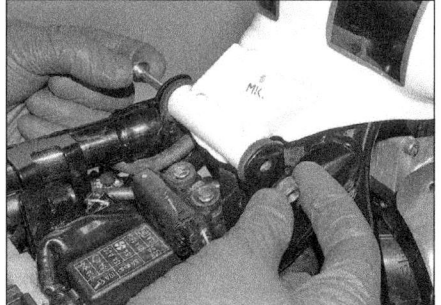

**2.4 Unscrew the nut and withdraw the bolt**

permissible levels of noise and of pollutants such as unburnt hydrocarbons, carbon monoxide etc. that can be emitted by those machines. All vehicles offered for sale must comply with legislation in force at the date of manufacture and must not subsequently be altered in any way which will affect their emission of noise or of pollutants.

**17** In practice, this means that adjustments may not be made to any part of the fuel, ignition or exhaust systems by anyone who is not authorised or mechanically qualified to do so, or who does not have the tools, equipment and data necessary to properly carry out the task. Also if any part of these systems is to be replaced it must be replaced with only genuine Triumph components or by components which are approved under the relevant legislation. The machine must never be used with any part of these systems removed, modified or damaged.

## 2  Fuel tank

⚠ *Warning: Refer to the precautions given in Section 1 before starting work.*

### Raise

**1** On all models except the Bobber remove the seat and the left-hand side panel (see Chapter 7).

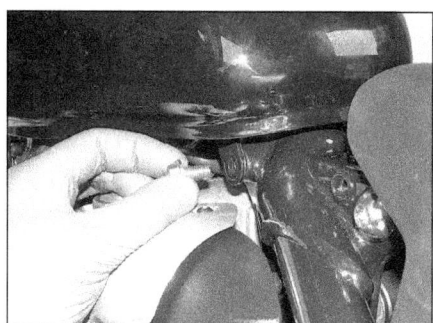

**2.5 Unscrew the bolt on each side**

**2** Disconnect the battery (see Chapter 8). Make sure the fuel cap is secure.

**3** Get a suitable prop such as a piece of 4 x 2 wood 8 to 10 inches long to place between the tank and the frame.

**4** On all models except the Bobber unscrew the nut on the tank mounting bolt and withdraw the bolt **(see illustration)**.

**5** On the Bobber unscrew the two tank mounting bolts **(see illustration)**.

**6** Draw the tank back a little, then lift the back of the tank and fit the piece of wood under it as shown **(see illustration)**.

### Removal

**Note:** *If the tank is full of fuel it will be quite heavy – either make sure the tank is nearly empty, or siphon any excess fuel out and into a suitable container before removal (siphons are cheaply available from a good automotive store), or have an assistant to help.*

**7** Make sure the fuel cap is secure. Have some rag to hand to catch any residual fuel in the connector and its union as the fuel hose is disconnected.

**8** Raise and support the tank as described above to access the hoses and connectors on the underside.

**9** On all models except the Bobber disconnect the fuel tank breather hose from the top of the roll-over valve and draw it out, noting its routing **(see illustration)**.

**10** On the Bobber release the fuel tank breather hose from the clip on the underside of the tank and disconnect the hose from the tank **(see illustration)**.

**2.6 Raise and support the rear of the tank**

**2.9 Pull the hose off the top of the valve**

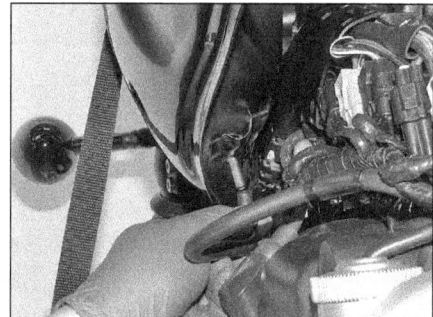

**2.10 Release and disconnect the hose**

2.11a Release the connectors from the bracket...

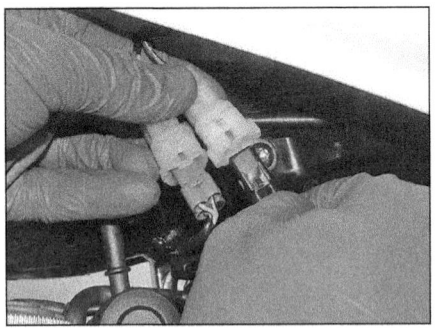

2.11b ...and disconnect them

2.12a Slide the cover across...

2.12b ...press the clips in...

2.12c ...and pull the hose connector off

**11** Release and disconnect the fuel pump (2-pin) and level sender (4-pin) wiring connectors **(see illustrations)**.
**12** Slide the fuel hose connector cover across to reveal the clips, then press the clips in and pull the hose off the fuel rail union **(see illustrations)**.
**13** Carefully lift the tank off the bike and remove it **(see illustration)**.
**14** Inspect the tank front support rubbers and the rear mounting rubbers for signs of damage or deterioration and fit new ones if necessary.

### Installation – all models

**15** Installation is the reverse of removal, noting the following:
● Make sure all mounting components are

correctly located before fitting the tank and stay located while fitting it.
● Initially position the tank in the raised position, with the front edge of the front support brackets located around each rubber **(see illustration 2.13)**.
● Make sure the connector is fully pushed onto the union until the clips locate, then push the connector cover across to cover the clips **(see illustration 2.15)** – if the cover won't push across the connector is not properly located.
● Make sure the electrical connectors are secure.
● Make sure the breather hose is correctly routed and secured **(see illustration 2.9 or 2.10)**.
● Reposition the tank so the front support

brackets are fully seated around the rubbers.
● On all models except the Bobber tighten the fuel tank mounting nut to 8 Nm.
● On the Bobber tighten the fuel tank mounting bolts to 30 Nm.
● Switch the ignition ON and check that there are no leaks around the fuel hose connector as the pump pressurises the system.

### Cleaning and repair

**16** All repairs to the fuel tank should be carried out by a professional who has experience in this critical and potentially dangerous work. Even after cleaning and flushing, explosive fumes can remain and ignite during repair of the tank.
**17** If the fuel tank is removed from the bike, it should not be placed in an area where sparks or open flames could ignite the fumes coming out of the tank. Be especially careful inside garages where a natural gas-type appliance is located, because the pilot light could cause an explosion.

---

### 3  Fuel pump, filter, and pressure regulator

> **Warning: Refer to the precautions given in Section 1 before starting work.**

### Fuel pump

#### Check

**1** The fuel pump is located inside the fuel tank.
**2** The fuel pump runs for a few seconds when the ignition is switched ON, then cuts out when the system is up to operating pressure, and cuts in again when the engine is started. If you can't hear anything, first check the engine management 15A fuse in the fusebox (see Chapter 8). Next check the wiring and wiring connectors in the fuel pump and relay circuit, referring to Section 2 for access to the pump wiring connector, and to Electrical system

2.13 Note how the front brackets seat around the rubber supports on the frame

2.15 Push the cover back over the clips

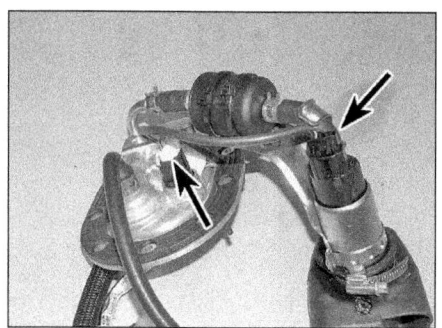

3.2 Make sure the wiring connectors (arrowed) are secure

3.6a Unscrew the mounting plate bolts

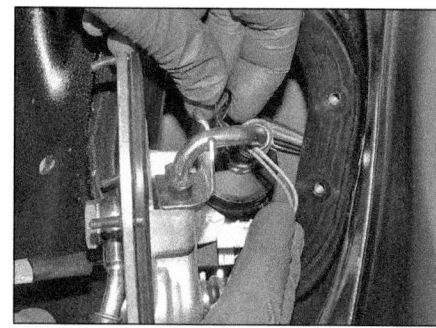

3.6b Lift the pump and disconnect the level sender connector, noting the routing of the wires

fault finding at the beginning of Chapter 8 and to the Wiring Diagram for your model at the end of it. Next, check the relay (see Chapter 8). If they are all good, remove the pump (see below) and check the internal wiring **(see illustration)**.

**3** Disconnect the connector from the top of the pump motor. Using a fully charged 12 volt battery and two insulated jumper wires, connect the negative (-) lead to the black wire terminal in the pump, then briefly touch the positive (+) lead to the violet/white wire terminal – the pump should operate. If the pump does not operate, replace the pump motor with a new one.

**4** If the pump operates but is thought to be delivering an insufficient amount of fuel, first check that the fuel tank breather hose is unobstructed, and that the fuel hose is in good condition and not pinched or trapped. If all is good, check the fuel pressure (Section 4).

### Removal

**5** Make sure the ignition is switched OFF. Using a siphon pump approved for petrol, drain

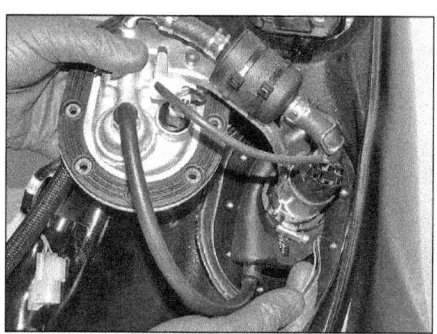

3.6c Carefully manoeuvre the pump out

the fuel from the tank into a suitable container. Remove the fuel tank (Section 2). Turn the tank upside down and rest it on some rag.

**6** Note the orientation of the fuel pump mounting plate **(see illustration)**. Unscrew the bolts, then displace the pump assembly, disconnect and release the internal fuel level sender wiring, and manoeuvre the pump out of the tank **(see illustrations)**.

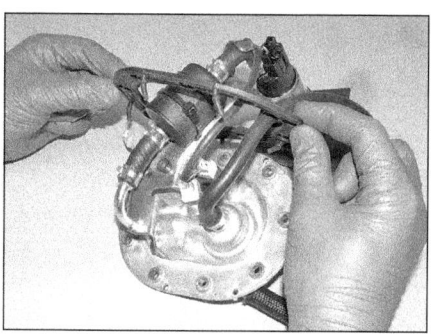

3.7 Remove the seal

**7** Remove the pump seal, noting which way round it fits **(see illustration)** – a new one must be used.

**8** To remove the pump motor, slacken the clamp around the base and detach the strainer housing **(see illustration)**. Undo the hose guide screw and remove the guide **(see illustration)**. Disconnect the wiring connector from the pump, then release the hose clamp

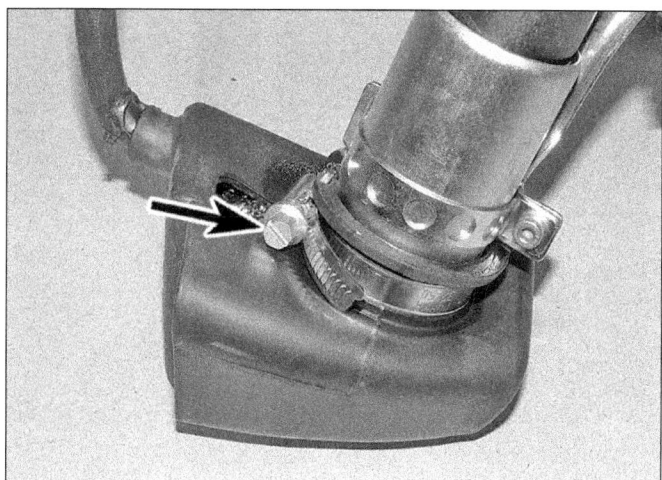

3.8a Slacken the strainer housing clamp screw (arrowed) and remove the housing

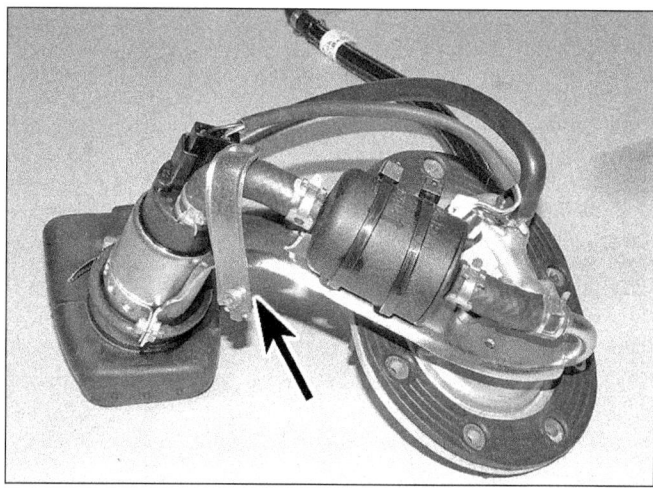

3.8b Hose guide screw (arrowed)

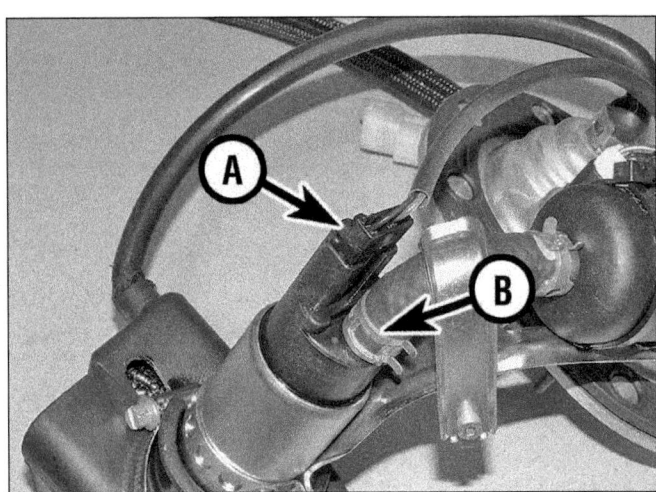

3.8c Pump wiring connector (A), hose clamp (B)

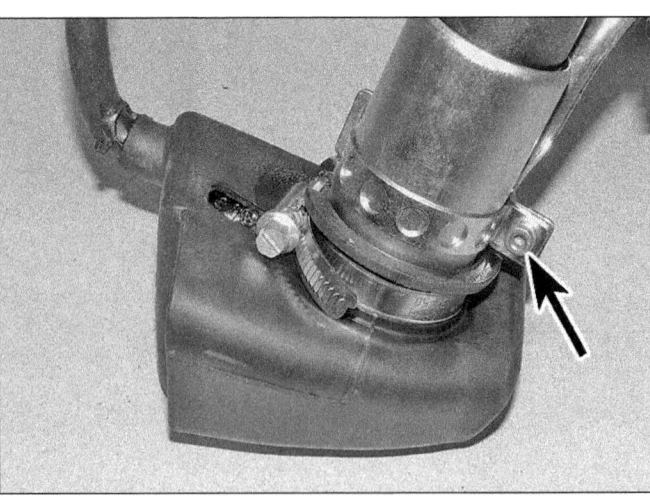

3.8d Pump clamp screw (arrowed)

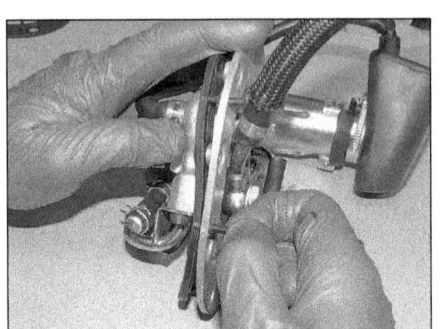

3.9 Fit a new seal, make sure it is the correct way up, and pull the tab ribs through

and slide it along the hose (see illustration). Undo the pump clamp screw and pull the pump out of the hose (see illustration). Fit the motor in reverse order, making sure the hose is fully pushed on and secured by the clamp and wiring connector is secure.

## Installation

9 Installation is the reverse of removal, noting the following:

● Make sure the fuel tank and pump mounting plate mating surfaces are clean.

● Fit a new seal onto the pump and pull the tabs through so the ribs seat on the outer side of the plate (see illustration 3.9).

● Manoeuvre the pump into the tank, making sure it is correctly orientated and the seal remains in place, and connect and secure the level sensor wiring, making sure it is correctly routed (see illustrations 3.6c and b).

● Make sure everything is correctly aligned and seated, then tighten the mounting plate bolts evenly and a little at a time in a criss-cross sequence to 5 Nm, then go round them again as sometimes the first bolt tightened will loosen slightly as the others are tightened.

● On completion, start the engine and check carefully that there is no leakage from around the pump mounting plate.

### Fuel filter replacement

10 Remove the pump from the tank (see above).
11 Undo the hose guide screw and remove the guide (see illustration 3.8b). Cut the cable ties around the filter, then release the hose clamps and slide them along the hoses (see illustration). Detach the hoses and remove the filter.
12 Fit the new filter with the arrow pointing in the direction of fuel flow, i.e. away from the pump, towards the mounting plate (see illustration 3.11). Make sure the hoses are fully pushed on to the unions and are secured with the clamps. Fit the bracket and new cable-ties.

### Fuel pressure regulator

13 Make sure the ignition is switched OFF. Using a siphon pump approved for petrol, drain the fuel from the tank into a suitable container. Remove the fuel tank (Section 2). Turn the tank upside down and rest it on some rag.
14 Release the circlip and pull the regulator out of the pump base (see illustrations).

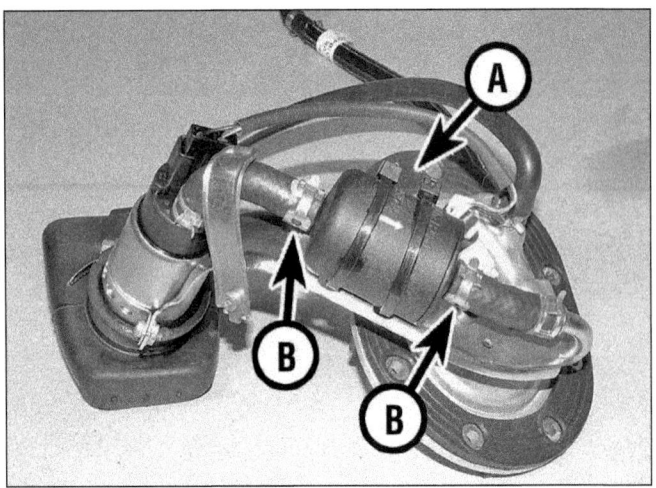

3.11 Cut the cable-ties (A), then release and displace the hose clamps (B)

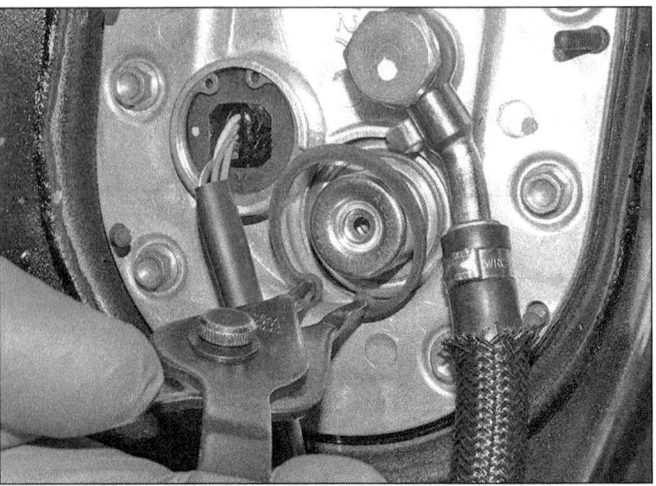

3.14a Release the circlip...

3.14b ...and pull the regulator out

3.14c O-rings (arrowed)

5.4 Fuel level sender (arrowed)

Remove the O-rings **(see illustration)** – the small one may be in the pump base. New ones must be used. Check the circlip for deformation and use a new one if necessary.

**15** Fit new O-rings onto the regulator and smear them with grease, then push the regulator all the way in so the O-rings are seated and secure it with the circlip **(see illustrations 3.14c, b and a).**

### 4  Fuel pressure check

 *Warning: Refer to the precautions given in Section 1 before starting work.*

**Special tool:** *To check the fuel pressure, the Triumph tool (Pt. No. T3880001) is needed. The tool comprises a gauge and two adapter hoses, marked A and B – use adapter hose A. A commercial pressure gauge will not be of any use. If required you can also use the wiring harness adapter (Pt. No. 3880391) that allows the fuel pump to be connected to the wiring loom with the fuel tank removed and supported next to the bike – this allows easier connection and use of the gauge and hose adapter, but is not essential.*

**1** Make sure the ignition switch is in the OFF position. If the wiring harness adapter is not being used, refer to Section 2, raise the tank and disconnect the fuel hose from the fuel rail. If the wiring harness adapter is being used, refer to Section 2 and remove the tank and place it on a suitable support next to the bike.

**2** Connect the adapter hose between the bike's fuel hose and the fuel rail union. Press each connector onto its union until it is felt and heard to click into place. Fit the pressure gauge into its union, again until it is felt to click into place.

**3** If the tank has been removed connect the pump using the wiring harness adapter.

**4** Turn the ignition switch ON and check the pressure reading on the gauge. Start the engine and allow it to idle. The operating pressure should be as given in the Specifications.

**5** Turn the ignition OFF. Have some rag ready to catch residual fuel in the adapter

hose. Release the pressure gauge by sliding its outer ferrule down – the gauge will spring out of the union. Release the adapter hose by pressing the clips on the connectors in. Install the fuel tank (Section 2).

**6** If the pressure is too low, either the pressure regulator is stuck open, the fuel pump is faulty, the strainer or filter is blocked, or there is a leak in the system, probably from a hose joint. Firstly check the system for leaks, which should be obvious because of the smell of fuel. Next clean the strainer and fit a new fuel filter, and if that does not solve the problem fit a new regulator, and then a new pump – refer to Section 3 for details.

**7** If the pressure is too high, the pressure regulator could be stuck closed, or the fuel pump check valve could be faulty. First check the fuel rail and injectors (Section 7). If the pressure is still too high fit a new regulator, and then a new pump – refer to Section 3 for details.

### 5  Fuel level sender

 *Warning: Refer to the precautions given in Section 1 before starting work.*

#### *Check*

**1** If the low fuel level warning light fails to come on either when the ignition is first turned on or if the fuel level is low, check the level sender **(see illustration 2.11b)** and instrument cluster wiring connectors (see Section 2 and Chapter 8 respectively), then check the wiring between the connectors for continuity, referring to the Electrical system fault finding at the beginning of Chapter 8 and to the wiring diagrams at the end of it.

**2** No values are given for the sender resistance. All that can be done is to inspect the sender's internal wiring and connectors once the pump has been removed.

#### *Removal and installation*

**3** Remove the fuel pump (Section 3).

**4** Reach inside the tank and release the clip on the top of the sensor, then slide the sensor up the bracket to release the two locating lugs

from the holes in the bracket and manoeuvre the sensor out, taking care not to snag the float arm **(see illustration)**.

**5** Fit the new sensor onto the bracket, aligning the lugs with the holes, then slide the sensor down until the clip engages **(see illustration)**.

**6** Install the fuel pump (Section 3).

### 6  Throttle body

 *Warning: Refer to the precautions given in Section 1 before starting work.*

#### *Removal*

**T100, Street Twin, Street Cup, Scrambler**

**1** Remove the fuel tank (Section 2).

**2** Remove the side panels (see Chapter 7).

**3** On the Scrambler undo the exhaust shield screws, noting the collars, and remove the outer and inner shields.

**4** Remove the throttle body cover (single screw) and its mounting piece (two screws) from each side.

**5** Disconnect the throttle actuator wiring connector.

**6** Disconnect the MAP sensor hose from the front vacuum take-off union on the top of the intake manifold, and where fitted disconnect the EVAP hose from the rear union.

**7** Fully undo the air duct clamp screw and remove the clamp from around the duct.

**8** Unscrew the four bolts securing the throttle body to the intake manifold, noting the washers. Ease the throttle body out to the right. Remove the sealing ring from the intake manifold – a new one must be used.

**9** Unless you are removing the intake manifold plug the duct with clean rag. To remove the manifold unscrew the four bolts. Remove the sealing rings – new ones must be used. Plug the intake ducts in the cylinder head with clean rag.

**10** Do not attempt to disassemble the throttle body.

**T120, Bobber, Thruxton, Thruxton R**

**11** Remove the fuel tank (Section 2).

6.13a On the T120 undo the air duct cover screw...

6.13b ...then release the slot from the tab

6.13c On the Bobber, Thruxton and Thruxton R undo the air duct cover screw and pull the pegs from the grommets

6.13d Undo the two screws and remove the mounting piece

6.14 Undo the screws and remove the trim piece

12 Remove the side panels (see Chapter 7).

13 Remove the air duct cover (single screw) and its mounting piece (two screws) from each side (see illustrations).

14 On the Bobber remove the trim piece from the front of the air filter housing on each side (see illustration).

15 Remove the crankcase breather hose, then undo the breather separator screw and remove the separator with its upper hose (see illustrations).

16 Disconnect the throttle actuator wiring connector (see illustration).

17 Release and disconnect the throttle position sensor wiring connector (see illustration).

6.15a Release and remove the hose

6.15b Undo the screw (arrowed)...

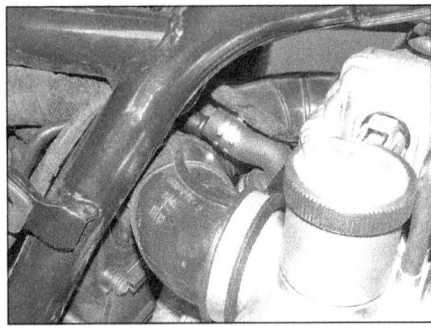

6.15c ...release the upper hose and remove the separator

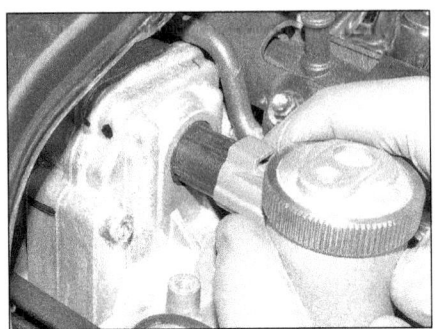

6.16 Disconnect the actuator wiring

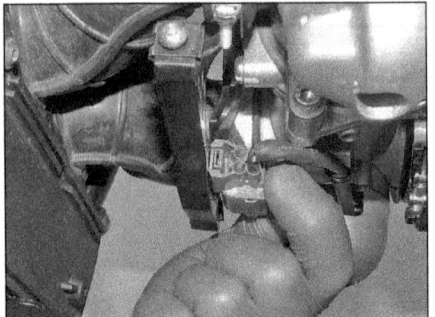

6.17a Release the connector from its holder...

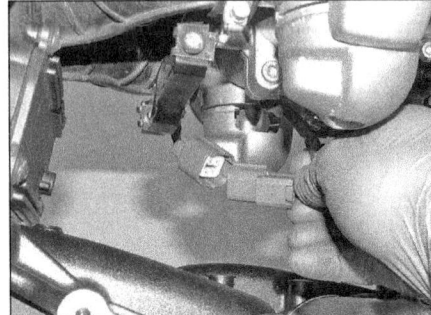

6.17b ...then disconnect it

**6.18a Disconnect the MAP sensor hose from each side**

**6.18b Disconnect the EVAP hose from the T-piece**

**6.19a Slacken the intake duct clamp screw (arrowed) on each side**

**18** Disconnect the MAP sensor hose from the outer vacuum take-off union on the top of each throttle bore, and where fitted disconnect the EVAP hose from the T-piece above the throttle body **(see illustrations)**.

**19** Slacken the intake duct clamp screws, then fully undo the air duct clamp screws and remove the clamps from around the ducts **(see illustrations)**.

**20** Ease the throttle body out to the right **(see illustrations)**.

**21** Unless you are removing the intake pieces plug each duct with clean rag. To remove the intake pieces unscrew the three bolts securing each one **(see illustration)**. Plug the intake ducts in the cylinder head with clean rag.

**22** Do not attempt to disassemble the throttle body.

### Cleaning

*Caution: Use only a dedicated spray cleaner (such as a carburettor and injector cleaner) for throttle body cleaning.*

**23** Spray the cleaner over the metal parts of the throttle body to remove any dirt and grime, using a nylon brush if required – be careful not to let any dirt get into the inside of the body.

### Inspection

**24** Check the throttle body for cracks or any other damage that may result in air getting in.

**25** Check that the throttle butterflies and the inside of the body is completely clean.

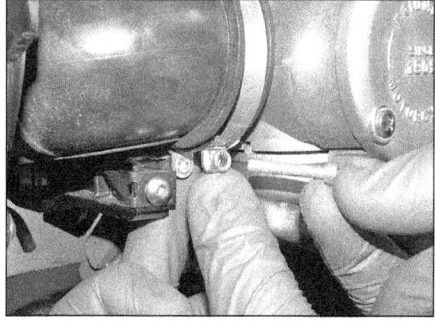

**6.19b Undo the air duct screw clamp screws...**

### Installation

**26** Installation is the reverse of removal, noting the following:

#### T100, Street Twin, Street Cup, Scrambler

**Note:** *On models up to VIN 783907 with an EVAP system, if you are fitting a new intake manifold, you will also need to fit a new EVAP system purge valve hose – this is because after that VIN the restrictor was moved from the hose to the manifold, and if you fit a new manifold with a restrictor and also have a restrictor in the hose the system will not purge correctly and the canister will be damaged.*

● Do not forget to remove the rag from the intakes, or from the manifold if not removed.

**6.19c ...and remove the clamps**

● If the intake manifold was removed make sure the manifold and cylinder head mating surfaces are clean, and fit new sealing rings into the grooves in the manifold. Fit the manifold and tighten the bolts to 9 Nm.

● Make sure the throttle body and manifold mating surfaces are clean, and fit a new sealing ring into the groove in the manifold. Fit the throttle body, making sure it seats in the air duct correctly, and tighten the bolts to 9 Nm.

● Make sure the air duct is fully seated around the throttle body before tightening the clamp.

● Make sure the wiring connector is secure.

● Make sure the MAP sensor hose, and where fitted the EVAP system hose, are pushed fully onto their unions.

**6.20a Pull the air ducts off and aside...**

**6.20b ...and remove the throttle bodies as shown**

**6.21 Intake piece bolts (arrowed)**

**T120, Bobber, Thruxton, Thruxton R**

● Do not forget to remove the rag from the intakes.
● If the intake pieces were removed make sure they and the cylinder head mating surfaces are clean. Tighten the bolts to 9 Nm.
● Make sure the throttle body is seated fully in each intake piece before tightening the clamps.
● Make sure each air duct is fully seated around the throttle body before tightening the clamps.
● Make sure the wiring connectors are secure.
● Make sure the MAP sensor hoses, and where fitted the EVAP system hose, are pushed fully onto their unions.

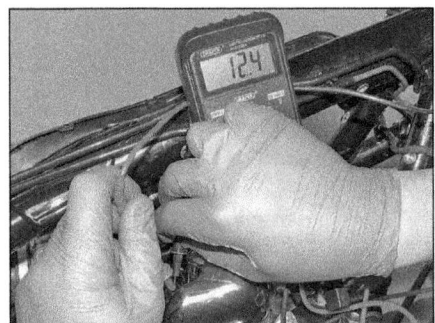

**7.2 Measure the resistance between the terminals**

**7.7 Disconnect the wiring**

## 7 Fuel rail and injectors

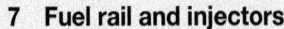 

⚠ *Warning: Refer to the precautions given in Section 1 before proceeding.*

### Check

**1** If the MIL light has come on, and you suspect an injector to be faulty, you can either have a Triumph dealer confirm this using the diagnostic tool or you can confirm it yourself

using an aftermarket OBD2 tool (see Section 11), or, if the engine runs, start it and allow it to idle, then check the operation of each injector in the throttle bodies using a sounding rod held against the injector – an injector will emit a 'clicking' noise when functioning. If an injector is silent, either the injector or its wiring harness is faulty.

**2** If the engine does not run, remove the fuel tank (Section 2). Disconnect the wiring connector from each injector in turn **(see illustration 7.7)**. Connect an ohmmeter between the terminals of the injector and measure the resistance **(see illustration)**. Compare each reading to that given in the Specifications. If the resistance of either injector differs greatly from that specified fit a new one.

**3** If the injectors are good check for continuity

in the wiring from each injector to the ECM and the EMS (engine management system) relay, referring to electrical system fault finding at the beginning of Chapter 8 and to the wiring diagram for your model at the end of it. If all is good, check the engine management 15A fuse (see Chapter 8), the EMS relay (Chapter 8), then the ECM (Section 12).

### Removal

**4** Remove the fuel tank (Section 2).
**5** On the T100, Street Twin, Street Cup and Scrambler remove the throttle body cover (single screw) and its mounting piece (two screws) from each side.
**6** On The T120, Bobber, Thruxton and Thruxton R remove the throttle body (Section 6).
**7** Disconnect the wiring connector from each injector **(see illustration)** – the connector for the right-hand injector (No. 2 cylinder) is identified by a band of red tape.
**8** Undo the fuel rail bolts and remove the rail covers and the spacers, then ease the fuel rail and injectors off the cylinder head **(see illustrations)**. A new O-ring must be fitted to the bottom of each injector on installation.
**9** If required release the injector retaining clip(s), noting how they locate, and carefully pull the injector(s) out of the fuel rail, as required **(see illustrations)**. A new O-ring must be fitted to the top of the injector on installation.

**7.8a Unscrew the bolts...**

**7.8b ...remove the covers and spacers...**

**7.8c ...and the fuel rail and injectors**

**7.9a Release the clip...**

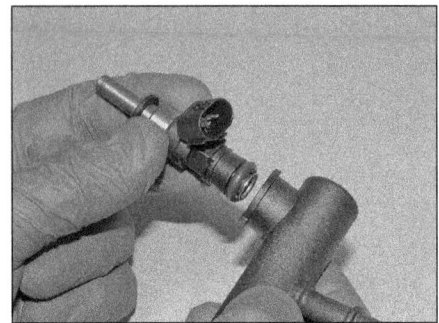

**7.9b ...and ease the injector out**

**10** Modern fuels contain detergents that should keep the rail and injectors clean and free of gum or varnish from residue fuel. Clean the rail in a dedicated cleaner, following the manufacturer's instructions. If an injector is suspected of being blocked have it ultrasonically cleaned by a specialist.

### Installation

**11** Fit a new O-ring smeared with oil onto the top of each injector removed from the fuel rail – the top O-rings are black, the bottom ones are brown **(see illustration)**. Push each injector into its socket in the fuel rail, with the wiring socket on the opposite side to the bolts holes in the rail, and aligning the retaining clip tabs **(see illustration 7.9b)**. Fit the clip, seating it around the tabs **(see illustration 7.9a)**.

**12** Fit a new brown O-ring smeared with oil into the groove around the bottom of each injector body **(see illustration)**. Fit the fuel rail and injector assembly onto the cylinder head, making sure each injector seats correctly **(see illustration 7.8c)**. Position the spacers and covers, then fit the fuel rail bolts and tighten them to 6 Nm **(see illustrations 7.8b and a)**.

**13** Connect the wiring connectors **(see illustration 7.7)** – the connector with the red tape around its wiring is for the right-hand (No. 2 cylinder) injector.

**14** Install the remaining components in reverse order of removal.

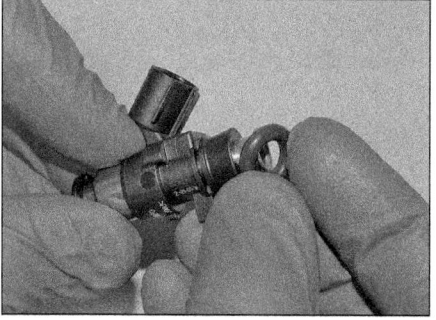

7.11 Fit the black O-ring onto the top of the injector

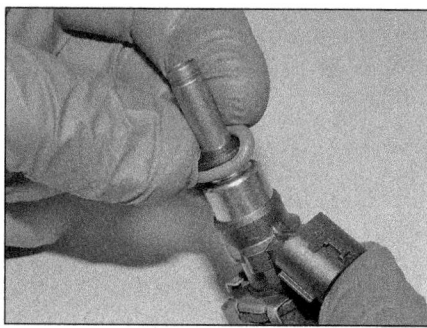

7.12 Fit the brown O-ring onto the bottom of the injector body

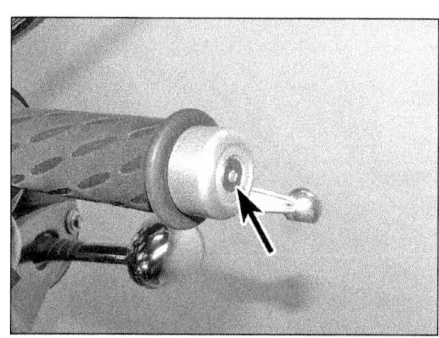

8.2 End-weight screw (arrowed)

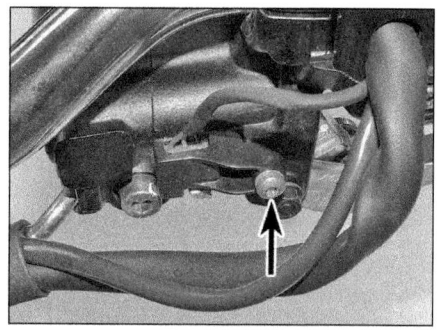

8.4 Undo the switch holder screw (arrowed) and displace the switch

## 8  Throttle system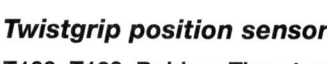

### Twistgrip position sensor

#### T100, T120, Bobber, Thruxton

**1** Disconnect the battery (see Chapter 8).

**2** On the T100 and T120 undo the handlebar end-weight screw and remove the weight **(see illustration)**.

**3** On the Bobber and Thruxton remove the right-hand mirror (see Chapter 7).

**4** Displace the brake light switch from the bottom of the master cylinder **(see illustration)**.

**5** Undo the switch housing screws and detach the housing face **(see illustration)**. Undo the twist grip sensor screws, and on the T120 disconnect the heated grip wiring connector **(see illustration)**.

**6** Undo the master cylinder clamp bolts and displace the master cylinder, supporting it upright **(see illustration)**.

**7** Slide the twistgrip off the handlebar, noting its alignment with and how it locates in the position sensor, and on the T120 taking care when drawing the heated grip wiring out of the handlebar and noting its routing **(see illustration)**.

**8** On the T100, T120 and Thruxton remove the headlight from its shell (see Chapter 8). Undo

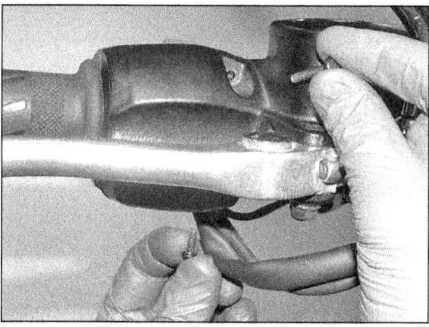

8.5a Undo the housing screws...

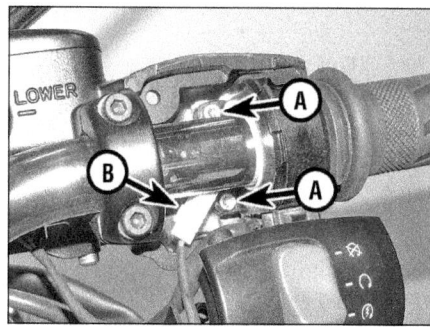

8.5b ...and detach the face, then undo the sensor screws (A), and on the T120 disconnect the wiring connector (B)

8.6 Remove the clamp and detach the master cylinder from the handlebar

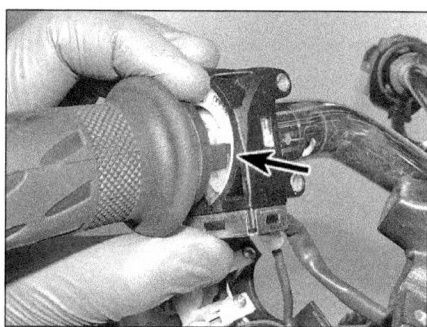

8.7 Note how the tab on the twistgrip locates in the sensor (arrowed)

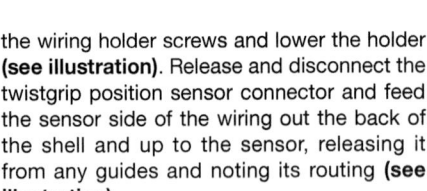

8.8a Undo the screws and lower the holder...

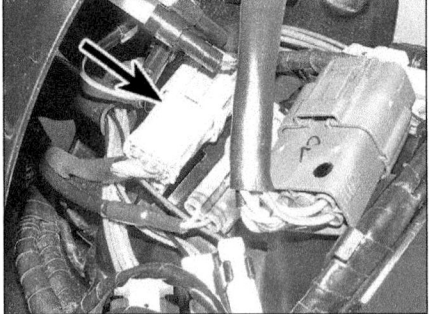

8.8b ...to access the twistgrip position sensor wiring connector (arrowed)

8.9 Twistgrip position sensor wiring connector (arrowed)

the wiring holder screws and lower the holder **(see illustration)**. Release and disconnect the twistgrip position sensor connector and feed the sensor side of the wiring out the back of the shell and up to the sensor, releasing it from any guides and noting its routing **(see illustration)**.

**9** On the Bobber remove the fuel tank (Section 2). Remove the wiring harness cover. Release and disconnect the twistgrip position sensor connector and feed the sensor side of the wiring up to the sensor, releasing it from any guides and noting its routing **(see illustration)**.

**10** Slide the sensor off the handlebar.

### Street Twin, Street Cup, Scrambler, Thruxton R

**11** Disconnect the battery (see Chapter 8).

**12** On the Street Twin and Scrambler undo the handlebar end-weight screw and remove the weight.

**13** On the Street Cup and Thruxton R remove the right-hand mirror (see Chapter 7).

**14** Remove the headlight from its shell (see Chapter 8). Undo the wiring holder screws and lower the holder **(see illustration 8.8a)**. Release and disconnect the twistgrip position sensor connector and feed the sensor side of the wiring out the back of the shell and up to the sensor, releasing it from any guides and noting its routing **(see illustration 8.8b)**.

**15** Undo the twistgrip sensor housing screws and detach the top of the housing from the handlebar **(see illustration)**.

**16** Release the twistgrip from the position sensor, noting its alignment and how the cut-out in the grip locates over the lug in the housing, and slide the twistgrip off the handlebar.

**17** Slide the sensor housing off the handlebar. Do not attempt to remove the sensor from the housing.

### Installation – all models

**18** Installation is the reverse of removal, noting following:

● On the T120 align the heated grip wiring with the flat section on the underside of the handlebar, feed it into the first hole and draw it out of the second hole as you slide the grip on, taking care not to twist it, and making sure the sensor is positioned on the twistgrip side of the second hole.

● Make sure the twistgrip engages correctly in the sensor.

● On the T100, T120, Bobber and Thruxton locate the pin on the master cylinder in the hole in the front of the handlebar **(see illustration)**. Tighten the clamp bolts to 12 Nm, tightening the top bolt first.

● On the Street Twin, Street Cup, Scrambler and Thruxton R locate the pin on the top of the twistgrip housing in the hole in the handlebar.

### Throttle actuator

**19** The throttle actuator is an integral part of the throttle body and is not available separately. Do not attempt to separate it

from the body or to loosen any of the yellow-painted screws or bolts – Triumph say that if you do you will have to fit a new throttle body as there is no way of resetting the motor to its correct position.

## 9  Exhaust system

**Warning: If the engine has been running the exhaust system will be very hot. Allow the system to cool before carrying out any work.**
*Caution: The exhaust downpipe assembly incorporates a catalytic converter and oxygen sensor. Take care when handling it, and do not strike or drop it because the delicate catalytic converter element could be damaged.*
**Note:** *Exhaust system bolts, studs and clamps tend to corrode easily – apply a penetrating lubricant with anti-rust properties before loosening them, and before fitting them clean off any rust from the threads using a wire brush and apply copper grease.*

### T100, T120, Street Twin, Street Cup, Thruxton, Thruxton R

#### Silencers

**1** Note the orientation of the clamp securing the silencer to the intermediate pipe, then slacken the bolt or nut, according to model **(see illustration)**.

8.15 Twistgrip housing screws (arrowed)

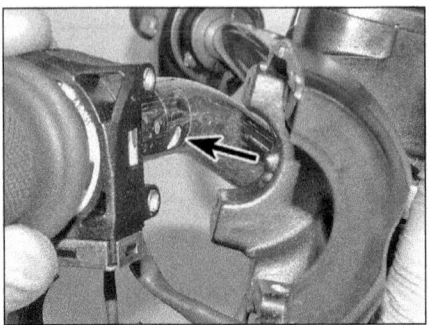

8.18 Locate the pin in the hole (arrowed)

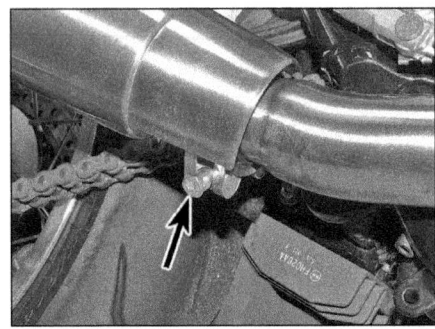

9.1 Slacken the clamp bolt (arrowed)

9.2 Left-hand silencer has a front mounting bolt and nut

9.4a Unscrew the nut...

9.4b ...and withdraw the footrest holder/bolt

2 When removing the left-hand silencer unscrew the nut on the front mount and withdraw the bolt **(see illustration)**.

3 On all except Thruxton and Thruxton R single-seat models remove the passenger footrest (see Chapter 5).

4 Unscrew the nut on the silencer mounting bolt **(see illustration)**. Support the silencer, then on all except Thruxton and Thruxton R single-seat models remove the footrest holder with the bolt, and on Thruxton and Thruxton R single-seat models remove the bolt, and draw the silencer out of the intermediate pipe **(see illustration)**. Remove the collar(s) and rubber bush(es) and washer(s) for safekeeping if required **(see illustration)**.

5 Check the condition of the sealing ring between the silencer and intermediate pipe and replace it with a new one if necessary **(see illustration)** – unless it is obviously in need of renewal it is best to leave it in place as it will be ruined when you dig it out.

6 Installation is the reverse of removal. Fit a new sealing ring into the silencer if necessary **(see illustration 9.5)**. Make sure the rubber bush, washer and collar are fitted into each mount. When fitting the silencer make sure the seal does not catch on the rim of the intermediate pipe as it is easily damaged. Make sure the clamp is correctly orientated and located. When fitting the footrest holder make sure the pin locates in the hole **(see illustration 9.4b)**. Run the engine and check that there are no leaks from the exhaust system.

### Header pipe/intermediate pipe assemblies

### Removal

7 Remove the silencer (see above).

8 Remove the fuel tank (Section 2).

9 Release and disconnect the oxygen sensor wiring connector **(see illustration)** – the connector for the right-hand header pipe sensor (No. 2 cylinder) is the upper of the two connectors and is identified by a band of red tape.

10 When removing the right-hand header pipe assembly unscrew the nut and withdraw the bolt securing the intermediate pipe to the frame cradle **(see illustration)**.

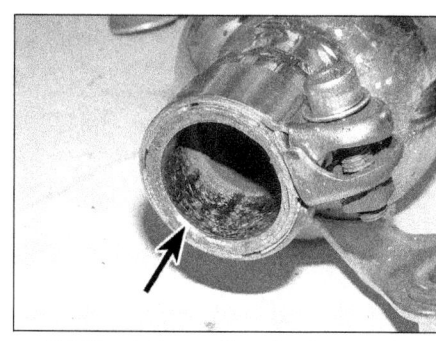

9.4c Remove the collar(s) and rubber bush(es) as required

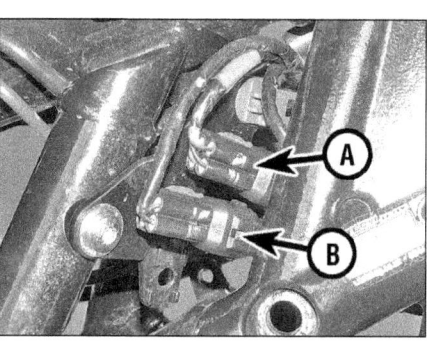

9.9 Oxygen sensor wiring connectors – right hand sensor connector (A), left-hand sensor connector (B)

11 On the Thruxton and Thruxton R slacken the clamp on the header balance pipe, and when removing the left-hand header

9.5 Check the sealing ring (arrowed)

9.10 Right-hand header pipe assembly bolt/nut (arrowed)

pipe assembly unscrew the bolt securing the intermediate pipe to the frame **(see illustrations)**.

9.11a Header balance pipe clamps (arrowed)

9.11b Left-hand header pipe assembly bolt (arrowed)

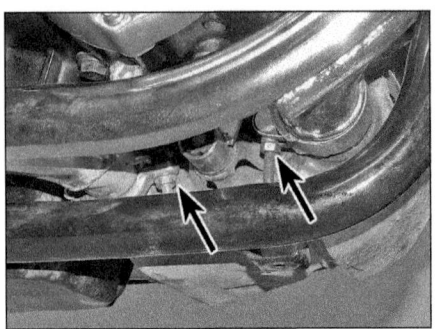

9.12 Slacken the clamps (arrowed)

9.13a Unscrew the nuts...

9.13b ...and draw the flanges off, noting how the inner one locates around the sensor...

9.13c ...and how they fit together

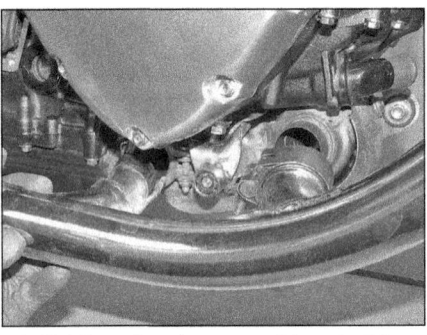

9.13d Ease the pipe assembly out of the collector box...

9.13e ...and off the head

**12** Slacken the clamps securing the header pipe and intermediate pipe in the collector box **(see illustration)**.

**13** Unscrew the header pipe flange nuts and remove the flanges, noting how they fit together **(see illustrations)**. Draw the header pipe and intermediate pipe out of the collector box and off the cylinder head **(see illustrations)**.

**14** Remove the gasket from the port in the cylinder head **(see illustration)** – a new one must be fitted. Check the condition of the sealing ring between the header pipe and collector box and replace it with a new one if necessary **(see illustration)** – unless it is obviously in need of renewal it is best to leave it in place as it will be ruined when you dig it out. Also check the intermediate pipe gasket in the collector box clamp (see below). If

required remove the oxygen sensor (Section 13).

**15** If required separate the intermediate pipe from the header pipe by unscrewing the clamp bolt(s), and on Street and Thruxton models removing the heat shield.

**Installation**

**16** If the intermediate pipe was separated from the header pipe fit them together but leave the clamp(s) loose enough for them to align themselves correctly when fitted into the collector box.

**17** Fit a new gasket into the cylinder head port **(see illustration)** – they have small tabs on them to keep them in place, but if required apply a smear of grease to assist. Fit a new sealing ring into the header pipe if necessary **(see illustration 9.14b)**. Fit a new gasket into

the intermediate pipe clamp on the collector box if necessary (see below). On Thruxton models fit a new sealing ring into the balance pipe if necessary. Make sure the rubber bush, washer and collar are fitted into the mount for the right intermediate pipe in the frame cradle, and into the mount for the left intermediate pipe on the Thruxton.

**18** Install the oxygen sensor if removed (Section 13).

**19** The header pipe flanges are marked so they cannot be fitted incorrectly – the flanges for the right-hand pipe are marked UR and LR, upper right and lower right, and those for the left-hand pipe are marked UL and LL, upper left and lower left.

**20** Manoeuvre the assembly into position so that the head of each header pipe locates in its port in the cylinder head first **(see**

9.14a Remove the old gasket

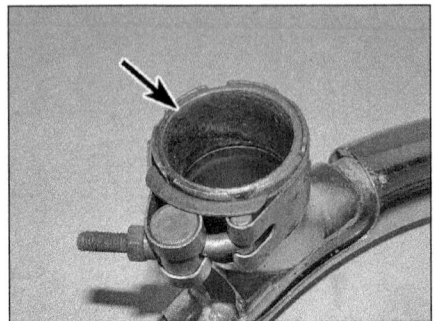

9.14b Check the sealing ring (arrowed)

9.17 Fit the new gaskets with the tabs innermost

9.20 The prong locates between the clamp ends

9.27a Release the wiring from the band...

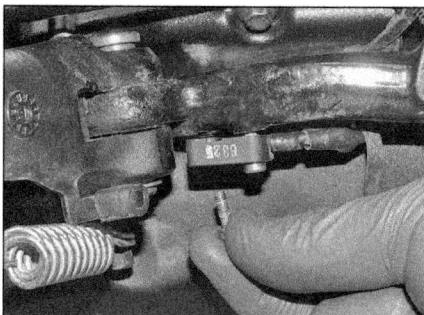

9.27b ...then undo the switch screws

9.27c Disconnect the horn wiring

9.27d Release the cable and wiring clips as described

illustration 9.10 or 9.11b). If the intermediate pipe was separated from the header pipe tighten the clamp bolt that joins them.

22  Reconnect the sensor wiring connector **(see illustration 9.9)** – make sure the wiring is correctly routed and secured, with the right sensor wiring going into the upper connector with the red-banded wiring and the left sensor going to the lower connector.

23  Install the fuel tank (Section 2).

24  Install the silencer (see above).

25  Run the engine and check that there are no leaks from the exhaust system.

## Collector box

### Removal

26  Remove the silencers and header/ intermediate pipe assemblies (see above).

27  Displace the sidestand switch from the left-hand frame cradle **(see illustrations)**. Disconnect the horn wiring connectors **(see illustration)**. Release the clutch cable and wiring clips from the left-hand cradle by pushing one side in and pulling them out **(see illustration)**.

28  Unscrew the nuts and remove the bolts securing the rear, middle and top of the right-hand frame cradle, then lower the cradle to release the peg from the radiator mount **(see illustrations)**.

**illustration 9.13e)**, on the Thruxton and Thruxton R the balance pipe locates, and the header pipe and intermediate pipe locate in the collector box **(see illustration 9.13d)** – make sure the header pipe seal, and on the Thruxton and Thruxton R the balance pipe seal, does not catch on the rim of the collector box or balance pipe as it is easily damaged, and make sure the prong on the intermediate pipe seats between the open ends of the clamp on the box **(see illustration)**. Fit the right intermediate pipe mounting bolt, but do not yet tighten the nut **(see illustration 9.10)**. On the Thruxton and Thruxton R fit the

left intermediate pipe bolt finger-tight **(see illustration 9.11b)**. Fit the header pipe flanges onto the studs as described in the previous Step, making sure they interlock correctly, then fit the nuts and tighten them to 19 Nm **(see illustrations 9.13c, b and a)**.

21  Tighten the header pipe clamp bolt and the intermediate pipe clamp bolt **(see illustration 9.12)**, and on the Thruxton and Thruxton R tighten the clamp on the header balance pipe **(see illustration 9.11a)**, and then tighten the right intermediate pipe mounting bolt nut, and on the Thruxton and Thruxton R the left intermediate pipe bolt **(see**

9.28a Right-hand cradle rear mounting bolt/nut (arrowed)

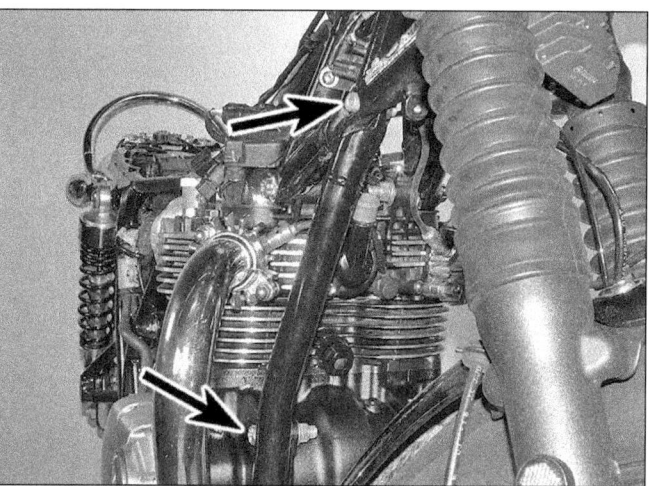

9.28b Right-hand cradle middle and top mounting bolts/nuts (arrowed)

9.29a Unscrew the rear bolts and remove the nut plate

9.29b Left-hand cradle middle and top mounting bolts/nuts (arrowed)

9.30a Unscrew the bolts...

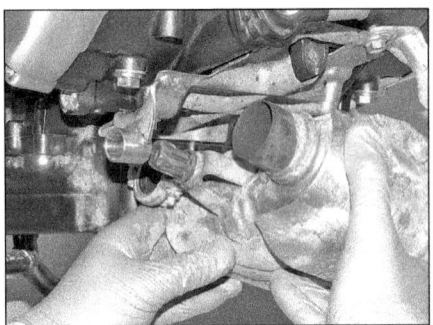

9.30b ...and release the rubbered lug

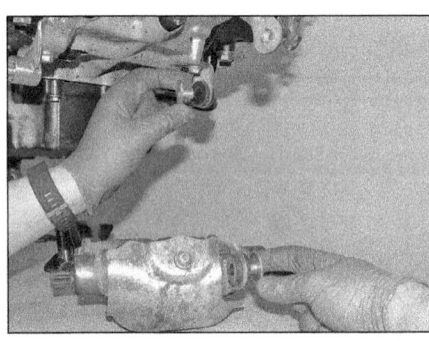

9.30c Remove the collars if required

9.31 Unscrew the bolts (arrowed) to remove the bracket

**29** Unscrew the bolts securing the rear of the left-hand frame cradle and collect the nut plate, then unscrew the nuts and remove the bolts securing the middle and top of the cradle, then lower it to release the peg from the radiator mount **(see illustrations)**.

**30** Unscrew the collector box bolts, noting the washers **(see illustration)**. Lower the left side of the box and draw the rubbered lug on the right out of the bracket **(see illustration)**. Note the collar in each bolt mount **(see illustration)**.

**31** If required remove the collector box bracket from the sump **(see illustration)**.

### Installation

**32** Installation is the reverse of removal, noting the following:
● Check the condition of the intermediate

pipe seal in the clamp, and if necessary open the clamp, remove the seal and replace with a new one **(see illustration)**. Make sure the rubbers are in good condition and the collars are fitted in the bolt mounts **(see illustration 9.30c)**.
● When fitting the frame cradles, make sure the lug locates correctly in the radiator mounting grommet. Fit all cradle nuts and bolts finger-tight only at first, then tighten the top bolt to 40 Nm, the rear bolt(s) to 40 Nm, and the middle bolt to 105 Nm, in that order.

### Bobber

### Silencers

### Removal

**33** To remove the right-hand silencer first remove the header pipe (see below)

**34** To remove the left-hand silencer unscrew the cover clamp bolt and remove the cover **(see illustration)**.

**35** Slacken the clamp securing the silencer in the collector box **(see illustration 9.20)**.

**36** Unscrew the silencer mounting bolt and draw the silencer out of the collector box **(see illustration)**. Remove the collar and rubber bush and washer for safekeeping if required.

**37** Check the condition of the silencer pipe seal in the collector box clamp, and if necessary open the clamp, remove the seal and replace with a new one **(see illustration 9.32)**. Make sure the rubber bushes and washers are in good condition and the collars are fitted.

### Installation

**38** Installation is the reverse of removal. Make sure the rubber bush, washer and

9.32 Open the clamp to release the seal

9.34 Cover clamp bolt (arrowed)

9.36 Silencer mounting bolt (arrowed)

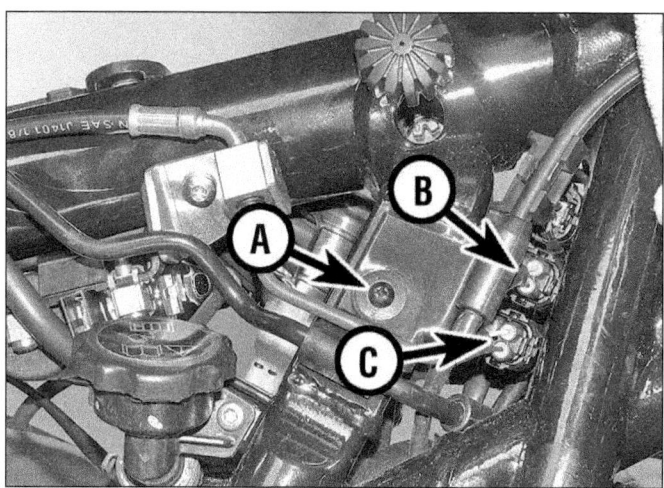

9.40 Undo the screw (A). Right-hand oxygen sensor connector (B), left-hand oxygen sensor connector (C)

9.41 Unscrew the clamp bolt (arrowed)

collar are fitted into each mount. Make sure the clamp is correctly orientated and located and the prong on the silencer locates between the open ends of the clamp **(see illustration 9.20)**. Run the engine and check that there are no leaks from the exhaust system.

### Header pipes

### Removal

**39** Remove the fuel tank (Section 2).
**40** Undo the wiring connector holder screw on the right-hand side of the frame, then release and disconnect the oxygen sensor wiring connector **(see illustration)** – the connector for the right-hand header pipe sensor is the upper of the two connectors and is identified by a band of red tape.
**41** To remove the right-hand header pipe unscrew the clamp bolt securing the pipe extension to the silencer **(see illustration)**.
**42** To remove the left-hand header pipe unscrew the cover clamp bolt and remove the cover **(see illustration 9.34)**.
**43** Slacken the clamp securing the header pipe in the collector box **(see illustration 9.13d)**.
**44** Unscrew the header pipe flange nuts and remove the flanges, noting how they fit together **(see illustrations 9.13a, b and c)**. Draw the pipe out of the collector box and off the cylinder head.
**45** Remove the gasket from the port in the cylinder head **(see illustration 9.14a)** – a new one must be fitted. Check the condition of the sealing ring between the pipe and collector box and replace it with a new one if necessary **(see illustration 9.14b)** – unless it is obviously in need of renewal it is best to leave it in place as it will be ruined when you dig it out, and bear in mind it is easy to damage a new one when fitting it. If required remove the sensor (Section 13).

### Installation

**46** Fit a new gasket into the cylinder head

port **(see illustration 9.17)** – they have small tabs on them to keep them in place, but if required apply a smear of grease to assist. Fit a new sealing ring into the header pipe if necessary **(see illustration 9.14b)**.
**47** Install the oxygen sensor if removed (Section 13).
**48** The header pipe flanges are marked so they cannot be fitted incorrectly – the flanges for the right-hand downpipe are marked UR and LR, upper right and lower right, and those for the left-hand downpipe are marked UL and LL, upper left and lower left.
**49** Manoeuvre the assembly into position so that the head of each header pipe locates in its port in the cylinder head first, and the bottom of the pipe locates in the collector box – make sure the seal does not catch on the rim of the collector box pipe as it is easily damaged. Fit the header pipe flanges onto the studs as described in the previous Step, making sure they interlock correctly, then fit the nuts and tighten them to 19 Nm **(see illustrations 9.13c, b and a)**.
**50** Tighten the header pipe clamp on the collector box.
**51** Reconnect the sensor wiring connector **(see illustration 9.40)** – make sure the wiring is correctly routed and secured, with the right

sensor wiring going into the upper connector with the red-banded wiring and the left sensor going to the lower connector. Fit the connector holder screw.
**52** Install the fuel tank (Section 2).
**53** Tighten the header pipe extension clamp on the right-hand pipe, and fit the cover on to the left-hand pipe **(see illustration 9.41 and 9.34)**.
**54** Run the engine and check that there are no leaks from the exhaust system.

### Collector box

### Removal

**55** Remove the silencers and header pipes.
**56** Displace the sidestand switch from the left-hand frame cradle **(see illustrations 9.27a and b)**. Disconnect the horn wiring connectors **(see illustration 9.27c)**. Release the clutch cable and wiring clips from the left-hand cradle by pushing one side in and pulling them out **(see illustration 9.27d)**.
**57** Remove the brace from the front of the cradles **(see illustration)**.
**58** To remove the right-hand cradle unscrew the footrest/brake pedal assembly bracket bolts and support the assembly with a cable-tie **(see illustration)**.
**59** To remove the left-hand cradle unscrew

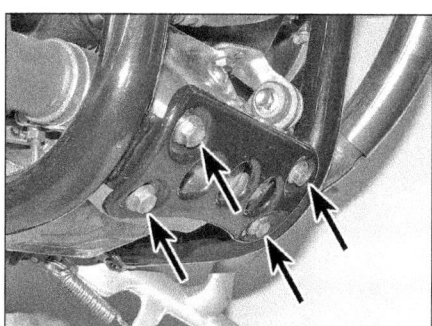

9.57 Unscrew the bolts (arrowed) and remove the brace

9.58 Displace the footrest/brake pedal bracket from the right-hand cradle

**9.59 Displace the footrest/gearchange lever bracket from the left-hand cradle**

**9.60a Frame cradle rear bolts (arrowed)**

**9.60b Frame cradle top bolts (arrowed)**

the footrest/gearchange lever assembly bracket bolts and support the assembly with a cable-tie **(see illustration)**.

**60** Unscrew the bolts securing the rear and top of the cradle and collect the nut plates **(see illustrations)**, then unscrew the nut and remove the bolt securing the middle of the cradle, then lower it to release the peg from the radiator mount.

**61** Unscrew the collector box bolts, noting the washers **(see illustration 9.30a)**. Lower the left side of the box and draw the rubbered lug on the right out of the bracket **(see illustration 9.30b)**. Note the collar in each bolt mount **(see illustration 9.30c)**.

**62** If required remove the collector box bracket from the sump **(see illustration 9.31)**.

### Installation

**63** Installation is the reverse of removal, noting the following:

● When fitting the frame cradles, make sure the lug locates correctly in the radiator mounting grommet. Fit all cradle nuts and bolts finger-tight only at first, then tighten the top bolts to 40 Nm, the rear bolts to 40 Nm, and the middle bolt to 105 Nm, in that order.

● Tighten the footrest/brake pedal and footrest/gearchange lever bracket bolts to 24 Nm.

## *Scrambler*

### Silencers

### Removal

**64** Remove the seat and the right-hand side panel (see Chapter 7).

**65** Unscrew the centre heat shield bolts, noting the collars, and remove the outer and inner shields.

**66** Slacken the clamp securing the silencer in the collector box.

**67** Unscrew the bolt joining the silencers at the back.

**68** Unscrew the silencer mounting bolt and draw the silencer out of the collector box. Remove the collars and rubber bushes for safekeeping if required. Check the condition of the bushes.

**69** Check the condition of the sealing ring between the silencer and collector box and replace it with a new one if necessary **(see illustration 9.5)** – unless it is obviously in need of renewal it is best to leave it in place as it will be ruined when you dig it out, and bear in mind it is easy to damage a new one when fitting it.

### Installation

**70** Installation is the reverse of removal. Fit a new sealing ring into the silencer if necessary **(see illustration 9.5)**. Make sure the rubber bush, washer and collar are fitted into each mount. When fitting the silencer make sure the seal does not catch on the rim of the collector box pipe as it is easily damaged. Make sure the clamp is correctly orientated and located. Make sure the rubber bushes and collars are fitted into each mount. Fit all bolts loosely at first, then tighten the clamps first. Run the engine and check that there are no leaks from the exhaust system.

### Header pipes/collector box

### Removal

**71** Remove the fuel tank (Section 2).

**72** Remove the silencers (see above).

**73** Release and disconnect the oxygen sensor wiring connectors **(see illustration 9.9)** – the connector for the right-hand header pipe sensor is the upper of the two connectors and is identified by a band of red tape.

**74** Slacken the clamp bolt securing the left-hand header pipe to the collector box pipe. Unscrew the left-hand header pipe flange nuts and remove the flanges, noting how they fit together **(see illustrations 9.13a, b and c)**. Draw the header pipe off the cylinder head and out of the pipe.

**75** Support the collector box, unscrew the right-hand header pipe flange nuts and remove the flanges, noting how they fit together. Draw the header pipe off the cylinder head.

**76** Remove the gasket from each port in the cylinder head **(see illustration 9.14a)** – new ones must be fitted. Check the condition of the sealing ring between the left-hand header pipe and collector box pipe and

replace it with a new one if necessary **(see illustration 9.14b)** – unless it is obviously in need of renewal it is best to leave it in place as it will be ruined when you dig it out, and bear in mind it is easy to damage a new one when fitting it. If required remove the sensors (Section 13).

### Installation

**77** Fit a new gasket into each cylinder head port **(see illustration 9.17)** – they have small tabs on them to keep them in place, but if required apply a smear of grease to assist. Fit a new sealing ring into the collector box pipe if necessary **(see illustration 9.14b)**.

**78** Install the oxygen sensors if removed (Section 13).

**79** The header pipe flanges are marked so they cannot be fitted incorrectly – the flanges for the right-hand downpipe are marked UR and LR, upper right and lower right, and those for the left-hand downpipe are marked UL and LL, upper left and lower left.

**80** Manoeuvre the collector box/right-hand header pipe into position so that the head of the downpipe locates in its port in the cylinder head. Fit the header pipe flanges onto the studs as described in the previous Step, making sure they interlock correctly, then fit the nuts and tighten them to 19 Nm **(see illustrations 9.13c, b and a)**.

**81** Manoeuvre the left-hand header pipe into position so that the head of the pipe locates in its port in the cylinder head, and the end locates in the collector box pipe – make sure the pipe does not catch on the rim of the seal in the collector box pipe as it is easily damaged. Fit the header pipe flanges onto the studs as described above, making sure they interlock correctly, then fit the nuts and tighten them to 19 Nm. Tighten the clamp bolt.

**82** Reconnect the sensor wiring connectors **(see illustration 9.9)** – make sure the wiring is correctly routed and secured, with the right sensor wiring going into the upper connector with the red-banded wiring and the left sensor going to the lower connector.

**83** Install the fuel tank (Section 2).

**84** Run the engine and check that there are no leaks from the exhaust system.

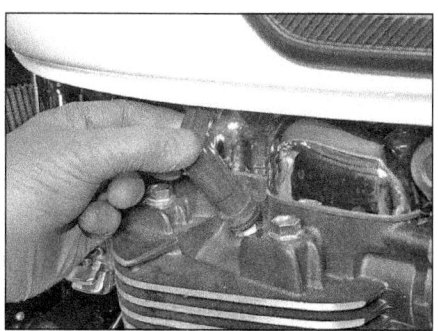

10.2 Pull the cap off the plug

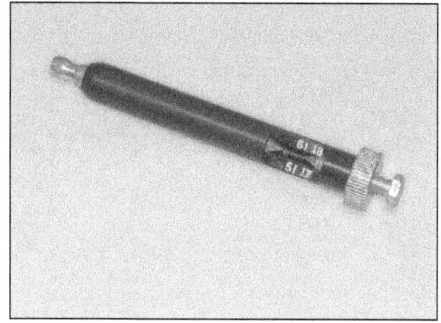

10.4 A typical ignition spark testing tool

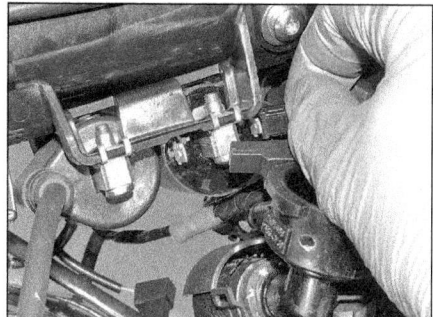

10.6 Disconnect the primary wiring

## 10 Ignition coils

**Warning: The energy levels in electronic systems can be very high. On no account should the ignition be switched on whilst the coils are connected and being held. Shocks from the HT circuit can be most unpleasant. Secondly, it is vital that the plugs are soundly earthed (grounded) when the system is checked for sparking. The ignition system components can be seriously damaged if the HT circuit becomes isolated.**

1 Each cylinder has its own ignition coil, mounted under the frame above the engine. The front coil is for the left-hand (No. 1) cylinder, the rear coil for the right-hand (No. 2) cylinder.

### Ignition system check

2 Pull the caps off the spark plugs **(see illustration)**. Fit a new spark plug into the cap for the coil being tested and hold the cap so the plug threads rest against the cylinder head.

**Warning: Do not remove the spark plugs from the engine to perform this check – atomised fuel being pumped out of the open spark plug hole could ignite, causing severe injury!**

3 Check that the kill switch is in the RUN position and the transmission is in neutral, then turn the ignition switch ON, pull the clutch lever in and turn the engine over on the starter motor. If the system is in good condition a regular, thick blue spark should be evident at the plug electrodes. If the spark appears thin or yellowish, or is non-existent, further investigation will be necessary. Turn the ignition OFF. Repeat the check for the other coil.

4 The ignition system must be able to produce a spark that is capable of jumping a particular size gap. Triumph provide no specification, but a healthy system should produce a spark capable of jumping at least 6 mm. Ignition spark gap testing tools are available from good suppliers **(see illustration)** – follow the manufacturer's instructions.

5 If the system is in good condition a regular, thick blue spark should be seen to jump the gap on the tool. If the test results are good the entire ignition system can be considered good. If the spark appears thin or yellowish, or is non-existent, further investigation is necessary.

6 Remove the fuel tank (Section 2). Disconnect the primary circuit wiring connectors from the coil being tested **(see illustration)**.

7 Using an ohmmeter or multimeter set to the ohms x 1 scale, measure the primary circuit resistance between the terminals on the coil **(see illustration)**. The resistance should be as given in the Specifications at the beginning of the Chapter. If not, the coil is faulty. Unscrew the plug cap from the end of the HT lead **(see illustration)**. Set the ohmmeter or multimeter to the K-ohms scale and measure

the secondary circuit resistance between one of the terminals on the coil and the wire core in the lead **(see illustration)**. Triumph does not specify a resistance but the coil we tested showed just over 18.5 K-ohms. If the value deviates from this figure by +/- 10%, the coil is faulty. The coil is a sealed unit and cannot therefore be repaired. If the resistances of the coil are correct, measure the resistance of the plug cap **(see illustration)** – it should be around 5 K-ohms. If not the cap is faulty. If all is good thread the cap back onto the lead until it goes tight, but do not try to overtighten it.

8 If the coils and spark plugs are good, then there is a fault elsewhere in the system. The likely faults are listed below, starting with the most probable source of failure. Work through the list systematically, referring to the subsequent sections for full details of the necessary checks and tests. Before checking the following items

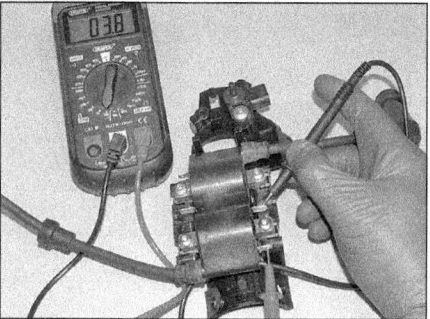

10.7a To test the coil primary resistance, connect the meter as shown

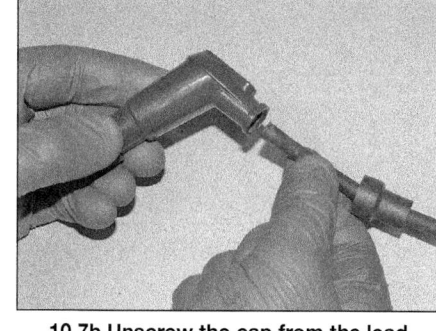

10.7b Unscrew the cap from the lead

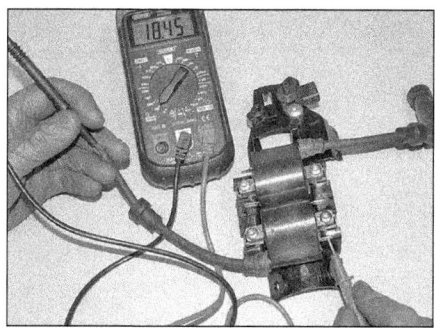

10.7c To test the coil secondary resistance, connect the meter as shown

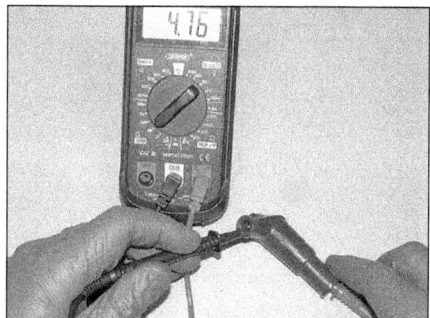

10.7d To test the cap connect the meter as shown

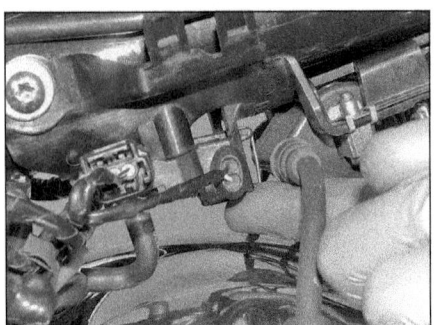

10.13 Release the ECT sensor connector

10.14 Disconnect the wiring and the hose (arrowed) from the MAP sensor

check that the battery is fully charged and that all fuses are in good condition.

a) Loose, corroded or damaged wiring connections, broken or shorted wiring between any of the component parts of the ignition system – refer to 'Electrical system fault finding' at the beginning of Chapter 8 and to the wiring diagram for your model at the end of it.

b) Blown EMS fuse or faulty EMS relay (Chapter 8).

c) Faulty ignition switch or engine kill switch (see Chapter 8).

d) Faulty clutch, neutral or sidestand switch (see Chapter 8).

e) Faulty crankshaft position sensor (Section 13).

f) Faulty ECM.

9 If the above checks don't reveal the cause of the problem, have the engine management system tested by a dealer equipped with the Triumph diagnostic tool that can perform a complete analysis of the engine management system. Refer to Sections 1 and 11 for more information.

### Removal

10 Remove the fuel tank (see Section 2).

11 Pull the spark plug caps off the plugs (see illustration 10.2).

12 Disconnect the primary circuit wiring connectors from the coils (see illustration 10.6). Note that the wiring that connects to the right-hand side of the front coil has red tape around it, and that the terminals on each coil are different sizes so the wiring cannot be wrongly connected.

13 Release the ECT sensor wiring connector from the coil holder (see illustration).

14 Disconnect the MAP sensor wiring connector and pull the hose off its union (see illustration).

15 Release the fuel pump wiring from its guide.

16 Undo the coil holder screws, noting the washers, and draw the coil assembly out to the right (see illustrations).

17 If required remove the coils from the bracket – each is secured by two screws, and the coil for the left-hand (No. 1) cylinder fits at the front of the bracket and has a longer HT lead (see illustration).

10.15 Release the pump wiring

10.16a Undo the two screws...

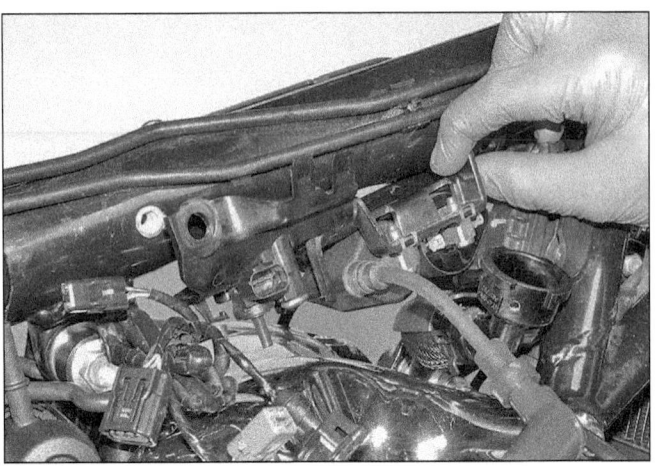

10.16b ...and remove the coil assembly

10.17 Each coil is held by two screws (arrowed)

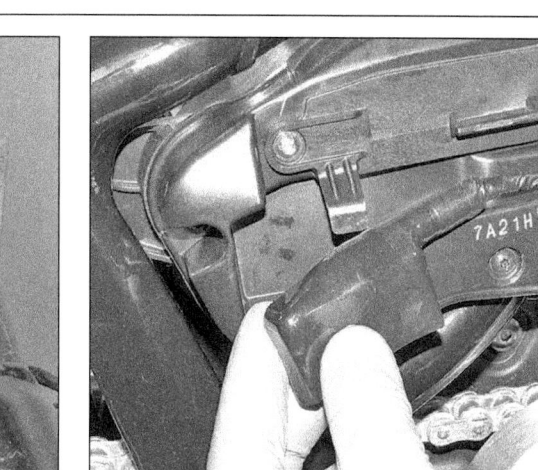

11.4a Fault code reader socket – all models except the Bobber

11.4b Fault code reader socket – Bobber

## Installation

18 Installation is the reverse of removal – make sure the coils are mounted correctly on the bracket as shown and the coil with the longer HT lead is at the front **(see illustration 10.17)**. Make sure the primary wiring with the red tape is connected to the terminals on the right-hand side of the front coil **(see illustration 10.6)**.

11 Engine management system

 *Warning: Refer to the precautions given in Section 1 before starting work.*

1 For a general description of the system see Section 1.

## Diagnostic tools and fault codes

2 To diagnose the exact cause of a failure in the system, either the Triumph diagnostic tool or an EOBD (OBD2) fault code reader is essential – both of these plug into a dedicated socket, located under the seat on all models except the Bobber, and behind the right-hand side panel on the Bobber **(see illustration 11.4a or b)**.

3 The ECM has in-built diagnostic functions which record and store all data should a permanent fault occur. Diagnostic trouble codes (DTCs) can then be read using the diagnostic tool, which lists a P-code to indicate the exact fault. Should a fault occur, the malfunction indicator light or symbol (MIL) in the instrument cluster illuminates. If this happens, the management system switches itself into 'limp home' mode, so that in theory you should not be left stranded. Depending on the problem, it is possible that you will notice no difference in the running of the motorcycle.

4 On all models except the Bobber remove the seat, and on the bobber remove the right-hand side panel (see Chapter 7). With the ignition off, plug the code reader into the socket **(see illustrations)**. Turn the ignition on and allow the code reader to process any stored fault codes – these will be displayed as a four digit number prefixed by the letter P. Turn off the ignition and disconnect the code reader once the P-code has been noted. Refer to the accompanying table to link the code with the faulty circuit. Once the fault has been rectified the code reader can be used to delete the stored code from the ECM's memory.

5 If you don't have access to a code reader it is possible to perform certain tests and checks to identify a particular fault, but the difficulty is knowing in which part of the system the fault has occurred, and therefore where to start checking. Further details on the functions of and checks that

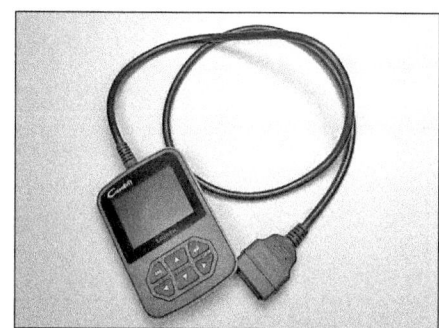

11.4c This OBD2 code reader is suitable for extracting P codes

can be made to the individual sensors and components and the wiring between them are detailed overleaf and in other Sections of this Chapter.

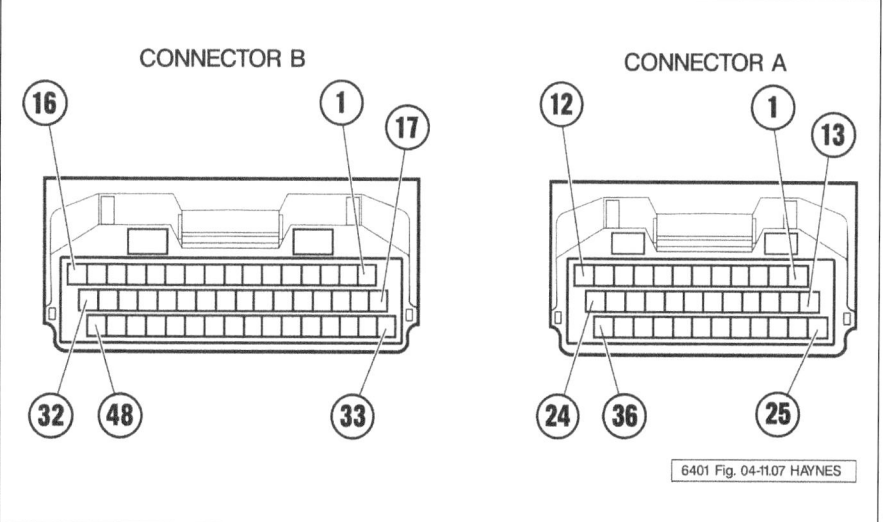

11.7 ECM wiring connector pin identification

| P-code | Circuit affected |
|--------|------------------|
| P0030 | Oxygen sensor heater cyl 1 – open circuit or short to earth |
| P0032 | Oxygen sensor heater cyl 1 – short circuit to battery |
| P0050 | Oxygen sensor heater cyl 2 – open circuit or short to earth |
| P0052 | Oxygen sensor heater cyl 2 – short circuit to battery |
| P0105 | MAP sensor open circuit or short circuit to 5V supply |
| P0107 | MAP sensor short circuit to earth |
| P0110 | Intake air temperature sensor open circuit or short circuit to 5V supply |
| P0112 | Intake air temperature sensor short circuit to earth |
| P0115 | Engine coolant temperature open circuit or short circuit to 5V supply |
| P0117 | Engine coolant temperature short circuit to earth |
| P0120 | Throttle position sensor 1 open circuit or short circuit to battery |
| P0122 | Throttle position sensor 1 short circuit to earth |
| P0130 | Oxygen sensor cyl 1 open circuit or short circuit to battery |
| P0131 | Oxygen sensor cyl 1 short to earth |
| P0150 | Oxygen sensor cyl 2 open circuit or short circuit to battery |
| P0151 | Oxygen sensor cyl 2 short circuit to earth |
| P0201 | Injector cyl 1 circuit fault |
| P0202 | Injector cyl 2 circuit fault |
| P0220 | Throttle position sensor 2 open circuit or short circuit to battery |
| P0222 | Throttle position sensor 2 short circuit to earth |
| P0335 | Crankshaft position sensor circuit fault |
| P0351 | Ignition coil circuit fault cyl 1 |
| P0352 | Ignition coil circuit fault cyl 2 |
| P0443 | EVAP purge control valve short circuit to earth or open circuit |
| P0459 | EVAP purge control valve short circuit to battery |
| P0460 | Fuel level sensor circuit fault |
| P0500 | Speed sensor fault |
| P0560 | System voltage problem – battery circuit malfunction |
| P056C | Cruise control cancel switch fault |
| P0571 | Brake light switch 1 fault |
| P0603 | EEPROM error |
| P0606 | ECM internal fault |
| P0616 | Starter relay coil short circuit to earth or open circuit |
| P0617 | Starter relay short circuit to battery+ |
| P0654 | Tachometer circuit fault |
| P0917 | Gear position sensor circuit fault |
| P1105 | MAP sensor vacuum hose fault |
| P1131 | Oxygen sensors connected wrong way round |
| P1135 | No TCS due to ABS fault |

| P-code | Circuit affected |
|--------|------------------|
| P1231 | Fuel pump relay short circuit to earth or open circuit |
| P1232 | Fuel pump relay short circuit to battery+ |
| P1508 | Immobiliser and ECM unmatched |
| P1520 | ABS modulator ID incompatible |
| P1521 | No signal to ABS modulator |
| P1552 | Cooling fan – short or open circuit |
| P1553 | Cooling fan – short to battery voltage/over temperature |
| P1571 | Brake light switch 2 fault |
| P1574 | Cruise control prevented due to other fault |
| P1575 | Cruise control disabled until button press sequence completed |
| P1576 | Brake light switch 1 correlation error with switch 2 |
| P1577 | Brake light switch 2 correlation error with switch 1 |
| P1604 | ECM tamper detected – contact Triumph |
| P1605 | ECM locked by tune lock function |
| P1607/8 | ECM ride by wire internal error |
| P1614 | ECM and instruments incorrect matched |
| P1619 | Headlight relay short circuit to earth or open circuit |
| P1620 | Headlight relay short circuit to battery |
| P1631 | Tip-over sensor short circuit to earth |
| P1632 | Tip-over sensor circuit short circuit to battery |
| P1650 | CAN-bus network communication fault with immobiliser ECM |
| P1659 | Ignition voltage supply circuit fault |
| P1685 | EMS relay fault |
| P1690 | CAN-bus network fault |
| P1695 | CAN-bus network communication fault with instruments |
| P1698 | 5 volt sensor supply circuit fault |
| P2100 | Throttle actuator open circuit |
| P2102 | Throttle actuator internal relay fault |
| P2103 | Throttle actuator internal relay stuck on |
| P2111 | Throttle valve drive stuck open |
| P2119 | Throttle valve drive error |
| P2120 | Twist grip position sensor 1 short circuit to earth or open circuit |
| P2123 | Twist grip position sensor 1 short circuit to battery |
| P2125 | Twist grip position sensor 2 short circuit to earth or open circuit |
| P2128 | Twist grip position sensor 2 short circuit to battery |
| P2135 | Throttle position sensor 1 correlation error with sensor 2 |
| P2138 | Twist grip position sensor 1 correlation error with sensor 2 |
| P2226 | Atmospheric pressure sensor open circuit or short circuit to 5V supply |
| P2228 | Atmospheric pressure sensor short circuit to earth |

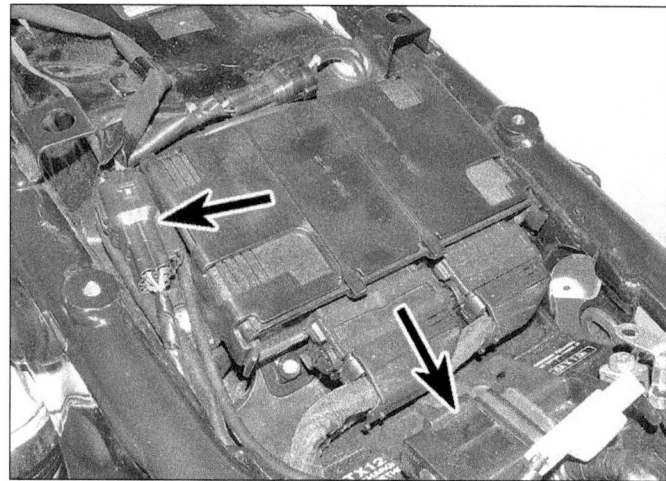

12.4a Displace the wiring connector and USB socket (arrowed)

12.4b Undo the ECM holder screw...

## Fault tracing

**Note:** *Refer to 'Electrical system fault finding' at the beginning of Chapter 8 and to the wiring diagram for your model at the end of it.*

**6** If a fault is indicated, check the wiring and connectors to and from the ECM (electronic control module) and the various sensors and all their related components – see Section 12 for access to the ECM and its connectors. It may be that a connector is dirty or corroded or has come loose – a dirty or corroded terminal or connector will affect the resistance in that circuit, which will upset the information going to the ECM, and therefore affect the decisions it makes in controlling the system. Electrical contact cleaners are available in aerosol cans from good suppliers.

**7** A wire could be pinched and is shorting out – a continuity test of all wires from connector to connector will locate this. Albeit a fiddly and laborious task, the only way to determine any wiring faults is to systematically work through the Wiring Diagrams at the end of Chapter 8 and test each individual wire and connector for continuity – all wires are colour-coded. When making continuity checks, isolate the wire being tested by disconnecting the wiring connectors at each end. The Wiring Diagrams show the pinout terminal identification for each wire on the ECM with the letter given on the wiring diagram indicating the relevant ECM connector, and the number referring to the terminal within that connector, as shown **(see illustration)** – match these to the terminals on the ECM connector(s) when making the tests.

**8** If all the wiring and connectors appear good, remove the relevant sensor and make sure its sensing tip or head is clean and undamaged, as this can often be the cause of inaccurate signals being sent to the ECM.

## Engine adaption

**9** The engine management system is adaptive, meaning it constantly reacts to changing operating conditions, either in riding style or in its operating environment.

**10** An adaption procedure can be easily carried out. The engine must be cold to do this, and the bike must be outside.

**11** Without touching the throttle, start the engine and allow it to idle until the cooling fan comes on, then leave it to idle for twelve minutes more. That's all there is to it!

## 12 ECM

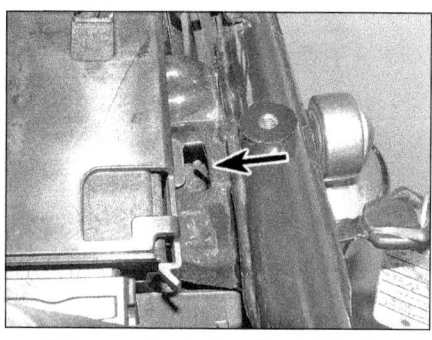

12.4c ...and note how the holder tab locates (arrowed)

## Removal

**Note:** *Before removing the ECM, make sure the ignition has been switched OFF for at least one minute to allow the system to power down before disconnecting the battery.*

**1** The ECM is mounted under the seat on all models except the Bobber, and behind the engine and under the air filter housings on the Bobber.

**2** Remove the seat (see Chapter 7).

**3** Disconnect the battery (see Chapter 8).

**4** On the T100, T120, Street Twin, Street Cup and Scrambler, release the tail light wiring connector from the ECM holder, then release the USB socket and move it aside so the wiring is clear of the screw **(see illustration)**. Undo the screw and displace the ECM assembly, noting how the tab locates, then release and disconnect the wiring connectors **(see illustrations)**. If required release and remove the holder from the ECM.

**5** On the Bobber remove the swingarm (see Chapter 5). Remove the ECM cover **(see illustration)**. Displace the ECM, then release and disconnect the wiring connectors **(see illustration)**.

12.5a Unscrew the bolt and remove the cover

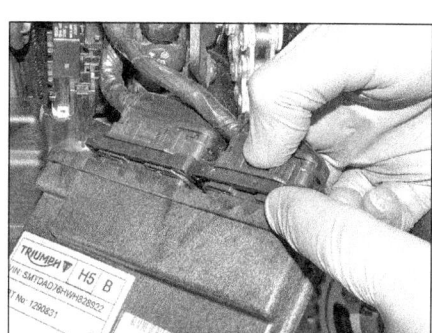

12.5b Lift the ECM out then release and disconnect the wiring

**6** On the Thruxton and Thruxton R release the ECM holder locking tabs **(see illustration)**. Release the ECM and tail light wiring from the holder **(see illustration)**. Release the front of the holder and remove it **(see illustration)**. Lift the ECM and release and disconnect the wiring connectors **(see illustration)**.

### Installation

**7** Installation is the reverse of removal. Check the terminal pins and connectors for damage and corrosion. Make sure the connectors are pushed fully on so the locking tabs engage.

## 13 Sensors

**Note:** *Before disconnecting the wiring connector from any sensor, make sure the ignition is switched OFF, and disconnect the battery (see Chapter 8).*

### Atmospheric pressure (AP) sensor

**1** The sensor reads the atmospheric (barometric) pressure (i.e. air density). The ECM combines this with other information to determine fuelling requirements.

**2** On the T100, T120, Street Twin, Street Cup and Scrambler remove the left-hand side cover (see Chapter 7). Disconnect the sensor wiring connector, then undo the screw, displace the sensor and disconnect the hose from the underside **(see illustration)** – if you

13.2 Atmospheric pressure sensor (arrowed) – T100, T120, Street Twin, Street Cup and Scrambler

13.4 Atmospheric pressure sensor (arrowed) – Thruxton and Thruxton R

12.6a Release the tabs...

12.6c ...then remove the holder, noting how it locates at the front

don't have the correct tools to access the sensor screw, undo the sensor bracket screws and displace the bracket.

**3** On the Bobber remove the left-hand air filter housing (Section 14). Disconnect the

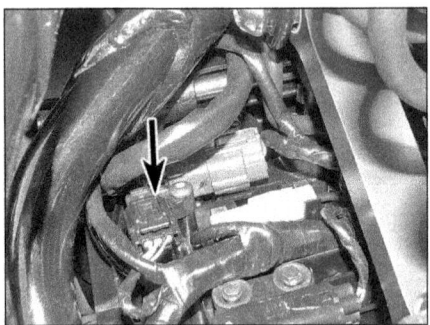

13.3 Atmospheric pressure sensor (arrowed) – Bobber

13.9 ECT sensor (arrowed)

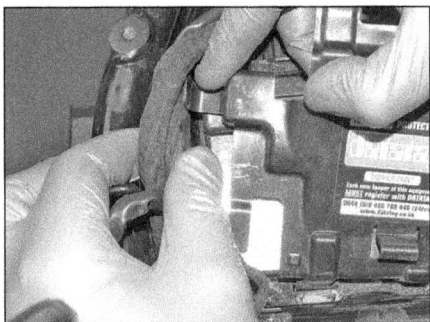

12.6b ...and the wiring...

12.6d Release and disconnect the wiring

sensor wiring connector, then undo the screw and remove the sensor **(see illustration)**.

**4** On the Thruxton and Thruxton R remove the seat (see Chapter 7). Disconnect the sensor wiring connector, then undo the screw and remove the sensor **(see illustration)**.

**5** Installation is the reverse of removal.

### Crankshaft position (CKP) sensor

**6** The sensor reads the position of the crankshaft and how fast it is turning; this information is used by the ECM to determine which cylinder is on its ignition stroke and when it should fire. The ECM combines engine speed with information from other sensors to determine fuelling and ignition requirements.

**7** The sensor is mounted in the alternator cover and is wired into the stator sub-loom; it is not available separately from it. Remove the alternator stator and replace it with a new one (see Chapter 8).

### Engine coolant temperature (ECT) sensor

#### Function

**8** The sensor reads the temperature of the engine coolant, and the ECM uses the information to determine fuelling requirements, particularly for hot and cold starting. It also provides input data for the operation of the high temperature warning light via the ECM.

#### Test

**9** The sensor is located in the front of the cylinder head **(see illustration)**.

**10** Remove the fuel tank to access the wiring connector (Section 2). Release the connector from the coil bracket **(see illustration 10.13)**. Push the wire clip in and disconnect it **(see illustration)**.

**11** Measure the resistance between the sensor terminals using an ohmmeter or multimeter set to the relevant scale for the temperature of the engine if warm, or the air if the engine is cold – see Specifications. It is best to take the first reading with the engine cold, and then take another reading with the engine warm to confirm the sensor is working correctly. If the results are not as specified, the sensor is faulty.

### Removal and installation

**12** The sensor is located in the front of the cylinder head **(see illustration 13.9)**. Drain the cooling system (see Chapter 1).

**13** Refer to Step 10 and disconnect the sensor wiring connector. Pull the rubber cover off the sensor then unscrew it. Remove the sealing washer – a new one must be used.

**14** Fit a new sealing washer onto the sensor, then thread it into the head and tighten it to 18 Nm. Reconnect and secure the wiring connector.

**15** Fill the cooling system (see Chapter 1).

### Gear position (GP) sensor

**16** The sensor is on the right-hand side of the engine. It signals the ECM which gear the engine is in, and the ECM then operates the neutral light and gear position indicator in the instrument cluster.

**17** Remove the right-hand side cover (see Chapter 7) and the front sprocket cover (see Chapter 6).

**18** On the T100, T120, Street Twin, Street Cup and Scrambler, undo the rear brake

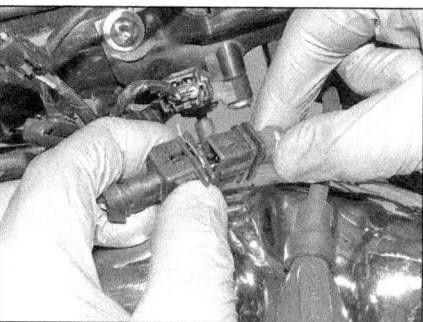

**13.10 Push the clip in to release the connector**

fluid reservoir screw, the brake hose guide bolt and the rider's footrest/brake pedal/master cylinder bracket bolts and displace the assembly, supporting it clear **(see illustrations)**. Release and disconnect the

**13.18a Displace the reservoir...**

**13.18b ..and release the hose guide...**

**13.18c ...then unscrew the bracket bolts and displace the assembly**

**13.18d GP sensor connector**

13.18e Wiring guide bolts (arrowed)

13.18f Draw the wiring out and release it from the guide

13.19a Unscrew the nuts and displace the coolant reservoir...

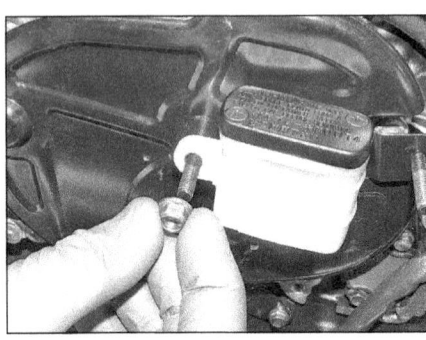

13.19b ...and the brake fluid reservoir

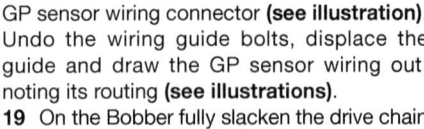

GP sensor wiring connector (see illustration). Undo the wiring guide bolts, displace the guide and draw the GP sensor wiring out, noting its routing (see illustrations).

**19** On the Bobber fully slacken the drive chain (see Chapter 1). Displace the coolant reservoir and brake fluid reservoir and support them upright and clear (see illustrations). Remove the reservoir mounting plate (see illustrations). Disengage the chain from the front sprocket and lay it over the front of the swingarm (see illustration). Remove the inner cover (see illustrations). Remove the wiring guide, noting the routing of the wiring in it, then unscrew the

13.19c Unscrew the mounting plate bolts...

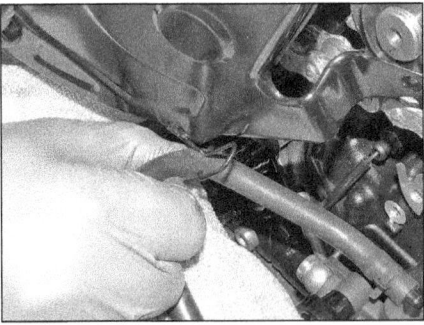

13.19d ...then release the hoses and remove the plate

13.19e Slip the chain off the sprocket

13.19f Undo the screws (arrowed)...

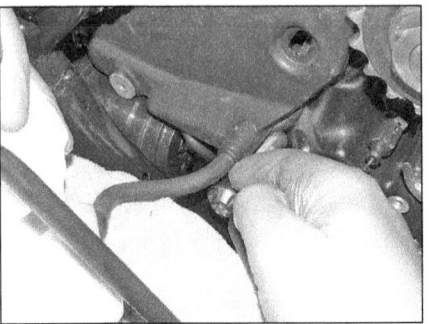

13.19g ...release the hose...

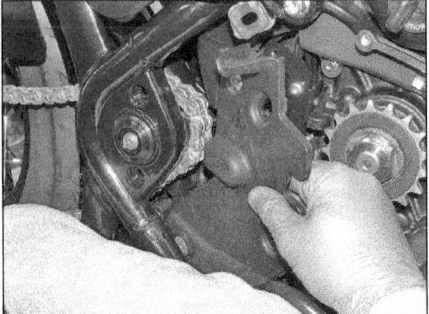

13.19h ...and remove the inner cover

13.19i Displace the relay bracket

13.19j GP sensor wiring connector (arrowed)

starter relay bracket bolts and displace the relay assembly (see illustration). Release and disconnect the GP sensor wiring connector (see illustration). Draw the GP sensor wiring out, noting its routing.

20 On the Thruxton and Thruxton R displace the coolant reservoir and support it upright and clear (see illustration). Remove the reservoir mounting plate (see illustrations). Undo the rear brake fluid reservoir screw and support the reservoir upright (see illustration 13.18a). Release and disconnect the GP sensor wiring connector (see illustration 13.18d). Undo the wiring guide bolt,

displace the guide and draw the GP sensor wiring out, noting its routing (see illustration). 21 Unscrew the bolts and remove the sensor (see illustration). Remove the O-rings – new ones should be used (see illustration 13.22). 22 Check that the contact pin is not damaged, and that the switch plate turns freely in the body (see illustration). 23 Fit the sensor using new O-rings smeared with petroleum jelly (Vaseline) or grease, locating the contact pin in the offset hole in the end of the selector drum (see illustration). Clean the threads of the bolts and apply some fresh threadlock. Tighten the bolts to 5 Nm.

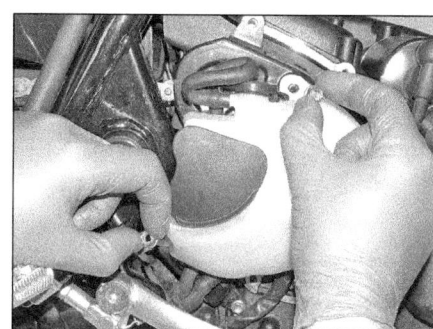

13.20a Unscrew the nuts and displace the reservoir

13.20b Unscrew the bolts...

13.20c ...release the wiring and remove the plate

13.20d Wiring guide bolt (arrowed)

13.21 Unscrew the two bolts

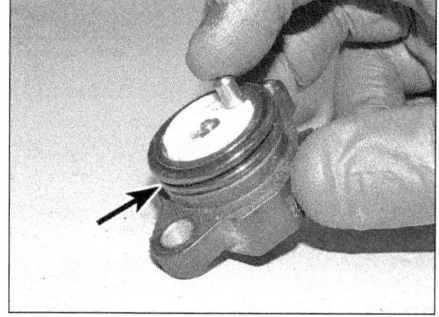

13.22 Check the pin and the switch plate. Sensor O-rings (arrowed)

13.23 Align the pin with the offset hole

**13.25 Route the hoses in the guide as shown**

**13.27 IAT sensor wiring connector (A) and screw (B)**

**13.32 MAP sensor screw (arrowed)**

24 Seat the wiring in the guide, aligning the white tape with the hole in the guide, route it to the connector and reconnect it **(see illustration 13.18f or 13.19j)**. Check the operation of the neutral light and gear position readout.

25 Install all remaining components in reverse order of removal according to model. On the T100, T120, Street Twin, Street Cup and Scrambler tighten the rider's footrest/brake pedal/master cylinder bracket bolts to 24 Nm. On the Bobber make sure the reservoir hoses are correctly routed in the mounting plate guide **(see illustration)**.

### Intake air temperature (IAT) sensor

#### Function

26 The sensor reads the temperature of the air in the air filter housing (left-hand on the Bobber). As changes in temperature affect air density, the ECM uses the information to determine fuelling requirements.

#### Test, removal and installation

27 On all models except the Bobber remove the seat (see Chapter 7). On the Thruxton and Thruxton R remove the fuel tank (Section 2). Disconnect the sensor wiring connector **(see illustration)**.
28 On the Bobber remove the left-hand air filter housing (Section 14).
29 Measure the resistance between the sensor terminals using an ohmmeter or multimeter set to the appropriate ohms or K-ohms scale. If the result is not as

given in the Specifications for the relevant temperature, the sensor is faulty.
30 To remove the sensor, undo the screw. Installation is the reverse of removal.

### Manifold absolute pressure (MAP) sensor

#### Function

31 The sensor reads the pressure of the air in the throttle body. The ECM combines this with other information to determine engine load and adjusts fuelling requirements accordingly.

#### Removal and installation

32 The sensor is mounted on the underside of the coil holder. Remove the coil assembly (Section 10). Undo the screw and remove the sensor **(see illustration)**.
33 Installation is the reverse of removal. Make sure the vacuum hoses are in good condition and securely fitted at each end.

### Oxygen (lambda) sensors

#### Function

34 The sensor measures oxygen left in the un-burnt exhaust gases and generates a signal voltage that is fed back to the ECM. In this way the ECM can correct the mixture supplied to the engine to ensure that the oxygen content of the exhaust gases remains within a narrow range and suitable for the operation of the catalytic converter. This type of system is called closed-loop control.

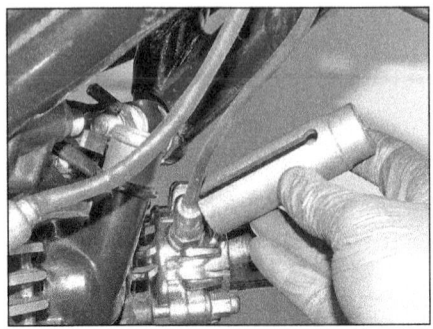

**13.38 Purpose-made sockets to accommodate the wiring are available, and mean the sensor can be tightened to the correct torque on installation**

#### Removal and installation

35 There is a sensor in each exhaust header pipe **(see illustration)**.
36 Remove the fuel tank (Section 2).
37 Release and disconnect the oxygen sensor wiring connector **(see illustration 9.9 or 9.40)** – the connector for the right-hand header pipe sensor is the upper of the two connectors and is identified by a band of red tape.
38 Unscrew and remove the sensor **(see illustration)** – the sensor is fragile so care must be taken not to apply undue force. If the sensor is difficult to unscrew or the area around it is badly corroded, apply a penetrating fluid and allow time for it to soak in.
39 When installing the sensor, apply copper grease to the sensor threads and tighten it to 25 Nm if the correct socket is available **(see illustration 13.38)**. Reconnect the sensor wiring connector – make sure the wiring is correctly routed and secured, with the right sensor wiring going into the upper connector with the red-banded wiring and the left sensor going to the lower connector.

### Throttle position (TP) sensor

40 The sensor reads the amount of throttle being used, and the ECM uses this in conjunction with the information from other sensors to determine fuelling and ignition requirements.
41 The sensor is an integral part of the throttle body and is not available separately. Do not attempt to separate it from the body or to loosen any of the yellow-painted screws or bolts because they have been factory set. Triumph say that if you do you will have to fit a new throttle body as there is no way of resetting the motor to its correct position.

### Tip-over (TO) sensor

#### Function

42 The sensor is basically a safety switch that tells the ECM if the bike has fallen over, in which case the ECM will shut down the fuel pump and stop the engine. The switch can be reset by picking the bike up and turning the ignition off, then on again.

**13.35 Oxygen sensors (arrowed)**

## Removal and installation

**43** On all models except the Bobber remove the seat (see Chapter 7). Unscrew the sensor bolts, displace the sensor and disconnect the wiring **(see illustration)**.

**44** On the Bobber remove the left-hand air filter housing (Section 14). Unscrew the sensor bolts, displace the sensor and disconnect the wiring **(see illustration)**.

**45** Clean the threads of the bolts and apply some fresh threadlock. Fit the sensor with the UP mark at the top and tighten the bolts to 3 Nm. Never remount the sensor; its position is critical to correct operation.

**13.43 Tip-over sensor (arrowed)**

**13.44 Tip-over sensor (arrowed)**

## 14  Air filter housings – Bobber

### *Removal*

### Right-hand housing

**1** Remove the right-hand side cover (see Chapter 7).

**2** Remove the fuel tank (Section 2).

**3** Remove the air duct cover **(see illustration)**.

**4** Remove the trim piece from the front of the air filter housing **(see illustration)**.

**5** Release the diagnostic connector and let it dangle by its wiring **(see illustration 11.4b)**.

**6** Disconnect the crankcase breather hose **(see illustration)**.

**7** Undo the air duct clamp screw and move the clamp forwards **(see illustration)**.

**14.3 Undo the screw then pull the pegs from the grommets**

**8** Undo the two screws securing the front of the housing and the bolt at the rear, noting the collar **(see illustrations)**. Ease the front of the housing out of the duct and the rear out of the frame **(see illustrations)**.

**14.4 Undo the screws and remove the trim piece**

### Left-hand housing

**9** Remove the left-hand side cover (see Chapter 7).

**10** Remove the fuel tank (Section 2).

**14.6 Release the clamp and pull the hose off**

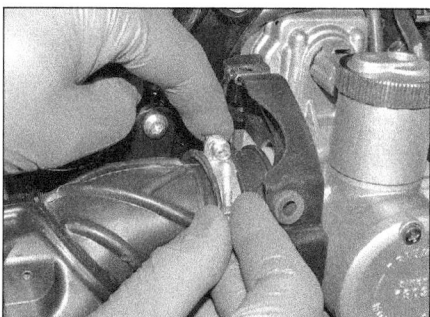

**14.7 Fully undo the clamp screw so the clamp can be moved forwards**

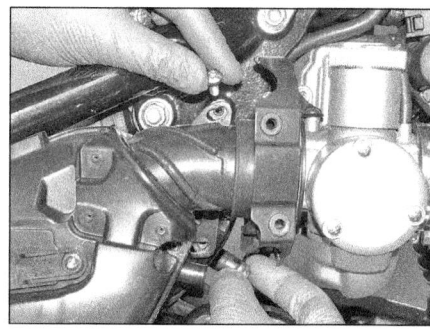

**14.8a Undo the front screws...**

**14.8b ...and the rear screw**

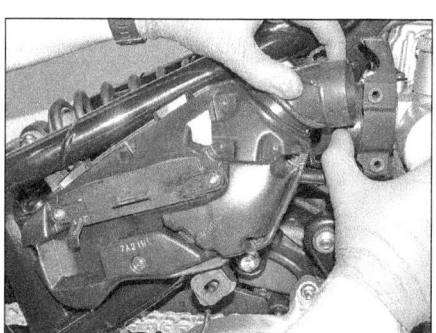

**14.8c Ease the front out of the duct...**

**14.8d ...and remove the housing**

14.13a Release the main fuse holder from the front of the housing...

14.13b ...and the fusebox from the back

**11** Remove the air duct cover **(see illustration 14.3).**
**12** Remove the trim piece from the front of the air filter housing **(see illustration 14.4).**
**13** Release the fuse boxes and let them dangle by the wiring **(see illustrations).**
**14** Disconnect the crankcase breather hose **(see illustration 14.6).**
**15** Undo the air duct clamp screw and move the clamp forwards **(see illustration 14.7).**
**16** Undo the two screws securing the front of the housing and the bolt at the rear, noting the collar **(see illustrations 14.8a and b).** Ease the front of the housing out of the duct and the rear out of the frame **(see illustration 14.8c and d),** then disconnect the IAT sensor wiring connector **(see illustration).**

### *Installation*

**17** Installation is the reverse of removal.

## 15 EVAP system

**1** This system prevents the escape of fuel vapour into the atmosphere by storing it in a charcoal-filled canister, located under the air filter housing on all models except the Bobber, and at the back of the frame low down on the right-hand side on the Bobber **(see illustrations).**
**2** When the engine is stopped, fuel vapour from the tank passes down the tank breather hose via a roll-over valve and into the canister where it is absorbed and stored whilst the motorcycle is standing. When the engine is started, the purge control valve, behind the left-hand side cover on all models except

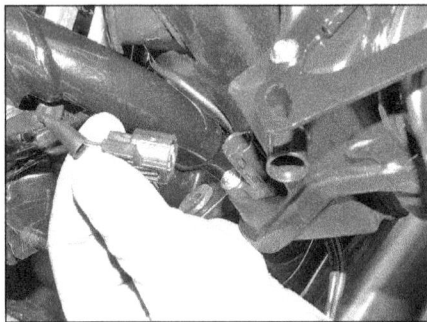

14.16 Disconnect the IAT sensor wiring

the Bobber, and next to the canister on the Bobber, opens and the vapours stored in the canister are sucked into the throttle body to

15.1a Canister is secured to the bottom of the air filter housing on all models except the Bobber

15.1b EVAP canister (arrowed) – Bobber

be burned during the normal combustion process **(see illustrations)**.

**3** The roll-over valve closes and prevents any fuel from escaping through it in the event of the bike falling over. The tank filler cap has a one-way valve that allows air into the tank as the volume of fuel decreases, but prevents any fuel vapour from escaping.

**4** The system is not adjustable and requires no servicing other than to check that all the hoses are in good condition and are securely connected at each end. Replace any hoses that are cracked, split or generally deteriorated with new ones. For access to the hoses on the Bobber **(see illustration 15.2c)** refer to the gear position sensor removal procedure in Section 13, referring to the relevant Steps.

**5** You can check the purge valve by disconnecting the wiring connector and measuring the resistance of the valve using an ohmmeter. If the result is not as given in the Specifications at the beginning of the Chapter, in particular if there is infinite or no resistance, the valve is faulty.

**15.2a Roll-over valve (arrowed)...**

## 16 Catalytic converter

### General information

**1** The catalytic converter minimises the level of exhaust pollutants released into the atmosphere. It consists of a canister containing a fine mesh impregnated with a catalyst material, over which the hot exhaust gases pass. The catalyst speeds up the oxidation of harmful carbon monoxide, unburned hydrocarbons and soot, effectively reducing the quantity of harmful products released into the atmosphere via the exhaust gases.

**2** The catalytic converter is housed in the exhaust collector box, located under the engine on all models except the Scrambler, and on the right-hand side of the engine as part of the right-hand header pipe assembly on the Scrambler – see Section 9.

**3** It operates under closed-loop control with an oxygen (Lambda) sensor feeding back gas oxygen content information to the ECM; information on the sensor can be found in Section 13.

### Precautions

**4** The catalytic converter is a reliable and simple device which needs no maintenance in itself, but there are some precautions the owner should note if the converter is to function properly for its full service life.

● DO NOT use leaded or lead replacement petrol (gasoline) – the additives will coat the precious metals, reducing their converting efficiency and will eventually destroy the catalytic converter.

● Always keep the ignition and fuel systems well-maintained in accordance with the manufacturer's schedule – if the fuel/air mixture is suspected of being incorrect

have it checked on an exhaust gas analyser.

● If the engine develops a misfire, do not ride the bike at all (or at least as little as possible) until the fault is cured.

● DO NOT use fuel or engine oil additives – these may contain substances harmful to the catalytic converter.

● DO NOT continue to use the bike if the engine burns oil to the extent of leaving a visible trail of blue smoke.

● Remember that the catalytic converter is FRAGILE – do not strike it with tools during servicing work.

## 17 Immobiliser

### General information

**Note:** *The immobiliser control unit also controls the tyre pressure monitoring system (TPMS), if fitted. Refer to Chapter 6 for details on the TPMS.*

**1** The immobiliser system will only allow the engine to be started if the signal sent from a transponder in the ignition key is recognised by the ECM. The signal from the transponder is picked up and transmitted by a receiver fitted around the top of the ignition switch to the immobiliser control unit, which in turn corresponds with the ECM. The system has its own self-diagnostic function. New immobiliser system components must be paired with the ECM and this can only be done using the Triumph diagnostic tool. The bike comes from the factory with two paired keys. A further two keys can be paired with the system.

**2** An immobiliser light in the instrument cluster flashes for twenty-four hours when the immobiliser is active. When the ignition

**15.2b ...and purge control valve – all models except the Bobber**

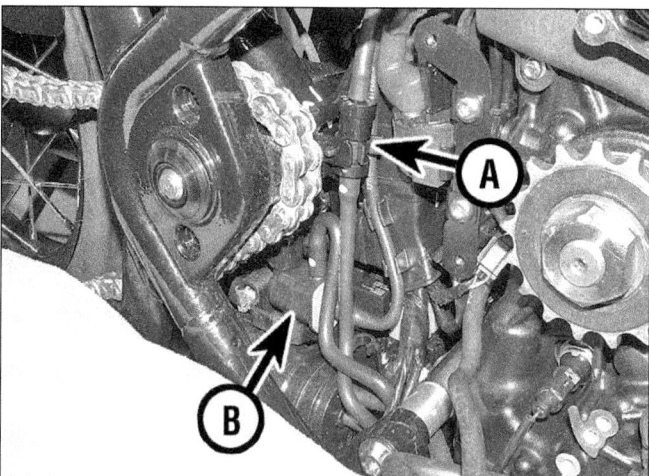

**15.2c Roll-over valve (A), purge control valve (B) – Bobber**

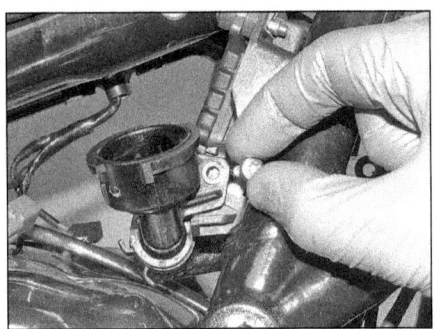

**17.6 Undo the screw**

**17.8a Immobiliser control unit – all models except the Bobber**

**17.8b Immobiliser control unit – Bobber**

is turned on, and the key transponder is recognised by the ECM, the light goes out.

**3** If the light comes on and stays on when the ignition is turned on there is a fault in the system. The Triumph diagnostic tool is required for fault code retrieval.

### Immobiliser control unit

**4** The immobiliser control unit is mounted behind the steering head on all models except the Bobber, and behind the engine and under the air filter housings on the Bobber.

**5** Disconnect the battery (see Chapter 8).

**6** On all models except the Bobber remove the fuel tank (Section 2), then displace the ignition coil assembly (Section 10) – there is no need to disconnect the wiring. Undo the cooling system filler neck screw **(see illustration)**.

**7** On the Bobber remove the ECM (Section 12).

**8** Slacken the control unit screws, then undo the control unit bracket screws, displace the bracket and disconnect the wiring connector **(see illustrations)**. Undo the control unit screws and remove the unit from the bracket.

**9** Installation is the reverse of removal.

### Immobiliser receiver

**10** The receiver is an integral part of the ignition switch and is not available separately. Refer to Chapter 8 for removal and installation of the switch.

# Chapter 5
# Frame and suspension

## Contents

## Degrees of difficulty

| Easy, suitable for novice with little experience 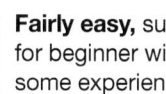 | Fairly easy, suitable for beginner with some experience | Fairly difficult, suitable for competent DIY mechanic | Difficult, suitable for experienced DIY mechanic | Very difficult, suitable for expert DIY or professional  |

## Specifications

### Front forks

Fork oil type
   All models except the Thruxton R . . . . . . . . . . . . . . . . . . . . . . . . . KHL34-G10 or equivalent 10W fork oil
   Thruxton R . . . . . . . . . . . . . . . . . . . . . . . . . . . . . . . . . . . . . . . . . . Showa SS47
Fork oil capacity
   T100 and Scrambler. . . . . . . . . . . . . . . . . . . . . . . . . . . . . . . . . . . 488 cc
   T120 . . . . . . . . . . . . . . . . . . . . . . . . . . . . . . . . . . . . . . . . . . . . . . . 434 cc
   Bobber . . . . . . . . . . . . . . . . . . . . . . . . . . . . . . . . . . . . . . . . . . . . . 447 cc
   Street Twin and Street Cup. . . . . . . . . . . . . . . . . . . . . . . . . . . . . . 478 cc
   Thruxton . . . . . . . . . . . . . . . . . . . . . . . . . . . . . . . . . . . . . . . . . . . . 405 cc
   Thruxton R . . . . . . . . . . . . . . . . . . . . . . . . . . . . . . . . . . . . . . . . . . 582 cc
Fork oil level*
   T100 and Scrambler. . . . . . . . . . . . . . . . . . . . . . . . . . . . . . . . . . . 105 mm
   T120
      Right-hand fork. . . . . . . . . . . . . . . . . . . . . . . . . . . . . . . . . . . . 126 mm
      Left-hand fork . . . . . . . . . . . . . . . . . . . . . . . . . . . . . . . . . . . . 165 mm
   Bobber . . . . . . . . . . . . . . . . . . . . . . . . . . . . . . . . . . . . . . . . . . . . . 109 mm
   Street Twin and Street Cup. . . . . . . . . . . . . . . . . . . . . . . . . . . . . . 97 mm
   Thruxton
      Right-hand fork. . . . . . . . . . . . . . . . . . . . . . . . . . . . . . . . . . . . 129 mm
      Left-hand fork . . . . . . . . . . . . . . . . . . . . . . . . . . . . . . . . . . . . 161 mm
   Thruxton R . . . . . . . . . . . . . . . . . . . . . . . . . . . . . . . . . . . . . . . . . . 68 mm

*Oil level is measured from the top of the tube with the fork spring removed and the leg fully compressed.

## Torque wrench settings

| | |
|---|---|
| Clutch lever bracket clamp bolts | 12 Nm |
| Clutch lever pivot bolt nut | 3.5 Nm |
| Fork clamp bolts | |
|    Bottom yoke | |
|       T100, T120, Street Twin, Street Cup, Scrambler | 45 Nm |
|       Bobber, Thruxton, Thruxton R | 25 Nm |
|    Top yoke | |
|       T100, T120, Bobber, Street Twin, Street Cup, Scrambler. | 24 Nm |
|       Thruxton and Thruxton R | 20 Nm |
| Fork damper bolt | 30 Nm |
| Fork rod guide (Thruxton R) | 90 Nm (but see Section 7) |
| Fork top bolt | |
|    T100, T120, Bobber, Street Twin, Street Cup, Scrambler, Thruxton . | 22 Nm |
|    Thruxton R | 35 Nm |
| Front brake lever pivot bolt | 1 Nm |
| Front brake lever pivot bolt nut | 6 Nm |
| Handlebars | |
|    T100, T120, Bobber, Street Twin, Street Cup, Scrambler | |
|       Handlebar holder bolts | 38 Nm |
|       Handlebar clamp bolts | 24 Nm |
|       Bar clamp bolts in centre piece – Street Cup | 8.5 Nm |
|    Thruxton and Thruxton R | |
|       Handlebar clamp bolts | 8.5 Nm |
|       Handlebar holder clamp bolts | 20 Nm |
|       Handlebar holder positioning bolts. | 8 Nm |
| Rear shock absorber bolts – T100, T120, Street Twin, | |
|    Street Cup and Scrambler | 28 Nm |
| Rear shock absorber bolts – Thruxton and Thruxton R | |
|    Upper bolt | 28 Nm |
|    Lower bolt/nut | 48 Nm |
| Rear shock absorber and suspension linkage bolts/nuts – Bobber . . . | see Section 11 and Section 12 |
| Steering head bearing adjuster nut | |
|    Initial setting | 40 Nm |
|    Final setting | 15 Nm |
| Steering head bearing adjuster locknut | 40 Nm |
| Steering stem nut | 90 Nm |
| Swingarm pivot bolt nut | 110 Nm |

## 1  General Information

1 All models have a steel twin cradle frame.

2 On all models except the Thruxton R front suspension is by a pair of 41 mm telescopic forks with internal coil springs. On the T100, Street Twin, Street Cup and Scrambler both forks having a conventional damper,on the T120 the right-hand fork has a cartridge damper and the left-hand fork has a conventional damper, and on the Thruxton both forks have a cartridge damper. The forks are not adjustable.

3 On the Thruxton R front suspension is by a pair of 43 mm Showa 'big piston' USD forks. The forks have adjustable spring pre-load and both rebound and compression damping.

4 On all models except the Bobber rear suspension is by a swingarm acting on a pair of shock absorbers that have adjustable spring pre-load on all models, and also adjustable rebound and compression damping on the Thruxton R.

5 On the Bobber the swingarm acts on a single shock absorber via a rising-rate linkage. The shock absorber is not adjustable.

## 2  Frame

1 The frame should not require attention unless accident damage has occurred. In most cases, fitting a new frame is the only satisfactory remedy for such damage. A few frame specialists have the jigs and other equipment necessary for straightening the frame to the required standard of accuracy, but even then there is no simple way of assessing to what extent the frame may have been over-stressed.

2 After the machine has covered a high mileage, the frame should be examined closely for signs of cracking or splitting at the welded joints. Loose engine mount bolts can cause ovaling or fracturing of the mounts themselves. Minor damage can often be repaired by welding, depending on the extent and nature of the damage, but this is a task for an expert.

3 Remember that a frame that is out of alignment will cause handling problems. If misalignment is suspected as the result of an accident, first check the wheel alignment (see Chapter 6). To have the frame checked thoroughly it will be necessary to strip the machine completely.

## 3  Footrests, gearchange lever and rear brake pedal

### Footrests

1 To remove the rider's footrests, remove the E-clip from the pivot pin, then pull the pin

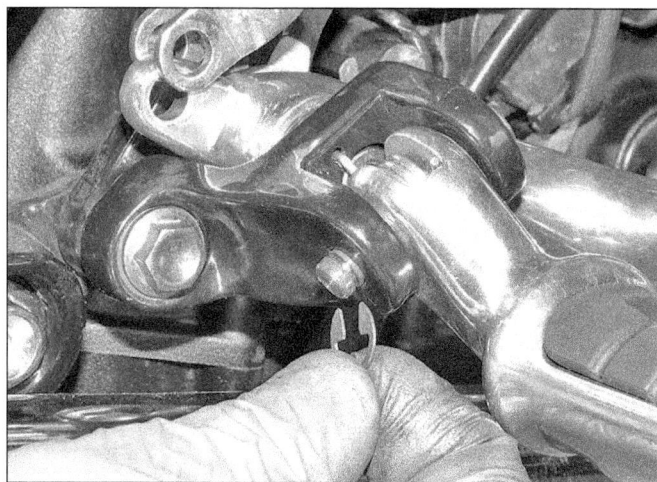

3.1a Remove the E-clip...

3.1b ...and withdraw the pin

out and remove the footrest, noting how the return spring ends locate **(see illustrations)**.

**2** To remove the passenger footrests remove the E-clip from the pivot pin then pull the pin out and remove the footrest, keeping a finger on the spring-loaded ball and detent plate located between the footrest and its bracket to secure the footrest in the UP position when not in use **(see illustrations)**. Remove the plate, ball and spring when the footrest is removed **(see illustration)**.

**3** On the T100, T120, Bobber, Street Twin, Street Cup, and Thruxton the footrest rubbers can be replaced with new ones if necessary –

undo the two screws on the underside of the footrest and remove the rubber, then remove the nut plate from inside the rubber **(see illustration)**.

**4** On the Scrambler the rider's footrest rubbers can be removed for extra grip on the footrest, or replaced with new ones if necessary, by releasing pegs on the rubber from the holes in the footrest. The passenger footrest rubbers can replaced in the same way as for other models as described in Step 3.

**5** Installation is the reverse of removal. Apply a smear of grease to the pivot pin and to the

contact areas between the footrest and its holder, and the detent plate on the passenger footrests.

### *Gearchange lever and linkage*

#### Removal

#### T100, T120, Street Twin, Street Cup, Scrambler

**6** Note the alignment of the punch mark on the gearchange shaft with the slit in the lever clamp, then unscrew the pinch bolt and slide the lever off **(see illustrations)**.

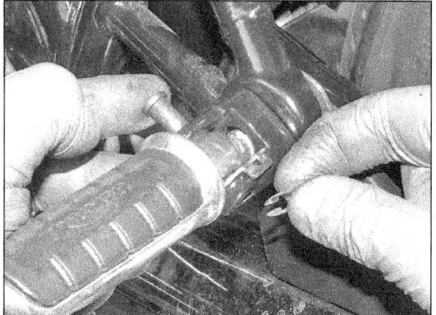

3.2a Remove the E-clip and withdraw the pin...

3.2b ...then ease the footrest out, holding the plate in place

3.2c Remove the plate, ball and spring

3.3 Footrest rubber screws (arrowed)

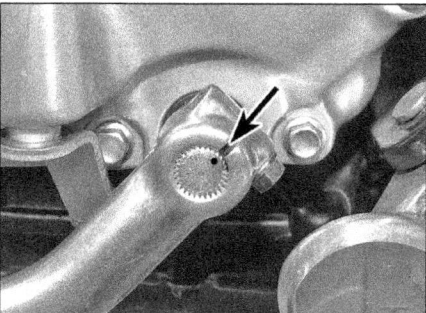

3.6a Note the alignment...

3.6b ...then unscrew the bolt and remove the lever

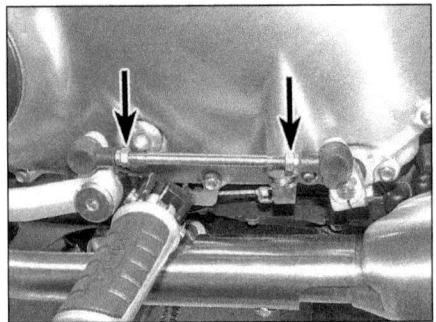

3.7a Linkage rod locknuts (arrowed) – Bobber

3.7b Linkage rod locknuts (arrowed) – Thruxton and Thruxton R

3.8a Lever pivot bolt (arrowed) – Bobber

3.8b Lever pivot bolt (arrowed) – Thruxton and Thruxton R

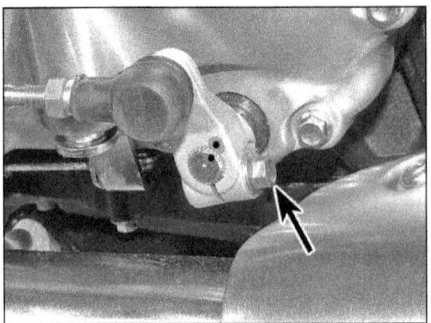

3.9a Linkage arm/shaft alignment and pinch bolt (arrowed) – Bobber

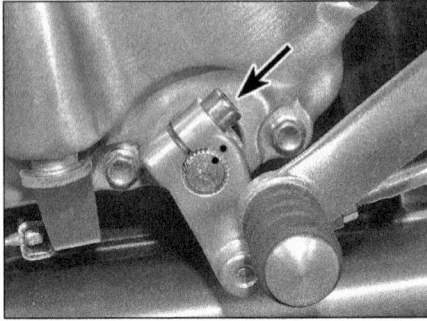

3.9b Linkage arm/shaft alignment and pinch bolt (arrowed) – Thruxton and Thruxton R

### Bobber, Thruxton, Thruxton R

7  To separate the gearchange lever from the linkage rod, measure and note the amount of exposed thread on each end of the rod (this determines the height of the lever relative to the footrest), then hold the flats on the joint piece and slacken the linkage rod locknuts, turning the rear nut on the Bobber and the front nut on the Thruxton and Thruxton R clockwise as they have left-hand threads **(see illustrations)**. Unscrew the rod and separate it from the lever and the arm – as the rod is reverse-threaded on the linkage arm end it will simultaneously unscrew from both lever and arm when turned in the one direction.

8  Unscrew the gearchange lever pivot bolt and remove the lever **(see illustrations)**.

9  Note the alignment of the punch marks on the gearchange shaft and linkage arm, then unscrew the pinch bolt and slide the arm off the shaft **(see illustrations)**.

10  If the toe rubber is worn remove it and fit a new one – on all models except the Thruxton and Thruxton R unscrew the toe rubber holder from the lever to do this, and on Thruxton and Thruxton R just slide the rubber off.

### Installation

11  Installation is the reverse of removal, noting the following:

● Align the punch mark on the gearchange shaft with the slit in the lever clamp or the punch mark on the linkage arm, according to model **(see illustration 3.6a, 3.9a or 3.9b)**.

● Clean any old grease off the lever pivot and the pivot bolt, then apply fresh grease.

● On the Bobber, Thruxton and Thruxton R adjust the gear lever height as required by slackening the locknuts and screwing the linkage rod in or out of the lever and arm as described in Step 7, then tighten the locknuts.

### *Rear brake pedal*

#### Removal

#### T100, T120, Street Twin, Street Cup, Scrambler

12  Remove the clip from the inner end of the master cylinder pushrod clevis pin, then withdraw the pin **(see illustrations)**.

13  Remove the footrest (see above).

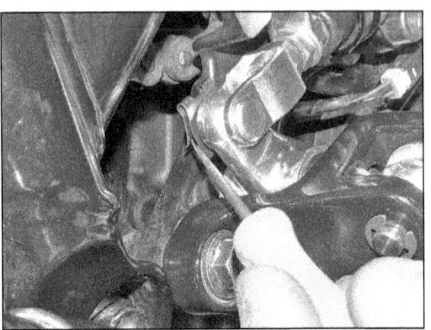

3.12a Push the sprung leaf of the clip out so it clears the end of the pin...

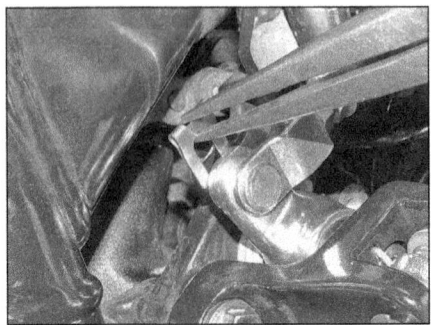

3.12b ...then slide it up and off...

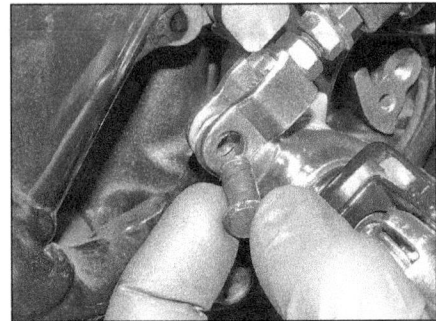

3.12c ...and withdraw the pin

3.14 Remove the footrest holder

3.15a Remove the pedal...

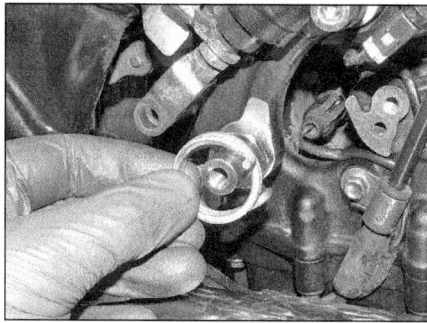

3.15b ...and the spring

**14** Unscrew the footrest holder bolts and remove the holder **(see illustration)**.
**15** Slide the brake pedal off the pivot then remove the return spring, noting how its ends locate **(see illustrations)**.

### Bobber

**16** Either secure the footrest in its raised position, or remove it (see above).
**17** Note the alignment of the punch marks on the shaft and pedal **(see illustration)**. Unscrew the pedal pinch bolt, slide the pedal off and remove the return spring, noting how its ends locate **(see illustrations)**.
**18** To remove the pivot shaft, unscrew the footrest/brake pedal bracket bolts and displace the assembly **(see illustration)**. Remove the clip from the inner end of the master cylinder pushrod clevis pin, then withdraw the pin **(see illustration and 3.12a, b and c)**. Remove the E-clip and washer and draw the pivot shaft out, noting the wave washer that sits between it and the bracket.

### Thruxton and Thruxton R

**19** Unhook the pedal return spring **(see illustration)**.
**20** Remove the clip from the inner end of the master cylinder pushrod clevis pin, then withdraw the pin **(see illustrations 3.18b and 3.12a, b and c)**.
**21** Unscrew the brake pedal pivot bolt and remove the pedal **(see illustration)**.

### Installation

**22** Installation is the reverse of removal, noting the following:

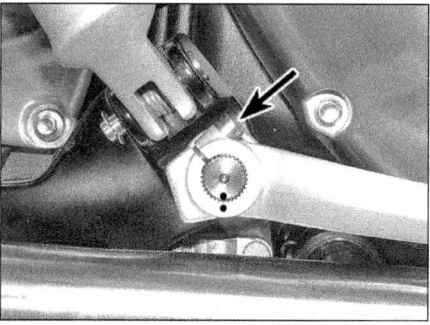

3.17a Note the alignment of the punch marks. Pedal pinch bolt (arrowed)

3.18a Use a ball-ended hex key to unscrew the bracket bolts

● Clean any old grease off the pedal pivot and apply fresh grease.
● On the Bobber clean any rust of the pivot shaft and pedal splines and apply a smear of grease. Fit the wave washer between

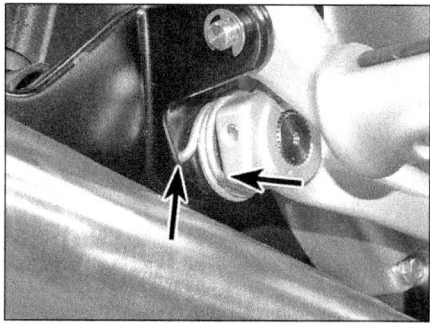

3.17b Note how the return spring ends (arrowed) locate

3.18b Remove the clip (arrowed) then withdraw the pin and detach the pushrod

the inner end of the pivot shaft and the footrest/pedal bracket.
● Make sure the spring ends are correctly located **(see illustration)**.

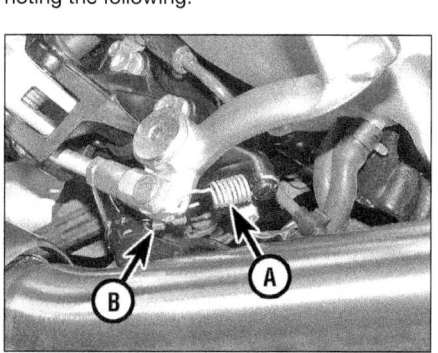

3.19 Pedal return spring (A), clevis pin clip (B)

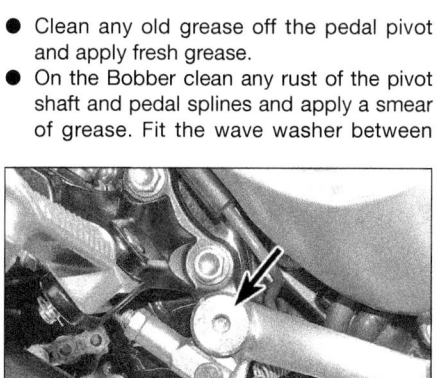

3.21 Pedal pivot bolt (arrowed)

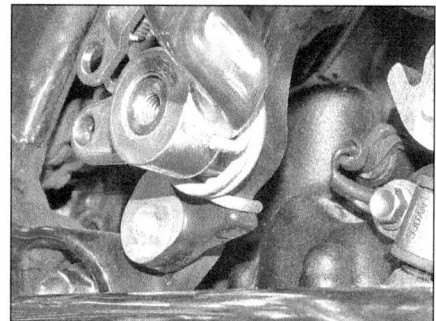

3.22 Spring end location – T100, T120, Street Twin, Street Cup and Scrambler

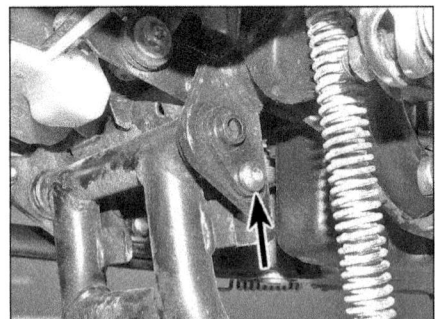

4.3 Use a spring hook to unhook the springs. Sidestand pivot E-clip (arrowed)

4.8 Stand spindle screw (arrowed)

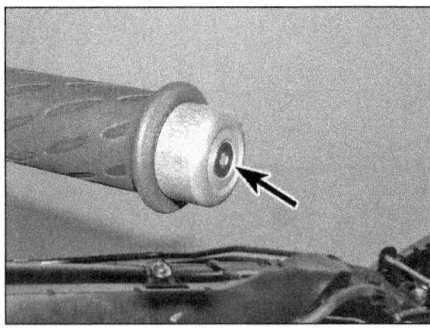

5.4 Undo the screw (arrowed) to remove the end-weight

## 4 Sidestand and centrestand

### Sidestand

**1** Support the motorcycle securely in an upright position using the centrestand on the T120 and an auxiliary stand on all other models. Tie the front brake on.
**2** On the T100, T120, Street Twin, Street Cup, Thruxton and Thruxton R refer to Chapter 4, Section 9, Steps 27 and 29, and remove the left-hand frame cradle.
**3** With the stand in the raised position, unhook the springs using a spring hook **(see illustration)**.
**4** Remove the E-clip from the bottom of the pivot pin, then push the pin out and remove the stand **(see illustration 4.3)**.
**5** Installation is the reverse of removal, noting the following points:
● Clean off all dirt and old grease from the pivot pin, stand and frame, then apply lithium-based grease.
● Check the springs hold the stand securely up against the stop in the raised position. Fit new ones if necessary – they come as a pair.
● Refer to Chapter 4, Section 9, Step 32 to fit the frame cradle.
● Check the operation of the sidestand

switch and starter safety circuit (see Chapter 1).

### Centrestand – T120

**6** Support the motorcycle on the sidestand or an auxiliary stand. Tie the front brake on.
**7** With the stand in the raised position, unhook the springs using a spring hook.
**8** Unscrew the stand spindle screw **(see illustration)**. Support the stand, withdraw the spindle and remove the stand. Remove the collar from each side of the stand.
**9** Installation is the reverse of removal, noting the following points:
● Clean off all dirt and old grease from the collars, spindle and the mounts on the frame, then apply lithium-based grease.
● Check the springs hold the stand securely up against the stop in the raised position. Fit new ones if necessary – they come as a pair.

## 5 Handlebars and levers

### Handlebars

#### Removal

**Note:** *The handlebars can be displaced without having to remove the throttle twistgrip, switch assemblies or levers, but take care to*

*avoid straining the handlebar wiring. Support or tie the handlebar assembly using rags to cushion it and anything it sits against. Also cover the front brake master cylinder with rag in case of leakage.*
**1** Remove the mirrors (see Chapter 7).
**2** Remove the throttle twistgrip and position sensor (see Chapter 4).
**3** On the Street Twin, Street Cup, Scrambler and Thruxton R displace the front brake master cylinder (see Chapter 6) – there is no need to drain the brake fluid, remove the lever or disconnect the brake hose. Keep the reservoir upright to prevent fluid spillage and make sure no strain is placed on the hose. Displace the right-hand switch housing (see Chapter 8).
**4** On the T100, T120, Street Twin and Scrambler remove the end-weight from the left-hand side **(see illustration)**.
**5** On all models except the T120 pull the left-hand grip off the handlebar – push a plastic tool or screwdriver covered with tape between the grip and the bar and use spray lubricant (see Caution) and/or compressed air to loosen the grip. If the grip has been bonded in place you may need to cut it free, in which case you will need a new one.
***Caution: Wear eye protection when using a spray lube for this purpose – it can spray back into your face.***
**6** On the T120 undo the heated grip button housing screws and displace the housing halves **(see illustrations)**. On the T100, T120,

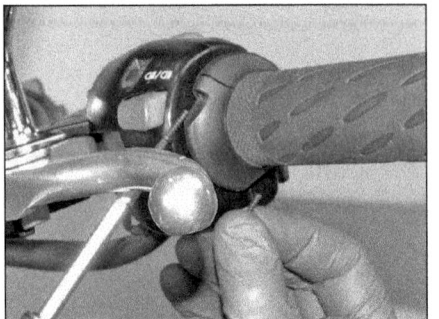

5.6a On the T120 undo the screws...

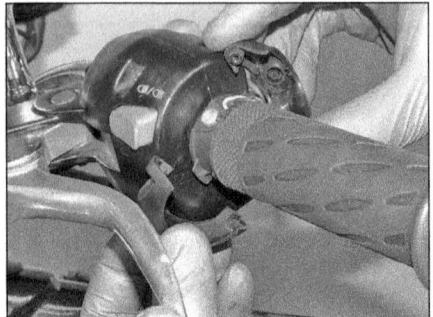

5.6b ...and displace the housing

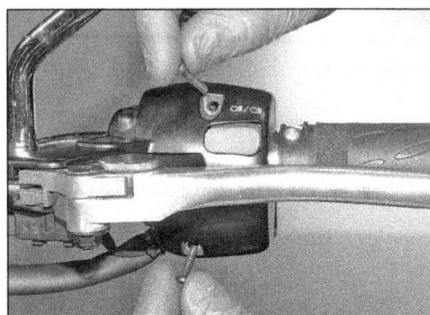

5.6c Undo the screws and displace the face of the switch

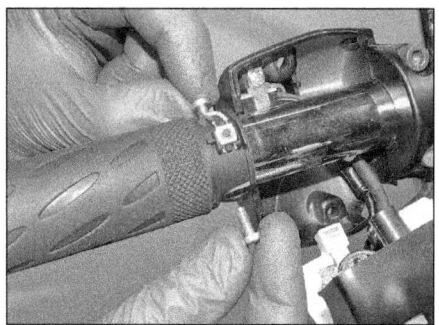

**5.6d On the T120 undo the heated grip screws**

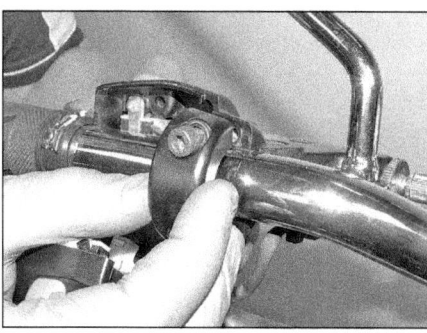

**5.6e Unscrew the clamp bolts and displace the housing/lever bracket assembly**

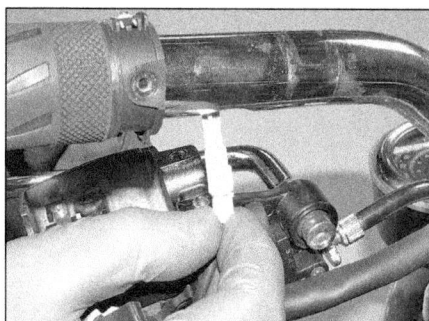

**5.6f On the T120 draw the connector out and disconnect it, then remove the grip**

Bobber and Thruxton displace the face of the left-hand switch housing from the handlebar, on the T120 also undo the heated grip screws, then on all models displace the switch housing/clutch lever bracket assembly **(see illustrations)**. On the T120 slide the heated grip towards the middle of the handlebar to draw the grip wiring connector out of the hole, disconnect it and slide the grip off **(see illustration)**.

**7** On the Street Twin, Street Cup, Scrambler and Thruxton R displace the clutch lever assembly **(see illustration)**. Displace the left-hand switch housing (see Chapter 8).

**8** On the Bobber release the bands from the handlebar **(see illustration)**.

**9** On the T100, T120, Bobber, Street Twin, Street Cup and Scrambler, support the handlebars, unscrew the clamps bolts and remove the clamp, then lift the handlebars off **(see illustration)**. Fit the clamp back onto the holders and fit the bolts finger-tight to keep the holders aligned. If required unscrew the bolts on the underside of the top yoke, noting how they secure the cable guide on the T100, T120 and Scrambler, and the washers fitted with the bolts on the Bobber, Street Twin and Street Cup, and remove the holders, the top washers, the rubbers and the sleeves, noting how they fit **(see illustrations)**. On the Street Cup the bars can be separated from the centre piece if required by slackening the clamp bolts.

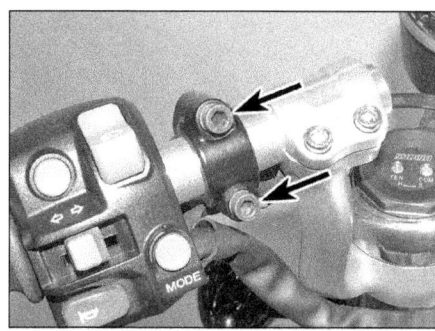

**5.7 Unscrew the clamp bolts (arrowed) and displace the lever bracket**

**5.8 Release the bands (arrowed)**

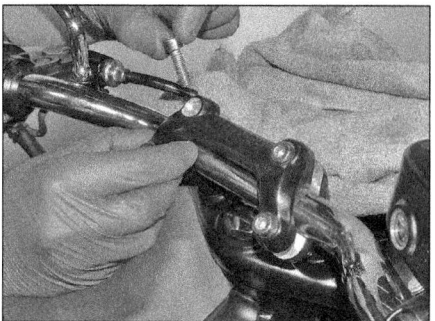

**5.9a Remove the clamp...**

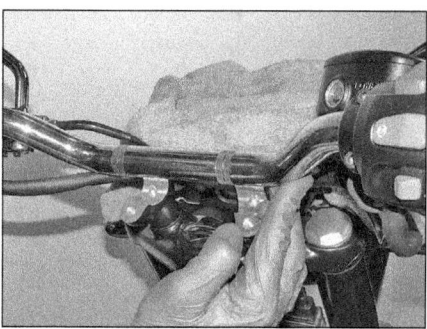

**5.9b ...then displace the handlebars from the holders**

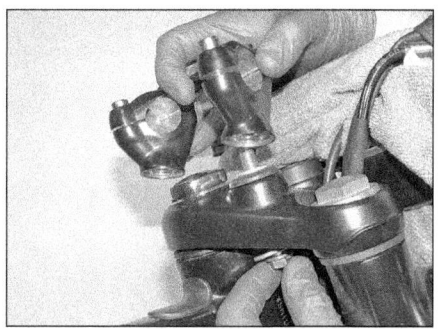

**5.9c Unscrew the bolts and remove the holders...**

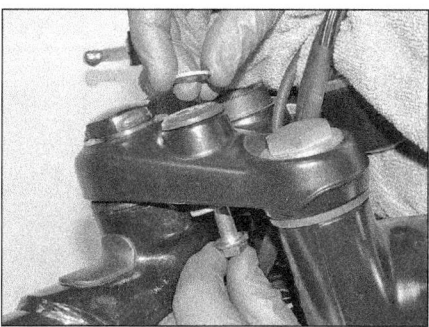

**5.9d ...the top washers...**

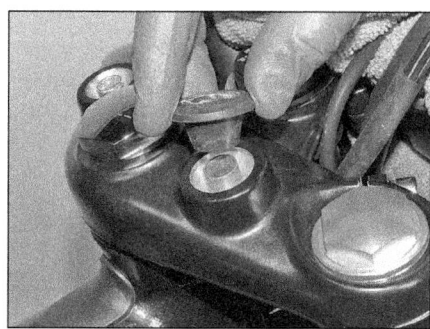

**5.9e ...rubbers and sleeves**

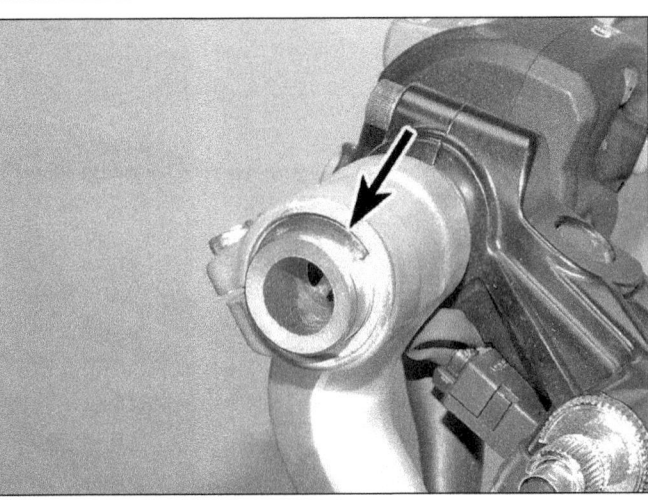

5.10a Slacken the clamp bolts (arrowed)...

5.10b ...then release the clip (arrowed)

**10** On the Thruxton and Thruxton R slacken the handlebar clamp bolts, then slide the bar in towards the centre until the retaining clip is exposed **(see illustrations)**. Release the clip and slide the bar out of the holder.

## Installation

**11** On the Thruxton and Thruxton R the right

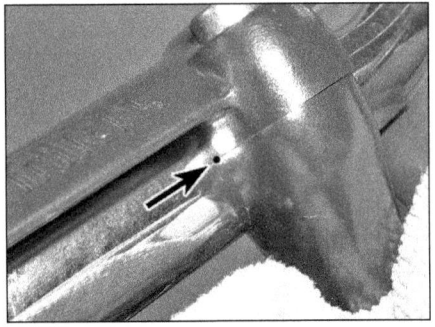

5.12 Align the clamp mating surfaces with the punch mark (arrowed) – T100, T120, Bobber, Street Twin type shown

handlebar has one alignment punch mark on its inner end, the left has two – make sure you fit them the correct way round. Slide the handlebar into the holder and fit a new retaining clip into the groove, then draw the handlebar out so the clip seats against the holder, aligning the bar so the punch mark(s) on the bar is/are between the split of the clamp, and tighten the clamp bolts to 8.5 Nm **(see illustrations 5.10b and a)**.

**12** On the T100, T120, Bobber, Street Twin, Street Cup and Scrambler, fit the handlebar holder rubbers and sleeve, washers, holders and bolts if removed, making sure the clamp is fitted onto the holders so they are correclty aligned, and that the bolts secure the cable guide on the T100, T120 and Scrambler, and are fitted with their washers on the Bobber, Street Twin and Street Cup, and tighten the holder bolts to 38 Nm **(see illustrations 5.9e, d and c)**. Remove the clamp and position the handlebars centrally, aligning the punch mark

on the front of the bar with the top edge of the inner side of the left-hand holder on the T100, T120, Bobber and Street Twin and the outer edge of the left-hand holder on the Street Cup, and the inner edge of the right-hand holder on the Scrambler **(see illustration)**. Fit the clamp and tighten the front bolts first, then the rear, to 24 Nm.

**13** On the Street Cup, if the bars were separated from the centre piece, slide the bar into the clamp so the punch mark is aligned with and between the outer edges of the split in the clamp, and tighten the clamp bolts to 8.5 Nm.

**14** Install the remaining components in the reverse order of removal, referring to the relevant Chapters where directed, and noting the following.

● Align the clutch lever bracket mating surfaces with the punch mark on the top of the handlebar **(see illustration 5.14a or b)**. Fit the clamp, where present with the UP mark facing up, and tighten the clamp bolts, top one first to 12 Nm.

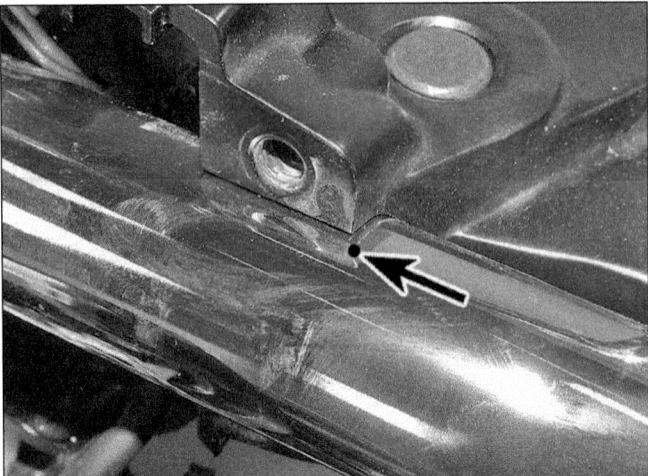

5.14a Align the clamp mating surfaces with the punch mark (arrowed) – T100, T120, Bobber and Thruxton type

5.14b Align the clamp mating surfaces with the punch mark (arrowed) – Thruxton R shown

5.16a Unscrew the nut...

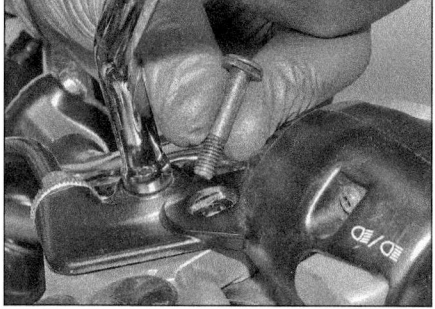

5.16b ... withdraw the bolt...

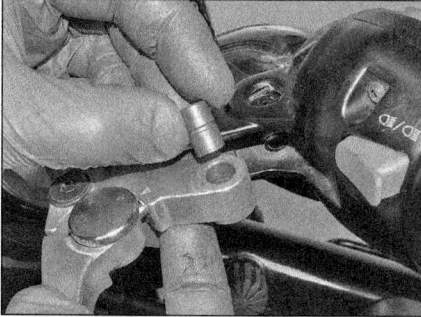

5.16c ...displace the lever and remove the sleeve...

● Check and adjust clutch cable freeplay (see Chapter 1).
● Check the operation of all switches, the front brake and clutch before taking the machine on the road.

### Clutch lever

**15** Create some slack in the cable (see Chapter 1, Section 10).

**16** Unscrew the lever pivot bolt nut, then push the pivot bolt out of the bracket, displace the lever and remove the sleeve if loose, then disconnect the clutch cable **(see illustrations)**.

**17** Installation is the reverse of removal. Apply grease to the pivot bolt shaft and sleeve and to the contact areas between the lever and its bracket, and to the inner clutch cable end. Align the flats on the underside of the pivot bolt head with those in the bolt head seat **(see illustration 5.16b)**. Tighten the nut to 3.5 Nm. Adjust the clutch cable freeplay (see Chapter 1).

### Front brake lever

**18** Counter-hold the head of the lever pivot bolt and unscrew the locknut **(see illustration)**. Unscrew the pivot bolt and remove the lever, noting how it locates against the master cylinder pushrod **(see illustrations)**.

**19** Installation is the reverse of removal. Apply silicone grease to the pivot bolt shaft and to the contact areas between the lever and its bracket and where the pushrod locates in the cup in the lever. Tighten the pivot bolt to 1 Nm, then hold the pivot bolt and tighten the locknut nut to 6 Nm **(see illustration 5.18a)**.

### 6 Fork removal and installation

### Removal

**1** Support the motorcycle upright on level ground so that the front wheel is off the ground.

**2** Remove the front wheel (see Chapter 6).

**3** Remove the front mudguard (see Chapter 7).

**4** Displace the wheel speed sensor from the bottom of the left-hand fork, noting the shim between it and the fork **(see illustration)**.

5.16d ... and disconnect the cable

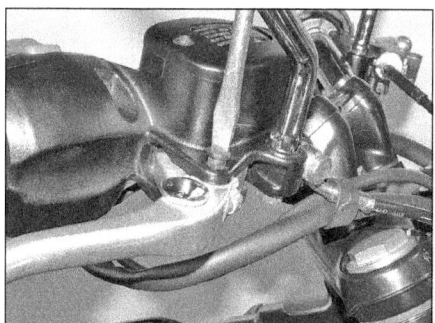

5.18b Unscrew the pivot bolt...

**5** Work on each fork leg individually. Note which fork fits on which side. Note the routing of the cables, wiring and hoses around the forks.

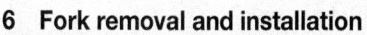

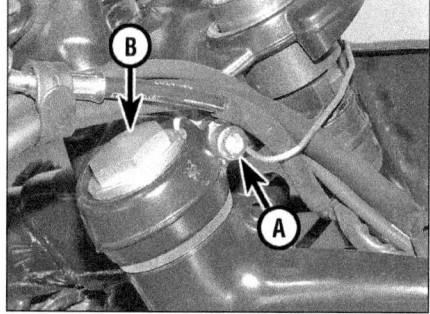

6.4 Undo the screw and displace the sensor, noting the shim (arrowed)

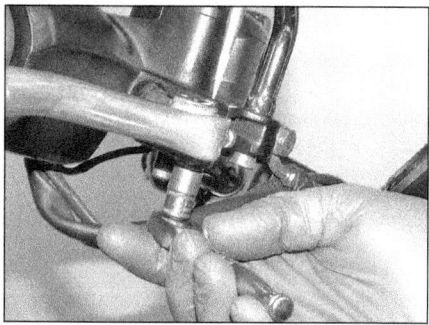

5.18a Counter-hold the pivot bolt when unscrewing and tightening the locknut

5.18c ...and remove the lever

**6** Note the alignment between the top of the fork outer tube and the top yoke, then loosen the fork clamp bolt in the top yoke **(see illustration)**. If the fork leg is to be

6.6 Slacken the clamp bolt (A) in the top yoke, then slacken the fork top bolt (B) if required

**6.7a Turn signal clamp bolt (A). Bottom yoke clamp bolts (B) – Bobber**

**6.7b Cable guide clamp bolt (arrowed) – Bobber**

disassembled, or if the fork oil is being changed, loosen the fork top bolt – on the Thruxton R the hex on the top bolt is shallow so you need to unscrew it using a 45mm socket without a chamfered edge for best grip, such as the Triumph tool part no.T3880186, or its after-market equivalent specifically for Showa's 43 mm big-piston forks.

**7** On the Bobber, Street Twin and Scrambler loosen the turn signal clamp bolt, and on the Bobber loosen the cable guide clamp bolt **(see illustrations)**.

**8** On the Thruxton and Thruxton R loosen the handlebar holder clamp bolt **(see illustration)**.

**9** Support the fork leg, then loosen the fork clamp bolt(s) in the bottom yoke and remove the fork by twisting it and pulling it

downwards, supporting the turn signal where necessary according to model as you do, and noting the routing of the turn signal wiring on the Bobber, Street Twin and Scrambler **(see illustrations)**. On T100 and T120 models make sure the headlight/turn signal assembly brackets remain seated between the yokes **(see illustration)**.

## Installation

**10** Remove all traces of corrosion from the fork tubes and the yokes.

**11** On T100 and T120 models make sure the headlight/turn signal assembly brackets are correctly seated and aligned between the yokes.

**12** Make sure the fork gaiter is in place.

**13** Slide the fork leg up through the bottom yoke, through the turn signal clamp, making sure the wiring is routed in the cut-out, on the Bobber, Street Twin and Scrambler, through the cable guide when fitting the left-hand fork on the Bobber, and through the handlebar holder clamp on the Thruxton and Thruxton R, and into the top yoke, making sure the wiring, cables and hoses are the correct side of the leg as noted on removal. Align the top of the fork tube with the top yoke as noted for your model, making sure each fork is the same **(see illustration 6.6, 6.7b or 6.8)**. Tighten the fork clamp bolt(s) in the bottom yoke to 45 Nm on the T100, T120, Street Twin, Street Cup and Scrambler, and to 25 Nm on the Bobber, Thruxton and Thruxton R.

**14** If the fork has been dismantled or if the oil has been changed, tighten the top bolt to 22 Nm on all models except the Thruxton R, and to 35 Nm on the Thruxton R **(see illustration 6.6)**.

**15** On the T100, T120, Bobber, Street Twin, Street Cup and Scrambler tighten the fork clamp bolt in the top yoke to 24 Nm **(see illustration 6.6)**.

**16** On the Thruxton and Thruxton R tighten the fork clamp bolt in the top yoke to 20 Nm. Tighten the handlebar holder clamp bolt to 20 Nm **(see illustration 6.8)**.

**17** If the fork gaiter was removed or the clamp loosened, seat the top of the gaiter against the underside of the bottom yoke and tighten the clamp **(see illustration)**.

**18** Install the remaining components in the reverse order of removal. Do not forget the shim between the wheel speed sensor and the fork, and when fitted check the air gap (see Chapter 6, Section 17).

**19** Check the operation of the front forks and brakes before taking the machine on the road.

## 7  Fork oil change

**1** After a high mileage the fork oil will deteriorate and its damping and lubrication qualities will be impaired. Always change the oil in both fork legs.

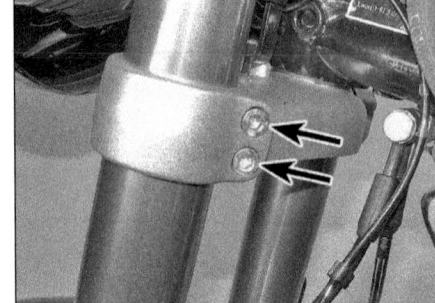

**6.8 Handlebar holder clamp bolt (arrowed)**

**6.9a Bottom yoke clamp bolt (arrowed) – T100, T120, Street Twin, Street Cup and Scrambler**

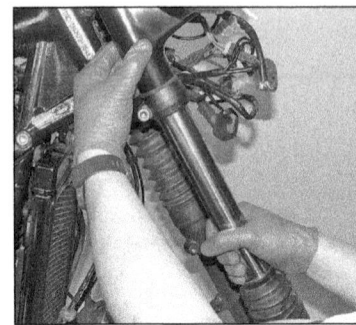

**6.9c Draw the fork down and out of the yokes, on the T100 and T120 making sure you do not dislodge the headlight/turn signal bracket**

**6.17 Push the gaiter up against the yoke and tighten the clamp**

**6.9b Bottom yoke clamp bolts (arrowed) – Thruxton R**

7.3 Remove the gaiter

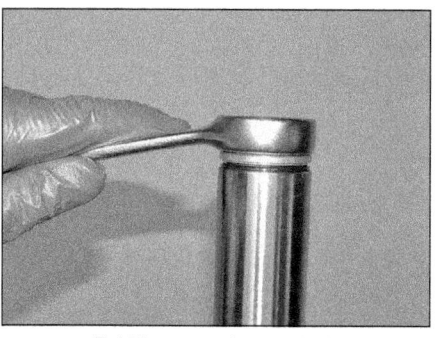

7.4 Unscrew the top bolt

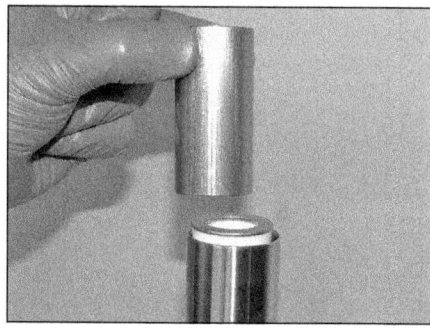

7.6a Remove the upper spacer...

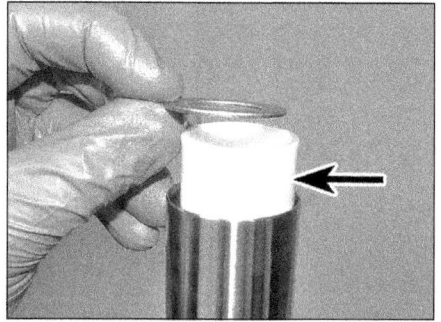

7.6b ...the washer and the lower spacer (arrowed)

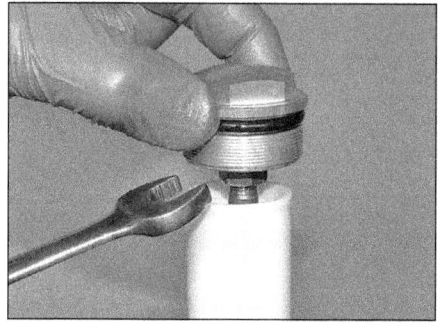

7.7a Fit a spanner onto the locknut...

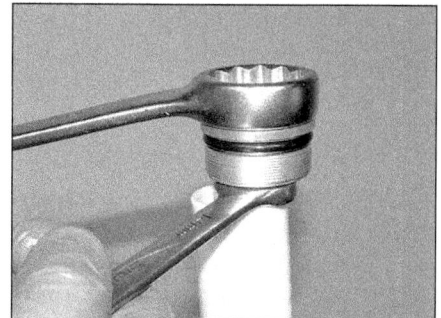

7.7b ...and the top bolt...

**2** Remove the fork (Section 6) – make sure you loosen the top bolt while the leg is still clamped in the bottom yoke.

### T100, T120, Bobber, Street Twin, Street Cup, Scrambler, Thruxton

**3** Slacken the fork gaiter clamp and slide the gaiter off **(see illustration)**.
**4** Unscrew the fork top bolt from the top of the inner tube – on the T100, Bobber, Street Twin, Street Cup and Scrambler, and on the left-hand fork on the T120, the bolt is under pressure from the fork spring, so if available use a ratchet tool so it does not need to be removed from the bolt as you unscrew it, and maintain some downward pressure on it, particularly as you come to the end of the threads, or alternatively hold the tool still and twist the fork tube to unthread it from the bolt **(see illustration)**.
**5** On the T100, Bobber, Street Twin, Street Cup, and Scrambler, remove the spacer **(see illustration 7.7d)**.
**6** On the left-hand fork on the T120, remove the upper spacer, the upper washer and the lower spacer **(see illustrations)**.
**7** On the right-hand fork on the T120, and on both forks on the Thruxton, hold the top bolt up and fit a spanner onto the locknut underneath it, then fit another spanner onto the top bolt and unscrew it until the locknut is at the bottom of the threads and the top bolt comes off **(see illustrations)**. Remove the spacer **(see illustration)**.
**8** Invert the fork over a suitable container for

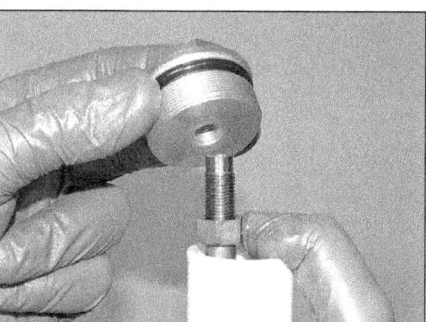

7.7c ...and thread the locknut all the way down and the top bolt off

the oil and catch the washer and the spring as they come out with the oil **(see illustration)**. Pump the inner tube, and the damper rod on the T120 left-hand forkand Thruxton forks,

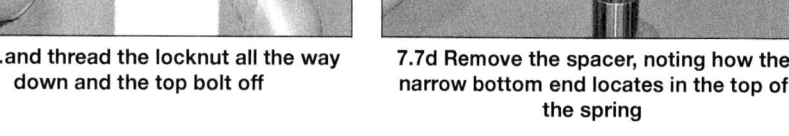

7.8a Tip the oil out and remove the washer and spring...

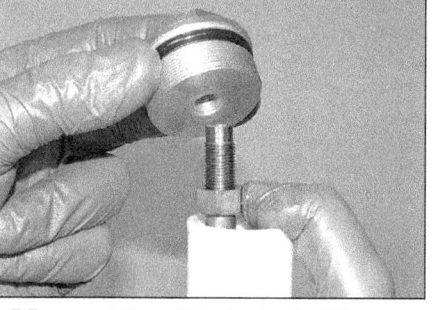

7.7d Remove the spacer, noting how the narrow bottom end locates in the top of the spring

several times to expel as much fork oil as possible **(see illustration)**. Support the fork upside down in the container for a while to allow as much oil as possible to drain, then

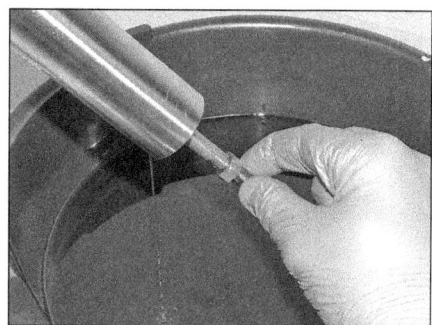

7.8b ... then pump the tube, and the damper rod as shown where fitted

**7.9a Fill the fork slowly to prevent air bubbles and overfilling**

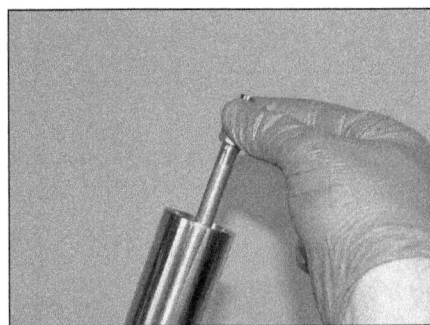

**7.9b Pump the tube, and the damper rod as shown where fitted**

**7.9c Measure the distance from the top of the tube to the oil**

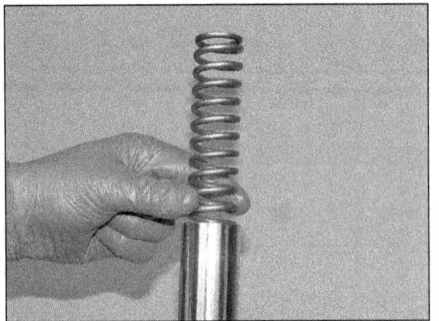

**7.10a Fit the spring...**

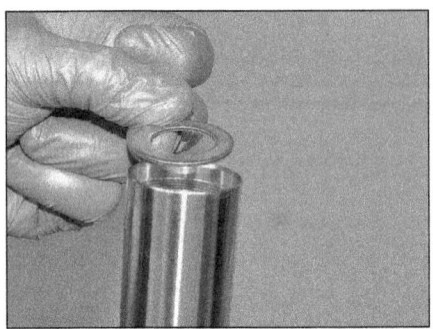

**7.10b ...and seat the washer on top of it**

pump again. If the fork oil contains metal particles inspect the fork bushes for wear (Section 8). Wipe any excess oil off the spring and spacer(s).

**9** Stand the fork upright. Slowly pour in the correct quantity and grade of fork oil as given in the Specifications **(see illustration)**. Now pump the inner tube, and the damper rod on the T120 right-hand fork and both Thruxton forks, slowly at least ten times to distribute the oil evenly and expel all air **(see illustration)**. Slide the inner tube down gently until it seats on the bottom. Measure the oil level from the top of the tube **(see illustration)**. Add or subtract oil until it is at the level given in the Specifications at the beginning of this Chapter for your model.

**10** Pull the inner tube out, then fit the spring

(see illustration). Fit the washer on top of the spring **(see illustration)**.

**11** On the T100, Bobber, Street Twin, Street Cup, and Scrambler fit the shouldered spacer with the shoulder facing down so it fits into the washer and the top of the spring **(see illustration 7.13)**.

**12** On the left fork on the T120 fit the shouldered spacer with the shoulder facing down so it fits into the washer and the top of the spring **(see illustration 7.13)**. Fit the upper washer and spacer **(see illustrations 7.6b and a)**.

**13** On the right fork on the T120, and on both forks on the Thruxton, lift the damper rod out and keep it extended, then fit the shouldered spacer with the shoulder facing down so it fits into the washer and the top of the spring

(see illustration). Make sure the locknut is at the bottom of the threads on the damper rod, then thread the top bolt on until its seats **(see illustration 7.7c)**. Thread the locknut up against the underside of the top bolt, then hold the top bolt and tighten the locknut **(see illustration 7.7b)**.

**14** If the top bolt O-ring is damaged or has deteriorated fit a new one **(see illustration)**. Smear some fork oil onto the O-ring.

**15** Extend the inner tube and thread the top bolt into it, making sure it does not cross-thread, and tighten it as much as possible while holding the inner tube **(see illustration 7.4)** – you can tighten the bolt to the specified torque setting when the fork has been installed in the bike and is held in the bottom yoke, but before the top yoke clamp bolt is tightened.

**16** On all models except the Street Cup fit the gaiter onto the fork, seating the bottom over the top of the outer tube. Do not yet tighten the clamp – do this after the fork has been installed so the top can be set at the correct height.

**17** Install the fork (Section 6).

### Thruxton R

**18** Adjust spring pre-load to its minimum setting (Section 14).

**19** Unscrew the fork top bolt from the top of the outer tube using the same 45mm socket referred to in the previous Section **(see illustration)**. The bolt will remain on the

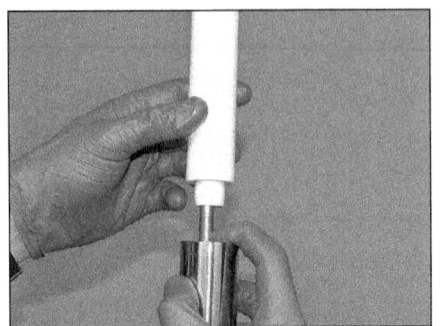

**7.13 Fit the shouldered end of the spacer through the washer and into the top of the spring**

**7.14 Check the O-ring (arrowed)**

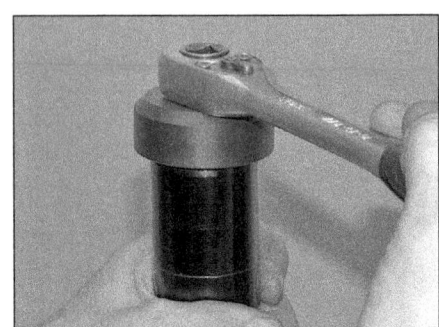

**7.19 Unscrew the top bolt**

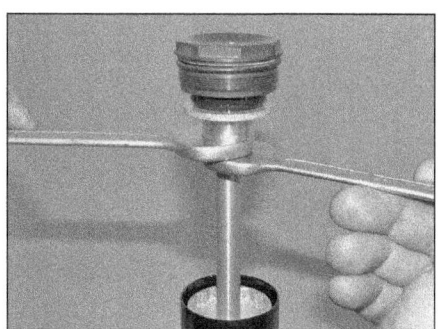
7.20a Hold the locknut and loosen the top bolt...

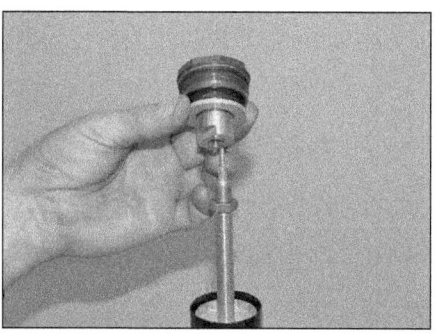
7.20b ...then unscrew the top bolt...

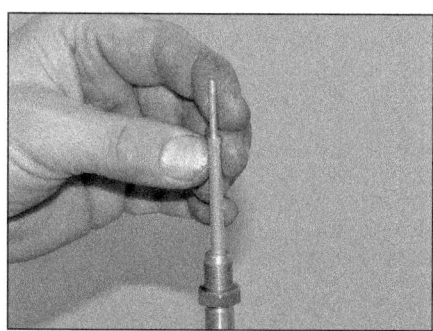
7.20c ...and draw the adjuster rods out

damper rod, held by the locknut on its top. Slide the outer tube down gently until it seats on the bottom.

**20** Counter-hold the locknut using one spanner and loosen the top bolt assembly using another spanner on the flats just above the locknut, then thread the top bolt off **(see illustrations)**. Draw the damping adjuster rods out **(see illustration)**. The top bolt should not be disassembled.

**21** Next you need either the Triumph service tool, Pt. No. T3880634, or an equivalent home-made set-up as shown **(see illustration)**, to fit into the bi-hex in the top of the rod guide in the top of the inner tube – the tool shown comprises two 35 mm nuts with circular flanges braised (or welded) onto each end of a piece of steel tube with an OD of 42 mm and 150 mm long. Place the bottom of the fork in a vice with pieces of wood to protect it as shown, then unscrew and remove the rod guide and damper assembly **(see illustrations)**.

**22** Get a suitable container to hold the oil, then tip the fork over it, drain the oil and remove the upper collar and the spring **(see illustrations)**.

**23** Support the fork upside down in the container for a while to allow as much oil as possible to drain. If the fork oil contains metal particles inspect the fork bushes for wear (Section 8). Wipe any excess oil off the spring and collar. Note that there is a lower collar that

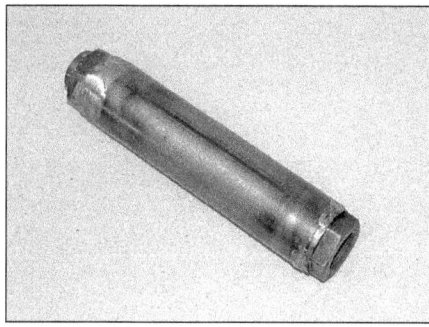
7.21a Home-made tool for unscrewing the rod guide

7.21b Secure the bottom of the fork in a vice...

7.21c ...then unscrew the guide...

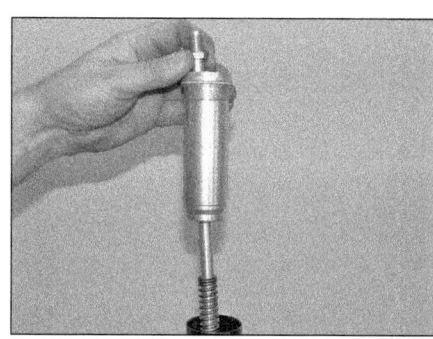
7.21d ...and remove the damper assembly

7.22a Drain the oil...

7.22b...and remove the upper collar...

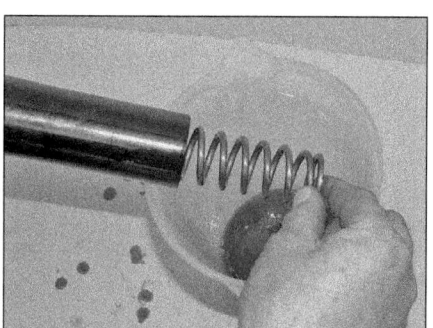
7.22c ...and the spring

**7.24a If removed, fit the lower collar**

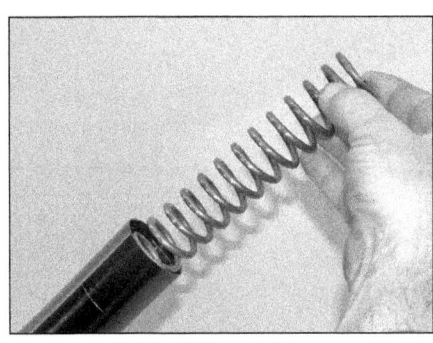

**7.24b Fit the spring...**

**7.24c ...and the upper collar**

may come out when you tip out the oil, though it didn't on the fork shown.

**24** If the lower collar came out, fit it with the rounded end at the bottom **(see illustration)**.

**7.25a Add the oil...**

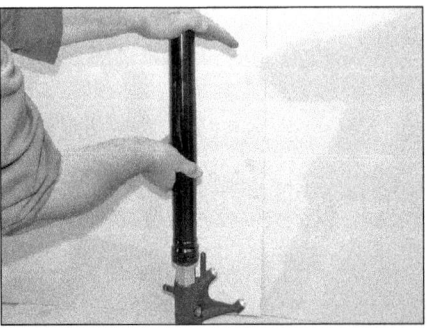

**7.25c ...then bleed the fork of air as described**

Fit the spring and the upper collar **(see illustrations)**.

**25** Stand the fork upright and slide the outer tube down gently until it seats on the bottom.

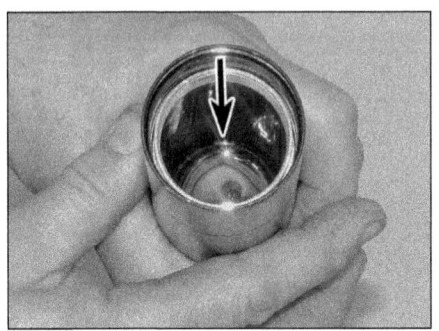

**7.25b ...up to the holes (arrowed)...**

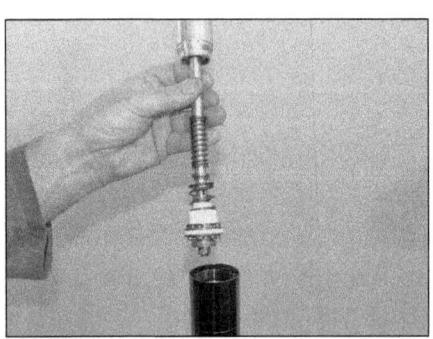

**7.26a Fit the damper assembly into the fork...**

Slowly pour in most of the specified quantity of fork oil, until it is up to the level of the holes in the inner tube **(see illustrations)**. Draw the outer tube up about 25 cm, then cover the top with your hand and slowly push it down **(see illustration)**. Remove your hand and draw it up, and repeat eight to ten times – this distributes the oil and expels all air.

**26** Place the bottom of the fork in a vice with pieces of wood to protect it as before **(see illustration 7.21b)**. Fit the damper assembly and rod guide into the top of the fork, then thread the rod guide into the inner tube and tighten it to 90 Nm if using the home-made tool described **(see illustrations)**. If you are using the Triumph tool that has an offset where the torque wrench fits into the tool, you need to calculate the reduced torque setting on the wrench so it takes into account the extra torque that the offset of the tool gives. To do this measure the length of the torque wrench from the end that is fitted into the tool to the centre of the handle and multiply by 90, then divide the result by the length of the torque wrench plus 25 mm (the extra length provided by the Triumph tool) – the result should give a figure of less than 90 Nm, and this is the figure that you must set the torque wrench to. For example if the torque wrench length is 300 mm, the torque setting required is 300 x 90 /325, giving a set torque of 83 Nm.

**27** Fit the damping adjuster rods into the damper rod **(see illustration)**.

**7.26b ...then thread the rod guide in...**

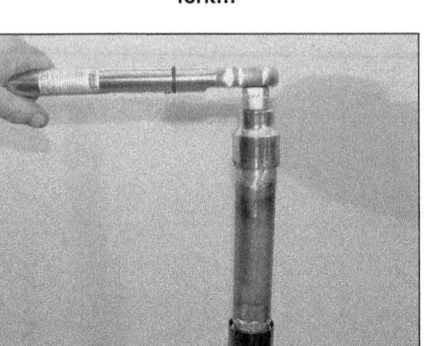

**7.26c ...and tighten to the specified torque**

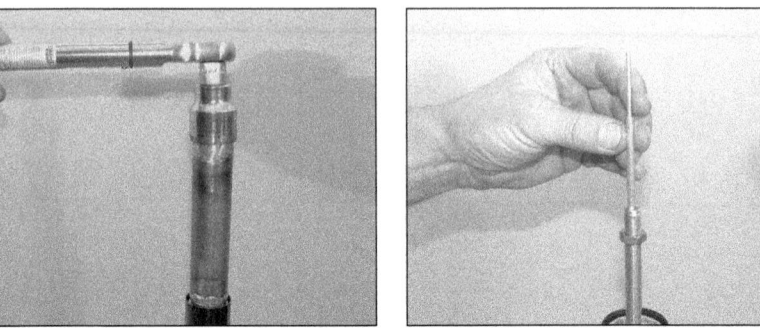

**7.27 Fit the adjuster rods into the damper rod**

7.28 Add the remaining oil

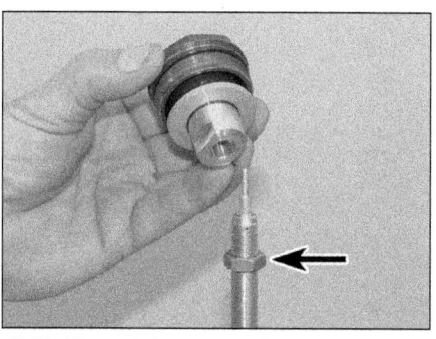

7.29a Thread the locknut (arrowed) all the way down, then thread the top bolt on until seated

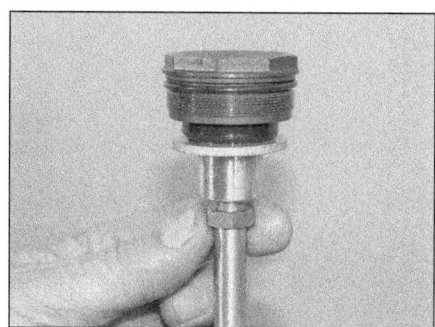

7.29b Thread the nut up against the top bolt...

7.29c ...then hold the top bolt and tighten the locknut against it

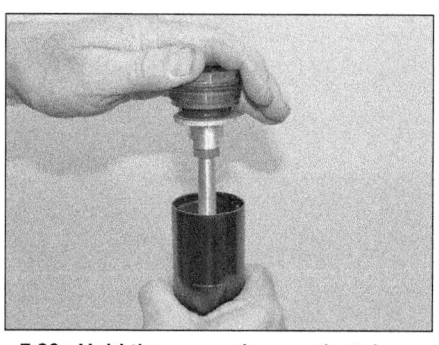

7.30a Hold the cap and pump the tube...

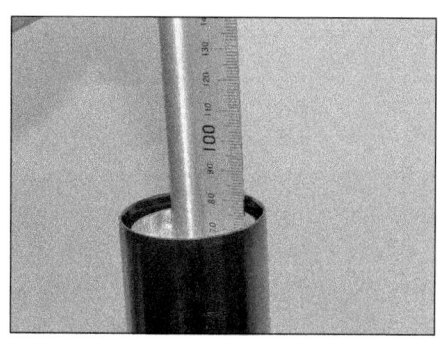

7.30b ...then measure the oil level

**28** Tip the remaining fork oil into the rod guide **(see illustration)**.

**29** Thread the damper rod locknut down to the bottom of its threads, then thread the top bolt onto the damper rod until it seats **(see illustration)**. Thread the locknut up against the top bolt, then counter-hold the top bolt using a spanner on the flats as before and tighten the locknut securely against it **(see illustrations)**.

**30** Hold the fork cap and pump the outer tube up and down several times, then slide it fully down **(see illustration)**. Measure the oil level from the top of the tube **(see illustration)**. Add or subtract oil until it is at the level specified at the beginning of this Chapter.

**31** If the top bolt O-ring is damaged or has deteriorated fit a new one **(see illustration)**.

Smear some fork oil onto the O-ring. Extend the outer tube and thread the top bolt into it, making sure it does not cross-thread, and tighten it as much as possible holding the tube by hand **(see illustration)**. Tighten the top bolt to the specified torque setting when the fork has been installed in the bike and is held in the bottom yoke, but before the top yoke clamp bolt is tightened.

**32** Install the fork (Section 6). Set the spring pre-load as noted or required (Section 14).

## 8  Fork overhaul

**Special tool:** *A dedicated fork bush and seal*

*driver is a good tool to have for this procedure, though not essential – an alternative method is given.*

**1** Remove the fork – make sure you loosen the top bolt while the leg is still clamped in the bottom yoke (Section 6). Always dismantle the fork legs separately to avoid interchanging parts and thus causing an accelerated rate of wear. Store all components in separate, clearly marked containers.

### *T100, T120, Bobber, Street Twin, Street Cup, Scrambler, Thruxton*

#### Disassembly

**2** When working on the right-hand fork remove the wheel axle clamp bolt **(see illustration)**.

7.31a Check and lubricate the O-ring (arrowed)...

7.31b ...then thread the top bolt into the tube

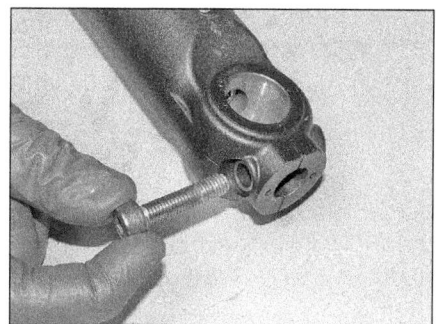

8.2 Remove the clamp bolt from the right-hand fork

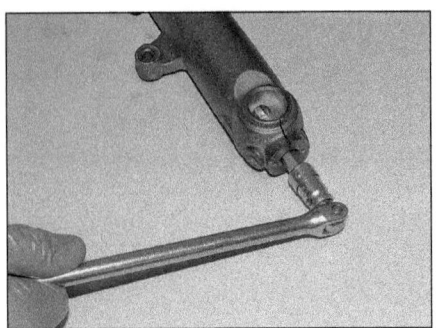

**8.4a Slacken the damper rod bolt as described**

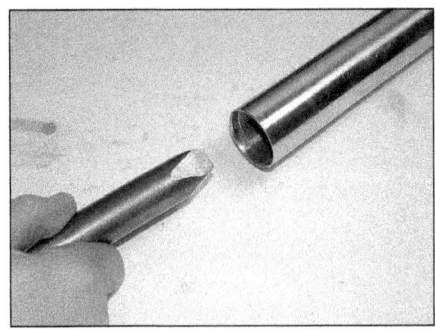

**8.4b Steel rod with end ground as shown to fit in the top of the damper rod**

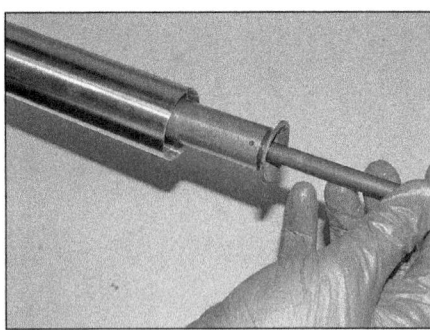

**8.6a Tip the damper out**

**8.6b Pump the rod to fully drain the cartridge**

**8.7 Prise out the dust seal using a flat-bladed screwdriver**

**3** On the Street Cup remove the fork protector, noting how it locates.

**4** Slacken then lightly retighten the damper cylinder/cartridge bolt in the base of the outer tube **(see illustration)**. If the damper turns with the bolt, compress the fork so the pressure of the spring holds the damper while the bolt is loosened. Alternatively use an impact wrench, if available. If the bolt cannot be loosened at this stage, for the right-hand fork on the T120, and for both forks on the the Thruxton, Triumph produce a holding tool, Part No. T3880633 which can be inserted down over the damper rod and onto the top of the cartridge once the spring has been removed – the tool has a shaped head that fits

in the top end of the damper cartridge to hold it while the bolt is loosened. For the forks on all other models you can try a broom handle tapered at the end and inserted so it fits in the top of the damper cylinder, and it usually does the job, or make a tool by shaping the end of a steel rod **(see illustration)**; stand this on the ground with its shaped end upwards and slide the fork over the tool, pressing it down onto it while unscrewing the bolt.

**5** Refer to Section 7 and drain the oil from the fork.

**6** Remove the damper bolt and its copper sealing washer from the bottom of the outer tube, using a holding tool as described in

Step 4 if necessary **(see illustration 8.4a)**. A new sealing washer must be used on reassembly. Tip the damper out **(see illustration)**. Note the rebound spring, which is loose on forks with a cylinder, and fitted on forks with a cartridge. On forks with a damper cartridge pump the rod to expel any residual oil **(see illustration)**.

**7** Carefully prise out the dust seal from the top of the outer tube **(see illustration)**. A new seal must be used on installation.

**8** Carefully remove the retaining clip, taking care not to scratch the surface of the tube **(see illustration)**.

**9** To separate the inner tube from the outer tube it is necessary to displace the oil seal and top bush from the top of the outer tube. The bottom bush on the inner tube will not pass through the top bush in the outer tube, and this can be used to good effect. Slide the inner tube in, then pull it quickly out so the bottom bush strikes the top bush **(see illustration)**. Repeat this operation until the seal and top bush are tapped out of the outer tube and the inner tube can be fully withdrawn **(see illustration)**.

**10** Slide the oil seal, washer and top bush off the inner tube, noting which way round they fit. A new oil seal must be used, but unless you have a dedicated seal installation tool keep the old one to use as an interface when driving the new seal in to prevent damage.

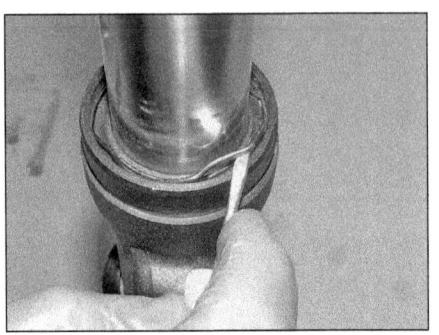

**8.8 Prise out the retaining clip using a flat-bladed screwdriver**

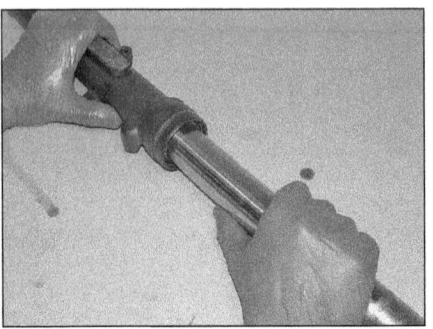

**8.9a Repeatedly draw the tubes apart...**

**8.9b ... until the seal and bush are displaced**

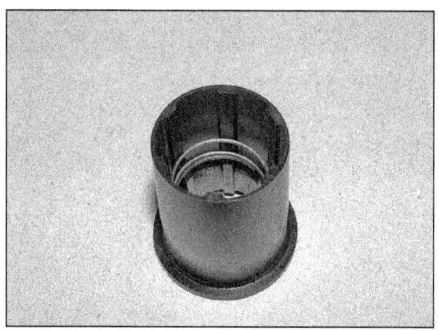

8.11a Retrieve the damper rod seat...

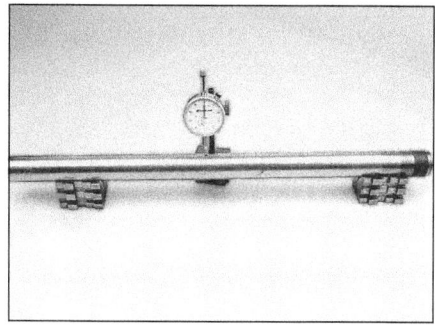

8.11b ... on some models there is a spring fitted in it

8.13 Checking the fork tube for runout

**11** Remove the damper seat – if it is not in the bottom of the inner tube, tip it out of the outer tube **(see illustrations)**.

### Inspection

**12** Clean all parts in solvent and blow them dry with compressed air, if available. Check the inner fork tube for score marks, scratches, rust spots and flaking of the chrome finish. Any such damage will result in premature seal failure. Fork inner tubes can be re-chromed using hard chrome, or replace them with new ones. Check the fork seal seat for nicks, gouges and scratches. If damage is evident, leaks will occur.

**13** Check the inner tube for runout using V-blocks and a dial gauge **(see illustration)**. A figure isn't given for runout but anything more than 0.2 mm should be considered beyond the limit.

 *Warning: If the tube is bent or exceeds the runout limit, it should not be straightened; replace it with a new one.*

**14** Check the working surface of each bush for wear **(see illustration)** – the surface should be Teflon grey all over. If the Teflon has worn to expose the material below the bush is worn. Only the top bushes are listed as being available separately, and they are not expensive, but the bottom bush is not listed and may only be available along with a new inner tube; check with a Triumph dealer as to availability of the bottom bushes. Do not

remove the bottom bush from its recess in the inner tube unnecessarily.
**15** Check the main spring for cracks and distortion. If necessary replace the spring in each fork with a new one – never replace only one spring.
**16** Check the damper cylinder or cartridge, and in particular the ring in the head of the damper cylinder, and the rebound spring for damage and wear. On forks with a cartridge make sure the rod moves smoothly and freely in and out. Check the damper seat, and its spring where fitted, for damage.

### Reassembly

**17** On forks with a damper cylinder fit the rebound spring if removed, and make sure the

piston ring is correctly seated in its groove.
**18** Slide the damper cylinder or cartridge all the way down into the inner tube so it protrudes from the bottom **(see illustration)**. Where fitted check the spring is correctly located in the damper seat **(see illustration 8.11b)**. Fit the seat onto the bottom of the rod, then push the seat up inside the tube **(see illustrations)**.
**19** Make sure the bottom bush is seated in its recess on the inner tube and lubricate it with new fork oil. Insert the tube into the outer tube and slide it fully down until it contacts the bottom **(see illustration)**.
**20** Lay the fork flat on the bench. Fit a new copper sealing washer onto the damper

8.14 Check the working surface of each bush for wear

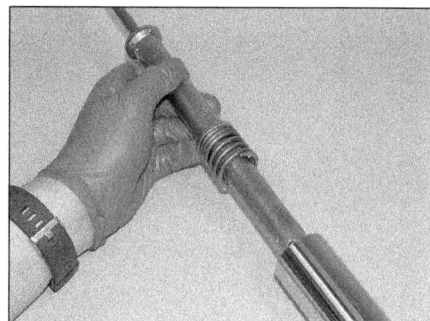

8.18a Slide the damper rod into the top of the tube...

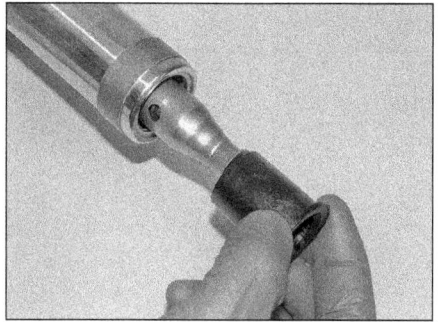

8.18b ... so it protrudes from the bottom, then fit the seat...

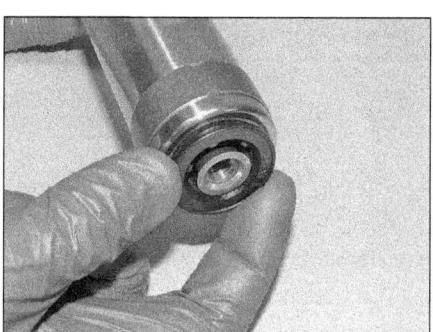

8.18c ... and push it into the bottom of the tube

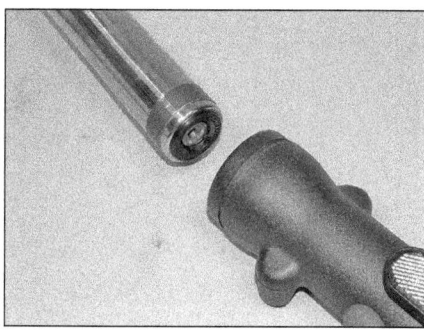

8.19 Fit the inner tube into the outer tube

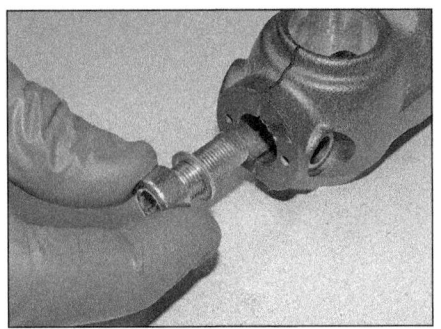

8.20 Fit a new sealing washer and apply threadlock

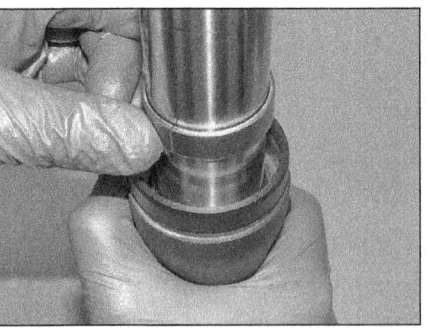

8.21a Slide the bush on...

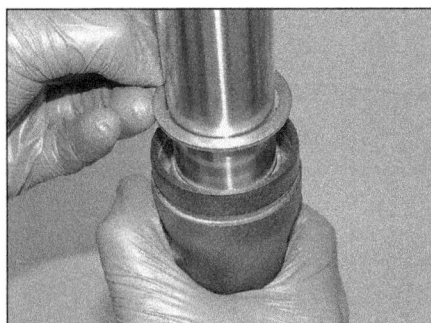

8.21b ... then seat the washer on it

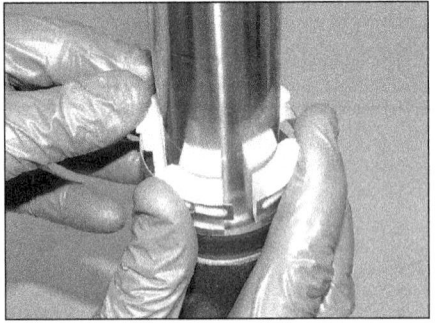

8.21c If using a proper fork seal installation tool fit the drive piece over the inner tube, into the top of the outer tube and onto the washer...

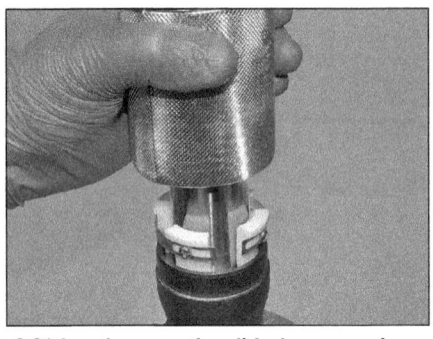

8.21d ... then use the slide-hammer piece to drive the bush in

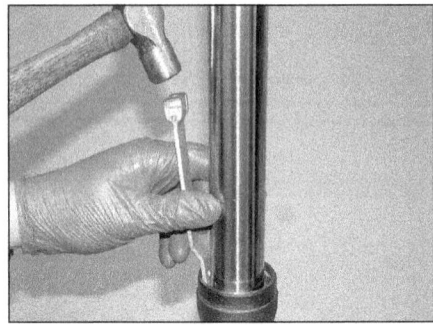

8.21e You can also drive the bush into place using a suitable drift – the one shown was specially shaped

8.21f Lift the washer to check the bush is fully recessed

bolt and apply a few drops of a suitable non-permanent thread locking compound (see illustration). Fit the bolt into the bottom of the outer tube, thread it into the damper and tighten it to 30 Nm. If the rod rotates inside the tube as you tighten the bolt, use the same holding method as on disassembly, or wait until the fork is fully reassembled and tighten it then (the pressure of the spring on the rod will prevent it from turning).

21 Lubricate the top bush with fork oil and slide it down the inner tube and into the outer tube (see illustration). Slide the washer down the tube and onto the bush (see illustration). Carefully drive the bush onto its seat in the outer tube using a dedicated fork seal tool if available, or a suitable drift, against the washer (which acts as an interface to prevent damage to the softer bush), turning the fork so the bush enters squarely if using a drift (see illustrations). Take care not to let the drift slip against the inner tube. You will know when the bush is seated as the tone of the impact changes, but lift the washer off to check (see illustration).

22 Lubricate the lips of the new oil seal with fork oil, then slide it down the inner tube and into the outer tube – make sure the marked side of the seal faces out (see illustration). Carefully drive the seal in and onto its seat using the same seal installation tool or drift (see illustrations 8.21d and e) – if using a drift slide the old seal onto the new one to act as an interface to prevent damage, then use a screwdriver to lift the old seal out when the new one is seated. The new seal is seated when the retaining clip groove is fully exposed (see illustration).

23 Fit the retaining ring into its groove (see illustration).

8.22a Slide the oil seal on

8.22b Check the retaining ring groove is fully exposed

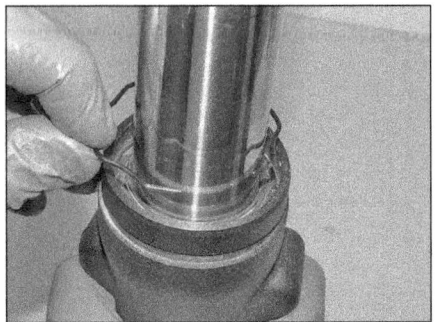

8.23 Make sure the ring seats fully in its groove

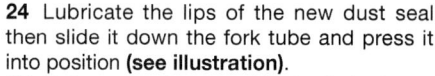

**8.24 Slide the dust seal down and press it into the outer tube**

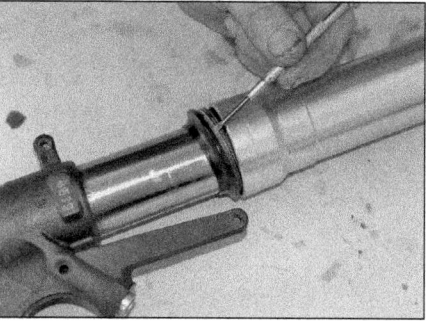

**8.31 Prise out the dust seal using a flat-bladed screwdriver**

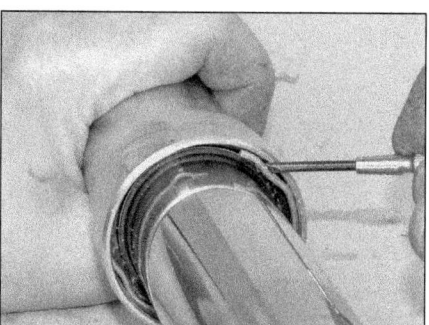

**8.32 Prise out the retaining clip using a flat-bladed screwdriver**

24 Lubricate the lips of the new dust seal then slide it down the fork tube and press it into position **(see illustration)**.

25 Refer to Section 7 and fill the fork with oil and finish reassembly.

26 If the damper bolt requires tightening (see Step 20), place the fork upside down on the floor, using a rag to protect it, then have an assistant compress the fork so that maximum spring pressure is placed on the damper rod head while tightening the bolt to 30 Nm.

27 On the Street Cup fit the fork protector, aligning the tab with the cut-out.

28 Fit the axle clamp bolt loosely into the right-hand fork **(see illustration 8.2)**.

29 Install the fork (Section 6).

### *Thruxton R*

#### Disassembly

30 Refer to Section 7 and drain the oil form the fork.

31 Carefully prise out the dust seal from the bottom of the outer tube **(see illustration)**.

32 Carefully prise out the oil seal retaining clip, taking care not to scratch the surface of the inner tube **(see illustration)**.

33 To separate the inner and outer tubes it is necessary to displace the bottom bush and oil seal from the bottom of the outer tube. The top bush on the inner tube will not pass through the bottom bush, and this can be used to good effect. Grasp the inner tube in one hand and the outer tube in the other and compress them slightly, then pull them apart so that the top bush strikes the bottom bush

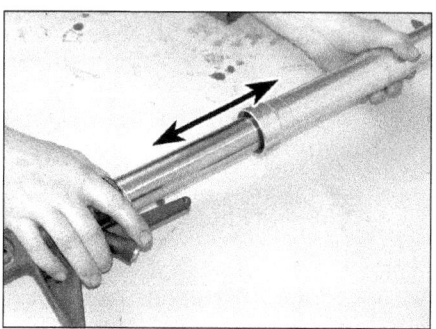

**8.33a To separate the tubes pull them apart firmly several times...**

**(see illustration)**. Repeat this operation until the bottom bush and seal are tapped out **(see illustration)**.

34 If the lower collar did not come out when draining the oil tip it out of the inner tube now **(see illustration)**.

35 Remove the top bush from its recess by levering its ends apart using a screwdriver **(see illustration)**. Slide the bottom bush, the oil seal washer, the oil seal, the retaining ring and the dust seal off the inner tube, noting which way up they fit. New bushes and a new oil seal and dust seal must be used.

#### Inspection

36 Clean all parts in solvent and blow them dry with compressed air, if available.

37 Check the fork inner tube for score marks, dents, pitting, scratches, flaking of its surface and excessive or abnormal wear. Fit a new

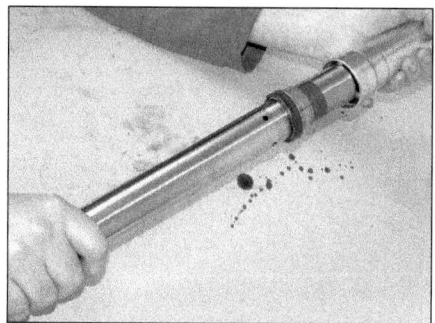

**8.33b...the slide-hammer effect will displace the oil seal, washer and bush**

tube if any are found. Check the inner tube for runout using V-blocks and a dial gauge.

 *Warning: If the inner tube is bent fit a new one.*

38 Check the fork outer tube for cracks. Check the fork seal seat and housing for nicks, gouges and scratches. If damage is evident, leaks will occur. Also check the oil seal washer for damage or distortion.

39 Check the spring for cracks and distortion. Note that spring length specifications are not given by Triumph. If necessary replace the springs in both forks with new ones. Never renew only one spring.

40 Check the condition of the piston ring in the bottom of the damper assembly and fit a new one if necessary **(see illustration)**. Also check the ring in the top of the rod guide **(see**

**8.34 Tip the lower collar out**

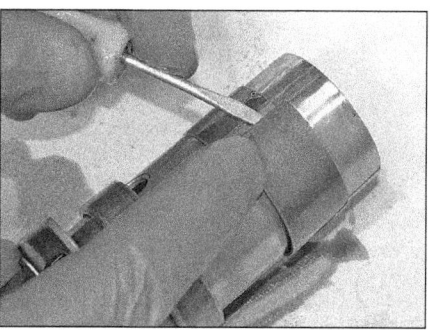

**8.35 Carefully lever the ends apart to expand it over the edge of its recess**

**8.40a Check the piston ring (arrowed)...**

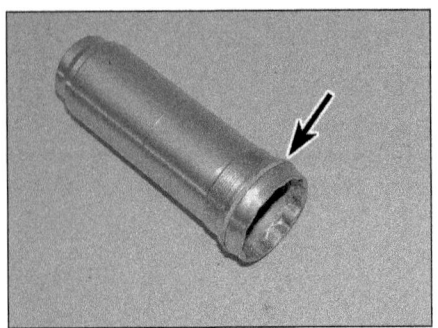

**8.40b ...and the ring (arrowed) in the guide**

**8.41a Use insulating tape to cover sharp edges...**

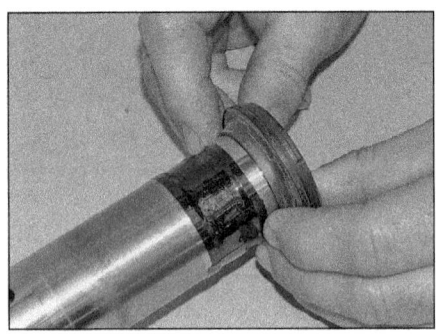

**8.41b...then slide the dust seal...**

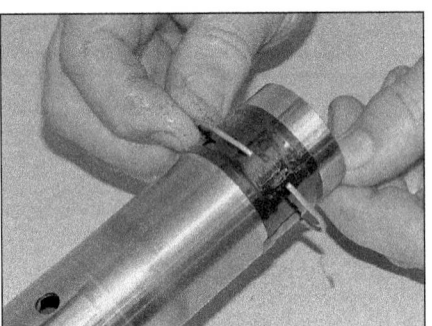

**8.41c ...retaining clip...**

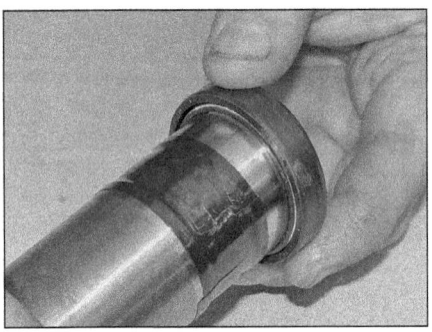

**8.41d ...oil seal...**

**8.41e ...and oil seal washer on**

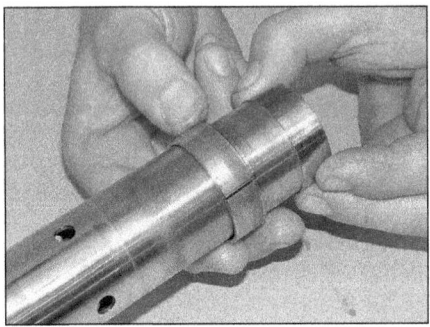

**8.41f Slide the bottom bush on...**

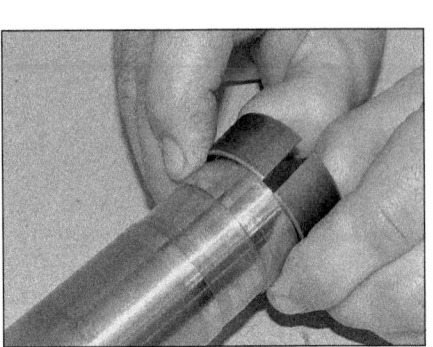

**8.41g ...then fit the top bush into its recess**

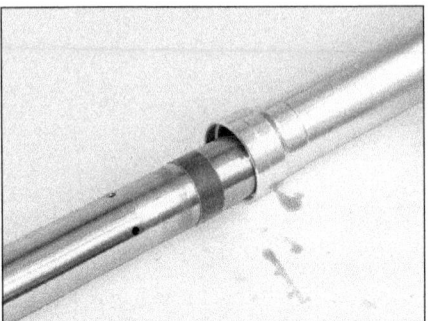

**8.42a Slide the inner tube into the outer tube**

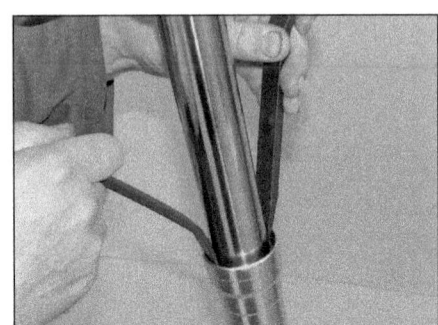

**8.42b Slide the top bush down and into the outer tube, squeezing its ends together to fit it**

illustration). Check all other components on the damper assembly for signs of wear and damage and if necessary fit a complete new assembly – the rings are the only components available separately. Make sure the damping rod and the damping adjuster rods are straight.

### Reassembly

41 Wrap one layer of thin insulating tape over the edges of the recess for the top bush in the inner tube to protect the seal lips **(see illustration)**. Smear some fork oil over the tape, and also over the oil seal lips. Slide the new dust seal, retaining clip, new oil seal, and oil seal washer onto the inner tube, making sure they are the correct way round **(see illustrations)**. Remove the tape, then lubricate the inner surface of the new bottom bush and slide it on **(see illustration)**. Fit the new top bush into its recess in the inner tube **(see illustration)**. Apply a smear of fork oil to the bushes.

42 Slide the inner tube fully into the outer tube **(see illustration)**. Support the fork upside down, and have an assistant hold the inner tube and the components on it up. Slide the bottom bush into the bottom of the outer tube, then squeeze the ends together using two suitable plastic or wooden tools to close the gap to allow the bush the drop in (if you are lucky), or at least to start to go in **(see illustration)**.

43 To get the bush fully in slide the oil seal

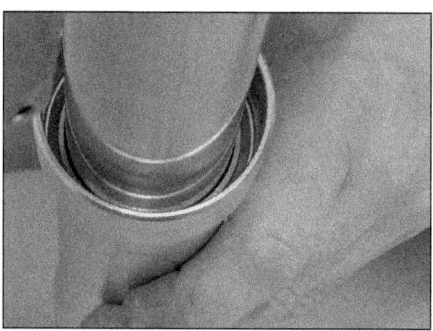

8.43a Use a drift to drive the bush in, with the washer as an interface…

8.43b…until the bush is fully seated

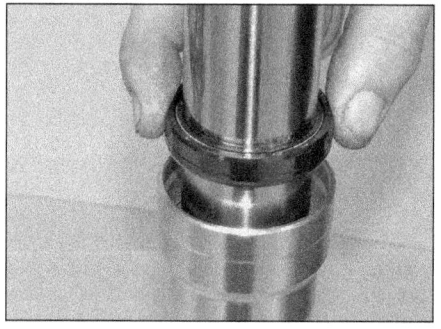

8.44 Fit the washer onto the bush

washer onto it **(see illustration 8.44)**. Using a fork seal driver tool **(see illustration 8.21d)**, or a suitable drift, carefully drive the bottom bush fully into its recess until the bush and washer seat – the washer prevents damaging the edges of the bush **(see illustrations)**. If using a drift, wrap tape around it to prevent scratching the inner tube. Make sure the bush enters the recess squarely. It is best to make sure that the inner tube is withdrawn as much as possible from the outer tube so that any accidental scratching is confined to the area that does not affect the oil seal. Lift the washer to check the bush is seated fully and squarely in its recess in the slider, then wipe the recess clean.

44 Slide the oil seal washer onto the bush **(see illustration)**.

45 Slide the new oil seal down and into the outer tube **(see illustration)**. Push the seal into place, driving it in as in Step 43 if you have the tool, until the retaining clip groove is visible. If you don't have the tool cut the old seal in half and use it as an interface between the drift and the new seal, and then push the seal in or use a piece of wood as a drift **(see illustrations)**. When the old seal is flush with the rim of the fork tube the new seal is seated – remove the pieces of old seal and check the retaining clip groove is visible **(see illustrations)**.

46 Fit the retaining clip, making sure it is correctly located in its groove **(see illustration)**.

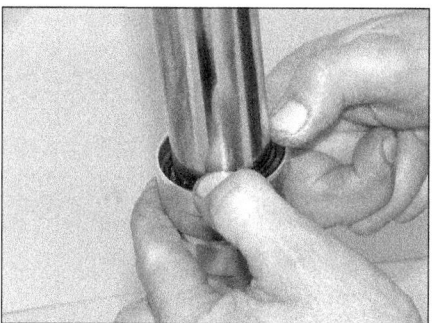

8.45a Slide the seal down and into the outer tube

8.45b Cut the old seal in half…

8.45c…and use it to push the new seal in…

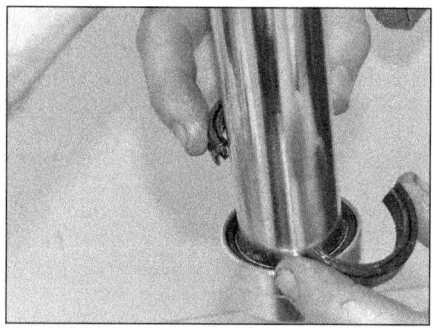

8.45d …or to protect it if driving it in …

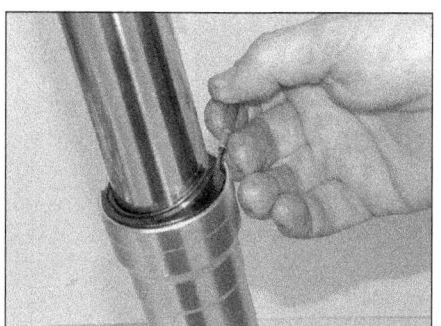

8.45e…then use a small screwdriver to retrieve it

8.45f Make sure the retaining clip groove (arrowed) is fully exposed

8.46 Fit the retaining clip in its groove…

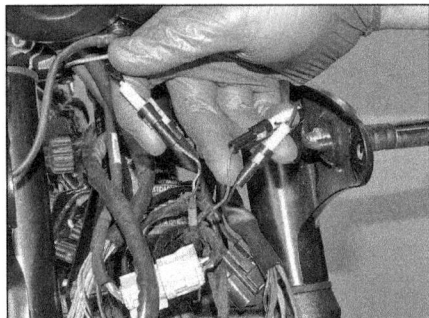

**8.47...then press the dust seal in**

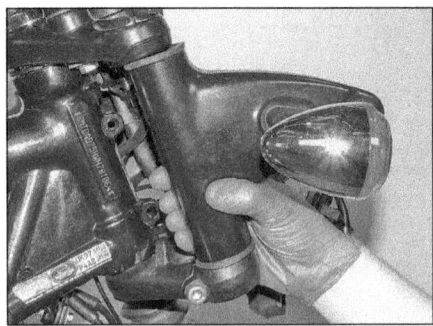

**9.5a Disconnect the turn signal wiring...**

**9.5b ...then ease the brackets out**

**47** Press the dust seal into the outer tube **(see illustration)**.
**48** Refer to Section 7 to fill the fork with oil and finish reassembly.
**49** Install the fork (Section 6). Set the spring pre-load as noted or required (Section 14).

## 9  Steering stem

**Special tool:** *Either the Triumph peg spanner, Part No. T3880023, or its equivalent bought commercially, is useful, but not essential, for slackening and tightening the adjuster nut and its locknut. The advantage of using a peg spanner is that the correct torque settings can be applied. If you are not using the peg spanner you need a C-spanner of the correct size, or an adjustable one, and the bearings must be adjusted by feel. You also need a 37mm socket or spanner to loosen and tighten the steering stem nut – this is not a common size, but they are available from good tool suppliers, or you can use a large adjustable spanner. The socket is preferable as the nut can then be tightened to the correct torque.*

### Removal

**1** Support the motorcycle upright on level ground so that the front wheel is off the ground. Remove the fuel tank (see Chapter 4).
**2** Remove the headlight and the instruments (see Chapter 8).
**3** On all models except the Thruxton and Thruxton R displace the handlebars (Section 5) – tie or support them clear of the yokes. If you are using a spanner to slacken and tighten the steering stem nut, you may also need to remove the handlebar holders and the top rubber dampers for clearance, depending on the type of spanner used (Section 5).
**4** Remove the front forks (Section 6).
**5** On the T100 and T120 disconnect the turn signal wiring connectors and remove the headlight/turn signal brackets from between the yokes, noting the rubber bushes **(see illustrations)**.
**6** On the T100, T120, Street Twin, Street Cup and Scrambler remove the regulator/rectifier (see Chapter 8).
**7** Stick some masking tape onto the top yoke and around the steering stem nut to protect its finish. Unscrew the nut, and on the Bobber remove the washer **(see illustration)**. Lift the top yoke, along with the handlebars on the

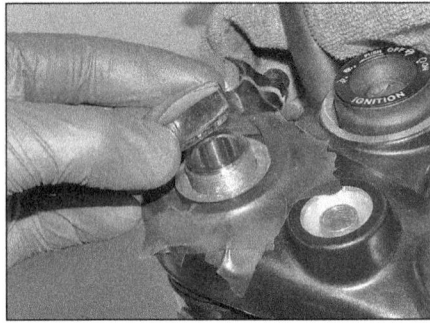

**9.7 Unscrew the steering stem nut then lift the yoke off**

Thruxton and Thruxton R, up off the steering stem and support it to one side.
**8** On the Street Cup, Thruxton and Thruxton R disconnect the turn signal wiring connectors. On the Street Twin, Street Cup, Scrambler, Thruxton and Thruxton R unscrew the bolts or nuts on the underside of the bottom yoke and remove the headlight/turn signal brackets, noting how they fit.
**9** Using either the Triumph service tool (Part No. T3880023) or a C-spanner, unscrew the locknut, then lift off the tabbed washer **(see illustrations)**.

**9.9a Unscrew and remove the locknut...**

**9.9b ...then remove the washer, noting how the tab locates in the slot**

9.10a Unscrew and remove the adjuster nut and bearing cover...

9.10b ... and remove the bottom yoke/steering stem

**10** Support the bottom yoke, then unscrew the bearing adjuster nut and gently lower the bottom yoke and steering stem out of the frame **(see illustrations)**. The bearing cover should come away with the nut, but if not remove it from the top of the steering head.
**11** Remove the dust seal, the inner race and upper bearing from the top of the steering head **(see illustrations)**.
**12** Remove the lower bearing from the bottom of the steering stem **(see illustration)**.
**13** Use a suitable solvent to remove all traces of old grease from the bearings and races and check them for wear or damage as described in Section 10.Do not remove the races from the steering head or the steering stem unless they are to be replaced with new ones – do not re-use the races if they have been removed.

### Installation

**14** Make sure the threads on the steering stem and in the adjuster nut are clean.
**15** Smear a liberal quantity of heavy duty lithium-based grease (Triumph recommend Castrol LCX222) onto the bearing outer races in the steering head. Work grease well into the upper and lower bearings. Fit the lower bearing onto the steering stem **(see illustration 9.12)**. Fit the upper bearing and its inner race and the dust seal into the top of the

steering head **(see illustrations 9.11b and a)**.
**16** If separated fit the bearing cover onto the bottom of the adjuster nut. Carefully lift the steering stem/bottom yoke up through the steering head, holding the upper bearing assembly so you don't accidently knock it out, and support it **(see illustration 9.10b)**. Thread the nut onto the steering stem and tighten it finger-tight **(see illustration)**.
**17** Triumph specify a torque setting for the adjuster nut, which can only be applied using their service tool or its equivalent (see Note above). With the tool fitted to a torque wrench, apply a torque of 40 Nm to the adjuster nut –

this will preload the bearings. Now slacken the nut and tighten it to the final torque setting of 15 Nm.
**18** If a tool isn't available tighten the adjuster nut using a C-spanner until all freeplay is removed, then tighten it a little more **(see illustration)**. This pre-loads the bearings. Now slacken the nut, then tighten it again, setting it so that all freeplay is just removed yet the steering is able to move smoothly (though it may feel a bit tight, but this is normal as the weight of the forks and wheel is not influencing the feel) from lock-to-lock. To do this, tighten the nut only a little at a time,

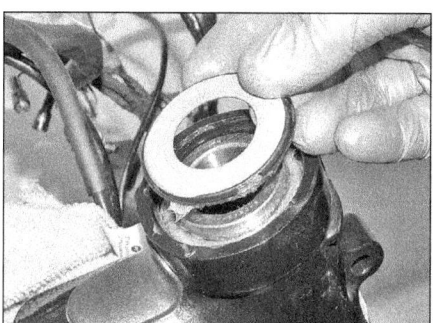

9.11a Remove the seal...

9.11b ... and the inner race and upper bearing

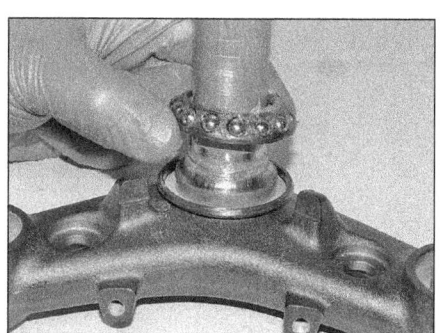

9.12 Remove the lower bearing

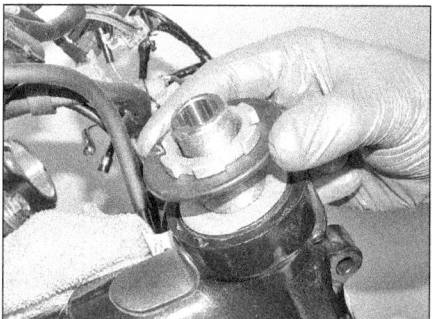

9.16 Thread the adjuster nut onto the stem

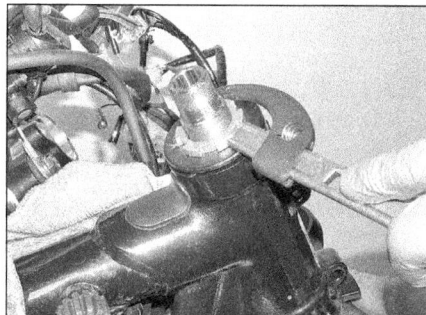

9.18 Using a C-spanner to tighten the adjuster nut

9.19 Thread the locknut onto the stem

9.20 When fitting the top yoke, where applicable make sure the rubber on the top of each headlight/turn signal bracket locates in the hole in the underside of the top yoke (arrowed – Thruxton R shown)

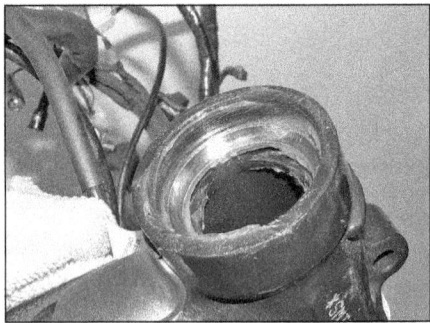

10.2 Check the inner and outer races for wear and damage

and after each tightening repeat the checks for freeplay and freedom of movement until the bearings are correctly set. The object is to set the adjuster nut so that the bearings are under a very light loading, just enough to remove any freeplay.

**19** Fit the tabbed washer, locating the tab in the slot **(see illustration 9.9b)**. Fit the locknut and tighten it to 40 Nm if the tool is available, or using a C-spanner if not **(see illustration)**.

**20** Install all components and assemblies, with the exception of the fuel tank, in reverse order of removal, referring to the relevant Sections and Chapters as directed above **(see illustration)**. Tighten the steering stem nut to 90 Nm.

**21** Carry out a final check of the steering head bearing freeplay as described in Chapter 1, and if necessary re-adjust – this is especially important if the correct torque

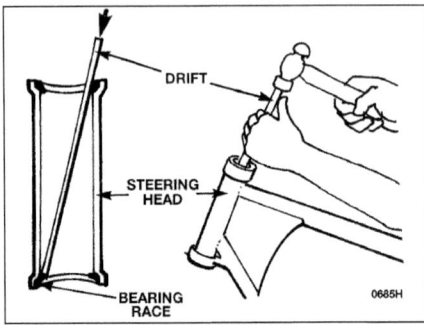

10.3a Drive the outer races from the steering head using a drift...

10.3b ... located in the cut-outs provided

settings were not applied to the adjuster nut and locknut as the extra weight and inertia of the forks, front wheel and handlebars will make a difference to the feel of the freeplay and movement checks.

## 10 Steering head bearings

### Inspection

**1** Remove the steering stem (Section 9). Using a suitable solvent, remove all traces of old grease from the bearings and races.

**2** Check for wear or damage – the races should be polished and free from indentations **(see illustration)**. Inspect the bearing balls for signs of wear, damage or discoloration, and examine their retainer cages for distortion, cracks or splits. Spin the bearing balls by hand. They should spin freely and smoothly. If there are signs of wear on any of the above

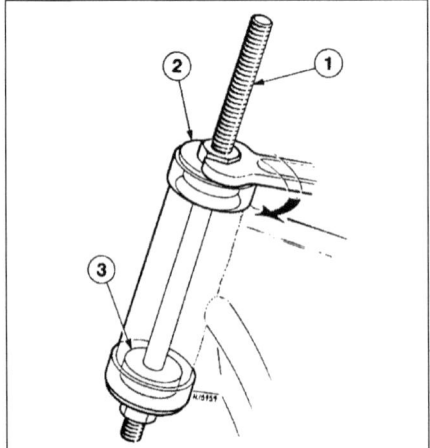

10.5 Drawbolt arrangement for fitting steering stem bearing races

*1 Long bolt or threaded bar*
*2 Thick washer*
*3 Guide for lower race*

components, both upper and lower bearing assemblies must be replaced with a new set. Do not remove the races from the steering head or the steering stem unless they are to be replaced with new ones – do not re-use the races if they have been removed.

### Renewal

**3** The outer races are an interference fit in the steering head and can be tapped out with a suitable drift located in the cut-outs in the head **(see illustrations)**. Alternate between the cut-outs so that the race is driven out squarely. It may prove advantageous to curve the end of the drift slightly to improve access.

**4** Alternatively, the races can be removed using a slide-hammer type bearing extractor – these can often be hired from tool shops.

**5** The new outer races can be fitted using a drawbolt arrangement **(see illustration)**, or by using a suitable tubular drift or socket that bears only on the outer flat rim of the race, and does not touch the sloping bearing surface of the race itself. Freezing the races first to shrink them will make them easier to fit.

**6** To remove the lower bearing race from the steering stem, first thread the nut onto the top of the stem to protect the threads, they lay the stem over on its side and use a punch or chisel under the base of the bearing seal to drive the seal and race up off the bottom yoke, taking great care not to damage the yoke – heating the race first with a hot-air gun should expand it a little to ease removal **(see illustration)**. Work the chisel around to ensure the race lifts squarely. Once there is clearance

10.6a Displace and remove the bearing inner race...

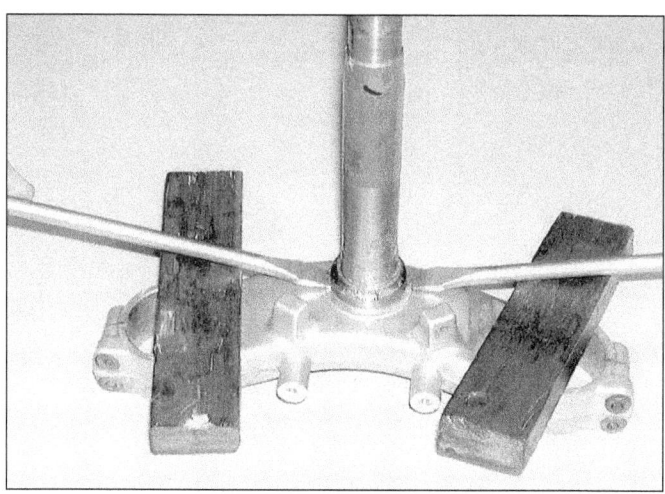

10.6b... using one or more of the methods described, as necessary

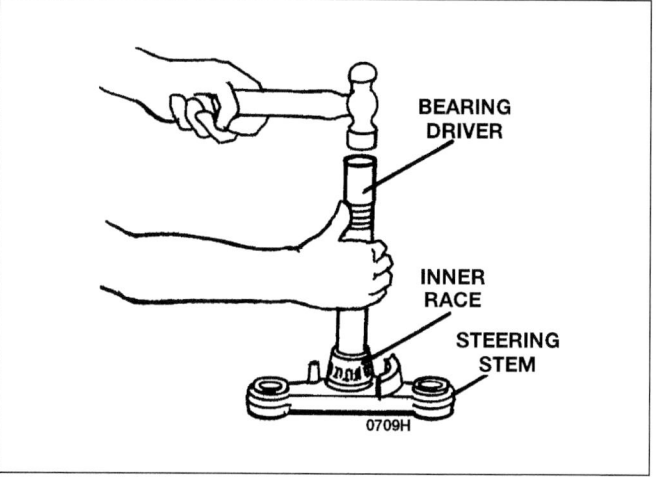

10.7 Drive the new bearing on using a suitable driver or a length of pipe

beneath the seal and race, use two levers placed on opposite sides of the race to work it free, using blocks of wood to improve leverage and protect the yoke **(see illustration)**. If the race is firmly in place, carefully cut it off using a Dremel or angle grinder – you will probably not need to cut all the way through, as often the race may crack after a groove has been cut, or you can work a screwdriver or chisel in the groove to finally split it. Alternatively, take the steering stem to a Triumph dealer.

7 Fit the new seal and lower race onto the steering stem. A length of tubing with an internal diameter slightly larger than the steering stem that bears only on the inner top flat rim of the race, and does not touch the sloping bearing surface of the race itself, will be needed to tap the new race into position **(see illustration)**. Heating the race first to expand it and cooling the stem in a freezer will make it easier to fit.

8 Install the steering stem (Section 9).

## 11 Rear shock absorber(s)

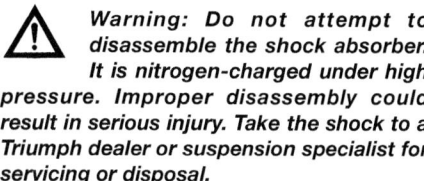

⚠ *Warning: Do not attempt to disassemble the shock absorber. It is nitrogen-charged under high pressure. Improper disassembly could result in serious injury. Take the shock to a Triumph dealer or suspension specialist for servicing or disposal.*

### Removal

#### All models except the Bobber

1 If possible remove and install the shock absorbers one at a time to avoid having to support the bike – one shock absorber maintains support while the other is removed. If you are removing both shocks at the same time support the motorcycle upright on level ground on an auxiliary stand or stands (but

not a rear paddock stand) – make sure that no weight is transmitted through any part of the rear suspension. You can use blocks of wood under the back of the frame **(see illustration 11.5a)** – use a rear paddock stand to initially raise the rear of the bike, then put the blocks under the frame, then remove the paddock stand. If you don't have a stand have an assistant tilt the bike to one side and place blocks under the high side, then carefully lift the bike onto the blocks and place blocks under the other side. Position a block or blocks of wood under the rear wheel so that it does not drop when the second shock is removed **(see illustration 11.5b)**. Tie the front brake lever on so the bike can't roll forward.

2 On the Street Twin, Street Cup, Thruxton and Thruxton R remove the silencer (see Chapter 4).

3 On the T100, T120, Street Twin, Street Cup and Scrambler unscrew the shock absorber bolts, noting the washers, and draw the shock off its mounts **(see illustrations)**.

11.3a Unscrew the bolts...

11.3b ... and remove the shock

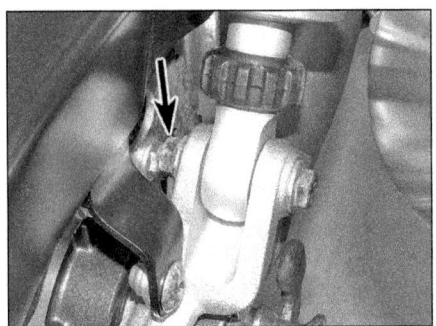

**11.4 Unscrew the nut (arrowed) then withdraw the bolt**

**11.5a Bike supported using blocks under the frame**

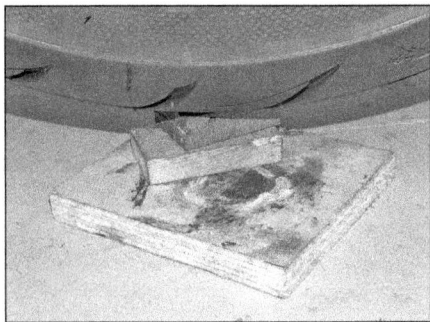

**11.5b Support the wheel using wood as shown**

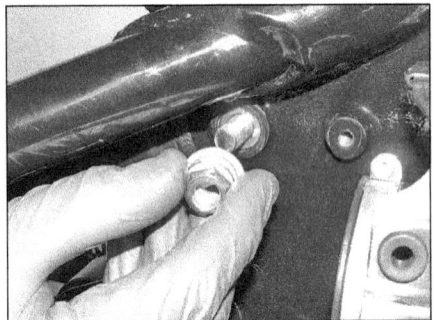

**11.8a Unscrew the nut and remove the washer**

**11.8b Slacken the adjuster sleeve a few turns**

**11.9 Unscrew the nut and withdraw the bolt**

**4** On the Thruxton and Thruxton R unscrew the nut on the shock absorber lower mounting bolt, then withdraw the bolt **(see illustration)**. Unscrew the upper mounting bolt, noting the washer, and draw the shock off its mounts. Note the sleeve in the lower mount.

### Bobber

**5** Support the motorcycle upright on level ground on an auxiliary stand or stands (but not a rear paddock stand) – make sure that no weight is transmitted through any part of the rear suspension. You can use blocks of wood under the back of the frame, but make sure they are clear of the regulator/rectifier and its wiring **(see illustration)** – if in doubt remove the regulator/rectifier (see Chapter 8). Use a rear paddock stand to initially raise the rear of the bike, then put the blocks under the

frame, then remove the paddock stand. If you don't have a stand have an assistant tilt the bike to one side and place blocks under the high side, then carefully lift the bike onto the blocks and place blocks under the other side. Position a block or blocks of wood under the rear wheel so that it does not drop when the suspension is detached **(see illustration)**. Tie the front brake lever on so the bike can't roll forward.
**6** Remove the seat (see Chapter 7).
**7** Remove the air filter housings (see Chapter 4).
**8** Unscrew the nut and remove the washer from the front mounting bolt **(see illustration)**. Push the bolt in a bit so the end is clear of the adjuster sleeve in the frame, but do not remove the bolt yet. Unscrew the adjuster sleeve a few turns using either the Triumph

tool (T3880166) or an equivalent tool that engages the slots in the rim **(see illustration)**.
**9** Unscrew the nut on the rear mounting bolt, then withdraw the bolt **(see illustration)**. Loosen the nut on the bolt securing the drop links to the swingarm **(see illustration 12.3a)**.
**10** Withdraw the front mounting bolt and remove the shock absorber **(see illustration)**.

### Inspection

**11** Inspect the body of the shock absorber for obvious physical damage and the coil spring for looseness, cracks or signs of fatigue.
**12** Inspect the shock damper rod for signs of bending, pitting and oil leakage **(see illustration)**.
**13** On all models except the Bobber inspect the pivot bush in each mounting for wear **(see illustration)**. No replacement parts are available.

**11.10 Withdraw the bolt and remove the shock**

**11.12 Check the damper rod (arrowed)**

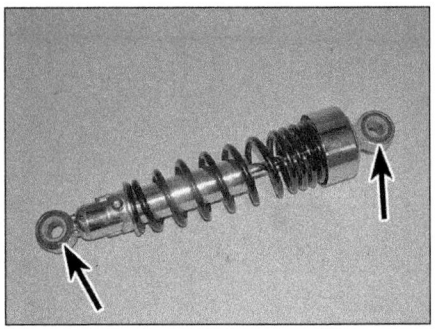

**11.13 Check the bushes (arrowed)**

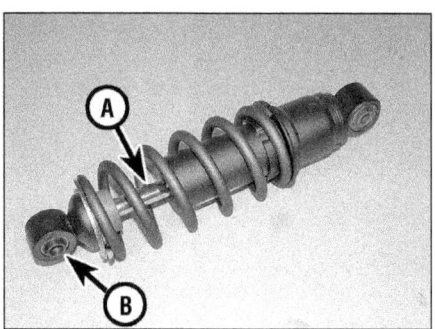

11.14a Damper rod (A), rear mounting bush (B)

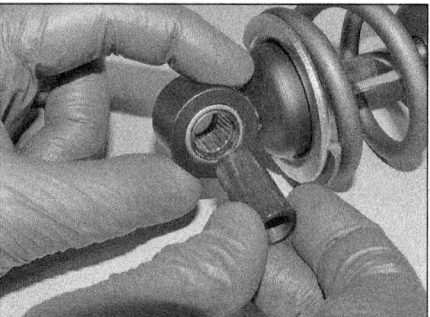

11.14b Withdraw the sleeve to check the seals and bearing

12.2 Unscrew the nut and withdraw the drop link-to-drag link bolt

**14** On the Bobber check the bush in the rear mounting for wear **(see illustration)**. Withdraw the sleeve from the front mounting and check the sleeve, seals and needle bearing **(see illustration)**. New seals can be fitted if required – lever them out with a screwdriver or seal hook, and push the new ones in with your fingers or a socket. A new sleeve can be fitted, but the bearing is not available. Clean off all old grease.

### *Installation*

**15** Installation is the reverse of removal, noting the following:

#### All models except the Bobber

● Smear some grease onto the mounting spigots.
● On all models except the Thruxton R fit the shock absorber with the pre-load adjuster lug facing out **(see illustration 11.3b)**.
● Clean the threads of the bolts and apply some fresh threadlock.
● On the T100, T120, Street Twin, Street Cup and Scrambler make sure the washers are fitted with the bolts, and tighten the bolts to 28 Nm.
● On the Thruxton and Thruxton R make sure the sleeve is fitted in the lower mount and the washer is fitted with the upper bolt. Tighten the upper bolt to 28 Nm and the lower bolt/nut to 48 Nm.

#### Bobber

● Withdraw the spacer and smear some grease onto the bearing and seals, and onto the outside of the spacer, then refit it **(see illustration 11.13b)**. Smear some grease onto the mounting bolt shanks.
● Fit the shock absorber with the label facing down.
● Insert the front bolt from the left, but do not yet fit the washer and nut **(see illustration 11.10)**. Insert the rear bolt from the right, fit the nut and tighten it finger-tight **(see illustration 11.9)**.
● Take up any slack in the rear suspension by lifting the rear wheel and supporting it in that position.
● Tighten the nut on the drop link-to-swingarm bolt to 80 Nm.

● Push the front bolt in a bit so the end is clear of the adjuster sleeve in the frame, and tighten the sleeve to 3 Nm using either the Triumph tool (T3880166) or an equivalent tool that engages the slots in the rim **(see illustration 11.7b)**.
● Fit the washer and nut onto the front bolt and tighten the front and rear bolts/nuts to 48 Nm.

### 12 Rear suspension linkage – Bobber

#### *Removal*

**1** Remove the shock absorber (Section 11).
**2** Unscrew the nut and withdraw the bolt

12.3a Unscrew the nut...

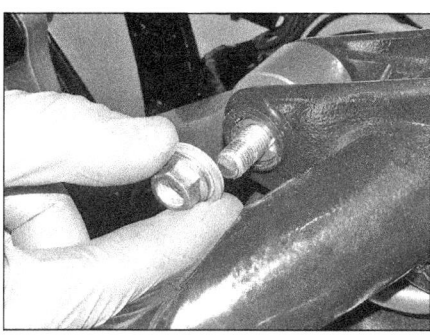

12.4a Unscrew the nut and remove the washer

joining the drop links to the drag link **(see illustration)**.
**3** Unscrew the nut on the bolt securing the drop links to the swingarm, then withdraw the bolt and remove the drop links **(see illustrations)**.
**4** Unscrew the nut and remove the washer from the bolt securing the drag link to the frame **(see illustration)**. Push the bolt in a bit so the end is clear of the adjuster sleeve in the frame, but do not remove the bolt yet. Unscrew the adjuster sleeve a few turns using either the Triumph tool (T3880166) or an equivalent tool that engages the slots in the rim **(see illustration 11.8b)**. Withdraw the bolt and remove the drag link **(see illustration)**.

### *Inspection*

**5** Withdraw the sleeve from each pivot of

12.3b ...withdraw the bolt and remove the drop links

12.4b Remove the drag link

12.5a Withdraw the sleeves from the drag link...

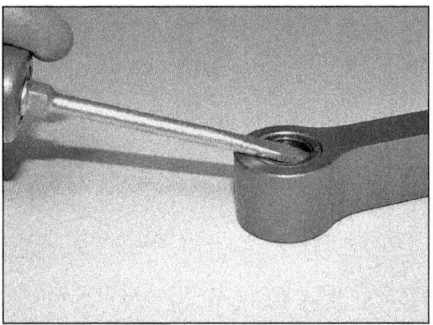

12.5b ... and the swingarm

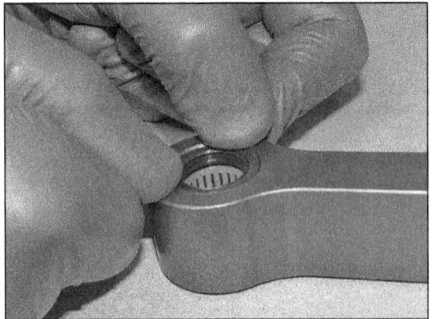

12.8 Lever the seals out

12.11 You should be able to press the new seals in with your thumbs

12.16 Tighten the adjuster sleeves to the specified torque

the drag link, and from the drop link pivot in the swingarm **(see illustrations)**. Thoroughly clean all components with a suitable solvent, removing all traces of dirt, corrosion and grease.

**6** Inspect all components closely, looking for obvious signs of wear such as heavy scoring, or for damage such as cracks or distortion. Inspect the bolt holes in the drop link ends for elongation.

**7** Check the condition of the needle bearings in the drag link and swingarm. Refer to *Tools and Workshop Tips* in the Reference section for more information on bearings. Slip each sleeve back into its bearing and check that there is not an excessive amount of freeplay between them.

**8** If the seals are obviously in bad condition, or if you are fitting new bearings, lever the seals out **(see illustration)**. Once removed

they cannot be reused – new ones must be fitted.

**9** Worn bearings can be driven or drawn out of their bores, but note that once removed they cannot be reused – new bearings must be fitted. The new bearings should be pressed or drawn into their bores rather than driven into position. In the absence of a press, a suitable drawbolt tool can be made up as described in *Tools and Workshop Tips* in the Reference section. When fitting the new bearings make sure they are central in their bores.

**10** Lubricate the bearings, sleeves and seal lips with multi-purpose lithium-based grease.

**11** Press and/or drive the new seals squarely into place with the marked side facing out **(see illustration)**.

### Installation

**12** If not already done, withdraw the sleeve

from each pivot of the drag link and from the drop link pivot in the swingarm, then clean the sleeves, seals and bearings, and apply multi-purpose lithium grease **(see illustrations 12.5a and b)**. Refit the sleeves.

**13** Install the drag link, drop links and shock absorber (Section 11) in reverse order of removal, but do not fit the washers or nuts onto the front bolts securing the drag link and shock absorber to the frame, and tighten all other bolts/nuts finger-tight only – insert the front bolts for the drag link and shock absorber from the left-hand side and the rear bolts and the drop link-to-swingarm bolt from the right.

**14** Take up any slack in the rear suspension by lifting the rear wheel and supporting it in that position.

**15** Tighten the nut on the drop link-to-swingarm bolt to 80 Nm.

**16** Push the drag link and shock absorber front bolts in a bit so the ends are clear of the adjuster sleeves in the frame, and tighten the sleeves to 3 Nm using either the Triumph tool (T3880166) or an equivalent tool that engages the slots in the rim **(see illustration)**. Fit the washers and nuts onto the front bolts and tighten them to 48 Nm.

**17** Tighten the drop link-to-drag link bolt/nut and then the shock absorber rear bolt/nut to 48 Nm.

**18** Install the air filter housings (see Chapter 4) and the seat (see Chapter 7), then remove the supports and if removed install the regulator/rectifier (see Chapter 8).

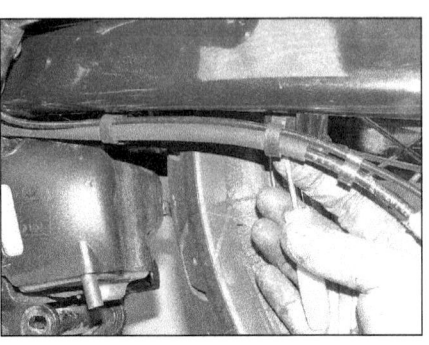

13.2 Release the hose guide clips by pushing one side in using a small screwdriver

13.3 Undo the two screws and remove the chain guard

### 13 Swingarm

### Removal

#### All models except the Bobber

**1** Refer to Section 11 and support the bike as described.

**2** Release the rear brake hose and the ABS rear wheel sensor wire from the swingarm **(see illustration)**.

**3** Remove the chain guard **(see illustration)**.

**4** Remove the rear wheel (see Chapter 6).
**5** Remove the shock absorbers (Section 11).
**6** Lay the drive chain over the outside of the swingarm with some rag between them.
**7** Remove the front sprocket cover (see Chapter 6).
**8** On the Thruxton and Thruxton R remove the left-hand heel guard, then unscrew the footrest bracket bolts and displace the footrest/gearchange lever assembly.
**9** Remove the swingarm pivot cover from the left-hand side of the frame **(see illustration)**. On the right-hand side unscrew the swingarm pivot bolt nut and remove the washer **(see illustration)**. Withdraw the swingarm pivot with its washer from the left-hand side, then slide it part-way into the right-hand side so it keeps the swingarm in position but does not go all the way through the adjuster sleeve in the left-hand side of the frame **(see**

13.9a Remove the cover

13.9b Unscrew the nut and remove the washer

**illustrations)**. Unscrew the adjuster sleeve a few turns using either the Triumph tool (T3880104) or an equivalent tool that engages the slots in the rim **(see illustration)**.
**10** Support the swingarm, then withdraw

the pivot bolt with its washer and remove the swingarm **(see illustration)**.

**Bobber**

**11** Refer to Section 11 and support the bike as described.

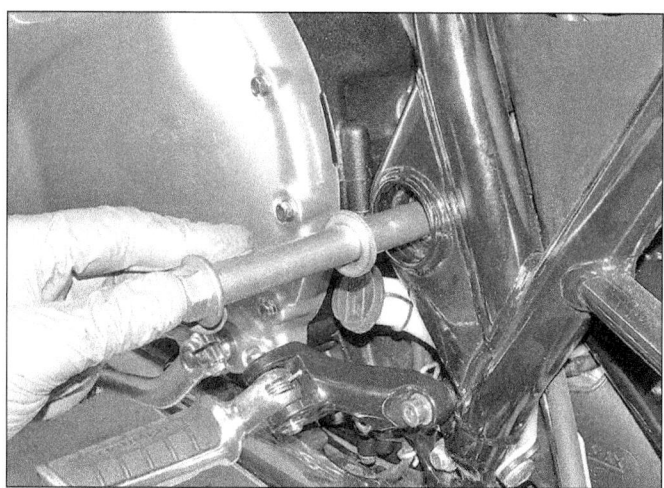

13.9c Withdraw the bolt from the left...

13.9d ...and refit it from the right

13.9e Unscrew the adjuster sleeve a few turns

13.10 Withdraw the bolt and remove the swingarm

13.12 Undo the hose guide screw

13.13 Chainguard is retained by two screws

13.17a Remove the cover from each side

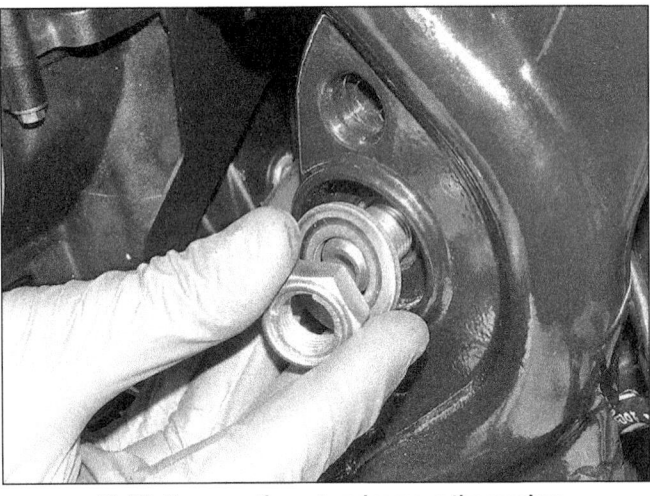

13.17b Unscrew the nut and remove the washer

13.17c Unscrew the adjuster sleeve a few turns

12  Release the rear brake hose and the ABS rear wheel sensor wire from the swingarm **(see illustration)**.

13  Remove the chain guard **(see illustration)**.

14  Remove the rear wheel (see Chapter 6).

15  Remove the rear mudguard (see Chapter 7).

16  Remove the suspension linkage drop link-to-swingarm bolt **(see illustrations 12.3a and b)**.

17  Slacken each swingarm pivot cover screw until the covers can be removed **(see illustration)**. On the left-hand side unscrew the swingarm pivot bolt nut and remove the washer **(see illustration)**. Push the swingarm pivot bolt in so the end is clear of the adjuster sleeve in the frame. Unscrew the adjuster sleeve a few turns using either the Triumph tool (T3880104) or an equivalent tool that engages the slots in the rim **(see illustration)**.

18  Support the swingarm, then withdraw the pivot bolt with its washer and remove the swingarm **(see illustrations)**.

13.18a Withdraw the bolt...

13.18b ... and remove the swingarm

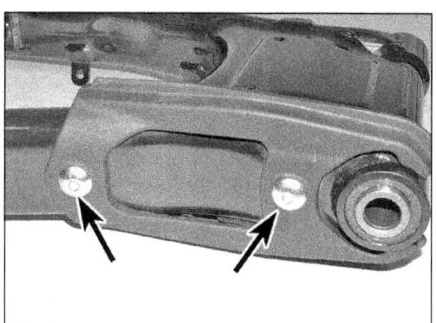

**13.19a Chain slider screws (arrowed) – all models except the Bobber**

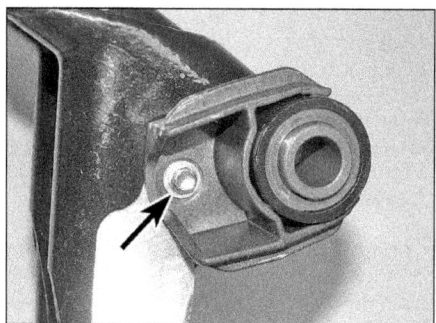

**13.19b Chain slider screw (arrowed)...**

**13.19c ...and swingarm protector screw (arrowed) – Bobber**

## Inspection

**19** If required remove the chain slider, along with the swingarm protector on the Bobber **(see illustrations)**. If the slider is badly worn or damaged fit a new one. On the Bobber also remove the bottom chain slider.

**20** Thoroughly clean the swingarm, removing all traces of dirt, corrosion and grease. Check the swingarm for cracks or distortion due to accident damage.

**21** Withdraw the bearing sleeve from the right-hand side and the spacer from the left **(see illustrations)**. Clean all old grease off the sleeve, spacer and the seals and bearings in each pivot.

**22** Inspect the bearings for signs of wear such as pitting and heavy scoring **(see illustration)**. Replace them with new ones if necessary (see below).

**23** Remove any old grease and corrosion from the swingarm pivot bolt. Check the bolt is straight by rolling it on a flat surface such as a piece of plate glass.

## Seal and bearing renewal

**24** If not already done withdraw the bearing sleeve from the right-hand side and the spacer from the left **(see illustrations 13.21a and b)**. Withdraw the central sleeve from the right-hand side **(see illustration)**.

**25** Lever the seal out from each side using a screwdriver or seal hook **(see illustration)**.

**26** A needle roller bearing is fitted in the right-hand side and two identical ball bearings secured by a circlip are in the left side. On the Thruxton and Thruxton R there is an inner seal fitted behind the needle bearing. Remove the circlip from the left side **(see illustration)**. Referring to the information in *Tools and*

*Workshop Tips* in the Reference section if required, first drive out the ball bearings using a long drift inserted from the right. Drive the needle bearing out, along with the inner seal on the Thruxton and Thruxton R, in the same way with the drift inserted from the left. Alternatively you can use a knife-edge puller with slide-hammer attachment to remove the bearings.

**27** Inspect the bearing seats and remove any scoring or corrosion carefully with steel wool or a suitable scraper.

**28** On the Thruxton and Thruxton R first fit the inner seal against its seat with its marked side facing out – the seal is lightly narrower than the outer seal.

**29** Fit the new bearings with the marked sides facing out. The new needle bearing must be pressed or drawn into the right-hand side, and not driven in as the impact will

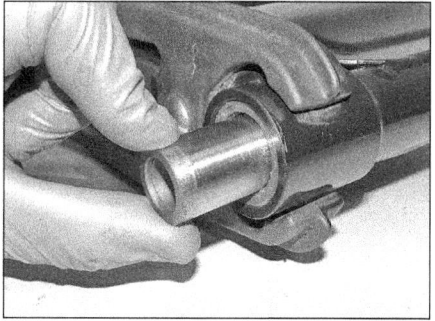

**13.21a Withdraw the sleeve...**

**13.21b ... and remove the spacer**

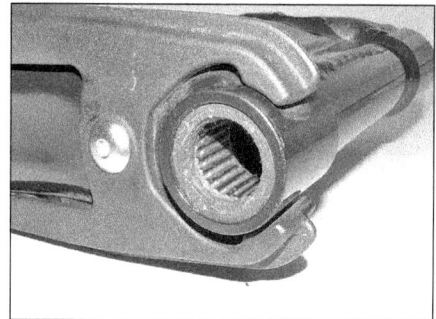

**13.22 Check the bearing(s) in each pivot**

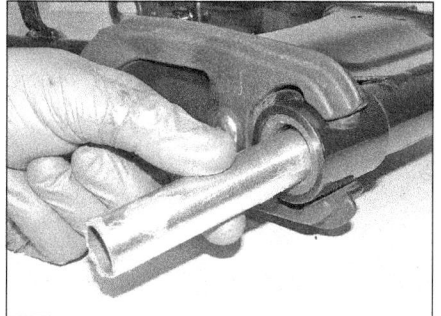

**13.24 Draw the sleeve out from between the bearings**

**13.25 Remove the seals**

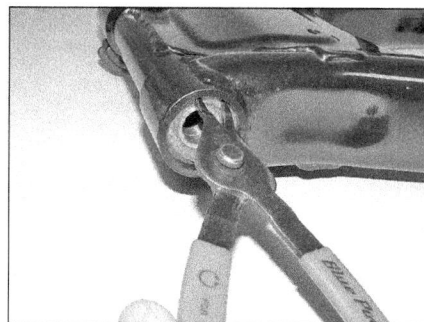

**13.26 Remove the circlip**

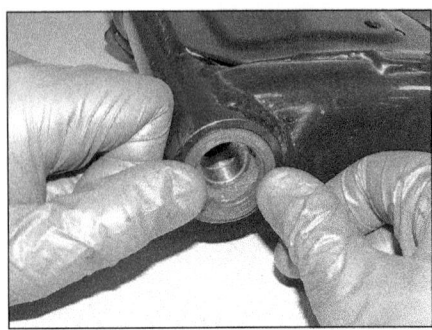

**13.31 Push the seal in with your thumbs and set it flush**

damage the cage. In the absence of a press, a suitable drawbolt arrangement can be made up as described in *Tools and Workshop Tips* in the Reference section. The ball bearings can be driven in using a socket or bearing driver that locates on the outer race of the bearing, not the inner race. Drive them in until seated, then fit the circlip into its groove, using a new one if the old one distorted on removal **(see illustration 13.26)**. Lubricate the bearings with lithium-based grease.

**30** Insert the central sleeve from the right-hand side **(see illustration 13.24)**.

**31** Fit a new seal into each side with the marked side facing out, setting them flush **(see illustration)**.

### *Installation*

**32** If removed, fit the chain slider, and the protector on the Bobber **(see illustrations 13.19a, b and c)**.

**33** Grease the sleeve and spacer, the bearings and the seal lips with lithium-based grease. Fit the sleeve into the right-hand side and the spacer into the left **(see illustrations 13.21a and b)**.

**34** Slide the washer onto the pivot bolt if

removed. Lubricate the bolt with lithium-based grease.

**35** Manoeuvre the swingarm into position and slide the pivot bolt in from the right-hand side, far enough for it to fully support the swingarm but so the adjuster sleeve in the left-hand side can be accessed for tightening **(see illustration 13.9d or 13.18a)**.

**36** On all models except the Bobber, using either the Triumph tool (T3880104) or equivalent tighten the adjuster sleeve in the left-hand side of the frame to 6 Nm **(see illustration 13.9e)**. Support the swingarm, then withdraw the pivot bolt with its washer from the right-hand side and slide it all the way though from the left-hand side **(see illustrations 13.9d and 13.9c)**. Fit the washer and a new nut onto the right-hand end, counter-hold the bolt head and tighten the nut to 110 Nm **(see illustration 13.9b)**. Fit the pivot cover **(see illustration 13.9a)**.

**37** On the Bobber, using either the Triumph tool (T3880104) or equivalent tighten the adjuster sleeve in the left-hand side of the frame to 6 Nm **(see illustration 13.17c)**. Push the bolt all the way in from the right-hand side. Fit the washer and a new nut onto the left-hand end, counter-hold the bolt head and tighten the nut to 110 Nm **(see illustration 13.17b)**. Fit the pivot covers and tighten the screws until the covers are secure **(see illustration 13.17a)**.

**38** Check that the swingarm moves up and down freely.

**39** On the Bobber align the swingarm with the the drop links, insert the bolt from the right and tighten the nut to 80 Nm **(see illustrations 12.3b and a)**.

**40** Install the remaining components in the reverse order of removal. Check and adjust the drive chain slack (see Chapter 1), and check the operation of the rear suspension and brake before taking the machine on the road.

## 14 Suspension adjustment

*Caution: Never attempt to turn the adjuster beyond the minimum or maximum setting.*

### *Front forks – Thruxton R*

**1** The front forks have adjustable spring pre-load and both rebound and compression damping. Always make sure both forks are set equally.

**2** Spring pre-load is adjusted using the hex key stored in the right-hand side cover to turn the adjuster bolt in the bottom of the fork **(see illustration)**. Turn the adjuster clockwise to increase pre-load and anti-clockwise to decrease it. To set the standard position, turn the adjuster fully anti-clockwise until it stops, then turn it clockwise 7 turns.

**3** Rebound damping is adjusted using a screwdriver to turn the adjuster marked TEN in the fork top bolt **(see illustration)**. Turn it clockwise to increase damping and anti-clockwise to decrease it. To set the standard position, turn the adjuster fully clockwise until it stops, then turn it anti-clockwise 5 turns.

**4** Compression damping is adjusted using a screwdriver to turn the adjuster marked COM in the fork top bolt **(see illustration 14.3)**. Turn it clockwise to increase damping and anti-clockwise to decrease it. To set the standard position, turn the adjuster fully clockwise until it stops, then turn it anti-clockwise 5-1/4 turns.

### *Rear shock absorbers – T100, T120, Street Twin, Street Cup, Scrambler, Thruxton*

**5** The rear shock absorbers have adjustable spring pre-load.

**6** Spring pre-load is adjusted using the tool stored in the right-hand side panel to turn

**14.2 Spring pre-load adjuster (arrowed)**

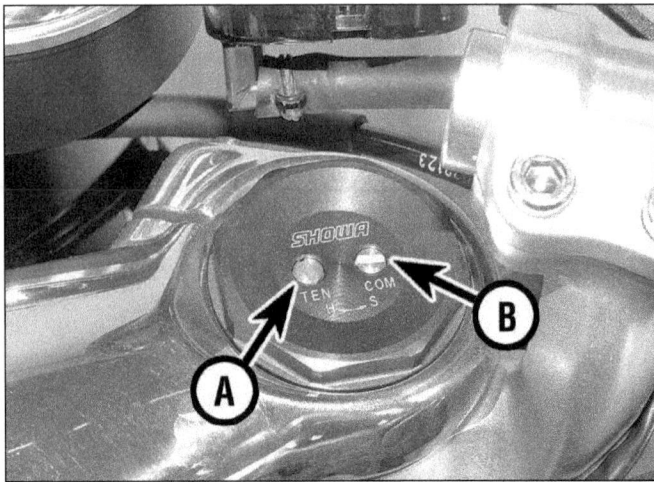

**14.3 Rebound damping adjuster (A), compression damping adjuster (B)**

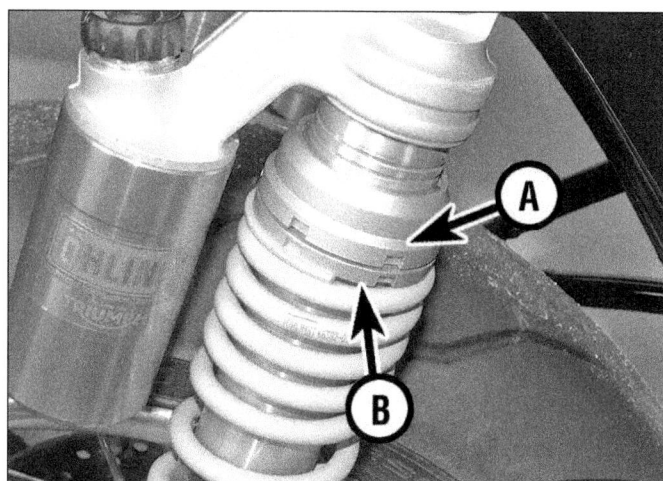

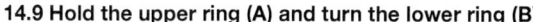

14.9 Hold the upper ring (A) and turn the lower ring (B)

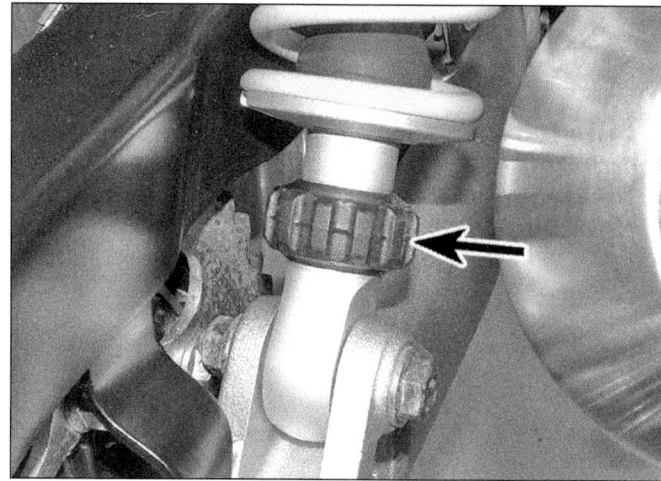

14.10 Rebound damping adjuster ring (arrowed)

the adjuster ring at the bottom of the shock absorber. Fit the tool into the hole in the adjuster lug and turn the adjuster clockwise to increase pre-load and anti-clockwise to decrease it.

**7** There are five positions. Position 1 is the minimum (softest) and standard setting, position 5 is the maximum (hardest) setting for when carrying a passenger and luggage. Align the setting required with the adjustment stopper.

### Rear shock absorbers – Thruxton R

**8** The shock absorbers have adjustable spring pre-load and both rebound and compression damping.

**9** Spring pre-load is adjusted using the C-spanners stored under the seat. Use one C-spanner to hold the upper ring and the other spanner to turn the lower ring on the top of the spring **(see illustration)**. Turn the lower ring clockwise (as viewed from above) to decrease pre-load and anti-clockwise to increase it. There are 3 defined settings. The standard setting is setting 1, i.e fully clockwise.

**10** Rebound damping is adjusted by turning the adjuster ring on the bottom of the shock absorber **(see illustration)**. Turn it anti-clockwise (as viewed from above) to increase damping and clockwise to decrease it. To set the standard position, turn the adjuster fully anti-clockwise until it stops, then turn it clockwise 24 clicks.

**11** Compression damping is adjusted by turning the adjuster knob on the top of the reservoir **(see illustration)**. Turn it clockwise (as viewed from above) to increase damping and anti-clockwise to decrease it. To set

the standard position, turn the adjuster fully clockwise until it stops, then turn it anti-clockwise 16 clicks.

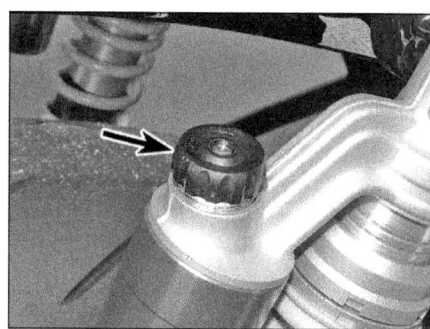

14.11 Compression damping adjuster knob

# Notes

# Chapter 6
# Brakes, wheels and final drive

## Contents

## Degrees of difficulty

| Easy, suitable for novice with little experience  | Fairly easy, suitable for beginner with some experience | Fairly difficult, suitable for competent DIY mechanic | Difficult, suitable for experienced DIY mechanic | Very difficult, suitable for expert DIY or professional |

## Specifications

### Brakes

| | |
|---|---|
| Brake fluid type . . . . . . . . . . . . . . . . . . . . . . . . . . . . . . . . . . . . . . . | DOT 4 |
| Brake pad minimum thickness. . . . . . . . . . . . . . . . . . . . . . . . . . . . . | 1.5 mm |
| Front caliper piston OD | |
|     T100, T120, Bobber, Street Twin, Street Cup, Scrambler, Thruxton . | 27.0 mm |
|     Thruxton R . . . . . . . . . . . . . . . . . . . . . . . . . . . . . . . . . . . . . . . . | 34.0 mm |
| Front disc diameter . . . . . . . . . . . . . . . . . . . . . . . . . . . . . . . . . . . . | 310 mm |
| Front disc thickness | |
|     T100, Street Cup | |
|         Standard . . . . . . . . . . . . . . . . . . . . . . . . . . . . . . . . . . . . | 5.0 mm |
|         Service limit . . . . . . . . . . . . . . . . . . . . . . . . . . . . . . . . . | 4.5 mm |
|     T120, Bobber, Street Twin, Scrambler, Thruxton | |
|         Standard . . . . . . . . . . . . . . . . . . . . . . . . . . . . . . . . . . . . | 5.5 mm |
|         Service limit . . . . . . . . . . . . . . . . . . . . . . . . . . . . . . . . . | 5.0 mm |
|     Thruxton R | |
|         Standard . . . . . . . . . . . . . . . . . . . . . . . . . . . . . . . . . . . . | 4.5 mm |
|         Service limit . . . . . . . . . . . . . . . . . . . . . . . . . . . . . . . . . | 4.0 mm |

## Brakes (continued)

| | |
|---|---|
| Front disc maximum runout . . . . . . . . . . . . . . . . . . . . . . . . . . . . . . . . . . . | 0.25 mm |
| Front master cylinder bore ID | |
|     T100, Street Twin, Street Cup, Scrambler . . . . . . . . . . . . . . . . . . . | 11.0 mm |
|     T120, Bobber, Thruxton . . . . . . . . . . . . . . . . . . . . . . . . . . . . . . | 14.0 mm |
|     Thruxton R . . . . . . . . . . . . . . . . . . . . . . . . . . . . . . . . . . . . . . . | 18.0 mm |
| Rear caliper piston OD . . . . . . . . . . . . . . . . . . . . . . . . . . . . . . . . . . . . . . | 27.0 mm |
| Rear disc diameter | |
|     T100, T120, Bobber, Street Twin, Street Cup, Scrambler . . . . . . . . | 255 mm |
|     Thruxton, Thruxton R . . . . . . . . . . . . . . . . . . . . . . . . . . . . . . . . . | 220 mm |
| Rear disc thickness | |
|     T100, T120, Bobber, Street Twin, Street Cup, Scrambler | |
|         Standard . . . . . . . . . . . . . . . . . . . . . . . . . . . . . . . . . . . . . | 5.5 mm |
|         Service limit . . . . . . . . . . . . . . . . . . . . . . . . . . . . . . . . . . | 5.0 mm |
|     Thruxton, Thruxton R | |
|         Standard . . . . . . . . . . . . . . . . . . . . . . . . . . . . . . . . . . . . . | 5.0 mm |
|         Service limit . . . . . . . . . . . . . . . . . . . . . . . . . . . . . . . . . . | 4.5 mm |
| Rear disc maximum runout | |
|     T100, T120, Bobber, Street Twin, Street Cup, Scrambler . . . . . . . . | 0.25 mm |
|     Thruxton, Thruxton R . . . . . . . . . . . . . . . . . . . . . . . . . . . . . . . . . | 0.50 mm |
| Rear master cylinder bore ID | |
|     T100, T120, Street Twin, Street Cup, Scrambler . . . . . . . . . . . . . . . | 14.0 mm |
|     Bobber, Thruxton, Thruxton R . . . . . . . . . . . . . . . . . . . . . . . . . . . | 12.7 mm |

## ABS components

| | |
|---|---|
| Wheel speed sensor air gap . . . . . . . . . . . . . . . . . . . . . . . . . . . . . . . . . | 0.4 to 1.2 mm |

## Wheels

| | |
|---|---|
| Runout – axial (side-to-side) and radial (out-of round) | |
|     T100, T120, Street Twin, Street Cup, Scrambler, Thruxton, Thruxton R. . | 0.6 mm max |
|     Bobber . . . . . . . . . . . . . . . . . . . . . . . . . . . . . . . . . . . . . . . . . . | 1.0 mm max |

## Tyres

| | |
|---|---|
| Tyre pressures . . . . . . . . . . . . . . . . . . . . . . . . . . . . . . . . . . . . . . . . . . | see *Pre-ride checks* |
| Tyre sizes* | |
|     T100, T120 | |
|         Front . . . . . . . . . . . . . . . . . . . . . . . . . . . . . . . . . . . . . . . . | 100/90-18 56H tubed |
|         Rear . . . . . . . . . . . . . . . . . . . . . . . . . . . . . . . . . . . . . . . . | 150/70R17 69H tubed |
|     Bobber | |
|         Front . . . . . . . . . . . . . . . . . . . . . . . . . . . . . . . . . . . . . . . . | 100/90-19 tubed |
|         Rear . . . . . . . . . . . . . . . . . . . . . . . . . . . . . . . . . . . . . . . . | 150/80R16 tubed |
|     Street Twin, Street Cup | |
|         Front . . . . . . . . . . . . . . . . . . . . . . . . . . . . . . . . . . . . . . . . | 100/90-18 56H tubeless |
|         Rear . . . . . . . . . . . . . . . . . . . . . . . . . . . . . . . . . . . . . . . . | 150/70R17 69H tubeless |
|     Scrambler | |
|         Front . . . . . . . . . . . . . . . . . . . . . . . . . . . . . . . . . . . . . . . . | 100/90-19 tubed |
|         Rear . . . . . . . . . . . . . . . . . . . . . . . . . . . . . . . . . . . . . . . . | 150/70R17 tubed |
|     Thruxton, Thruxton R | |
|         Front . . . . . . . . . . . . . . . . . . . . . . . . . . . . . . . . . . . . . . . . | 120/70ZR17 58W tubed |
|         Rear . . . . . . . . . . . . . . . . . . . . . . . . . . . . . . . . . . . . . . . . | 160/60ZR17 69W tubed |

*Refer to the owner's handbook, the tyre information label on the swingarm or chainguard, or your Triumph dealer or a tyre specialist for approved tyre brands and ratings.*

## Final drive

| | |
|---|---|
| Chain size (OE fitment) | |
|     T100, Street Twin, Street Cup, Scrambler . . . . . . . . . . . . . . . . . . . | 520, 102 links (DID 520 VM2) |
|     T120 . . . . . . . . . . . . . . . . . . . . . . . . . . . . . . . . . . . . . . . . . . . | 525, 100 links (EK525MVXZ2) |
|     Bobber . . . . . . . . . . . . . . . . . . . . . . . . . . . . . . . . . . . . . . . . . . | 525, 108 links (RK525GXW) |
|     Thruxton, Thruxton R . . . . . . . . . . . . . . . . . . . . . . . . . . . . . . . . . | 525, 100 links (EK525ZVX3) |
| Drive chain slack and stretch limit . . . . . . . . . . . . . . . . . . . . . . . . . . . | see Chapter 1 |
| Sprocket sizes | |
|     T100, Street Twin, Street Cup, Scrambler . . . . . . . . . . . . . . . . . . . | 17T front, 41T rear |
|     T120, Bobber . . . . . . . . . . . . . . . . . . . . . . . . . . . . . . . . . . . . . . | 17T front, 37T rear |
|     Thruxton, Thruxton R . . . . . . . . . . . . . . . . . . . . . . . . . . . . . . . . . | 16T front, 42T rear |

## Torque wrench settings

ABS components

| | |
|---|---|
| Front wheel pulse ring/brake disc bolts . . . . . . . . . . . . . . . . . . . . . . | 22 Nm |
| Rear wheel pulse ring bolts . . . . . . . . . . . . . . . . . . . . . . . . . . . | 5 Nm |
| Wheel speed sensor bolt . . . . . . . . . . . . . . . . . . . . . . . . . . . . . | 9 Nm |
| Brake hose banjo bolts. . . . . . . . . . . . . . . . . . . . . . . . . . . . . . | 25 Nm |

Footrest/brake pedal/master cylinder bracket bolts

| | |
|---|---|
| Bobber . . . . . . . . . . . . . . . . . . . . . . . . . . . . . . . . . . . . . . | 24 Nm |
| Thruxton and Thruxton R . . . . . . . . . . . . . . . . . . . . . . . . . . . . . | 25 Nm |

Front brake caliper mounting bolts

| | |
|---|---|
| All models except Thruxton R . . . . . . . . . . . . . . . . . . . . . . . . . . . | 21 Nm |
| Thruxton R . . . . . . . . . . . . . . . . . . . . . . . . . . . . . . . . . . . . | 55 Nm (but see Section 2) |
| Front brake disc bolts . . . . . . . . . . . . . . . . . . . . . . . . . . . . . . | 22 Nm |

Front brake master cylinder clamp bolts

| | |
|---|---|
| All models except the Thruxton R . . . . . . . . . . . . . . . . . . . . . . . . | 12 Nm |
| Thruxton R . . . . . . . . . . . . . . . . . . . . . . . . . . . . . . . . . . . . | 8.5 Nm |
| Front brake pad retaining pin . . . . . . . . . . . . . . . . . . . . . . . . . . . | 18 Nm |
| Front sprocket cover bolts . . . . . . . . . . . . . . . . . . . . . . . . . . . . . | 9 Nm |
| Front sprocket nut . . . . . . . . . . . . . . . . . . . . . . . . . . . . . . . . | 180 Nm |
| Front wheel axle . . . . . . . . . . . . . . . . . . . . . . . . . . . . . . . . . | 65 Nm |
| Front wheel axle clamp bolt(s) . . . . . . . . . . . . . . . . . . . . . . . . . . | 22 Nm |

Rear brake caliper mounting bolts

| | |
|---|---|
| All models except the Bobber . . . . . . . . . . . . . . . . . . . . . . . . . . . | 40 Nm |

Bobber

| | |
|---|---|
| Upper . . . . . . . . . . . . . . . . . . . . . . . . . . . . . . . . . . . . . . | 24 Nm |
| Lower . . . . . . . . . . . . . . . . . . . . . . . . . . . . . . . . . . . . . . | 29 Nm |
| Rear brake disc bolts . . . . . . . . . . . . . . . . . . . . . . . . . . . . . . . | 22 Nm |

Rear brake master cylinder bolts

| | |
|---|---|
| T100, T120, Street Twin, Street Cup, Scrambler . . . . . . . . . . . . . . . | 24 Nm |
| Bobber . . . . . . . . . . . . . . . . . . . . . . . . . . . . . . . . . . . . . . | 16 Nm |
| Thruxton and Thruxton R . . . . . . . . . . . . . . . . . . . . . . . . . . . . . | 18 Nm |
| Rear brake pad retaining pin(s) . . . . . . . . . . . . . . . . . . . . . . . . . . | 18 Nm |
| Rear sprocket nuts . . . . . . . . . . . . . . . . . . . . . . . . . . . . . . . . | 55 Nm |
| Rear wheel axle nut . . . . . . . . . . . . . . . . . . . . . . . . . . . . . . . . | 110 Nm |

## 1  General Information

**1** The T100, T120, Bobber, Scrambler, Thruxton and Thruxton R have steel rimmed spoke wheels with tubed tyres. The Street Twin and Street Cup are fitted with cast alloy wheels with tubeless tyres.

**2** Both front and rear brakes are hydraulically-operated disc brakes. The T100, Street Twin, Street Cup and Scrambler have a single disc front and rear each with a twin piston sliding caliper. The T120 and Thruxton have twin discs at the front and a single disc at the rear, each with a twin piston sliding caliper. The Bobber has a single disc front and rear, with a twin piston sliding caliper at the front and a single piston sliding caliper at the rear. The Thruxton R has twin discs at the front with opposed four-piston calipers, and a single disc at the rear with a twin piston sliding caliper. ABS (anti-lock braking system) and TCS (traction control system) is fitted as standard.

**3** Drive from the gearbox to the rear wheel is by chain and sprockets.

## 2  Front brake pads

**1** Release the brake hose from the mudguard, and from the clips holding the ABS sensor wire on the left-hand side, to give more freedom of movement **(see illustration)**.

**2** On all models except the Thruxton R unscrew the pad pin plug, then slacken the pad pin **(see illustration)**. Unscrew the caliper mounting bolts and slide the caliper off the disc **(see illustration)**. Unscrew the

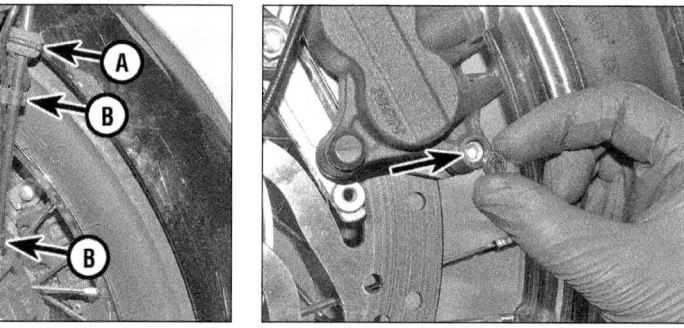

2.1 Release the hose from the guide (A), and on the left from the clips (B)

2.2a Unscrew the plug and slacken the pin (arrowed)

2.2b Unscrew the bolts and displace the caliper

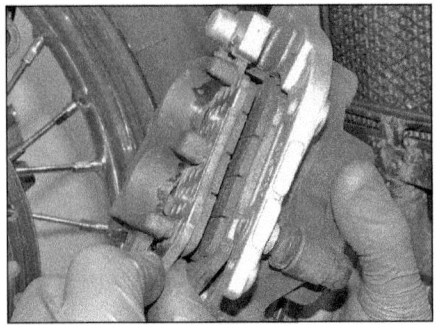

2.2c Remove the pin and lift the pads out

2.3a Unscrew the bolts and displace the caliper

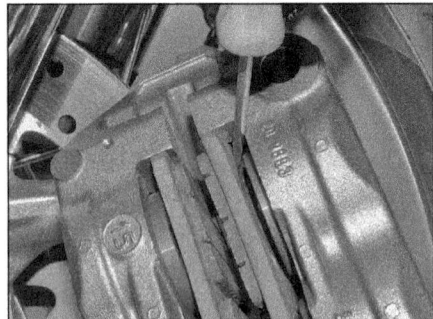

2.3b Ease the pads across...

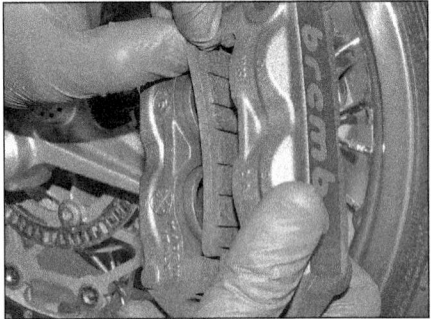

2.3c ...and lift them out

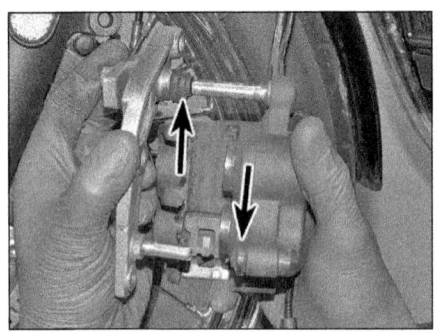

2.7a Slide the caliper and bracket apart. Clean and check the pins and rubber boots (arrowed)

2.7b Clean the spring...

pad pin and remove the pads **(see illustration)**.

**3** On the Thruxton R unscrew the caliper mounting bolts and slide the caliper off the disc **(see illustration)**.Ease each pad in turn to the middle until the end tabs are clear of the lugs then lift the pad out **(see illustrations)**.

**4** Inspect the surface of each pad for contamination and check that the friction material has not worn down to the service limit (see Chapter 1, Section 13). If either pad is worn down to, or beyond the limit, is fouled with oil or grease, or is heavily scored or damaged, both pads in each caliper must be replaced with new ones. It is not possible to degrease the friction material – if the pads are contaminated in any way fit new ones.

**5** Check that each pad has worn evenly. If uneven wear is noticed, one of the pistons is probably sticking in the caliper, in which case the caliper must be overhauled (Section 3).

**6** If the pads are in good condition clean them carefully, using a fine wire brush that is completely free of oil and grease, to remove all traces of road dirt and corrosion. Using a pointed instrument, dig out any embedded particles of foreign matter. Spray the pads with brake system cleaner.

**7** On all models except the Thruxton R separate the bracket from the caliper by sliding them apart **(see illustration)**. Clean off all traces of corrosion and hardened grease from the slider pins and rubber boots. Check the rubber boots. If they are damaged, deformed or deteriorated, they should be replaced with new ones. Note how the pad spring is fitted and remove it for cleaning if required **(see illustration)**. Also clean the

pad guide on the bracket **(see illustration)**. Remove any corrosion from the pad pin.

**8** On the Thruxton R note how the pad spring is fitted and remove it for cleaning if required **(see illustration)**.

**9** Spray the inside of the caliper with brake system cleaner, paying particular attention to the exposed section of each piston to remove any dirt or debris that could cause the seals to be damaged. Remove any traces of corrosion that might cause sticking of the pads in the caliper.

**10** If new pads are being fitted, push the pistons all the way back into the caliper to create room for them, and if you are refitting the same pads push the pistons in a little way **(see illustration)**- push the pistons using finger pressure or a piece of wood as leverage, or place the old pads back in the caliper and

2.7c ...and the guide

2.8 Clean the pad spring (arrowed)

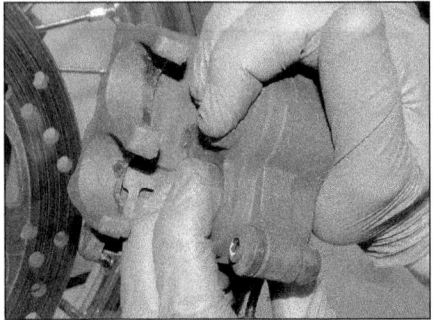

2.10 You should be able to push the pistons in using finger pressure

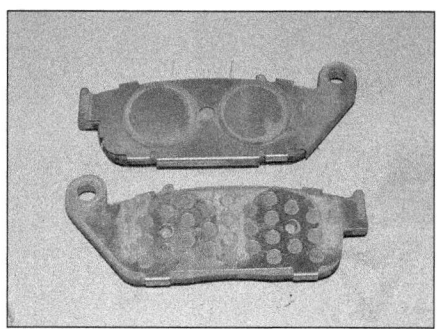

2.14a Clean and check the shims

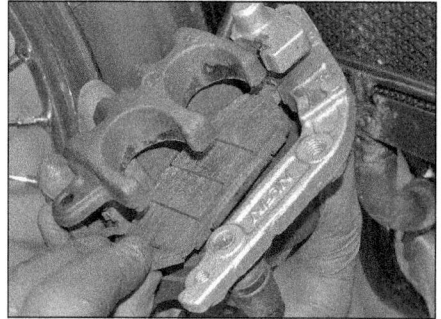

2.14b Fit the pads into the caliper...

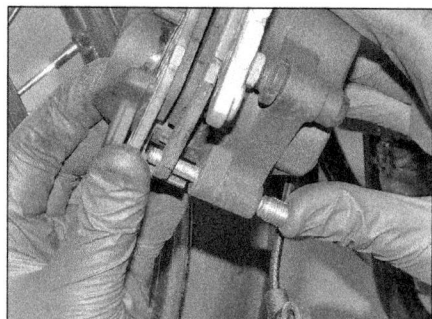

2.14c ... then press them up against the spring and fit the pin

use a large, flat-bladed screwdriver inserted between them. Alternatively obtain a piston retracting tool from a good tool supplier.

**11** As the pistons are pushed into the caliper, brake fluid will be displaced back into the reservoir on the master cylinder. Depending on the initial level, it may be necessary to remove the reservoir cap, plate and diaphragm, and remove some fluid (see *Pre-ride checks*).

**12** If a piston appears to be sticking in the caliper, the caliper must be overhauled (Section 3).

**13** Check the condition of the brake disc (Section 4).

**14** On all models except the Thruxton R make sure the pad spring is clean and correctly fitted in the caliper, and the pad guide is clean and correctly fitted on the bracket **(see illustrations 2.7b and c)**. Apply a smear of silicone based grease to the slider pins and inside the boots **(see illustration 2.7a)**. Slide the caliper onto the bracket, making sure each boot rim seats correctly around the base of its pin. Check that the caliper is able to slide freely. Clean the shim on the back of each pad, and make sure it is correctly seated **(see illustration)**. Smear the pad pin lightly with copper-based grease. Fit the pads into the caliper, making sure their ends locate against the guide on the bracket **(see illustration)**. Press the pads against the spring to align the holes, insert the pad pin and tighten it finger-tight **(see illustration)**. Slide the caliper onto the disc, making sure the pads sit squarely on each side **(see illustration 2.2b)**. Fit the caliper bolts and tighten them to 21 Nm. Now tighten the retaining pin to 18 Nm. Smear the pad pin plug threads with copper grease and fit the plug **(see illustration 2.2a)**.

**15** On the Thruxton R seat the tab on one end of the pad under its lug in the caliper, then push the other end of the pad against the spring to align the other tab with the lug and slide it across **(see illustration)**. Repeat for the other pad. Slide the caliper onto the disc, making sure the pads sit squarely on each side **(see illustration 2.3a)**. Fit the bolts and tighten them lightly so the caliper is seated but is still able to move slightly from side to side. Using a feeler gauge check that for each caliper the clearance between each brake pad lug and the disc (therefore making four

checks per caliper) is equal and at least 0.3 mm **(see illustrations)** – use the small amount of side-to-side movement in the caliper to achieve this. With the clearances equal tighten the caliper bolts first to 10 Nm, and then to 55 Nm. If you cannot get the clearance on each caliper above 0.3 mm, without touching the front brake position the bike so the front wheel is against a solid upright structure such as a wall, then loosen the axle clamp bolts on the bottom of the right-hand fork **(see illustration)**. Without touching the front brake, push down on the handlebars to pump the forks twice to align them on the axle, then tighten the clamp bolts to 22 Nm. Repeat the caliper clearance measurements. If you cannot get the clearance greater than 0.3 mm on either or both calipers seek professional advice from a Triumph dealer.

**16** Secure the brake hose, and on the left-hand side the ABS wire **(see illustration 2.1)**.

**17** Pump the brake lever several times to bring the pads into contact with the discs.

**18** Check the fluid level in the master cylinder reservoir (see *Pre-ride checks*).

**19** Check the operation of the brake before riding the bike.

### 3 Front brake caliper(s)

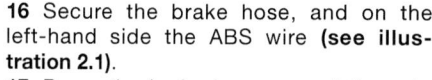

 *Warning: Caliper overhaul must be done in a spotlessly clean work area to avoid contamination and possible failure of the brake hydraulic system components. Do not, under any*

2.15a Fit the pads as described

2.15b Check the clearance (arrowed) between each lug on each caliper...

2.15c ...using a feeler gauge

2.15d Axle clamp bolts (arrowed)

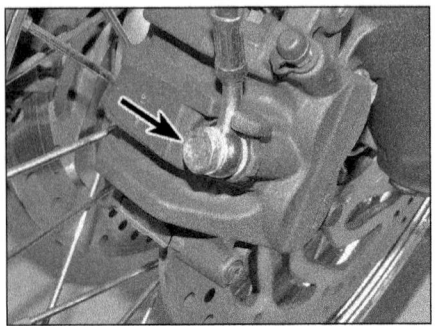

**3.2a Brake hose banjo bolt – all models except the Thruxton R**

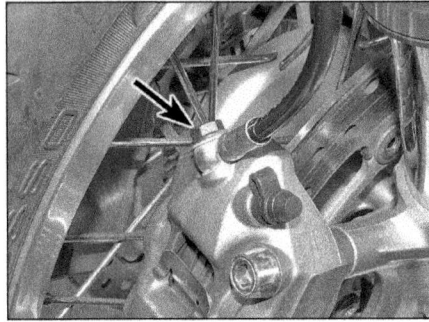

**3.2b Brake hose banjo bolt – Thruxton R**

**3.2c Seal the banjo using a nut and bolt and the sealing washers...**

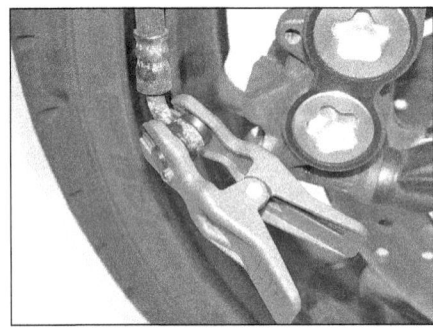

**3.2d... or using a dedicated tool**

circumstances, use petroleum-based solvents to clean brake parts. Use clean DOT 4 brake fluid, dedicated brake cleaner or denatured alcohol only, as described. To prevent damage from spilled brake fluid, always cover paintwork when working on the braking system.

**Note:** *If the caliper is being overhauled (usually due to sticking pistons or fluid leaks) read through the entire procedure first and make sure that you have a new seal kit and some new DOT 4 brake fluid.*

**Note:** *On all models except the Thruxton R, due to the shape of the brake hose banjo bolt heads, which have slightly rounded corners, you need to use a hex socket to slacken and tighten them rather than a bi-hex one.*

### Removal

**1** To displace the caliper (e.g. for wheel removal) release the brake hose from the mudguard, and from the clips holding the ABS sensor wire on the left-hand side, to give more freedom of movement **(see illustration 2.1)**. Unscrew the caliper mounting bolts and slide the caliper off the disc **(see illustration 2.2b or 2.3a)**. Secure the caliper to the bike with a bungee or cable-tie so it is out of the way and not hanging by the hose. Do not operate the brake lever while the caliper is off the disc.

**2** To remove the caliper (but see Step 3 if the caliper is being overhauled), note the alignment of the brake hose banjo fitting, then unscrew the banjo bolt and detach the hose,

noting the positions of the sealing washers **(see illustrations)**. Be prepared with a rag to catch any drops of brake fluid. Seal the banjo union with a suitable nut and bolt and the two sealing washers or using a dedicated tool, or support it upright and cover it in rag **(see illustrations)**. Note that new sealing washers must be used on reassembly. Unscrew the caliper mounting bolts and slide the caliper off the disc **(see illustration 2.2b or 2.3a)**. Remove the brake pads if required (Section 2).

**3** On all models except the Thruxton R, if the caliper is being overhauled first remove the brake pads (Section 2). Use the brake lever to pump the pistons most of the way out (as far as the point where the disc runs), but make sure they don't come all the way out **(see illustration 3.4)**. Refit the caliper and tighten the bolts enough to hold it, then disconnect the hose as described in Step 2. Unscrew the bolts and remove the caliper, then slide the caliper and bracket apart **(see illustration 2.7a)**.

**4** On the Thruxton R, if the caliper is being overhauled it must be done in two stages, one side of the caliper first, then the other. First remove the brake pads (Section 2). Push the pistons on one side of the caliper in and hold them so they can't move, then use the brake lever to pump the opposite pistons most of the way out (as far as the point where the disc runs), but make sure they don't come all the way out **(see illustration)**. Refit the caliper and tighten the bolts enough to hold it, then disconnect the hose as described in Step 2. Unscrew the bolts and remove the caliper.

### Overhaul

**Note:** *If a piston sticks in its bore and cannot be displaced, the caliper will have to be replaced with a new one.*

**5** Remove the displaced pistons and drain the fluid out of the caliper, taking care to note which caliper bore the pistons came from so they can be returned to their original location **(see illustrations)**. Clean the exterior of the caliper with brake system cleaner.

**6** Remove the dust seals and the piston seals from the piston bores using a wooden

**3.4 Hold the pistons on one side fully in and displace the pistons on the other side as described**

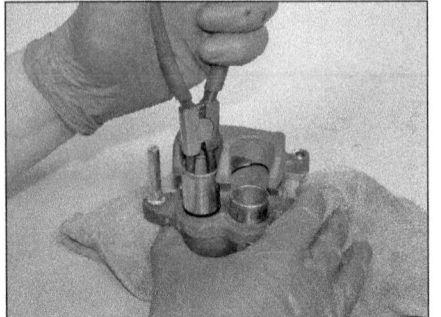

**3.5a Removing a piston on all models except the Thruxton R – you can use external circlip pliers as shown if you can't pull the piston out with your fingers**

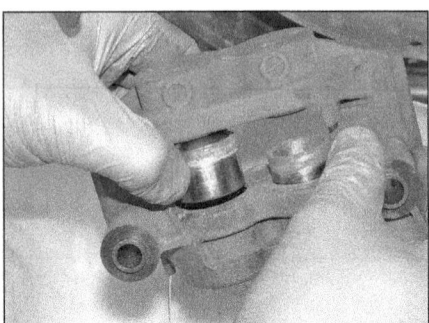

**3.5b Removing a piston on the Thruxton R**

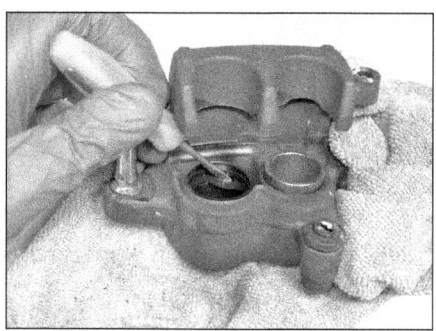

**3.6 Remove the seals and discard them**

**3.8 Check the surfaces of the pistons and bores – the plating on this piston is lifting off**

**3.9a Lubricate the new piston seals with brake fluid...**

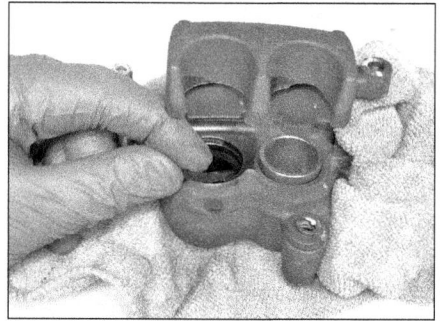

**3.9b ...then fit them into their grooves**

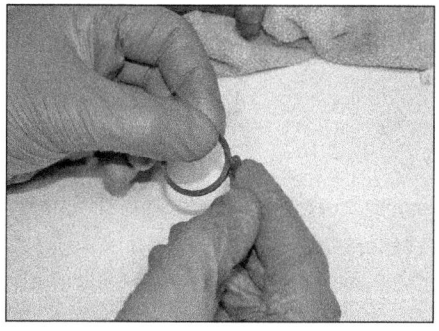

**3.10a Lubricate the new dust seals with brake fluid or silicone grease...**

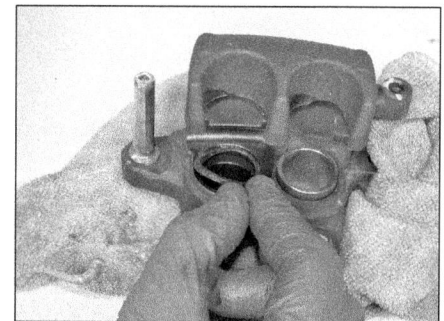

**3.10b... then fit them into their grooves**

or plastic tool to avoid scratching the bores **(see illustration)**. New seals must be fitted on reassembly.

**7** Clean the pistons and bores with clean DOT 4 brake fluid. Blow compressed air through the fluid passages in the caliper to ensure they are clear (make sure the air is filtered and unlubricated).

*Caution: Do not, under any circumstances, use a petroleum-based solvent to clean brake parts.*

**8** Inspect the caliper bores and pistons for signs of corrosion, nicks and burrs and loss of plating **(see illustration)**. If surface defects are present, the pistons and/or caliper assembly must be replaced with a new one. If the caliper is in bad shape the master cylinder should also be checked.

**9** Lubricate the new piston seals with new DOT 4 brake fluid, then fit them into the lower grooves in the caliper bores **(see illustrations)**.

**10** Lubricate the new dust seals with the brake fluid or silicone grease, then fit them into the upper grooves in the caliper bores **(see illustrations)**.

**11** Lubricate the pistons with the brake fluid and fit them, closed-end first, into the caliper bores **(see illustration)**; if refitting the original pistons make sure they are returned to the same bores. Using your thumbs, push the pistons all the way in, making sure they enter the bores squarely and do not displace the seals. Wipe away any excess fluid as it will attract dirt.

**12** On the Thruxton R hold the pistons in on the side that was just overhauled (cable-ties

work well) and use compressed directed into the fluid inlet to extract the pistons on the other side of the caliper.

### Installation

**13** Refer to Section 2 to clean and check the caliper components, to fit the brake pads if removed, and to install the caliper – if the pads weren't removed ease them apart slightly if necessary for extra clearance around the disc using a large flat-bladed screwdriver or similar tool, making sure you do not damage the friction material surface.

**14** Connect the brake hose using new sealing washers on each side of the banjo fitting **(see illustration 9.33b)**. Align the fitting as noted on removal **(see illustration 3.2a or b)**. Tighten the banjo bolt to 25 Nm.

**15** Top-up the brake fluid reservoir with new DOT 4 brake fluid and bleed the system as described in Section 11.

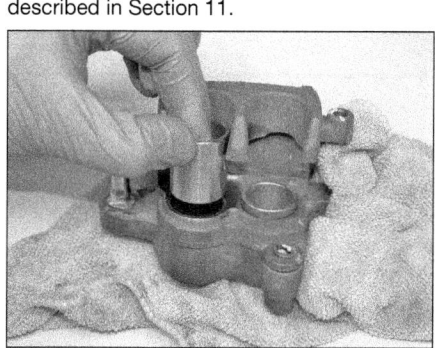

**3.11 Lubricate the pistons with brake fluid and push them all the way in**

**16** Check that there are no fluid leaks and test the brake before riding the bike.

### 4 Front brake disc(s)

### Inspection

**1** Inspect the surface of each disc for score marks and other damage. Light scratches are normal after use and will not affect brake operation, but deep grooves and heavy score marks will reduce braking efficiency and accelerate pad wear. If a disc is badly grooved it must be replaced with a new one.

**2** The disc must not be allowed to wear down to a thickness less than the service limit given in the Specifications. Check the thickness of the disc with a micrometer **(see illustration)**.

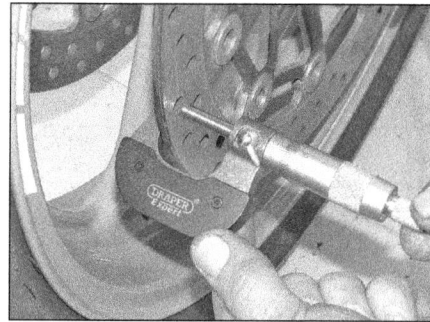

**4.2 Using a micrometer to measure disc thickness**

4.3 Set up a dial gauge with the probe contacting the brake disc, then rotate the wheel to check for runout

If the thickness is less than the service limit, fit a new one.

**3** To check disc runout, support the bike upright so that the front wheel is raised off the ground. Mount a dial gauge to a fork leg, with the plunger on the gauge touching the surface of the disc about 10 mm (1/2 in) from the outer edge **(see illustration)**. Rotate the wheel and watch the gauge needle, comparing the reading with the limit listed in the Specifications. If the runout exceeds the service limit, check the wheel bearings for play (see Chapter 1). If the bearings are worn, fit new ones (Section 16) and repeat this check. If disc runout is still excessive, fit a new one.

### Removal

**4** Remove the front wheel (Section 14).
*Caution: Don't lay the wheel down and allow it to rest on either disc – they could become warped. Set the wheel on wood blocks so the wheel rim supports the weight of the wheel.*

**5** If you are not replacing the disc with a new one, mark the relationship of the disc to the wheel so that it can be installed in the same position. Unscrew the disc bolts, loosening them evenly and a little at a time in a criss-cross pattern to avoid distorting the disc, remove the ABS wheel speed sensor rotor (left-hand disc only on twin disc models), and remove disc from the wheel **(see illustration)**. Note that Triumph specify to use new bolts when fitting the disc.

4.5 Unscrew the bolts (arrowed) and remove the rotor and the disc

**6** On the T100, T120, Bobber, Scrambler and Thruxton remove the disc damper from the wheel, noting which way round it fits – it can only fit one way due to its taper, but mark the outer face to avoid confusion when fitting it. Check the damper for cracks and distortion and fit a new one if necessary.

### Installation

**7** Before fitting the disc, make sure there is no dirt or corrosion where it seats on the hub, or where the damper fits into the wheel on the T100, T120, Bobber, Scrambler and Thruxton, particularly right in the angle of the seat. If the disc does not sit flat when it is bolted down, it will appear to be warped when checked or when the front brake is used.

**8** Before seating the ABS rotor on the disc, make sure there is no dirt or corrosion between the mating surfaces as this will not allow the ring to sit flat when bolted down and it will be warped and could cause the ABS system to indicate a fault.

**9** On the T100, T120, Bobber, Scrambler and Thruxton fit the disc damper onto the wheel, making sure it is the correct way round as noted on removal and seats correctly.

**10** Fit the disc onto the wheel – align the previously applied register marks if you are refitting the original disc. Seat the ABS rotor on the disc (left-hand disc on twin disc models).

**11** Either use new bolts, or clean the threads of the original bolts and apply a suitable

non-permanent thread locking compound. Fit the bolts and tighten them evenly and a little at a time in a criss-cross pattern to 22 Nm. If a new disc has been fitted remove any protective coating from its working surfaces. Clean the disc using acetone or brake system cleaner. If a new disc or discs have been fitted, fit new brake pads.

**12** Install the front wheel (Section 14).

**13** Operate the brake lever several times to bring the pads into contact with the discs. Check the operation of the brake carefully before riding the motorcycle.

## 5  Front brake master cylinder

⚠️ **Warning: Any work on the internal components of the master cylinder must be done in a spotlessly clean work area to avoid contamination and possible failure of the brake hydraulic system. Do not, under any circumstances, use petroleum-based solvents to clean brake parts. Use clean DOT 4 brake fluid, dedicated brake cleaner or denatured alcohol only, as described. To prevent damage from spilled brake fluid, always cover paintwork when working on the braking system.**

**Note:** *On all models except the Thruxton R, if you are overhauling the master cylinder this can be done without removing it from the handlebar. All you need to do is remove the front brake lever. If the master cylinder is being overhauled (usually due to sticking or poor action, or fluid leaks) read through the entire procedure first and make sure that you have a new piston set and some new DOT 4 brake fluid. On the Thruxton R an overhaul kit is not available for the master cylinder.*

**Note:** *On all models except the Thruxton R, due to the shape of the brake hose banjo bolt heads, which have slightly rounded corners, you need to use a hex socket to slacken and tighten them rather than a bi-hex one.*

### Removal

**1** Remove the brake fluid from the reservoir and wipe the reservoir with a clean rag (see Section 11 – fluid change).

**2** On the T100, T120, Street Twin, Street Cup and Scrambler remove the right-hand mirror (see Chapter 7).

**3** Remove the brake lever (see Chapter 5).

**4** On the T100, T120, Bobber and Thruxton undo the brake light switch holder screw and displace the holder and switch from the bottom of the master cylinder **(see illustration)**. On the Street Twin, Street Cup and Scrambler undo the brake light switch screw and displace the switch from the bottom of the master cylinder. On the Thruxton R ease the brake light switch evenly off the bottom of the master cylinder **(see illustration)** – it has two pegs that are a push fit into holes.

**5** Note the alignment of the brake hose banjo

5.4a Brake light switch holder screw (arrowed) – T100, T120, Bobber and Thruxton

5.4b Brake light switch (arrowed) – Thruxton R

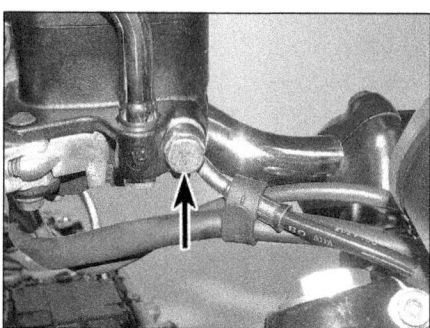

5.5a Brake hose banjo bolt (arrowed) –
T100, T120, Bobber and Thruxton

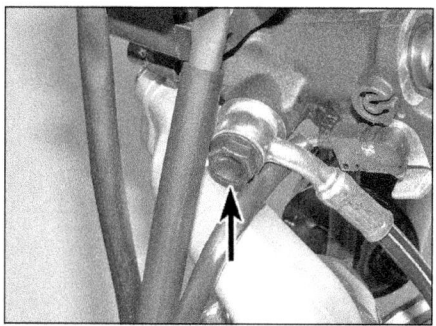

5.5b Brake hose banjo bolt (arrowed) –
Thruxton R

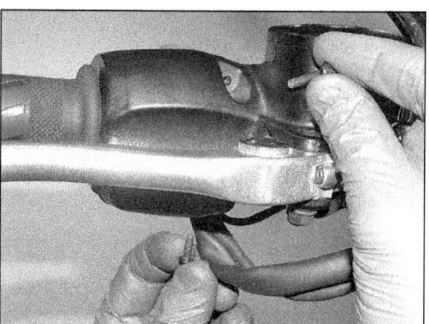

5.6a Undo the screws and detach the
switch face

5.6b Undo the sensor screws (arrowed)

5.6c Unscrew the clamp bolts and remove
the master cylinder

5.7 Master cylinder clamp bolts (arrowed) –
Thruxton R shown

fitting, then unscrew the banjo bolt and detach the hose, noting the positions of the sealing washers **(see illustration)**. Be prepared with a rag to catch any drops of brake fluid. Seal the banjo union with a suitable nut and bolt and the two sealing washers or using a dedicated tool, or support it upright and cover it in rag **(see illustration 3.2c or d)**. Note that new sealing washers must be used on reassembly.
**6** On the T100, T120, Bobber and Thruxton, undo the switch housing screws and detach the housing face **(see illustration)**. Undo the twistgrip sensor screws **(see illustration)**. Undo the master cylinder clamp bolts and remove the master cylinder **(see illustration)**.
**7** On the Street Twin, Street Cup, Scrambler and Thruxton R undo the master cylinder

clamp bolts and remove the master cylinder **(see illustration)**. If required remove the reservoir and hose from the master cylinder. Check the hose for cracks and fit a new one if necessary.

### Overhaul

**8** Remove the rubber boot **(see illustration)**.
**9** The piston assembly is secured by a circlip. Remove the circlip using circlip pliers, then draw out the piston and spring assembly **(see illustrations)**.
**10** Clean inside the master cylinder with fresh DOT 4 brake fluid. If compressed air is available, blow it through the fluid passages to ensure they are clear (make sure the air is filtered and unlubricated).

*Caution: Do not, under any circumstances, use a petroleum-based solvent to clean brake parts.*
**11** Check the master cylinder bore for corrosion, scratches, nicks and score marks. If damage or wear is evident, the master cylinder must be replaced with a new one. If the master cylinder is in poor condition, then the caliper(s) should be checked as well.
**12** The rubber boot, circlip, piston (with seals) and spring are included in the master cylinder rebuild kit. Use all of the new parts, regardless of the apparent condition of the old ones. On the T100, T120, Bobber and Thruxton, if the piston set components are not pre-assembled fit the seal onto the piston and the cup onto

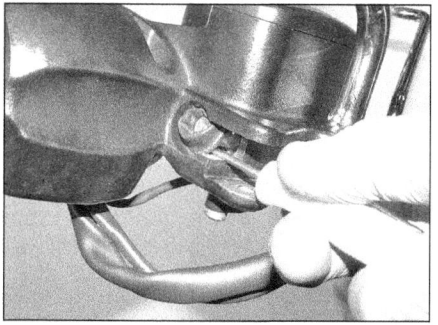

5.8 Remove the rubber boot, noting how it
locates

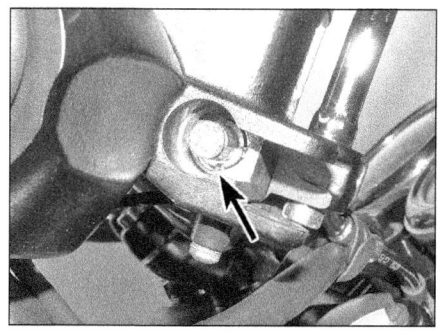

5.9a Release the circlip (arrowed)...

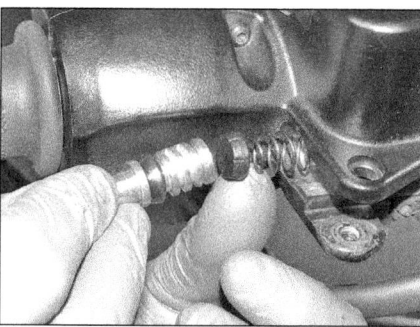

5.9b ...and draw out the piston and spring

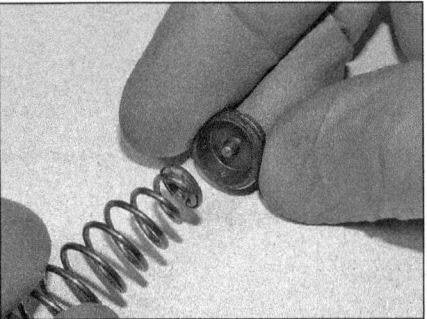

5.12a Fit the seal onto the piston as shown

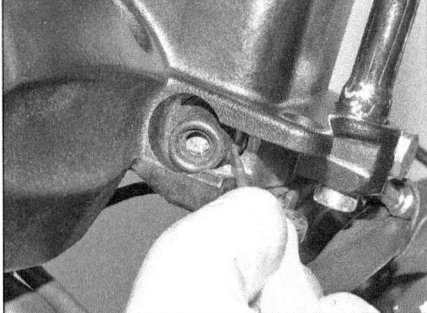

5.12b Fit the peg on the underside of the cup into the hole in the top of the spring

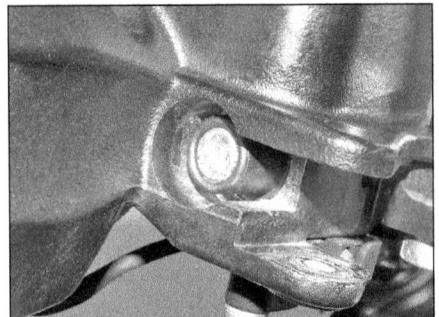

5.14a Carefully push the wide lip into the bore...

5.14b ...and seat the narrow lip in the groove

5.15 Locate the pin in the hole (arrowed)

5.16 Align the mating surfaces of the clamp with the punch mark (arrowed) on the handlebar – Thruxton R shown

the spring (see illustrations). On the Street Twin, Street Cup and Scrambler the piston set should come assembled, but if not fit the seal, cup and spring onto the piston using the old piston set as a guide. Do not fit the rubber boot onto the piston, and if it is already in place remove it.

13  Insert the spring and piston and push the piston in, making sure the cup and seal lips do not turn inside out, and fit the new circlip, making sure it is properly located in the groove (see illustrations 5.9b and a).

14  Push the wide outer lip on the inner end of the boot into place and seat the narrow inner lip on the outer end in its groove in the end of the piston (see illustrations).

### Installation

15  On the T100, T120, Bobber and Thruxton position the master cylinder on the handlebar, locating the pin on the master cylinder in the hole in the front of the handlebar (see illustration). Tighten the clamp bolts to 12 Nm, tightening the top bolt first (see illustration 5.6c). Fit the twistgrip sensor screws and switch housing face (see illustrations 5.6b and a).

16  On the Street Twin, Street Cup, Scrambler and Thruxton R, position the master cylinder on the handlebar, aligning the inner side of the clamp joint on the Street Twin, Scrambler and Thruxton R and the outer side on the Street Cup with the punch mark on the top of the handlebar (see illustration). Fit the back of the clamp with its UP mark or triangle pointing up, then fit the

clamp bolts and tighten them to 12 Nm on the Street Twin, Street Cup and Scrambler, and to 8.5 Nm on the Thruxton R, tightening the top bolt first (see illustration 5.7). Fit the reservoir and hose if removed – make sure the hose is fully pushed onto its union at each end and is secured by the clamps.

17  Connect the brake hose using new sealing washers on each side of the banjo fitting (see illustration 9.33b). Align the fitting as noted on removal (see illustration 5.5a or b). Tighten the banjo bolt to 25 Nm.

18  Install the brake lever (see Chapter 5).

19  Fit the brake light switch (see illustration 5.4a or b).

20  Fit the mirror where removed (see Chapter 7).

21  Fill the master cylinder reservoir with new DOT 4 brake fluid and bleed the air from the system as described in Section 11.

22  Check that there are no fluid leaks and test the brake and brake light before riding the bike.

### 6  Rear brake pads

1  On the T100 and T120 remove the left-hand silencer (see Chapter 4).

2  On all models except the Bobber release the brake hose and ABS wheel sensor wire from the swingarm to give more freedom of movement (see illustration).

3  On the T100, T120, Street Twin, Street Cup and Scrambler displace the wheel speed sensor from the bracket (Section 17). Slacken the pad retaining pins, then unscrew the caliper bolts and slide the caliper assembly off (see illustration). Unscrew and remove

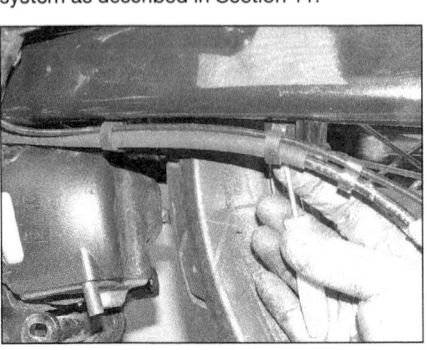

6.2 Release the hose guide clips by pushing one side in using a small screwdriver

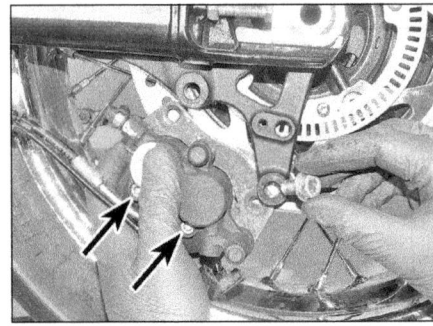

6.3a Slacken the pins (arrowed), then unscrew the bolts and displace the caliper

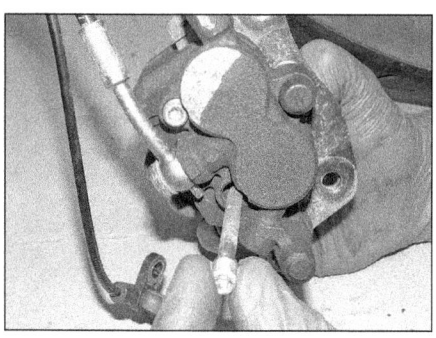

6.3b Unscrew the pins

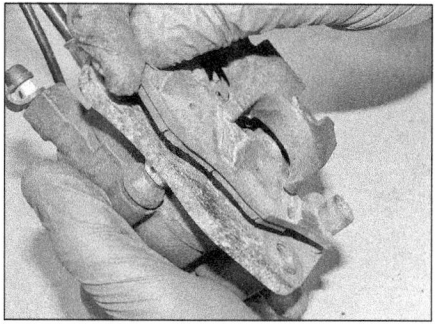

6.3c Remove the inner pad, noting how it locates round the post...

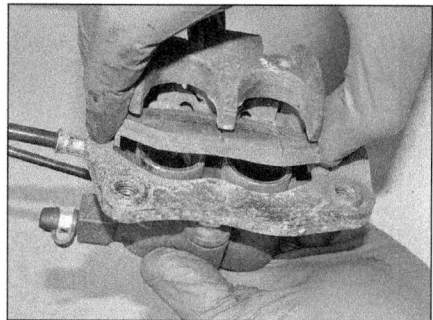

6.3d ...then remove the outer pad

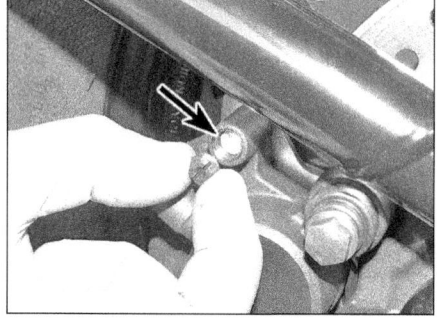

6.4a Remove the plug and slacken the pin (arrowed)

6.4b Unscrew the bolts...

6.4c ...and slide the caliper off

the pad pins, then pivot the inner pad up and remove it, then remove the outer pad (see illustrations).

4 On the Bobber unscrew the pad retaining pin plug, then slacken the pad pin (see illustration). Unscrew the caliper bolts and slide the caliper off (see illustration). Unscrew and remove the pad pin, then remove the pads, noting how they fit (see illustrations).

5 On the Thruxton and Thruxton R slacken the pad retaining pins. Remove the rear wheel (Section 15). Pivot the inner pad up and remove it, then remove the outer pad (see illustrations 6.3c and d).

6 Inspect the surface of each pad for contamination and check that the friction material has not worn down to the service limit of 1.5 mm or the base of the wear grooves (see Chapter 1, Section 13). If either pad is worn down to, or beyond the limit, is fouled with oil or grease, or is heavily scored or damaged, fit a new set of pads. It is not possible to degrease the friction material – if the pads are contaminated in any way fit new ones.

7 If the pads are in good condition clean them carefully, using a fine wire brush that is completely free of oil and grease, to remove all traces of road dirt and corrosion. Using a pointed instrument, dig out any embedded particles of foreign matter. Spray the pads with brake system cleaner.

8 On all models except the Bobber separate the bracket from the caliper by sliding them apart (see illustration). On all models clean

6.4d Remove the pin...

6.4e ...and lift the pads out

off all traces of corrosion and hardened grease from the slider pins and rubber boots. Check the rubber boots – if they are damaged, deformed or deteriorated, they should be replaced with new ones, but on the Bobber

check with a Triumph dealer as they are not shown as being available separately from the caliper. Note how the pad spring is fitted and remove it for cleaning if required (see illustration). On the Bobber also clean the

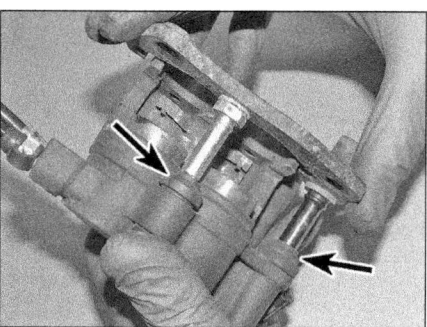

6.8a Slide the caliper off the bracket. Clean and check the pins and boots (arrowed)

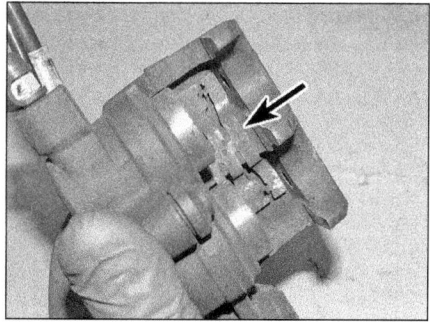

6.8b Pad spring (arrowed) – all models except the Bobber

6.8c Pad spring (arrowed)...

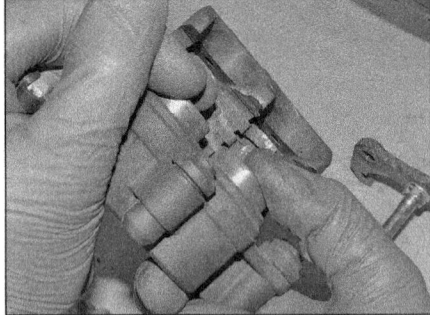

6.8d ...and pad guide (arrowed) on the Bobber

6.10 You should be able to push the piston in using finger pressure

pad guide on the bracket **(see illustration)**. Remove any corrosion from the pad pin(s).

**9** Spray the inside of the caliper with brake system cleaner, paying particular attention to the exposed section of the piston(s) to remove any dirt or debris that could cause the seals to be damaged.

**10** If new pads are being fitted, push the piston(s) all the way back into the caliper to create room for them. Push the piston(s) using finger pressure or a piece of wood as leverage, or place the old pads back in the caliper and use a large, flat-bladed screwdriver inserted between them **(see illustration)**. Alternatively obtain a piston retracting tool from a good tool supplier.

**11** As the piston(s) is/are pushed into the caliper, brake fluid will be displaced back through the master cylinder and into the reservoir. Depending on the initial level, it may be necessary to remove the reservoir cover, plate and diaphragm, and siphon out some fluid (see *Pre-ride checks*).

**12** If a piston appears to be sticking in the caliper, the caliper must be overhauled (Section 7).

**13** Check the condition of the brake disc (Section 8).

**14** Make sure the pad spring is clean and correctly fitted in the caliper, and on the Bobber the pad guide is clean and correctly fitted on the bracket **(see illustration 6.8b or 2.8c and d)**. Apply a smear of silicone based grease to the slider pins and inside the boots **(see illustration 6.8a)**. On all models except the Bobber slide the caliper onto the bracket, making sure each boot rims seats correctly around the base of its pin. Smear the pad pin(s) lightly with copper-based grease.

**15** On the T100, T120, Street Twin, Street Cup and Scrambler, seat the outer pad against the pistons, then hook the inner pad around the post and pivot it down into the caliper **(see illustrations 6.3d and c)**. Push the pads up against the spring to align the holes and insert the pads pins, tightening them finger-tight **(see illustration 6.3b)**. Slide the caliper onto the disc, fit the bolts and tighten to 40 Nm **(see illustration 6.3a)**. Now tighten the pads pins to 18 Nm. Fit the wheel speed sensor (Section 17).

**16** On the Bobber fit the pads into the caliper **(see illustration 6.4e)**. Press the pads against the spring to align the holes, slide the pad pin through and tighten it finger-tight **(see illustration 6.4d)**. Slide the caliper onto the disc, making sure the pads sit squarely on each side, and the lower ends seat against the guide on the bracket **(see illustration 6.4c)**. Fit the caliper bolts and tighten the upper one to 24 Nm and the lower to 29 Nm **(see illustration 6.4b)**. Now tighten the retaining pin to 18 Nm. Smear the pad pin plug threads with copper grease and fit the plug **(see illustration 6.4a)**.

**17** On the Thruxton and Thruxton R, seat the outer pad against the pistons, then hook the inner pad around the post and pivot it down into the caliper **(see illustrations 6.3d and c)**. Press the pads up against the spring to align the holes and insert the pads pins, tightening them finger-tight. Install the rear wheel (Section 15). Now tighten the pads pins to 18 Nm.

**18** On all models except the Bobber secure the brake hose and ABS wire to the swingarm **(see illustration 6.2)**.

**19** Operate the brake pedal several times to bring the pads into contact with the disc.

**20** Check the fluid level in the master cylinder reservoir (see *Pre-ride checks*).

**21** Check the brake before riding the bike.

## 7 Rear brake caliper

⚠️ *Warning: Caliper overhaul must be done in a spotlessly clean work area to avoid contamination and possible failure of the brake hydraulic system components. Do not, under any circumstances, use petroleum-based solvents to clean brake parts. Use clean DOT 4 brake fluid, dedicated brake cleaner or denatured alcohol only, as described. To prevent damage from spilled brake fluid, always cover paintwork when working on the braking system.*

**Note:** *If the caliper is being overhauled (usually due to a sticking piston or fluid leaks) read*

*through the entire procedure first and make sure that you have a new seal kit and some new DOT 4 brake fluid.*

**Note:** *Due to the shape of the brake hose banjo bolt heads, which have slightly rounded corners, you need to use a hex socket to slacken and tighten them rather than a bi-hex one.*

### Removal

**1** To remove the caliper (but see Step 2 if the caliper is being overhauled), note the alignment of the brake hose banjo fitting, then unscrew the banjo bolt and detach the hose, noting the positions of the sealing washers. Be prepared with a rag to catch any drops of brake fluid. Seal the banjo union with a suitable nut and bolt and the two sealing washers or using a dedicated tool, or support it upright and cover it in rag **(see illustrations 3.2c and d)**. Note that new sealing washers must be used on reassembly. Remove the brake pads (Section 6) – this covers removing the caliper.

**2** if the caliper is being overhauled first remove the brake pads (Section 6). Operate the brake pedal to pump the piston(s) most of the way out **(see illustration 3.4)**. Refit the caliper and tighten the bolts enough to hold it, or on the Thruxton and Thruxton R slide the rear axle through the swingarm and caliper bracket, then disconnect the hose as described in Step 1. Remove the caliper, then on all models except the Bobber slide the caliper and bracket apart **(see illustration 6.8a)**.

**3** On the Bobber, if required remove the rear wheel (Section 15), then remove the caliper bracket.

### Overhaul

**Note:** *If a piston sticks in its bore and cannot be displaced, the caliper will have to be replaced with a new one.*

**4** Remove the displaced piston(s) and drain the fluid out of the caliper **(see illustration 3.5a)**. Clean the exterior of the caliper with brake system cleaner.

**5** Remove the dust seal(s) and the piston

seal(s) from the piston bore(s) using a wooden or plastic tool to avoid scratching the bore(s) **(see illustration 3.6)**. New seals must be fitted on reassembly.

**6** Clean the piston(s) and bore(s) with clean DOT 4 brake fluid. Blow compressed air through the fluid passages in the caliper to ensure they are clear (make sure the air is filtered and unlubricated).

*Caution: Do not, under any circumstances, use a petroleum-based solvent to clean brake parts.*

**7** Inspect the caliper bore(s) and piston(s) for signs of corrosion, nicks and burrs and loss of plating **(see illustration 3.8)**. If surface defects are present, the piston(s) and/or caliper assembly must be replaced with a new one. If the caliper is in bad shape the master cylinder should also be checked.

**8** Lubricate the new piston seal(s) with new DOT 4 brake fluid, then fit it/them into the lower groove(s) in the caliper bore(s) **(see illustrations 3.9a and b)**.

**9** Lubricate the new dust seal(s) with the brake fluid or silicone grease, then fit it/them into the upper groove(s) in the caliper bore(s) **(see illustrations 3.10a and b)**.

**10** Lubricate the piston(s) with the brake fluid and fit it/them, closed-end first, into the caliper bore(s) **(see illustration 3.11)**. Using your thumbs, push the piston(s) all the way in, making sure it/they enter the bore(s) squarely and do not displace the seals. Wipe away any excess fluid as it will attract dirt.

## Installation

**11** On the Bobber, if removed, fit the caliper bracket and install the rear wheel (see Section 15).

**12** Refer to Section 6 to clean and check all components and to fit the brake pads, ignoring any Steps that do not apply following a caliper overhaul.

**13** Connect the brake hose using new sealing washers on each side of the banjo fitting **(see illustration 9.33b)**. Align the fitting as noted on removal. Tighten the banjo bolt to 25 Nm.

**14** Top-up the brake fluid reservoir with new DOT 4 brake fluid and bleed the system as described in Section 11.

**15** Check that there are no fluid leaks and test the brake before riding the bike.

## 8  Rear brake disc

### Inspection

**1** Refer to Section 4 of this Chapter. To check the disc runout, support the bike upright so that the rear wheel is raised off the ground. Mount the dial gauge to the swingarm.

**8.4 Rear brake disc bolts (arrowed)**

### Removal

**2** Remove the rear wheel (Section 15).

**3** Remove the ABS wheel speed sensor rotor (Section 17).

*Caution: Don't lay the wheel down and allow it to rest on the disc or the sprocket – they could become warped. Set the wheel on wood blocks so the wheel rim supports the weight of the wheel.*

**4** If you are not replacing the disc with a new one, mark the relationship of the disc to the wheel so that it can be installed in the same position. Unscrew the disc bolts, loosening them evenly and a little at a time in a criss-cross pattern to avoid distorting the disc, then remove the disc from the wheel **(see illustration)**. Note that Triumph specify to use new bolts when fitting the disc.

### Installation

**5** Before fitting the disc, make sure there is no dirt or corrosion where the disc seats on the hub, particularly right in the angle of the seat. If the disc does not sit flat when it is bolted down, it will appear to be warped when checked or when the rear brake is used.

**6** Fit the disc onto the wheel; align the previously applied register marks if you are reinstalling the original disc.

**7** Either fit new bolts or clean the threads of the original bolts and apply a suitable non-permanent thread locking compound. Fit the bolts and tighten them evenly and a little at a time in a criss-cross pattern to 22 Nm. If a new disc has been fitted remove any protective coating from its working surfaces. Clean the disc using acetone or brake system cleaner. If a new disc has been fitted, fit new brake pads.

**8** Install the ABS wheel speed sensor rotor (Section 17).

**9** Install the rear wheel (Section 15).

**10** Operate the brake pedal several times to bring the pads into contact with the disc. Check the operation of the brake carefully before riding the motorcycle.

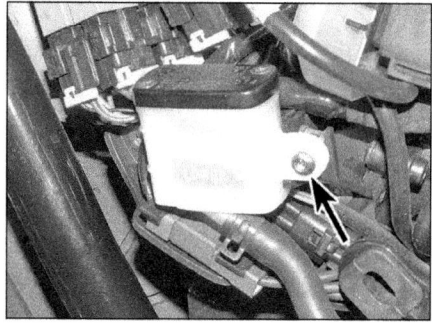

**9.3 Reservoir screw (arrowed)**

## 9  Rear brake master cylinder

⚠ *Warning: Any work on the internal components of the master cylinder must be done in a spotlessly clean work area to avoid contamination and possible failure of the brake hydraulic system. Do not, under any circumstances, use petroleum-based solvents to clean brake parts. Use clean DOT 4 brake fluid, dedicated brake cleaner or denatured alcohol only, as described. To prevent damage from spilled brake fluid, always cover paintwork when working on the braking system.*

**Note:** *On all models except the Thruxton and Thruxton R, if you are overhauling the master cylinder (usually due to sticking or poor action, or fluid leaks) read through the entire procedure first and make sure that you have a new piston set, circlip, and if the rubber boot is damaged a new pushrod assembly (the boot is not available separately), and some new DOT 4 brake fluid. On the Thruxton and Thruxton R no piston set is available for the master cylinder.*

**Note:** *Due to the shape of the brake hose banjo bolt heads, which have slightly rounded corners, you need to use a hex socket to slacken and tighten them rather than a bi-hex one.*

### Removal

#### T100, T120, Street Twin, Street Cup and Scrambler

**1** Remove the right-hand side cover (see Chapter 7). Remove the front sprocket cover (Section 20).

**2** On the Scrambler remove the upper exhaust silencer (see Chapter 4).

**3** Remove the brake fluid from the reservoir and wipe the reservoir with a clean rag (see Section 11 – fluid change). Undo the reservoir screw **(see illustration)**.

**4** On the Street Twin up to VIN 737936, undo the brake light switch bracket screws and displace the switch assembly.

9.5a Undo the screw...

9.5b ...push the bracket down and release it from the lug

9.6a Push the sprung leaf of the clip out so it is clear of the end of the pin...

9.6b ...then slide it up and off...

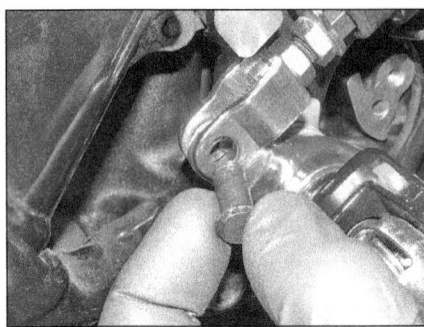

9.6c ...and withdraw the pin

5 On the T100, T120, Street Twin from VIN 737937, Street Cup and Scrambler, undo the brake light switch bracket screw then slide the bracket down to free the slot from the lug head and displace the switch assembly **(see illustrations)**.

6 Remove the clip from the inner end of the master cylinder pushrod clevis pin and withdraw the pin **(see illustrations)**.

7 Note the alignment of the brake hose banjo fitting, then unscrew the banjo bolt and detach the hose, noting the positions of the sealing washers **(see illustration)**. Be prepared with a rag to catch any drops of brake fluid. Seal the banjo union with a suitable nut and bolt or using a dedicated tool, or support it upright and cover it in rag **(see illustrations 3.2c or d)**. Note that new sealing washers must be used on reassembly.

8 Unscrew the master cylinder bolts and remove the master cylinder and reservoir **(see illustration)**.

### Bobber

9 Remove the front sprocket cover (Section 20).

10 Disconnect the rear brake light switch wiring connector **(see illustration)**.

11 Displace the coolant reservoir and support it upright to one side **(see illustrations)**.

12 Remove the brake fluid from the reservoir and wipe the reservoir with a clean rag (see

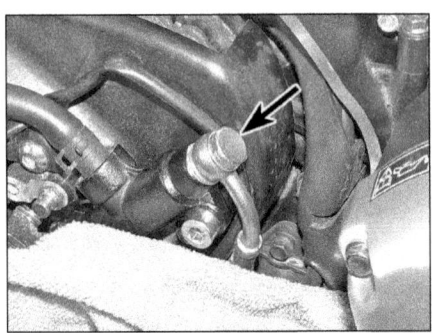

9.7 Brake hose banjo bolt (arrowed)

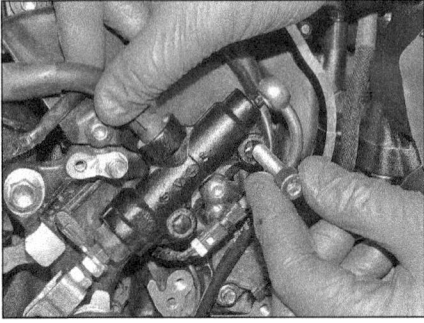

9.8 Unscrew the bolts and remove the master cylinder

9.10 Rear brake light switch wiring connector (arrowed)

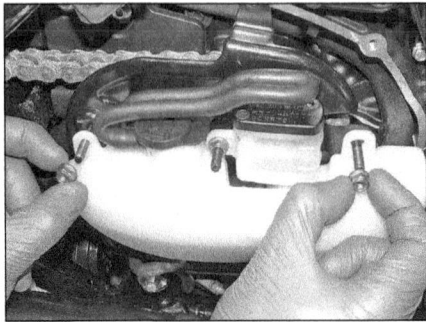

9.11a Unscrew the nuts, displace the reservoir...

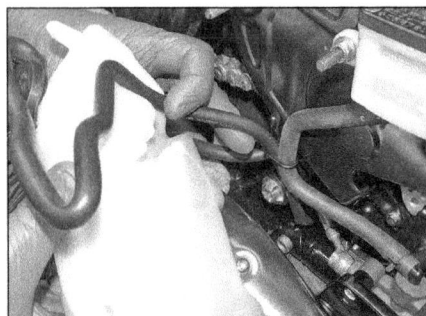

9.11b ...and release the hose

9.12 Unscrew the nut

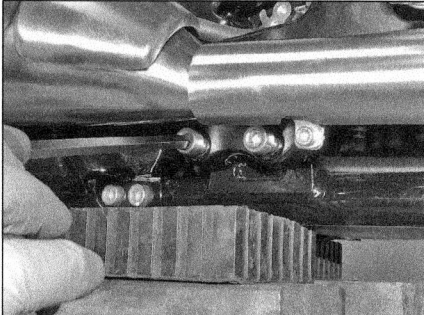

9.13 Brake hose banjo bolt (arrowed)

9.14a Unscrew the bolts using a ball-ended hex key...

9.14b ... and lift the assembly out

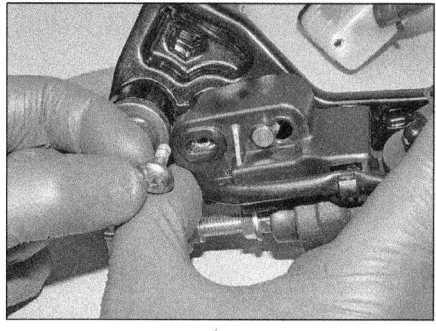

9.15 Undo the screw and displace the bracket

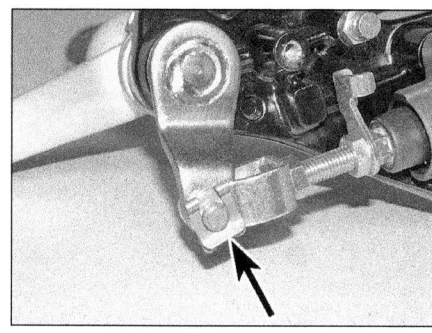

9.16 Remove the clip (arrowed) then withdraw the clevis pin

Section 11 – fluid change). Undo the reservoir nut (see illustration).

**13** Note the alignment of the brake hose banjo fitting, then unscrew the banjo bolt and detach the hose, noting the positions of the sealing washers (see illustration). Be prepared with a rag to catch any drops of brake fluid. Seal the banjo union with a suitable nut and bolt or using a dedicated tool, or support it upright and cover it in rag (see illustrations 3.2c or d). Note that new sealing washers must be used on reassembly.

**14** Unscrew the footrest/brake pedal/master cylinder bracket bolts and lift the complete assembly out, noting the routing of the brake light switch wire (see illustrations).

**15** Undo the brake light switch bracket screw then slide the bracket to free the slot from the lug head and displace the switch assembly (see illustration).

**16** Remove the clip from the inner end of the master cylinder pushrod clevis pin and withdraw the pin (see illustration and 9.6a, b and c).

**17** Unscrew the master cylinder bolts and remove the master cylinder and reservoir from the bracket (see illustrations).

### Thruxton and Thruxton R

**18** Remove the right-hand side cover (see Chapter 7). Remove the front sprocket cover (Section 20).

**19** Remove the brake fluid from the reservoir and wipe the reservoir with a clean rag (see Section 11 – fluid change). Undo the reservoir screw (see illustration 9.3).

**20** Unscrew the brake hose guide bolt (see illustration). Note the alignment of the brake hose banjo fitting, then unscrew the banjo bolt and detach the hose, noting the positions

9.17a One bolt (arrowed) is on the inner side...

9.20a Brake hose guide bolt (arrowed)

of the sealing washers (see illustration). Be prepared with a rag to catch any drops of brake fluid. Seal the banjo union with a suitable nut and bolt or using a dedicated

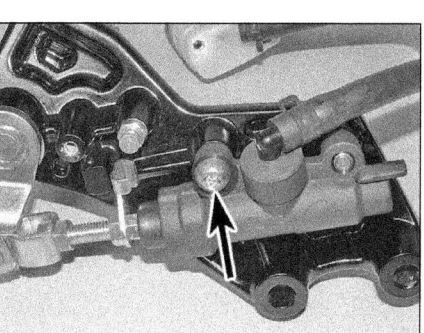

9.17b ...and one on the outer side of the bracket

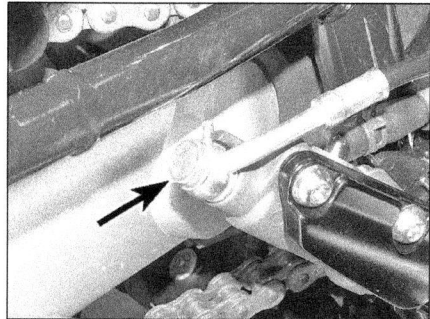

9.20b Brake hose banjo bolt (arrowed)

**9.21 Unscrew the bracket bolts (arrowed)**

**9.24 Front bolt/nut (A), rear bolt (B)**

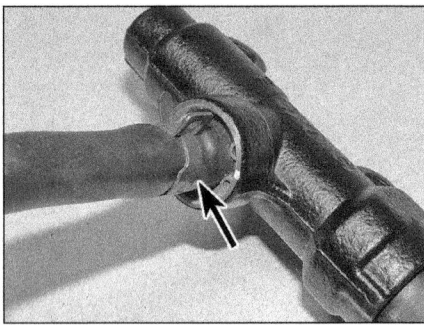

**9.25 Reservoir hose clamp (arrowed)**

**9.26a Pull the boot out...**

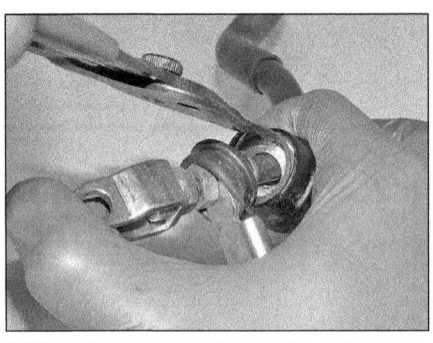

**9.26b ...then release the circlip and remove the pushrod assembly...**

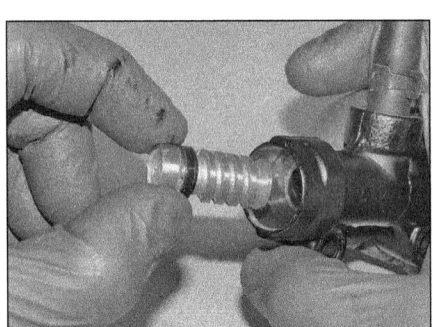

**9.26c ...and the piston...**

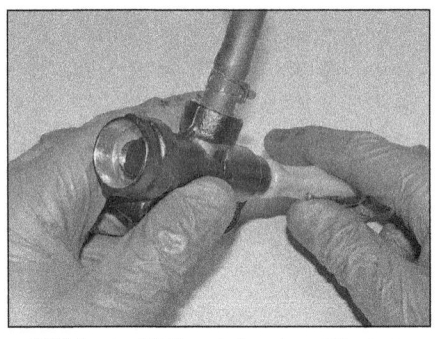

**9.26d ...and if the spring doesn't come with the piston push it out as shown**

**9.29a Fit the seal onto the piston as shown**

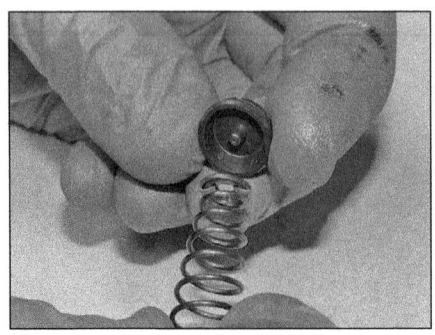

**9.29b Fit the peg on the underside of the cup into the hole in the top of the spring**

tool, or support it upright and cover it in rag **(see illustrations 3.2c or d).** Note that new sealing washers must be used on reassembly.
21 Unscrew the footrest/brake pedal/master cylinder bracket bolts and lift the complete assembly out, then disconnect the brake light switch wiring connector **(see illustration)**.
22 Undo the brake light switch bracket screw then slide the bracket to free the slot from the lug head and displace the switch assembly **(see illustration 9.15)**.
23 Remove the clip from the inner end of the master cylinder pushrod clevis pin and withdraw the pin **(see illustrations 9.16 and 9.6a, b and c)**.
24 Unscrew the nut on the master cylinder front bolt and remove the bolt, then unscrew the rear bolt and remove the master cylinder and reservoir from the bracket **(see illustration)**.

### Overhaul – T100, T120, Bobber, Street Twin, Street Cup and Scrambler

25 If required release the clamp securing the reservoir hose to the union on the master cylinder and detach the hose **(see illustration)**. Unless there are signs that the reservoir hose union seal is leaking, do not remove the union – the union assembly comes as a set and the seal is not available by itself.
26 Pull back the boot from the end of the master cylinder to reveal the retaining circlip **(see illustration)**. Depress the pushrod and use circlip pliers to remove the circlip, then remove the pushrod, the piston and spring **(see illustrations)** – if necessary push the spring and cup out using a screwdriver inserted from the top **(see illustration)**.
27 Clean inside the master cylinder with fresh DOT 4 brake fluid. If compressed air is available, blow it through the fluid passages to ensure they are clear (make sure the air is filtered and unlubricated).

*Caution: Do not, under any circumstances, use a petroleum-based solvent to clean brake parts.*

28 Check the master cylinder bore for corrosion, scratches, nicks and score marks. If damage or wear is evident, the master cylinder must be replaced with a new one. If the master cylinder is in poor condition, then the caliper should be checked as well.
29 The piston, seal, cup and spring are included in the piston set. Use all of the new parts, regardless of the apparent condition of the old ones. Fit the seal onto the piston and the cup into the narrow end of the spring **(see illustrations)**. Lubricate the cup, seal and piston with clean brake fluid. Smear some silicone grease onto the rounded end of the pushrod.

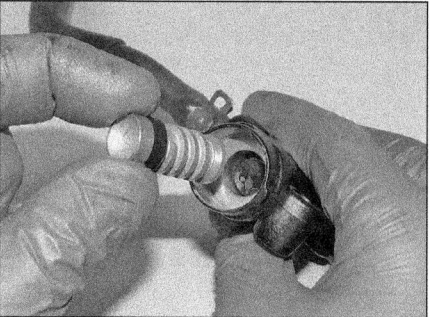

9.30a Fit the spring...

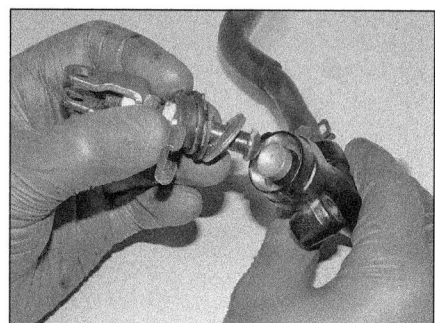

9.30b ... and the piston...

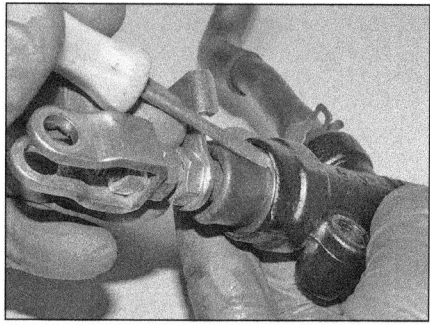

9.30c ...and push them in using the pushrod...

30  Insert the wide end of the spring then ease the cup in, making sure its lip does not catch as it enters the bore (see illustration). Seat the piston against the cup, then seat the pushrod against the piston and push it in to compress the spring, making sure the seal lip does not catch (see illustrations). Hold the pushrod and fit the circlip into its groove (see illustration).

31  Push the boot into place with its wider end located inside the master cylinder (see illustration).

32  Check the reservoir, cap, diaphragm plate and diaphragm and fit new ones as required if they are damaged or deteriorated. Check the reservoir hose for cracks or splits and replace it with a new one if necessary. Check the hose clips and use new ones if they are strained or corroded. Push the reservoir hose fully onto its union and secure it with the clip (see illustration 9.25).

### Installation

33  Installation is the reverse of removal, noting the following:
● On the T100, T120, Street Twin, Street Cup and Scrambler tighten the master cylinder bolts to 24 Nm.
● On the Bobber tighten the master cylinder bolts to 16 Nm and the bracket bolts to 24 Nm.
● On the Thruxton and Thruxton R tighten the master cylinder bolts to 18 Nm – Triumph specify to use a new locknut with the front bolt. Tighten the bracket bolts to 25 Nm.

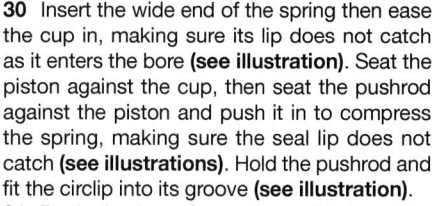

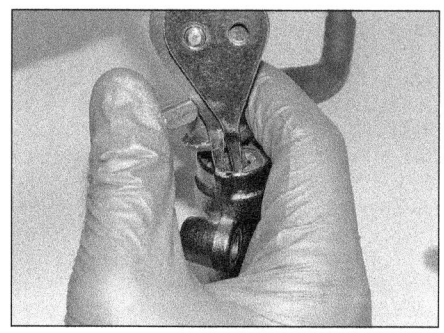

9.30d ...and fit the circlip

● Push on the brake light switch bracket so the switch button is against and pushed in by the actuation plate on the pushrod before tightening the screw(s) (see illustration 9.33a). After tightening the screw(s) push the brake pedal down or the pushrod in and check that you can hear the switch button click as the switch closes and then again as it opens when the pedal or pushrod is released.
● Fit the brake hose banjo bolt using a new sealing washer on each side of the banjo union (see illustration 9.33b). Align the hose on the master cylinder, then tighten the bolt to 25 Nm (see illustration 9.7, 9.13 or 9.24).
● Make sure the flat side of the clevis pin clip locates correctly in its groove and the

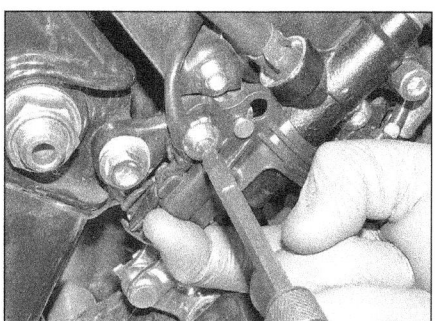

9.33a Push on the bracket to ensure the lug head is fully seated in the narrow section of the slot and the switch button is against the plate

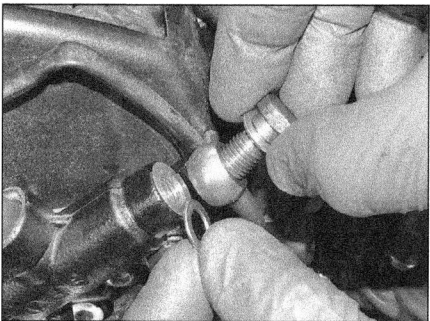

9.33b Use new sealing washers, one on each side of the banjo union

9.31 Seat the wide lip of the boot in the master cylinder

shaped side seats around the end of the pin (see illustration 9.16).

34  Fill the fluid reservoir with new DOT 4 brake fluid and bleed the air from the system as described in Section 11.

35  Check that there are no fluid leaks and test the brake and brake light before riding the bike.

## 10  Brake hoses and fittings

**Note:** *Due to the shape of the brake hose banjo bolt heads, which have slightly rounded corners, you need to use a hex socket to slacken and tighten them rather than a bi-hex one.*

### Inspection

1  Brake hose and pipe condition should be checked regularly and the hoses replaced with new ones at the specified interval (see Chapter 1).

### Renewal

**Note:** *With ABS, before draining the brake fluid from the system, changing the fluid, or disconnecting any brake hose or pipe, bear in mind that the system must be bled on completion of work, and although this is done initially in the same way as models without ABS, to complete the procedure effectively the Triumph Diagnostic tool must be used to open and close the solenoids within the ABS modulator, and this can only be carried out by a dealer with the diagnostic tool. The bike should be transported, not ridden, to the dealer.*

**2** The brake hoses have banjo fittings on each end. For access to the ABS modulator see Section 17. Trace the hose being removed from end to end and remove all parts necessary as required according to model to be able to release and remove the hose, referring to the relevant Chapter(s).

**3** Flush the old brake fluid from the system (Section 11).

**4** Cover the surrounding area with plenty of rags to catch any drops of brake fluid. Release the hose from any clips and guides as required according to model, noting the routing. Note the alignment of the banjo fitting. Unscrew the banjo bolt at each end of the hose.

**5** Position the new hose or hose/pipe, making sure it is correctly aligned and not twisted or otherwise strained, and ensure that it is correctly routed through any clips or guides and is clear of all moving components.

**6** Check that the banjo fittings align correctly, then fit the banjo bolts, using a new sealing washer on each side of the fitting **(see illustration 9.33)**.

**7** Tighten the banjo bolts to 25 Nm.

**8** Refill the system with new brake fluid and bleed out all air (Section 11). Check that there are no fluid leaks and thoroughly test the operation of the brake before riding the motorcycle.

## 11 Brake system bleeding and fluid change

**Special tool:** *The brake bleeding equipment described in Step 3 will be required – ready-made bleeding kits are cheaply available from automotive stores.*

**Note:** *Before draining the brake fluid from the system, changing the fluid, or disconnecting any brake hoses or pipes from the master cylinders and ABS modulator or between them, bear in mind that the system must be bled on completion of work. To complete the procedure*

*effectively the Triumph Diagnostic tool must be used to open and close the solenoids within the ABS modulator, and this can only be carried out by a dealer with the diagnostic tool. The bike should be transported, not ridden, to the dealer. It is OK to disconnect the hoses from the calipers, provided they are supported upright to minimise fluid loss and air ingress, as they come after the modulator in the system and so any air that gets into the end of the hose or caliper does not have to bleed through the modulator.*

### Bleeding

**1** Bleeding a brake is the process of removing aerated brake fluid from the master cylinder, the hose(s)/pipe(s) and the brake caliper(s). Bleeding is necessary whenever a brake system hydraulic connection is loosened, after a component or hose is replaced with a new one, when a master cylinder or caliper is overhauled, or when there is a spongy feel to the lever and it travels all the way back to the handlebar, and where braking force is less than it should be, and it is not due to any mechanical fault in the system (i.e. a sticking piston in the caliper, or a pad that is not moving as it should due to corrosion, for example on the pad pin). Leaks in the system may also allow air to enter, but leaking brake fluid will reveal their presence and warn you of the need for repair.

**2** Brake bleeding is considered by some as a bit of a black art – seasoned professionals sometimes have trouble getting a good firm feel in the brake lever, while a first timer may have no trouble at all. One of the problems, particularly with the front brakes, is that you are working against natural principles – science dictates that air bubbles in a liquid will rise to the top, but the process entails pumping the brake fluid and any air bubbles it contains down, from the master cylinder at the top to the bleed valve in the caliper at the bottom, so while the fluid is moving down the air bubbles will want to rise. Air bubbles can also get trapped, particularly where there

are high points in its path, and when there are extra components and pipes as on ABS models.

**3** To bleed the brakes using the conventional method, you will need some new DOT 4 brake fluid, a length of clear flexible hose, a small container partially filled with clean brake fluid, some rags, and a ring spanner to fit the brake caliper bleed valve. Bleeding kits that include the hose, a one-way valve and a container are available relatively cheaply from a good auto store, and simplify the task **(see illustration)**. You may also need a block of wood as a support for the fluid container.

**4** Cover painted components to prevent damage in the event that brake fluid is spilled. *Caution: Brake fluid attacks painted finishes and plastics – to prevent damage from spilled fluid, always cover paintwork when working on the braking system, and clean up any spills immediately using brake cleaner.*

### Front brake system

**5** Turn the handlebars so the reservoir is level. Refer to *Pre-ride checks* and remove the reservoir cover, diaphragm plate (where fitted) and diaphragm. Slowly pump the brake lever a few times to dislodge any fine air bubbles from the small hole in the bottom of the reservoir. Now hold the lever in to force any large air bubbles out of the large hole – you can tie the lever to the handlebar and leave it pressurised for a while to prevent having to hold it, then release it and slowly pump it a few times. You can tell when all the air is gone as the large hole appears completely dark, whereas if there is any air left it will appear to have a silvery rim that is actually the edge of an air bubble.

**6** On the Thruxton R the front brake system has three bleed points, one on the master cylinder and one on each caliper. Bleed the master cylinder first **(see illustration)**. On twin disc models there is a bleed valve on each caliper.

**11.3 Brake bleeding kit set-up**

**11.6 Master cylinder bleed valve (arrowed) – Thruxton R**

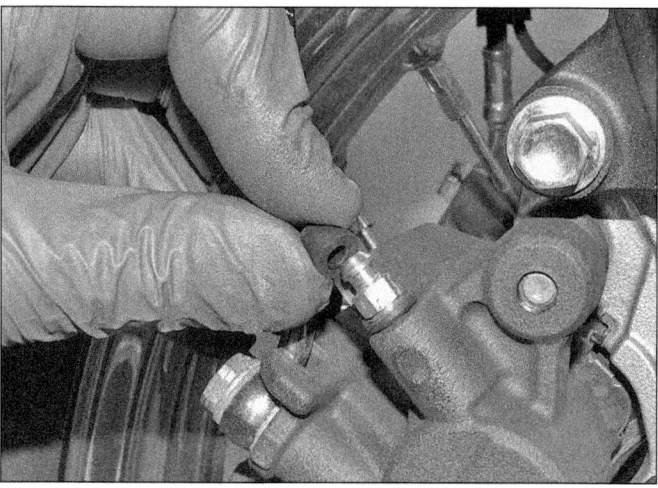

11.7a Pull the cap off the bleed valve

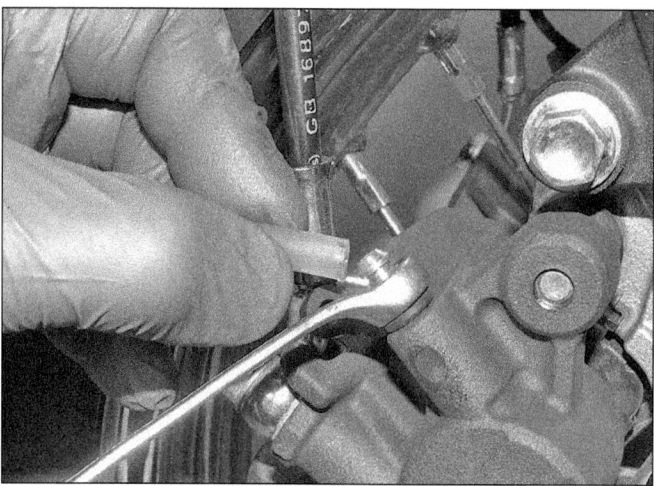

11.7b Fit the ring spanner over the valve then connect the hose

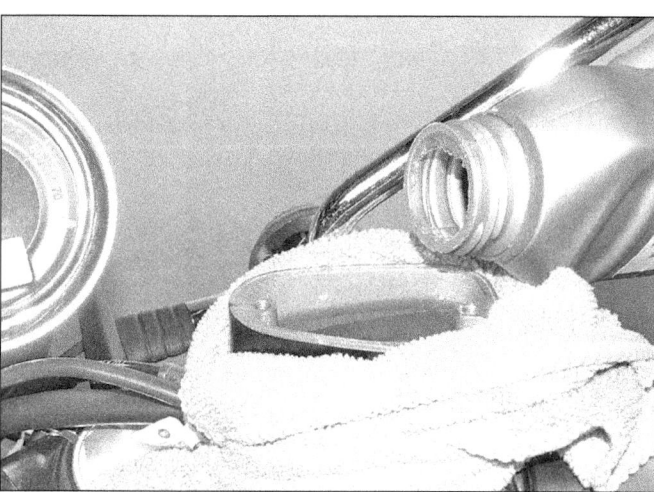

11.8 Keep the reservoir topped up

11.9 Bleed the front brake as described

**7** Pull the dust cap off the bleed valve **(see illustration)**. If using a ring spanner (which is preferable to an open-ended one) fit it onto the valve. Attach one end of the bleeding hose to the bleed valve and, if not using a kit, submerge the other end in the clean brake fluid in the container **(see illustration)**.

**8** Check the fluid level in the reservoir – keep it topped up and do not allow the level to drop below the lower level line during the procedure **(see illustration)**.

**9** Slowly pump the brake lever a few times, then hold it in and open the bleed valve a quarter turn **(see illustration)**. When the valve is opened, brake fluid will flow out of the bleed valve into the clear tubing, and the lever will move to the handlebar. If there is air in the system there will be air bubbles in the brake fluid coming out of the valve, but not necessarily on the first pump.

**10** Tighten the bleed valve, then release the brake lever. Repeat the process until no air

bubbles have been seen for a few pumps, and the lever is firm when applied, topping the reservoir up when necessary. On completion tighten the bleed valve and remove the equipment, then fit the dust cap.

**11** On twin disc models and the Thruxton R transfer the equipment to the next bleed valve and repeat the bleeding procedure.

**12** When the system has been successfully bled there should be a good and progressively firm feel as the lever is applied, and the lever should not be able to travel all the way back to the handlebar.

**13** When you've completed bleeding, refer to *Pre-ride checks* and top-up the reservoir, then fit the diaphragm, diaphragm plate, and cover according to model. Check for spilled brake fluid and clean up as required.

**14** Refer to the Note above and if necessary take the bike to a Triumph dealer to complete the bleeding of the modulator. Check that there are no fluid leaks and test the brake before riding the bike.

**Rear brake system**

**15** On the T100 and T120 remove the left-hand silencer (see Chapter 4). On all models except the Bobber remove the right-hand side cover (see Chapter 7). On the Bobber remove the front sprocket cover (Section 20).

**16** Refer to *Pre-ride checks* and remove the reservoir cover screws and remove the cover, diaphragm plate and diaphragm. Slowly pump the brake pedal a few times to dislodge any fine air bubbles from the small hole in the bottom of the reservoir. Now hold the lever in to force any large air bubbles out of the large hole – you can support a weight on the pedal and leave it pressurised for a while to prevent having to hold it, then release it and slowly pump it a few times. You can tell when all the air is gone as the large hole appears completely dark, whereas if there is any air left it will appear to have a silvery rim that is actually the edge of an air bubble.

**17** Pull the dust cap off the bleed valve on

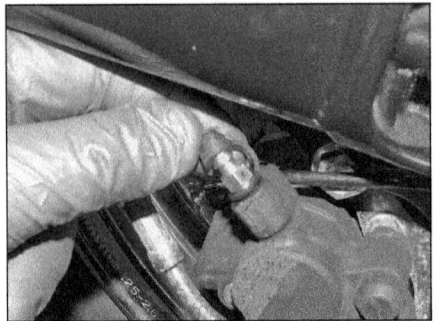

**11.17a Pull the cap off the bleed valve**

**11.17b Fit the ring spanner over the valve then connect the hose**

**11.18 Keep the reservoir topped up**

the caliper **(see illustration)**. If using a ring spanner (which is preferable to an open-ended one) fit it onto the valve. Attach one end of the bleeding hose to the bleed valve and, if not using a kit, submerge the other end in the clean brake fluid in the container **(see illustration)**.

**18** Check the fluid level in the reservoir – keep it topped up and do not allow the level to drop below the lower level line during the procedure **(see illustration)**.

**19** Slowly pump the brake pedal a few times, then hold it down and open the bleed valve a quarter turn **(see illustration)**. When the valve is opened, brake fluid will flow out of the bleed valve into the clear tubing, and the pedal will move down. If there is air in the system there will be air bubbles in the brake fluid coming out of the valve, but not necessarily on the first pump.

**20** Tighten the bleed valve, then release the brake pedal. Repeat the process until no air bubbles have been seen for a few pumps, and the pedal is firm when applied, topping the reservoir up when necessary.

**21** When the system has been successfully bled there should be a good and progressively firm feel as the pedal is applied, and the pedal should not be able to travel all the way down to its stop.

**Note:** *Following a master cylinder overhaul on a T120 the system would not bleed, evident by the fact that the fluid level in the reservoir did not drop however much the pedal was pumped. This was because the top of the master cylinder was full of air. If this happens slacken the brake hose banjo bolt and slowly pump the pedal until air stops bubbling out and just fluid comes out, at which point tighten the banjo bolt to 25 Nm, then bleed the system as normal.*

**22** When you've completed bleeding tighten the bleed valve and remove the equipment, then fit the dust cap. Refer to *Pre-ride checks* and top-up the reservoir to between the level marks, then fit the diaphragm, diaphragm plate, and cover. Check for spilled brake fluid and clean up as required.

**23** Refer to the Note above and if necessary take the bike to a Triumph dealer to complete the bleeding of the modulator. Check that there are no fluid leaks and test the brake before riding the bike.

**Both systems**

**24** If it is not possible to produce a firm feel to the lever or pedal, the fluid may be full of many tiny air bubbles rather than a few big ones. To remedy this apply some pressure to the system, for the front brake by tying the front brake lever lightly back to the handlebar,

and for the rear by tying a weight to the brake pedal – do not apply too much pressure or the cup and seals in the master cylinder and caliper may fail. Let the fluid stabilise for a few hours, after which the tiny bubbles should either have risen to the top in the reservoir, or have formed into one or more big bubbles that can be more easily bled out by repeating the bleeding procedure.

**25** If you are still having trouble look for any high point in the system in which a pocket of air may become trapped. Displace and agitate the hose or pipe so the bubble can be dislodged (but take care not to bend a pipe) – tapping it may help. If necessary displace the master cylinder and/or the caliper(s), and free the brake hose(s) from guides and move the parts around to dislodge the air and encourage it towards a bleed valve – refer to the relevant Sections as required to displace components. If you cannot get the system to bleed correctly take the bike to a Triumph dealer.

**26** If bleeding the system using the conventional tools and methods stated does not give satisfactory results, or if otherwise preferred, you can use a commercially available vacuum-type brake bleeding tool, such as the Mity-vac, following the manufacturer's instructions **(see illustration)**.

**11.19 Bleed the rear brake as described**

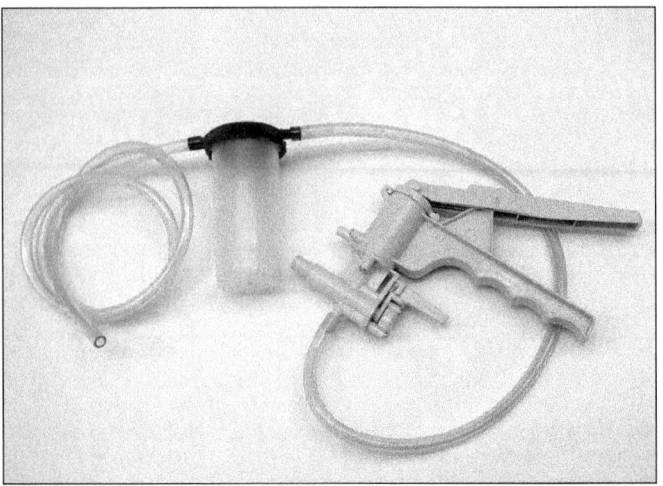

**11.26 Vacuum-type brake bleeding tool**

This type of tool literally sucks the fluid out by creating a vacuum at the bleed valve. Users of such tools often get confused by the amount of air that appears to be in the brake fluid – more often than not this is caused by the vacuum sucking air past the bleed valve threads (air provides less resistance to the vacuum than the brake fluid) where it mixes with the fluid being drawn out. If this is the case the vacuum applied may be too great, or the bleed valve may have been loosened too much. One way to get round this is to remove the bleed valve and thread some PTFE tape around its threads, but note that doing so will be a bit messy, so have some rag to hand.

### Fluid change

**27** Changing the brake fluid is a similar process to bleeding the brakes and requires the same materials plus a suitable tool (such as a syringe, or alternatively lots of absorbent rag or paper) for siphoning the fluid out of the reservoir.
**28** Cover painted components and fit the equipment to the relevant caliper following the appropriate Steps in the bleeding procedure given above. Remove the reservoir cover or cap, diaphragm plate and diaphragm (Step 5 or 16). Remove the fluid from the reservoir into a suitable container, either by sucking it up using a tool as shown, drawing it out into a syringe, or soaking it up in some paper towel. Wipe the reservoir clean. Fill the reservoir with new brake fluid. Squeeze or press the brake lever or pedal and open the bleed valve **(see illustrations 11.9 and 11.19)**. When the valve is opened, brake fluid will flow out of the caliper into the clear tubing, and the lever will move toward the handlebar, or the pedal will move down.
**29** Tighten the bleed valve, then slowly release the brake lever or pedal. Keep the reservoir topped-up with new fluid at all times or air may enter the system and greatly increase the length of the task. Repeat the process until new fluid can be seen emerging from the caliper bleed valve.
**30** On completion tighten the bleed valve and remove the equipment, then fit the dust cap. Top-up the reservoir to the mark, then fit the diaphragm, diaphragm plate, and cover or cap. Check for spilled brake fluid and clean up as required.
**31** Refer to the Note above and take the bike to a Triumph dealer to complete the bleeding of the modulator. Check that there are no fluid leaks and test the brake before riding the bike.

### Draining the system for overhaul

**32** Draining the brake fluid is again a similar process to bleeding the brakes. The quickest and easiest way is to use a commercially available vacuum-type brake bleeding tool (see Step 26) – follow the manufacturer's instructions. Otherwise follow the procedure

described above for changing the fluid, but quite simply do not put any new fluid into the reservoir – the system fills itself with air instead.
**33** When it comes to refilling the system start by adding new fluid from a sealed container to the reservoir, then perform the bleeding procedure as described above until the fluid comes out of the bleed valve, and keep at it until you are certain there is no more air left in the system.

## 12 Wheel inspection and repair

**1** In order to carry out a proper inspection of the wheels, it is necessary to support the bike securely in an upright position so that the wheel being inspected is raised off the ground. Clean the wheels thoroughly to remove mud and dirt that may interfere with the inspection procedure or mask defects. Make a general check of the wheels (see Chapter 1) and tyres (see *Pre-ride checks*).
**2** Attach a dial gauge to the fork or the swingarm and position its tip against the side of the wheel rim **(see illustration)**. Spin the wheel slowly and check the axial (side-to-side) runout at the rim.
**3** In order to accurately check radial (out of round) runout with the dial gauge, remove the wheel from the machine, and the tyre from the wheel. With the axle clamped in a vice and the dial gauge positioned on the top of the rim,

**12.2 Check the wheel for radial (out-of-round) runout (A) and axial (side-to-side) runout (B)**

the wheel can be rotated to check the runout.
**4** An easier, though slightly less accurate, method is to attach a stiff wire pointer to the fork or the swingarm and position the end a fraction of an inch from the edge of the wheel rim where the wheel and tyre join. If the wheel is true, the distance from the pointer to the rim will be constant as the wheel is rotated. If wheel runout is excessive, check the wheel bearings very carefully before renewing the wheel.
**5** If wheel runout is excessive, first check the wheel bearings. If they are good, on spoke wheeled models it should be possible to realign the wheel by adjusting the spokes, but to do this accurately takes some knowledge and skill, and should be left to an experienced wheel builder. On cast alloy wheeled models you will have to renew the wheel.
**6** The cast wheels should also be inspected for cracks, flat spots on the rim and other damage. Look very closely for dents in the area where the tyre bead contacts the rim. Dents in this area may prevent complete sealing of the tubeless tyre against the rim, which leads to deflation of the tyre over a period of time. If damage is evident, the wheel will have to be renewed. Never attempt to repair a damaged cast alloy wheel.

## 13 Wheel alignment check

**1** Misalignment of the wheels due to a bent frame or forks can cause strange and possibly serious handling problems. If the frame or forks are at fault, repair by a frame specialist or replacement with new parts are the only options.
**2** To check wheel alignment you will need an assistant, a length of string or a perfectly straight piece of wood and a ruler. A plumb bob or spirit level for checking that the wheels are vertical will also be required.
**3** In order to make a proper check of the wheels it is necessary to support the bike in an upright position on an auxiliary stand. First ensure that the chain adjuster markings coincide on each side of the swingarm (see Chapter 1, Section 3). Next, measure the width of both tyres at their widest points. Subtract the smaller measurement from the larger measurement, then divide the difference by two. The result is the amount of offset that should exist between the front and rear tyres on both sides of the machine.
**4** If a string is used, have your assistant hold one end of it about halfway between the floor and the rear axle, with the string touching the back edge of the rear tyre sidewall.
**5** Run the other end of the string forward and pull it tight so that it is roughly parallel to the

floor **(see illustration)**. Slowly bring the string into contact with the front edge of the rear tyre sidewall, then turn the front wheel until it is parallel with the string. Measure the distance from the front tyre sidewall to the string.

**6** Repeat the procedure on the other side of the motorcycle. The distance from the front tyre sidewall to the string should be equal on both sides.

**7** As previously mentioned, a perfectly straight length of wood or metal bar may be substituted for the string **(see illustration)**.

**8** If the distance between the string and tyre is greater on one side, or if the rear wheel appears to be out of alignment, have your machine checked by a Triumph dealer or motorcycle frame specialist.

**9** If the front-to-back alignment is correct, the wheels still may be out of alignment vertically.

**10** Using a plumb bob or spirit level, check the rear wheel to make sure it is vertical. To do this, hold the string of the plumb bob against the tyre upper sidewall and allow the weight to settle just off the floor. If the string touches both the upper and lower tyre sidewalls and is perfectly straight, the wheel is vertical. If it is not, adjust the stand until it is.

**11** Once the rear wheel is vertical, check that the front wheel is vertical also. If both wheels are not perfectly vertical, the frame and/or major suspension components are bent.

## 14 Front wheel

### *Removal*

**1** Support the bike on the centrestand on the T120 and on a rear paddock stand on all other models, then raise the front using a jack under the engine with a piece of wood between them to spread the load, so the forks are fully extended and the front wheel is just on the ground.

**2** Displace the front brake caliper(s) (Section 3).

**3** Slacken the axle clamp bolt(s) on the bottom of the right-hand fork, then unscrew the axle **(see illustration)**.

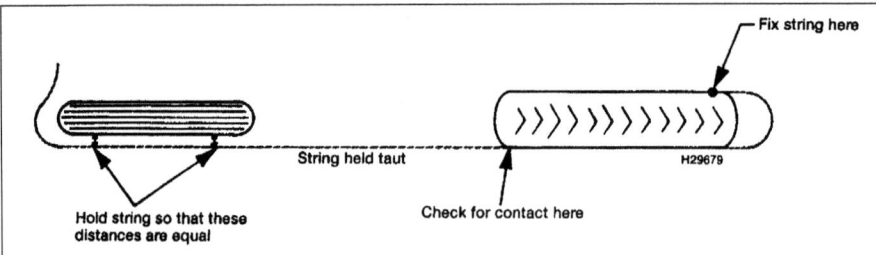

13.5 Wheel alignment check using string

**4** Support the wheel, then withdraw the axle and remove the wheel from between the forks **(see illustration)**.

**5** Remove the spacer from each side of the wheel, noting how they fit inside the bearing seals **(see illustration)**.

*Caution: Don't lay the wheel down and allow it to rest on either brake disc – they could become warped. Set the wheel on wood blocks so the wheel rim supports the weight of the wheel, or keep the wheel upright. Don't operate the brake lever with the wheel removed.*

**6** Wipe any old grease off the bearing seals and check the condition of the seals and the wheel bearings (Section 16).

**7** Clean the axle and remove any corrosion using steel wool. Check the axle is straight by rolling it on a flat surface such as a piece of plate glass. If available, place the axle in V-blocks and check for runout using a dial gauge. If the axle is bent, fit a new one.

**8** Clean the spacers and remove any corrosion with steel wool. The spacers should be perfectly smooth where they locate in the seals.

### *Installation*

**9** Apply lithium-based grease to the insides of the bearing seals. Fit a spacer into the seal on each side **(see illustration 14.5)**.

**10** Apply a thin coat of lithium-based grease to the axle. Position the wheel between the forks, making sure the directional arrow on the tyre points in the direction of normal rotation and the spacers remain in place.

**11** Align and support the wheel, slide the axle in from the right-hand side and into the

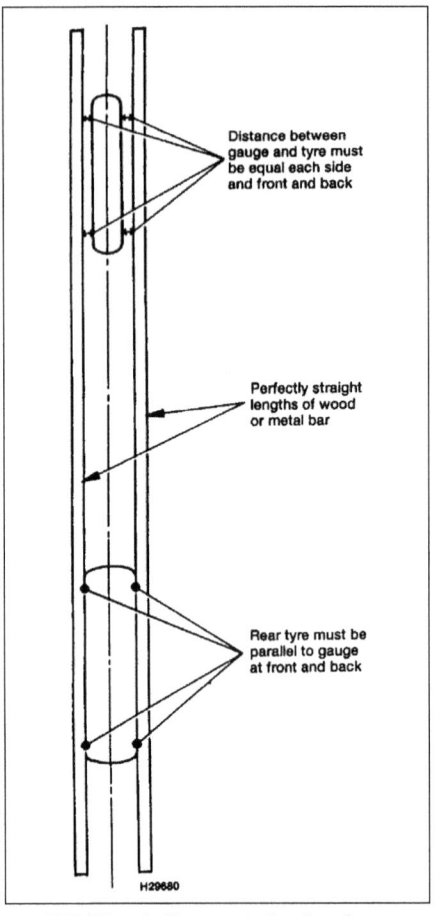

13.7 Wheel alignment check using a straight-edge

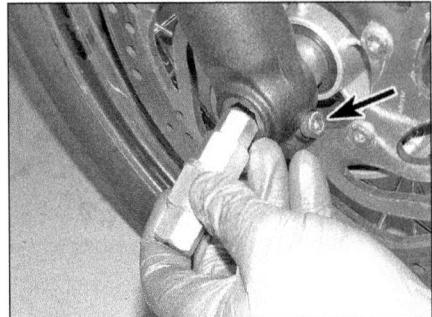

14.3 Slacken the clamp bolt(s) (arrowed) then unscrew the axle using a hex tool – this shows a multi-sized axle tool available from good tool suppliers

14.4 Withdraw the axle and remove the wheel

14.5 Remove the spacer from each side

bottom of the left-hand fork, and tighten it to 65 Nm **(see illustration 14.4)**.

**12** Install the brake caliper(s) (Section 3). Apply the front brake to bring the pads back into contact with the discs. Take the bike off its stand and pump the forks by applying the brake and pressing down on the handlebars.

**13** Tighten the clamp bolt(s) on the bottom of the right-hand fork to 22 Nm **(see illustration 14.3)**.

**14** Check the operation of the front brake before riding the motorcycle.

## 15 Rear wheel and sprocket coupling

### *Removal*

**1** Support the bike on the centrestand on the T120 and on a rear paddock stand on all other models except the Bobber. Place a support under the wheel that just takes up the gap without pushing up on it **(see illustration)**. On the Bobber you need to raise the back of the bike sufficiently for the rear wheel to clear the rear mudguard – we placed 170 mm of blocks

**15.1a Take up the gap using blocks of wood**

**15.1b Bobber supported under the frame**

under the frame on each side, removed the sprocket coupling and tilted the wheel to get it out **(see illustration)**. To fit the blocks have an assistant tilt the bike to one side and place blocks under the high side, then carefully lift the bike onto the blocks and place blocks under the other side – make sure the blocks are clear of the regulator/rectifier, or remove it if necessary (see Chapter 8). On all models tie the front brake lever on so the bike can't roll forward.

**2** On the T100, T120 and Street Twin remove the silencers (see Chapter 4).

**3** Remove the chain guard **(see illustration)**.

**4** Create some slack in the chain (see Chapter 1).

**5** Unscrew the axle nut and remove the washer and the right-hand adjuster plate **(see illustrations)**.

**6** Support the wheel, then withdraw the axle with the left-hand adjuster plate **(see illustration)**. The left and right adjuster plates differ so do not muddle them up.

**15.3 Undo the two screws and remove the guard**

**15.5a Remove the axle nut and washer...**

**15.5b... and the adjuster plate**

**15.6 Withdraw the axle and the adjuster plate**

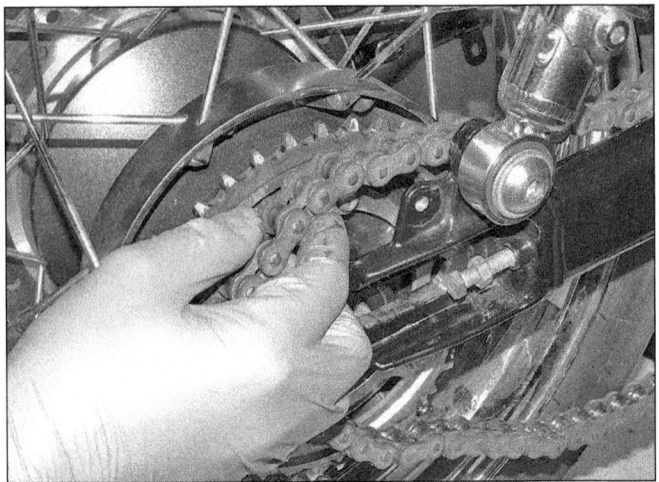

15.7 Slip the chain off the rear sprocket

15.8a On all models except the Bobber draw the wheel back a bit then displace the caliper bracket from its lug on the swingarm

15.8b On the Bobber slide the caliper bracket forwards, noting how its rib locates in the slot...

15.8c ...and remove the sprocket coupling and dampers...

15.8d ...and tilt the wheel as required for clearance

15.9a Remove the plain spacer from the right-hand side...

15.9b ... and the shouldered spacer from the left

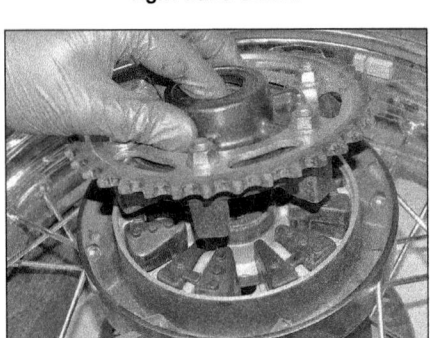

15.10a Lift the sprocket coupling out...

15.10b ...and remove the dampers

7 Disengage the chain from the rear sprocket and lay it on some rag over the swingarm (see illustration).

8 Draw the wheel back and displace the brake caliper bracket, noting how it locates on the swingarm, and support it out of the way (see illustrations). On the Bobber, if necessary remove the sprocket coupling and dampers from the right-hand side and tilt the wheel as shown to get it out (see illustration).

9 Remove the spacer from the each side of the wheel, noting how they fit inside the bearing seals (see illustrations).

*Caution: Don't lay the wheel down and allow it to rest on the disc or the sprocket – they could become warped. Set the wheel on wood blocks so the wheel rim supports the weight of the wheel, or keep the wheel upright. Don't operate the brake pedal with the wheel removed.*

10 Check for any rotational play between the sprocket coupling and the wheel (refit the dampers and coupling on the Bobber if removed) – play indicates worn rubber dampers, and a new set must be fitted. If required lift the sprocket coupling out of the hub and remove the dampers (see illustrations). Note the spacer fitted in

15.10c A spacer fits into the inner side of the bearing as shown

15.18 Correct fitted position of adjuster plate and axle head

the coupling **(see illustration)**. Check the coupling for cracks or any obvious signs of damage. Also check the sprocket studs for looseness, wear or damage.

**11** Wipe any old grease off the bearing seals and check the condition of the seals and the wheel bearings in both the wheel and the sprocket coupling (Section 16).

**12** Clean the axle and remove any corrosion using steel wool. Check the axle is straight by rolling it on a flat surface such as a piece of plate glass. If available, place the axle in V-blocks and check for runout using a dial gauge. If the axle is bent, replace it with a new one.

**13** Clean the spacers and remove any corrosion with steel wool. The spacers should be perfectly smooth where they locate in the seals.

### Installation

**14** If removed, and with the exception of the Bobber if necessary for clearance when fitting the wheel, fit the rubber dampers, using a new set if necessary **(see illustration 15.10b)**. Make sure the spacer is in place in the sprocket coupling bearing, then press the sprocket coupling firmly into the hub, making sure it is fully and evenly seated **(see illustrations 15.10c and a)**.

**15** Apply lithium-based grease to the insides of the bearing seals. Fit the plain spacer into the right-hand side of the wheel and the shouldered spacer into the left, making sure they fit inside the bearing seals **(see illustrations 15.9a and b)**.

**16** Manoeuvre the wheel and the caliper bracket into place, on all models except the Bobber making sure that the slot in the bracket sits over the rib on the inside of the swingarm **(see illustration 15.8a)**, and on the Bobber fitting the rubber dampers and sprocket coupling if removed, making sure the spacer is fitted **(see illustration 15.10c)**,

and making sure the rib on the caliper bracket locates in the slot on the swingarm **(see illustrations 15.8d, c and b)**.

**17** Fit the drive chain around the sprocket **(see illustration 15.7)**.

**18** Slide the left-hand adjuster plate onto the axle and seat the flats on the axle head in it **(see illustration)**.

**19** Lubricate the axle with a smear of grease. Align the wheel, making sure the spacers and caliper bracket remain in place, and slide the axle through from the left-hand side **(see illustration 15.6)** – make sure the adjuster plate and axle head seat correctly **(see illustration 15.18)**.

**20** Seat the right-hand adjuster plate over the end of the axle with the raised section facing out and towards the adjuster bolt, then fit the washer and the axle nut **(see illustrations 15.5b and a)**.

**21** Follow the procedure in Chapter 1 and adjust the chain tension, then tighten the axle nut to 110 Nm.

**22** Fit the chain guard. Install the silencers on the T100, T120 and Street Twin (see Chapter 4).

**23** Apply the rear brake to bring the pads into contact with the disc. Test the rear brake before riding the bike.

16.3 Lever out the seals

## 16 Wheel and sprocket coupling bearings

### Wheel bearings

**Note:** *Always fit the wheel bearings in sets, never individually.*

**1** Remove the wheel (Section 14 or Section 15). If not already done lift the sprocket coupling out of the rear wheel and remove the rubber dampers **(see illustrations 15.10a and b)**. Lay the wheel rim on wood blocks. A caged ball bearing is fitted in each side of the wheel, with a circlip securing the bearing in the left-hand side.

**2** Inspect the seal(s) and bearings – check that each bearing inner race turns smoothly and that the outer race is a tight fit in the hub (see *Tools and Workshop Tips* in the Reference Section). Do not remove the bearings unless they are going to be replaced with new ones.

**3** Lever out the bearing seal from each side of the hub on the front wheel and from the left-hand side of the rear wheel using a flat-bladed screwdriver or a seal hook **(see illustration)**. Take care not to damage the hub. New seals must be fitted on reassembly.

**4** Remove the circlip from the left-hand side **(see illustration)**. A new circlip should be used.

16.4 Release the circlip using internal circlip pliers

16.5a Move the spacer to the side to expose the inner race...

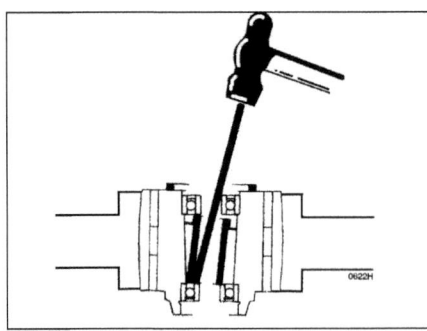

16.5b ...then locate the drift on it and drive the bearing out

16.5c Locate the knife edge of the puller in the gap between the bearing and the spacer, then expand it...

16.5d ...and use the slide-hammer to dislodge the bearing

16.7 A socket can be used to drive the new bearing in

**5** Move the bearing spacer aside to expose the inner race on the lower bearing **(see illustration)**. Using a metal rod (preferably a brass punch) inserted through the centre of the upper bearing and spacer and onto the lower bearing's inner race (do not locate the drift on the top of the spacer) drive the lower bearing from the hub, moving the spacer around and relocating the drift so it's driven out squarely **(see illustration)**. The bearing spacer will also come out. Turn the wheel over so that the remaining bearing faces down. Drive the bearing out of the wheel using a socket on the inner race and an extension bar. If you can't move the spacer, or if you can't get sufficient purchase with the drift, remove the bearings using an internal expanding puller with slide-hammer attachment, which can be obtained commercially – select the

correct attachment and locate it between the inner race of the upper bearing and the spacer, then tighten the inner bolt to expand and lock the puller **(see illustration)**. Attach the slide-hammer, hold the wheel firmly down and jar the bearing out **(see illustration)**.

**6** Thoroughly clean the hub area of the wheel and inspect the bearing housings for damage. If a housing is damaged, consult a Triumph dealer or wheel specialist before reassembling the wheel.

**7** Fit the new bearings with the marked side facing out. Drive the first bearing in using a bearing driver or suitable socket that bears only on the outer race, and make sure the bearing fits squarely and all the way onto its seat **(see illustration)**. Alternatively draw it in using a drawbolt arrangement (see *Tools and Workshop Tips*).

**8** Turn the wheel over then fit the bearing spacer and the other new bearing.

**9** Fit the new circlip into the left-hand side, making sure it seats in the groove **(see illustration 16.4)**.

**10** Fit the new seal(s), marked side facing out, into the hub using finger pressure or a suitable driver that bears on the outer rim, setting them flush with the hub **(see illustration)**. Smear the seal lips with grease.

**11** Clean the disc(s) using acetone or brake system cleaner, then install the wheel.

### Sprocket coupling bearing

**12** Remove the rear wheel (Section 15). If not already done lift the sprocket coupling out of the wheel and remove the rubber dampers **(see illustrations 15.10a and b)**. Remove the spacer from the coupling **(see illustration 15.10c)**.

**13** Inspect the seal and bearing – check that the bearing inner races turn smoothly and that the outer race is a tight fit in the coupling (see *Tools and Workshop Tips* in the Reference Section). Do not remove the bearing unless it is being replaced with a new one.

**14** If new components are needed lever out the bearing seal using a flat-bladed screwdriver or a seal hook **(see illustration)**. Take care not to damage the rim of the coupling. Discard the seal – a new one must be fitted.

**15** Remove the circlip **(see illustration)**. A new circlip should be used.

**16** Support the coupling on blocks of wood,

16.10 Fit the new seal and press or tap it into place

16.14 Lever out the seal

16.15 Release the circlip using internal circlip pliers

**16.16 Drive the bearing out from the inside**

**16.18 A socket can be used to drive in the new bearing**

**16.20 Press or drive the seal into the coupling**

sprocket side down, and drive the bearing out from the inside using a bearing driver or socket **(see illustration)**.

**17** Thoroughly clean the sprocket coupling and inspect the bearing housing for damage. If the housing is damaged, consult a Triumph dealer or wheel specialist before reassembling the wheel.

**18** Fit the new bearing with the marked side facing out. Drive the bearing in using a bearing driver or suitable socket that bears only on the outer race, and make sure the bearing fits squarely and all the way onto its seat **(see illustration)**.

**19** Fit the new circlip into the left-hand side, making sure it seats in the groove **(see illustration 16.15)**.

**20** Fit the new seal, marked side facing out, into the coupling using finger pressure or a suitable driver that bears on the outer rim, setting it flush with the hub **(see illustration)**. Smear the seal lips with grease.

**21** Push the spacer into the inner side of the bearing **(see illustration 15.10c)**.

**22** Clean the brake disc using acetone or brake system cleaner then install the wheel (Section 15).

## 17 ABS and TCS

### System operation

  *Warning: The system works by comparing the relative speed of the wheels, and is programmed using the wheel and tyre sizes specified and fitted as standard by Triumph. If non-specified wheels or tyres are fitted the control unit may become confused and the system will not function correctly.*

### ABS (Anti-lock Braking System)

**1** The anti-lock braking system (ABS) prevents the wheels from locking up under hard braking or on uneven road surfaces. A sensor on each wheel picks up information about the speed of wheel rotation from a pulse ring mounted on the wheel and transmits to an electronic control unit in the modulator,

and if it senses that a wheel is about to lock, it activates the solenoids in the modulator which releases brake pressure momentarily to that wheel, preventing a skid. When the system is active a pulsing can be felt through the lever or pedal as the fluid pressure is released and reapplied as required. The front and rear systems are entirely independent of each other, even though they function through the same control module and modulator.

**2** When the ignition switch is turned on, the ABS indicator light on the instrument panel come on, then goes off when a speed of 6 mph (10 km/h) is reached. If the indicator light stays on, or comes on while riding, then there is probably a fault in the system, in which case it will record a fault code (see Chapter 4 Section 11). Stop the motorcycle and switch the ignition switch off. Switch it on again, start the engine and ride the bike – if the light goes off then the system is OK and will work, but the fault code is still stored. Depending on the severity or continuity of a fault the system may or may not switch itself off, but if it doesn't, if the fault still exists when the bike is next ridden, it will not switch itself on. If the light remains on or comes on again, take the machine to a Triumph dealer for further investigation. It is possible to turn ABS off on the Thruxton, Thruxton R and Street Scrambler models. Details can be found in the owner's manual. ABS will default to ON when the ignition is next switched on.

### TCS (Traction Control System)

**3** The TCS helps prevent slipping or loss of traction of the rear wheel under hard

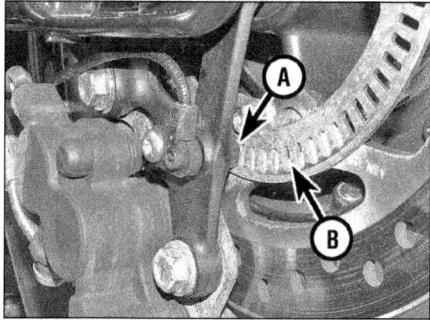

**17.5a Check the sensor tip (A) and rotor poles (B) are clean**

acceleration or poor road conditions. In the event that loss of traction is detected the ECM reduces engine power until it is restored.

**4** TCS works in conjunction with ABS. If there is an ABS fault, the TCS will not function and warning lights for ABS, TCS disabled, and the MIL warning light will be displayed. It is possible to turn TCS off via the scroll button and instrument menu. TCS will default to ON when the ignition is next switched on. Refer to the owner's manual for details.

### Checks

**5** The only actions the owner can take in the case of a fault, and the only maintenance that can be applied, is firstly to make sure there is no dirt or debris on each wheel speed sensor tip or between the poles on the sensor rotor **(see illustration)**. Secondly check the air gap between the sensor tip and one of the poles on the rotor, though once set, this is unlikely to change. Check the gap by inserting a feeler gauge between the sensor and the tip of one of the poles **(see illustrations)**. Check the gap in different places by rotating the wheel. If the gap is not between 0.4 and 1.2 mm, displace the sensor (see below) and adjust the air gap by inserting a shim of the required thickness to bring the gap within specifications **(see illustration 17.12 or 17.16)**. Shims are available in sizes of 0.5, 1.0, 1.5 and 2.0 mm. On completion tighten the bolt to 9 Nm.

**6** Also make a check of all the system wiring and connectors (see below for access), looking for chafed wires or broken connector pins, damp or corroded terminals, and if required refer to electrical system fault finding

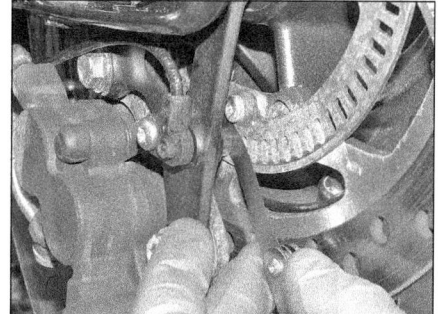

**17.5b Checking the air gap on the rear sensor**

17.9 Front wheel speed sensor (arrowed)

17.10a Undo the screws and displace the holder...

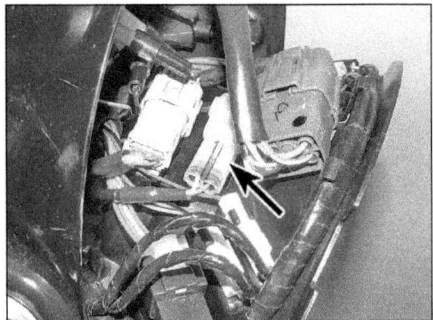

17.10b ...to access the sensor wiring connector (arrowed)

at the beginning of Chapter 8, and to the wiring diagrams at the end of it and check all wiring for continuity. Make sure the ignition

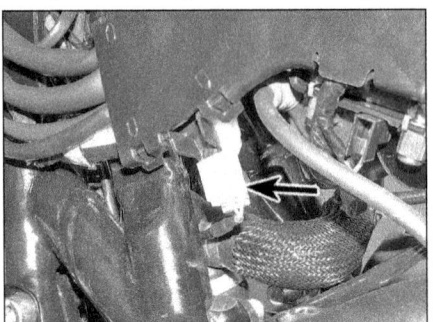

17.11 Front wheel sensor connector (arrowed)

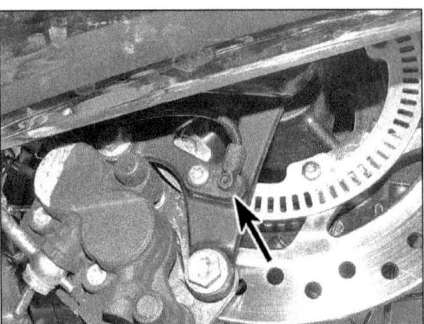

17.14a Rear wheel speed sensor (arrowed) – T100, T120, Street Twin, Street Cup, Scrambler, Thruxton and Thruxton R similar

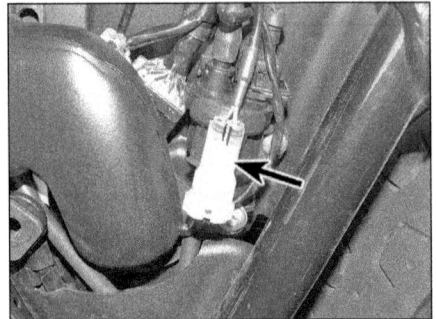

17.15a Rear wheel sensor connector (arrowed) – all models except the Bobber

is OFF before disconnecting any wiring connectors or making any tests.

**7** If the indicator light does not come on when

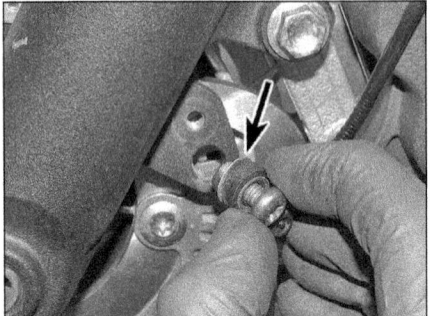

17.12 The shim (arrowed) fits between the sensor and the fork

17.14b Rear wheel speed sensor (arrowed) – Bobber

17.15b Rear wheel sensor connector (arrowed) – Bobber

the ignition is switched on, check the ABS fuse (see Chapter 8) and the instrument panel and the control module wiring connectors. If all is good, take the machine to a Triumph dealer for testing.

**8** Fault diagnosis and any other work on the system, including the final stage of bleeding it and changing the brake fluid, must be undertaken by a Triumph dealer.

### Component removal and installation

#### Front wheel sensor

**9** The sensor is mounted in the bottom of the left-hand fork **(see illustration)**.

**10** On all models except the Bobber remove the headlight from its shell (see Chapter 8). Undo the wiring holder screws and lower the holder **(see illustration)**. Release and disconnect the front wheel sensor connector and feed the sensor side of the wiring out the back of the shell and down to the sensor, releasing it from any guides and noting its routing **(see illustration)**.

**11** On the Bobber remove the fuel tank (see Chapter 4). Release and disconnect the front wheel sensor connector and feed the sensor side of the wiring down to the sensor, releasing it from any guides and noting its routing **(see illustration)**.

**12** Undo the screw securing the sensor and withdraw it from the fork, collecting the shim fitted between them **(see illustration)**.

**13** Installation is the reverse of removal. Make sure the sensor tip is clean and undamaged, and that the mounting surfaces and shim are clean. Make sure any shim previously fitted is positioned between the sensor and the fork. Tighten the screw to 9 Nm. Check the air gap (see Step 5).

#### Rear wheel sensor

**14** The sensor is mounted in the rear brake caliper bracket **(see illustrations)**.

**15** On all models except the Bobber remove the left-hand side cover (see Chapter 7). On the Bobber remove the battery (see Chapter 8). Disconnect the sensor wiring connector **(see illustrations)**. Free the wiring from any ties and the clips and feed it down to the sensor, noting its routing.

**17.16 The shim (arrowed) fits between the sensor and the bracket**

**17.21 Rear wheel rotor screws (arrowed)**

**16** Undo the screw securing the sensor and withdraw it from the bracket, collecting the shim fitted between them **(see illustration)**.

**17** Installation is the reverse of removal. Make sure the sensor tip is clean and undamaged, and that the mounting plate is not distorted. Make sure any shim previously fitted is positioned between the mounting plate and the caliper bracket. Tighten the bolt to 9 Nm. Check the air gap (see Step 5).

### Front wheel rotor

**18** Refer to Section 4 – the brake disc bolts also secure the rotor.

**19** Before seating the rotor on the disc, make sure there is no dirt or corrosion between the mating surfaces as this will not allow the ring to sit flat when bolted down and it will be warped and could cause the ABS system to indicate a fault. Tighten the bolts evenly in a criss-cross pattern to the torque setting specified at the beginning of the Chapter.

### Rear wheel rotor

**20** Remove the wheel (Section 15).

**21** Undo the rotor screws and lift it off **(see illustration)**.

**22** Before fitting the rotor, make sure there is no dirt or corrosion between the mating surfaces as this will not allow the rotor to sit flat when screwed down and it will be warped and could cause the ABS system to indicate a fault. Clean the threads of the screws and apply threadlock or use new screws, and tighten them evenly in a criss-cross pattern to 5 Nm.

### Modulator

**Note:** *Due to the shape of the brake hose banjo bolt heads, which have slightly rounded corners, you need to use a hex socket to slacken and tighten them rather than a bi-hex one.*

**Note:** *Before removing the modulator, bear in mind that the system must be bled on*

completion of work, and although this is done initially in the same way as models without ABS, to complete the procedure the Triumph Diagnostic tool must be used to open and close the solenoids within the modulator, and this can only be carried out by a dealer. The bike should be transported, not ridden, to the dealer.

**23** Have some clean rag to hand to catch any spilled brake fluid and some clingfilm to wrap around the end of each pipe as it is disconnected. Drain the brake fluid from both front and rear brake systems (Section 11).

**24** Disconnect the battery (see Chapter 8).

**25** Remove the swingarm (see Chapter 5).

**26** On the T100, T120, Street Twin, Street Cup and Scrambler remove the coolant reservoir cover then displace the reservoir and support it upright to one side **(see illustrations)**.

**27** On the Bobber, Thruxton and Thruxton R remove the regulator/rectifier (see Chapter 8).

**17.26a Undo the screws and remove the cover...**

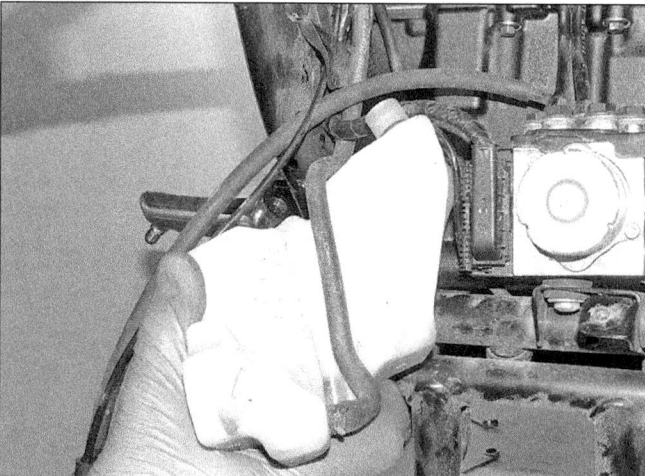

**17.26b ...and displace the reservoir**

17.28a Undo the screws (arrowed)

17.28b Push up on the underside to release the centre clip, then release the inner tabs...

17.28c ... and lift the tray off the outer hook

17.28d Unscrew the bolts (arrowed)...

17.28e ...release the box from the lug (arrowed)...

17.28f ...and manoeuvre it out

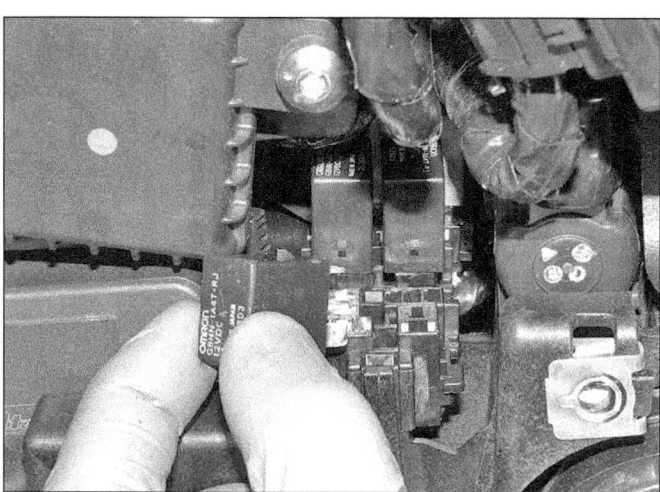

17.28g Remove the relays...

17.28h ...then release the relay holder clips...

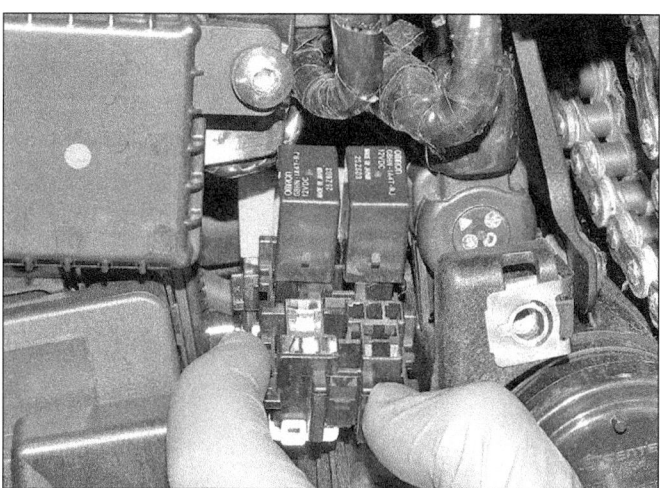

17.28i ...and displace them

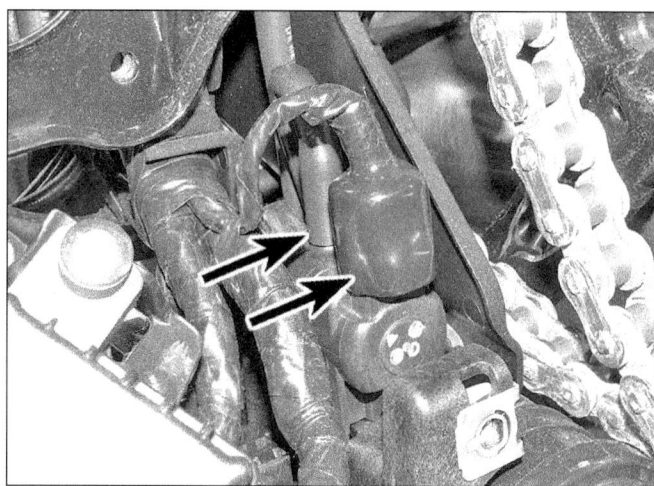

17.28j Disconnect the hose and wiring (arrowed) from the valve

**28** On the Bobber remove the air filter housings, the ECM, and the immobiliser control unit (see Chapter 4). Undo the battery box lid screws **(see illustration)**. Release and remove the battery tray, noting how it locates **(see illustrations)**. Unscrew the battery box bolts and remove the box **(see illustrations)**. Remove the relays, then release the relay holders from the modulator bracket **(see illustrations)**. Disconnect the wiring connector and hose from the EVAP system purge control valve **(see illustration)**.

**29** Release the security clip and disconnect the wiring connector from the control module **(see illustration)**.

**30** Note the arrangement and alignment of the brake hoses/pipe on the top of the modulator, then unscrew the bolts, detach the banjo unions and remove the sealing washers, being prepared with some rag to catch any residual fluid **(see illustrations)**. New sealing

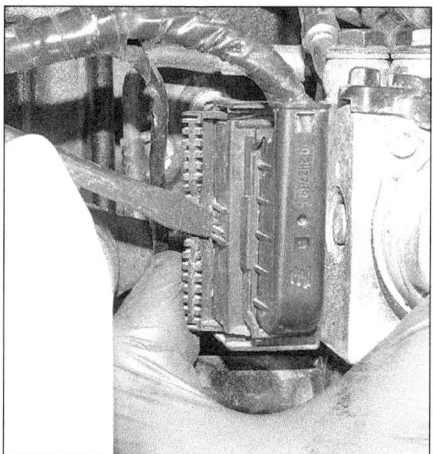

17.29 Push the clip in then pull the lever to release the connector

17.30a Brake hose/pipe arrangement on all models except the Bobber

17.30b Brake hose/pipe arrangement on the Bobber

17.31 Modulator screws (arrowed)

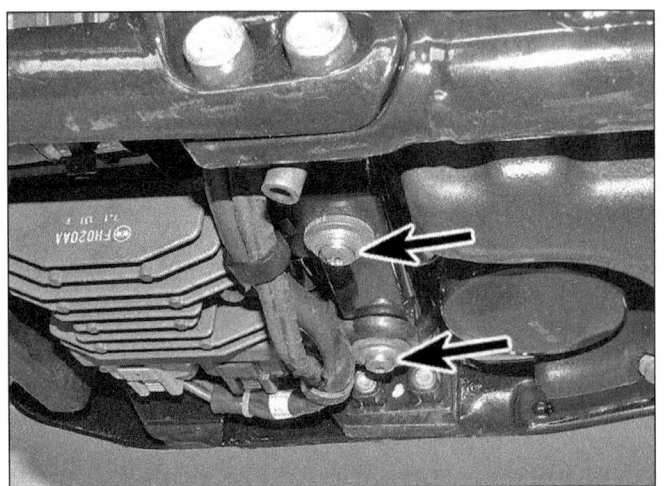

17.32a Undo the screws underneath (arrowed)...

17.32b ...the screws at the back (arrowed)...

17.32c ...the screw from the left side (arrowed but hidden)...

17.32d ...and the lower bolt

washers must be used on installation. Cover the unions with clean rag and move them aside.

**31** On the T100, T120, Street Twin, Street Cup, Scrambler, Thruxton and Thruxton R, undo the modulator screws and remove the modulator. If required undo the hose positioning plate screw and remove the plate from the modulator.

**32** On the Bobber, undo the modulator bracket screws on the underside, at the back and on the left-hand side, and undo the inner cover lower bolt on the right-hand side **(see illustrations)**. Lift the rear of the modulator bracket and manoeuvre the modulator out. If required undo the screw on the underside and remove the modulator from the bracket. If required undo the hose positioning plate screw and remove the plate from the modulator.

**33** Installation is the reverse of removal. Clean the threads of the modulator/modulator

bracket screws and apply threadlock, or use new screws. Use new sealing washers on each side of each banjo union and tighten the banjo bolts to 25 Nm.

**34** Bleed the hydraulic system following the procedure in Section 11, then transport the bike to a Triumph dealer for bleeding of the modulator. Check the operation of both front and rear brakes carefully before riding the motorcycle.

## 18 Tyres

### General information

**1** The wire spoked wheels on the T100, T120, Bobber, Scrambler, Thruxton and Thruxton R are designed to take tubed tyres. The cast

alloy wheels on the Street Twin and Street Cup are designed to take tubeless tyres. Tyre sizes are given in the Specifications at the beginning of this chapter.

**2** Refer to the *Pre-ride checks* listed at the beginning of this manual for tyre maintenance.

**3** When selecting new tyres, refer to the tyre information in the Owner's Handbook. Ensure that front and rear tyre types are compatible, the correct size and correct speed rating; if necessary seek advice from a Triumph dealer or motorcycle tyre fitting specialist **(see illustration)**.

### *Tubeless tyres – cast alloy wheels*

**4** Have the tyres fitted by a motorcycle tyre specialist rather than attempting to do it yourself. The force required to break the seal between the wheel rim and tyre bead is substantial, and is usually beyond the

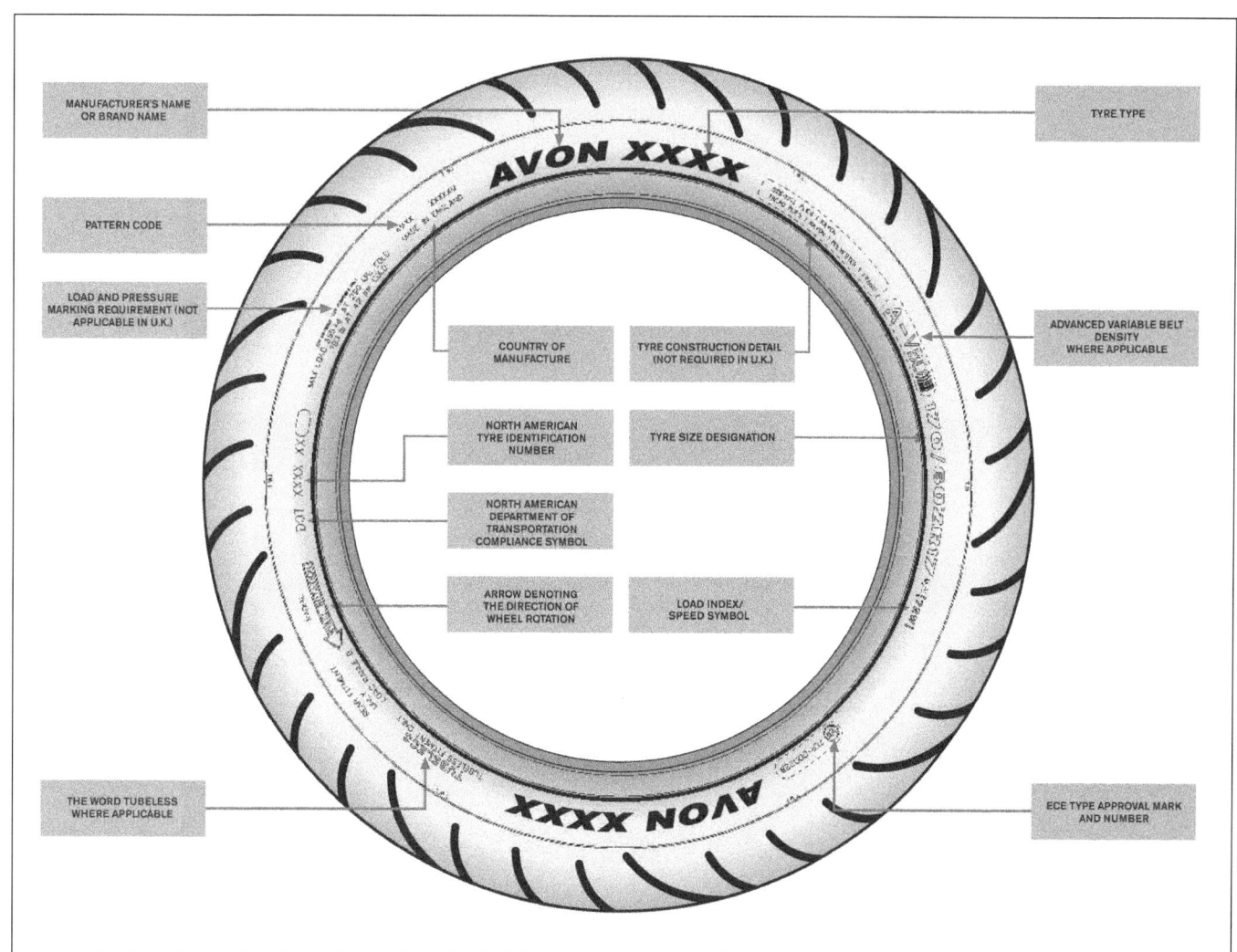

**18.3 Common tyre sidewall markings**

**18.9 Deflate the tyre. After pushing the tyre beads away from rim flanges push the tyre bead into the well of the rim at the point opposite the valve. Insert a tyre lever adjacent to the valve and work the bead over the edge of the rim**

capabilities of an individual working with normal tyre levers, also initial sealing of the tyre is difficult with workshop equipment. Additionally, the specialist will be able to balance the wheels after tyre fitting.

**5** If a tyre pressure monitor system is fitted (Section 19) make sure the tyre fitter is made aware of this and don't rely on the rim sticker giving the information. The pressure sensors on the inner side of the valve could be damaged if care isn't taken.

**6** Note that punctured tubeless tyres can in some cases be repaired. External repairs made using a repair kit should only ever be considered as a temporary measure to get you to a dealer for a new tyre, and riding at speed or with any extra load should be avoided. Internal repairs carried out by a motorcycle tyre fitting specialist are better. Make sure a wheel with a repaired tyre is balanced before it is fitted back on the bike. Seek advice from the tyre specialist about reduced speeds and loads which may apply on a repaired tyre.

### Tubed tyres – wire spoked wheels

**7** Tyre changing is a specialist task. If you attempt it at home you'll need at least two motorcycle tyre levers and some rim protectors. The rim protectors will prevent

damage to the rims by the tyre levers. Following tyre renewal, the wheel should be balanced by a tyre specialist. The following procedure is illustrated with a generic cast alloy wheel.

### Removal

**8** Begin by removing the wheel from the motorcycle. If the tyre is going to be re-used, mark it next to the valve stem with chalk.

**9** Deflate the tyre by removing the valve stem core. When it is fully deflated, push the bead of the tyre away from the rim on both sides. In some extreme cases, this can only be accomplished with a bead breaking tool, but most often it can be carried out with tyre levers **(see illustration)**. Riding on a deflated tyre to break the bead is not recommended, as damage to the rim and tyre will occur.

**10** Dismounting a tyre is easier when the tyre is warm, so an indoor tyre change is recommended in cold climates. The rubber gets very stiff and is difficult to manipulate when cold.

**11** Place the wheel on a thick pad or old blanket. This will help keep the wheel and tyre from slipping around. Take care to protect the disc/sprocket from damage – if necessary, remove it.

**12** Once the bead is completely free of the rim, lubricate the inside edge of the rim and the tyre bead with soap and water or rubber lubricant (do not use any type of petroleum-based lubricant, as it will cause the tyre to deteriorate). Remove the locknut and push the tyre valve through the rim.

**13** Insert one of the tyre levers under the bead of the tyre at the valve stem and lift the bead up over the rim. This should be fairly easy. Take care not to pinch the inner tube as this is done. If it is difficult to pry the bead up, make sure that the rest of the bead opposite the valve stem is in the dropped centre section of the rim **(see illustration)**.

**14** Hold the tyre lever down with the bead over the rim, then move about 1 or 2 inches to either side and insert the second tyre lever. Be careful not to cut or slice the bead or the tyre may split when inflated. Also, take care not to catch or pinch the inner tube as the second tyre lever is levered over. For this reason, tyre

levers are recommended over screwdrivers or other implements.

**15** With a small section of the bead up over the rim, one of the levers can be removed and reinserted 1 or 2 inches farther around the rim until about 1/4 of the tyre bead is above the rim edge. Make sure that the rest of the bead is in the dropped centre of the rim. At this point, the bead can usually be pulled up over the rim by hand.

**16** Once all of the first bead is over the rim, the inner tube can be withdrawn from the tyre and rim **(see illustration)**. Push in on the valve stem, lift up on the tyre next to the stem, reach inside the tyre and carefully pull out the inner tube. It is usually not necessary to completely remove the tyre from the rim to fit a new the inner tube, however it is recommended because checking for foreign objects in the tyre is difficult while it is still mounted on the rim.

**17** To remove the tyre completely, make sure the bead is broken all the way around on the remaining edge, then stand the tyre and wheel up on the tread and grab the wheel with one hand. Push the tyre down over the same edge of the rim while pulling the rim away from the tyre **(see illustration)**. If the bead is correctly positioned in the dropped centre of the rim, the tyre should roll off and separate from the rim very easily. If tyre levers are used to work this last bead over the rim, the outer edge of the rim may be marred. If a tyre lever is necessary, be sure to protect the rim as described earlier.

### Inspection

**18** Fit a new inner tube when fitting a new tyre and also if the existing inner tube is punctured. Puncture repair kits are available, but the expense of a new inner tube is minimal.

**19** Check the rim for sharp edges or damage. Make sure the rubber trim band is in good condition and properly installed before inserting the inner tube.

**20** Check the inside of the tyre to make sure the object that caused the puncture is not still inside. Also check the outside of the tyre, particularly the tread area, to make sure nothing is projecting through the tyre that may cause another puncture.

**18.13 Use two levers to work the bead over the edge of the rim. Note the use of rim protectors**

**18.16 Remove the inner tube from the tyre**

**18.17 When the first bead is clear remove tyre as shown**

## Installation

**21** Fitting a tyre is basically the reverse of removal. Some tyres have a balance mark and/or directional arrows molded into the tyre sidewall. Look for these marks so that the tyre can be installed properly. The dot should be aligned with the valve stem.

**22** If the tyre was not removed completely to fit the inner tube, the inner tube should be inflated just enough to make it round **(see illustrations)**. Sprinkle it with talcum powder, which acts as a dry lubricant, then carefully lift up the tyre edge and install the new inner tube with the valve stem next to the hole in the rim. Once the inner tube is in place, push the valve stem through the rim and start the locknut on the stem.

**23** Lubricate the tyre bead, then push it over the rim edge and into the dropped centre section opposite the inner tube valve stem. Work around each side of the rim, carefully pushing the bead over the rim **(see illustrations)**. The last section may have to be levered on with tyre levers. If so, take care not to pinch the inner tube as this is done.

**24** Once the bead is over the rim edge, check to see that the inner tube valve stem is pointing to the centre of the hub. If it's angled slightly in either direction, rotate the tyre on the rim to straighten it out. Thread the locknut the rest of the way onto the stem but don't tighten it completely.

**25** Inflate the inner tube to approximately 40 psi (2.7 Bar) and check to make sure the guidelines on the tyre sidewalls are the same distance from the rim around the circumference of the tyre.

 *Warning: Do not overinflate the inner tube or the tube may burst.*

**26** After the tyre bead is correctly seated on the rim, adjust the tyre pressure to the correct amount (see *Pre-ride checks* at the beginning of the manual), then tighten the valve stem locknut securely and tighten the cap.

**27** It is recommended that a motorcycle tyre specialist balances the wheel.

## 19 Tyre pressure monitoring system (TPMS)

### General information

**1** A tyre pressure monitoring system (TPMS) may be fitted as an optional extra on the Street Twin and Street Cup only with tubeless tyres – the system cannot be fitted to models with tubed tyres. A sensor inside each wheel measures the pressure of air in the tyre and transmits to a read-out on the instrument panel via the immobiliser/TPMS control unit (covered in Chapter 4). The system will only transmit a read-out when the bike reaches a speed of 12 mph (20 km/h) – until then the read-out will only show two dashes. Each

**18.22a Partially inflate the inner tube and insert it in the tyre**

**18.23a Check the inner tube is correctly positioned and work the second bead over the rim, starting at a point opposite the valve**

sensor is powered by its own internal battery, but as the sensors are sealed units new sensors must be fitted when the batteries run out.

**2** The system monitors real-time pressures, so as the tyre warms up with use the pressure displayed will increase. Tyre pressures should always be checked and set when the tyres are cold, so do not re-adjust the pressure when the tyre is warm because the read-out says it is higher than it should be. The cold pressures specified by Triumph take into account the fact that pressures will increase as the tyres warm.

**3** Triumph state that cold tyre pressures should only be set using an accurate tyre gauge, and not using the TPMS read-out. Refer to the *Pre-ride checks* listed at the beginning of this manual for tyre pressure check details and tyre maintenance.

**4** The system performs its own self-diagnosis, and in the event of a fault the read warning light will come on and the tyre symbol will flash. The Triumph diagnostic tool is required for fault code retrieval.

**5** It is advisable to inform whoever may be fitting new tyres of the presence of a sensor in each wheel, as they are easily damaged – an adhesive label on each wheel rim identifies the position of the sensor, but the label may well have come off, or been taken off. Note that the use of 'get-you-home'

**18.22b Work the first bead over rim and feed the valve through the hole in the rim. Partially screw on the retaining ring to hold the valve in place**

**18.23b Work the final bead over rim while pushing valve inwards to ensure the inner tube is not trapped**

puncture repair sealants injected via the valve may well damage the sensor beyond use.

## 20 Front sprocket cover

### Removal

**1** On the Thruxton and Thruxton R remove the heel plate from the cover if required **(see illustration)** – the cover can be removed with the heel plate attached.

**2** Unscrew the bolts and remove the cover

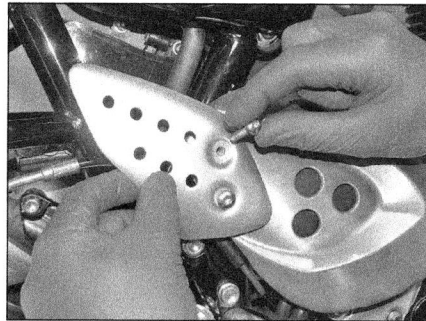

**20.1 Remove the heel plate from the sprocket cover**

20.2 Sprocket cover bolts (arrowed)

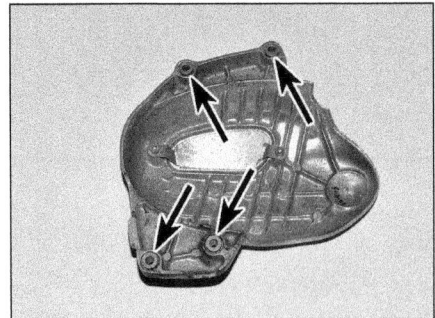

20.3a Check the collars and grommets (arrowed)

20.3b Make sure the buffer is fitted over the swingarm pivot

(see illustration). Note the collars in the grommets and remove them if required. Clean all old chain lube and dirt from inside the cover.

### Installation

3 Installation is the reverse of removal. Make sure the grommets and collars are in place (see illustration). On all models except the Bobber make sure the swingarm pivot buffer is in place (see illustration). Tighten the bolts to 9 Nm.

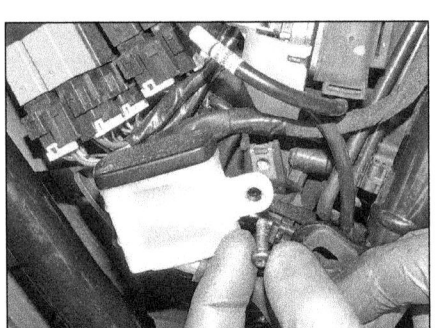

21.6a Displace the reservoir...

## 21 Chain and sprockets

Note: The chain and sprockets should always be replaced as a set – running a new chain on old sprockets or vice versa will rapidly increase chain and sprocket wear. Refer to Chapter 1 for details of routine chain maintenance and checks.

### Chain cleaning

1 Refer to Chapter for details of routine cleaning with the chain installed on the sprockets.
2 If the chain is extremely dirty remove it (see below) and soak it in paraffin (kerosene) for approximately five or six minutes, then clean it using a soft brush.
Caution: Don't use petrol, solvent or other cleaning fluids that might damage its internal sealing properties. Don't use high-pressure water. Remove the chain, wipe it off, then blow dry it with compressed air immediately. The entire process shouldn't take longer than ten

minutes – if it does, the O-rings in the chain rollers could be damaged.

### Chain and sprocket removal

Note: The drive chain has a riveted-type soft (joining) link so it can be split using one of several commercially-available chain cutting/staking tools (but the cheap ones are best avoided). The soft joining link can be recognised by the sideplate's different colour, as well as by the riveted ends of the link's two pins which look as if they have been deeply centre-punched, instead of peened over as with all the other pins.
3 Identify the soft link in the chain and move the bike so the link is in a suitable position to work on.
4 On all models except the Bobber remove the right-hand side cover (see Chapter 7).
5 Remove the front sprocket cover (Section 20).
6 On the T100, T120, Street Twin, Street Cup and Scrambler, undo the rear brake fluid reservoir screw, the brake hose guide bolt and the rider's footrest/brake pedal/master cylinder bracket bolts and displace the assembly, supporting it clear (see illustrations).

21.6b ...and release the hose guide...

21.6c ...then unscrew the bracket bolts and displace the assembly

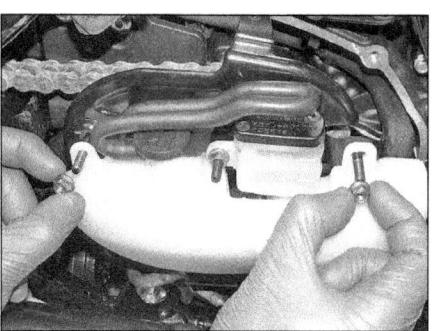

**21.7a Unscrew the nuts and displace the coolant reservoir...**

**21.7b ...and the brake fluid reservoir**

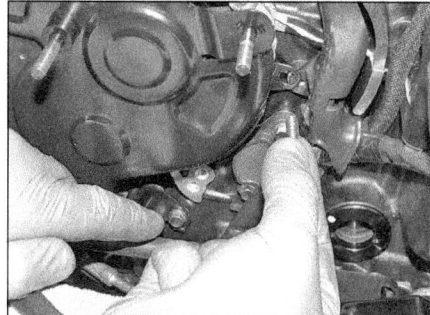

**21.7c Unscrew the mounting plate bolts...**

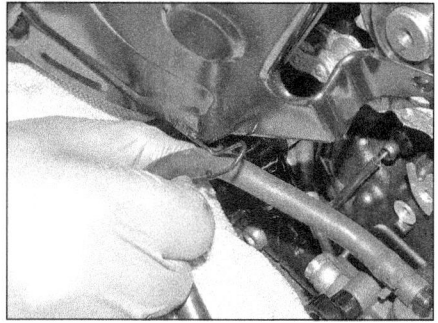

**21.7d ...then release the hoses and remove the plate**

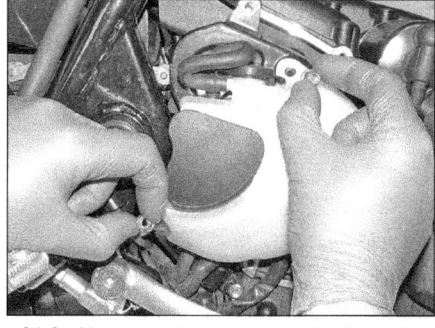

**21.8a Unscrew the nuts and displace the reservoir**

**21.8b Unscrew the bolts...**

**7** On the Bobber fully slacken the drive chain (see Chapter 1). Displace the coolant reservoir and brake fluid reservoir and support them upright and clear **(see illustrations)**. Remove the reservoir mounting plate **(see illustrations)**.

**8** On the Thruxton and Thruxton R displace the coolant reservoir and support it upright and clear **(see illustration)**. Remove the reservoir mounting plate **(see illustrations)**. Undo the rear brake fluid reservoir screw and support the reservoir upright. Release and disconnect the GP sensor wiring connector. Undo the wiring guide bolt, displace the guide

and draw the GP sensor wiring out, noting its routing **(see illustration)**.

**9** Bend the raised tab of the lockwasher off the front sprocket nut so the nut can turn **(see illustration)**. Engage a high gear and have an assistant sit on the seat and apply the front brake, then slacken the sprocket nut.

**10** Remove the rear wheel (Section 15).

**11** Slip the chain off the front sprocket **(see illustration)**. Split the chain at the soft link using a chain breaker tool – refer to *Tools and Workshop Tips* in the Reference section at the end of this manual for details of how to use the tool, or follow the tool manufacturer's

**21.8c ...release the wiring and remove the plate**

**21.9 Bend the tab flat**

**21.11 Slip the chain off the sprocket**

21.13 Rear sprocket nuts (arrowed)

21.15a Slide the sprocket on...

21.15b ...then fit the new washer...

21.15c ...and thread the nut on

21.20 Lock the nut by bending the rim of the washer up against it

21.22 Route the hoses in the guide as shown

instructions. Remove the chain from the bike, noting its routing around the swingarm. Note that it is essential to use a new soft link when re-joining the chain.

**12** Unscrew the front sprocket nut, remove the washer and slide the sprocket off the shaft **(see illustrations 21.15c, b and a)**. A new washer should be used.

**13** Rest the rear wheel sprocket side up on some blocks of wood placed under the tyre. Unscrew the rear sprocket nuts and lift the sprocket off the studs **(see illustration)**. Triumph specify to use new nuts.

### Chain and sprocket installation

**14** Fit the rear sprocket over the studs and onto the hub with the marked side facing out **(see illustration 21.13)**. Fit new nuts and tighten them evenly and in a criss-cross sequence to 55 Nm.

**15** Slide the front sprocket onto the shaft with

the marked side facing out **(see illustration)**. Fit the new lockwasher with the dished side facing out, then fit the nut and tighten finger-tight **(see illustrations)**.

**16** Route the drive chain around the sprocket **(see illustration 21.11)**, leaving the two ends mid-way along the bottom run.

**17** Referring to *Tools and Workshop Tips* in the Reference Section, fit the new joining link from the inside using new O-rings. Fit the new sideplate using new O-rings and with its identification marks facing out. Using the chain tool to press the sideplate into position. Stake the new link using the chain tool, following carefully the instructions of both the chain manufacturer and the tool manufacturer. DO NOT re-use old joining link components.

**18** After riveting, check the soft link and pin ends for any signs of cracking. If there is any evidence of cracking, the soft link, O-rings,

and sideplate must be replaced with new ones.

**19** Install the rear wheel (Section 15) – take up some of the slack in the chain but tighten the axle nut finger-tight only at this stage.

**20** Engage a high gear and have an assistant sit on the seat and apply the front brake, then tighten the front sprocket nut to 180 Nm. Bend the rim of the lockwasher up against one flat of the nut **(see illustration)**.

**21** Adjust and lubricate the chain (see Chapter 1).

**22** Install all remaining components in reverse order of removal according to model. On the T100, T120, Street Twin, Street Cup and Scrambler tighten the rider's footrest/brake pedal/master cylinder bracket bolts to 24 Nm. On the Bobber make sure the reservoir hoses are correctly routed in the mounting plate guide **(see illustration)**.

# Chapter 7
# Bodywork

## Contents

## Degrees of difficulty

| **Easy,** suitable for novice with little experience  | **Fairly easy,** suitable for beginner with some experience | **Fairly difficult,** suitable for competent DIY mechanic | **Difficult,** suitable for experienced DIY mechanic | **Very difficult,** suitable for expert DIY or professional |
|---|---|---|---|---|

## 1  General Information

**1** This Chapter covers the procedures necessary to remove and install the bodywork. Since many service and repair operations on these motorcycles require the removal of the body panels, the procedures are grouped here and referred to from other Chapters.

**2** In the case of damage to the bodywork, it is usually necessary to remove the broken component and replace it with a new (or used) one. Note that there are however some companies that specialise in 'plastic welding' and there are a number of DIY bodywork repair kits available.

**3** When attempting to remove any body panel, first study it closely, noting any fasteners and associated fittings, to be sure of returning everything to its correct place on installation. Once the evident fasteners have been removed, try to withdraw the panel as described but DO NOT FORCE IT – if it will not release, check that all fasteners have been removed and try again.

**4** When installing a body panel, first study it closely, noting any fasteners and associated fittings removed with it, to be sure of returning everything to its correct place. Check that all fasteners are in good condition, including the rubber mounts; replace any faulty fasteners with new ones before the panel is reassembled. Check also that all mounting brackets are straight and repair them or replace them with new ones if necessary before attempting to install the panel.

**5** Tighten the fasteners securely, but be careful not to overtighten any of them or the panel may break (not always immediately) due to the uneven stress.

## 2  Seat(s)

### *T100, T120, Street Twin, Street Cup, Thruxton, Thruxton R*

**1** Unlock the seat using the ignition key in the lock on the left-hand side, turning it anti-clockwise and pushing down on the back of the seat, then lift the back of the seat and draw it back **(see illustration)**.

**2** To fit the seat locate the tab at the front under the tank bracket and the hooks in the middle under the bridges on the top of the frame, then push the back of the seat down to engage the lock, which you will hear click into place **(see illustration)**. Check the lock has engaged by trying to lift the back of the seat.

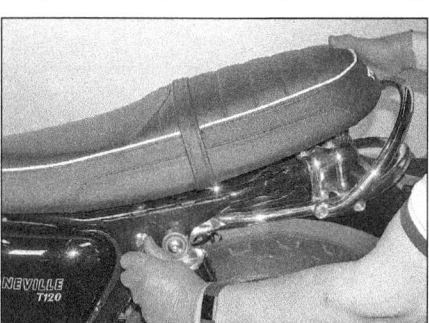

**2.1 Insert and turn the key, then lift the rear of the seat and remove it**

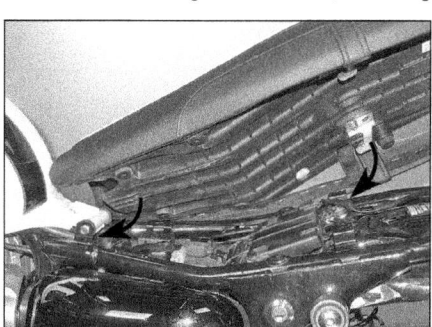

**2.2 Locate the tab under the tank bracket and the hooks under the bridges**

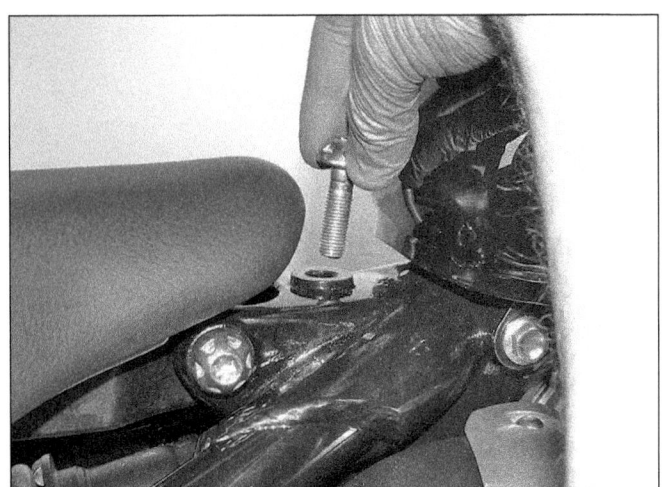

2.3a Unscrew the front bolt...

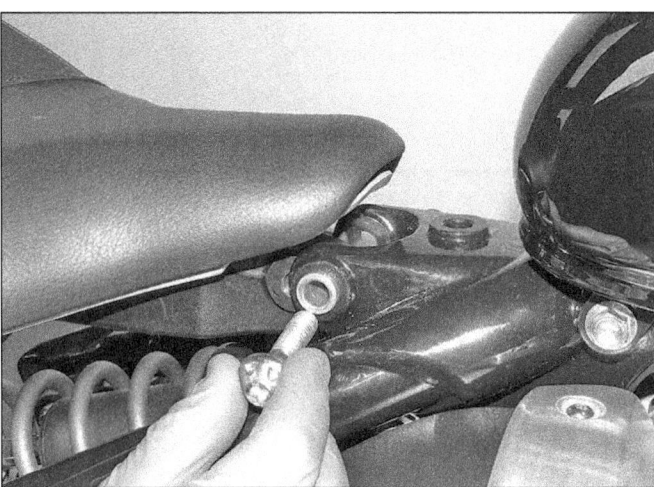

2.3b ...and the bolt on each side

## Bobber

3 Unscrew bolt at the front of the seat and the bolt on each side, then draw the seat back out of the frame (see illustrations). Note the collar fitted into the inner side of the right-hand side mount.

4 If required release the seat from the bracket by unscrewing the nuts on the underside, noting the washers.

5 Installation is the reverse of removal – make sure the collar is fitted into the inner side of the right-hand mount, then tighten the right-hand bolt first, then the left-hand, then the front, all to 48 Nm. If the nuts on the underside were loosened tighten them to 38 Nm after positioning the seat as required (see Step 6).

6 The seat can be adjusted to suit rider preference – slacken the nuts on the underside and slide the seat forwards or backwards along the bracket to the desired position,

then tighten the nuts to 38 Nm (see illustration).

## Scrambler

### Passenger seat (if fitted)

7 Unscrew the bolt at the back, then lift the back of the seat and draw it back.

8 To fit the seat align the two posts at the front with the slots in the luggage rack sub-frame, then push the seat forwards so the rear lugs seats in its hole. Secure the seat with the bolt.

### Rider's seat

9 Remove the passenger seat if fitted.

10 Unlock the seat using the ignition key in the lock on the left-hand side, turning it anti-clockwise and pushing down on the back of the seat, then lift the back of the seat and draw it back.

11 To fit the seat locate the tab at the front under the tank bracket, then push the back of the seat down to engage the lock, which you

will hear click into place. Check the lock has engaged by trying to lift the back of the seat.

### 3 Side panels

### T100, T120, Street Twin, Street Cup, Thruxton, Thruxton R

1 To remove a side panel carefully pull the panel evenly away to release the three pegs from the grommets (see illustration).

2 To fit a side panel align the pegs with the grommets and push the panel evenly in – smear a little oil in each grommet to ease installation if required.

### Bobber

3 To remove a side panel carefully pull the lower edge away to release the peg from the grommet, then slide it to the rear to release

2.6 Slacken the nuts (arrowed) to adjust the seat

3.1 Each panel is held by three pegs that locate in grommets in the frame

**3.3a Pull the bottom away to release the peg...**

**3.3b ...slide the panel to the rear...**

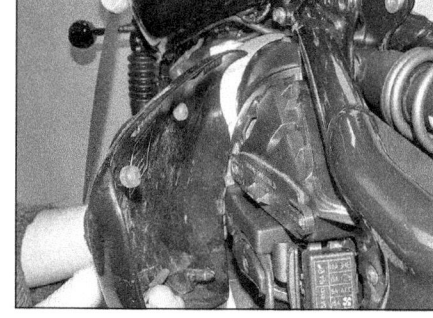

**3.3c ...and remove it**

the slots in the top from the locating tangs and lift it off **(see illustrations)**.

**4** To fit a side panel align the slots in the top of the panel to the rear of the tangs on the frame and slide the panel forwards to engage them, then align the peg with the grommet and push the panel in **(see illustrations 3.3c and a)** – smear a little oil in the grommet to ease installation if required.

### Scrambler

#### Right-hand panel

**5** To remove the panel carefully pull the top of the panel away to release the two pegs from the grommets, then lift the panel to release the slot from the bottom grommet.

**6** To fit the panel seat the slot over the bottom grommet, align the top pegs with the grommets and push the panel evenly in – smear a little oil in each grommet to ease installation if required.

#### Left-hand panel

**7** To remove the panel carefully pull the panel evenly away to release the three pegs from the grommets.

**8** To fit the panel align the pegs with the grommets and push the panel evenly in – smear a little oil in each grommet to ease installation if required.

### 4  Mudguard(s)

#### Front – all models

**1** Release the brake hose(s) from the mudguard as required according to model.

**2** On all models except the Thruxton R remove the wheel (see Chapter 6). Undo the

screws on each side, then manoeuvre the mudguard out **(see illustrations)**.

**3** On the Thruxron R undo the two screws on each side and draw the mudguard forwards **(see illustration)**.

**4** Installation is the reverse of removal.

#### Rear – Bobber

**5** Remove the battery (see Chapter 8).

**6** Disconnect the tail light assembly wiring connector and feed it out to the mudguard, releasing it from the clip **(see illustration)**.

**4.2a Undo the three screws on each side on the T100 and T120 (shown), and the two screws on all other models except the Thruxton R...**

**4.2b ...and remove the mudguard**

**4.3 Mudguard screws (arrowed)**

**4.6 Tail light wiring connector (arrowed)**

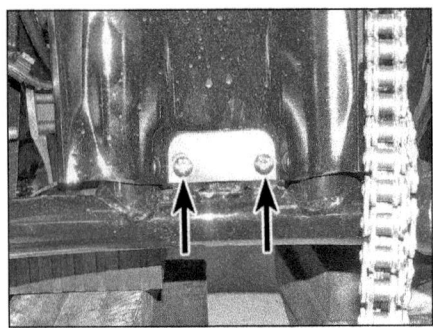

4.8 Undo the front screws (arrowed)

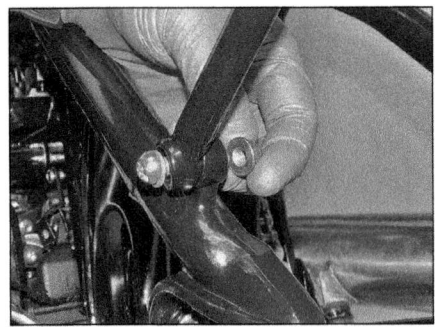

4.9 Unscrew the nut and withdraw the bolt on each side

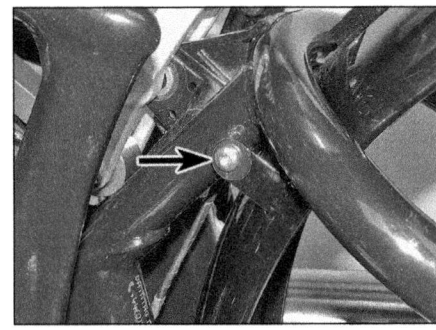

4.10a Undo the screw (arrowed) on each side...

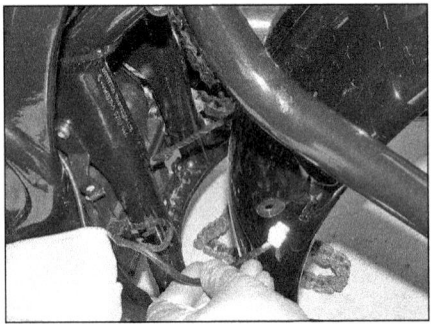

4.10b ...and remove the mudguard, feeding the wiring out

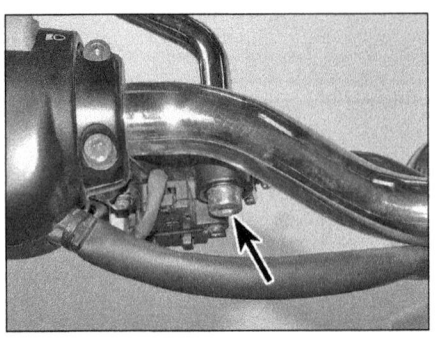

5.1 Mirror bolt (arrowed) – note the arrangement of the washers

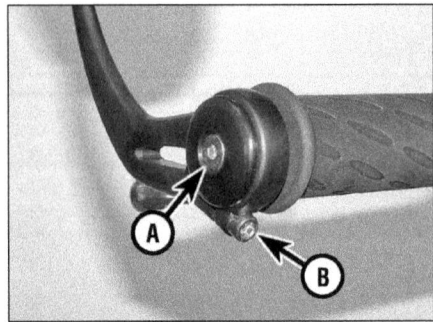

5.8 End-weight bolt (A), mirror clamp bolt (B)

**7** Remove the rear wheel (see Chapter 6).
**8** Undo the two screws at the front, noting the washers **(see illustration)**.
**9** Unscrew the nut and withdraw the bolt on each side at the back, noting the washer **(see illustration)**.
**10** Undo the screw on each side at the front and manoeuvre the mudguard out, noting the routing of the wiring **(see illustrations)**.
**11** Installation is the reverse of removal – fit all bolts/nuts loosely at first, then tighten the front screws to 12 Nm and the rear nuts/bolts to 30 Nm.

## 5  Mirrors

### T100, T120

**1** Unscrew the bolt on the underside and remove the two washers, then lift the mirror off and remove the two washers from the seat **(see illustration)**.
**2** Installation is the reverse of removal – position the mirror as required then tighten the bolt to 20 Nm.

### Street Twin, Scrambler

**3** Lift the rubber boot off the base.
**4** To remove the mirror leaving the mounting boss in place, slacken the locknut, turning it clockwise as it has left-hand threads, then turn the mirror the same way to unscrew it from the boss.
**5** To remove the complete mirror, unscrew the mounting boss from the master cylinder/clutch lever bracket clamp, turning it anticlockwise.
**6** Installation is the reverse of removal.
**7** To adjust the position of the mirror lift the rubber boot, then slacken the locknut, turning it clockwise, reposition the mirror as required and tighten the locknut.

### Bobber, Street Cup, Thruxton, Thruxton R

**8** Unscrew the handlebar end-weight bolt and remove the weight **(see illustration)**.
**9** Slacken the mirror clamp bolt and slide the mirror off.
**10** Installation is the reverse of removal – position the mirror as required then tighten the clamp bolt.

## 6  Windshield – Street Cup

**1** Undo the four screws and remove the screen from the brackets.
**2** To remove the brackets first remove the headlight (see Chapter 8). Unscrew the headlight bracket upper nuts/bolts and slacken the lower bolts to release the fly screen brackets.
**3** Installation is the reverse of removal. Check the condition of the rubber wellnuts for the fly screen bolts and fit new ones if necessary. Apply some copper grease to the bolt threads.

## 7  Belly-pan – Scrambler

**1** To remove the guard unscrew the four bolts.
**2** To remove the bracket unscrew the three bolts.
**3** Installation is the reverse of removal. Tighten the bracket bolts to 19 Nm and the belly-pan bolts to 9 Nm.

# Chapter 8
# Electrical system

## Contents

## Degrees of difficulty

| | | | | |
|---|---|---|---|---|
| **Easy,** suitable for novice with little experience 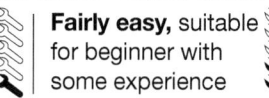 | **Fairly easy,** suitable for beginner with some experience | **Fairly difficult,** suitable for competent DIY mechanic | **Difficult,** suitable for experienced DIY mechanic | **Very difficult,** suitable for expert DIY or professional  |

## Specifications

### Battery

| | |
|---|---|
| Capacity | |
| All models except the Bobber | 12V, 10Ah |
| Bobber | 12V, 8Ah |
| Type | |
| All models except the Bobber | Yuasa YTX12-BS |
| Bobber | Yuasa YTX9-BS |
| Charge condition | |
| Fully charged | 12.8V |
| Half-charged | 12.4V |
| Discharged | 12V or less |
| Charging time | Until fully charged (12.8V) (see Section 4) |

### Charging system

| | |
|---|---|
| Alternator nominal output | 46.5 Amps @ 3000 rpm |
| Alternator stator coil resistance | 0.14 to 0.18 ohms |
| Current leakage | 1mA (max) |
| Unregulated voltage | 15 to 25 V AC @ 850 rpm, 35 to 40 V AC @ 4000 – 5000 rpm |
| Regulated voltage output @ 2000 rpm | 13.5 to 15.0V DC |

### Fuses

| | |
|---|---|
| Main | 30A |
| USB socket (except Bobber) | 5A |
| Headlight | 15A |
| Ignition/starter | 10A |
| Auxiliary lights | 10A |
| Engine management system (EMS) | 15A |
| Accessory socket | 5A |
| Cooling fan | 15A (see Note in Section 5) |
| ABS | 25A |
| Diagnostics/alarm | 15A |

## Bulbs

| | |
|---|---|
| Headlight . . . . . . . . . . . . . . . . . . . . . . . . . . . . . . . . . . . . . . . . . . . . . . . | 60/55W halogen (H4) |
| Sidelight | |
|     T100, Bobber, Street Twin, Street Cup, Scrambler . . . . . . . . . . . . . | 5W |
|     T120, Thruxton, Thruxton R . . . . . . . . . . . . . . . . . . . . . . . . . . . . | LED |
| Brake/tail/licence plate light. . . . . . . . . . . . . . . . . . . . . . . . . . . . . . . . | LED |
| Turn signal lights | |
|     All models except the Bobber . . . . . . . . . . . . . . . . . . . . . . . . . . . | 10W |
|     Bobber . . . . . . . . . . . . . . . . . . . . . . . . . . . . . . . . . . . . . . . . . . . . | LED |
| Instrument cluster illumination and warning lights. . . . . . . . . . . . . . . . | LED |

## Torque wrench settings

| | |
|---|---|
| Alternator cover bolts. . . . . . . . . . . . . . . . . . . . . . . . . . . . . . . . . . . . . . | 10 Nm |
| Alternator rotor bolt | |
|     Stage 1 . . . . . . . . . . . . . . . . . . . . . . . . . . . . . . . . . . . . . . . . . . . . | 85 Nm |
|     Stage 2 . . . . . . . . . . . . . . . . . . . . . . . . . . . . . . . . . . . . . . . . . . . . | 120 Nm |
| Alternator stator bolts. . . . . . . . . . . . . . . . . . . . . . . . . . . . . . . . . . . . . | 12 Nm |
| CKP sensor screws . . . . . . . . . . . . . . . . . . . . . . . . . . . . . . . . . . . . . . . | 6 Nm |
| Rider's footrest/brake pedal/master cylinder bracket bolts. . . . . . . . . | 24 Nm |
| Oil pressure switch. . . . . . . . . . . . . . . . . . . . . . . . . . . . . . . . . . . . . . . . | 15 Nm |
| Starter motor mounting bolts. . . . . . . . . . . . . . . . . . . . . . . . . . . . . . . | 7 Nm |

### 1 General Information

**1** All models have a 12 volt electrical system charged by a three-phase alternator mounted on the right-hand end of the crankshaft, with a separate regulator/rectifier.

**2** The regulator maintains the charging system output within the specified range to prevent overcharging, and the rectifier converts the ac (alternating current) output of the alternator to dc (direct current) to power the lights and other components and to charge the battery.

**3** The starting system includes the starter motor, the battery, the relay and the various wires and switches. If the engine stop switch is in the RUN position and the ignition switch is ON, the starter relay allows the starter motor to operate only if the transmission is in neutral and the clutch lever is pulled in. The starter lockout system prevents the starter motor from operating if the engine is in gear and the sidestand is down. If will also stop the engine if the sidestand is extended in gear. The starter motor is mounted on the top of the crankcase.

**Note:** *Keep in mind that electrical parts, once purchased, cannot be returned. To avoid unnecessary expense, make very sure the faulty component has been positively identified before buying a replacement part.*

### 2 Electrical system fault finding

⚠️ **Warning: To prevent the risk of short circuits, the battery negative (-ve) terminal should be disconnected before any of the bike's other electrical components are disturbed. Don't forget to reconnect the terminal securely once work is finished or if battery power is needed for circuit testing.**

**1** A typical electrical circuit consists of an electrical component, the switches, relays, etc, related to that component and the wiring and connectors that link the component to the battery and the frame.

**2** Before tackling any troublesome electrical circuit, first study the wiring diagram thoroughly to get a complete picture of what makes up that individual circuit. Trouble spots, for instance, can often be narrowed down by noting if other components related to that circuit are operating properly or not. If several components or circuits fail at one time, chances are the fault lies either in the fuse or in a common earth (ground) connection, as several circuits are often routed through the same fuse and earth (ground) connections.

**3** Electrical problems often stem from simple causes, such as loose or corroded connections or a blown fuse. Prior to any electrical fault finding, always visually check the condition of the fuse, wires and connections in the problem circuit. Intermittent failures can be especially frustrating, since you can't always duplicate the failure when it's convenient to test. In such situations, a good practice is to clean all connections in the affected circuit, whether or not they appear to be good. All of the connections and wires should also be wiggled to check for looseness which can cause intermittent failure.

**4** If you don't have a multimeter it is highly advisable to obtain one – they are not expensive and will enable a full range of electrical tests to be made **(see illustration)**. Go for a modern digital one with LCD display as they are easier to use. A continuity tester

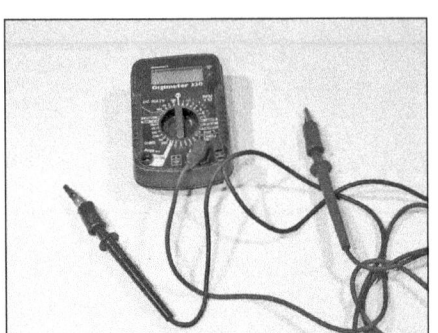

**2.4a A digital multimeter can be used for all electrical tests**

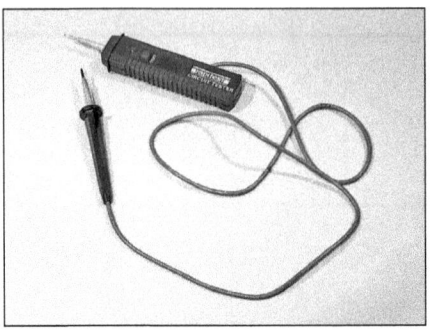

**2.4b A battery-powered continuity tester**

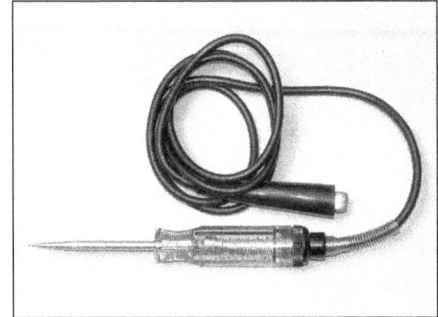

**2.4c A simple test light is useful for voltage tests**

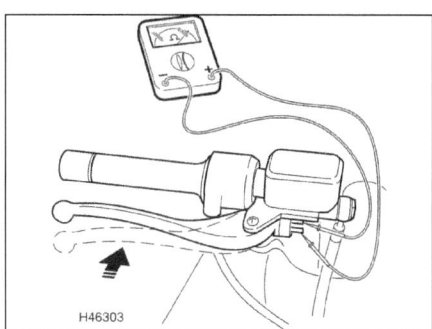

2.10 Continuity should be indicated across switch terminals when lever is operated

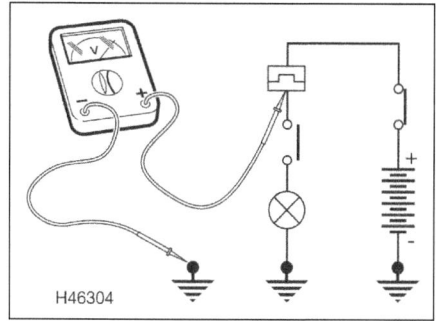

2.12 Wiring continuity check. Connect the meter probes across each end of the same wire

2.15 Voltage check. Connect the meter positive probe to the component and the negative probe to earth

and/or test light are useful for certain electrical checks as an alternative, though are limited in their usefulness compared to a multimeter (see illustrations).

## Continuity checks

5 The term continuity describes the uninterrupted flow of electricity through an electrical circuit. Continuity can be checked with a multimeter set either to its continuity function (a beep is emitted when continuity is found), or to the resistance (ohms/Ω) function, or with a dedicated continuity tester. Both instruments are powered by an internal battery, therefore the checks are made with the ignition OFF. As a safety precaution, always disconnect the battery negative (-) lead before making continuity checks, particularly if ignition system checks are being made.

6 If using a multimeter, select the continuity function if it has one, or the resistance (ohms) function. Touch the meter probes together and check that a beep is emitted or the meter reads zero, which indicates continuity. If there is no continuity there will be no beep or the meter will show infinite resistance. After using the meter, always switch it OFF to conserve its battery.

7 A continuity tester can be used in the same way – its light should come on or it should beep to indicate continuity in the switch ON position, but should be off or silent in the OFF position.

8 Note that the polarity of the test probes doesn't matter for continuity checks, although care should be taken to follow specific test procedures if a diode or solid-state component is being checked.

### Switch continuity checks

9 If a switch is at fault, trace its wiring to the wiring connectors. Separate the connectors and inspect them for security and condition. A build-up of dirt or corrosion here will most likely be the cause of the problem – clean up and apply a water dispersant such as WD40, or alternatively use a dedicated contact cleaner and protection spray.

10 If using a multimeter, select the continuity function if it has one, or the resistance (ohms)

function, and connect its probes to the terminals in the connector (see illustration). Simple ON/OFF type switches only have two wires whereas combination switches have three or more wires. Study the wiring diagram to ensure that you are connecting to the correct pair of wires. Continuity should be indicated with the switch ON and no continuity with it OFF.

### Wiring continuity checks

11 Many electrical faults are caused by damaged wiring, often due to incorrect routing or chaffing on frame components. Loose, wet or corroded wire connectors can also be the cause of electrical problems.

12 A continuity check can be made on a single length of wire by disconnecting it at each end and connecting the meter or continuity tester probes to each end of the wire (see illustration). Continuity should be indicated if the wire is good. If no continuity is shown, suspect a broken wire.

13 To check for continuity to earth in any earth wire connect one probe of your meter or tester to the earth wire terminal in the connector and the other to the frame, engine, or battery earth (-) terminal. Continuity should be indicated if the wire is good. If no continuity is shown, suspect a broken wire or corroded or loose earth point (see below).

## Voltage checks

14 A voltage check can determine whether power is reaching a component. Use a multimeter set to the dc (direct current) voltage scale to check for power from the battery or regulator/rectifier, or set to the ac (alternating current) voltage scale to check for power from the alternator. A test light can be used to check for dc voltage. The test light is the cheaper component, but the meter has the advantage of being able to give a voltage reading.

15 Connect the meter or test light in parallel, i.e. across the load (see illustration).

16 First identify the relevant wiring circuit by referring to the wiring diagram at the end of this manual. If other electrical components share the same power supply (i.e. are fed from the same fuse), take note whether they are

working correctly – this is useful information in deciding where to start checking the circuit.

17 If using a meter, check first that the meter leads are plugged into the correct terminals on the meter (red to positive (+), black to negative (-)). Set the meter to the appropriate volts function (dc or ac), where necessary at a range suitable for the battery voltage – 0 to 20 vdc. Connect the meter red probe (+) to the power supply wire and the black probe to a good metal earth (ground) on the motorcycle's frame or directly to the battery negative terminal. Battery voltage, or the specified voltage, should be shown on the meter with the ignition switch, and if necessary any other relevant switch, ON.

18 If using a test light (see illustration 2.4c), connect its positive (+) probe to the power supply terminal and its negative (-) probe to a good earth (ground) on the motorcycle's frame. With the switch, and if necessary any other relevant switch, ON, the test light should illuminate.

19 If no voltage is indicated, work back towards the power source continuing to check for voltage. When you reach a point where there is voltage, you know the problem lies between that point and your last check point.

## Earth (ground) checks

20 Earth connections are made either directly to the engine or frame (such as the starter motor or ignition coil which only have a positive feed) or by a separate wire into the earth circuit of the wiring harness. Alternatively a short earth wire is sometimes run from the component directly to the motorcycle's frame.

21 Corrosion is a common cause of a poor earth connection, as is a loose earth terminal fastener.

22 If total or multiple component failure is experienced, check the security of the main earth lead from the negative (-) terminal of the battery, the earth lead bolted to the engine, and the main earth point(s) on the frame. If corroded, dismantle the connection and clean all surfaces back to bare metal. Remake the connection and prevent further corrosion from forming by smearing battery terminal grease over the connection.

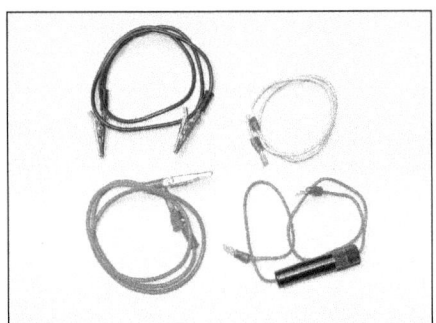

**2.23 A selection of insulated jumper wires**

**23** To check the earthing of a component, use an insulated jumper wire to temporarily bypass its earth connection **(see illustration)** – connect one end of the jumper wire to the earth terminal or metal body of the component and the other end to the motorcycle's frame. If the circuit works with the jumper wire installed, the earth circuit is faulty.

**24** To check an earth wire first check for corroded or loose connections, then check the wiring for continuity (Step 13) between each connector in the circuit in turn, and then to its earth point, to locate the break.

## 3 Battery

*Caution: Be extremely careful when handling or working around the battery. The electrolyte is very caustic and an explosive gas (hydrogen) is given off when the battery is charging.*

## *Removal and installation*

### All models except the Bobber

**1** Remove the seat (see Chapter 7).

**2** On the T100, T120, Street Twin, Street Cup and Scrambler displace the ECM and position it aside (see Chapter 4) – there is no need to disconnect the wiring.

**3** Undo the negative (-) terminal screw first and disconnect the lead from the battery **(see illustrations)**. Lift up the insulating cover to access the positive (+) terminal, then undo the screw and disconnect the lead.

**4** Unhook the rubber strap, and on the T100, T120, Street Twin, Street Cup and Scrambler remove the USB socket holder, then lift the battery out **(see illustrations)**.

**5** Installation is the reverse of removal. Clean the battery terminals and lead ends with a wire brush, fine sandpaper or steel wool.

**3.3a On the T100, T120, Street Twin, Street Cup and Scrambler disconnect the negative terminal first, then the positive terminal (arrowed)**

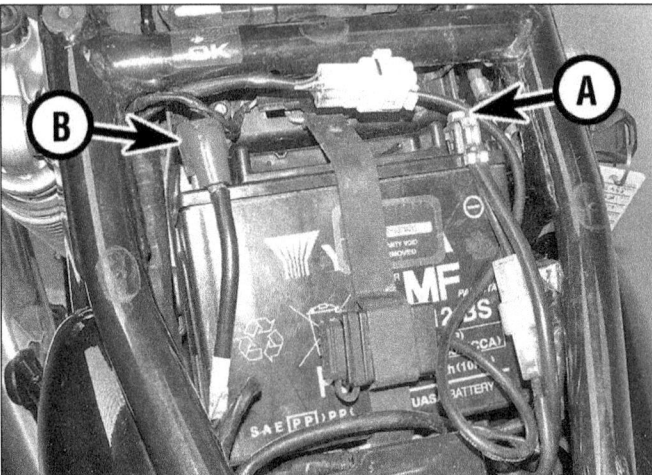

**3.3b Negative terminal (A), positive terminal (B) - Thruxton and Thruxton R**

**3.4a Unhook the strap and remove the holder (arrowed) where fitted...**

**3.4b and carefully lift the battery out – it is quite heavy**

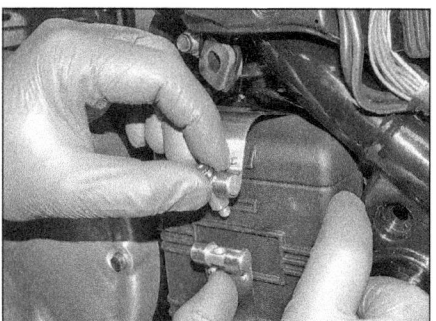

**3.7a Undo the screw...**

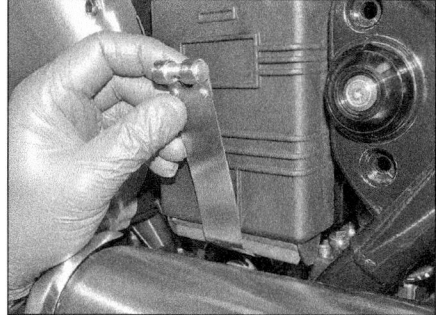

**3.7b ...and remove the strap...**

**3.7c ...and the cover**

Reconnect the leads, connecting the positive (+) terminal first.

### Bobber

**6** Remove the left-hand side panel (see Chapter 7).

**7** Undo the battery cover retaining strap screw and remove the upper and lower sections of the strap **(see illustrations)** – note the spacer and O-ring fitted with the screw **(see illustration 3.11)**. Remove the battery cover **(see illustration)**.

**8** Lift the rubber cover off the negative (-) lead terminal on the engine, undo the screw and disconnect the lead, then cover the terminal with the rubber boot to prevent it contacting the engine **(see illustration)**.

**9** Lift up the insulating cover to access the positive (+) terminal, then undo the screw and disconnect the lead **(see illustration)**.

**10** Unhook the rubber strap, then slide the battery out **(see illustrations)**.

**11** Installation is the reverse of removal. Clean the battery terminals and lead ends with a wire brush, fine sandpaper or steel wool. Reconnect the leads, connecting the positive (+) terminal first. Make sure the O-ring and spacer are in place on the retaining strap screw **(see illustration)**.

### Inspection and maintenance

**12** The battery is a maintenance free (sealed) type, therefore requiring no regular maintenance. However, the following checks should still be performed.

**13** Check the state of charge by measuring the voltage at the battery terminals **(see illustration)**. Connect the voltmeter positive (+) probe to the battery positive (+) terminal, and the negative (–) probe to the battery negative (–) terminal. When fully charged there should be 12.8 volts present. If the voltage falls below 12 volts remove the battery (see above), and recharge it as described below in Section 4.

**14** Check the battery terminals and leads are tight and free of corrosion. If corrosion is evident, clean the terminals as described in Step 5, then protect them from further corrosion.

**15** Keep the battery case clean to prevent current leakage, which can discharge the battery over a period of time (especially when it sits unused). Wash the outside of the case

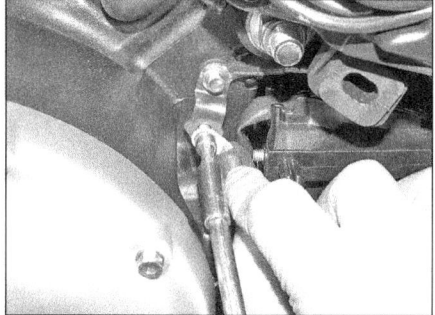

**3.8 Release the negative lead terminal from the engine**

**3.9 Disconnect the positive terminal**

**3.10a Unhook the strap...**

**3.10b and slide the battery out – it is quite heavy**

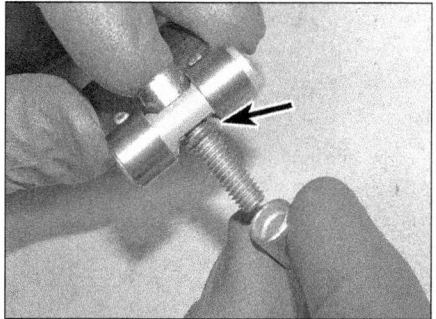

**3.11 Check the O-ring (arrowed) and spacer are fitted**

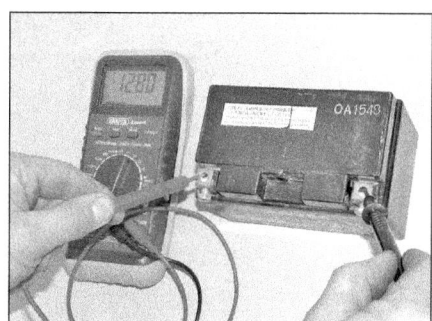

**3.13 Checking battery voltage**

with a solution of baking soda and water. Rinse the battery thoroughly, then dry it.

**16** Look for cracks in the case and replace the battery with a new one if any are found. If acid has been spilled on the frame or battery box, neutralise it with a baking soda and water solution, then dry it thoroughly.

**17** If the motorcycle sits unused for long periods of time, disconnect the leads from the battery terminals, negative (–) terminal first. Refer to Section 4 and charge the battery once every month to six weeks.

## 4  Battery charging

**Caution: Be extremely careful when handling or working around the battery. The electrolyte is very caustic and an explosive gas (hydrogen) is given off when the battery is charging.**

**1** Check the charger is rated for a 12V battery.

**2** Remove the battery (Section 3). If not already done, refer to Section 3, Step 13, and check the open circuit voltage of the battery. Triumph recommends charging the battery if terminal voltage is less than 12.7 volts.

**3** Connect the charger to the battery BEFORE switching the charger ON. Make sure that the positive (+) lead on the charger is connected to the positive (+) terminal on the battery, and the negative (-) lead is connected to the negative (-) terminal **(see illustration)**.

**4** It is best to use a dedicated motorcycle battery charger, preferably one of the 'intelligent' ones that constantly monitors the state of charge and controls its output accordingly. If a normal car type charger is used check that after a probable initial peak, the charge rate falls to a safe level consistent with the charge rate specified on the battery. If the battery becomes hot during charging stop. Further charging will cause damage. Many motorcycle chargers are designed for the maintenance and recovery of heavily discharged MF batteries. They are not expensive, and are a worthwhile investment, especially if the bike is not used over winter. Follow the manufacturer's instructions.

**5** If the recharged battery discharges rapidly when left disconnected it is likely that an internal short caused by physical damage or sulphation has occurred. A new battery will be required. A sound battery will tend to lose its charge at about 1% per day.

**6** Install the battery (Section 3).

**7** If the motorcycle sits unused for long periods of time, charge the battery once every month to six weeks and leave it disconnected. Note that many chargers contain a means of trickle charging the battery, allowing it to remain connected.

## 5  Fuses

**Note:** *Early T120 and Street Twin models were fitted with a 10A cooling fan fuse – this has since been uprated to 15A. If a 10A fuse is fitted on your bike and it fails, a kit is available containing a new 15A fuse and a sticker for the fusebox lid showing the new rating.*

**1** The electrical system as a whole is protected by the main fuse, and individual circuits are protected by other fuses of different ratings (see Specifications).

**2** On all models except the Bobber the main fuse is housed in the starter relay, which is behind the right-hand side panel, and all other fuses are housed in the fusebox, which is under the seat. Remove the side panel or seat for access (see Chapter 7). To access the main fuse displace the starter relay, then release and remove the cover **(see illustrations)**. To access the fusebox fuses unclip the fusebox lid – the identity, location and specified rating of each fuse is marked on the lid, and each fuse is marked with its rating **(see illustrations)**.

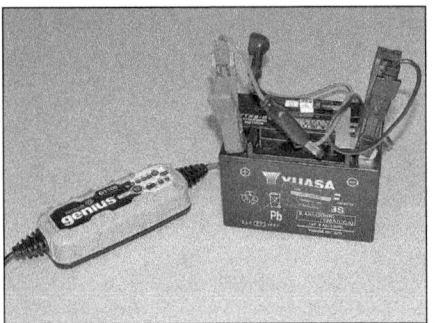

**4.3 Battery connected to a charger**

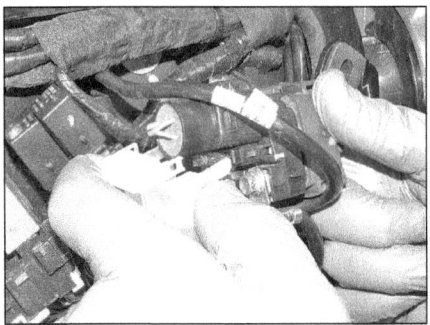

**5.2a Displace the relay and remove the cover...**

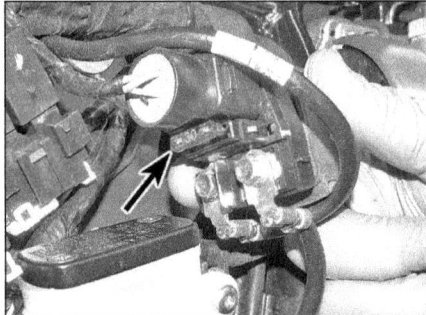

**5.2b ... to access the main fuse (arrowed)**

**5.2c Fuse layout and ratings are marked on the lid**

**5.2d Open the lid to access the fuses**

5.3a Open the lid to access the main fuse

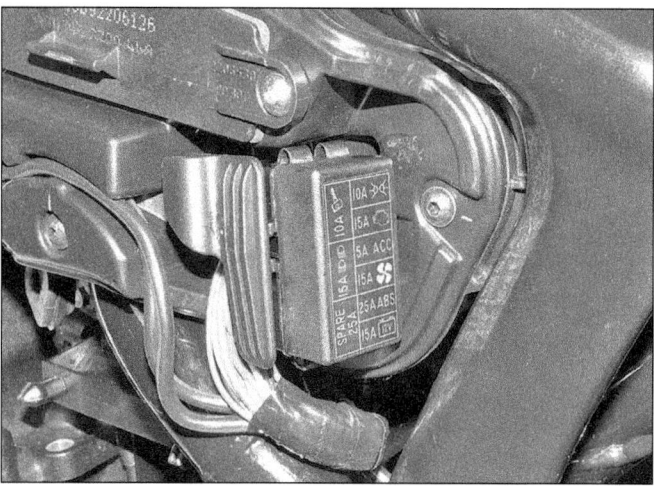

5.3b Fuse layout and ratings are marked on the lid

5.3c Open the lid to access the fuses

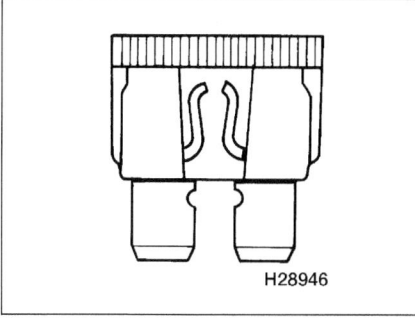

5.4 A blown fuse can be identified by a break in its element

**3** On the Bobber the main fuse is in a holder behind the left-hand side panel, and all other fuses are housed in the fusebox, also behind the left-hand side panel. Remove the side panel for access (see Chapter 7). To access the main fuse unclip the fuse holder lid **(see illustration)**. To access the fusebox fuses unclip the fusebox lid – the identity, location and specified rating of each fuse is marked on the lid, and each fuse is marked with its rating **(see illustrations)**.

**4** The fuses can be removed and checked visually. If you can't pull the fuse out with your fingertips, use a suitable pair of pliers. A blown fuse is easily identified by a break in the element **(see illustration)**, or can be tested for continuity using an ohmmeter or continuity tester – if there is no continuity, it has blown. Each fuse is clearly marked with its rating and must only be replaced by a fuse of the same rating. It is advisable to carry a spare fuse of each rating on the bike at all times.

 *Warning: Never put in a fuse of a higher rating or bridge the terminals with any other substitute, however temporary it may be. Serious damage may be done to the circuit, or a fire may start.*

**5** If the new fuse blows, you need to check the relevant circuit and its components carefully for evidence of a short-circuit. Look for bare wires and chafed, melted or burned insulation.

**6** Sometimes fuses blow for no specific reason, in which case replacing it with a new one is the only action required. Also corrosion of the fuse ends and fusebox terminals may occur and cause poor fuse contact. If this happens, remove the corrosion with a wire brush or emery paper, then spray the fuse end and terminals with electrical contact cleaner.

## 6 Lighting system check

**Note:** *Refer to Electrical system fault finding (Section 2) and to the Wiring Diagrams at the end of the Chapter when making electrical tests on any part of the system.*

**1** If a light fails first check the bulb (see relevant Section), the bulb terminals in the holder, and the wiring connector. Bulbs are used for the headlight on all models, the

sidelight on the T100, Bobber, Street Twin, Street Cup and Scrambler, and for the turn signal lights on all models except the Bobber. When checking for a blown filament in a bulb, it is advisable to back up a visual check with a continuity test of the filament as it is not always apparent that a bulb has blown. When testing for continuity, remember that on single terminal bulbs it is the metal body of the bulb that is the earth (ground).

**2** LEDs (Light Emitting Diodes) are used for the brake/tail/licence plate light and instrument lights on all models, for the position light (or daytime running light) on the T120, Thruxton and Thruxton R, and for the turn signal lights on the Bobber. If the light does not work check the wiring connector. If an individual LED fails it cannot be replaced with a new one, but the rest should continue to function. If none of them work, it is more likely to be a circuit problem.

**3** Also check the relevant fuse (Section 5). If no fault can be found check the wiring and connectors in the circuit. If no problem can be found for a headlight fault refer to Section 13 and check the headlight relay, and if that is good check the starter circuit relay. Make sure each relay is secure in its connector and that the terminals are corrosion free and not bent or broken. Then check the function of the relay itself as described. Note that the turn signal relay is incorporated in the instruments.

## 7 Headlight bulb and sidelight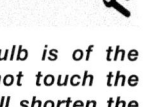

*Caution: The headlight bulb is of the quartz-halogen type. Do not touch the bulb glass as skin acids will shorten the bulb's service life. If the bulb is accidentally touched, it should be wiped carefully when cold with a rag soaked in methylated spirit and dried before fitting.*

**7.1a Remove the screw on each side of the shell**

**7.1b Disconnect the headlight wiring...**

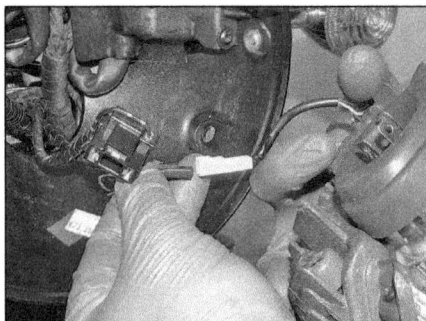

**7.1c ... and the sidelight wiring**

### *Headlight bulb*

#### All models except the Bobber

**1** Undo the screw on each side of the headlight and displace the headlight from the shell, then disconnect the headlight and sidelight wiring connectors and remove the headlight **(see illustrations)**.

**2** Remove the rubber cover from the back of the headlight **(see illustration)**.
**3** Release the bulb retaining clip, noting how it fits, then remove the bulb **(see illustrations)**.
**4** Fit the new bulb, bearing in mind the information in the Caution above. Make sure the tabs on the bulb flange are aligned with the slots in the back of the headlight, and

secure the bulb in position with the retaining clip **(see illustrations 7.3b and a)**.
**5** Fit the rubber cover **(see illustration 7.2)**.
**6** Reconnect the wiring **(see illustrations 7.1c and b)**. Fit the headlight into the shell, locating the tab on the top behind the rib on the shell **(see illustration)**. Fit the screws **(see illustration 7.1a)**. Check the operation of the headlight.

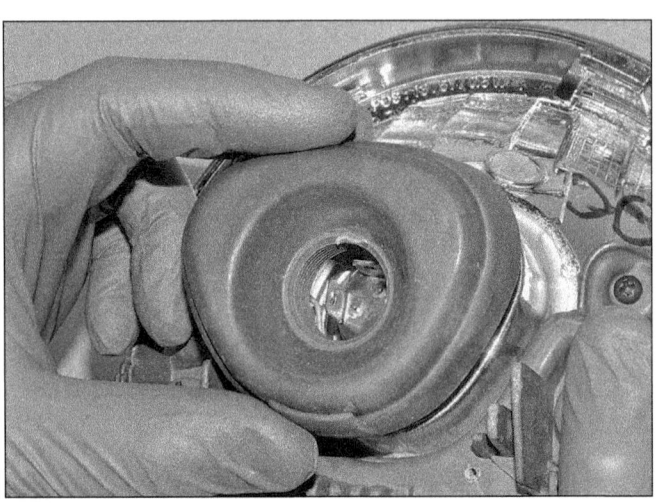

**7.2 Remove the cover**

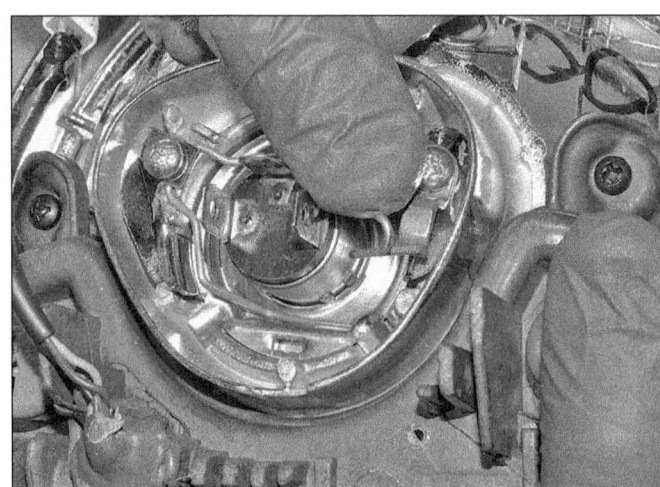

**7.3a Release the clip...**

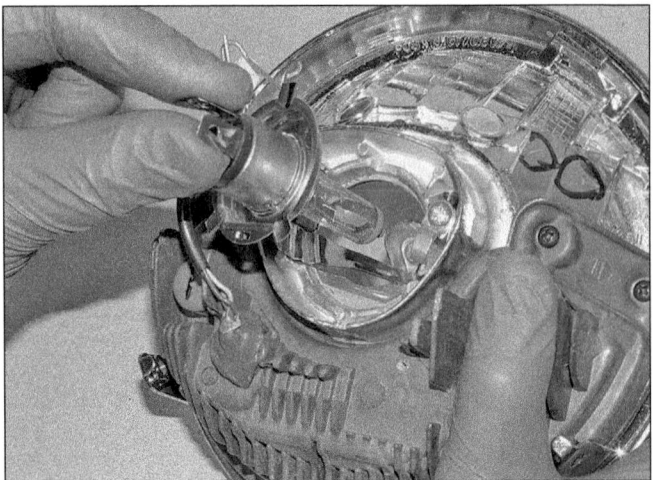

**7.3b ...and remove the bulb**

**7.6 Tab at top locates behind rib inside the shell via the cut-out in the wiring holder**

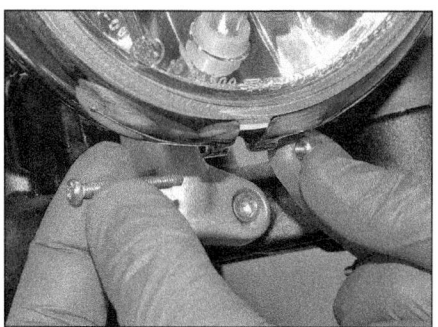

7.7a Undo the nut and remove the screw...

7.7b ...then remove the rim

7.7c Displace the headlight...

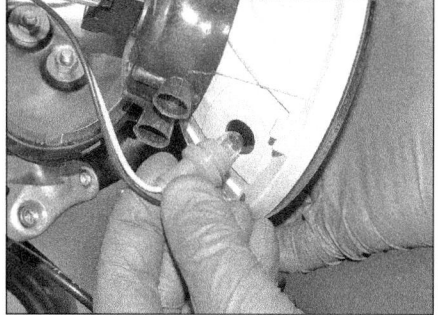

7.7d ...remove the sidelight bulb holder...

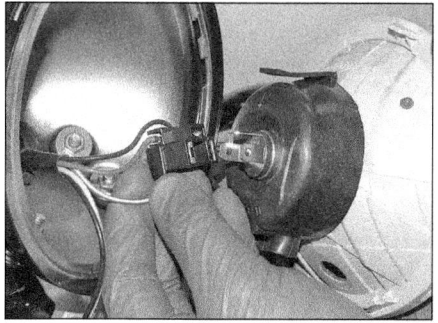

7.7e ... and disconnect the headlight wiring

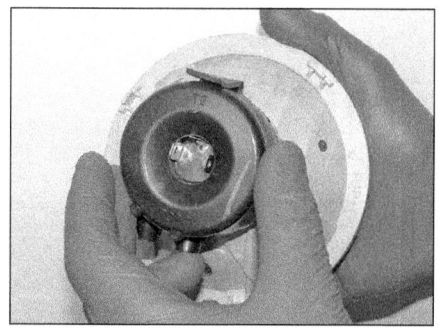

7.8 Remove the cover

### Bobber

7  Undo the nut on the headlight rim clamp screw, withdraw the screw and remove the rim **(see illustrations)**. Displace the headlight from the shell, then pull the sidelight bulb holder out, disconnect the headlight wiring connector, and remove the headlight **(see illustrations)**.

8  Remove the rubber cover from the back of the headlight **(see illustration)**.

9  Release the bulb retaining clip, noting how it fits, then remove the bulb **(see illustrations)**.

10  Fit the new bulb, bearing in mind the information in the Caution above. Make sure the tabs on the bulb flange are aligned with the slots in the back of the headlight, and secure the bulb in position with the retaining clip **(see illustrations 7.9b and a)**.

11  Fit the rubber cover **(see illustration 7.8)**.

12  Reconnect the wiring and fit the sidelight bulb holder **(see illustrations 7.7e and d)**. Fit the headlight into the shell, then fit and secure the rim **(see illustrations 7.7c, b and a)**. Check the operation of the headlight.

### Sidelight bulb – T100, Bobber, Street Twin, Street Cup and Scrambler

13  Undo the screw on each side and displace the headlight from the shell **(see illustration 7.1a)**. Pull the sidelight bulb holder out. Seat the headlight back in the shell.

14  On the Bobber undo the nut on the headlight rim clamp screw, withdraw the screw and remove the rim **(see illustrations 7.7a and b)**. Displace the headlight from the shell, then pull the sidelight bulb holder out **(see illustrations 7.7c and d)**. Seat the headlight back in the shell.

15  Pull the sidelight bulb out of its holder **(see illustration)**.

16  Align the new bulb with its socket in the bulbholder and press it into place. Fit the bulbholder into the headlight.

17  Fit the headlight into the shell, either locating the tab on the top behind the rib on the shell and fitting the screws **(see illustrations 7.6 and 7.1a)**, or fitting and securing the rim according to model **(see illustration 7.7c, b and a)**. Check the operation of the sidelight.

### Sidelight LED unit – T120, Thruxton and Thruxton R

18  The sidelight LED unit is part of the headlight. If the LED unit fails remove the headlight from the shell (see Step 1) and replace it with a new one.

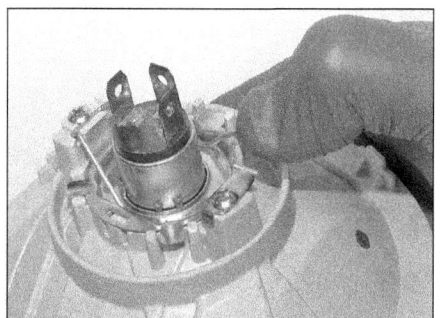

7.9a Release the clip...

7.9b ...and remove the bulb

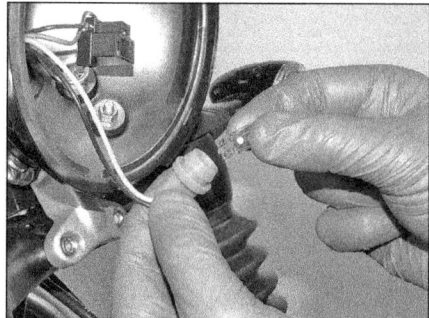

7.15 ...and pull the bulb from the holder

8.2a Undo the screws...

8.2b ...displace the holder and release the connectors

8.3a Unscrew the bolt on each side...

8.3b ... and draw the wiring out

## 8  Headlight, headlight aim

### Headlight removal and installation

#### All models except the Bobber

**1** Undo the screw on each side of the headlight and displace the headlight from the shell, then disconnect the headlight and sidelight wiring connectors and remove the headlight **(see illustrations 7.1a, b, and c)**.
**2** Undo the wiring holder screws and lower the holder **(see illustration)**. Release all the wiring connectors from the wiring holder, noting which fits where, and remove the holder **(see illustration)**.
**3** Unscrew the bolt securing each side of the shell, noting the washer **(see illustration)**. Draw the shell forwards and feed the wiring out through the back of the shell **(see illustrations)**.

#### Bobber

**4** Remove the fuel tank (see Chapter 4). Remove the wiring harness cover. Release and disconnect the headlight connector and feed the wiring to the headlight, releasing it from any guides and noting its routing **(see illustration)**.

**5** Unscrew the headlight bracket bolts and remove the headlight **(see illustration)**.

#### Installation – all models

**6** Installation is the reverse of removal. Make sure all the wiring is correctly connected and secured. Check the operation of the headlight and sidelight. Check the headlight aim.

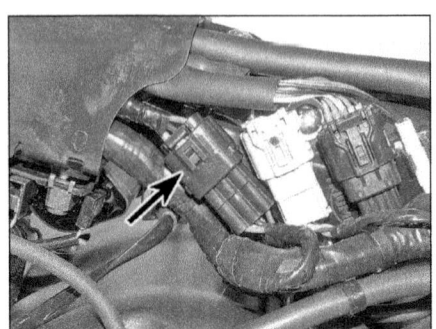

8.4 Headlight connector (arrowed)

8.5 Headlight bracket bolts (arrowed)

8.9 Slacken the nut (arrowed) to adjust the headlight

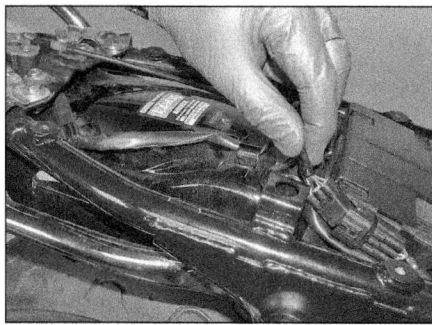

9.2a Disconnect and release the wiring

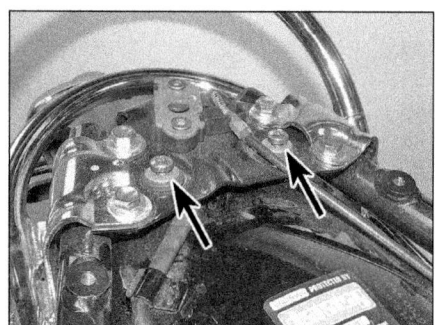

9.2b Slacken the screws (arrowed)

### Headlight aim adjustment

**Note:** *An improperly adjusted headlight may cause problems for oncoming traffic or provide poor, unsafe illumination of the road ahead. Before adjusting the headlight aim, be sure to consult with local traffic laws and regulations – for UK models refer to MOT Test Checks in the Reference section.*

**7** The headlight beam can adjusted vertically. Before making any adjustment, check that the tyre pressures are correct. Make any adjustments to the headlight aim with the machine on level ground, with the fuel tank half full and with an assistant sitting on the seat. If the bike is usually ridden with a passenger on the back, have a second assistant to do this. Set the headlight on low beam.

**8** On all models except the Bobber slacken the bolt securing each side of the headlight shell **(see illustration 8.3a)** to the bracket and pivot the headlight up or down as required, then tighten the bolts.

**9** On the Bobber slacken the nut on the headlight pivot bolt and pivot the headlight up or down as required, then tighten the nut **(see illustration)**.

## 9  Tail light

### T100, T120, Thruxton, Thruxton R

**1** Remove the seat (see Chapter 7).
**2** Disconnect the tail light wiring connector, and release the wiring from the guide **(see illustration)**. Slacken the mudguard rear screws **(see illustration)**.
**3** Unscrew the three bolts and the nut/ screw bolts securing the tail light/turn signal bracket assembly to the mudguard, then lift it off and draw the wiring out, pushing the mudguard down for clearance **(see illustrations)**. Note the arrangement of the collars and grommets in the bracket mounts **(see illustration)**.
**4** Remove the wiring cover **(see illustration)**. Disconnect the turn signal wiring connectors **(see illustration)** – note that the wires on the harness side of the connectors for the right-hand turn signal have red sleeves so they cannot be wrongly connected.
**5** Undo the tail light cover screws and remove the cover **(see illustration)**. Release the wiring

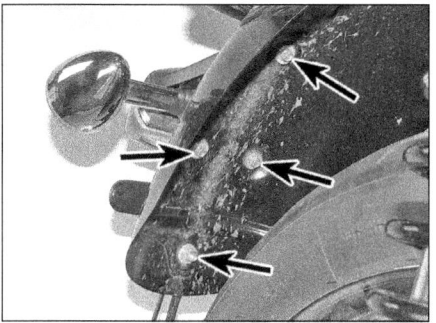

9.3a Unscrew the three bolts and the nut and screw at the bottom (arrowed)

9.3b Lift the assembly off and draw the wiring out

9.3c Note which way the collars are fitted

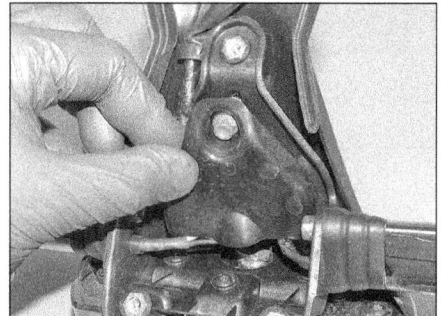

9.4a Remove the cover...

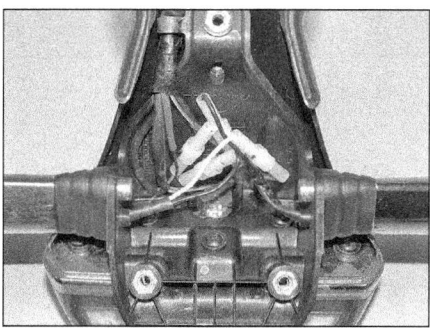

9.4b ...and disconnect the turn signal wiring

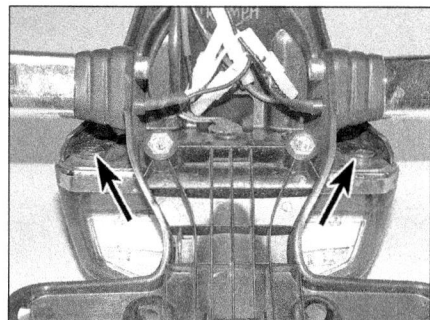

9.5a Tail light cover screws (arrowed)

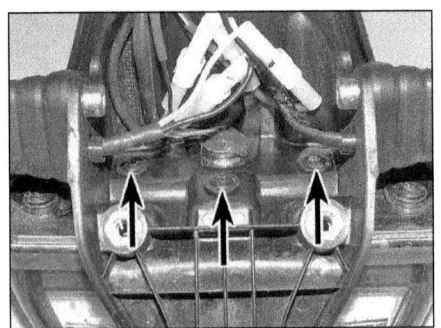

9.5b Tail light screws (arrowed)

harness from the guide. Undo the tail light screws and remove the light **(see illustration)**.
6 Installation is the reverse of removal. Check the grommets are in good condition and the sleeves are fitted in them. Check the operation of the tail light, brake light, and turn signals.

### Street Twin, Street Cup, Scrambler

7 Remove the seat and on Scrambler models also remove the luggage rack and its mounting plate (see Chapter 7).

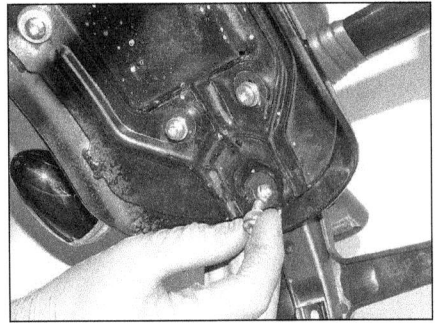

9.14a Undo the screws and displace the tail light assembly...

8 Disconnect the tail light wiring connector **(see illustration 9.2a)**.
9 Undo the four mudguard screws and remove the mudguard.
10 Undo the three screws securing the wiring cover to the support bracket on the underside of the mudguard and remove the cover. Unscrew the two bolts and remove the support bracket from the mudguard – the bolts also secure the tail light.
11 Undo the remaining tail light bolt and remove the light. The separate licence plate light on the Scrambler and Street Twin is mounted to the lower part of the support bracket.
12 Installation is the reverse of removal. Check the operation of the tail light, brake light and licence plate light.

### Bobber

13 Remove the rear wheel (see Chapter 6).
14 Undo the three screws securing the tail light/turn signal bracket assembly to the mudguard, noting the washers, then lift it off and draw the wiring out of the channel **(see illustration)** – if there is not enough slack in the wiring release the rubber holder from the front of the mudguard to give more **(see illustration)**.
15 Disconnect the tail light, licence plate light and turn signal wiring connectors and remove the assembly **(see illustration)** – note that the wires for the right-hand turn signal have red sleeves so they cannot be wrongly connected.
16 Undo the tail light screws and remove the light **(see illustration 9.15)**. Note the collars in the rubber pad. Unbolt the licence plate and reflector brackets to access the licence plate light mountings.
17 Installation is the reverse of removal. Check the collars are fitted. Check the operation of the tail light, licence plate light, brake light and turn signals.

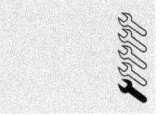

### 10 Turn signals

### Bulb replacement – all models except the Bobber

1 Most turn signal problems are the result of a burned out bulb or corroded socket. This is especially true when the turn signals function properly in one direction, but fail to flash in the other direction. Check the bulbs and the sockets as follows.
2 On the T100, T120, Street Cup, Thruxton and Thruxton R, carefully twist the turn signal lens clockwise to release the tabs and remove the lens.
3 On the Street Twin and Scrambler undo the turn signal lens screw and remove the lens, noting how the tab locates.
4 Push the bulb into the holder and twist it anti-clockwise to remove it.
5 Check the socket and terminal for corrosion, if necessary scrape them clean and spray with electrical contact cleaner before a new bulb is fitted. Line up the pins of the new bulb with the slots in the socket (noting that on amber bulbs the pins are offset), then push the bulb in and turn it clockwise until it locks into place.
6 On the T100, T120, Street Cup, Thruxton and Thruxton R, align the tabs on the lens with the slots in the housing and carefully twist the lens anti-clockwise to lock the tabs.
7 On the Street Twin and Scrambler locate the tab on the lens on the inner side of the signal body and tighten the screw – do not overtighten it as it is easy to crack the lens or strip the threads.
8 Check the operation of the turn signals.

### LED unit replacement – Bobber

9 The LED unit is available separately although check its cost – you may find it

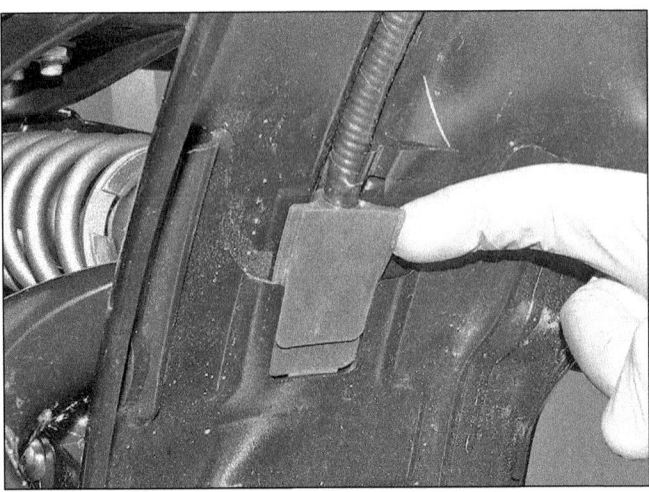

9.14b ...releasing the rubber from the mudguard allows more slack in the wiring

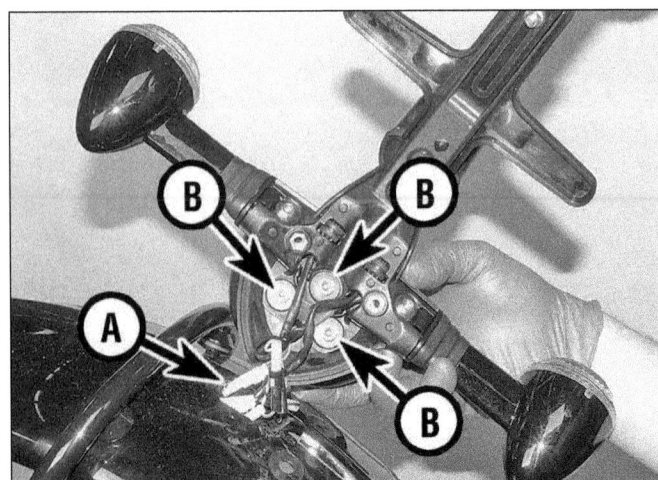

9.15 Tail assembly wiring connectors (A). Tail light screws (B)

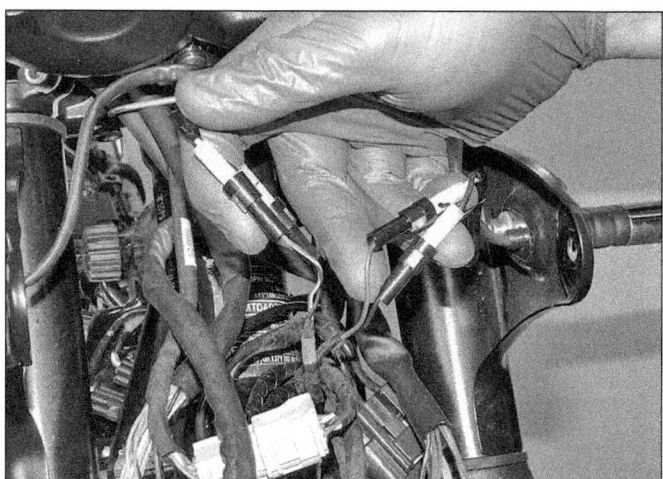

10.10a Turn signal wiring connectors

10.10b Turn signal screw (arrowed)

better to replace the complete turn signal as described below.

## Turn signal removal and installation

### Front turn signals

**10** On the T100, T120, Street Cup, Thruxton and Thruxton R remove the headlight (Section 8). Disconnect the turn signal wiring connectors **(see illustration)** – note that the wires on the harness side of the connectors for the right-hand turn signal have red sleeves so they cannot be wrongly connected. Undo the screw, noting the washer where fitted, and remove the turn signal **(see illustration)**.

**11** On the Bobber remove the fuel tank (see Chapter 4). Trace the wiring from the turn signal and disconnect it at the connector, then feed the wiring to the turn signal, releasing it from any guides and noting its routing – note that the wires on the harness side of the connectors for the right-hand turn signal have red sleeves so they cannot be wrongly

connected. Refer to Chapter 5 to displace the front fork, and slide the turn signal off the top of the fork when it is between the yokes – there is no need to remove the fork completely from the bottom yoke. If required undo the screw and remove the turn signal from the clamp, noting the routing of the wiring.

**12** On the Street Twin and Scrambler remove the headlight from its shell, then undo the wiring holder screws and lower the holder **(see illustrations 7.1a, b and c and 8.2a)**. Disconnect the turn signal wiring connectors **(see illustration)** – note that the wires on the harness side of the connectors for the right-hand turn signal have red sleeves so they cannot be wrongly connected. Refer to Chapter 5 to displace the front fork, and slide the turn signal off the top of the fork when it is between the yokes – there is no need to remove the fork completely from the bottom yoke. If required undo the screw and remove the turn signal from the clamp, noting the routing of the wiring.

**13** Installation is the reverse of removal. Check the operation of the turn signals.

### Rear turn signals

**14** On the T100, T120, Thruxton and Thruxton R refer to Section 9, Steps 1 to 4 to remove the tail light/turn signal assembly, wiring cover and to disconnect the turn signal wiring connectors. Undo the turn signal screw and remove the turn signal **(see illustration)**.

**15** On the Bobber remove the tail light and its rubber pad (Section 9). Remove the rear reflector and bracket from the main bracket. Undo the three screws and separate the main bracket from the tail light bracket. Undo the turn signal screw and remove the turn signal from the tail light bracket.

**16** On the Street Twin, Street Cup and Scrambler undo the three screws securing the wiring cover to the support bracket on the underside of the mudguard and remove the cover. Disconnect the turn signal wiring connectors – note that the wires on the harness side of the connectors for the right-hand turn

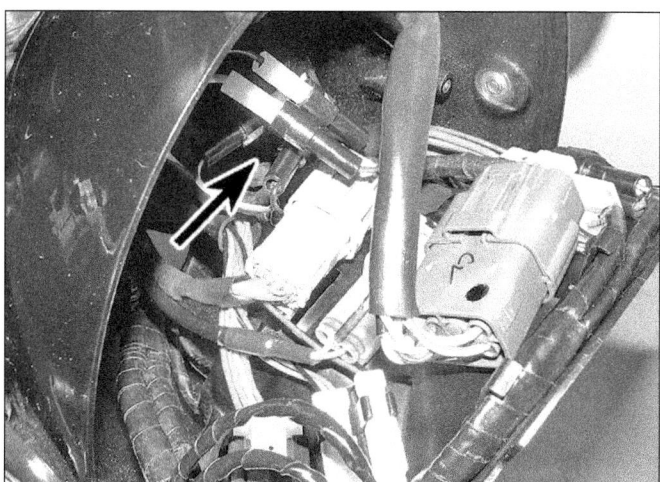

10.12 Turn signal wiring connectors (arrowed)

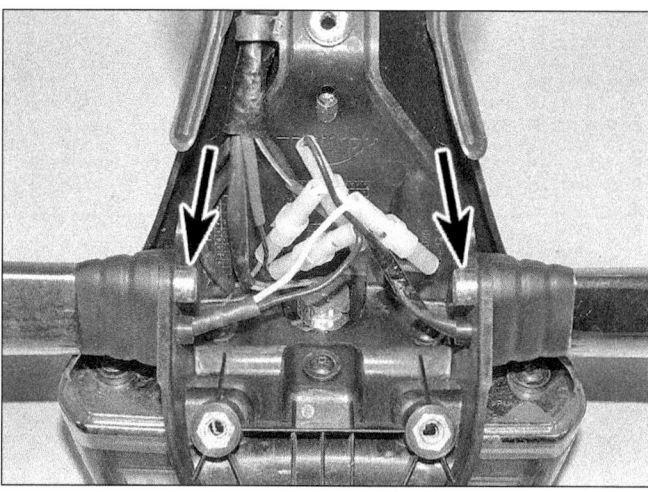

10.14 Turn signal screws (arrowed)

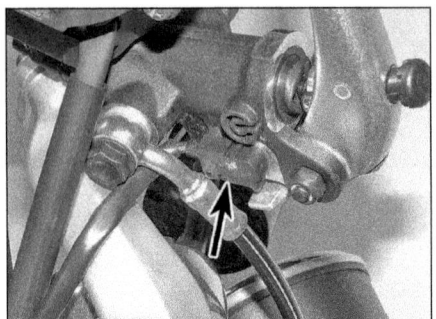

**11.5 Front brake light switch (arrowed)**

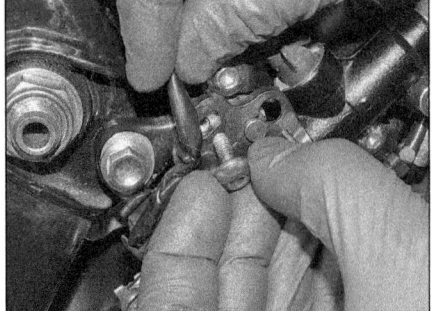

**11.9a Undo the screw...**

**11.9b ...push down and displace the bracket**

signal have red sleeves so they cannot be wrongly connected. Unscrew the nut, withdraw the bolt and remove the turn signal.

**17** Installation is the reverse of removal. Check the operation of the turn signals.

## 11 Brake light switches

### *Check*

**Note:** *On the Thruxton and Thruxton R Triumph has added a self-adhesive foam pad to the rear brake light switch body to reduce the clearance between it and the master cylinder bracket – if on your bike the rear brake light flickers, and the switch does not have the foam pad, obtain one from you dealer (part No. T3660288) and stick it onto the switch.*

**1** Before checking the switches, check the brake light circuit. Also check that you can hear the switch button click as you pull the brake lever in or push the pedal down, and click again as you release it. If not check the switch is securely mounted and correctly positioned so the lever or pedal contact plate is holding the switch button in at rest, and releasing it when pulled in or pushed down.

**2** Refer below for access to the switch wiring connector, then test the switch as described in Section 2.

### *Removal and installation*

#### Front brake light switch

**3** The front brake light switch is mounted on the underside of the brake master cylinder.

**4** On all models except the Thruxton R the switch is wired into the right-hand switch housing on the handlebar and is not available separately – refer to Section 15 for access to the wiring connectors and to remove the switch assembly.

**5** On the Thruxton R remove the headlight from its shell, then undo the wiring holder screws and lower the holder **(see illustrations 7.1a, b and c and 8.2a)**. Disconnect the brake light switch wiring connector. Feed the switch side of the connector out of the headlight and to the switch, noting its routing. Ease the switch evenly off the bottom of the master

**11.10a Release the wiring...**

cylinder **(see illustration)** – it has two pegs that are a push fit into holes.

**6** Installation is the reverse of removal. Check the operation of the brake light.

#### Rear brake light switch

#### T100, T120, Street Twin, Street Cup and Scrambler

**7** Remove the front sprocket cover(see Chapter 6).

**8** On the Street Twin up to VIN 737936, undo the brake light switch bracket screws and displace the switch assembly, then disconnect the wiring connector.

**9** On the T100, T120, Street Twin from VIN 737937, Street Cup and Scrambler, undo the brake light switch bracket screw then slide the bracket down to free the slot from the lug head and displace the switch assembly,

**11.11 Push on the bracket to ensure the lug head is fully seated in the narrow section of the slot and the switch button is against the plate**

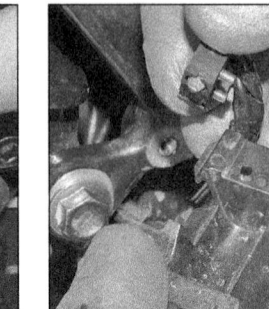

**11.10b ... then ease the switch off to release the pegs from the holes**

then disconnect the wiring connector **(see illustrations)**.

**10** Release the switch wiring from its guide on the bracket, then release the switch from the bracket, noting how it locates **(see illustrations)**.

**11** Installation is the reverse of removal – push on the brake light switch bracket so the switch button is against and pushed in by the actuation plate on the pushrod before tightening the screw(s) **(see illustration)**. After tightening the screw(s) push the brake pedal down and check that you can hear the switch button click as the switch closes and then again as it opens when the pedal is released. Check the operation of the brake light.

#### Bobber

**12** Remove the front sprocket cover (see Chapter 6).

**13** Disconnect the rear brake light switch wiring connector **(see illustration)**.

**11.13 Rear brake light switch wiring connector (arrowed)**

11.14a Unscrew the nuts, displace the reservoir...

11.14b ...and release the hose

11.15a Unscrew the bolts using a ball-ended hex key...

**14** Displace the coolant reservoir and support it upright to one side **(see illustrations)**.

**15** Unscrew the footrest/brake pedal/master cylinder bracket bolts and lift the complete assembly out, noting the routing of the brake light switch wire **(see illustrations)**.

**16** Undo the brake light switch bracket screw then slide the bracket to free the slot from the lug head and displace the switch assembly **(see illustration)**.

**17** Release the switch wiring from its guide on the bracket, then release the switch from the bracket, noting how it locates **(see illustrations)**.

**18** Installation is the reverse of removal – push on the brake light switch bracket so the switch button is against and pushed in by the actuation plate on the pushrod before tightening the screw **(see illustration)**. After tightening the screw push the brake pedal down and check that you can hear the switch button click as the switch closes and then again as it opens when the pedal is released. Check the operation of the brake light.

### Thruxton and Thruxton R

**19** Remove the heel guard from the front sprocket cover **(see illustration)**.

**20** Unscrew the footrest/brake pedal/master cylinder bracket bolts and lift the complete assembly out, then disconnect the brake light switch wiring connector **(see illustration)**.

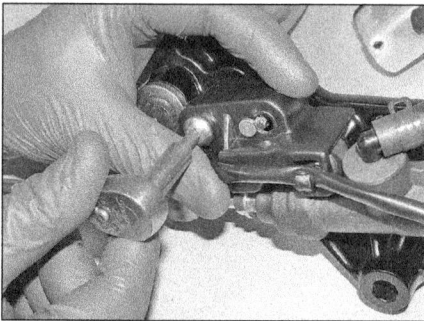

11.15b ... and lift the assembly out

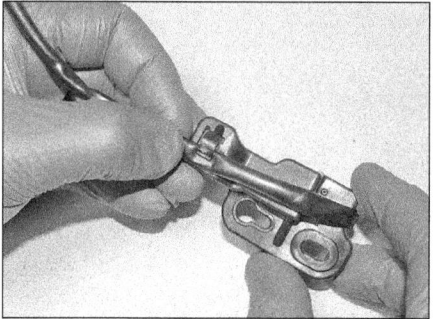

11.16 Undo the screw and displace the bracket

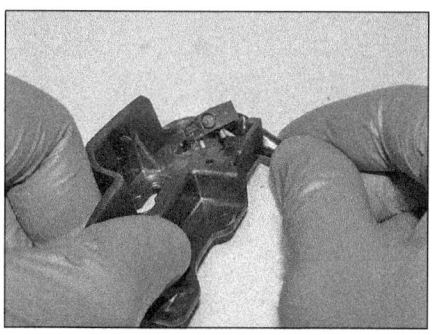

11.17a Release the wiring...

11.17b ...then ease the switch off to release the pegs from the holes

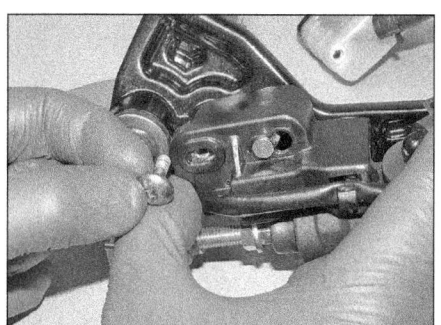

11.18 Push on the bracket to ensure the lug head is fully seated in the narrow section of the slot and the switch button is against the plate

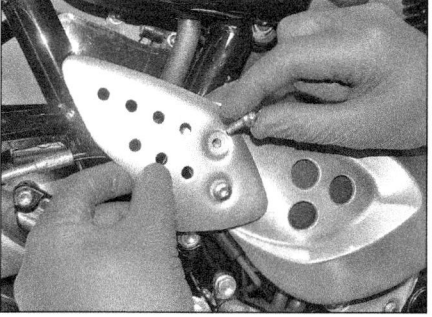

11.19 Undo the screws and remove the guard

11.20 Unscrew the bracket bolts (arrowed)

12.5a Remove the cover...

12.5b ...and disconnect the wiring

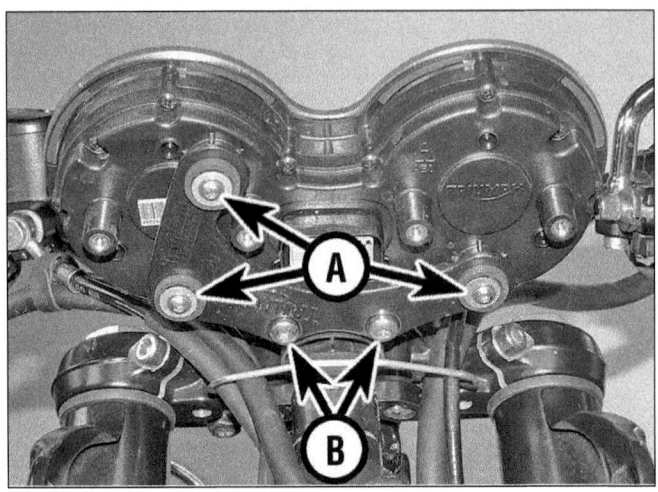

12.5c Instrument screws (A), instrument bracket screws (B)

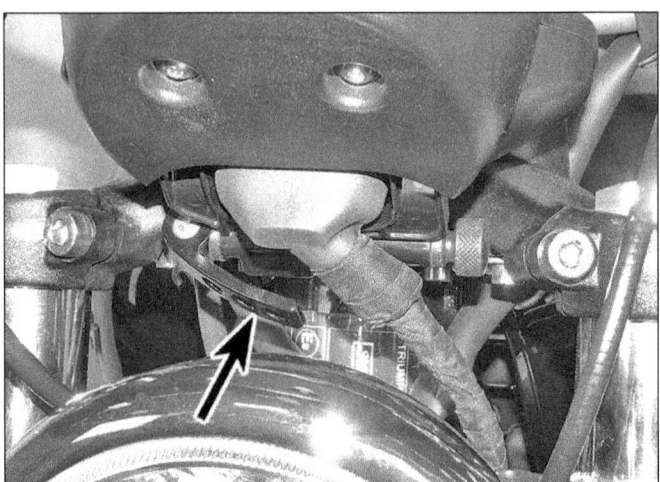

12.6a Pull the lever (arrowed) down to release the adjuster

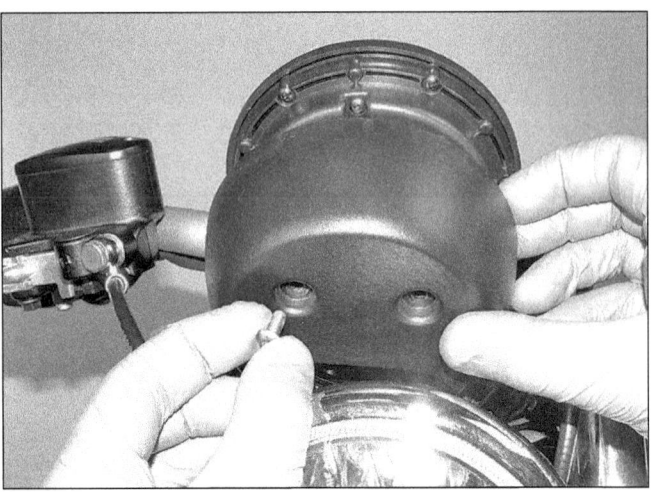

12.6b Remove the cover...

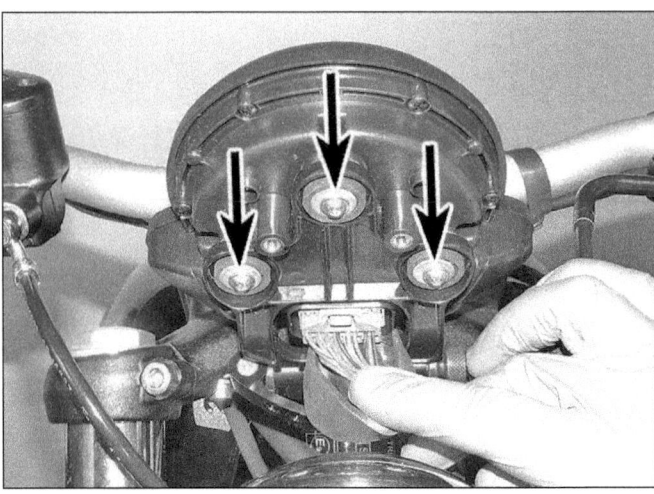

12.6c ...and disconnect the wiring. Instrument screws (arrowed)

**21** Undo the brake light switch bracket screw then slide the bracket to free the lug head from the slot and displace the switch assembly.

**22** Release the switch wiring from its guide on the bracket, then release the switch from the bracket, noting how it locates.

**23** Installation is the reverse of removal – push on the brake light switch bracket so the switch button is against and pushed in by the actuation plate on the pushrod before tightening the screw **(see illustration 11.11)**. After tightening the screw push the brake pedal down and check that you can hear the switch button click as the switch closes and then again as it opens when the pedal is released. Check the operation of the brake light.

## 12 Instruments

### Check

**1** Specific test data for the instruments is not available. Refer below for access to the wiring connector and check that it is securely connected to the instrument cluster, and also refer to the relevant Section of this Chapter or to other Chapters and check that the other end of the wiring is securely connected to its source (i.e. gear position switch, oil pressure switch, fuel level sender, coolant temperature sensor etc). Check all wires for continuity from pin to pin, referring to electrical system fault finding (Section 2) and to the wiring diagrams.

**2** Check that all earth wires have a good connection. If all the wiring is good, it is possible that there are faults in the switches or sensors or the electronic control module (ECM) of the engine management system, which provide much of the information to the instruments. If all checks point at faulty instruments rather than wiring or the engine management system, take the instrument cluster to a Triumph dealer for further assessment.

**3** All of the warning and instrument lights are LEDs. If the cause of any problem (i.e. neutral light not coming on) cannot be traced it is possible the LED has failed, in which case a new instrument cluster must be fitted.

### Removal and installation

**4** Disconnect the battery negative (-) terminal (Section 3).

**5** On the T100, T120, Street Cup, Thruxton and Thruxton R remove the headlight (Section 8). Undo the instrument cover screws and remove the cover from the back of the instrument cluster **(see illustration)**. Pull the rubber boot back and disconnect the wiring connector **(see illustration)**. Undo the screws, noting the washers, and detach the instrument cluster from the bracket, noting how the pegs locate in the grommets **(see illustration)**. If required remove the bracket from the yoke.

**6** On the Bobber release the instrument angle adjuster and pivot the instruments up as far as they go **(see illustration)**. On the Bobber, Street Twin and Scrambler, undo the instrument cover screws and remove the cover from the back of the instrument cluster **(see illustration)**. Pull the rubber boot back and disconnect the wiring connector **(see illustration)**. Undo the screws, noting the washers, and detach the instrument cluster from the bracket, noting how the pegs locate in the grommets.

**7** Installation is the reverse of removal. Check the rubber grommets for cracks and deterioration and fit new ones if necessary. Make sure the wiring connector is secure.

## 13 Relays

**Note:** *Before disconnecting a relay, make sure the ignition has been switched OFF for at least one minute to allow the system to power down, then disconnect the battery (Section 3). Refer to the Wiring Diagrams for relay terminal identification.*

**1** The following circuit relays are fitted: headlight main relay, headlight DIP/DRL relay (market specific), starter circuit relay, cooling fan relay, engine management system (EMS) relay and fuel pump relay. For the starter motor relay see Section 20.

**2** To access the relays on all models except the Bobber remove the right-hand side cover (see Chapter 7). The relays are located as shown **(see illustration)**.

**3** To access the relays on the Bobber remove the left-hand air filter housing (see Chapter 4). Undo the battery box lid screws **(see illustration)**. Release and remove the battery tray, noting how it locates **(see illustrations)**. Unscrew the battery box bolts and remove the box **(see illustrations)**. The relays are located as shown **(see illustration)**.

**4** To remove a relay pull it up out of its socket. Check the terminals and sockets for damage and corrosion.

**5** To test a black (4 terminal) relay, and referring to the Wiring Diagrams for terminal identification, connect a continuity tester or a multimeter set to the ohms x 1 scale between the No. 3 and No. 5 wire terminals on the relay – there should be no continuity or infinite resistance. If there is continuity or zero resistance replace the relay with a new one. Using a fully-charged 12 volt battery and two insulated jumper wires, connect the positive (+) terminal of the battery to the No. 1 wire terminal on the relay, and the negative (–) terminal to the No. 2 wire terminal on the

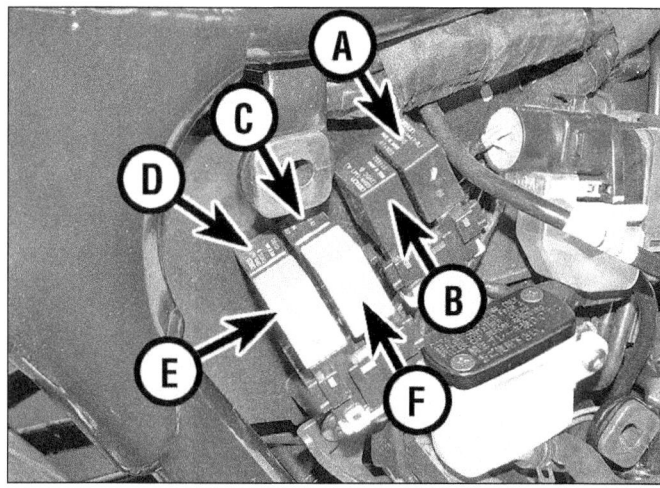

13.2 Cooling fan relay (A), headlight main relay (B), fuel pump relay (C), EMS relay (D), starter circuit relay (E), headlight DIP/DRL relay (F)

13.3a Undo the screws (arrowed)

13.3b Push up on the underside to release the centre clip, then release the inner tabs...

13.3c ...and lift the tray off the outer hook

13.3d Unscrew the bolts (arrowed)...

13.3e ...release the box from the lug (arrowed)...

13.3f ...and manoeuvre it out

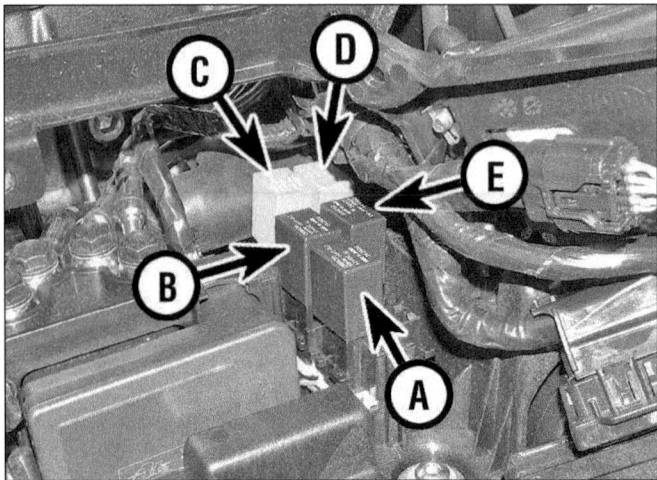

13.3g Cooling fan relay (A), fuel pump relay (B), starter circuit relay (C), headlight main relay (D), EMS relay (E)

relay. At this point the relay should be heard to click and there should be continuity or zero resistance between No. 3 and No. 5 terminals. If this is the case the relay is proved good. If the relay does not click when battery voltage is applied and the tester or meter indicates no continuity (infinite resistance), the relay is faulty and must be replaced with a new one.

6  To test a blue (5 terminal) relay, and referring to the Wiring Diagrams 10 for terminal identification, connect a continuity tester or a multimeter set to the ohms x 1 scale between the No. 3 and No. 4 wire terminals on the relay – there should be continuity or zero resistance. If there is no continuity or infinite resistance replace the relay with a new one. Now connect between No. 3 and No. 5 – there should be no continuity or infinite resistance. If there is continuity or zero resistance replace the relay with a new one. Using a fully-charged 12 volt battery and two insulated jumper wires, connect the positive (+) terminal of the battery to the No. 1 wire terminal on the relay, and the negative (–) terminal to the No. 2 wire terminal on the relay. At this point the relay should be heard to click and there should be continuity or zero resistance between No 3. and No. 5, and no continuity between No. 3 and No. 4. If this is the case the relay is proved good. If the relay does not click when battery voltage is applied and the tester or meter does not indicate what it should, the relay is faulty and must be replaced with a new one.

## 14  Ignition switch

 **Warning: To prevent the risk of short circuits, disconnect the battery negative (–) lead before making any ignition switch checks.**

### Check

1  On all models except the Bobber remove the headlight from its shell, then undo the wiring holder screws and lower the holder **(see illustrations 7.1a, b and c and 8.2a)**. Release and disconnect the ignition switch connector **(see illustration)**.
2  On the Bobber remove the left-hand air filter housing (see Chapter). Disconnect the ignition switch wiring connector **(see illustration)**.
3  Using a multimeter or a continuity tester, make the checks on the switch side of the connector. Check the continuity of the connector terminal pairs (see Wiring Diagrams). Continuity should exist between the terminals connected by a solid line on the diagram when the switch key is turned to the indicated position.
4  If the switch fails any of the tests, replace it with a new one.

### Removal

5  Disconnect the battery negative (–) lead (Section 3).

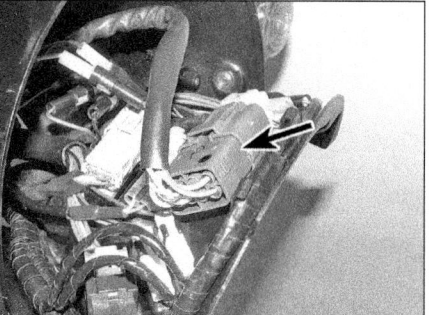

**14.1 Ignition switch wiring connector (arrowed)**

### All models except the Bobber

6  Disconnect the ignition switch wiring (see Step 1).
7  Either remove the fuel tank (see Chapter 4), or cover it in plenty of rag.
8  Remove the headlight (Section 8) and the instruments (Section 12). Displace or remove the headlight and instrument bracket(s) and/or wiring/cable/hose guide(s) as required according to model from the underside of the top yoke or from between the yokes.
9  On all models except the Thruxton and Thruxton R displace the handlebars from the top yoke (see Chapter 5) – tie or support them clear of the yoke. If you are using a spanner to slacken and tighten the steering stem nut, you may also need to remove the handlebar holders and the top rubber dampers for clearance, depending on the type of spanner used (see Chapter 5).

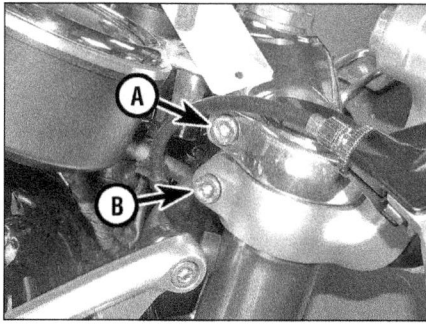

**14.10 Fork clamp bolt (A), handlebar clamp bolt (B)**

**14.11b ... and remove the top yoke**

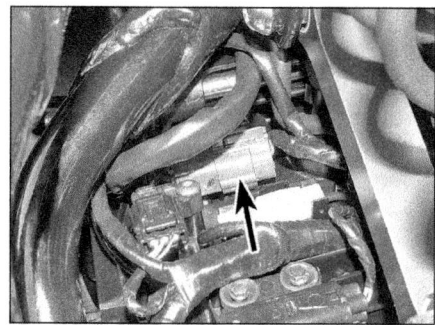

**14.2 Ignition switch wiring connector (arrowed)**

10  Slacken the fork clamp bolts in the top yoke, and on the Thruxton and Thruxton R also slacken the handlebar clamp bolts **(see illustration)**.
11  Check that everything except the ignition switch is free and clear of the top yoke so it can be removed. Stick some masking tape onto the top yoke and around the steering stem nut to protect its finish. Unscrew the steering stem nut **(see illustration)**. Lift the top yokeup off the forks and steering stem, noting how the headlight brackets locate (except on the T100 and T120), then on the Thruxton and Thruxton R unscrew the handlebar positioning bolts and displace the handlebars from the yoke **(see illustration)**.
12  Two single-use shear-head security bolts mount the ignition switch to the underside of the top yoke **(see illustration)**. The heads of the bolts must be tapped around using a suitable drift such as a cold chisel, or drilled

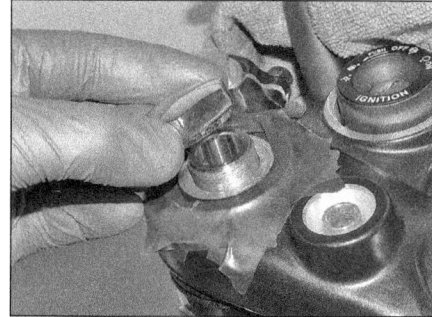

**14.11a Unscrew the nut...**

**14.12 Ignition switch shear-head bolts (arrowed)**

off, before the switch can be removed. To do this, mount the yoke in a vice equipped with padded soft jaws to avoid damaging the yoke. Remove the bolts then withdraw the switch from the yoke. New bolts must be used.

### Bobber

**13** On the Bobber remove the left-hand air filter housing (see Chapter 4). Disconnect the ignition switch wiring connector **(see illustration 14.2)**.

**14** Unscrew the ignition switch bolts, noting the collars in the grommets and the threaded sleeves, and displace the switch from the bracket **(see illustration)**.

**15** Refer to Chapter 2 and displace the engine from the frame enough to remove the switch, noting the routing of the wiring.

### *Installation*

**16** Installation is the reverse of removal, noting the following:
● On all models except the Bobber obtain the correct type shear-head bolts from a Triumph dealer – do not use another type of bolt. Tighten the bolts until their heads shear off.

Refer to Chapter 5, Section 5 and Section 9 for installation details and torque settings related to the top yoke and handlebars.
● Make sure the wiring is securely connected and correctly routed.

## 15 Handlebar switches

### *Check*

**1** Generally speaking, the handlebar switch units are reliable and trouble-free. Most problems are caused by dirty or corroded contacts, but wear and breakage of internal parts is a possibility that should not be overlooked. If breakage does occur, the entire switch unit and related wiring harness will have to be replaced with a new one, as individual parts are not available. The switches can be checked for continuity using a multimeter or a continuity tester.

**2** On the T100, T120, Street Twin, Street Cup, Scrambler, Thruxton and Thruxton R

**14.14 Ignition switch bolts (arrowed)**

remove the headlight from its shell, then undo the wiring holder screws and lower the holder **(see illustrations 7.1a, b and c and 8.2a)**. Trace the wiring from the switch and release and disconnect the relevant switch connector(s) **(see illustrations)**.

**3** On the Bobber remove the fuel tank (see Chapter 4). Trace the wiring from the switch and release and disconnect the relevant switch connector(s) **(see illustrations)**.

**15.2a Right-hand switch connectors**

**15.2b Left-hand switch connectors**

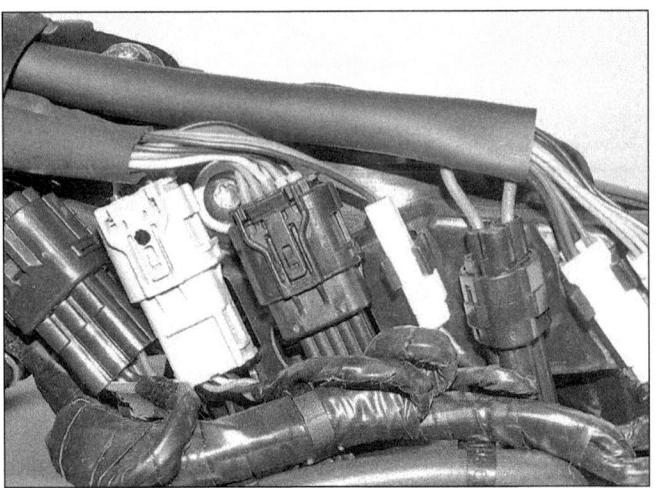

**15.3a Right-hand switch wiring connectors**

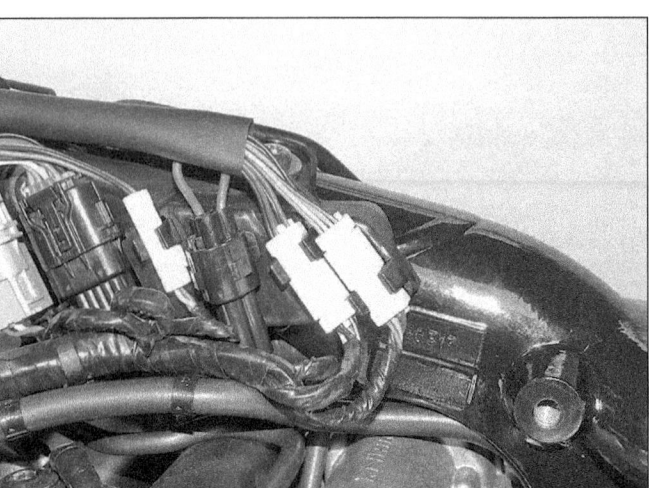

**15.3b Left-hand switch wiring connectors**

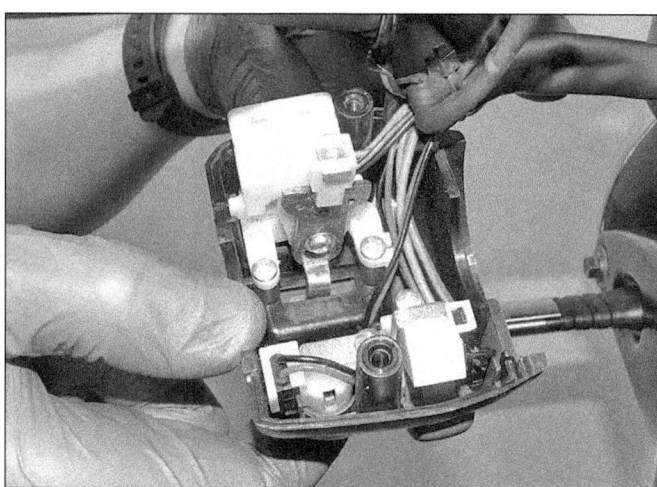

15.5 Check for loose or broken wires or broken switch components

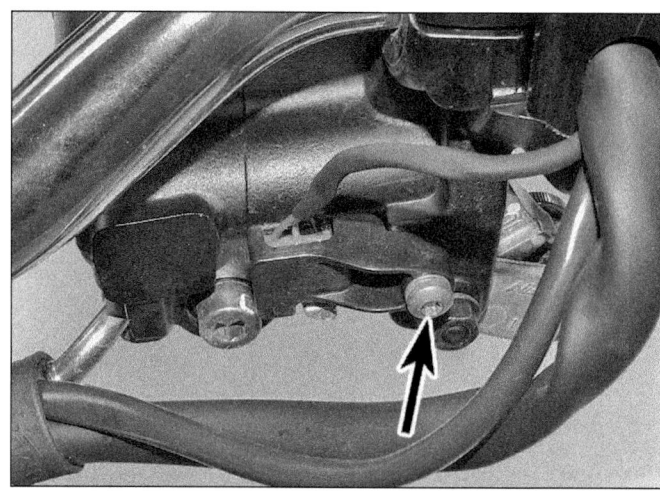

15.9 Undo the screw (arrowed) to release the switch

**4** Check for continuity between the terminals of the switch harness with the switch in the various positions (i.e. switch OFF – no continuity, switch ON – continuity).

**5** If the continuity check indicates a problem exists displace the switch from the handlebar. Spray the inside of the switch with electrical contact cleaner, and check for any broken or damaged components **(see illustration)**.

**6** If they are accessible, the contacts can be scraped clean with a penknife or polished with steel wool. If wiring connections are weak or broken, they could be re-soldered. If any components are damaged or broken a new switch must be fitted.

### Removal

**7** On the T100, T120, Street Twin, Street Cup, Scrambler, Thruxton and Thruxton R refer to Step 2 for access and release and disconnect the relevant switch connector(s), then feed the sensor switch of the wiring out the back of the shell and up to the switch, releasing it from any guides and noting its routing.

**8** On the Bobber remove the fuel tank (see Chapter 4). Remove the wiring harness cover. Release and disconnect the relevant switch connectors and feed the switch side of the wiring up to the switch, releasing it from any guides and noting its routing **(see illustrations 15.3a and b).**

**9** When removing the right-hand switch, on the T100, T120, Bobber and Thruxton undo the brake light switch holder screw and displace the holder and switch from the bottom of the master cylinder **(see illustration)**, and on the Street Twin, Street Cup and Scrambler undo the brake light switch screw and displace the switch from the bottom of the master cylinder.

**10** On the T100, T120, Bobber, and Thruxton, to remove the right-hand switch undo the switch housing screws and detach the switch face **(see illustrations)**. To remove the left-hand switch refer to Chapter 5, Section 5 – the front section of the switch is part of the clutch lever bracket assembly.

**11** On the Street Twin, Street Cup, Scrambler

and Thruxton R undo the switch housing screws, noting which fits where if they are different, and separate the two halves of the switch, noting how the pin locates in the hole in the handlebar **(see illustration)** – the clutch switch is part of the handlebar switch and must be released from the clutch lever bracket when removing the left-hand switch.

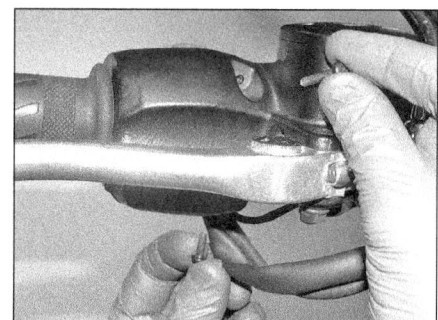

15.10a Undo the two screws...

15.10b ...and remove the switch face from the housing

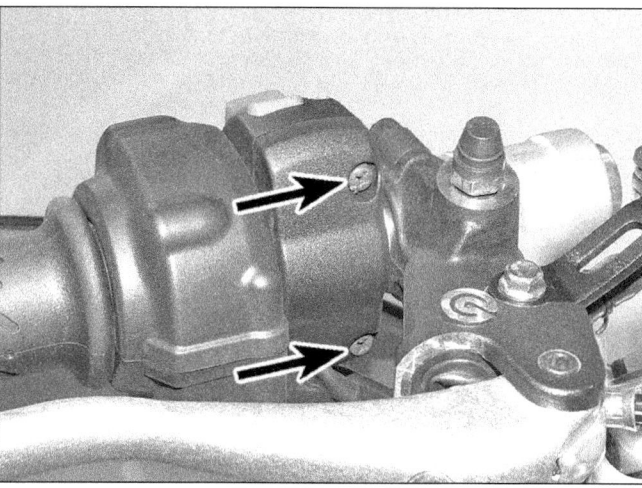

15.11 Right-hand switch housing screws (arrowed)

**16.2a Sidestand switch connector (arrowed) - all models except the Bobber**

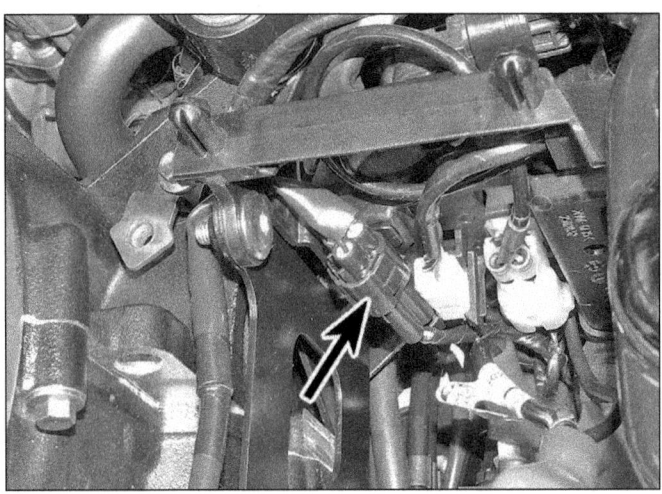

**16.2b Sidestand switch connector (arrowed) - Bobber**

**16.2c Release the wiring from the band**

**16.3 The switch is secured by two screws**

### *Installation*

**12** Installation is the reverse of removal. Make sure the wiring is securely connected and correctly routed. Check the operation of all switches before riding the motorcycle.

## 16 Sidestand switch

**1** The sidestand switch is mounted on the underside of the left-hand frame cradle. The switch is part of the safety circuit, which prevents or stops the engine running if the transmission is in gear whilst the sidestand is down, and prevents the engine from starting if the transmission is in gear unless the sidestand is up and the clutch lever is pulled in.

**2** To access the switch wiring connector, on all models except the Bobber remove the left-hand side panel (see Chapter 7), and on the Bobber remove the battery (Section 3). Disconnect the connector **(see illustrations)**. Feed the wiring down to the switch, releasing it from the guide and noting its routing **(see illustration)**.

**3** Undo the screws and remove the switch **(see illustration)**.

**4** Installation is the reverse of removal.

## 17 Clutch switch

**1** The clutch switch is mounted on the underside of the clutch lever bracket. The switch is part of the safety circuit and prevents the engine from starting unless the clutch lever is pulled in. The switch is part of the left-hand switch housing – refer to Section 15 to access the wiring connector.

**2** To test the clutch switch disconnect the switch housing wiring connectors **(see illustration 15.2b or 15.3b)**. Check the operation of the clutch switch using a multimeter or continuity tester. Refer to the Wiring Diagram for your model and connect the meter probes to the clutch switch wire terminals in the relevant connector. With the lever pulled in there should be continuity (zero resistance) between the terminals, and with the lever out there should be no continuity (infinite resistance). If not fit a new switch housing.

## 18 Horn

**1** The horn is mounted on the frame downtube on the left-hand side.

### *Check*

**2** Pull the wiring connectors off the horn

terminals **(see illustration)**. Using two jumper wires and a fully charged 12V battery, apply voltage directly to the terminals on the horn. If the horn sounds, check the button in the switch housing (Section 15) and the wiring between the switch and the horn (see Section 2 and the Wiring Diagrams at the end of this Chapter).

**3** If the horn sounds weak or distorted, the tone can be adjusted by turning the screw on the back.

**4** If the horn doesn't sound, or can't be adjusted, replace it with a new one.

### Removal and installation

**5** Pull the wiring connectors off the terminals **(see illustration 18.2)**.

**6** Unscrew the bolt and remove the horn **(see illustration)**.

**7** Fit the horn and tighten the bolt. Connect the wiring connectors and check the operation of the horn.

### 19 Oil pressure switch

**1** The switch is in the left-hand side of the engine, behind the front sprocket cover.

### Check

**2** The oil pressure warning light should come on when the ignition is switched ON, and then go off when the engine is started. If the light does not go off when the engine is started, or comes on while the engine is running, stop the engine immediately and check the oil level (see *Pre-ride checks*). If the level is correct check the switch as described below, and if the switch is

**18.2 Pull the wiring connectors off**

**18.6 Horn mounting bolt (arrowed)**

good carry out an oil pressure check (see Chapter 2).

**3** If the oil pressure warning light does not come on when the ignition is turned ON, but all other instrument functions work, access and disconnect the oil pressure switch wiring connector (see below). With the ignition switched ON, earth (ground) the connector against the crankcase using a piece of wire between them, and check that the warning light comes on. If the light comes on, the switch is faulty. To confirm the switch is faulty check for continuity between the switch terminal and the crankcase – with the engine off there should be continuity, with the engine running there should be no continuity.

**4** If the light still does not come on, check for voltage at the wire terminal with the ignition ON. If there is no voltage present check there is continuity in the wire between the switch and the instrument connector, referring to Section 12 for access. Repair the wiring if necessary. If the wiring is all good and the switch is good there is a fault in the instruments.

**5** If the warning light does not go out when

the engine is started or comes on whilst the engine is running, yet the oil pressure is satisfactory, access and disconnect the oil pressure switch wiring connector (see below). With the wiring disconnected and the ignition switched ON the light should be out. If it is illuminated, the wire between the switch and instrument cluster could be earthed (grounded) at some point. If the wiring is good, the switch must be assumed faulty and replaced with a new one.

### Removal

**Note:** *To minimise the amount of oil loss the bike should be on the sidestand when removing the switch.*

**6** Remove the front sprocket cover (see Chapter 6).

**7** On the T100, T120, Street Twin, Street Cup and Scrambler, undo the brake hose guide bolt and the rider's footrest/brake pedal/master cylinder bracket bolts and displace the assembly, supporting it clear **(see illustrations)**.

**8** On the Bobber displace the coolant reservoir and brake fluid reservoir and

**19.7a Undo the hose guide bolt...**

**19.7b ...and the footrest/brake assembly bracket bolts**

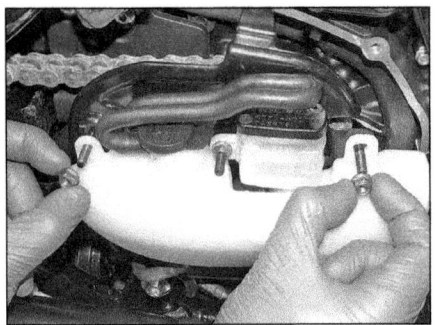

**19.8a Unscrew the nuts and displace the coolant reservoir...**

**19.8b ...and the brake fluid reservoir**

**19.8c Unscrew the mounting plate bolts...**

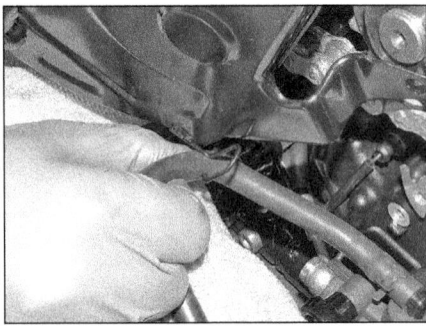

**19.8d ...release the hoses from the guide and remove the plate**

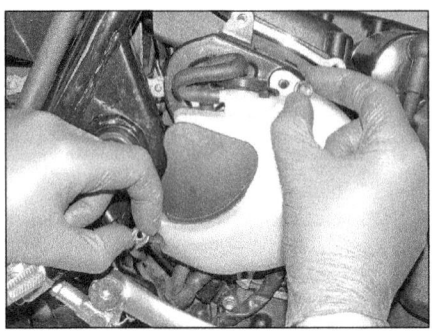

**19.9a Unscrew the nuts and displace the coolant reservoir**

**19.9b Unscrew the mounting plate bolts...**

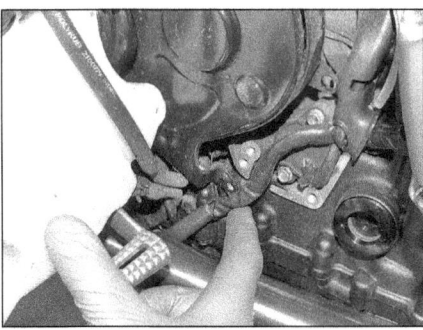

**19.9c ...release the wiring from the guide and remove the plate**

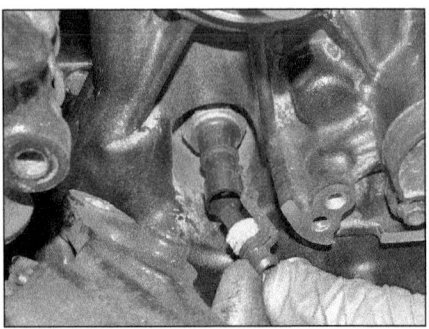

**19.10 Lift the catch then pull the connector off**

**19.14 Route the hoses in the guide as shown**

support them upright and clear **(see illustrations)**. Remove the reservoir mounting plate **(see illustrations)**.

9 On the Thruxton and Thruxton R displace the coolant reservoir and support it upright and clear **(see illustration)**. Remove the reservoir mounting plate **(see illustrations)**.

10 Release and disconnect the wiring connector from the oil pressure switch **(see illustration)**.

11 Unscrew and remove the switch – be prepared to catch any residual oil with a rag. Remove the sealing washer – a new one must be used

### Installation

12 Fit the switch using a new sealing washer and tighten to 15 Nm.

13 Connect the wiring connector, making sure it pushes fully on so the catch clicks into place **(see illustration 25.3)**.

14 Install all remaining components in reverse order of removal according to model. On the T100, T120, Street Twin, Street Cup and Scrambler tighten the rider's footrest/brake pedal/master cylinder bracket bolts to 24 Nm. On the Bobber make sure the reservoir hoses are correctly routed in the mounting plate guide **(see illustration)**.

15 Run the engine and check that the switch operates correctly and without leakage.

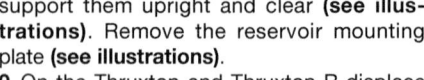

**20 Starter motor relay**

### Check

1 If the starter circuit is faulty, first check the main fuse and ignition/starter fuse (Section 5).

2 On all models except the Bobber remove the remove the right-hand side cover (see Chapter 7). Displace the relay and remove the plastic cover **(see illustration 5.2a)**.

3 On the Bobber remove the right-hand side cover (see Chapter 7) and the front sprocket cover (see Chapter 6). Fully slacken the drive chain (see Chapter 1). Displace the coolant reservoir and brake fluid reservoir and support them upright and clear **(see illus-**

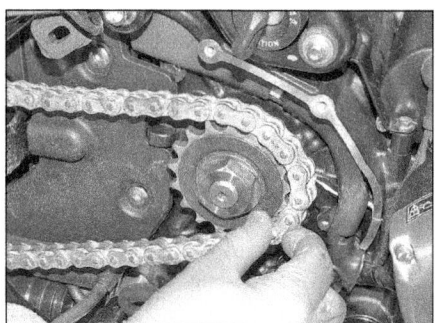

**20.3a Slip the chain off the sprocket**

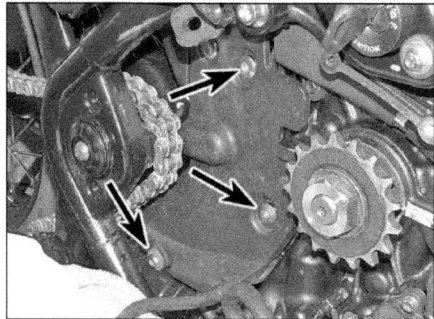

**20.3b Undo the screws (arrowed)...**

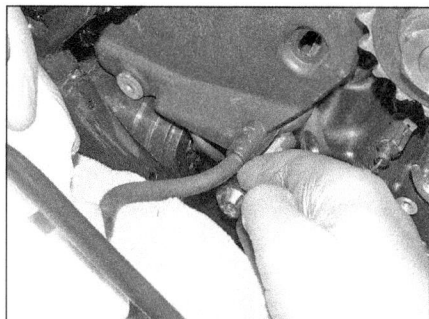

**20.3c ...release the hose from the guide...**

trations **19.8a and b)**. Remove the reservoir mounting plate **(see illustrations 19.8c and d)**. Disengage the chain from the front sprocket and lay it over the front of the swingarm **(see illustration)**. Remove the inner cover **(see illustrations)**. Displace the relay and lift the insulating covers off the main lead terminals **(see illustration)**.

**4** Unscrew the bolt securing the starter motor lead (the outer lead, marked M) to the relay; position the lead away from the terminal **(see illustrations)**. With the ignition switch ON, the engine kill switch in the RUN position, the transmission in neutral, and the clutch lever pulled in, press the starter button. The relay should be heard to click.

**5** If the relay doesn't click, switch the ignition OFF and remove the relay as described below; then test it as follows. Using a continuity tester or a multimeter set to the resistance (ohms) range, test for continuity between the relay's starter motor and battery lead terminals. There should be no continuity (infinite resistance). Now, using insulated jumper wires and a fully charged 12V battery, connect the battery positive (+) terminal to the white/red wire terminal on the relay and the battery negative (-) terminal to the black wire terminal. With voltage applied, the

**20.3d ...and remove the inner cover**

relay should be heard to click and continuity (0 ohms) should now be shown on the meter.

**6** If the relay is good, check for battery voltage at the white/red wire terminal on the loom side of the wiring connector with the ignition switch ON, the engine kill switch in the RUN position, the transmission in neutral, the clutch lever pulled in and the starter button pressed. If no voltage is present, check the other components and their wiring and connectors in the starter circuit from

**20.3e Undo the relay bracket screws and draw the relay out to access the leads**

the battery to the relay (see Wiring Diagrams at the end of this Chapter). If voltage is present, check the black wire for continuity to earth.

### Renewal

**7** On all models except the Bobber disconnect the battery (Section 3). Remove the remove the right-hand side cover (see Chapter 7). Displace the relay and remove the plastic cover **(see illustration 5.2a)**. Disconnect the relay wiring connector, then

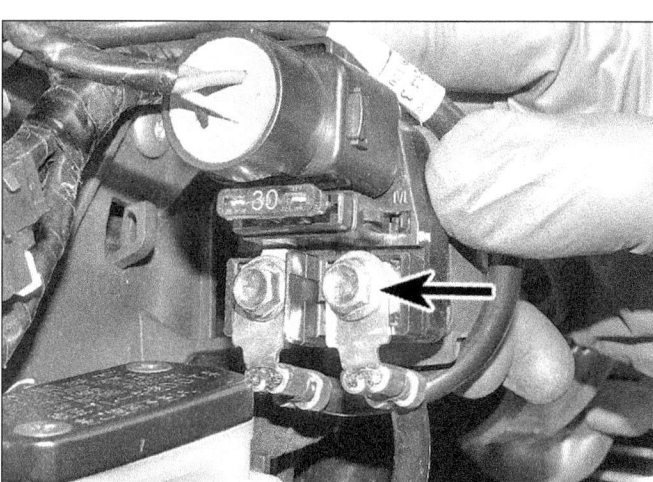

**20.4a Starter motor lead terminal (arrowed) - all models except the Bobber**

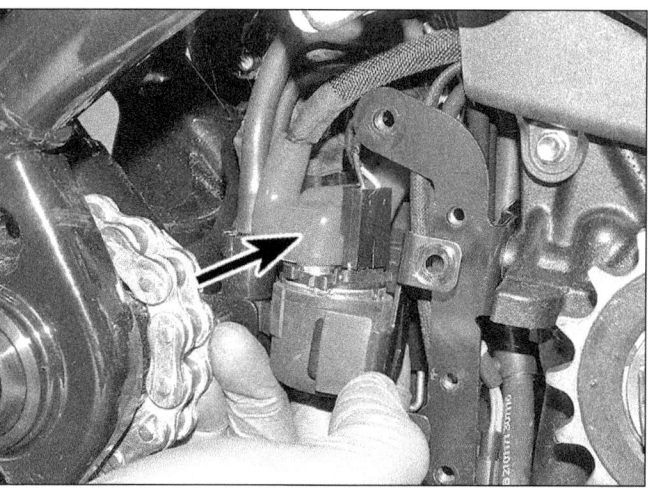

**20.4b Starter motor lead terminal (arrowed) - Bobber**

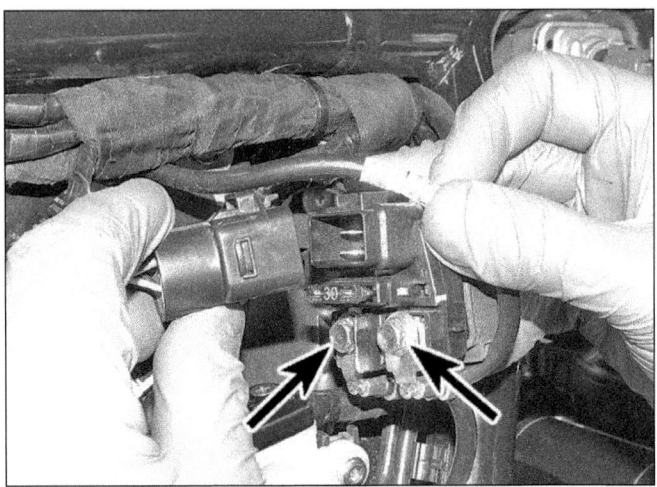

20.7 Disconnect the wiring, then unscrew the bolts (arrowed) and detach the leads

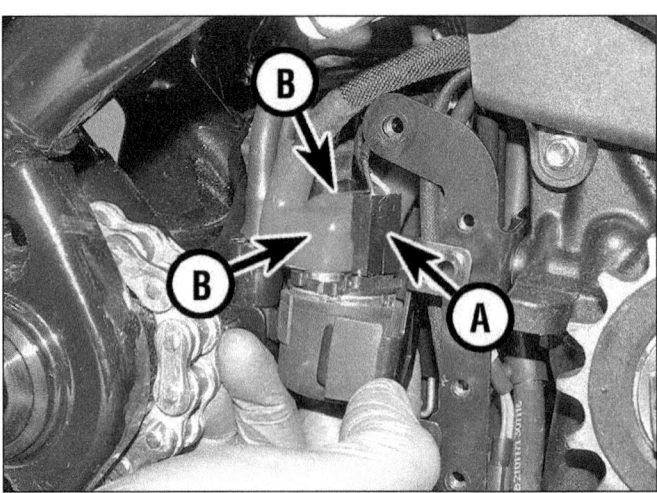

20.8 Disconnect the wiring connectors (A), then lift the covers (B), unscrew the bolts and detach the leads

unscrew the starter motor and battery lead bolts and detach the leads **(see illustration)**. If you are fitting a new relay remove the main fuse – the new relay should come with a fuse fitted, in which case keep the other as a spare.

**8** On the Bobber remove the battery (Section 3). Remove the right-hand side cover (see Chapter 7) and the front sprocket cover (see Chapter 6). Fully slacken the drive chain (see Chapter 1). Displace the coolant reservoir and brake fluid reservoir and support them upright and clear **(see illustrations 19.8a and b)**. Remove the reservoir mounting plate

(see illustrations 19.8c and d). Disengage the chain from the front sprocket and lay it over the front of the swingarm **(see illustration 20.3a)**. Remove the inner cover **(see illustrations 20.3b, c and d)**. Unscrew the relay bracket screws and displace the relay **(see illustration 20.3e)**. Disconnect the wiring connectors, then lift the rubber covers off the starter motor and battery lead terminals then unscrew the bolts and detach the leads **(see illustration)**. Remove the relay from its bracket.

**9** Installation is the reverse of removal. Make

sure the starter and battery lead bolts are tight.

## 21 Starter motor

### Check

**1** Remove the starter motor (see below). Cover one of the motor mounting lugs in rag and clamp it in a soft-jawed vice – do not overtighten it.

**2** Using a fully-charged 12 volt battery and two insulated jumper wires, connect the positive (+) terminal of the battery to the protruding terminal on the starter motor, and the negative (–) terminal to the exposed mounting lug. At this point the starter motor should spin freely. If this is the case the motor is proved good.

### Removal

**3** The starter motor is mounted on the crankcase, behind the cylinder block.

**4** Disconnect the battery negative (–) lead (Section 3).

**5** Peel back the terminal boot, unscrew the nut securing the lead to the starter motor terminal and detach the lead **(see illustration)**.

**6** Unscrew the two motor mounting bolts, and on the Bobber also unscrew the remaining ignition switch bracket bolt and position the switch assembly clear **(see illustrations)**. Draw the starter motor out of the crankcase **(see illustration 21.9)** – use a screwdriver to initially lever it out if required.

**7** Remove the O-ring on the end of the starter motor **(see illustration 21.8)** – a new one must be used.

### Installation

**8** Fit a new O-ring onto the end of the starter motor, making sure it is seated in its groove, and smear it with grease **(see illustration)**.

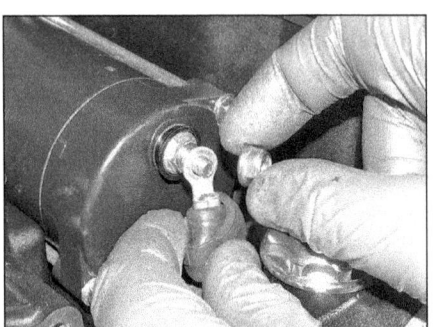

21.5 Unscrew the nut and detach the lead

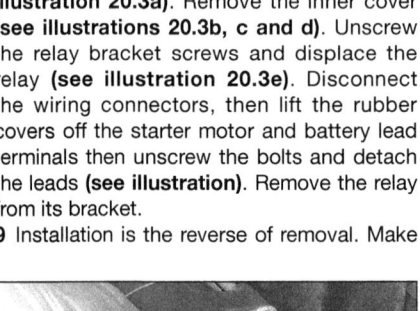

21.6a Unscrew the two bolts...

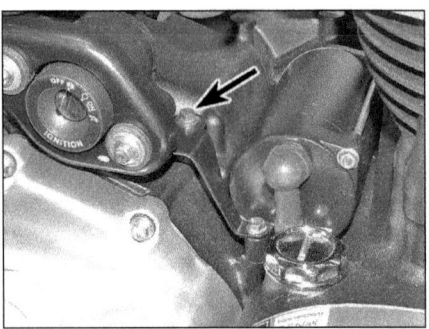

21.6b ...and on the Bobber unscrew the ignition switch bracket bolt (arrowed)

21.8 Fit a new O-ring and smear it with grease

**21.9 Manoeuvre the motor into place as shown**

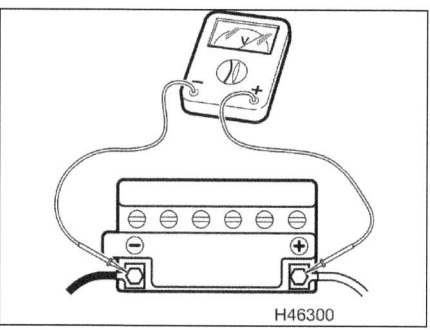

**22.5 Checking the charging system output – connect the voltmeter as shown**

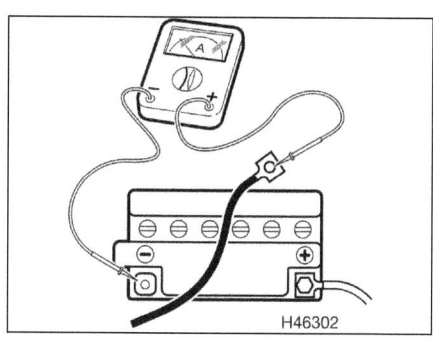

**22.9 Checking the charging system leakage rate – connect the ammeter as shown**

9 Manoeuvre the motor into position and slide it into the crankcase **(see illustration)**. Make sure that the starter motor teeth mesh correctly with those of the starter idler gear.

10 Fit the mounting bolts, and the ignition switch bracket on the Bobber, and tighten them to 7 Nm **(see illustrations 21.6a and b)**.

11 Connect the lead to the starter motor terminal and secure it with the nut **(see illustration 21.5)**. Fit the boot over the terminal.

12 Install all remaining components in reverse order of removal.

13 Connect the battery negative (–) lead.

## 22 Charging system testing

1 If the performance of the charging system is suspect, the system as a whole should be checked first, followed by testing of the individual components. Before beginning the checks, make sure the battery is fully charged and that all system connections are clean and tight.

2 Checking the output of the charging system and the performance of the various components within the charging system requires the use of a multimeter (with voltage, current and resistance checking facilities). If a multimeter is not available, the job of checking the charging system should be left to a Triumph dealer or automotive electrician.

3 When making the checks, follow the procedures carefully to prevent incorrect connections or short circuits, as irreparable damage to electrical system components may result if short circuits occur.

### *Output test*

4 Start the engine and warm it up to normal operating temperature. Refer to Section 3 for access to the battery terminals.

5 To check the regulated voltage output, allow the engine to idle and connect a multimeter set to the 0 to 20 volts DC scale (voltmeter) across the terminals of the battery, positive (+) lead to battery positive (+) terminal, negative (–) lead to battery negative (–) terminal **(see illustration)**. Slowly increase

the engine speed to 2000 rpm and note the reading obtained.

6 The regulated voltage should be as given in the Specifications. If the voltage is outside these limits, check the alternator, then the regulator/rectifier (Section 23and Section 24).

7 Stop the engine and disconnect the test meter.

### *Leakage test*

*Caution: Always connect an ammeter in series with the battery, never in parallel, otherwise it will be damaged. Do not turn the ignition ON or operate the starter motor when the ammeter is connected – a sudden surge in current will blow the meter's fuse.*

8 Turn the ignition switch OFF. Disconnect the lead from the battery negative (–) terminal (Section 3).

9 Set the multimeter to the Amps function – set the meter to a high amps range initially and then bring it down to the mA (milli Amps) range; if there is a high current flow in the circuit it may blow the meter's fuse. Connect the meter negative (–) probe to the battery negative (–) terminal, and the positive (+) probe to the disconnected negative (–) lead **(see illustration)**.

10 No current flow should be indicated. If current leakage is indicated (generally greater than 1mA, but may be more due to the alarm), there is a short circuit in the wiring. Using the wiring diagrams at the end of this Chapter, systematically disconnect individual electrical components, checking the meter each time until the source is identified.

11 If no leakage is indicated, disconnect the meter and connect the negative (–) lead to the battery.

## 23 Alternator

### *Check*

1 On the T100, T120, Street Twin, Street Cup and Scrambler remove the right-hand side panel (see Chapter 7). Release and disconnect the alternator wiring connector **(see illustration)**.

2 On the Bobber, Thruxton and Thruxton R refer to Section 24 for access and disconnect the grey wiring connector with the three wires from the regulator/rectifier.

3 Using a multimeter set to the ohms x 1 (ohmmeter) scale, measure the resistance between the centre wire and each of the other two on the alternator side of the connector, then between the outer two wires, taking a total of three readings, then check for continuity between each terminal and ground (earth). If the stator coil windings are in good condition the resistance readings should be within the range given in the Specifications, and there should be no continuity (infinite resistance) between the terminals and ground (earth). If not, check the fault is not due to damaged wiring between the connector and coils. If the wiring is good, the alternator stator coil assembly is at fault and should be replaced with a new one.

4 Set the multimeter to read AC voltage. With the engine idling, check the unregulated voltage output of the alternator between each pair of terminals in the alternator side of the connector, so taking a total of three readings, then raise engine speed to 4500 rpm and check again. If the stator coil windings are in good condition the three readings should be within the range shown in the Specifications at the start of this Chapter for each engine speed. If not, the alternator stator coil assembly is faulty and should be replaced with a new one, but first check the fault is not due to damaged wiring between the connector and the stator.

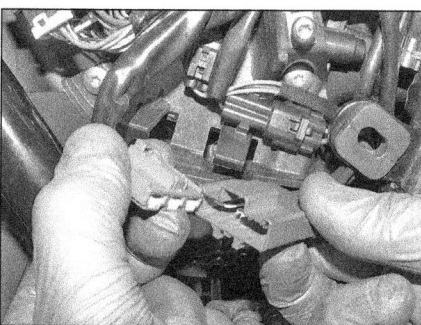

**23.1 Disconnect the alternator wiring connector**

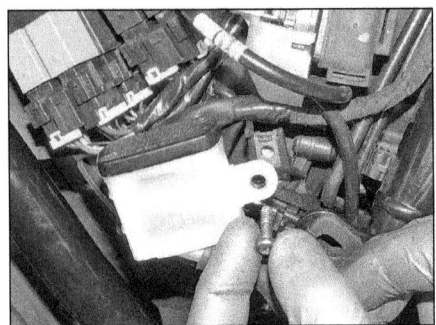

**23.7a Undo the screw**

**23.7b CKP sensor connector**

### Alternator cover removal

**Note:** *To minimise the amount of oil loss the bike should be on the sidestand when removing the switch.*

**5** Disconnect the battery negative (-) lead (Section 3).

**6** Remove the right-hand side cover (see Chapter 7) and the front sprocket cover (see Chapter 6).

**7** On the T100, T120, Street Twin, Street Cup and Scrambler, undo the rear brake fluid reservoir screw **(see illustration)**, the brake hose guide bolt and the rider's footrest/brake pedal/master cylinder bracket bolts and displace the assembly, supporting it clear **(see illustrations 19.7a and b)**. Release and disconnect the CKP sensor and alternator wiring connectors **(see illustration and 23.1)**.

Undo the wiring guide screws, displace the guide and draw the CKP sensor and alternator wiring out, noting its routing **(see illustrations)**.

**8** On the Bobber fully slacken the drive chain (see Chapter 1). Refer to Section 24 and disconnect the grey wiring connector with the three wires from the regulator/rectifier, and release the wiring from its ties. Displace the coolant reservoir and brake fluid reservoir and support them upright and clear **(see illustrations 19.8a and b)**. Remove the reservoir mounting plate **(see illustrations 19.8c and d)**. Disengage the chain from the front sprocket and lay it over the front of the swingarm **(see illustration 20.3a)**. Remove the inner cover **(see illustrations 20.3b, c and d)**. Remove the wiring guide, noting the routing of the wiring in it, then undo the starter relay bracket screws and displace the relay assembly **(see illustration)**. Release and disconnect the CKP sensor wiring connector **(see illustration)**. Draw the CKP sensor wiring out, noting its routing. Feed the alternator wiring to the cover, noting its routing.

**23.7c Undo the screws (arrowed)...**

**23.7d ...displace the guide and release the wiring from it**

**23.8a Undo the wiring guide and relay bracket screws (arrowed)**

**23.8b CKP sensor connector (arrowed)**

23.9 Wiring guide screw (arrowed)

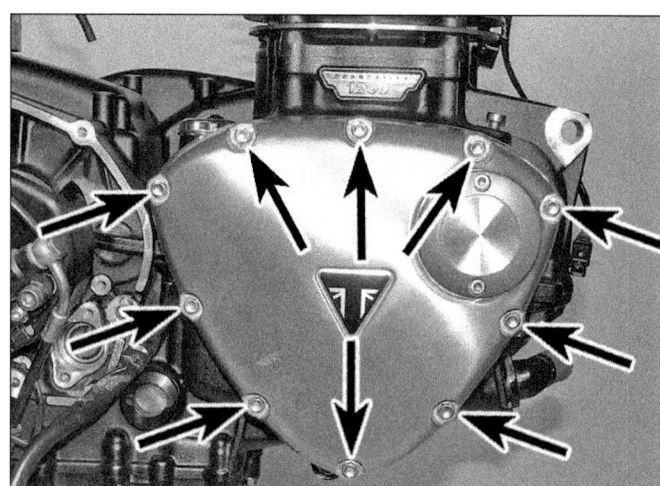

23.10 Alternator cover bolts (arrowed)

23.12 Using a rotor holder while unscrewing the bolt

23.13a Fit the puller onto the rotor...

**9** On the Thruxton and Thruxton R remove the regulator/rectifier (Section 24). Feed the alternator wiring connector with the three wires out, releasing the wiring from its ties and noting its routing. Displace the coolant reservoir and support it upright and clear **(see illustration 19.9a)**. Remove the reservoir mounting plate **(see illustrations 19.9b and c)**. Undo the rear brake fluid reservoir screw and support the reservoir upright **(see illustration 23.7a)**. Release and disconnect the CKP sensor wiring connector **(see illustration 23.7b)**. Undo the wiring guide screw, displace the guide and draw the CKP sensor wiring out, noting its routing **(see illustration)**. Feed the alternator wiring to the cover, noting its routing.

**10** Unscrew and remove the alternator cover bolts **(see illustration)**. Remove the cover, being prepared to catch any residual oil, and noting that you need to pull against the attraction of the magnets in the alternator rotor. If necessary break the gasket seal by tapping gently around the edge with a soft-faced hammer or block of wood – do not try to lever between the cover/crankcases mating surfaces as they could be damaged. Remove the gasket – a new one must be used. Remove the dowels from either the cover or the crankcase if they are loose **(see illustration 23.21a)**.

**11** Remove the two O-rings from the balancer deadshaft **(see illustration 23.20)** – new ones must be used.

### Alternator rotor and stator removal

**Special Tool:** *A puller is essential for removal of the alternator rotor from the crankshaft.*

**12** To remove the rotor bolt it is necessary to stop the rotor from turning. This is best achieved using a rotor holding tool, either Triumph Part Nos. T3880656 and T38806060, or there are several commercially available types. If a rotor strap is used keep the strap away from the timing triggers on the rotor. With the rotor held unscrew the rotor bolt and remove the washer **(see illustration)**.

**13** To remove the rotor from the shaft it is necessary to use a rotor puller, either the Triumph tool Part No. T3880365, or alternatively a similar tool can be obtained commercially. Fit the puller, using either the thrust pad supplied with the Triumph tool or a spacer between the puller bolt and the end of the crankshaft to protect the rotor bolt threads, hold the rotor as before, and tighten the puller centre bolt until the rotor is displaced from the shaft **(see illustrations)**.

23.13b ... then hold the rotor and tighten the puller bolt

23.14 Woodruff key (arrowed)

23.15 Alternator stator bolts and CKP sensor and wiring guide screws (arrowed)

23.17 Apply sealant to the groove in the grommet

23.18 Slide the rotor onto the shaft

23.19a Fit the bolt and washer...

23.19b...and tighten the bolt to the specified torque

**23.20 Fit new O-rings (arrowed)**

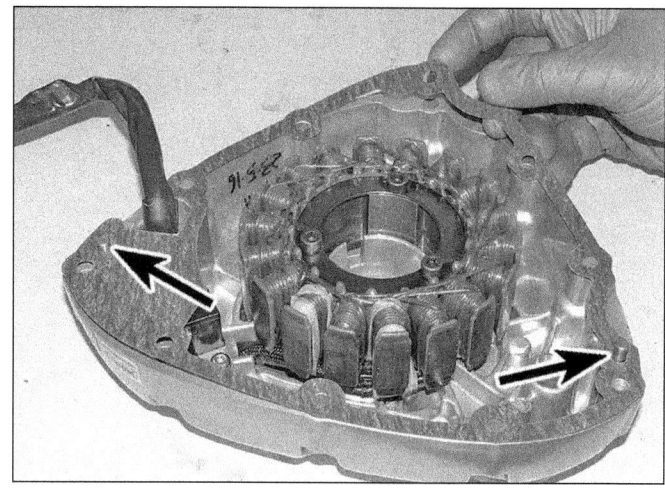

**23.21a Fit a new gasket onto the dowels (arrowed)...**

**14** Remove the Woodruff key from its slot in the end of the crankshaft if it is loose **(see illustration)**.

**15** To remove the stator from the cover, undo the screws securing the CKP sensor and the wiring guide and the bolts securing the stator, then remove the assembly, noting how the wiring grommet locates **(see illustration)**.

### Alternator rotor and stator installation

**16** Fit the stator, wiring guide and CKP sensor, aligning the wiring grommet with the recess in the alternator cover **(see illustration 23.15)**. Clean the sensor and wiring guide screw and stator bolt threads and apply a suitable non-permanent thread locking compound. Tighten the stator bolts to 12 Nm, the CKP sensor screws to 6 Nm and the wiring guide screw to 9 Nm.

**17** Apply a suitable sealant to the wiring grommet, then press it into the recess in the cover **(see illustration)**.

**18** Clean the tapered end of the crankshaft and the corresponding mating surface on the inside of the rotor with a suitable solvent. Fit the Woodruff key into its slot if removed **(see illustration 23.14)**. Make sure that no metal objects have attached themselves to the magnet on the inside of the rotor, then align the slot in the hub with the key and slide the rotor onto the shaft **(see illustration)**.

**19** Fit the washer onto the rotor bolt and thread the bolt in **(see illustration)**. Hold the rotor as on removal and tighten the bolt first to 85 Nm, and then to 120 Nm **(see illustration)**.

### Alternator cover installation

**20** Fit two new O-rings smeared with oil into the grooves in the balancer deadshaft **(see illustration)**.

**21** If removed, fit the dowels in the cover, then lay a new gasket over the dowels onto the cover **(see illustration)**. Fit the cover, noting that it will be forcibly drawn on by

the magnets, and make sure it is seated all around **(see illustration)**. Fit the bolts and tighten them evenly in a criss-cross sequence to 10 Nm **(see illustration 23.10)**.

**22** Feed the wiring back to the connectors and reconnect them, and install all components as required according to model in reverse order of removal.

**23** Check the engine oil level and add some if necessary (see *Pre-ride checks*).

## 24 Regulator/rectifier

**1** The regulator/rectifier is mounted on the bottom yoke on the T100, T120, Street Twin, Street Cup and Scrambler, and on the underside of the bike to the rear of the engine on the Bobber, Thruxton and Thruxton R.

### Check

**2** The internal circuitry of the regulator/rectifier consists of three diodes and three field-effect transistors (FET) – these can be tested using a multimeter set to the diode test function.

**3** Remove the regulator/rectifier (see below).

**4** To test the FETs connect the positive (+) lead of the meter to the right-hand terminal in the black socket (as viewed with the regulator/rectifier sockets facing you, black on the right and grey on the left), then connect the negative (-) lead to each of the three pins in the grey socket in turn, thereby taking three readings. In each case there should be a reading of 0.4 to 0.7 volts – if not, replace the regulator/rectifier with a new one. Now reverse the meter leads, so the negative is connected to the right-hand black socket terminal and the positive connects to the grey socket terminals in turn. In each case there should be a reading of more than 1.4 volts, or OL (open loop) should be displayed (according to meter

**23.21b ... then carefully fit the cover**

type) – if not, replace the regulator/rectifier with a new one.

**5** To test the diodes connect the negative (-) lead of the meter to the left-hand terminal in the black socket (as viewed with the regulator/rectifier sockets facing you, black on the right and grey on the left), then connect the positive (+) lead to each of the three pins in the grey socket in turn, thereby taking three readings. In each case there should be a reading of 0.1 to 0.3 volts – if not, replace the regulator/rectifier with a new one. Now reverse the meter leads, so the positive is connected to the left-hand black socket terminal and the negative connects to the grey socket terminals in turn. In each case there should be a reading of more than 1.4 volts, or OL (open loop) should be displayed (according to meter type) – if not, replace the regulator/rectifier with a new one.

**6** If all appears to be good check the power supply to the regulator/rectifier – there should be a constant battery voltage (i.e. voltage present with ignition switch on or off) at the black/red wire terminal in the loom side of the black connector. If there is none check for continuity in the wire to the main fuse, referring to Section 2 and Section 5 and to the Wiring diagrams at the end of the chapter. If

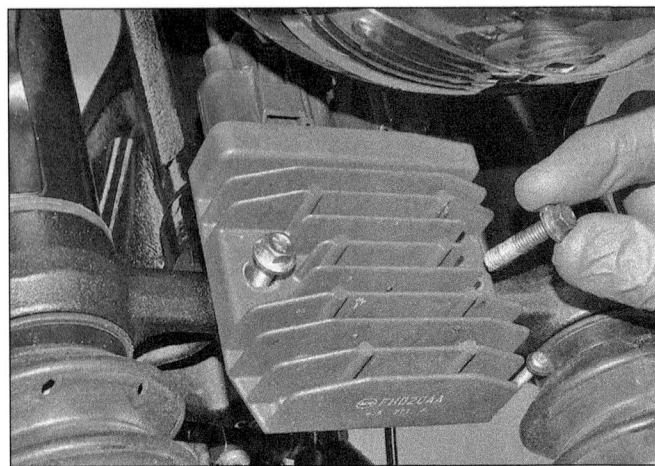

24.8a Unscrew the bolts...

24.8b ...then disconnect the wiring

there is voltage, check for continuity to earth in the black wire.

### Removal and installation

7 Disconnect the battery (Section 3).
8 On the T100, T120, Street Twin, Street Cup and Scrambler unscrew the regulator/rectifier bolts, then disconnect the wiring connectors **(see illustrations)**.
9 On the Bobber unscrew the regulator/rectifier bolts, then disconnect the wiring connectors **(see illustration)**.

10 On the Thruxton and Thruxton R undo the ABS modulator cover screws and displace the cover **(see illustrations)**. Unscrew the regulator/rectifier bolts, then disconnect the wiring connectors **(see illustration)**.
11 Installation is the reverse of removal.

24.9 Regulator/rectifier bolts (arrowed)

24.10a Undo the screw (arrowed)...

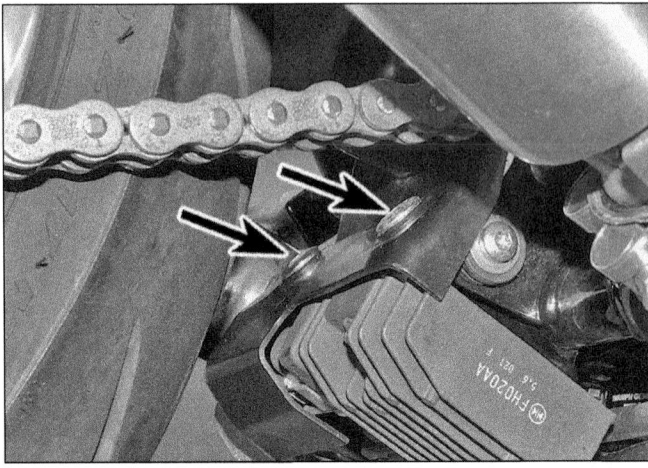

24.10b ...and the screws (arrowed) and displace the cover

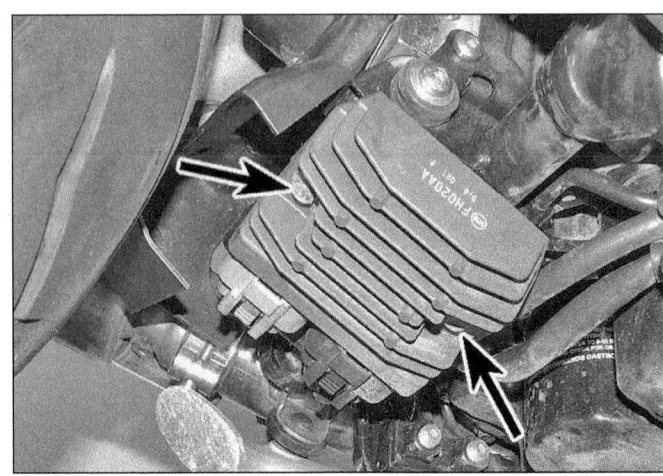

24.10c Regulator/rectifier bolts (arrowed)

## 25 Wiring diagrams

1  When using the colour wiring diagrams note the following.

2  Not all components shown will be fitted. Certain components, such as the alarm, daytime running lights (DRL), cruise control, heated grips and mode switch may be model specific, market specific or factory-fitted options.

3  The cylinders are identified as 1 (left-hand) and 2 (right-hand); the ignition coils, injectors and oxygen sensors are labelled accordingly. Many components on the right-hand side of the motorcycle have a red band around the wiring sleeve.

4  The ECM pinout numbers correspond with the wiring plug terminals **(see illustration)**. Connectors are labelled A and B.

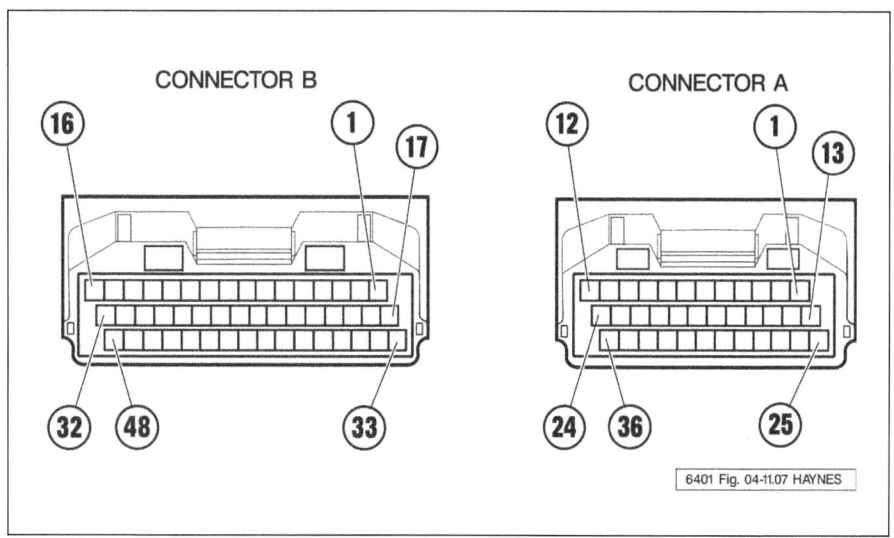

**25.4 ECM wiring connector pin identification**

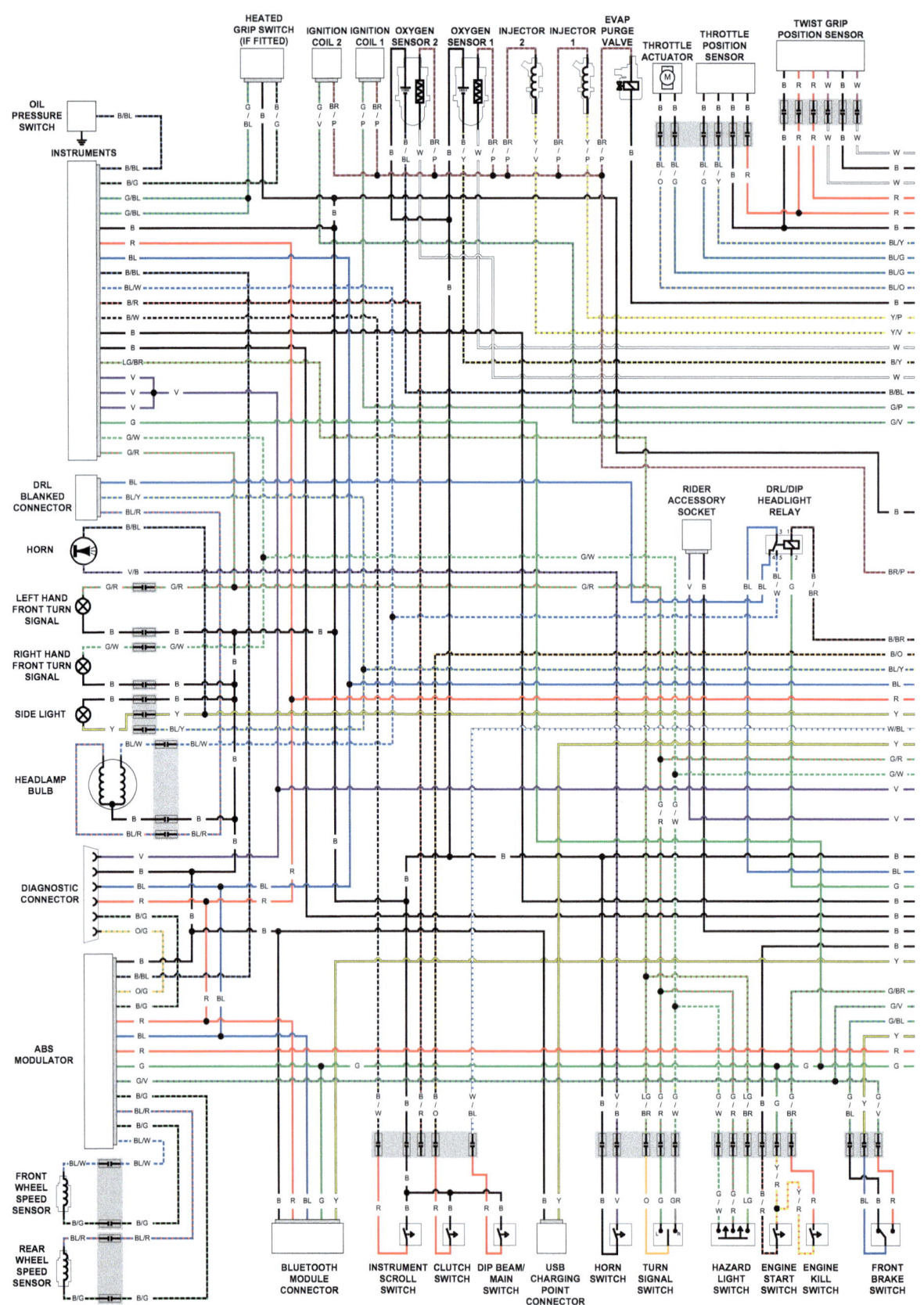

**Wiring diagram – Street Twin, Cup, Scrambler**

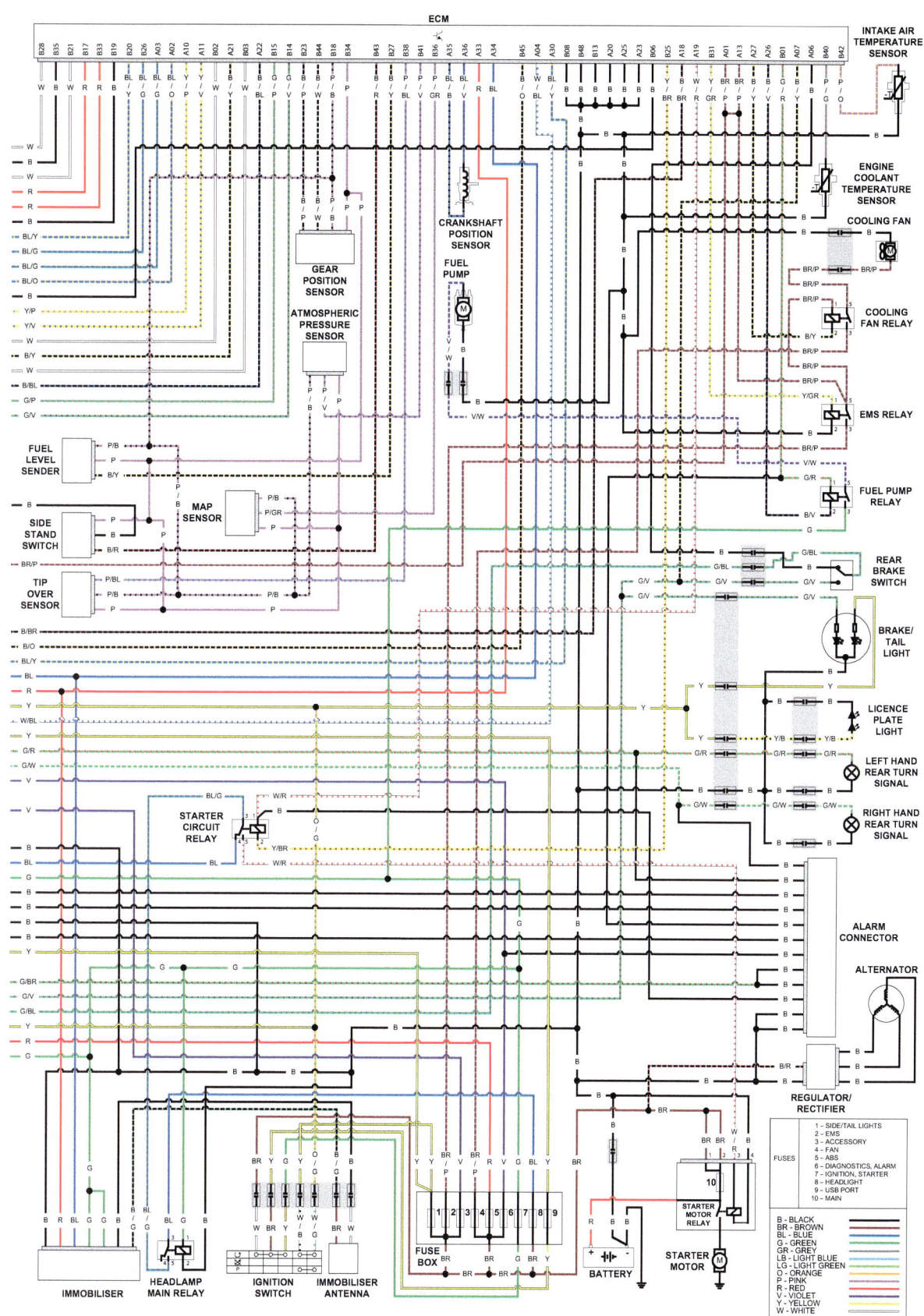

Wiring diagram – Street Twin, Cup, Scrambler (continued)

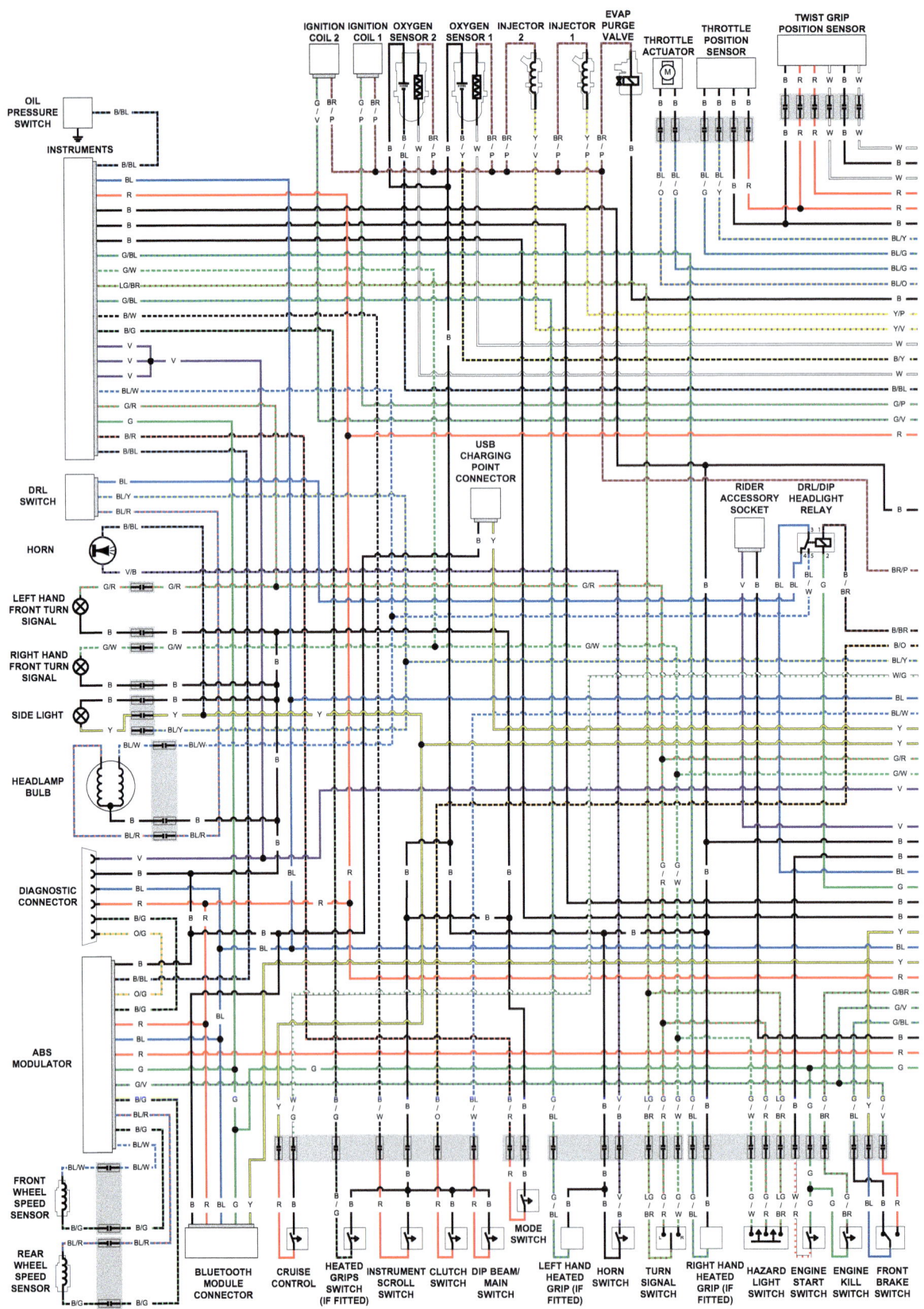

**Wiring diagram – T100**

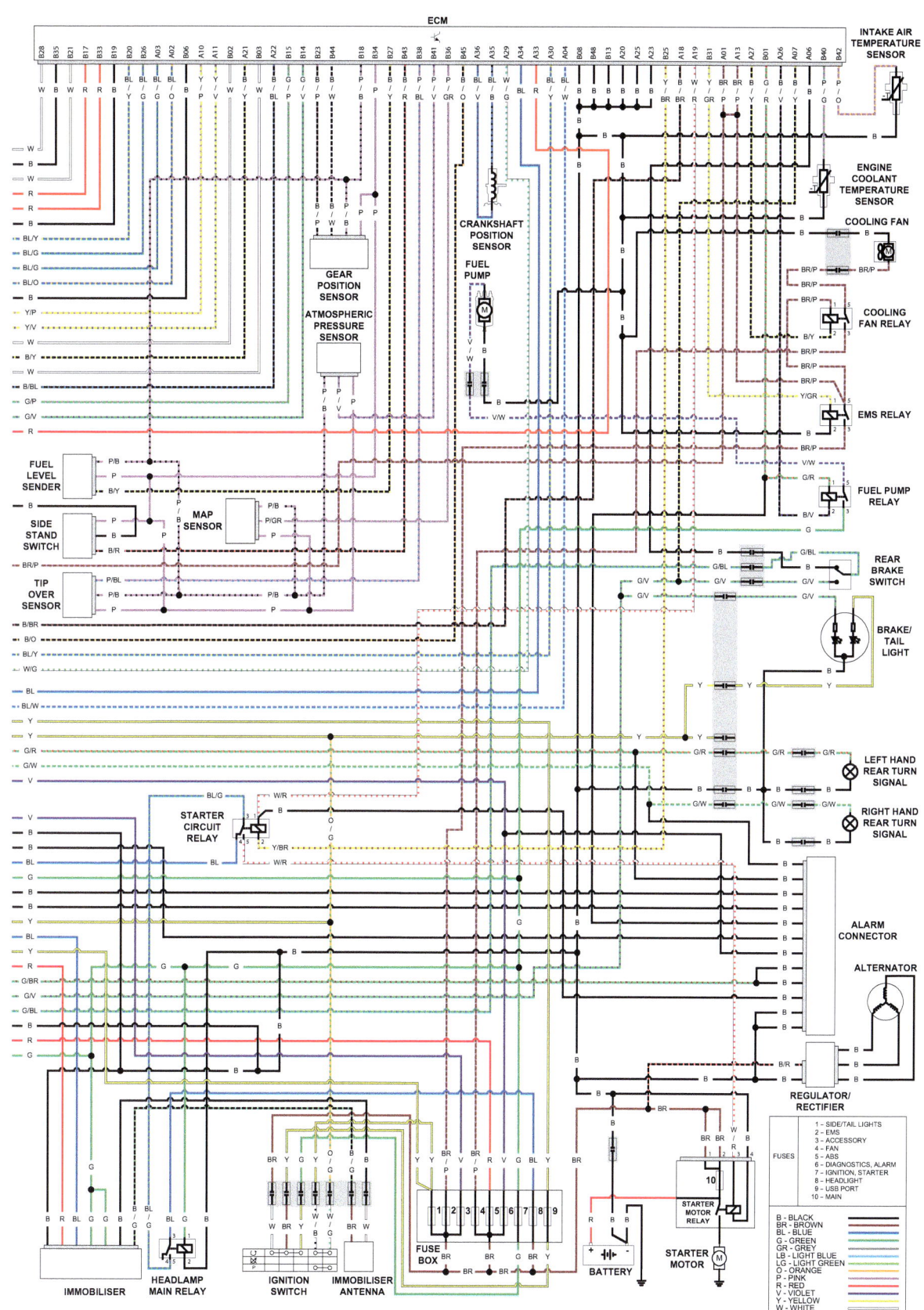

**Wiring diagram – T100 (continued)**

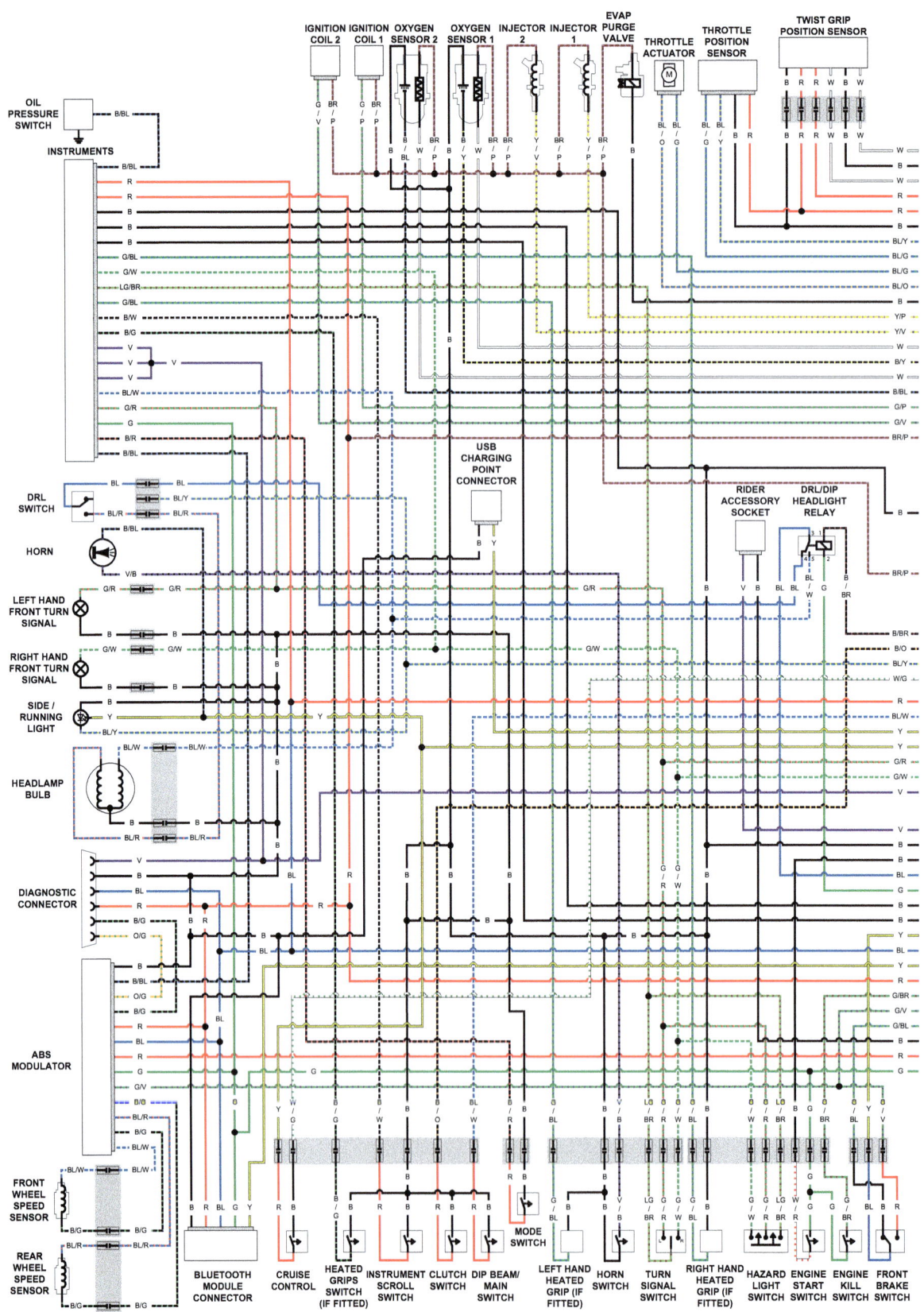

**Wiring diagram – T120**

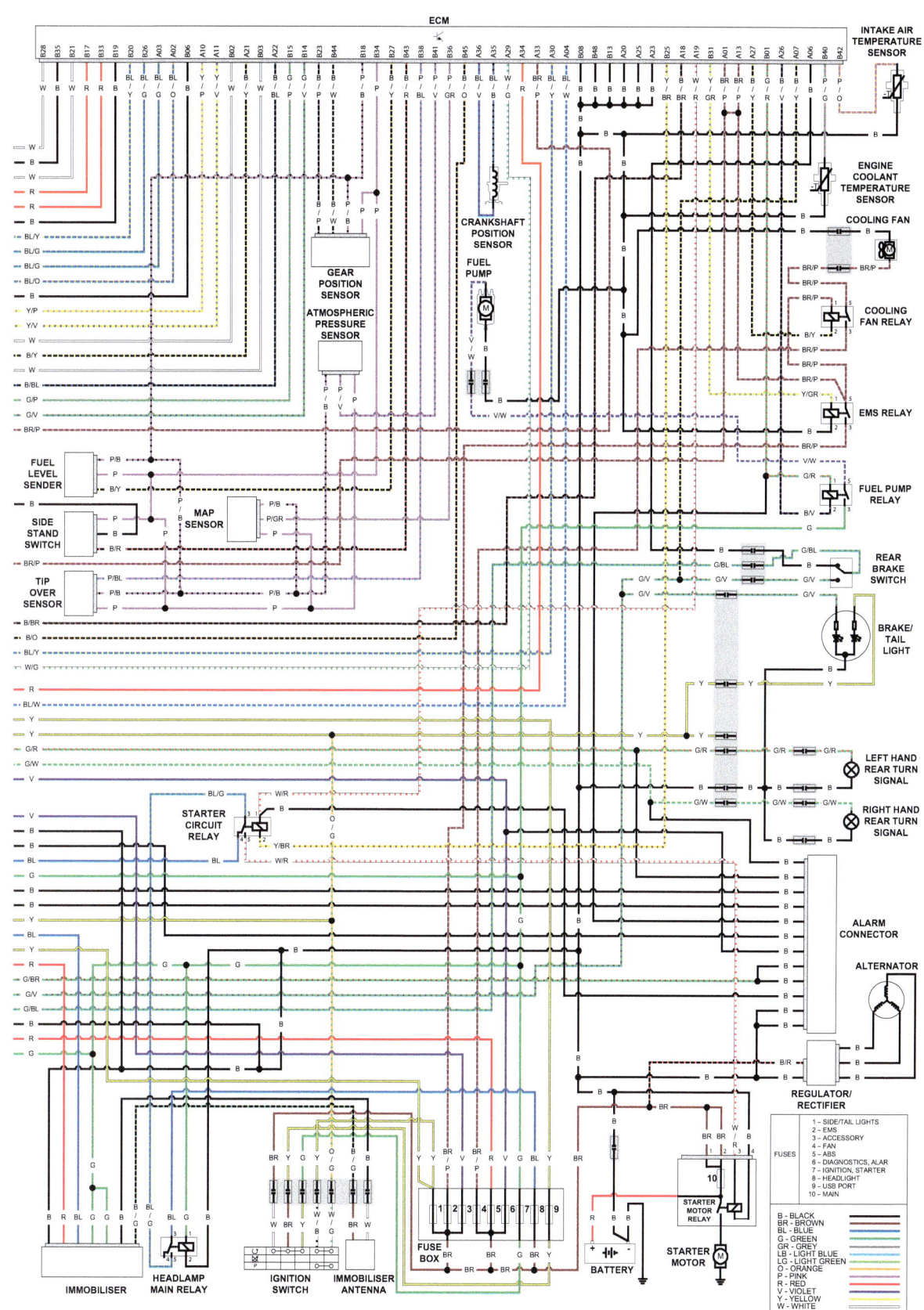

**Wiring diagram – T120 (continued)**

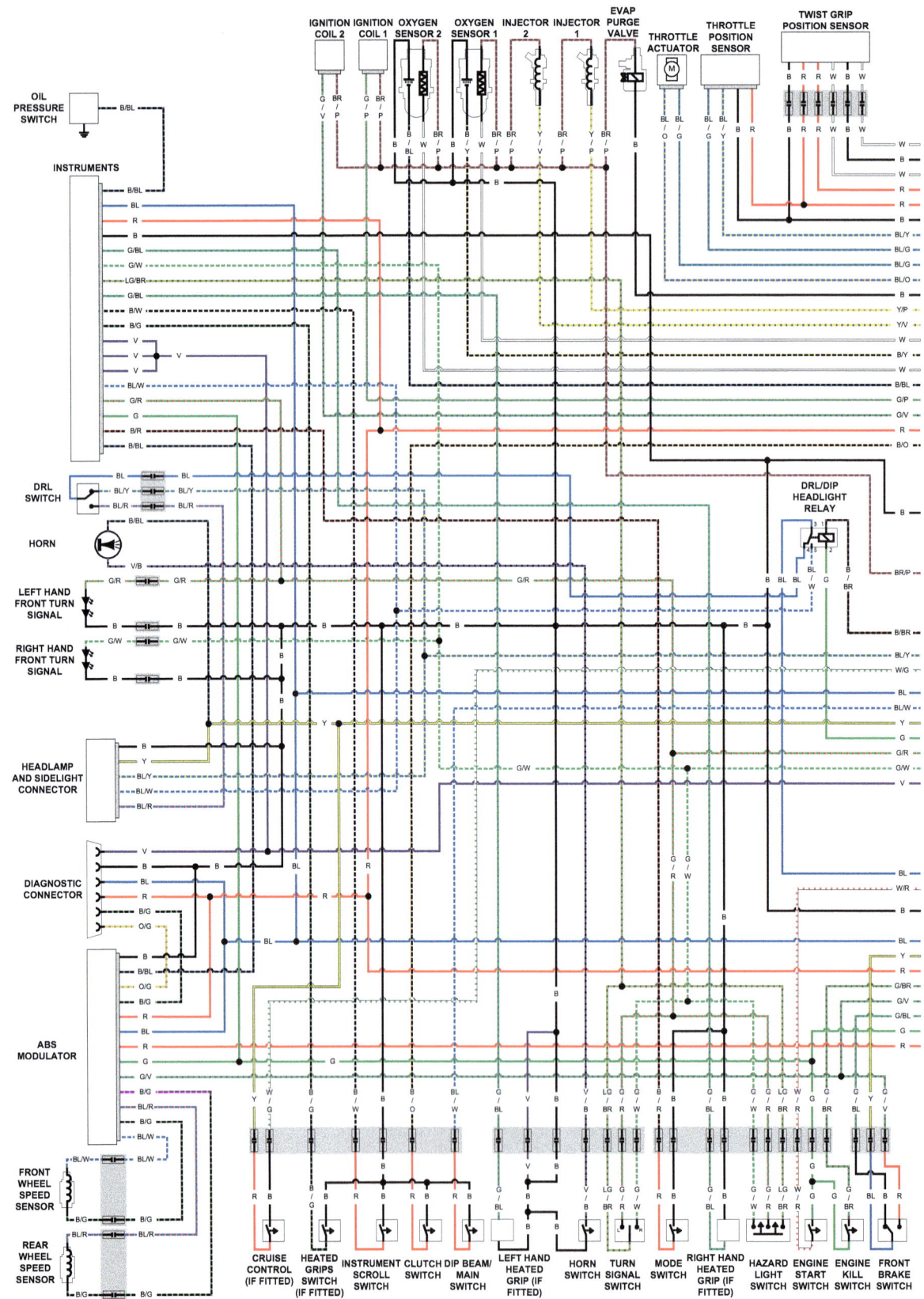

**Wiring diagram – Bobber**

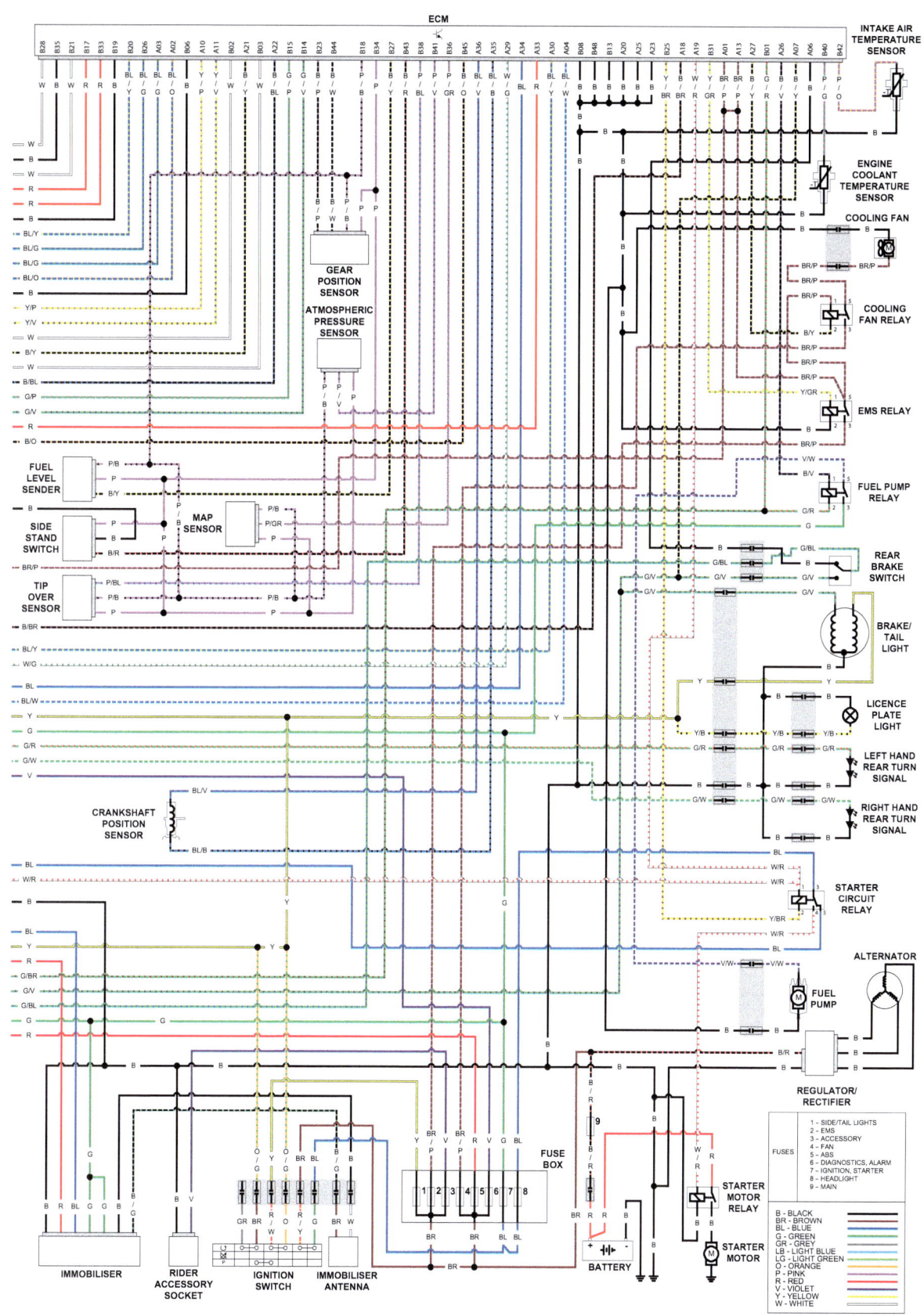

**Wiring diagram – Bobber (continued)**

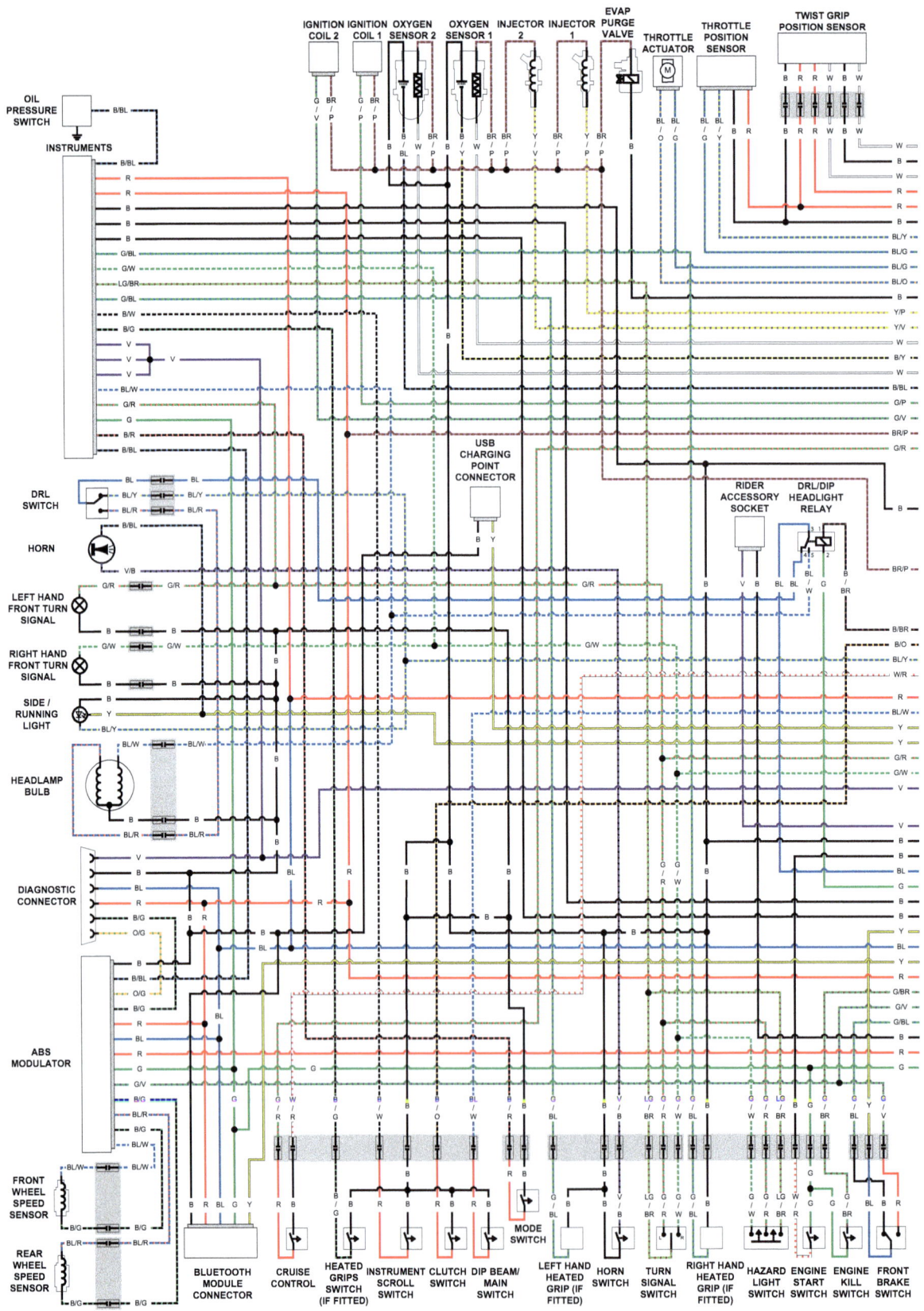

**Wiring diagram – Thruxton**

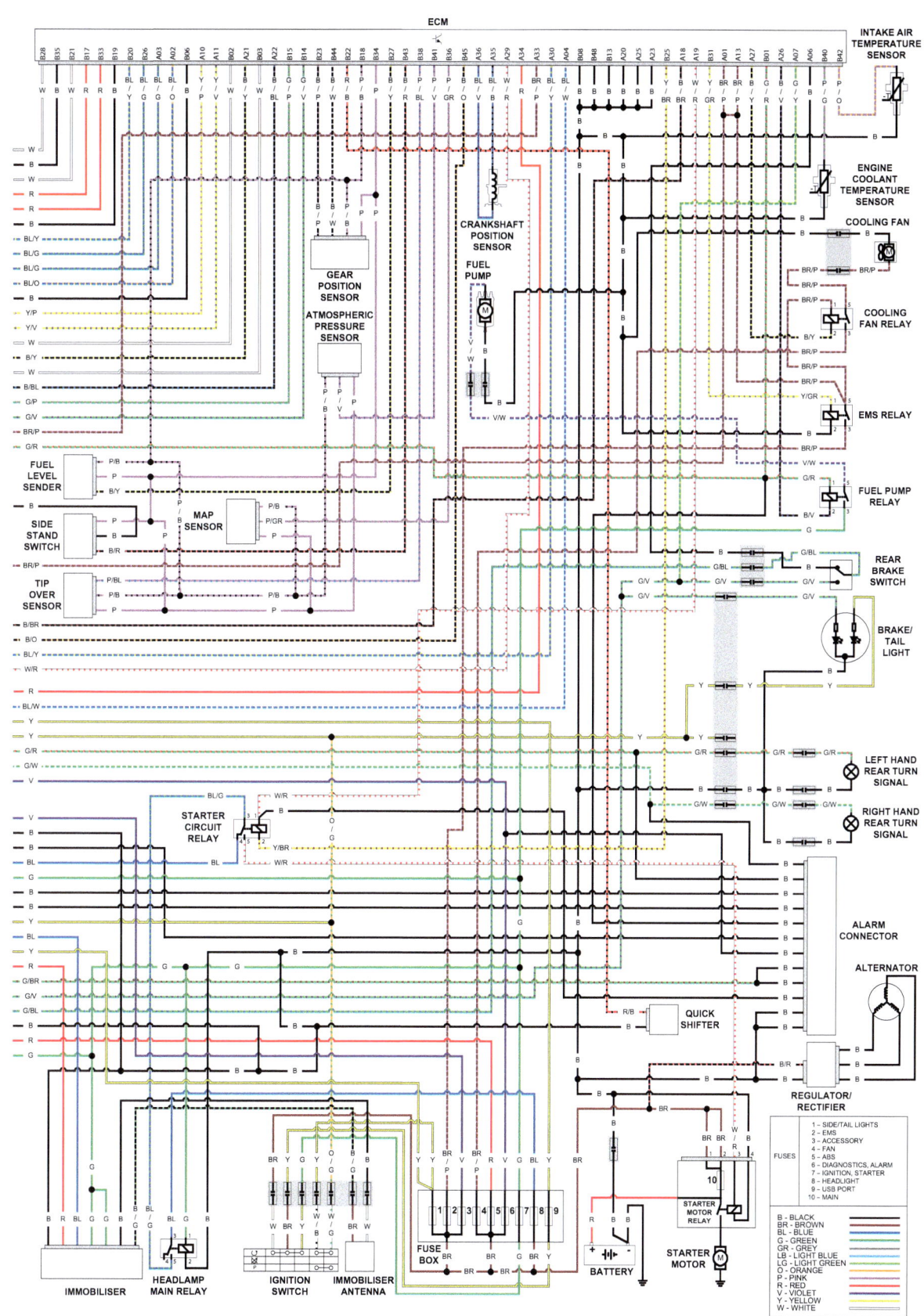

**Wiring diagram – Thruxton (continued)**

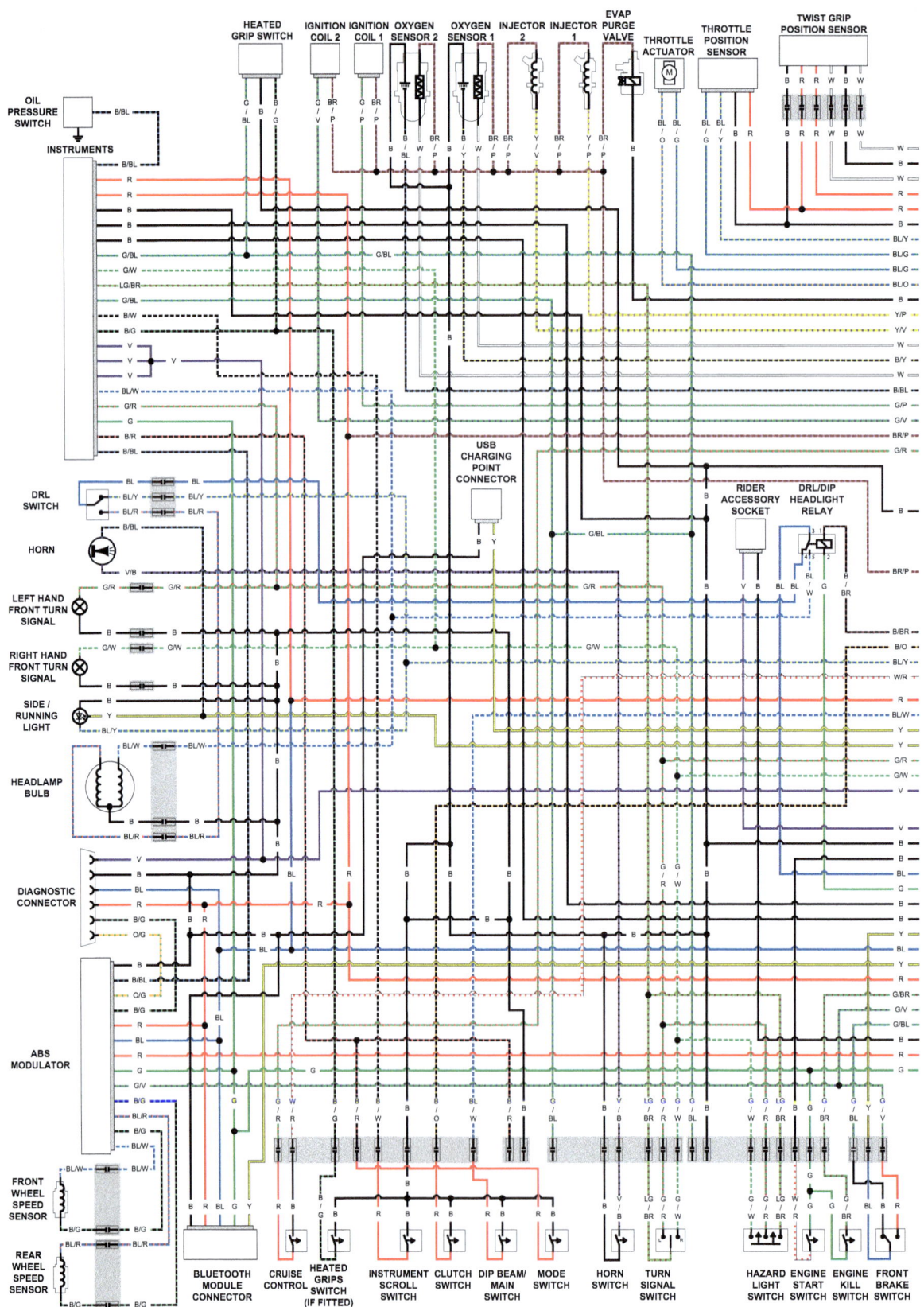

**Wiring diagram – Thruxton R**

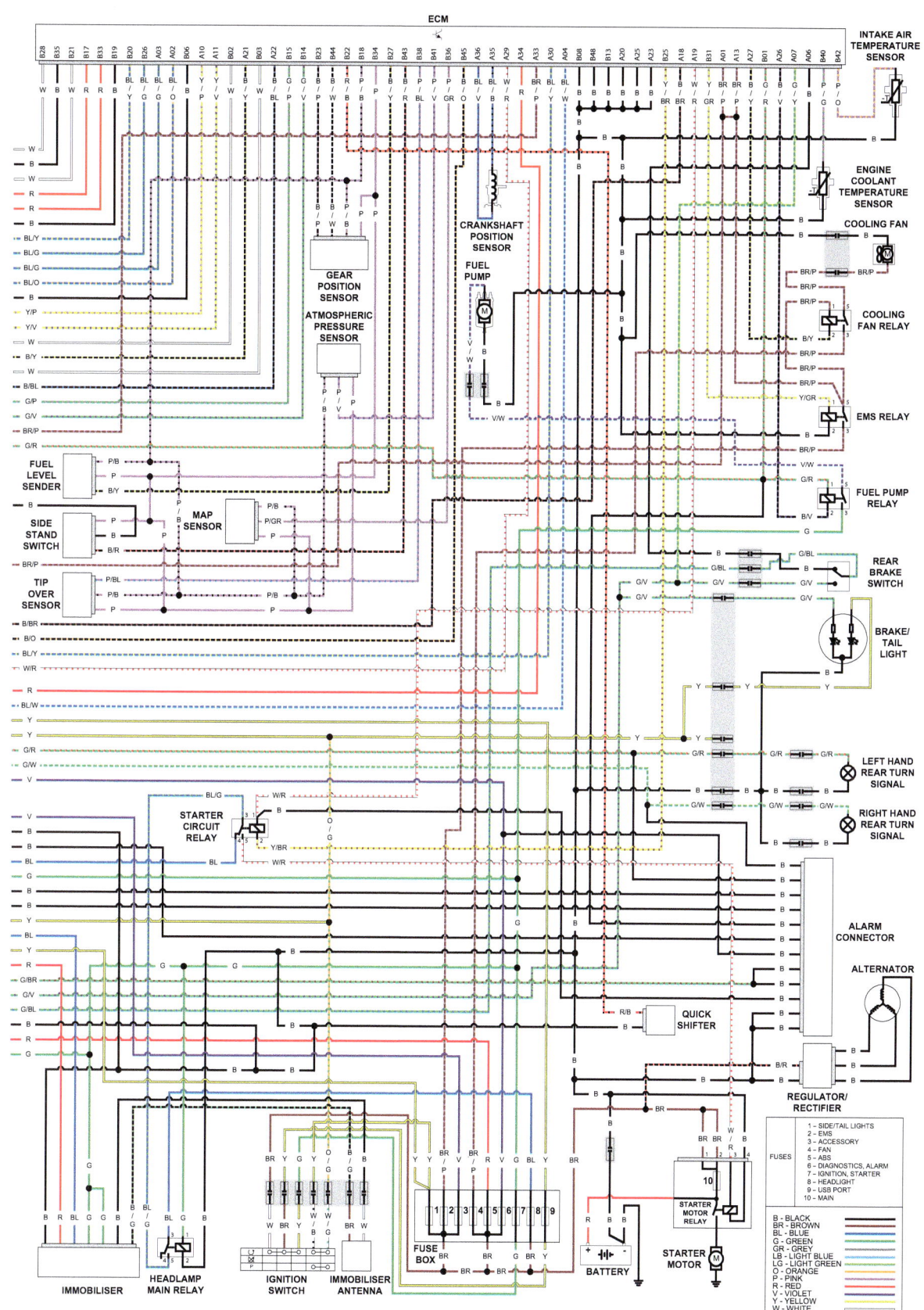

**Wiring diagram – Thruxton R (continued)**

# Reference

## Tools and Workshop Tips  REF•1

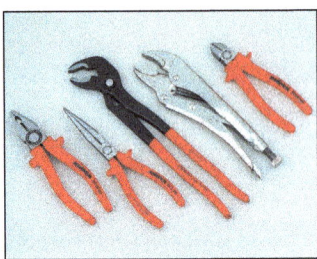

● Building up a tool kit and equipping your workshop ● Using tools ● Understanding bearing, seal, fastener and chain sizes and markings ● Repair techniques

## Security REF•19

● Locks and chains ● U-locks ● Disc locks ● Alarms and immobilisers ● Security marking systems ● Tips on how to prevent bike theft

## Lubricants and fluids  REF•22

● Engine oils ● Transmission (gear) oils ● Coolant/anti-freeze ● Fork oils and suspension fluids ● Brake/clutch fluids ● Spray lubes, degreasers and solvents

## MOT Test Checks REF•25

● A guide to the UK MOT test ● Which items are tested ● How to prepare your motorcycle for the test and perform a pre-test check

## Storage  REF•30

● How to prepare your motorcycle for going into storage and protect essential systems ● How to get the motorcycle back on the road

## Conversion Factors REF•33

$$34 \text{ Nm} \times 0.738 = 25 \text{ lbf ft}$$

● Formulae for conversion of the metric (SI) units used throughout the manual into Imperial measures

## Fault Finding REF•34

● Common faults and their likely causes ● Links to main chapters for testing and repair procedures

## Technical Terms Explained  REF•43

● Component names, technical terms and common abbreviations explained

## Index REF•47

## Buying tools

A toolkit is a fundamental requirement for servicing and repairing a motorcycle. Although there will be an initial expense in building up enough tools for servicing, this will soon be offset by the savings made by doing the job yourself. As experience and confidence grow, additional tools can be added to enable the repair and overhaul of the motorcycle. Many of the specialist tools are expensive and not often used so it may be preferable to hire them, or for a group of friends or motorcycle club to join in the purchase.

As a rule, it is better to buy more expensive, good quality tools. Cheaper tools are likely to wear out faster and need to be renewed more often, nullifying the original saving.

> **Warning: To avoid the risk of a poor quality tool breaking in use, causing injury or damage to the component being worked on, always aim to purchase tools which meet the relevant national safety standards.**

The following lists of tools do not represent the manufacturer's service tools, but serve as a guide to help the owner decide which tools are needed for this level of work. In addition, items such as an electric drill, hacksaw, files, soldering iron and a workbench equipped with a vice, may be needed. Although not classed as tools, a selection of bolts, screws, nuts, washers and pieces of tubing always come in useful.

For more information about tools, refer to the Haynes *Motorcycle Workshop Practice Techbook* (Bk. No. 3470).

## Manufacturer's service tools

Inevitably certain tasks require the use of a service tool. Where possible an alternative tool or method of approach is recommended, but sometimes there is no option if personal injury or damage to the component is to be avoided. Where required, service tools are referred to in the relevant procedure.

Service tools can usually only be purchased from a motorcycle dealer and are identified by a part number. Some of the commonly-used tools, such as rotor pullers, are available in aftermarket form from mail-order motorcycle tool and accessory suppliers.

# Maintenance and minor repair tools

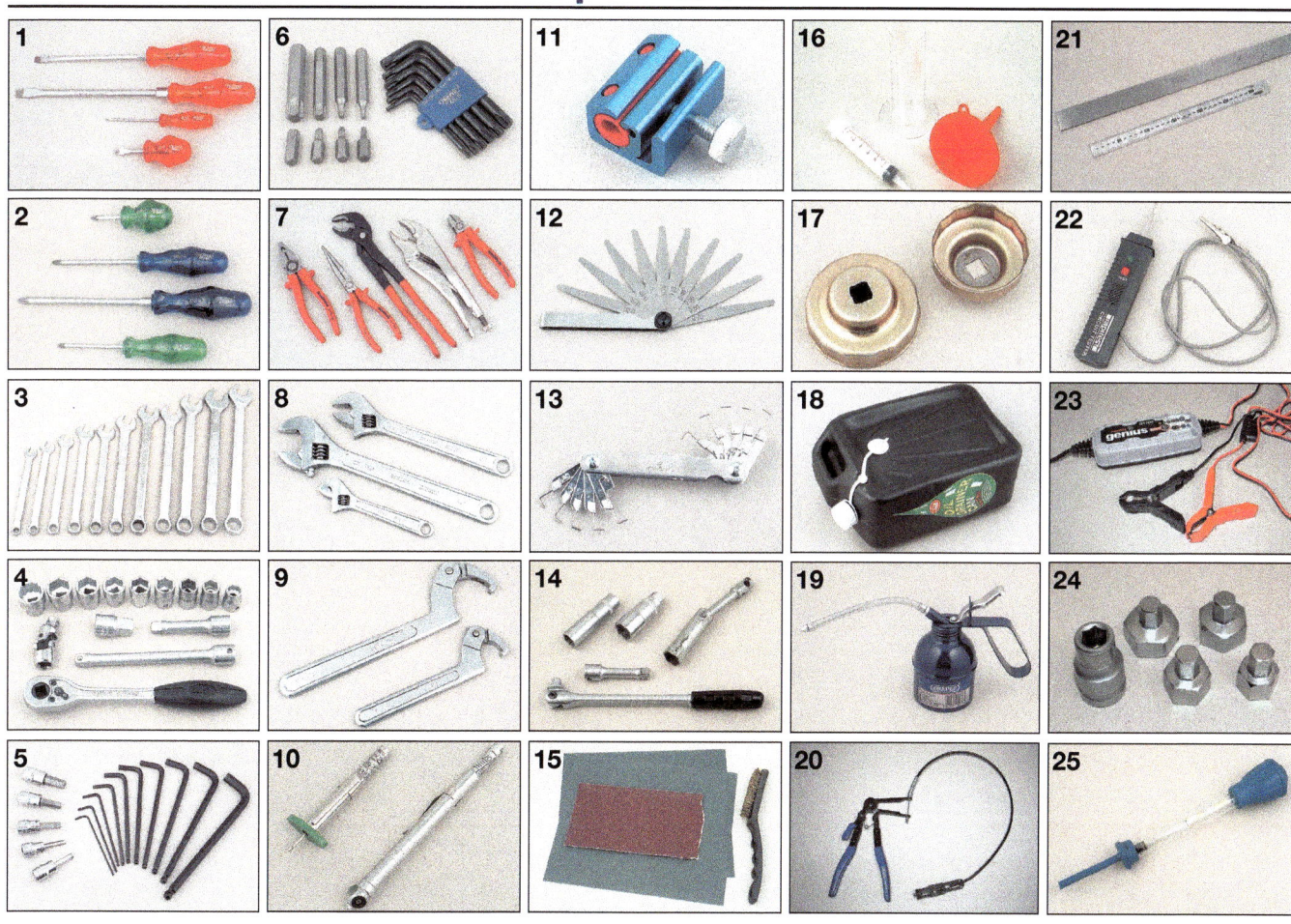

1 Set of flat-bladed screwdrivers
2 Set of Phillips head screwdrivers
3 Combination open-end and ring spanners
4 Socket set (3/8 inch or 1/2 inch drive)
5 Set of Allen keys or bits
6 Set of Torx keys or bits
7 Pliers, cutters and self-locking grips (Mole grips)
8 Adjustable spanners
9 C-spanners
10 Tread depth gauge and tyre pressure gauge
11 Cable oiler clamp
12 Feeler gauges
13 Spark plug gap measuring tool
14 Spark plug spanner or deep plug sockets
15 Wire brush and emery paper
16 Calibrated syringe, measuring vessel and funnel
17 Oil filter adapters
18 Oil drainer can or tray
19 Pump type oil can
20 Hose clamp pliers
21 Straight-edge and steel rule
22 Continuity tester
23 Battery charger
24 Large hex-bit set
25 Anti-freeze tester (for liquid-cooled engines)

# Repair and overhaul tools

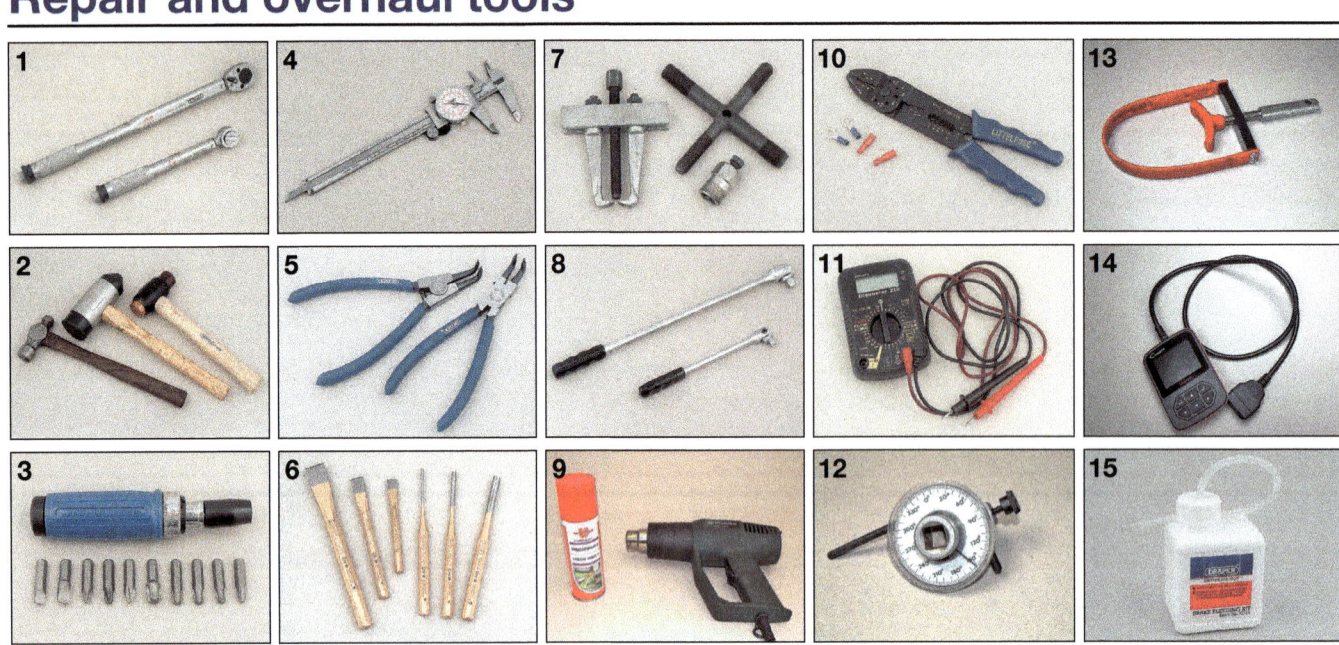

1 Torque wrench
   (small and mid-ranges)
2 Conventional, plastic or
   soft-faced hammers
3 Impact driver set

4 Vernier gauge
5 Circlip pliers (internal and
   external, or combination)
6 Set of cold chisels
   and punches

7 Selection of pullers
8 Breaker bars
9 Freeze spray and heat
   gun

10 Wire stripper and
   crimper tool
11 Multimeter (measures
   amps, volts and ohms)
12 Angle gauge

13 Strap wrench
14 OBD2 fault code reader
15 One-man brake/clutch
   bleeder kit

# Specialist tools

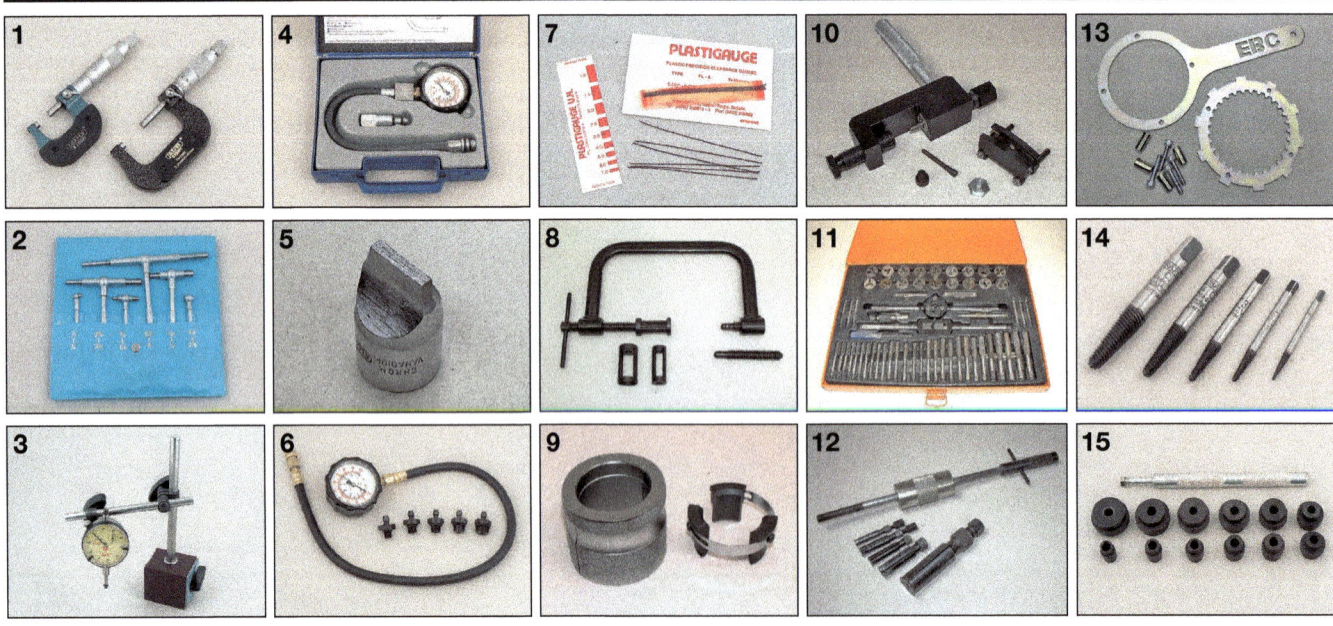

1 Micrometers
   (external type)
2 Telescoping gauges
3 Dial gauge

4 Cylinder
   compression gauge
5 Slotted tool for swingarm
   adjuster sleeve
6 Oil pressure gauge

7 Plastigauge kit
8 Valve spring compressor
9 Two-piece seal driver –
   ideal for fork seals

10 Chain riveting tool
11 Tap and die set
12 Slide-hammer with knife-
   edged bearing pullers

13 Clutch holding tool
14 Screw extractor set
15 Bearing driver set

## 1 Workshop equipment and facilities

### The workbench

● Work is made much easier by raising the bike up on a ramp - components are much more accessible if raised to waist level. The hydraulic or pneumatic types seen in the dealer's workshop are a sound investment if you undertake a lot of repairs or overhauls **(see illustration 1.1)**.

**1.1 Hydraulic motorcycle ramp**

● If raised off ground level, the bike must be supported on the ramp to avoid it falling. Most ramps incorporate a front wheel locating clamp which can be adjusted to suit different diameter wheels. When tightening the clamp, take care not to mark the wheel rim or damage the tyre - use wood blocks on each side to prevent this.

● Secure the bike to the ramp using tie-downs **(see illustration 1.2)**. If the bike has only a sidestand, and hence leans at a dangerous angle when raised, support the bike on an auxiliary stand.

**1.2 Tie-downs are used around the passenger footrests to secure the bike**

● Auxiliary (paddock) stands are widely available from mail order companies or motorcycle dealers and attach either to the wheel axle or swingarm pivot **(see illustration 1.3)**. If the motorcycle has a centrestand, you can support it under the crankcase to prevent it toppling whilst either wheel is removed **(see illustration 1.4)**.

**1.3 This auxiliary stand attaches to the swingarm pivot**

**1.4 Always use a block of wood between the engine and jack head when supporting the engine in this way**

### Fumes and fire

● Refer to the Safety first! page at the beginning of the manual for full details. Make sure your workshop is equipped with a fire extinguisher suitable for fuel-related fires (Class B fire - flammable liquids) - it is not sufficient to have a water-filled extinguisher.

● Always ensure adequate ventilation is available. Unless an exhaust gas extraction system is available for use, ensure that the engine is run outside of the workshop.

● If working on the fuel system, make sure the workshop is ventilated to avoid a build-up of fumes. This applies equally to fume build-up when charging a battery. Do not smoke or allow anyone else to smoke in the workshop.

### Fluids

● If you need to drain fuel from the tank, store it in an approved container marked as suitable for the storage of petrol (gasoline) **(see illustration 1.5)**. Do not store fuel in glass jars or bottles.

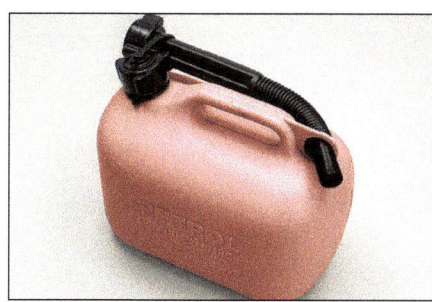

**1.5 Use an approved can only for storing petrol (gasoline)**

● Use proprietary engine degreasers or solvents which have a high flash-point, such as paraffin (kerosene), for cleaning off oil, grease and dirt - never use petrol (gasoline) for cleaning. Wear rubber gloves when handling solvent and engine degreaser. The fumes from certain solvents can be dangerous - always work in a well-ventilated area.

### Dust, eye and hand protection

● Protect your lungs from inhalation of dust particles by wearing a filtering mask over the nose and mouth. Many frictional materials still contain asbestos which is dangerous to your health. Protect your eyes from spouts of liquid and sprung components by wearing a pair of protective goggles **(see illustration 1.6)**.

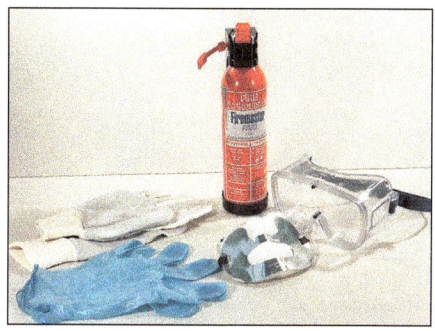

**1.6 A fire extinguisher, goggles, mask and protective gloves should be at hand in the workshop**

● Protect your hands from contact with solvents, fuel and oils by wearing rubber gloves. Alternatively apply a barrier cream to your hands before starting work. If handling hot components or fluids, wear suitable gloves to protect your hands from scalding and burns.

### What to do with old fluids

● Old cleaning solvent, fuel, coolant and oils should not be poured down domestic drains or onto the ground. Package the fluid up in old oil containers, label it accordingly, and take it to a garage or disposal facility. Contact your local authority for location of such sites or ring the oil care hotline.

**Note: It is antisocial and illegal to dump oil down the drain. To find the location of your local oil recycling bank in the UK, call 03708 506 506 or visit www.oilbankline.org.uk**

**In the USA, note that any oil supplier must accept used oil for recycling.**

## 2 Fasteners - screws, bolts and nuts

### *Fastener types and applications*

#### Bolts and screws

● Fastener head types are either of hexagonal, Torx or splined design, with internal and external versions of each type **(see illustrations 2.1 and 2.2)**; splined head fasteners are not in common use on motorcycles. The conventional slotted or Phillips head design is used for certain screws. Bolt or screw length is always measured from the underside of the head to the end of the item **(see illustration 2.11)**.

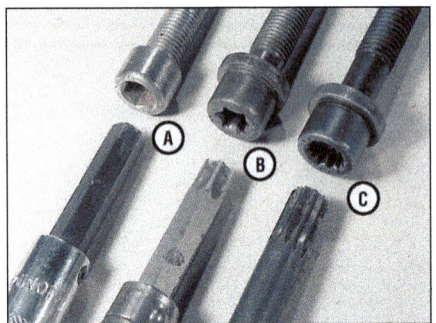

**2.1 Internal hexagon/Allen (A), Torx (B) and splined (C) fasteners, with corresponding bits**

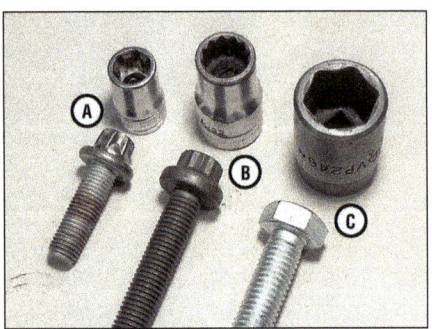

**2.2 External Torx (A), splined (B) and hexagon (C) fasteners, with corresponding sockets**

● Certain fasteners on the motorcycle have a tensile marking on their heads, the higher the marking the stronger the fastener. High tensile fasteners generally carry a 10 or higher marking. Never replace a high tensile fastener with one of a lower tensile strength.

#### Washers **(see illustration 2.3)**

● Plain washers are used between a fastener head and a component to prevent damage to the component or to spread the load when torque is applied. Plain washers can also be used as spacers or shims in certain assemblies. Copper or aluminium plain washers are often used as sealing washers on drain plugs.

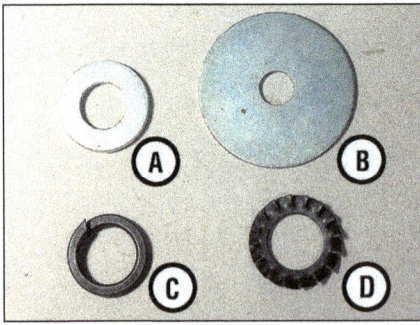

**2.3 Plain washer (A), penny washer (B), spring washer (C) and serrated washer (D)**

● The split-ring spring washer works by applying axial tension between the fastener head and component. If flattened, it is fatigued and must be renewed. If a plain (flat) washer is used on the fastener, position the spring washer between the fastener and the plain washer.
● Serrated star type washers dig into the fastener and component faces, preventing loosening. They are often used on electrical earth (ground) connections to the frame.
● Cone type washers (sometimes called Belleville) are conical and when tightened apply axial tension between the fastener head and component. They must be installed with the dished side against the component and often carry an OUTSIDE marking on their outer face. If flattened, they are fatigued and must be renewed.
● Tab washers are used to lock plain nuts or bolts on a shaft. A portion of the tab washer is bent up hard against one flat of the nut or bolt to prevent it loosening. Due to the tab washer being deformed in use, a new tab washer should be used every time it is disturbed.
● Wave washers are used to take up endfloat on a shaft. They provide light springing and prevent excessive side-to-side play of a component. Can be found on rocker arm shafts.

#### Nuts and split pins

● Conventional plain nuts are usually six-sided **(see illustration 2.4)**. They are sized by thread diameter and pitch. High tensile nuts carry a number on one end to denote their tensile strength.

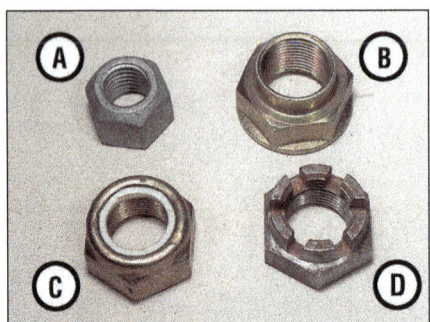

**2.4 Plain nut (A), shouldered locknut (B), nylon insert nut (C) and castellated nut (D)**

● Self-locking nuts either have a nylon insert, or two spring metal tabs, or a shoulder which is staked into a groove in the shaft - their advantage over conventional plain nuts is a resistance to loosening due to vibration. The nylon insert type can be used a number of times, but must be renewed when the friction of the nylon insert is reduced, ie when the nut spins freely on the shaft. The spring tab type can be reused unless the tabs are damaged. The shouldered type must be renewed every time it is disturbed.
● Split pins (cotter pins) are used to lock a castellated nut to a shaft or to prevent slackening of a plain nut. Common applications are wheel axles and brake torque arms. Because the split pin arms are deformed to lock around the nut a new split pin must always be used on installation - always fit the correct size split pin which will fit snugly in the shaft hole. Make sure the split pin arms are correctly located around the nut **(see illustrations 2.5 and 2.6)**.

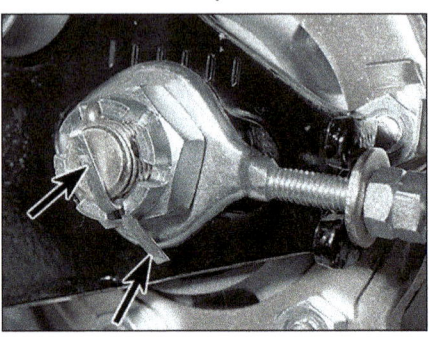

**2.5 Bend split pin (cotter pin) arms as shown (arrows) to secure a castellated nut**

**2.6 Bend split pin (cotter pin) arms as shown to secure a plain nut**

*Caution: If the castellated nut slots do not align with the shaft hole after tightening to the torque setting, tighten the nut until the next slot aligns with the hole - never slacken the nut to align its slot.*

● R-pins (shaped like the letter R), or slip pins as they are sometimes called, are sprung and can be reused if they are otherwise in good condition. Always install R-pins with their closed end facing forwards **(see illustration 2.7)**.

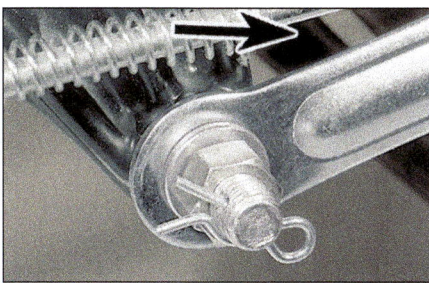

**2.7 Correct fitting of R-pin. Arrow indicates forward direction**

### Circlips (see illustration 2.8)

● Circlips (sometimes called snap-rings) are used to retain components on a shaft or in a housing and have corresponding external or internal ears to permit removal. Parallel-sided (machined) circlips can be installed either way round in their groove, whereas stamped circlips (which have a chamfered edge on one face) must be installed with the chamfer facing away from the direction of thrust load **(see illustration 2.9)**.

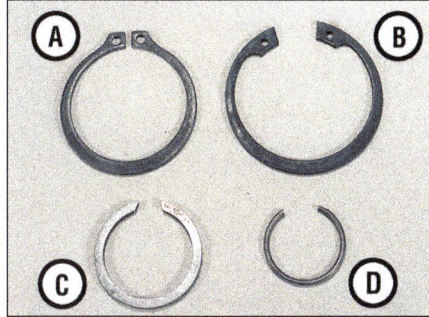

**2.8 External stamped circlip (A), internal stamped circlip (B), machined circlip (C) and wire circlip (D)**

● Always use circlip pliers to remove and install circlips; expand or compress them just enough to remove them. After installation, rotate the circlip in its groove to ensure it is securely seated. If installing a circlip on a splined shaft, always align its opening with a shaft channel to ensure the circlip ends are well supported and unlikely to catch **(see illustration 2.10)**.

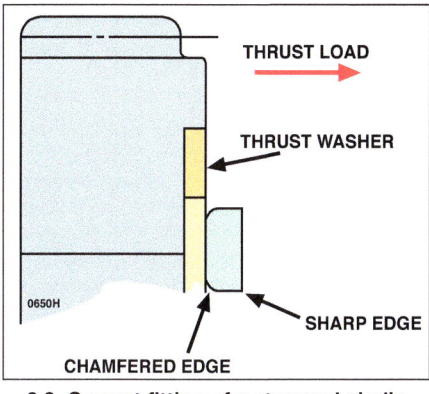

**2.9 Correct fitting of a stamped circlip**

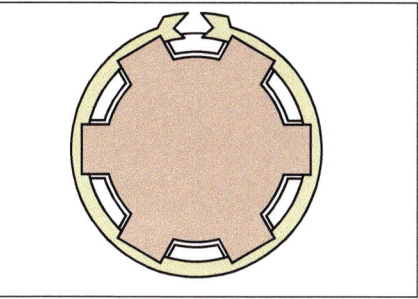

**2.10 Align circlip opening with shaft channel**

● Circlips can wear due to the thrust of components and become loose in their grooves, with the subsequent danger of becoming dislodged in operation. For this reason, renewal is advised every time a circlip is disturbed.

● Wire circlips are commonly used as piston pin retaining clips. If a removal tang is provided, long-nosed pliers can be used to dislodge them, otherwise careful use of a small flat-bladed screwdriver is necessary. Wire circlips should be renewed every time they are disturbed.

### Thread diameter and pitch

● Diameter of a male thread (screw, bolt or stud) is the outside diameter of the threaded portion **(see illustration 2.11)**. Most motorcycle manufacturers use the ISO (International Standards Organisation) metric system expressed in millimetres, eg M6 refers to a 6 mm diameter thread. Sizing is the same for nuts, except that the thread diameter is measured across the valleys of the nut.

● Pitch is the distance between the peaks of the thread **(see illustration 2.11)**. It is expressed in millimetres, thus a common bolt size may be expressed as 6.0 x 1.0 mm (6 mm thread diameter and 1 mm pitch). Generally pitch increases in proportion to thread diameter, although there are always exceptions.

● Thread diameter and pitch are related for conventional fastener applications and the accompanying table can be used as a guide. Additionally, the AF (Across Flats), spanner or socket size dimension of the bolt or nut **(see illustration 2.11)** is linked to thread and pitch specification. Thread pitch can be measured with a thread gauge **(see illustration 2.12)**.

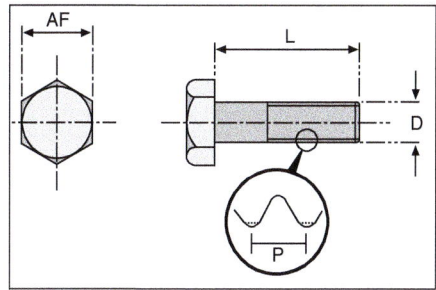

**2.11 Fastener length (L), thread diameter (D), thread pitch (P) and head size (AF)**

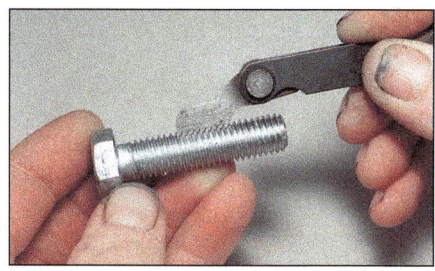

**2.12 Using a thread gauge to measure pitch**

| AF size | Thread diameter x pitch (mm) |
| --- | --- |
| 8 mm | M5 x 0.8 |
| 8 mm | M6 x 1.0 |
| 10 mm | M6 x 1.0 |
| 12 mm | M8 x 1.25 |
| 14 mm | M10 x 1.25 |
| 17 mm | M12 x 1.25 |

● The threads of most fasteners are of the right-hand type, ie they are turned clockwise to tighten and anti-clockwise to loosen. The reverse situation applies to left-hand thread fasteners, which are turned anti-clockwise to tighten and clockwise to loosen. Left-hand threads are used where rotation of a component might loosen a conventional right-hand thread fastener.

### Seized fasteners

● Corrosion of external fasteners due to water or reaction between two dissimilar metals can occur over a period of time. It will build up sooner in wet conditions or in countries where salt is used on the roads during the winter. If a fastener is severely corroded it is likely that normal methods of removal will fail and result in its head being ruined. When you attempt removal, the fastener thread should be heard to crack free and unscrew easily - if it doesn't, stop there before damaging something.

● A smart tap on the head of the fastener will often succeed in breaking free corrosion which has occurred in the threads **(see illustration 2.13)**.

● An aerosol penetrating fluid (such as WD-40) applied the night beforehand may work its way down into the thread and ease removal. Depending on the location, you may be able to make up a Plasticine well around the fastener head and fill it with penetrating fluid.

**2.13 A sharp tap on the head of a fastener will often break free a corroded thread**

● If you are working on an engine internal component, corrosion will most likely not be a problem due to the well lubricated environment. However, components can be very tight and an impact driver is a useful tool in freeing them **(see illustration 2.14)**.

**2.14 Using an impact driver to free a fastener**

● Where corrosion has occurred between dissimilar metals (eg steel and aluminium alloy), the application of heat to the fastener head will create a disproportionate expansion rate between the two metals and break the seizure caused by the corrosion. Whether heat can be applied depends on the location of the fastener - any surrounding components likely to be damaged must first be removed **(see illustration 2.15)**. Heat can be applied using a paint stripper heat gun or clothes iron, or by immersing the component in boiling water - wear protective gloves to prevent scalding or burns to the hands.

**2.15 Using heat to free a seized fastener**

● As a last resort, it is possible to use a hammer and cold chisel to work the fastener head unscrewed **(see illustration 2.16)**. This will damage the fastener, but more importantly extreme care must be taken not to damage the surrounding component.

*Caution: Remember that the component being secured is generally of more value than the bolt, nut or screw - when the fastener is freed, do not unscrew it with force, instead work the fastener back and forth when resistance is felt to prevent thread damage.*

**2.16 Using a hammer and chisel to free a seized fastener**

## Broken fasteners and damaged heads

● If the shank of a broken bolt or screw is accessible you can grip it with self-locking grips. The knurled wheel type stud extractor tool or self-gripping stud puller tool is particularly useful for removing the long studs which screw into the cylinder mouth surface of the crankcase or bolts and screws from which the head has broken off **(see illustration 2.17)**. Studs can also be removed by locking two nuts together on the threaded end of the stud and using a spanner on the lower nut **(see illustration 2.18)**.

**2.17 Using a stud extractor tool to remove a broken crankcase stud**

**2.18 Two nuts can be locked together to unscrew a stud from a component**

● A bolt or screw which has broken off below or level with the casing must be extracted using a screw extractor set. Centre punch the fastener to centralise the drill bit, then drill a hole in the fastener **(see illustration 2.19)**. Select a drill bit which is approximately half to three-quarters the diameter of the fastener

**2.19 When using a screw extractor, first drill a hole in the fastener . . .**

and drill to a depth which will accommodate the extractor. Use the largest size extractor possible, but avoid leaving too small a wall thickness otherwise the extractor will merely force the fastener walls outwards wedging it in the casing thread.

● If a spiral type extractor is used, thread it anti-clockwise into the fastener. As it is screwed in, it will grip the fastener and unscrew it from the casing **(see illustration 2.20)**.

**2.20 . . . then thread the extractor anti-clockwise into the fastener**

● If a taper type extractor is used, tap it into the fastener so that it is firmly wedged in place. Unscrew the extractor (anti-clockwise) to draw the fastener out.

⚠️ *Warning: Stud extractors are very hard and may break off in the fastener if care is not taken - ask an engineer about spark erosion if this happens.*

● Alternatively, the broken bolt/screw can be drilled out and the hole retapped for an oversize bolt/screw or a diamond-section thread insert. It is essential that the drilling is carried out squarely and to the correct depth, otherwise the casing may be ruined - if in doubt, entrust the work to an engineer.

● Bolts and nuts with rounded corners cause the correct size spanner or socket to slip when force is applied. Of the types of spanner/socket available always use a six-point type rather than an eight or twelve-point type - better grip

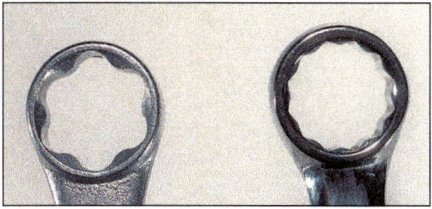

**2.21 Comparison of surface drive ring spanner (left) with 12-point type (right)**

is obtained. Surface drive spanners grip the middle of the hex flats, rather than the corners, and are thus good in cases of damaged heads **(see illustration 2.21)**.

● Slotted-head or Phillips-head screws are often damaged by the use of the wrong size screwdriver. Allen-head and Torx-head screws are much less likely to sustain damage. If enough of the screw head is exposed you can use a hacksaw to cut a slot in its head and then use a conventional flat-bladed screwdriver to remove it. Alternatively use a hammer and cold chisel to tap the head of the fastener around to slacken it. Always replace damaged fasteners with new ones, preferably Torx or Allen-head type.

**HAYNES HiNT**

*A dab of valve grinding compound between the screw head and screwdriver tip will often give a good grip.*

## Thread repair

● Threads (particularly those in aluminium alloy components) can be damaged by overtightening, being assembled with dirt in the threads, or from a component working loose and vibrating. Eventually the thread will fail completely, and it will be impossible to tighten the fastener.

● If a thread is damaged or clogged with old locking compound it can be renovated with a thread repair tool (thread chaser) **(see illustrations 2.22 and 2.23)**; special thread

**2.22 A thread repair tool being used to correct an internal thread**

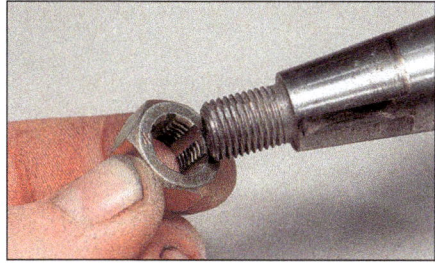

**2.23 A thread repair tool being used to correct an external thread**

chasers are available for spark plug hole threads. The tool will not cut a new thread, but clean and true the original thread. Make sure that you use the correct diameter and pitch tool. Similarly, external threads can be cleaned up with a die or a thread restorer file **(see illustration 2.24)**.

**2.24 Using a thread restorer file**

● It is possible to drill out the old thread and retap the component to the next thread size. This will work where there is enough surrounding material and a new bolt or screw can be obtained. Sometimes, however, this is not possible - such as where the bolt/screw passes through another component which must also be suitably modified, also in cases where a spark plug or oil drain plug cannot be obtained in a larger diameter thread size.

● The diamond-section thread insert (often known by its popular trade name of Heli-Coil) is a simple and effective method of renewing the thread and retaining the original size. A kit can be purchased which contains the tap, insert and installing tool **(see illustration 2.25)**. Drill out the damaged thread with the size drill specified **(see illustration 2.26)**. Carefully retap the thread **(see illustration 2.27)**. Install the

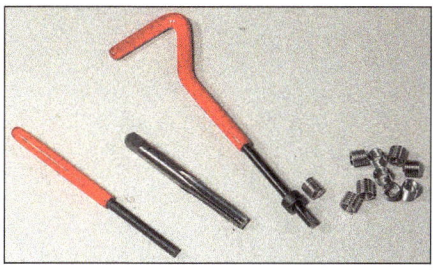

**2.25 Obtain a thread insert kit to suit the thread diameter and pitch required**

**2.26 To install a thread insert, first drill out the original thread . . .**

**2.27 . . . tap a new thread . . .**

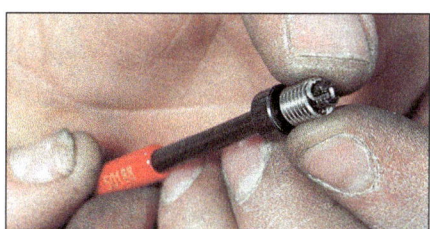

**2.28 . . . fit insert on the installing tool . . .**

**2.29 . . . and thread into the component . . .**

**2.30 . . . break off the tang when complete**

insert on the installing tool and thread it slowly into place using a light downward pressure **(see illustrations 2.28 and 2.29)**. When positioned between a 1/4 and 1/2 turn below the surface withdraw the installing tool and use the break-off tool to press down on the tang, breaking it off **(see illustration 2.30)**.

● There are epoxy thread repair kits on the market which can rebuild stripped internal threads, although this repair should not be used on high load-bearing components.

### Thread locking and sealing compounds

● Locking compounds are used in locations where the fastener is prone to loosening due to vibration or on important safety-related items which might cause loss of control of the motorcycle if they fail. It is also used where important fasteners cannot be secured by other means such as lockwashers or split pins.

● Before applying locking compound, make sure that the threads (internal and external) are clean and dry with all old compound removed. Select a compound to suit the component being secured - a non-permanent general locking and sealing type is suitable for most applications, but a high strength type is needed for permanent fixing of studs in castings. Apply a drop or two of the compound to the first few threads of the fastener, then thread it into place and tighten to the specified torque. Do not apply excessive thread locking compound otherwise the thread may be damaged on subsequent removal.

● Certain fasteners are impregnated with a dry film type coating of locking compound on their threads. Always renew this type of fastener if disturbed.

● Anti-seize compounds, such as copper-based greases, can be applied to protect threads from seizure due to extreme heat and corrosion. A common instance is spark plug threads and exhaust system fasteners.

### 3 Measuring tools and gauges

### Feeler gauges

● Feeler gauges (or blades) are used for measuring small gaps and clearances **(see illustration 3.1)**. They can also be used to measure endfloat (sideplay) of a component on a shaft where access is not possible with a dial gauge.

● Feeler gauge sets should be treated with care and not bent or damaged. They are etched with their size on one face. Keep them clean and very lightly oiled to prevent corrosion build-up.

**3.1 Feeler gauges are used for measuring small gaps and clearances - thickness is marked on one face of gauge**

● When measuring a clearance, select a gauge which is a light sliding fit between the two components. You may need to use two gauges together to measure the clearance accurately.

### Micrometers

● A micrometer is a precision tool capable of measuring to 0.01 or 0.001 of a millimetre. It should always be stored in its case and not in the general toolbox. It must be kept clean and never dropped, otherwise its frame or measuring anvils could be distorted resulting in inaccurate readings.

● External micrometers are used for measuring outside diameters of components and have many more applications than internal micrometers. Micrometers are available in different size ranges, eg 0 to 25 mm, 25 to 50 mm, and upwards in 25 mm steps; some large micrometers have interchangeable anvils to allow a range of measurements to be taken. Generally the largest precision measurement you are likely to take on a motorcycle is the piston diameter.

● Internal micrometers (or bore micrometers) are used for measuring inside diameters, such as valve guides and cylinder bores. Telescoping gauges and small hole gauges are used in conjunction with an external micrometer, whereas the more expensive internal micrometers have their own measuring device.

### External micrometer

**Note:** *The conventional analogue type instrument is described. Although much easier to read, digital micrometers are considerably more expensive.*

● Always check the calibration of the micrometer before use. With the anvils closed (0 to 25 mm type) or set over a test gauge

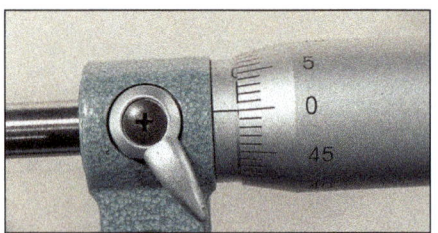

**3.2 Check micrometer calibration before use**

(for the larger types) the scale should read zero **(see illustration 3.2)**; make sure that the anvils (and test piece) are clean first. Any discrepancy can be adjusted by referring to the instructions supplied with the tool. Remember that the micrometer is a precision measuring tool - don't force the anvils closed, use the ratchet (4) on the end of the micrometer to close it. In this way, a measured force is always applied.

● To use, first make sure that the item being measured is clean. Place the anvil of the micrometer (1) against the item and use the thimble (2) to bring the spindle (3) lightly into contact with the other side of the item **(see illustration 3.3)**. Don't tighten the thimble down because this will damage the micrometer - instead use the ratchet (4) on the end of the micrometer. The ratchet mechanism applies a measured force preventing damage to the instrument.

● The micrometer is read by referring to the linear scale on the sleeve and the annular scale on the thimble. Read off the sleeve first to obtain the base measurement, then add the fine measurement from the thimble to obtain the overall reading. The linear scale on the sleeve represents the measuring range of the micrometer (eg 0 to 25 mm). The annular scale

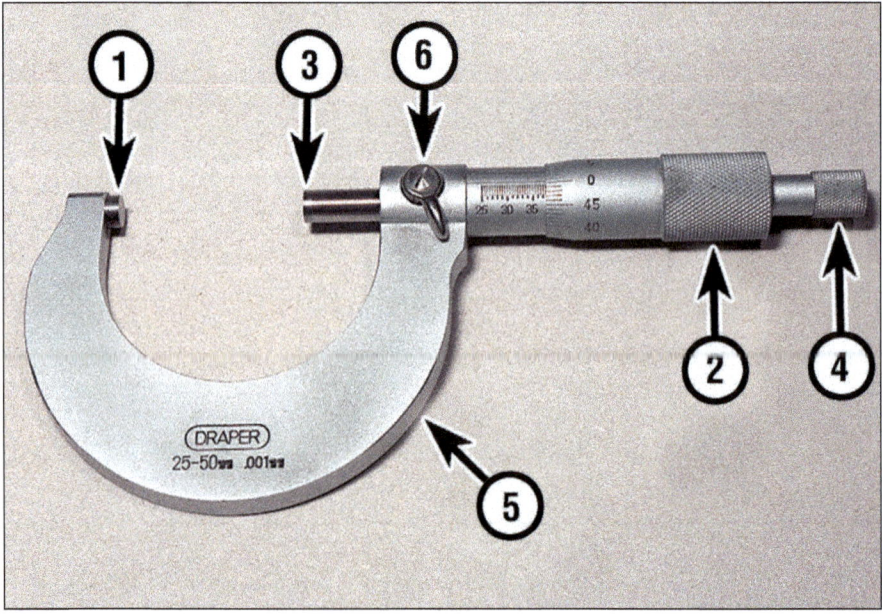

**3.3 Micrometer component parts**

| | | |
|---|---|---|
| 1 Anvil | 3 Spindle | 5 Frame |
| 2 Thimble | 4 Ratchet | 6 Locking lever |

on the thimble will be in graduations of 0.01 mm (or as marked on the frame) - one full revolution of the thimble will move 0.5 mm on the linear scale. Take the reading where the datum line on the sleeve intersects the thimble's scale. Always position the eye directly above the scale otherwise an inaccurate reading will result.

In the example shown the item measures 2.95 mm **(see illustration 3.4)**:

| | |
|---|---|
| **Linear scale** | 2.00 mm |
| **Linear scale** | 0.50 mm |
| **Annular scale** | 0.45 mm |
| **Total figure** | 2.95 mm |

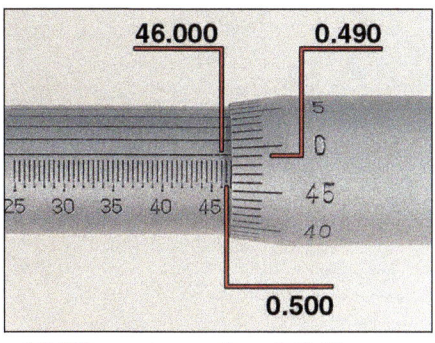

**3.5 Micrometer reading of 46.99 mm on linear and annular scales . . .**

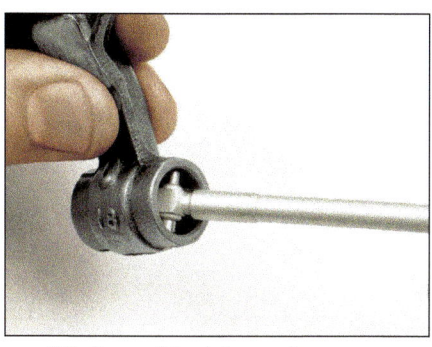

**3.7 Expand the telescoping gauge in the bore, lock its position . . .**

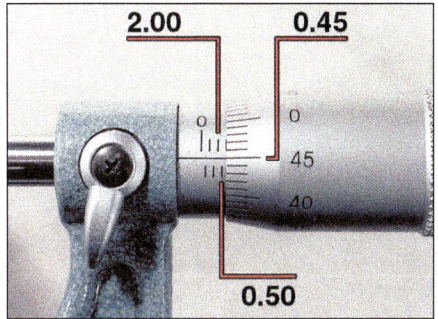

**3.4 Micrometer reading of 2.95 mm**

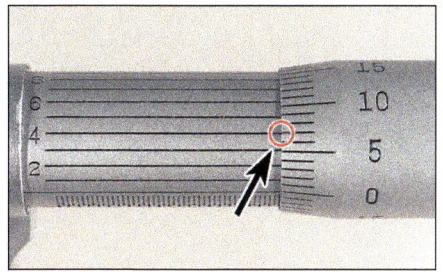

**3.6 . . . and 0.004 mm on vernier scale**

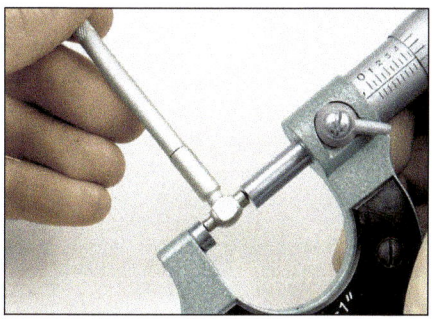

**3.8 . . . then measure the gauge with a micrometer**

Most micrometers have a locking lever (6) on the frame to hold the setting in place, allowing the item to be removed from the micrometer.
● Some micrometers have a vernier scale on their sleeve, providing an even finer measurement to be taken, in 0.001 increments of a millimetre. Take the sleeve and thimble measurement as described above, then check which graduation on the vernier scale aligns with that of the annular scale on the thimble **Note:** *The eye must be perpendicular to the scale when taking the vernier reading - if necessary rotate the body of the micrometer to ensure this.* Multiply the vernier scale figure by 0.001 and add it to the base and fine measurement figures.

In the example shown the item measures 46.994 mm **(see illustrations 3.5 and 3.6)**:

| | |
|---|---|
| **Linear scale (base)** | 46.000 mm |
| **Linear scale (base)** | 00.500 mm |
| **Annular scale (fine)** | 00.490 mm |
| **Vernier scale** | 00.004 mm |
| **Total figure** | 46.994 mm |

### Internal micrometer

● Internal micrometers are available for measuring bore diameters, but are expensive and unlikely to be available for home use. It is suggested that a set of telescoping gauges and small hole gauges, both of which must be used with an external micrometer, will suffice for taking internal measurements on a motorcycle.
● Telescoping gauges can be used to

measure internal diameters of components. Select a gauge with the correct size range, make sure its ends are clean and insert it into the bore. Expand the gauge, then lock its position and withdraw it from the bore **(see illustration 3.7)**. Measure across the gauge ends with a micrometer **(see illustration 3.8)**.
● Very small diameter bores (such as valve guides) are measured with a small hole gauge. Once adjusted to a slip-fit inside the component, its position is locked and the gauge withdrawn for measurement with a micrometer **(see illustrations 3.9 and 3.10)**.

### Vernier caliper

**Note:** *The conventional linear and dial gauge type instruments are described. Digital types are easier to read, but are far more expensive.*
● The vernier caliper does not provide the precision of a micrometer, but is versatile in being able to measure internal and external diameters. Some types also incorporate a depth gauge. It is ideal for measuring clutch plate friction material and spring free lengths.
● To use the conventional linear scale vernier, slacken off the vernier clamp screws (1) and set its jaws over (2), or inside (3), the item to be measured **(see illustration 3.11)**. Slide the jaw into contact, using the thumb-wheel (4) for fine movement of the sliding scale (5) then tighten the clamp screws (1). Read off the main scale (6) where the zero on the sliding scale (5) intersects it, taking the whole number to the left of the zero; this provides the base measurement. View along the sliding scale and select the division which

**3.9 Expand the small hole gauge in the bore, lock its position . . .**

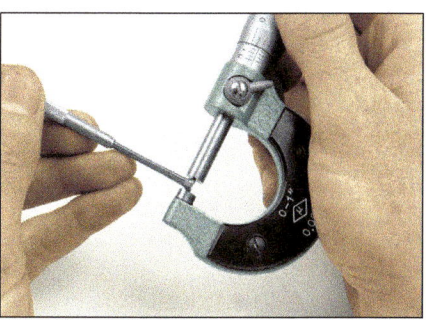

**3.10 . . . then measure the gauge with a micrometer**

lines up exactly with any of the divisions on the main scale, noting that the divisions usually represents 0.02 of a millimetre. Add this fine measurement to the base measurement to obtain the total reading.

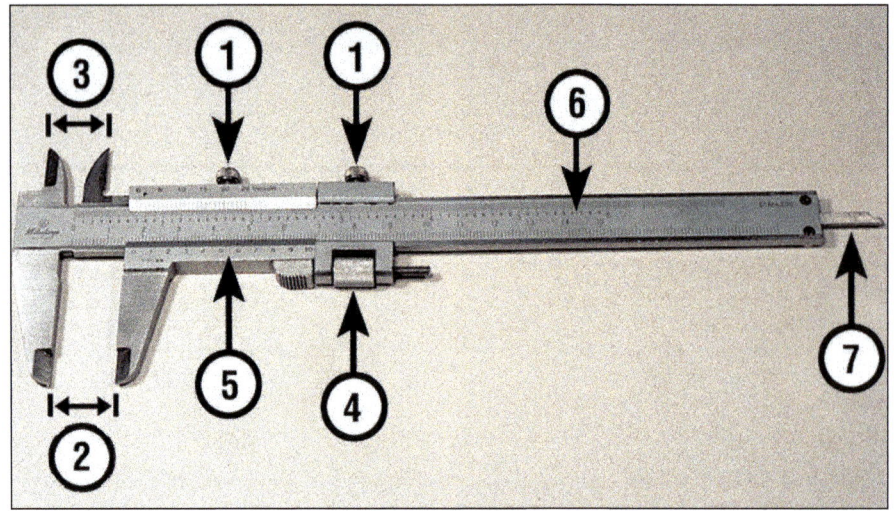

**3.11 Vernier component parts (linear gauge)**

| | | | | | |
|---|---|---|---|---|---|
| 1 | Clamp screws | 3 | Internal jaws | 5 | Sliding scale | 7 | Depth gauge |
| 2 | External jaws | 4 | Thumbwheel | 6 | Main scale | |

In the example shown the item measures

55.92 mm **(see illustration 3.12)**:

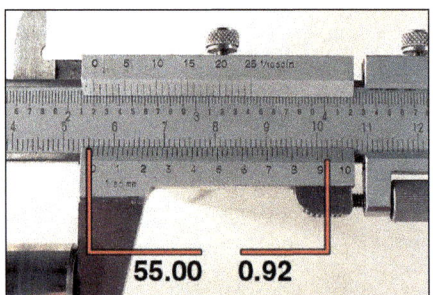

**3.12 Vernier gauge reading of 55.92 mm**

| Base measurement | 55.00 mm |
|---|---|
| Fine measurement | 00.92 mm |
| Total figure | 55.92 mm |

● Some vernier calipers are equipped with a dial gauge for fine measurement. Before use, check that the jaws are clean, then close them fully and check that the dial gauge reads zero. If necessary adjust the gauge ring accordingly. Slacken the vernier clamp screw (1) and set its jaws over (2), or inside (3), the item to be measured **(see illustration 3.13)**. Slide the jaws into contact, using the thumbwheel (4) for fine movement. Read off the main scale (5) where the edge of the sliding scale (6) intersects it, taking the whole number to the left of the zero; this provides the base measurement. Read off the needle position on the dial gauge (7) scale to provide the fine measurement; each division represents 0.05 of a millimetre. Add this fine measurement to the base measurement to obtain the total reading.

In the example shown the item measures 55.95 mm **(see illustration 3.14)**:

| Base measurement | 55.00 mm |
|---|---|
| Fine measurement | 00.95 mm |
| Total figure | 55.95 mm |

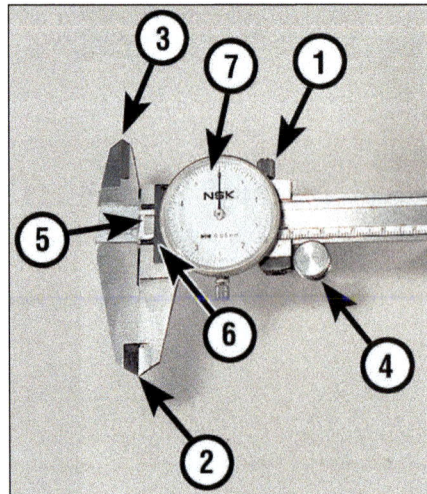

**3.13 Vernier component parts (dial gauge)**

| | | | |
|---|---|---|---|
| 1 | Clamp screw | 5 | Main scale |
| 2 | External jaws | 6 | Sliding scale |
| 3 | Internal jaws | 7 | Dial gauge |
| 4 | Thumbwheel | | |

**3.14 Vernier gauge reading of 55.95 mm**

## Plastigauge

● Plastigauge is a plastic material which can be compressed between two surfaces to measure the oil clearance between them. The width of the compressed Plastigauge is measured against a calibrated scale to determine the clearance.

● Common uses of Plastigauge are for measuring the clearance between crankshaft journal and main bearing inserts, between crankshaft journal and big-end bearing inserts, and between camshaft and bearing surfaces. The following example describes big-end oil clearance measurement.

● Handle the Plastigauge material carefully to prevent distortion. Using a sharp knife, cut a length which corresponds with the width of the bearing being measured and place it carefully across the journal so that it is parallel with the shaft **(see illustration 3.15)**. Carefully install both bearing shells and the connecting rod. Without rotating the rod on the journal tighten its bolts or nuts (as applicable) to the specified torque. The connecting rod and bearings are then disassembled and the crushed Plastigauge examined.

**3.15 Plastigauge placed across shaft journal**

● Using the scale provided in the Plastigauge kit, measure the width of the material to determine the oil clearance **(see illustration 3.16)**. Always remove all traces of Plastigauge after use using your fingernails.

*Caution: Arriving at the correct clearance demands that the assembly is torqued correctly, according to the settings and sequence (where applicable) provided by the motorcycle manufacturer.*

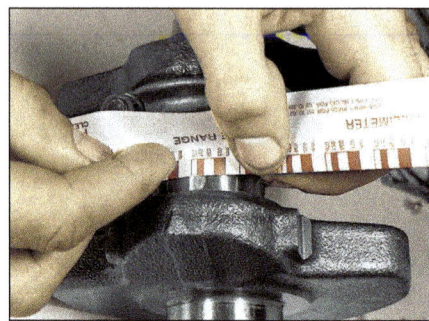

**3.16 Measuring the width of the crushed Plastigauge**

## Dial gauge or DTI (Dial Test Indicator)

● A dial gauge can be used to accurately measure small amounts of movement. Typical uses are measuring shaft runout or shaft endfloat (sideplay) and setting piston position for ignition timing on two-strokes. A dial gauge set usually comes with a range of different probes and adapters and mounting equipment.

● The gauge needle must point to zero when at rest. Rotate the ring around its periphery to zero the gauge.

● Check that the gauge is capable of reading the extent of movement in the work. Most gauges have a small dial set in the face which records whole millimetres of movement as well as the fine scale around the face periphery which is calibrated in 0.01 mm divisions. Read off the small dial first to obtain the base measurement, then add the measurement from the fine scale to obtain the total reading.

In the example shown the gauge reads 1.48 mm (see illustration 3.17):

| Base measurement | 1.00 mm |
| Fine measurement | 0.48 mm |
| Total figure | 1.48 mm |

3.17 Dial gauge reading of 1.48 mm

● If measuring shaft runout, the shaft must be supported in vee-blocks and the gauge mounted on a stand perpendicular to the shaft. Rest the tip of the gauge against the centre of the shaft and rotate the shaft slowly whilst watching the gauge reading (see illustration 3.18). Take several measurements along the length of the shaft and record the

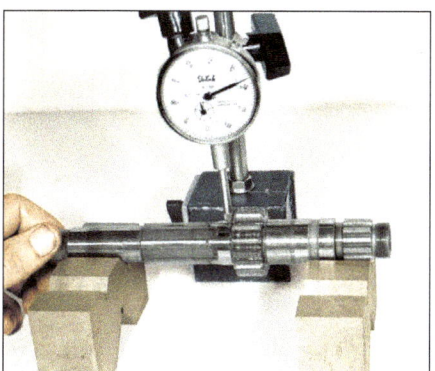

3.18 Using a dial gauge to measure shaft runout

maximum gauge reading as the amount of runout in the shaft. Note: *The reading obtained will be total runout at that point - some manufacturers specify that the runout figure is halved to compare with their specified runout limit.*

● Endfloat (sideplay) measurement requires that the gauge is mounted securely to the surrounding component with its probe touching the end of the shaft. Using hand pressure, push and pull on the shaft noting the maximum endfloat recorded on the gauge (see illustration 3.19).

3.19 Using a dial gauge to measure shaft endfloat

● A dial gauge with suitable adapters can be used to determine piston position BTDC on two-stroke engines for the purposes of ignition timing. The gauge, adapter and suitable length probe are installed in the place of the spark plug and the gauge zeroed at TDC. If the piston position is specified as 1.14 mm BTDC, rotate the engine back to 2.00 mm BTDC, then slowly forwards to 1.14 mm BTDC.

## Cylinder compression gauges

● A compression gauge is used for measuring cylinder compression. Either the rubber-cone type or the threaded adapter type can be used. The latter is preferred to ensure a perfect seal against the cylinder head. A 0 to 300 psi (0 to 20 Bar) type gauge (for petrol/gasoline engines) will be suitable for motorcycles.

● The spark plug is removed and the gauge either held hard against the cylinder head (cone type) or the gauge adapter screwed into the cylinder head (threaded type) (see illustration 3.20). Cylinder compression is measured with the engine turning over, but not running. The

3.20 Using a rubber-cone type cylinder compression gauge

gauge will hold the reading until manually released.

## Oil pressure gauge

● An oil pressure gauge is used for measuring engine oil pressure. Most gauges come with a set of adapters to fit the thread of the take-off point (see illustration 3.21). If the take-off point specified by the motorcycle manufacturer is an external oil pipe union, make sure that the specified replacement union is used to prevent oil starvation.

3.21 Oil pressure gauge and take-off point adapter (arrow)

● Oil pressure is measured with the engine running (at a specific rpm) and often the manufacturer will specify pressure limits for a cold and hot engine.

## Straight-edge and surface plate

● If checking the gasket face of a component for warpage, place a steel rule or precision straight-edge across the gasket face and measure any gap between the straight-edge and component with feeler gauges (see illustration 3.22). Check diagonally across the component and between mounting holes (see illustration 3.23).

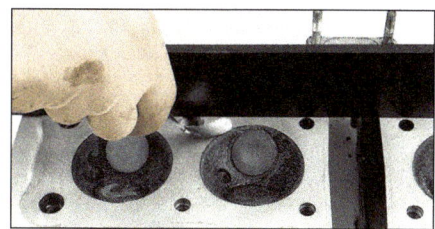

3.22 Use a straight-edge and feeler gauges to check for warpage

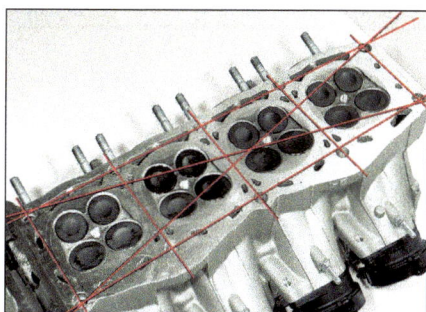

3.23 Check for warpage in these directions

● Checking individual components for warpage, such as clutch plain (metal) plates, requires a perfectly flat plate or piece or plate glass and feeler gauges.

## 4  Torque and leverage

### What is torque?

● Torque describes the twisting force about a shaft. The amount of torque applied is determined by the distance from the centre of the shaft to the end of the lever and the amount of force being applied to the end of the lever; distance multiplied by force equals torque.

● The manufacturer applies a measured torque to a bolt or nut to ensure that it will not slacken in use and to hold two components securely together without movement in the joint. The actual torque setting depends on the thread size, bolt or nut material and the composition of the components being held.

● Too little torque may cause the fastener to loosen due to vibration, whereas too much torque will distort the joint faces of the component or cause the fastener to shear off. Always stick to the specified torque setting.

### Using a torque wrench

● Check the calibration of the torque wrench and make sure it has a suitable range for the job. Torque wrenches are available in Nm (Newton-metres), kgf m (kilograms-force metre), lbf ft (pounds-feet), lbf in (inch-pounds). Do not confuse lbf ft with lbf in.

● Adjust the tool to the desired torque on the scale (see illustration 4.1). If your torque wrench is not calibrated in the units specified, carefully convert the figure (see Conversion Factors). A manufacturer sometimes gives a torque setting as a range (8 to 10 Nm) rather than a single figure - in this case set the tool midway between the two settings. The same torque may be expressed as 9 Nm ± 1 Nm. Some torque wrenches have a method of locking the setting so that it isn't inadvertently altered during use.

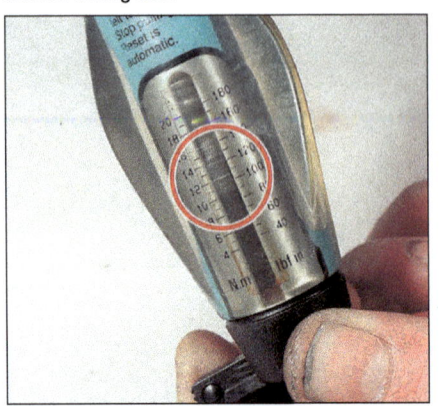

**4.1  Set the torque wrench index mark to the setting required, in this case 12 Nm**

● Install the bolts/nuts in their correct location and secure them lightly. Their threads must be clean and free of any old locking compound. Unless specified the threads and flange should be dry - oiled threads are necessary in certain circumstances and the manufacturer will take this into account in the specified torque figure. Similarly, the manufacturer may also specify the application of thread-locking compound.

● Tighten the fasteners in the specified sequence until the torque wrench clicks, indicating that the torque setting has been reached. Apply the torque again to double-check the setting. Where different thread diameter fasteners secure the component, as a rule tighten the larger diameter ones first.

● When the torque wrench has been finished with, release the lock (where applicable) and fully back off its setting to zero - do not leave the torque wrench tensioned. Also, do not use a torque wrench for slackening a fastener.

### Angle-tightening

● Manufacturers often specify a figure in degrees for final tightening of a fastener. This usually follows tightening to a specific torque setting.

● A degree disc can be set and attached to the socket (see illustration 4.2) or a protractor can be used to mark the angle of movement on the bolt/nut head and the surrounding casting (see illustration 4.3).

**4.2  Angle tightening can be accomplished with a torque-angle gauge . . .**

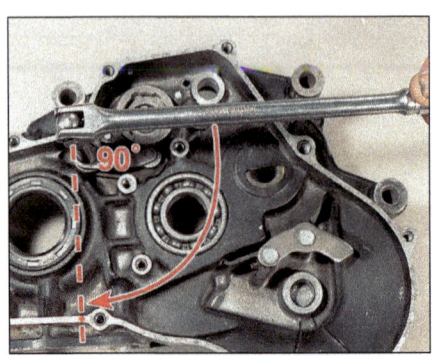

**4.3  . . . or by marking the angle on the surrounding component**

### Loosening sequences

● Where more than one bolt/nut secures a component, loosen each fastener evenly a little at a time. In this way, not all the stress of the joint is held by one fastener and the components are not likely to distort.

● If a tightening sequence is provided, work in the REVERSE of this, but if not, work from the outside in, in a criss-cross sequence (see illustration 4.4).

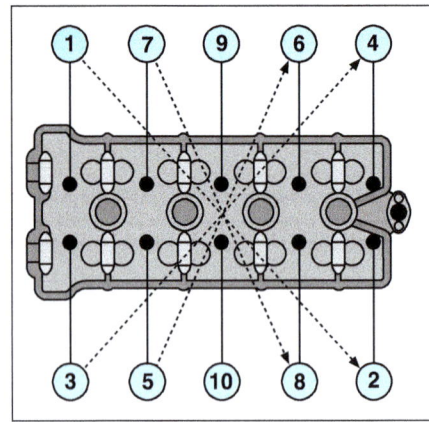

**4.4  When slackening, work from the outside inwards**

### Tightening sequences

● If a component is held by more than one fastener it is important that the retaining bolts/nuts are tightened evenly to prevent uneven stress build-up and distortion of sealing faces. This is especially important on high-compression joints such as the cylinder head.

● A sequence is usually provided by the manufacturer, either in a diagram or actually marked in the casting. If not, always start in the centre and work outwards in a criss-cross pattern (see illustration 4.5). Start off by securing all bolts/nuts finger-tight, then set the torque wrench and tighten each fastener by a small amount in sequence until the final torque is reached. By following this practice,

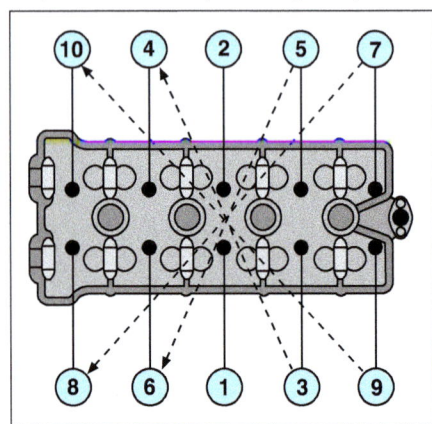

**4.5  When tightening, work from the inside outwards**

the joint will be held evenly and will not be distorted. Important joints, such as the cylinder head and big-end fasteners often have two- or three-stage torque settings.

### Applying leverage

● Use tools at the correct angle. Position a socket wrench or spanner on the bolt/nut so that you pull it towards you when loosening. If this can't be done, push the spanner without curling your fingers around it **(see illustration 4.6)** - the spanner may slip or the fastener loosen suddenly, resulting in your fingers being crushed against a component.

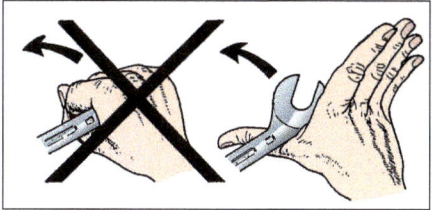

**4.6 If you can't pull on the spanner to loosen a fastener, push with your hand open**

● Additional leverage is gained by extending the length of the lever. The best way to do this is to use a breaker bar instead of the regular length tool, or to slip a length of tubing over the end of the spanner or socket wrench.
● If additional leverage will not work, the fastener head is either damaged or firmly corroded in place (see Fasteners).

## 5 Bearings

### Bearing removal and installation

#### Drivers and sockets

● Before removing a bearing, always inspect the casing to see which way it must be driven out - some casings will have retaining plates or a cast step. Also check for any identifying markings on the bearing and if installed to a certain depth, measure this at this stage. Some roller bearings are sealed on one side - take note of the original fitted position.
● Bearings can be driven out of a casing using a bearing driver tool (with the correct size head) or a socket of the correct diameter. Select the driver head or socket so that it contacts the outer race of the bearing, not the balls/rollers or inner race. Always support the casing around the bearing housing with wood blocks, otherwise there is a risk of fracture. The bearing is driven out with a few blows on the driver or socket from a heavy mallet. Unless access is severely restricted (as with wheel bearings), a pin-punch is not recommended unless it is moved around the bearing to keep it square in its housing.

● The same equipment can be used to install bearings. Make sure the bearing housing is supported on wood blocks and line up the bearing in its housing. Fit the bearing as noted on removal - generally they are installed with their marked side facing outwards. Tap the bearing squarely into its housing using a driver or socket which bears only on the bearing's outer race - contact with the bearing balls/rollers or inner race will destroy it **(see illustrations 5.1 and 5.2)**.
● Check that the bearing inner race and balls/rollers rotate freely.

**5.1 Using a bearing driver against the bearing's outer race**

**5.2 Using a large socket against the bearing's outer race**

#### Pullers and slide-hammers

● Where a bearing is pressed on a shaft a puller will be required to extract it **(see illustration 5.3)**. Make sure that the puller clamp or legs fit securely behind the bearing and are unlikely to slip out. If pulling a bearing

**5.3 This bearing puller clamps behind the bearing and pressure is applied to the shaft end to draw the bearing off**

off a gear shaft for example, you may have to locate the puller behind a gear pinion if there is no access to the race and draw the gear pinion off the shaft as well **(see illustration 5.4)**.

> **Caution: Ensure that the puller's centre bolt locates securely against the end of the shaft and will not slip when pressure is applied. Also ensure that puller does not damage the shaft end.**

**5.4 Where no access is available to the rear of the bearing, it is sometimes possible to draw off the adjacent component**

● Operate the puller so that its centre bolt exerts pressure on the shaft end and draws the bearing off the shaft.
● When installing the bearing on the shaft, tap only on the bearing's inner race - contact with the balls/rollers or outer race with destroy the bearing. Use a socket or length of tubing as a drift which fits over the shaft end **(see illustration 5.5)**.

**5.5 When installing a bearing on a shaft use a piece of tubing which bears only on the bearing's inner race**

● Where a bearing locates in a blind hole in a casing, it cannot be driven or pulled out as described above. A slide-hammer with knife-edged bearing puller attachment will be required. The puller attachment passes through the bearing and when tightened expands to fit firmly behind the bearing **(see illustration 5.6)**. By operating the slide-hammer part of the tool the bearing is jarred out of its housing **(see illustration 5.7)**.
● It is possible, if the bearing is of reasonable weight, for it to drop out of its housing if the casing is heated as described opposite.

**5.6 Expand the bearing puller so that it locks behind the bearing . . .**

**5.7 . . . attach the slide hammer to the bearing puller**

If this method is attempted, first prepare a work surface which will enable the casing to be tapped face down to help dislodge the bearing - a wood surface is ideal since it will not damage the casing's gasket surface. Wearing protective gloves, tap the heated casing several times against the work surface to dislodge the bearing under its own weight **(see illustration 5.8)**.

**5.8 Tapping a casing face down on wood blocks can often dislodge a bearing**

● Bearings can be installed in blind holes using the driver or socket method described above.

## Drawbolts

● Where a bearing or bush is set in the eye of a component, such as a suspension linkage arm or connecting rod small-end, removal by drift may damage the component. Furthermore, a rubber bushing in a shock absorber eye cannot successfully be driven out of position. If access is available to a engineering press, the task is straightforward. If not, a drawbolt can be fabricated to extract the bearing or bush.

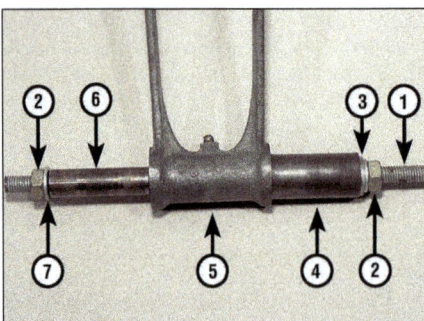

**5.9 Drawbolt component parts assembled on a suspension arm**

1  Bolt or length of threaded bar
2  Nuts
3  Washer (external diameter greater than tubing internal diameter)
4  Tubing (internal diameter sufficient to accommodate bearing)
5  Suspension arm with bearing
6  Tubing (external diameter slightly smaller than bearing)
7  Washer (external diameter slightly smaller than bearing)

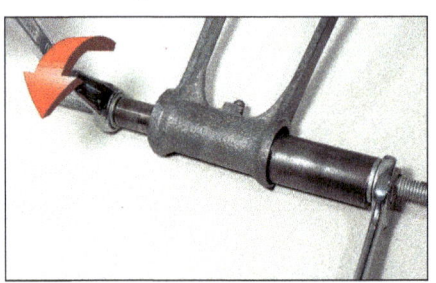

**5.10 Drawing the bearing out of the suspension arm**

● To extract the bearing/bush you will need a long bolt with nut (or piece of threaded bar with two nuts), a piece of tubing which has an internal diameter larger than the bearing/bush, another piece of tubing which has an external diameter slightly smaller than the bearing/bush, and a selection of washers **(see illustrations 5.9 and 5.10)**. Note that the pieces of tubing must be of the same length, or longer, than the bearing/bush.

● The same kit (without the pieces of tubing) can be used to draw the new bearing/bush back into place **(see illustration 5.11)**.

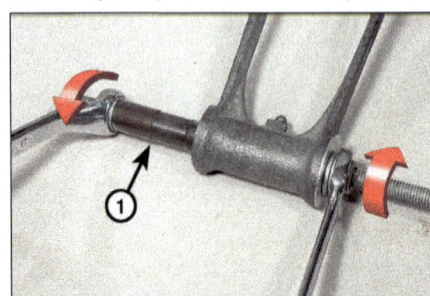

**5.11 Installing a new bearing (1) in the suspension arm**

## Temperature change

● If the bearing's outer race is a tight fit in the casing, the aluminium casing can be heated to release its grip on the bearing. Aluminium will expand at a greater rate than the steel bearing outer race. There are several ways to do this, but avoid any localised extreme heat (such as a blow torch) - aluminium alloy has a low melting point.

● Approved methods of heating a casing are using a domestic oven (heated to 100°C) or immersing the casing in boiling water **(see illustration 5.12)**. Low temperature range localised heat sources such as a paint stripper heat gun or clothes iron can also be used **(see illustration 5.13)**. Alternatively, soak a rag in boiling water, wring it out and wrap it around the bearing housing.

> ⚠️ **Warning: All of these methods require care in use to prevent scalding and burns to the hands. Wear protective gloves when handling hot components.**

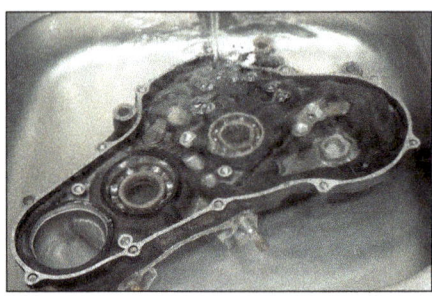

**5.12 A casing can be immersed in a sink of boiling water to aid bearing removal**

**5.13 Using a localised heat source to aid bearing removal**

● If heating the whole casing note that plastic components, such as the neutral switch, may suffer - remove them beforehand.

● After heating, remove the bearing as described above. You may find that the expansion is sufficient for the bearing to fall out of the casing under its own weight or with a light tap on the driver or socket.

● If necessary, the casing can be heated to aid bearing installation, and this is sometimes the recommended procedure if the motorcycle manufacturer has designed the housing and bearing fit with this intention.

Installation of bearings can be eased by placing them in a freezer the night before installation. The steel bearing will contract slightly, allowing easy insertion in its housing. This is often useful when installing steering head outer races in the frame.

## Bearing types and markings

Plain shell bearings, ball bearings, needle roller bearings and tapered roller bearings will all be found on motorcycles (see illustrations 5.14 and 5.15). The ball and roller types are usually caged between an inner and outer race, but uncaged variations may be found.

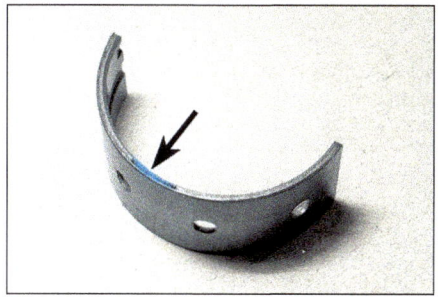

**5.14 Shell bearings are either plain or grooved. They are usually identified by colour code (arrow)**

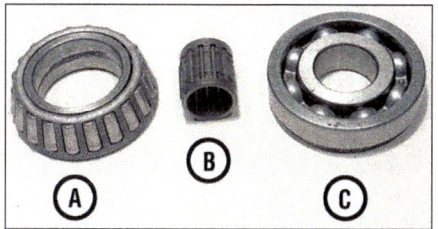

**5.15 Tapered roller bearing (A), needle roller bearing (B) and ball journal bearing (C)**

Shell bearings (often called inserts) are usually found at the crankshaft main and connecting rod big-end where they are good at coping with high loads. They are made of a phosphor-bronze material and are impregnated with self-lubricating properties.

Ball bearings and needle roller bearings consist of a steel inner and outer race with the balls or rollers between the races. They require constant lubrication by oil or grease and are good at coping with axial loads. Taper roller bearings consist of rollers set in a tapered cage set on the inner race; the outer race is separate. They are good at coping with axial loads and prevent movement along the shaft - a typical application is in the steering head.

Bearing manufacturers produce bearings to ISO size standards and stamp one face of the bearing to indicate its internal and external diameter, load capacity and type (see illustration 5.16).

Metal bushes are usually of phosphor-bronze material. Rubber bushes are used in suspension mounting eyes. Fibre bushes have also been used in suspension pivots.

**5.16 Typical bearing marking**

## Bearing fault finding

If a bearing outer race has spun in its housing, the housing material will be damaged. You can use a bearing locking compound to bond the outer race in place if damage is not too severe.

Shell bearings will fail due to damage of their working surface, as a result of lack of lubrication, corrosion or abrasive particles in the oil (see illustration 5.17). Small particles of dirt in the oil may embed in the bearing material whereas larger particles will score the bearing and shaft journal. If a number of short journeys are made, insufficient heat will be generated to drive off condensation which has built up on the bearings.

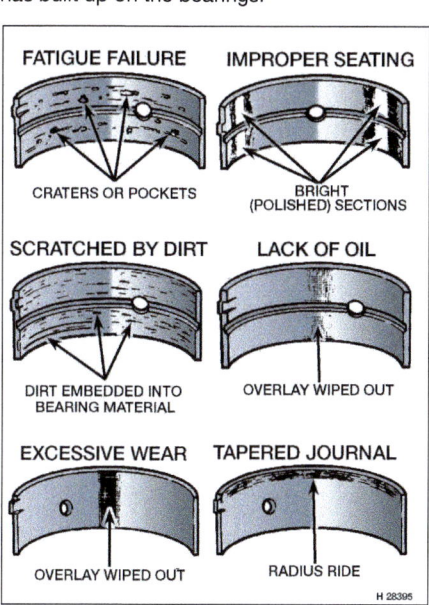

**5.17 Typical bearing failures**

Ball and roller bearings will fail due to lack of lubrication or damage to the balls or rollers. Tapered-roller bearings can be damaged by overloading them. Unless the bearing is sealed on both sides, wash it in paraffin (kerosene) to remove all old grease then allow it to dry. Make a visual inspection looking to dented balls or rollers, damaged cages and worn or pitted races (see illustration 5.18).

A ball bearing can be checked for wear by listening to it when spun. Apply a film of light oil to the bearing and hold it close to the ear - hold the outer race with one hand and spin the

**5.18 Example of ball journal bearing with damaged balls and cages**

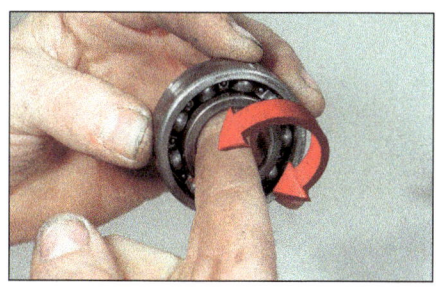

**5.19 Hold outer race and listen to inner race when spun**

inner race with the other hand (see illustration 5.19). The bearing should be almost silent when spun; if it grates or rattles it is worn.

## 6  Oil seals

## Oil seal removal and installation

Oil seals should be renewed every time a component is dismantled. This is because the seal lips will become set to the sealing surface and will not necessarily reseal.

Oil seals can be prised out of position using a large flat-bladed screwdriver (see illustration 6.1). In the case of crankcase seals, check first that the seal is not lipped on the inside, preventing its removal with the crankcases joined.

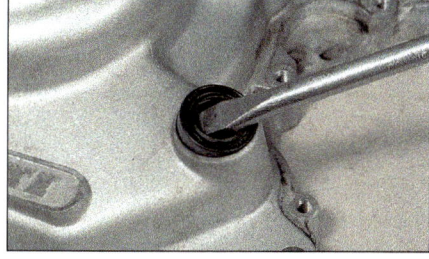

**6.1 Prise out oil seals with a large flat-bladed screwdriver**

New seals are usually installed with their marked face (containing the seal reference code) outwards and the spring side towards the fluid being retained. In certain cases, such as a two-stroke engine crankshaft seal, a double lipped seal may be used due to there being fluid or gas on each side of the joint.

● Use a bearing driver or socket which bears only on the outer hard edge of the seal to install it in the casing - tapping on the inner edge will damage the sealing lip.

### Oil seal types and markings

● Oil seals are usually of the single-lipped type. Double-lipped seals are found where a liquid or gas is on both sides of the joint.

● Oil seals can harden and lose their sealing ability if the motorcycle has been in storage for a long period - renewal is the only solution.

● Oil seal manufacturers also conform to the ISO markings for seal size - these are moulded into the outer face of the seal **(see illustration 6.2)**.

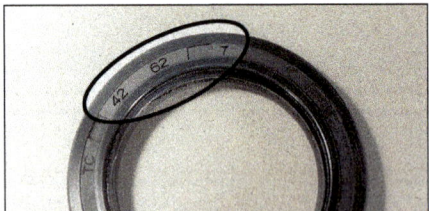

**6.2 These oil seal markings indicate inside diameter, outside diameter and seal thickness**

### 7 Gaskets and sealants

### Types of gasket and sealant

● Gaskets are used to seal the mating surfaces between components and keep lubricants, fluids, vacuum or pressure contained within the assembly. Aluminium gaskets are sometimes found at the cylinder joints, but most gaskets are paper-based. If the mating surfaces of the components being joined are undamaged the gasket can be installed dry, although a dab of sealant or grease will be useful to hold it in place during assembly.

● RTV (Room Temperature Vulcanising) silicone rubber sealants cure when exposed to moisture in the atmosphere. These sealants are good at filling pits or irregular gasket faces, but will tend to be forced out of the joint under very high torque. They can be used to replace a paper gasket, but first make sure that the width of the paper gasket is not essential to the shimming of internal components. RTV sealants should not be used on components containing petrol (gasoline).

● Non-hardening, semi-hardening and hard setting liquid gasket compounds can be used with a gasket or between a metal-to-metal joint. Select the sealant to suit the application: universal non-hardening sealant can be used on virtually all joints; semi-hardening on joint faces which are rough or damaged; hard setting sealant on joints which require a permanent bond and are subjected to high temperature and pressure. **Note:** Check first if the paper gasket has a bead of sealant

impregnated in its surface before applying additional sealant.

● When choosing a sealant, make sure it is suitable for the application, particularly if being applied in a high-temperature area or in the vicinity of fuel. Certain manufacturers produce sealants in either clear, silver or black colours to match the finish of the engine. This has a particular application on motorcycles where much of the engine is exposed.

● Do not over-apply sealant. That which is squeezed out on the outside of the joint can be wiped off, whereas an excess of sealant on the inside can break off and clog oilways.

### Breaking a sealed joint

● Age, heat, pressure and the use of hard setting sealant can cause two components to stick together so tightly that they are difficult to separate using finger pressure alone. Do not resort to using levers unless there is a pry point provided for this purpose **(see illustration 7.1)** or else the gasket surfaces will be damaged.

● Use a soft-faced hammer **(see illustration 7.2)** or a wood block and conventional hammer to strike the component near the mating surface. Avoid hammering against cast extremities since they may break off. If this method fails, try using a wood wedge between the two components.

**Caution: If the joint will not separate, double-check that you have removed all the fasteners.**

**7.1 If a pry point is provided, apply gently pressure with a flat-bladed screwdriver**

**7.2 Tap around the joint with a soft-faced mallet if necessary - don't strike cooling fins**

### Removal of old gasket and sealant

● Paper gaskets will most likely come away complete, leaving only a few traces stuck

*Most components have one or two hollow locating dowels between the two gasket faces. If a dowel cannot be removed, do not resort to gripping it with pliers - it will almost certainly be distorted. Install a close-fitting socket or Phillips screwdriver into the dowel and then grip the outer edge of the dowel to free it.*

on the sealing faces of the components. It is imperative that all traces are removed to ensure correct sealing of the new gasket.

● Very carefully scrape all traces of gasket away making sure that the sealing surfaces are not gouged or scored by the scraper **(see illustrations 7.3, 7.4 and 7.5)**. Stubborn deposits can be removed by spraying with an aerosol gasket remover. Final preparation of

**7.3 Paper gaskets can be scraped off with a gasket scraper tool . . .**

**7.4 . . . a knife blade . . .**

**7.5 . . . or a household scraper**

**7.6 Fine abrasive paper is wrapped around a flat file to clean up the gasket face**

**7.7 A kitchen scourer can be used on stubborn deposits**

the gasket surface can be made with very fine abrasive paper or a plastic kitchen scourer **(see illustrations 7.6 and 7.7)**.

● Old sealant can be scraped or peeled off components, depending on the type originally used. Note that gasket removal compounds are available to avoid scraping the components clean; make sure the gasket remover suits the type of sealant used.

## 8 Chains

### Breaking and joining final drive chains

● Drive chains for all but small bikes are continuous and do not have a clip-type connecting link. The chain must be broken using a chain breaker tool and the new chain securely riveted together using a new soft rivet-type link. Never use a clip-type connecting link instead of a rivet-type link, except in an emergency. Various chain breaking and riveting tools are available, either as separate tools or combined as illustrated in the accompanying photographs - read the instructions supplied with the tool carefully.

> ⚠ **Warning: The need to rivet the new link pins correctly cannot be overstressed - loss of control of the motorcycle is very likely to result if the chain breaks in use.**

● Rotate the chain and look for the soft link. The soft link pins look like they have been

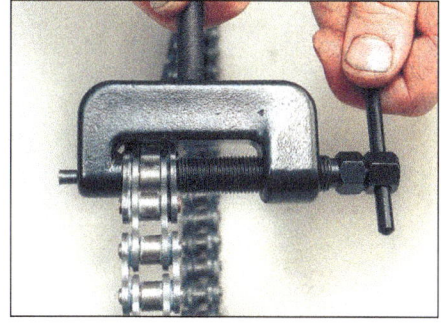

**8.1 Tighten the chain breaker to push the pin out of the link . . .**

**8.2 . . . withdraw the pin, remove the tool . . .**

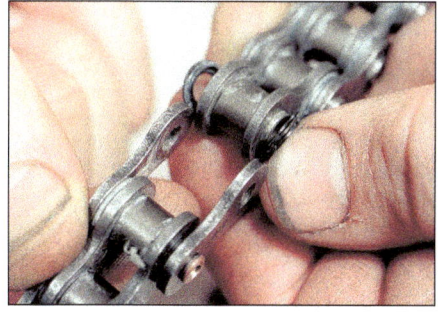

**8.3 . . . and separate the chain link**

deeply centre-punched instead of peened over like all the other pins **(see illustration 8.9)** and its sideplate may be a different colour. Position the soft link midway between the sprockets and assemble the chain breaker tool over one of the soft link pins **(see illustration 8.1)**. Operate the tool to push the pin out through the chain **(see illustration 8.2)**. On an O-ring chain, remove the O-rings **(see illustration 8.3)**. Carry out the same procedure on the other soft link pin.

> **Caution: Certain soft link pins (particularly on the larger chains) may require their ends to be filed or ground off before they can be pressed out using the tool.**

● Check that you have the correct size and strength (standard or heavy duty) new soft link - do not reuse the old link. Look for the size marking on the chain sideplates **(see illustration 8.10)**.

● Position the chain ends so that they are engaged over the rear sprocket. On an O-ring

**8.4 Insert the new soft link, with O-rings, through the chain ends . . .**

**8.5 . . . install the O-rings over the pin ends . . .**

**8.6 . . . followed by the sideplate**

chain, install a new O-ring over each pin of the link and insert the link through the two chain ends **(see illustration 8.4)**. Install a new O-ring over the end of each pin, followed by the sideplate (with the chain manufacturer's marking facing outwards) **(see illustrations 8.5 and 8.6)**. On an unsealed chain, insert the link through the two chain ends, then install the sideplate with the chain manufacturer's marking facing outwards.

● Note that it may not be possible to install the sideplate using finger pressure alone. If using a joining tool, assemble it so that the plates of the tool clamp the link and press the sideplate over the pins **(see illustration 8.7)**. Otherwise, use two small sockets placed over

**8.7 Push the sideplate into position using a clamp**

**8.8 Assemble the chain riveting tool over one pin at a time and tighten it fully**

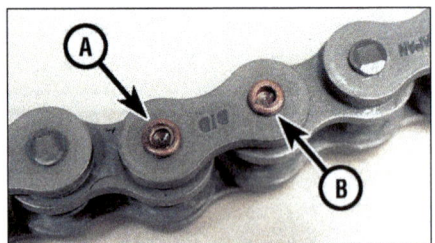

**8.9 Pin end correctly riveted (A), pin end unriveted (B)**

the rivet ends and two pieces of the wood between a G-clamp. Operate the clamp to press the sideplate over the pins.

● Assemble the joining tool over one pin (following the maker's instructions) and tighten the tool down to spread the pin end securely **(see illustrations 8.8 and 8.9)**. Do the same on the other pin.

> ⚠ **Warning: Check that the pin ends are secure and that there is no danger of the sideplate coming loose. If the pin ends are cracked the soft link must be renewed.**

### Final drive chain sizing

● Chains are sized using a three digit number, followed by a suffix to denote the chain type **(see illustration 8.10)**. Chain type is either standard or heavy duty (thicker sideplates), and also unsealed or O-ring/X-ring type.

● The first digit of the number relates to the pitch of the chain, ie the distance from the centre of one pin to the centre of the next pin **(see illustration 8.11)**. Pitch is expressed in eighths of an inch, as follows:

**8.10 Typical chain size and type marking**

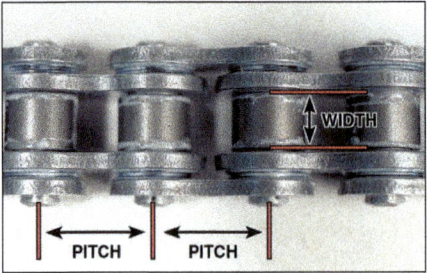

**8.11 Chain dimensions**

| Sizes commencing with a 4 (eg 428) have a pitch of 1/2 inch (12.7 mm) |
| Sizes commencing with a 5 (eg 520) have a pitch of 5/8 inch (15.9 mm) |
| Sizes commencing with a 6 (eg 630) have a pitch of 3/4 inch (19.1 mm) |

● The second and third digits of the chain size relate to the width of the rollers, again in imperial units, eg the 525 shown has 5/16 inch (7.94 mm) rollers **(see illustration 8.11)**.

### 9  Hoses

### Clamping to prevent flow

● Small-bore flexible hoses can be clamped to prevent fluid flow whilst a component is worked on. Whichever method is used, ensure that the hose material is not permanently distorted or damaged by the clamp.

a) A brake hose clamp available from auto accessory shops **(see illustration 9.1)**.

b) A wingnut type hose clamp **(see illustration 9.2)**.

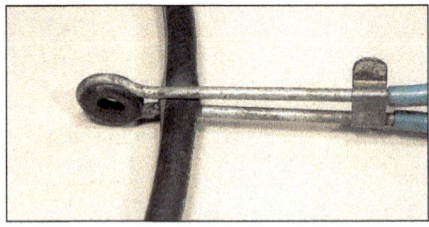

**9.1 Hoses can be clamped with an automotive brake hose clamp . . .**

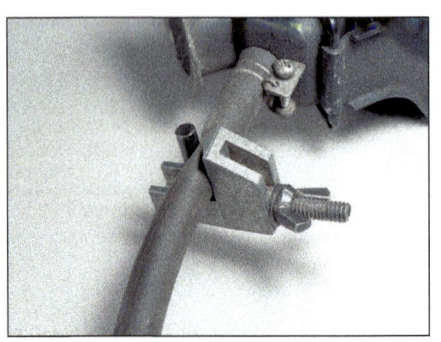

**9.2 . . . a wingnut type hose clamp . . .**

c) Two sockets placed each side of the hose and held with straight-jawed self-locking grips **(see illustration 9.3)**.

d) Thick card each side of the hose held between straight-jawed self-locking grips **(see illustration 9.4)**.

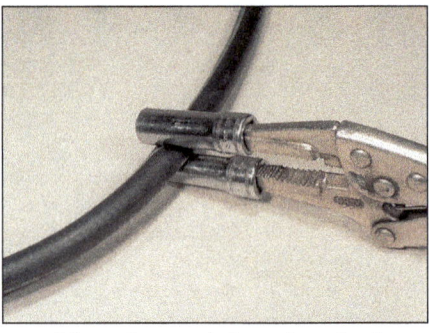

**9.3 . . . two sockets and a pair of self-locking grips . . .**

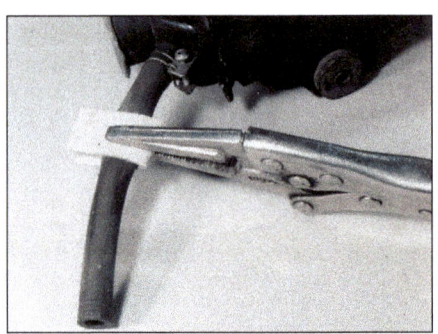

**9.4 . . . or thick card and self-locking grips**

### Freeing and fitting hoses

● Always make sure the hose clamp is moved well clear of the hose end. Grip the hose with your hand and rotate it whilst pulling it off the union. If the hose has hardened due to age and will not move, slit it with a sharp knife and peel its ends off the union **(see illustration 9.5)**.

● Resist the temptation to use grease or soap on the unions to aid installation; although it helps the hose slip over the union it will equally aid the escape of fluid from the joint. It is preferable to soften the hose ends in hot water and wet the inside surface of the hose with water or a fluid which will evaporate.

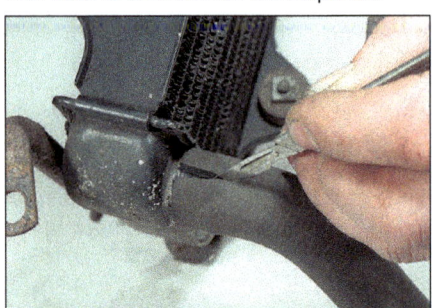

**9.5 Cutting a coolant hose free with a sharp knife**

## Introduction

In less time than it takes to read this introduction, a thief could steal your motorcycle. Returning only to find your bike has gone is one of the worst feelings in the world. Even if the motorcycle is insured against theft, once you've got over the initial shock, you will have the inconvenience of dealing with the police and your insurance company.

The motorcycle is an easy target for the professional thief and the joyrider alike and the official figures on motorcycle theft make for depressing reading; on average a motor-cycle is stolen every 16 minutes in the UK!

Motorcycle thefts fall into two categories, those stolen 'to order' and those taken by opportunists. The thief stealing to order will be on the look out for a specific make and model and will go to extraordinary lengths to obtain that motorcycle. The opportunist thief on the other hand will look for easy targets which can be stolen with the minimum of effort and risk.

Whilst it is never going to be possible to make your machine 100% secure, it is estimated that around half of all stolen motorcycles are taken by opportunist thieves. Remember that the opportunist thief is always on the look out for the easy option: if there are two similar motorcycles parked side-by-side, they will target the one with the lowest level of security. By taking a few precautions, you can reduce the chances of your motorcycle being stolen.

# Security equipment

There are many specialised motorcycle security devices available and the following text summarises their applications and their good and bad points.

Once you have decided on the type of security equipment which best suits your needs, we recommended that you read one of the many equipment tests regularly carried out by the motorcycle press. These tests

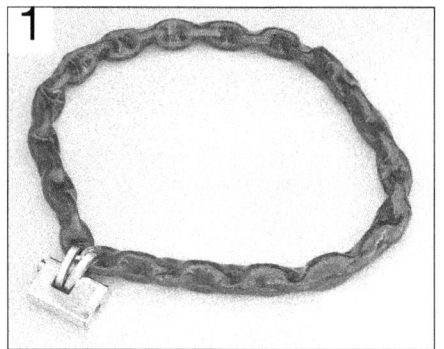

Ensure the lock and chain you buy is of good quality and long enough to shackle your bike to a solid object

compare the products from all the major manufacturers and give impartial ratings on their effectiveness, value-for-money and ease of use.

No one item of security equipment can provide complete protection. It is highly recommended that two or more of the items described below are combined to increase the security of your motorcycle (a lock and chain plus an alarm system is just about ideal). The more security measures fitted to the bike, the less likely it is to be stolen.

### Lock and chain

Pros: *Very flexible to use; can be used to secure the motorcycle to almost any immovable object. On some locks and chains, the lock can be used on its own as a disc lock (see below).*

Cons: *Can be very heavy and awkward to carry on the motorcycle, although some types*

*will be supplied with a carry bag which can be strapped to the pillion seat.*

● Heavy-duty chains and locks are an excellent security measure **(see illustration 1).** Whenever the motorcycle is parked, use the lock and chain to secure the machine to a solid, immovable object such as a post or railings. This will prevent the machine from being ridden away or being lifted into the back of a van.

● When fitting the chain, always ensure the chain is routed around the motorcycle frame or swingarm **(see illustrations 2 and 3).** Never merely pass the chain around one of the wheel rims; a thief may unbolt the wheel and lift the rest of the machine into a van, leaving you with just the wheel! Try to avoid having excess chain free, thus making it difficult to use cutting tools, and keep the chain and lock off the ground to prevent thieves attacking it with a cold chisel. Position the lock so that its lock barrel is facing downwards; this will make it harder for the thief to attack the lock mechanism.

Pass the chain through the bike's frame, rather than just through a wheel . . .

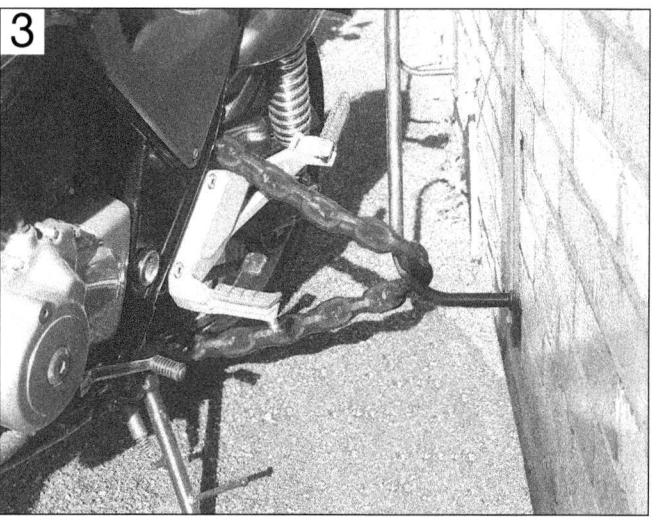

. . . and loop it around a solid object

## U-locks

**Pros:** *Highly effective deterrent which can be used to secure the bike to a post or railings. Most U-locks come with a carrier which allows the lock to be easily carried on the bike.*

**Cons:** *Not as flexible to use as a lock and chain.*

● These are solid locks which are similar in use to a lock and chain. U-locks are lighter than a lock and chain but not so flexible to use. The length and shape of the lock shackle limit the objects to which the bike can be secured **(see illustration 4)**.

## Disc locks

**Pros:** *Small, light and very easy to carry; most can be stored underneath the seat.*

**Cons:** *Does not prevent the motorcycle being lifted into a van. Can be very embarrassing if*

A typical disc lock attached through one of the holes in the disc

U-locks can be used to secure the bike to a solid object – ensure you purchase one which is long enough

you forget to remove the lock before attempting to ride off!

● Disc locks are designed to be attached to the front brake disc. The lock passes through one of the holes in the disc and prevents the wheel rotating by jamming against the fork/ brake caliper **(see illustration 5)**. Some are equipped with an alarm siren which sounds if the disc lock is moved; this not only acts as a theft deterrent but also as a handy reminder if you try to move the bike with the lock still fitted.

● Combining the disc lock with a length of cable which can be looped around a post or railings provides an additional measure of security **(see illustration 6)**.

## Alarms and immobilisers

**Pros:** *Once installed it is completely hassle-free to use. If the system is 'Thatcham' or 'Sold Secure-approved', insurance companies may give you a discount.*

**Cons:** *Can be expensive to buy and complex to install. No system will prevent the motorcycle from being lifted into a van and taken away.*

● Electronic alarms and immobilisers are available to suit a variety of budgets. There are three different types of system available: pure alarms, pure immobilisers, and the more expensive systems which are combined alarm/immobilisers **(see illustration 7)**.
● An alarm system is designed to emit an audible warning if the motorcycle is being tampered with.
● An immobiliser prevents the motorcycle being started and ridden away by disabling its electrical systems.
● When purchasing an alarm/immobiliser system, check the cost of installing the system unless you are able to do it yourself. If the motorcycle is not used regularly, another consideration is the current drain of the system. All alarm/immobiliser systems are powered by the motorcycle's battery; purchasing a system with a very low current drain could prevent the battery losing its charge whilst the motorcycle is not being used.

A disc lock combined with a security cable provides additional protection

A typical alarm/immobiliser system

Indelible markings can be applied to most areas of the bike – always apply the manufacturer's sticker to warn off thieves

Chemically-etched code numbers can be applied to main body panels . . .

. . . again, always ensure that the kit manufacturer's sticker is applied in a prominent position

## Security marking kits

**Pros:** *Very cheap and effective deterrent. Many insurance companies will give you a discount on your insurance premium if a recognised security marking kit is used on your motorcycle.*

**Cons:** *Does not prevent the motorcycle being stolen by joyriders.*

● There are many different types of security marking kits available. The idea is to mark as many parts of the motorcycle as possible with a unique security number **(see illustrations 8, 9 and 10)**. A form will be included with the kit to register your personal details and those of the motorcycle with the kit manufacturer. This register is made available to the police to help them trace the rightful owner of any motorcycle or components which they recover should all other forms of identification have been removed. Always apply the warning stickers provided with the kit to deter thieves.

## Ground anchors, wheel clamps and security posts

**Pros:** *An excellent form of security which will deter all but the most determined of thieves.*

**Cons:** *Awkward to install and can be expensive.*

● Whilst the motorcycle is at home, it is a good idea to attach it securely to the floor or a solid wall, even if it is kept in a securely locked garage. Various types of ground anchors, security posts and wheel clamps are available for this purpose **(see illustration 11)**. These security devices are either bolted to a solid concrete or brick structure or can be cemented into the ground.

Permanent ground anchors provide an excellent level of security when the bike is at home

# Security at home

A high percentage of motorcycle thefts are from the owner's home. Here are some things to consider whenever your motorcycle is at home:
● Where possible, always keep the motorcycle in a securely locked garage. Never rely solely on the standard lock on the garage door, these are usual hopelessly inadequate. Fit an additional locking mechanism to the door and consider having the garage alarmed. A security light, activated by a movement sensor, is also a good investment.

● Always secure the motorcycle to the ground or a wall, even if it is inside a securely locked garage.
● Do not regularly leave the motorcycle outside your home, try to keep it out of sight wherever possible. If a garage is not available, fit a motorcycle cover over the bike to disguise its true identity.
● It is not uncommon for thieves to follow a motorcyclist home to find out where the bike is kept. They will then return at a later date. Be aware of this whenever you are returning

home on your motorcycle. If you suspect you are being followed, do not return home, instead ride to a garage or shop and stop as a precaution.
● When selling a motorcycle, do not provide your home address or the location where the bike is normally kept. Arrange to meet the buyer at a location away from your home. Thieves have been known to pose as potential buyers to find out where motorcycles are kept and then return later to steal them.

# Security away from the home

As well as fitting security equipment to your motorcycle here are a few general rules to follow whenever you park your motorcycle.
● Park in a busy, public place.
● Use car parks which incorporate security features, such as CCTV.

● At night, park in a well-lit area, preferably directly underneath a street light.
● Engage the steering lock.
● Secure the motorcycle to a solid, immovable object such as a post or railings with an additional lock. If this is not possible,

secure the bike to a friend's motorcycle. Some public parking places provide security loops for motorcycles.
● Never leave your helmet or luggage attached to the motorcycle. Take them with you at all times.

# Lubricants and fluids

A wide range of lubricants, fluids and cleaning agents is available for motor-cycles. This is a guide as to what is available, its applications and properties.

## Four-stroke engine oil

● Engine oil is without doubt the most important component of any four-stroke engine. Modern motorcycle engines place a lot of demands on their oil and choosing the right type is essential. Using an unsuitable oil will lead to an increased rate of engine wear and could result in serious engine damage. Before purchasing oil, always check the recommended oil specification given by the manufacturer. The manufacturer will state a recommended 'type or classification' and also a specific 'viscosity' range for engine oil.

● The oil 'type or classification' is identified by its API (American Petroleum Institute) rating. The API rating will be in the form of two letters, e.g. SG. The S identifies the oil as being suitable for use in a petrol (gasoline) engine (S stands for spark ignition) and the second letter, ranging from A to J, identifies the oil's performance rating. The later this letter, the higher the specification of the oil; for example API SG oil exceeds the requirements of API SF oil. **Note:** *On some oils there may also be a second rating consisting of another two letters, the first letter being C, e.g. API SF/CD. This rating indicates the oil is also suitable for use in a diesel engines (the C stands for compression ignition) and is thus of no relevance for motorcycle use.*

● The 'viscosity' of the oil is identified by its SAE (Society of Automotive Engineers) rating. All modern engines require multigrade oils and the SAE rating will consist of two numbers, the first followed by a W, e.g. 10W/40. The first number indicates the viscosity rating of the oil at low temperatures (W stands for winter – tested at –20°C) and the second number represents the viscosity of the oil at high temperatures (tested at 100°C). The lower the number, the thinner the oil. For example an oil with an SAE 10W/40 rating will give better cold starting and running than an SAE 15W/40 oil.

● As well as ensuring the 'type' and 'viscosity' of the oil match the recommendations, another consideration to make when buying engine oil is whether to purchase a standard mineral-based oil, a semi-synthetic oil (also known as a synthetic blend or synthetic-based oil) or a fully-synthetic oil. Although all oils will have a similar rating and viscosity, their cost will vary considerably; mineral-based oils are the cheapest, the fully-synthetic oils the most expensive with the semi-synthetic oils falling somewhere in-between. This decision is very much up to the owner, but it should be noted that modern synthetic oils have far better lubricating and cleaning qualities than traditional mineral-based oils and tend to retain these properties for far longer. Bearing in mind the operating conditions inside a modern, high-revving motorcycle engine it is highly recommended that a fully synthetic oil is used. The extra expense at each service could save you money in the long term by preventing premature engine wear.

● As a final note always ensure that the oil is specifically designed for use in motorcycle engines. Engine oils designed primarily for use in car engines sometimes contain additives or friction modifiers which could cause clutch slip on a motorcycle fitted with a wet-clutch.

## Two-stroke engine oil

● Modern two-stroke engines, with their high power outputs, place high demands on their oil. If engine seizure is to be avoided it is essential that a high-quality oil is used. Two-stroke oils differ hugely from four-stroke oils. The oil lubricates only the crankshaft and piston(s) (the transmission has its own lubricating oil) and is used on a total-loss basis where it is burnt completely during the combustion process.

● The Japanese have recently introduced a classification system for two-stroke oils, the JASO rating. This rating is in the form of two letters, either FA, FB or FC – FA is the lowest classification and FC the highest. Ensure the oil being used meets or exceeds the recommended rating specified by the manufacturer.

● As well as ensuring the oil rating matches the recommendation, another consideration to make when buying engine oil is whether to purchase a standard mineral-based oil, a semi-synthetic oil (also known as a synthetic blend or synthetic-based oil) or a fully-synthetic oil. The cost of each type of oil varies considerably; mineral-based oils are the cheapest, the fully-synthetic oils the most expensive with the semi-synthetic oils falling somewhere in-between. This decision is very much up to the owner, but it should be noted that modern synthetic oils have far better lubricating properties and burn cleaner than traditional mineral-based oils. It is therefore recommended that a fully synthetic oil is used. The extra expense could save you money in the long term by preventing premature engine wear, engine performance will be improved, carbon deposits and exhaust smoke will be reduced.

Always ensure that the oil is specifically designed for use in an injector system. Many high quality two-stroke oils are designed for competition use and need to be pre-mixed with fuel. These oils are of a much higher viscosity and are not designed to flow through the injector pumps used on road-going two-stroke motorcycles.

## Transmission (gear) oil

On a two-stroke engine, the transmission and clutch are lubricated by their own separate oil bath which must be changed in accordance with the Maintenance Schedule.

Although the engine and transmission units of most four-strokes use a common lubrication supply, there are some exceptions where the engine and gearbox have separate oil reservoirs and a dry clutch is used.

Motorcycle manufacturers will either recommend a monograde transmission oil or a four-stroke multigrade engine oil to lubricate the transmission.

Transmission oils, or gear oils as they are often called, are designed specifically for use in transmission systems. The viscosity of these oils is represented by an SAE number, but the scale of measurement applied is different to that used to grade engine oils. As a rough guide a SAE90 gear oil will be of the same viscosity as an SAE50 engine oil.

## Shaft drive oil

On models equipped with shaft final drive, the shaft drive gears are will have their own oil supply. The manufacturer will state a recommended 'type or classification' and also a specific 'viscosity' range in the same manner as for four-stroke engine oil.

Gear oil classification is given by the number which follows the API GL (GL standing for gear lubricant) rating, the higher the number, the higher the specification of the oil, e.g. API GL5 oil is a higher specification than API GL4 oil. Ensure the oil meets or

exceeds the classification specified and is of the correct viscosity. The viscosity of gear oils is also represented by an SAE number but the scale of measurement used is different to that used to grade engine oils. As a rough guide an SAE90 gear oil will be of the same viscosity as an SAE50 engine oil.

If the use of an EP (Extreme Pressure) gear oil is specified, ensure the oil purchased is suitable.

## Fork oil and suspension fluid

Conventional telescopic front forks are hydraulic and require fork oil to work. To ensure the forks function correctly, the fork oil must be changed in accordance with the Maintenance Schedule.

Fork oil is available in a variety of viscosities, identified by their SAE rating; fork oil ratings vary from light (SAE 5) to heavy (SAE 30). When purchasing fork oil, ensure the viscosity rating matches that specified by the manufacturer.

Some lubricant manufacturers also produce a range of high-quality suspension fluids which are very similar to fork oil but are designed mainly for competition use. These fluids may have a different viscosity rating system which is not to be confused with the SAE rating of normal fork oil. Refer to the manufacturer's instructions if in any doubt.

## Brake and clutch fluid

All disc brake systems and some clutch systems are hydraulically operated. To ensure correct operation, the hydraulic fluid must be changed in accordance with the Maintenance Schedule.

Brake and clutch fluid is classified by its DOT rating with most motorcycle manufacturers specifying DOT 3 or 4 fluid. Both fluid types are glycol-based

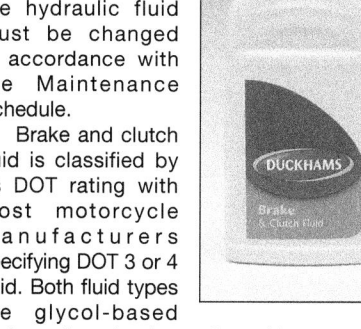

and can be mixed together without adverse effect; DOT 4 fluid exceeds the requirements

of DOT 3 fluid. Although it is safe to use DOT 4 fluid in a system designed for use with DOT 3 fluid, never use DOT 3 fluid in a system which specifies the use of DOT 4 as this will adversely affect the system's performance. The type required for the system will be marked on the fluid reservoir cap.

Some manufacturers also produce a DOT 5 hydraulic fluid. DOT 5 hydraulic fluid is silicone-based and is not compatible with the glycol-based DOT 3 and 4 fluids. Never mix DOT 5 fluid with DOT 3 or 4 fluid as this will seriously affect the performance of the hydraulic system.

## Coolant/antifreeze

When purchasing coolant/antifreeze, always ensure it is suitable for use in an aluminium engine and contains corrosion inhibitors to prevent possible blockages of the internal coolant passages of the system. As a general rule, most coolants are designed to be used neat and should not be diluted whereas antifreeze can be mixed with distilled water to provide a coolant solution of the required strength. Refer to the manufacturer's instructions on the bottle.

Ensure the coolant is changed in accordance with the Maintenance Schedule.

## Chain lube

Chain lube is an aerosol-type spray lubricant specifically designed for use on motorcycle final drive chains. Chain lube has two functions, to minimise friction between the final drive chain and sprockets and to prevent corrosion of the chain. Regular use of a good-quality chain lube will extend the life of the drive chain and sprockets and thus maximise the power being transmitted from the transmission to the rear wheel.

When using chain lube, always allow some time for the solvents in the lube to evaporate before riding the motorcycle. This will minimise the amount of lube which will 'fling' off from the chain when the motorcycle is used. If the motorcycle is equipped with an 'O-ring' chain, ensure the chain lube is labelled as being suitable for use on 'O-ring' chains.

## Degreasers and solvents

● There are many different types of solvents and degreasers available to remove the grime and grease which accumulate around the motorcycle during normal use. Degreasers and solvents are usually available as an aerosol-type spray or as a liquid which you apply with a brush. Always closely follow the manufacturer's instructions and wear eye protection during use. Be aware that many solvents are flammable and may give off noxious fumes; take adequate precautions when using them (see *Safety First!*).

● For general cleaning, use one of the many solvents or degreasers available from most motorcycle accessory shops. These solvents are usually applied then left for a certain time before being washed off with water.

**Brake cleaner** is a solvent specifically designed to remove all traces of oil, grease and dust from braking system components. Brake cleaner is designed to evaporate quickly and leaves behind no residue.

**Carburettor cleaner** is an aerosol-type solvent specifically designed to clear carburettor blockages and break down the hard deposits and gum often found inside carburettors during overhaul.

**Contact cleaner** is an aerosol-type solvent designed for cleaning electrical components. The cleaner will remove all traces of oil and dirt from components such as switch contacts or fouled spark plugs and then dry, leaving behind no residue.

**Gasket remover** is an aerosol-type solvent designed for removing stubborn gaskets from engine components during overhaul. Gasket remover will minimise the amount of scraping required to remove the gasket and therefore reduce the risk of damage to the mating surface.

## Spray lubricants

● Aerosol-based spray lubricants are widely available and are excellent for lubricating lever pivots and exposed cables and switches. Try to use a lubricant which is of the dry-film type as the fluid evaporates, leaving behind a dry-film of lubricant. Lubricants which leave behind an oily residue will attract dust and dirt which will increase the rate of wear of the cable/lever.

● Most lubricants also act as a moisture dispersant and a penetrating fluid. This means they can also be used to 'dry out' electrical components such as wiring connectors or switches as well as helping to free seized fasteners.

## Greases

● Grease is used to lubricate many of the pivot-points. A good-quality multi-purpose grease is suitable for most applications but some manufacturers will specify the use of specialist greases for use on components such as swingarm and suspension linkage bushes. These specialist greases can be purchased from most motorcycle (or car) accessory shops; commonly specified types include molybdenum disulphide grease, lithium-based grease, graphite-based grease, silicone-based grease and high-temperature copper-based grease.

## Gasket sealing compounds

● Gasket sealing compounds can be used in conjunction with gaskets, to improve their sealing capabilities, or on their own to seal metal-to-metal joints. Depending on their type, sealing compounds either set hard or stay relatively soft and pliable.

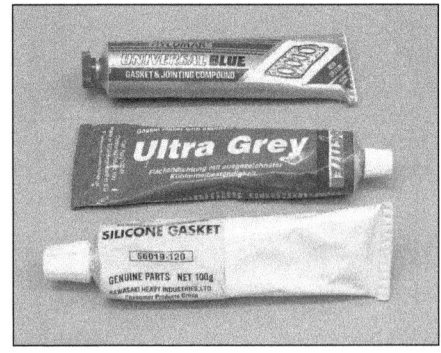

● When purchasing a gasket sealing compound, ensure that it is designed specifically for use on an internal combustion engine. General multi-purpose sealants available from DIY stores may appear visibly similar but they are not designed to withstand the extreme heat or contact with fuel and oil encountered when used on an engine (see *'Tools and Workshop Tips'* for further information).

## Thread locking compound

● Thread locking compounds are used to secure certain threaded fasteners in position to prevent them from loosening due to vibration. Thread locking compounds can be purchased from most motorcycle (and car) accessory shops. Ensure the threads of the both components are completely clean and dry before sparingly applying the locking compound (see *'Tools and Workshop Tips'* for further information).

## Fuel additives

● Fuel additives which protect and clean the fuel system components are widely available. These additives are designed to remove all traces of deposits that build up on the carburettors/injectors and prevent wear, helping the fuel system to operate more efficiently. If a fuel additive is being used, check that it is suitable for use with your motorcycle, especially if your motorcycle is equipped with a catalytic converter.

● Octane boosters are also available. These additives are designed to improve the performance of highly-tuned engines being run on normal pump-fuel and are of no real use on standard motorcycles.

## About the MOT Test

In the UK, all vehicles more than three years old are subject to an annual test to ensure that they meet minimum safety requirements. A current test certificate must be issued before a machine can be used on public roads, and is required before a road fund licence can be issued. Riding without a current test certificate will also invalidate your insurance.

For most owners, the MOT test is an annual cause for anxiety, and this is largely due to owners not being sure what needs to be checked prior to submitting the motorcycle for testing. The simple answer is that a fully roadworthy motorcycle will have no difficulty in passing the test.

This is a guide to getting your motorcycle through the MOT test. Obviously it will not be possible to examine the motorcycle to the same standard as the professional MOT tester, particularly in view of the equipment required for some of the checks. However, working through the following procedures will enable you to identify any problem areas before submitting the motorcycle for the test.

It has only been possible to summarise the test requirements here, based on the regulations in force at the time of printing. Test standards are becoming increasingly stringent, although there are some exemptions for older vehicles. More information about the test can be obtained from the MOT Inspection Manual for Motor Bicycle and Side Car Testing at www.gov.uk

Many of the checks require that one of the wheels is raised off the ground. If the motorcycle doesn't have a centre stand, note that an auxiliary stand will be required. Additionally, the help of an assistant may prove useful.

Certain exceptions apply to machines under 50 cc, machines without a lighting system, and Classic bikes - if in doubt about any of the requirements listed below seek confirmation from an MOT tester prior to submitting the motorcycle for the test.

Check that the frame number is clearly visible.

# Electrical System

### Lights, turn signals, horn and reflector

● With the ignition on, check the operation of the following electrical components. **Note:** *The electrical components on certain small-capacity machines are powered by the generator, requiring that the engine is run for this check.*

a) *Headlight and tail light. Check that both illuminate in the low and high beam switch positions.*
b) *Position lights. Check that the front position (or sidelight) and tail light illuminate in this switch position.*
c) *Turn signals. Check that all flash at the correct rate, and that the warning light(s) function correctly. Check that the turn signal switch works correctly.*
d) *Hazard warning system (where fitted). Check that all four turn signals flash in this switch position.*
e) *Brake stop light. Check that the light comes on when the front and rear brakes are independently applied. Models first used on or after 1st April 1986 must have a brake light switch on each brake.*
f) *Horn. Check that the sound is continuous and of reasonable volume.*

● Check that there is a red reflector on the rear of the machine, either mounted separately or as part of the tail light lens.
● Check the condition of the headlight, tail light and turn signal lenses.

### Headlight beam height

● The MOT tester will perform a headlight beam height check using specialised beam setting equipment **(see illustration 1)**. This equipment will not be available to the home mechanic, but if you suspect that the headlight is incorrectly set or may have been maladjusted in the past, you can perform a rough test as follows.
● Position the bike in a straight line facing a brick wall. The bike must be off its stand, upright and with a rider seated. Measure the height from the ground to the centre of the headlight and mark a horizontal line on the wall at this height. Position the motorcycle 3.8 metres from the wall and draw a vertical

**Headlight beam height checking equipment**

line up the wall central to the centreline of the motorcycle. Switch to dipped beam and check that the beam pattern falls slightly lower than the horizontal line and to the left of the vertical line **(see illustration 2)**.

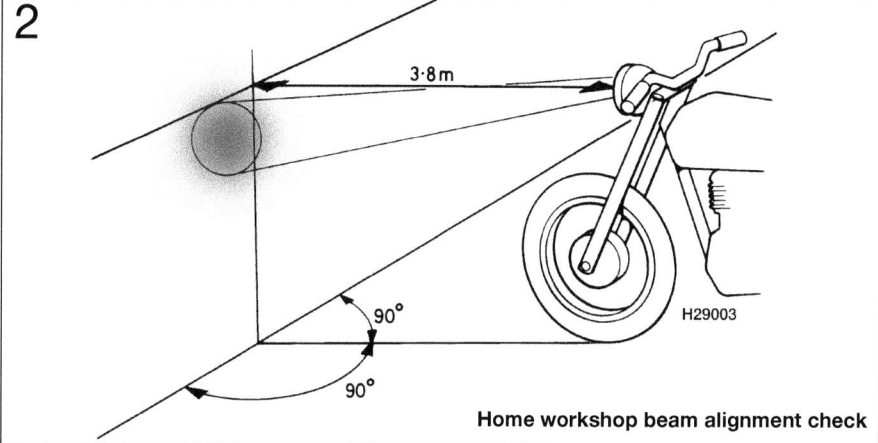

**Home workshop beam alignment check**

# Exhaust System and Final Drive

### Exhaust

● Check that the exhaust mountings are secure and that the system does not foul any of the rear suspension components.
● Start the motorcycle. When the revs are increased, check that the exhaust is neither holed nor leaking from any of its joints. On a linked system, check that the collector box is not leaking due to corrosion.

● Note that the exhaust decibel level ("loudness" of the exhaust) is assessed at the discretion of the tester. If the motorcycle was first used on or after 1st January 1985 the silencer must carry the BSAU 193 stamp, or a marking relating to its make and model, or be of OE (original equipment) manufacture. If the silencer is marked NOT FOR ROAD USE, RACING USE ONLY or similar, it will fail the MOT.

### Final drive

● On chain or belt drive machines, check that the chain/belt is in good condition and does not have excessive slack. Also check that the sprocket is securely mounted on the rear wheel hub. Check that the chain/belt guard is in place.
● On shaft drive bikes, check for oil leaking from the drive unit and fouling the rear tyre.

# Steering and Suspension

### Steering

● With the front wheel raised off the ground, rotate the steering from lock to lock. The handlebar or switches must not contact the fuel tank or be close enough to trap the rider's hand. Problems can be caused by damaged lock stops on the lower yoke and frame, or by the fitting of non-standard handlebars.
● When performing the lock to lock check, also ensure that the steering moves freely without drag or notchiness. Steering movement can be impaired by poorly routed cables, or by overtight head bearings or worn bvearings. The tester will perform a check of the steering head bearing lower race by mounting the front wheel on a surface plate, then performing a lock to

lock check with the weight of the machine on the lower bearing (see illustration 3).
● Grasp the fork sliders (lower legs) and attempt to push and pull on the forks

Front wheel mounted on a surface plate for steering head bearing lower race check

(see illustration 4). Any play in the steering head bearings will be felt. Note that in extreme cases, wear of the front fork bushes can be misinterpreted for head bearing play.
● Check that the handlebars are securely mounted.
● Check that the handlebar grip rubbers are secure. They should by bonded to the bar left end and to the throttle cable pulley on the right end.

### Front suspension

● With the motorcycle off the stand, hold the front brake on and pump the front forks up and down (see illustration 5). Check that they are adequately damped.

Checking the steering head bearings for freeplay

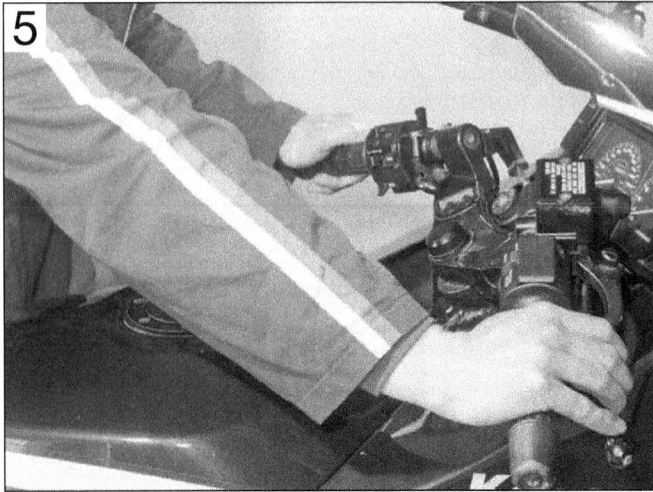

Hold the front brake on and pump the front forks up and down to check operation

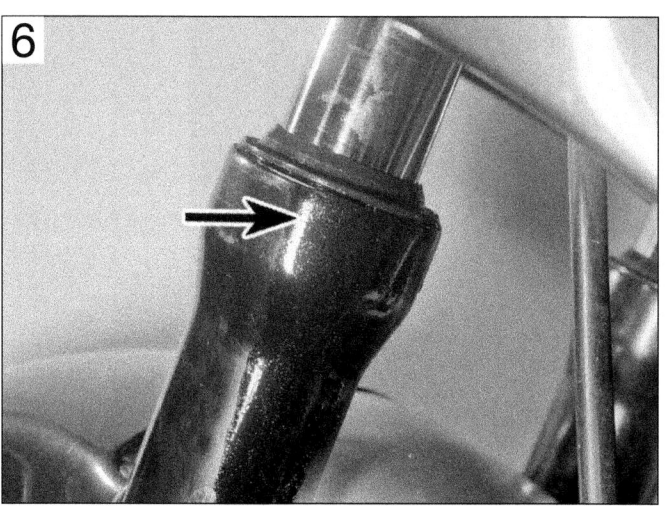

Inspect the area around the fork dust seal for oil leakage (arrow)

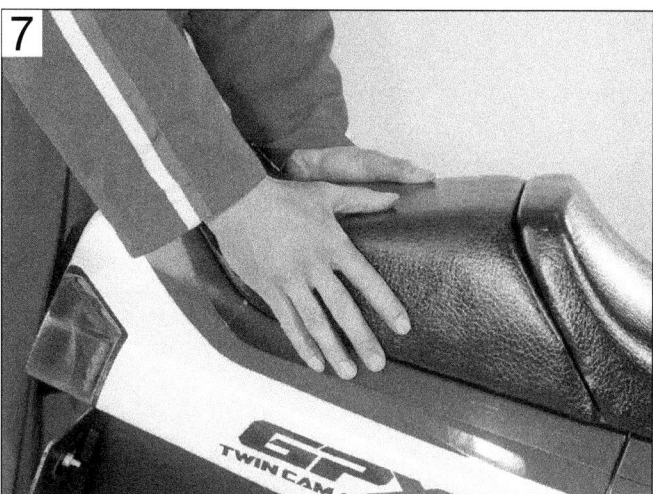

Bounce the rear of the motorcycle to check rear suspension operation

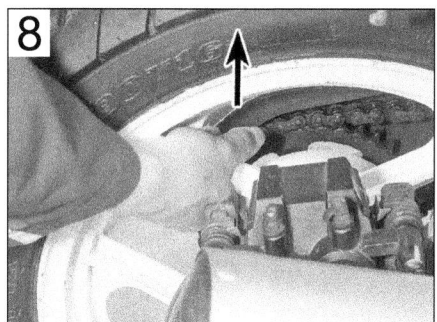

Checking for rear suspension linkage play

● Inspect the area above and around the front fork oil seals **(see illustration 6)**. There should be no sign of oil on the fork tube (stanchion) nor leaking down the slider (lower leg). On models so equipped, check that there is no oil leaking from the anti-dive units.
● On models with swingarm front suspension, check that there is no freeplay in the linkage when moved from side to side.

## Rear suspension

● With the motorcycle off the stand and an assistant supporting the motorcycle by its handlebars, bounce the rear suspension **(see illustration 7)**. Check that the suspension components do not foul on any of the cycle parts and check that the shock absorber(s) provide adequate damping.
● Visually inspect the shock absorber(s) and check that there is no sign of oil leakage from its damper. This is somewhat restricted on certain single shock models due to the location of the shock absorber.
● With the rear wheel raised off the ground, grasp the wheel at the highest point and attempt to pull it up **(see illustration 8)**. Any play in the swingarm pivot or suspension linkage bearings will be felt as movement. **Note:** *Do not confuse play with actual suspension movement.* Failure to lubricate suspension linkage bearings can lead to bearing failure **(see illustration 9)**.
● With the rear wheel raised off the ground, grasp the swingarm ends and attempt to move the swingarm from side to side and forwards and backwards - any play indicates wear of the swingarm pivot bearings **(see illustration 10)**.

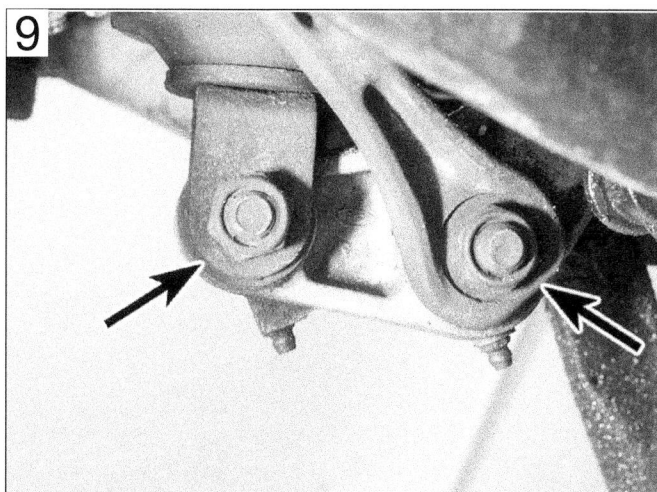

Worn suspension linkage pivots (arrows) are usually the cause of play in the rear suspension

Grasp the swingarm at the ends to check for play in its pivot bearings

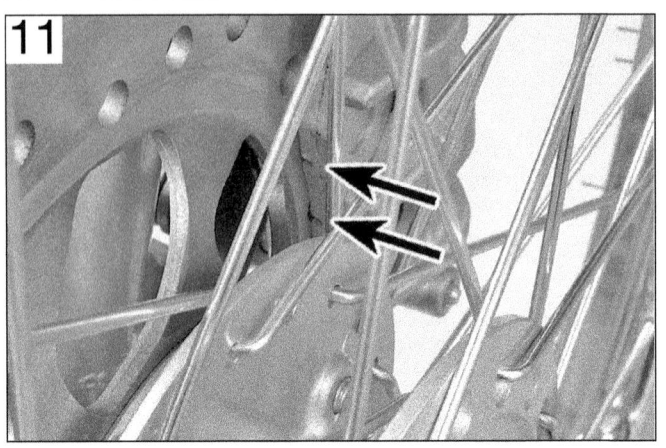

Brake pad wear can usually be viewed without removing the caliper. Most pads have wear indicator grooves (arrowed) and some also have indicator tangs or cut-outs.

On drum brakes, check the angle of the operating lever with the brake fully applied. Most drum brakes have a wear indicator pointer or scale.

# Brakes, Wheels and Tyres

## Brakes

● With the wheel raised off the ground, apply the brake then free it off, and check that the wheel is about to revolve freely without brake drag.

● On disc brakes, examine the disc itself. Check that it is securely mounted and not cracked.

● On disc brakes, view the pad material through the caliper mouth and check that the pads are not worn down beyond the limit **(see illustration 11)**.

● On drum brakes, check that when the brake is applied the angle between the operating lever and cable or rod is not too great **(see illustration 12)**. Check also that the operating lever doesn't foul any other components.

● On disc brakes, examine the flexible hoses from top to bottom. Have an assistant hold the brake on so that the fluid in the hose is under pressure, and check that there is no sign of fluid leakage, bulges or cracking. If there are any metal brake pipes or unions, check that these are free from corrosion and damage. Where a brake-linked anti-dive system is fitted, check the hoses to the anti-dive in a similar manner.

● Check that the rear brake torque arm is secure and that its fasteners are secured by self-locking nuts or castellated nuts with split-pins or R-pins **(see illustration 13)**.

● On models with ABS, check that the self-check warning light in the instrument panel works.

● The MOT tester will perform a test of the motorcycle's braking efficiency based on a calculation of rider and motorcycle weight. Although this cannot be carried out at home, you can at least ensure that the braking systems are properly maintained. For hydraulic disc brakes, check the fluid level, lever/pedal feel (bleed of air if its spongy) and pad material. For drum brakes, check adjustment, cable or rod operation and shoe lining thickness.

## Wheels and tyres

● Check the wheel condition. Cast wheels should be free from cracks and if of the built-up design, all fasteners should be secure. Spoked wheels should be checked for broken, corroded, loose or bent spokes.

● With the wheel raised off the ground, spin the wheel and visually check that the tyre and wheel run true. Check that the tyre does not foul the suspension or mudguards.

● With the wheel raised off the ground, grasp the wheel and attempt to move it about the axle (spindle) **(see illustration 14)**. Any play felt here indicates wheel bearing failure.

Brake torque arm must be properly secured at both ends

Check for wheel bearing play by trying to move the wheel about the axle (spindle)

Checking the tyre tread depth

Tyre direction of rotation arrow can be found on tyre sidewall

Castellated type wheel axle (spindle) nut must be secured by a split pin or R-pin

Two straightedges are used to check wheel alignment

● Check the tyre tread depth, tread condition and sidewall condition **(see illustration 15)**.
● Check the tyre type. Front and rear tyre types must be compatible and be suitable for road use. Tyres marked NOT FOR ROAD USE, COMPETITION USE ONLY or similar, will fail the MOT.

● If the tyre sidewall carries a direction of rotation arrow, this must be pointing in the direction of normal wheel rotation **(see illustration 16)**.
● Check that the wheel axle (spindle) nuts (where applicable) are properly secured. A self-locking nut or castellated nut with a split-pin or R-pin can be used **(see illustration 17)**.
● Wheel alignment is checked with the motorcycle off the stand and a rider seated. With the front wheel pointing straight ahead, two perfectly straight lengths of metal or wood and placed against the sidewalls of both tyres **(see illustration 18)**. The gap each side of the front tyre must be equidistant on both sides. Incorrect wheel alignment may be due to a cocked rear wheel (often as the result of poor chain adjustment) or in extreme cases, a bent frame.

# General checks and condition

● Check the security of all major fasteners, bodypanels, seat, fairings (where fitted) and mudguards.

● Check that the rider and pillion footrests, handlebar levers and brake pedal are securely mounted.

● Check for corrosion on the frame or any load-bearing components. If severe, this may affect the structure, particularly under stress.

# Sidecars

A motorcycle fitted with a sidecar requires additional checks relating to the stability of the machine and security of attachment and swivel joints, plus specific wheel alignment (toe-in) requirements. Additionally, tyre and lighting requirements differ from conventional motorcycle use. Owners are advised to check MOT test requirements with an official test centre.

# Preparing for storage

## Before you start

If repairs or an overhaul is needed, see that this is carried out now rather than left until you want to ride the bike again.

Give the bike a good wash and scrub all dirt from its underside. Make sure the bike dries completely before preparing for storage.

## Engine

● Remove the spark plug(s) and lubricate the cylinder bores with approximately a teaspoon of motor oil using a spout-type oil can **(see illustration 1)**. Reinstall the spark plug(s). Crank the engine over a couple of times to coat the piston rings and bores with oil. If the bike has a kickstart, use this to turn the engine over. If not, flick the kill switch to the OFF position and crank the engine over on the starter **(see illustration 2)**. If the nature on the ignition system prevents the starter operating with the kill switch in the OFF position, remove

the spark plugs and fit them back in their caps; ensure that the plugs are earthed (grounded) against the cylinder head when the starter is operated **(see illustration 3)**.

⚠️ **Warning: It is important that the plugs are earthed (grounded) away from the spark plug holes otherwise there is a risk of atomised fuel from the cylinders igniting.**

> **HAYNES HINT** *On a single cylinder four-stroke engine, you can seal the combustion chamber completely by positioning the piston at TDC on the compression stroke.*

● Drain the carburettor(s) otherwise there is a risk of jets becoming blocked by gum deposits from the fuel **(see illustration 4)**.

● If the bike is going into long-term storage, consider adding a fuel stabiliser to the fuel in the tank. If the tank is drained completely, corrosion of its internal surfaces may occur if left unprotected for a long period. The tank can be treated with a rust preventative especially for this purpose. Alternatively, remove the tank and pour half a litre of motor oil into it, install the filler cap and shake the tank to coat its internals with oil before draining off the excess. The same effect can also be achieved by spraying WD40 or a similar water-dispersant around the inside of the tank via its flexible nozzle.

● Make sure the cooling system contains the correct mix of antifreeze. Antifreeze also contains important corrosion inhibitors.

● The air intakes and exhaust can be sealed off by covering or plugging the openings. Ensure that you do not seal in any condensation; run the engine until it is hot,

Squirt a drop of motor oil into each cylinder

Flick the kill switch to OFF . . .

. . . and ensure that the metal bodies of the plugs (arrows) are earthed against the cylinder head

Connect a hose to the carburettor float chamber drain stub (arrow) and unscrew the drain screw

Exhausts can be sealed off with a plastic bag

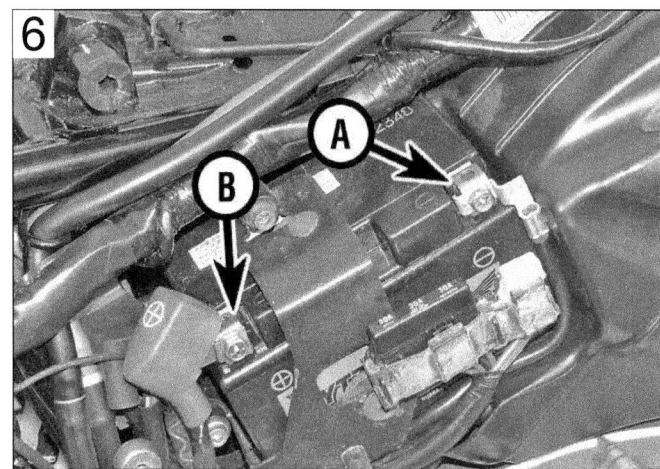

Disconnect the negative lead (A) first, followed by the positive lead (B)

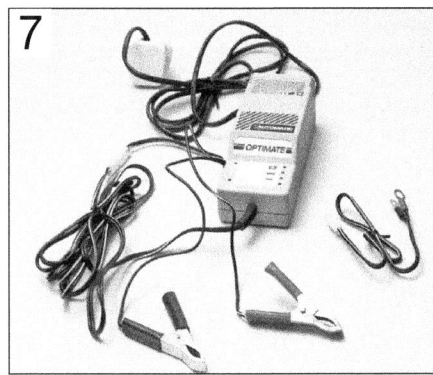

Use a suitable battery charger - this kit also assess battery condition

● Check the electrolyte level and top up if necessary (conventional refillable batteries). Clean the terminals.
● Store the battery off the motorcycle and away from any sources of fire. Position a wooden block under the battery if it is to sit on the ground.
● Give the battery a trickle charge for a few hours every month (see illustration 7).

## Tyres

● Place the bike on its centrestand or an auxiliary stand which will support the motorcycle in an upright position. Position wood blocks under the tyres to keep them off the ground and to provide insulation from damp. If the bike is being put into long-term storage, ideally both tyres should be off the ground; not only will this protect the tyres, but will also ensure that no load is placed on the steering head or wheel bearings.
● Deflate each tyre by 5 to 10 psi, no more or the beads may unseat from the rim, making subsequent inflation difficult on tubeless tyres.

## Pivots and controls

● Lubricate all lever, pedal, stand and footrest

pivot points. If grease nipples are fitted to the rear suspension components, apply lubricant to the pivots.
● Lubricate all control cables.

## Cycle components

● Apply a wax protectant to all painted and plastic components. Wipe off any excess, but don't polish to a shine. Where fitted, clean the screen with soap and water.
● Coat metal parts with Vaseline (petroleum jelly). When applying this to the fork tubes, do not compress the forks otherwise the seals will rot from contact with the Vaseline.
● Apply a vinyl cleaner to the seat.

## Storage conditions

● Aim to store the bike in a shed or garage which does not leak and is free from damp.
● Drape an old blanket or bedspread over the bike to protect it from dust and direct contact with sunlight (which will fade paint). This also hides the bike from prying eyes. Beware of tight-fitting plastic covers which may allow condensation to form and settle on the bike.

then switch off and allow to cool. Tape a piece of thick plastic over the silencer end(s) (see illustration 5). Note that some advocate pouring a tablespoon of motor oil into the silencer(s) before sealing them off.

## Battery

● Remove it from the bike - in extreme cases of cold the battery may freeze and crack its case (see illustration 6).

# Getting back on the road

## Engine and transmission

● Change the oil and replace the oil filter. If this was done prior to storage, check that the oil hasn't emulsified - a thick whitish substance which occurs through condensation.
● Remove the spark plugs. Using a spout-type oil can, squirt a few drops of oil into the cylinder(s). This will provide initial lubrication as the piston rings and bores comes back into contact. Service the spark plugs, or fit new ones, and install them in the engine.

● Check that the clutch isn't stuck on. The plates can stick together if left standing for some time, preventing clutch operation. Engage a gear and try rocking the bike back and forth with the clutch lever held against the handlebar. If this doesn't work on cable-operated clutches, hold the clutch lever back against the handlebar with a strong elastic band or cable tie for a couple of hours (see illustration 8).
● If the air intakes or silencer end(s) were blocked off, remove the bung or cover used.
● If the fuel tank was coated with a rust

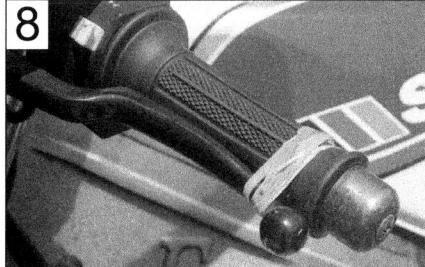

Hold clutch lever back against the handlebar with elastic bands or a cable tie

preventative, oil or a stabiliser added to the fuel, drain and flush the tank and dispose of the fuel sensibly. If no action was taken with the fuel tank prior to storage, it is advised that the old fuel is disposed of since it will go off over a period of time. Refill the fuel tank with fresh fuel.

## Frame and running gear

● Oil all pivot points and cables.
● Check the tyre pressures. They will definitely need inflating if pressures were reduced for storage.
● Lubricate the final drive chain (where applicable).
● Remove any protective coating applied to the fork tubes (stanchions) since this may well destroy the fork seals. If the fork tubes weren't protected and have picked up rust spots, remove them with very fine abrasive paper and refinish with metal polish.
● Check that both brakes operate correctly. Apply each brake hard and check that it's not possible to move the motorcycle forwards, then check that the brake frees off again once released. Brake caliper pistons can stick due to corrosion around the piston head, or on the sliding caliper types, due to corrosion of the slider pins. If the brake doesn't free after repeated operation, take the caliper off for examination. Similarly drum brakes can stick due to a seized operating cam, cable or rod linkage.
● If the motorcycle has been in long-term storage, renew the brake fluid and clutch fluid (where applicable).
● Depending on where the bike has been stored, the wiring, cables and hoses may have been nibbled by rodents. Make a visual check and investigate disturbed wiring loom tape.

## Battery

● If the battery has been previously removal and given top up charges it can simply be reconnected. Remember to connect the positive cable first and the negative cable last.
● On conventional refillable batteries, if the battery has not received any attention, remove it from the motorcycle and check its electrolyte level. Top up if necessary then charge the battery. If the battery fails to hold a charge and a visual checks show heavy white sulphation of the plates, the battery is probably defective and must be renewed. This is particularly likely if the battery is old. Confirm battery condition with a specific gravity check.
● On sealed (MF) batteries, if the battery has not received any attention, remove it from the motorcycle and charge it according to the information on the battery case - if the battery fails to hold a charge it must be renewed.

## Starting procedure

● If a kickstart is fitted, turn the engine over a couple of times with the ignition OFF to distribute oil around the engine. If no kickstart is fitted, flick the engine kill switch OFF and the ignition ON and crank the engine over a couple of times to work oil around the upper cylinder components. If the nature of the ignition system is such that the starter won't work with the kill switch OFF, remove the spark plugs, fit them back into their caps and earth (ground) their bodies on the cylinder head. Reinstall the spark plugs afterwards.
● Switch the kill switch to RUN, operate the choke and start the engine. If the engine won't start don't continue cranking the engine - not only will this flatten the battery, but the starter motor will overheat. Switch the ignition off and try again later. If the engine refuses to start, go through the fault finding procedures in this manual. **Note:** *If the bike has been in storage for a long time, old fuel or a carburettor blockage may be the problem. Gum deposits in carburettors can block jets - if a carburettor cleaner doesn't prove successful the carburettors must be dismantled for cleaning.*

● Once the engine has started, check that the lights, turn signals and horn work properly.

● Treat the bike gently for the first ride and check all fluid levels on completion. Settle the bike back into the maintenance schedule.

## Length (distance)

| | | | | |
|---|---|---|---|---|
| Inches (in) | x 25.4 | = Millimetres (mm) | x 0.0394 | = Inches (in) |
| Feet (ft) | x 0.305 | = Metres (m) | x 3.281 | = Feet (ft) |
| Miles | x 1.609 | = Kilometres (km) | x 0.621 | = Miles |

## Volume (capacity)

| | | | | |
|---|---|---|---|---|
| Cubic inches (cu in; in³) | x 16.387 | = Cubic centimetres (cc; cm³) | x 0.061 | = Cubic inches (cu in; in³) |
| Imperial pints (Imp pt) | x 0.568 | = Litres (l) | x 1.76 | = Imperial pints (Imp pt) |
| Imperial quarts (Imp qt) | x 1.137 | = Litres (l) | x 0.88 | = Imperial quarts (Imp qt) |
| Imperial quarts (Imp qt) | x 1.201 | = US quarts (US qt) | x 0.833 | = Imperial quarts (Imp qt) |
| US quarts (US qt) | x 0.946 | = Litres (l) | x 1.057 | = US quarts (US qt) |
| Imperial gallons (Imp gal) | x 4.546 | = Litres (l) | x 0.22 | = Imperial gallons (Imp gal) |
| Imperial gallons (Imp gal) | x 1.201 | = US gallons (US gal) | x 0.833 | = Imperial gallons (Imp gal) |
| US gallons (US gal) | x 3.785 | = Litres (l) | x 0.264 | = US gallons (US gal) |

## Mass (weight)

| | | | | |
|---|---|---|---|---|
| Ounces (oz) | x 28.35 | = Grams (g) | x 0.035 | = Ounces (oz) |
| Pounds (lb) | x 0.454 | = Kilograms (kg) | x 2.205 | = Pounds (lb) |

## Force

| | | | | |
|---|---|---|---|---|
| Ounces-force (ozf; oz) | x 0.278 | = Newtons (N) | x 3.6 | = Ounces-force (ozf; oz) |
| Pounds-force (lbf; lb) | x 4.448 | = Newtons (N) | x 0.225 | = Pounds-force (lbf; lb) |
| Newtons (N) | x 0.1 | = Kilograms-force (kgf; kg) | x 9.81 | = Newtons (N) |

## Pressure

| | | | | |
|---|---|---|---|---|
| Pounds-force per square inch (psi; lbf/in²; lb/in²) | x 0.070 | = Kilograms-force per square centimetre (kgf/cm²; kg/cm²) | x 14.223 | = Pounds-force per square inch (psi; lbf/in²; lb/in²) |
| Pounds-force per square inch (psi; lbf/in²; lb/in²) | x 0.068 | = Atmospheres (atm) | x 14.696 | = Pounds-force per square inch (psi; lbf/in²; lb/in²) |
| Pounds-force per square inch (psi; lbf/in²; lb/in²) | x 0.069 | = Bars | x 14.5 | = Pounds-force per square inch (psi; lbf/in²; lb/in²) |
| Pounds-force per square inch (psi; lbf/in²; lb/in²) | x 6.895 | = Kilopascals (kPa) | x 0.145 | = Pounds-force per square inch (psi; lbf/in²; lb/in²) |
| Kilopascals (kPa) | x 0.01 | = Kilograms-force per square centimetre (kgf/cm²; kg/cm²) | x 98.1 | = Kilopascals (kPa) |
| Millibar (mbar) | x 100 | = Pascals (Pa) | x 0.01 | = Millibar (mbar) |
| Millibar (mbar) | x 0.0145 | = Pounds-force per square inch (psi; lbf/in²; lb/in²) | x 68.947 | = Millibar (mbar) |
| Millibar (mbar) | x 0.75 | = Millimetres of mercury (mmHg) | x 1.333 | = Millibar (mbar) |
| Millibar (mbar) | x 0.401 | = Inches of water (inH₂O) | x 2.491 | = Millibar (mbar) |
| Millimetres of mercury (mmHg) | x 0.535 | = Inches of water (inH₂O) | x 1.868 | = Millimetres of mercury (mmHg) |
| Inches of water (inH₂O) | x 0.036 | = Pounds-force per square inch (psi; lbf/in²; lb/in²) | x 27.68 | = Inches of water (inH₂O) |

## Torque (moment of force)

| | | | | |
|---|---|---|---|---|
| Pounds-force inches (lbf in; lb in) | x 1.152 | = Kilograms-force centimetre (kgf cm; kg cm) | x 0.868 | = Pounds-force inches (lbf in; lb in) |
| Pounds-force inches (lbf in; lb in) | x 0.113 | = Newton metres (Nm) | x 8.85 | = Pounds-force inches (lbf in; lb in) |
| Pounds-force inches (lbf in; lb in) | x 0.083 | = Pounds-force feet (lbf ft; lb ft) | x 12 | = Pounds-force inches (lbf in; lb in) |
| Pounds-force feet (lbf ft; lb ft) | x 0.138 | = Kilograms-force metres (kgf m; kg m) | x 7.233 | = Pounds-force feet (lbf ft; lb ft) |
| Pounds-force feet (lbf ft; lb ft) | x 1.356 | = Newton metres (Nm) | x 0.738 | = Pounds-force feet (lbf ft; lb ft) |
| Newton metres (Nm) | x 0.102 | = Kilograms-force metres (kgf m; kg m) | x 9.804 | = Newton metres (Nm) |

## Power

| | | | | |
|---|---|---|---|---|
| Horsepower (hp) | x 745.7 | = Watts (W) | x 0.0013 | = Horsepower (hp) |

## Velocity (speed)

| | | | | |
|---|---|---|---|---|
| Miles per hour (miles/hr; mph) | x 1.609 | = Kilometres per hour (km/hr; kph) | x 0.621 | = Miles per hour (miles/hr; mph) |

## Fuel consumption*

| | | | | |
|---|---|---|---|---|
| Miles per gallon, Imperial (mpg) | x 0.354 | = Kilometres per litre (km/l) | x 2.825 | = Miles per gallon, Imperial (mpg) |
| Miles per gallon, US (mpg) | x 0.425 | = Kilometres per litre (km/l) | x 2.352 | = Miles per gallon, US (mpg) |

## Temperature

Degrees Fahrenheit = (°C x 1.8) + 32        Degrees Celsius (Degrees Centigrade; °C) = (°F - 32) x 0.56

*It is common practice to convert from miles per gallon (mpg) to litres/100 kilometres (l/100km), where mpg x l/100 km = 282*

This Section provides an easy reference-guide to the more common faults that are likely to afflict your machine. Obviously, the opportunities are almost limitless for faults to occur as a result of obscure failures, and to try and cover all eventualities would require a book. Indeed, a number have been written on the subject.

Successful troubleshooting is not a mysterious 'black art' but the application of a bit of knowledge combined with a systematic and logical approach to the problem. Approach any troubleshooting by first accurately identifying the symptom and then checking through the list of possible causes, starting with the simplest or most obvious and progressing in stages to the most complex.

Take nothing for granted, but above all apply liberal quantities of common sense.

The main symptom of a fault is given in the text as a major heading below which are listed the various systems or areas which may contain the fault. Details of each possible cause for a fault and the remedial action to be taken are given, in brief, in the paragraphs below each heading. Further information should be sought in the relevant Chapter.

### Engine doesn't start or is difficult to start

- [ ] Starter motor doesn't rotate
- [ ] Starter motor rotates but engine does not turn over
- [ ] Starter works but engine won't turn over (seized)
- [ ] No fuel flow
- [ ] Engine flooded
- [ ] No spark or weak spark
- [ ] Compression low
- [ ] Stalls after starting
- [ ] Rough idle

### Poor running at low speeds

- [ ] Spark weak
- [ ] Fuel/air mixture incorrect
- [ ] Compression low
- [ ] Poor acceleration

### Poor running or no power at high speed

- [ ] Firing incorrect
- [ ] Fuel/air mixture incorrect
- [ ] Compression low
- [ ] Knocking or pinking
- [ ] Miscellaneous causes

### Overheating

- [ ] Engine overheats
- [ ] Firing incorrect
- [ ] Fuel/air mixture incorrect
- [ ] Compression too high
- [ ] Engine load excessive
- [ ] Lubrication inadequate
- [ ] Miscellaneous causes

### Clutch problems

- [ ] Clutch slipping
- [ ] Clutch not disengaging completely

### Gearchanging problems

- [ ] Doesn't go into gear or lever doesn't return
- [ ] Jumps out of gear
- [ ] Overselects

### Abnormal engine noise

- [ ] Knocking or pinking
- [ ] Piston slap or rattling
- [ ] Valve noise
- [ ] Other noise

### Abnormal driveline noise

- [ ] Clutch noise
- [ ] Transmission noise
- [ ] Final drive noise

### Abnormal frame and suspension noise

- [ ] Front end noise
- [ ] Rear end noise
- [ ] Brake noise

### Engine lubrication system

- [ ] Oil pressure warning light comes on

### Excessive exhaust smoke

- [ ] White smoke
- [ ] Black smoke
- [ ] Brown smoke

### Poor handling or stability

- [ ] Handlebars hard to turn
- [ ] Handlebar shakes or vibrates excessively
- [ ] Machine pulls to one side
- [ ] Poor shock absorbing qualities

### Braking problems

- [ ] Brakes are spongy, don't hold
- [ ] Brake lever or pedal pulsates
- [ ] Brakes drag
- [ ] ABS system

### Electrical problems

- [ ] Battery dead or weak
- [ ] Battery overcharged

# Engine doesn't start or is difficult to start

## Starter motor doesn't rotate

☐ Engine kill switch OFF.
☐ Fuse blown. Check main fuse, ignition/starter fuse and EMS fuse (Chapter 8).
☐ Battery voltage low. Check battery condition and recharge or replace battery (Chapter 8).
☐ Loose or corroded battery connections/terminals. Tighten or clean connections (Chapter 8).
☐ Starter motor defective. Make sure the wiring to the starter is secure and free of corrosion. Replace or repair the motor if defective (Chapter 8).
☐ Starter motor relay defective. Make sure the wiring to relay is secure and free of corrosion. Test the operation of the relay, internal corrosion or arcing can cause the relay to not pass sufficient current to the starter motor even if it clicks when the start button is operated (Chapter 8).
☐ Starter switch not contacting. The contacts could be wet, corroded or dirty. Disassemble and clean the switch (Chapter 8).
☐ Wiring open or shorted. Check all wiring connections and harnesses to make sure that they are dry, tight and not corroded. Also check for broken or frayed wires that can cause a short to ground (earth) (see Wiring diagrams).
☐ Ignition or kill switch defective. This is usually caused by water, corrosion, damage or excessive wear. The switches can be disassembled and cleaned with electrical contact cleaner. If cleaning does not help, replace the switches (Chapter 8).
☐ Faulty gear position sensor, sidestand switch or clutch switch. Check the wiring to each switch and the switch itself (see Chapter 8).
☐ Faulty starter circuit relay (Chapter 8).
☐ Fuel injection system shutdown due to system fault (Chapter 4).

## Starter motor rotates but engine does not turn over

☐ Starter clutch defective. Inspect and repair or replace with a new one (see Chapter 2).
☐ Damaged idler or starter gears. Inspect and replace the damaged parts (see Chapter 2).

## Starter works but engine won't turn over (seized)

☐ Seized engine caused by one or more internally damaged components. Failure due to wear, abuse or lack of lubrication. Damage can include seized valves, camshaft, pistons, crankshaft, connecting rod bearings, or transmission gears or bearings. Refer to Chapter 2 for engine disassembly.

## No fuel flow

☐ No fuel in tank.
☐ Fuel tank breather hose obstructed (Chapter 4).
☐ Faulty fuel pump relay. Check the relay (see Chapter 8).
☐ Fuel pump or pressure regulator faulty, or the fuel filter is blocked (see Chapter 4).
☐ Engine control module (ECM) defective (Chapter 4).
☐ Ignition key not recognised by immobiliser system (where fitted) (Chapter 4).
☐ Fuel hose kinked. Fit a new hose (Chapter 4).
☐ Fuel rail or injector clogged (Chapter 4). For both injectors to be clogged, either a very bad batch of fuel with an unusual additive has been used, or some other foreign material has entered the tank. Check the fuel pump. In some cases, if a machine has been unused for several months, the fuel turns to a varnish-like liquid which can cause an injector needle to stick to its seat. Drain the tank and fuel system, ultrasonically clean or replace fuel injectors.

## Engine flooded

☐ Injector needle valve worn or stuck open. A piece of dirt, rust or other debris can cause the needle to seat improperly, causing excess fuel to be admitted to the throttle body. In this case, the injector should be cleaned and the needle and seat inspected (Chapter 4). If the needle and seat are worn, then the leaking will persist and the parts should be renewed.
☐ Starting technique incorrect. Under normal circumstances (i.e. if all the components of the fuel injection system are good) the machine should start with the throttle closed.

## No spark or weak spark

☐ Ignition switch OFF.
☐ Engine kill switch turned to the OFF position.
☐ Ignition or kill switch shorted. This is usually caused by water, corrosion, damage or excessive wear. The switches can be disassembled and cleaned with electrical contact cleaner. If cleaning does not help, replace the switches (Chapter 8).
☐ Battery voltage low. Check battery condition and recharge or replace battery (Chapter 8).
☐ Spark plug cap not making good contact. Make sure that the caps are pushed fully onto the spark plugs (Chapter 1).
☐ Spark plugs dirty, defective or worn out. Locate reason for fouled plugs using the firing end condition photos and follow the plug maintenance procedures (Chapter 1).
☐ Incorrect spark plugs. Wrong type or heat range. Check and install correct plugs (Chapter 1).
☐ Ignition coil, HT lead or spark plug cap faulty (Chapter 4).
☐ Fuel injection system shutdown due to system fault (Chapter 4).
☐ Crankshaft position (CKP) sensor defective (Chapter 4).
☐ EMS relay or tip-over sensor faulty (Chapter 4).
☐ Engine control module (ECM) defective (see Chapter 4).
☐ Wiring shorted or broken between: ignition switch and engine kill switch (or blown fuse); ECM and kill switch; ECM and ignition coils; ECM and CKP sensor. Make sure that all wiring connections are clean, dry and tight. Look for chafed and broken wires (see Chapter)

## Compression low

☐ Spark plugs loose. Remove the plugs and inspect their threads. Reinstall and tighten securely (see Chapter 1).
☐ Cylinder head not sufficiently tightened down. If the cylinder head is suspected of being loose, then there's a chance that the gasket or head is damaged if the problem has persisted for any length of time. The head bolts should be tightened to the proper torque and in the correct sequence (Chapter 2).
☐ Improper valve clearance. This means that the valve is not closing completely and compression pressure is leaking past the valve. Check and adjust the valve clearances (Chapter 1).
☐ Cylinder and/or piston worn. Excessive wear will cause compression pressure to leak past the rings. This is usually accompanied by worn rings as well. A top-end overhaul is necessary (Chapter 2).
☐ Piston rings worn, weak, broken, or sticking. Broken or sticking piston rings usually indicate a lubrication or fuelling problem that causes excess carbon deposits to form on the pistons and rings. Top-end overhaul is necessary (Chapter 2).
☐ Piston ring-to-groove clearance excessive. This is caused by excessive wear of the piston ring lands. Piston renewal is necessary (Chapter 2).
☐ Cylinder head gasket damaged. If a head is allowed to become loose, or if excessive carbon build-up on the piston crown and combustion chamber causes extremely high compression, the head gasket may leak. Retorquing the head is not always sufficient to restore the seal, so a new gasket is necessary (Chapter 2).
☐ Cylinder head warped. This is caused by overheating or improperly tightened head bolts. Machine shop resurfacing or a new head is necessary (Chapter 2).
☐ Valve spring broken or weak. Caused by component failure or wear; the springs must be replaced with new ones (Chapter 2).
☐ Valve not seating properly. This is caused by a bent valve (from over-revving or improper valve adjustment), burned valve or seat (incorrect air/fuel mixture) or an accumulation of carbon deposits on the seat. The valves must be cleaned and/or renewed and the seats very lightly lapped (Chapter 2).

# Engine doesn't start or is difficult to start (continued)

### Stalls after starting

- [ ] Ignition malfunction (Chapter 4).
- [ ] Fuel injection system malfunction (Chapter 4).
- [ ] Fuel contaminated. The fuel can be contaminated with either dirt or water, or can change chemically if the machine has been unused for several months. Drain the tank and fuel system (Chapter 4).
- [ ] Intake air leak. Check for loose throttle body-to-intake manifold/duct connections, disconnected or damaged MAP sensor or EVAP hose on throttle body (Chapter 4).

### Rough idle

- [ ] Ignition fault (Chapter 4).
- [ ] Throttle bodies not synchronised on 1200 engines (Chapter 1).
- [ ] Fuel injection system malfunction (Chapter 4).
- [ ] Fuel contaminated. The fuel can be contaminated with either dirt or water, or can change chemically if the machine has been unused for several months. Drain the tank and the fuel system (Chapter 4).
- [ ] Intake air leak. Check for loose throttle body-to-intake duct connections, disconnected or damaged MAP sensor or EVAP hose on throttle body (Chapter 4).
- [ ] Air filter clogged. Fit a new filter and clean its housing (Chapter 1).

# Poor running at low speeds

### Spark weak

- [ ] Battery voltage low. Check battery condition and recharge or replace battery (Chapter 8).
- [ ] Spark plug caps not making good contact. Make sure that the caps are pushed fully onto the spark plugs (Chapter 1).
- [ ] Spark plugs dirty, defective or worn out. Locate reason for fouled plugs and follow the plug maintenance procedures (see Chapter 1).
- [ ] Incorrect spark plugs. Wrong type or heat range. Check and install correct plugs (see Chapter 1).
- [ ] Ignition coil, HT lead or spark plug cap defective (Chapter 4).
- [ ] Loose or corroded coil wiring connectors. Check security and clean connections (Chapter 4).

### Fuel/air mixture incorrect

- [ ] Fuel tank breather hose obstructed (Chapter 4).
- [ ] Fuel pump or pressure regulator faulty, or the pump's filter is blocked (Chapter 4).
- [ ] Fuel hose kinked. Replace the fuel hose (Chapter 4).
- [ ] Fuel rail or injector clogged (Chapter 4).
- [ ] For both injectors to be clogged, either a very bad batch of fuel with an unusual additive has been used, or some other foreign material has entered the tank. Clean the fuel pump strainer and fit a new filter. In some cases, if a machine has been unused for several months, the fuel turns to a varnish-like liquid which can cause an injector needle to stick to its seat. Drain the tank and fuel system, ultrasonically clean or replace fuel injectors.Intake air leak. Check for loose throttle body-to-intake duct connections, disconnected or damaged MAP sensor or EVAP hose on throttle body (Chapter 4).
- [ ] Air filter clogged. Fit a new filter and clean its housing (Chapter 1).

### Compression low

**Note:** *Check by performing a compression test (see Chapter 2).*
- [ ] Spark plugs loose. Remove the plugs and inspect their threads. Reinstall and tighten securely (see Chapter 1).
- [ ] Cylinder head not sufficiently tightened down. If a cylinder head is suspected of being loose, then there's a chance that the gasket or head is damaged if the problem has persisted for any length of time. The head bolts should be tightened to the proper torque and in the correct sequence (Chapter 2).

- [ ] Improper valve clearance. This means that the valve is not closing completely and compression pressure is leaking past the valve. Check and adjust the valve clearances (Chapter 1).
- [ ] Cylinder and/or piston worn. Excessive wear will cause compression pressure to leak past the rings. This is usually accompanied by worn rings as well. A top-end overhaul is necessary (Chapter 2).
- [ ] Piston rings worn, weak, broken, or sticking. Broken or sticking piston rings usually indicate a lubrication or fuelling problem that causes excess carbon deposits to form on the pistons and rings. Top-end overhaul is necessary (Chapter 2).
- [ ] Piston ring-to-groove clearance excessive. This is caused by excessive wear of the piston ring lands. Piston renewal is necessary (Chapter 2).
- [ ] Cylinder head gasket damaged. If the head is allowed to become loose, or if excessive carbon build-up on the piston crown and combustion chamber causes extremely high compression, the head gasket may leak. Retorquing the head is not always sufficient to restore the seal, so a new gasket is necessary (Chapter 2).
- [ ] Cylinder head warped. This is caused by overheating or improperly tightened head bolts. Machine shop resurfacing or head renewal is necessary (Chapter 2).
- [ ] Valve spring broken or weak. Caused by component failure or wear; the springs must be renewed (Chapter 2).
- [ ] Valve not seating properly. This is caused by a bent valve (from over-revving or improper valve adjustment), burned valve or seat (improper fuelling) or an accumulation of carbon deposits on the seat (from fuelling or lubrication problems).
- [ ] The valves must be cleaned and/or renewed and the seats very lightly lapped (Chapter 2).

### Poor acceleration

- [ ] Throttle system faulty (Chapter 4)
- [ ] Timing not advancing. The crankshaft position sensor (CKP) or the engine control module (ECM) may be defective (Chapter 4).
- [ ] Engine oil viscosity too high. Using a heavier oil than that recommended in Chapter 1 can damage the oil pump or lubrication system and cause drag on the engine.
- [ ] Brakes dragging. Usually caused by corrosion behind dust seals, ingestion of dirt past a deteriorated seal or from a warped disc or bent axle (Chapter 6).

# Poor running or no power at high speed

## Firing incorrect

- ☐ Spark plug caps not making good contact. Make sure that the caps are pushed fully onto the spark plugs (Chapter 1).
- ☐ Spark plugs dirty, defective or worn out. Locate reason for fouled plugs using spark plug condition chart on the inside back cover and follow the plug maintenance procedures (see Chapter 1).
- ☐ Incorrect spark plugs. Wrong type or heat range. Check and install correct plugs (see Chapter 1).
- ☐ Ignition coil, HT lead or spark plug cap defective (Chapter 4).
- ☐ Faulty ECM (Chapter 4).

## Fuel/air mixture incorrect

- ☐ Fuel tank breather hose obstructed (Chapter 4).
- ☐ Fuel pump faulty or blocked fuel filter or strainer. Inspect and replace/clean as necessary (Chapter 4).
- ☐ Fuel hose kinked. Replace the fuel hose (Chapter 4).
- ☐ Fuel rail or injector clogged (Chapter 4). For both injectors to be clogged, either a very bad batch of fuel with an unusual additive has been used, or some other foreign material has entered the tank. Check the fuel pump, filter and strainer. In some cases, if a machine has been unused for several months, the fuel turns to a varnish-like liquid which can cause an injector needle to stick to its seat. Drain the tank and fuel system, ultrasonically clean or replace fuel injectors.Intake air leak. Check for loose throttle body-to-intake duct connections, disconnected or damaged MAP sensor or EVAP hose on throttle body (Chapter 4).
- ☐ Air filter clogged. Fit a new filter and clean its housing (Chapter 1).

## Compression low

**Note:** *Check by performing a compression test (see Chapter 2).*
- ☐ Spark plugs loose. Remove the plugs and inspect their threads. Reinstall and tighten securely (see Chapter 1).
- ☐ Cylinder head not sufficiently tightened down. If a cylinder head is suspected of being loose, then there's a chance that the gasket or head is damaged if the problem has persisted for any length of time. The head bolts should be tightened to the proper torque and in the correct sequence (Chapter 2).
- ☐ Improper valve clearance. This means that the valve is not closing completely and compression pressure is leaking past the valve. Check and adjust the valve clearances (Chapter 1).
- ☐ Cylinder and/or piston worn. Excessive wear will cause compression pressure to leak past the rings. This is usually accompanied by worn rings as well. A top-end overhaul is necessary (Chapter 2).
- ☐ Piston rings worn, weak, broken, or sticking. Broken or sticking piston rings usually indicate a lubrication or fuelling problem that causes excess carbon deposits to form on the pistons and rings. Top-end overhaul is necessary (Chapter 2).
- ☐ Piston ring-to-groove clearance excessive. This is caused by excessive wear of the piston ring lands. Piston renewal is necessary (Chapter 2).

- ☐ Cylinder head gasket damaged. If a head is allowed to become loose, or if excessive carbon build-up on the piston crown and combustion chamber causes extremely high compression, the head gasket may leak. Retorquing the head is not always sufficient to restore the seal, so a new gasket is necessary (Chapter 2).
- ☐ Cylinder head warped. This is caused by overheating or improperly tightened head bolts. Machine shop resurfacing or head renewal is necessary (Chapter 2).
- ☐ Valve spring broken or weak. Caused by component failure or wear; the springs must be replaced with new ones (Chapter 2).
- ☐ Valve not seating properly. This is caused by a bent valve (from over-revving or improper valve adjustment), burned valve or seat (improper fuelling) or an accumulation of carbon deposits on the seat (from fuelling or lubrication problems).
- ☐ The valves must be cleaned and/or renewed and the seats serviced (Chapter 2).

## Knocking or pinking

- ☐ Carbon build-up in combustion chamber. Use of a fuel additive that will dissolve the adhesive bonding the carbon particles to the piston crown and chamber is the easiest way to remove the build-up. Otherwise, the cylinder head will have to be removed and decarbonised (Chapter 2).
- ☐ Incorrect or poor quality fuel. Old or improper grades of fuel can cause detonation. This causes the pistons to rattle, thus the knocking or pinking sound. Drain old fuel and always use the recommended fuel grade.
- ☐ Spark plug heat range incorrect. Uncontrolled detonation indicates the plug heat range is too hot. The plug in effect becomes a glow plug, raising cylinder temperatures. Install the proper heat range plug (Chapter 1).
- ☐ Improper air/fuel mixture. This will cause the cylinders to run hot, which leads to detonation. A blockage in the fuel system or an air leak can cause this imbalance (see Chapter 4).

## Miscellaneous causes

- ☐ Throttle system faulty (Chapter 4).
- ☐ Clutch slipping due loose or worn clutch components (see Chapter 2).
- ☐ Timing not advancing. The crankshaft position sensor (CKP) or the engine control module (ECM) may be defective (Chapter 4). If so, they must be replaced with new ones.
- ☐ Engine oil viscosity too high. Using a heavier oil than the one recommended in Chapter 1 can damage the oil pump or lubrication system and cause drag on the engine.
- ☐ Brakes dragging. Usually caused by corrosion behind dust seals, ingestion of dirt past a deteriorated seal or from a warped disc or bent axle (Chapter 6).

# Overheating

### Engine overheats

☐ Coolant level low. Check and add coolant (Pre-ride checks).
☐ Leak in cooling system. Check cooling system hoses and radiator for leaks and other damage. Repair or renew parts as necessary (Chapter 3).
☐ Faulty thermostat. Check and renew as described in Chapter 3.
☐ Faulty radiator cap. Remove the cap and have it pressure tested (Chapter 3).
☐ Coolant passages clogged. Drain, flush and refill with fresh coolant (Chapter 1).
☐ Water pump defective (Chapter 2).
☐ Clogged or damaged radiator fins (see Chapter 1).
☐ Faulty cooling fan, relay or coolant temperature sensor (see Chapter 3).

### Firing incorrect

☐ Spark plugs dirty, defective or worn out. Locate reason for fouled plugs and follow the plug maintenance procedures (Chapter 1).
☐ Incorrect spark plugs. Wrong type or heat range. Check and install correct plugs (Chapter 1).
☐ Ignition coil, HT lead or spark plug cap defective (Chapter 4).
☐ Faulty ECM (Chapter 4).

### Fuel/air mixture incorrect

☐ Fuel tank breather hose obstructed (Chapter 4).
☐ Fuel pump faulty or blocked filter/strainer (Chapter 4).
☐ Fuel hose kinked. Replace the fuel hose (Chapter 4).
☐ Fuel rail or injector clogged (Chapter 4). For both injectors to be clogged, either a very bad batch of fuel with an unusual additive has been used, or some other foreign material has entered the tank. Check the fuel pump, filter and strainer. In some cases, if a machine has been unused for several months, the fuel turns to a varnish-like liquid which can cause an injector needle to stick to its seat. Drain the tank and fuel system, ultrasonically clean or replace fuel injectors.
☐ Intake air leak. Check for loose throttle body-to-intake duct connections, disconnected or damaged MAP sensor or EVAP hose on throttle body (Chapter 4).
☐ Air filter clogged. Fit a new filter and clean its housing (Chapter 1).

### Compression too high

**Note:** *Check by performing a compression test (see Chapter 2).*
☐ Carbon build-up in combustion chamber. Use of a fuel additive that will dissolve the adhesive bonding the carbon particles to the piston crown and chamber is the easiest way to remove the build-up. Otherwise, the cylinder head will have to be removed and decarbonised (Chapter 2).

### Engine load excessive

☐ Clutch slipping due loose or worn clutch components (see Chapter 2).
☐ Engine oil level too high. Too much oil will cause pressurisation of the crankcase and inefficient engine operation. Check Specifications and drain to proper level (Chapter 1 and Pre-ride checks).
☐ Engine oil viscosity too high. Using a heavier oil than the one recommended in Chapter 1 can damage the oil pump or lubrication system as well as cause drag on the engine.
☐ Brakes dragging. Usually caused by corrosion behind dust seals, ingestion of dirt past deteriorated seal or from a warped disc or bent axle (Chapter 6).

### Lubrication inadequate

☐ Engine oil level too low. Friction caused by intermittent lack of lubrication or from oil that is overworked can cause overheating. The oil provides a definite cooling function in the engine. Check the oil level (see Pre-ride checks).
☐ Low engine oil pressure. Check the pressure (see Chapter 2).
☐ Blocked oil filter (see Chapter 2).

### Miscellaneous causes

☐ Modification to exhaust system. Most aftermarket exhaust systems cause the engine to run leaner, which make them run hotter. When installing an aftermarket exhaust system, always check with the manufacturer/supplier as to whether the fuel system requires adjustment.

# Clutch problems

### Clutch slipping

☐ Insufficient clutch cable freeplay. Check and adjust (Chapter 1).
☐ Clutch plates worn or warped. Overhaul the clutch assembly (Chapter 2).
☐ Clutch springs broken or weak. Old or heat-damaged (from slipping clutch) springs should be replaced with new ones (Chapter 2).
☐ Clutch release mechanism faulty (Chapter 2).
☐ Clutch centre or housing worn. This causes improper engagement of the plates. Replace the damaged or worn parts (Chapter 2).
☐ Incorrect oil used in engine. Oils designed for car engines often contain friction modifiers, which if used in an engine with a wet clutch can promote clutch slip. Always use the correct oil designed for motorcycle engines (Pre-ride checks).

### Clutch not disengaging completely

☐ Excessive clutch cable freeplay. Check and adjust (Chapter 1).
☐ Clutch release mechanism faulty (Chapter 2).

☐ Clutch plates warped or damaged. This will cause clutch drag, which in turn will cause the machine to creep. Overhaul the clutch assembly (Chapter 2).
☐ Clutch springs fatigued or broken. Fit new springs (Chapter 2).
☐ Engine oil deteriorated. Old, thin oil will not provide proper lubrication for the plates, causing the clutch to drag. Change the oil and filter (Chapter 1).
☐ Engine oil viscosity too high. Using a heavier oil than recommended in Chapter 1 can cause the plates to stick together. Change to the correct weight oil.
☐ Clutch housing bearing seized on the transmission input shaft. Lack of lubrication, severe wear or damage can cause the bearing to seize. Overhaul of the clutch, and perhaps transmission, may be necessary to repair the damage (Chapter 2).
☐ Loose clutch centre nut. Causes housing and centre misalignment putting a drag on the engine. Engagement adjustment continually varies. Overhaul the clutch assembly (Chapter 2).

# Gearchanging problems

### Doesn't go into gear or lever doesn't return

- [ ] Clutch not disengaging (see above).
- [ ] Gearchange mechanism stopper arm spring weak or broken, or arm roller broken or worn. Replace the spring or arm with a new one (Chapter 2).
- [ ] Selector fork(s) bent, worn or seized. Overhaul the transmission (Chapter 2).
- [ ] Gear(s) stuck on shaft. Most often caused by a lack of lubrication or excessive wear in transmission bearings and bushes. Overhaul the transmission (see Chapter 2).
- [ ] Selector drum binding. Caused by lubrication failure or excessive wear. Replace the drum and/or its bearings with a new one (Chapter 2).
- [ ] Gearchange mechanism return spring weak or broken (Chapter 2).

- [ ] Gearchange linkage arm broken. Splines stripped out of arm or shaft, caused by a loose linkage arm pinch bolt or from dropping the bike (Chapter 2).

### Jumps out of gear

- [ ] Selector fork(s) worn (Chapter 2).
- [ ] Selector fork groove(s) in selector drum worn (Chapter 2).
- [ ] Gear pinion dogs or dog slots worn or damaged (Chapter 2).
- [ ] No attempt should be made to repair the worn parts.

### Overselects

- [ ] Gearchange mechanism stopper arm spring weak or broken, or arm roller broken or worn (Chapter 2).
- [ ] Gearchange mechanism spring(s) weak or broken (Chapter 2).

# Abnormal engine noise

### Knocking or pinking

- [ ] Carbon build-up in combustion chamber. Use of a fuel additive that will dissolve the adhesive bonding the carbon particles to the piston crown and chamber is the easiest way to remove the build-up. Otherwise, the cylinder head will have to be removed and decarbonised (Chapter 2).
- [ ] Incorrect or poor quality fuel. Old or improper grades of fuel can cause detonation. This causes the pistons to rattle, thus the knocking or pinking sound. Drain old fuel and always use the recommended fuel grade (Chapter 4).
- [ ] Spark plug heat range incorrect. Uncontrolled detonation indicates the plug heat range is too hot. The plug in effect becomes a glow plug, raising cylinder temperatures. Install the proper heat range plug (Chapter 1).
- [ ] Improper air/fuel mixture. This will cause the cylinders to run hot, which leads to detonation. A blockage in the fuel system or an air leak can cause this imbalance (Chapter 4).

### Piston slap or rattling

- [ ] Cylinder-to-piston clearance excessive. Cylinder and/or piston worn, usually accompanied by worn rings as well. A top-end overhaul is necessary (Chapter 2).
- [ ] Piston ring(s) worn, broken or sticking. Overhaul the top-end (Chapter 2).
- [ ] Piston pin, piston pin bore or connecting rod small-end worn from high mileage or seized due to lack of lubrication (Chapter 2).
- [ ] Piston seizure damage. Usually from lack of lubrication or overheating. Replace the pistons and cylinder block, as necessary (Chapter 2).
- [ ] Connecting rod big-end clearance excessive. Caused by excessive wear or lack of lubrication. Replace worn parts (Chapter 2).

- [ ] Connecting rod bent. Caused by over-revving, trying to start a badly flooded engine or from ingesting a foreign object into the combustion chamber. Replace the damaged parts (Chapter 2).

### Valve noise

- [ ] Incorrect valve clearances – check and adjust (Chapter 1).
- [ ] Valve spring broken or weak. Check and replace all valve springs (Chapter 2).
- [ ] Camshaft journals in the cylinder head worn or damaged. Lubrication failure at high rpm is usually the cause of damage due to insufficient oil or failure to change the oil at the recommended intervals. Since there are no replaceable bearings in the head, the camshaft and/or cylinder head and camshaft holders will have to be replaced with new ones (Chapter 2).

### Other noise

- [ ] Cylinder head gasket leaking. Check around the joint for blowing with the engine running.
- [ ] Exhaust pipe leaking at cylinder head connection. Caused by incorrect fit of pipe(s), loose exhaust flange or damaged gasket. All exhaust system fasteners should be tightened evenly and carefully to avoid leaks (Chapter 4).
- [ ] Crankshaft runout excessive (Chapter 2).
- [ ] Caused by a bent crankshaft (from over-revving) or damage from an upper cylinder component failure. Can also be attributed to dropping the machine on either of the crankshaft ends.
- [ ] Engine mounting bolts loose – ensure all the bolts are tightened to the specified torque settings (Chapter 2).
- [ ] Crankshaft bearings worn (Chapter 2).
- [ ] Cam chain rattle, due to worn chain or defective tensioner. Also worn chain tensioner/guide blades (see Chapter 2).

# Abnormal driveline noise

### Clutch noise

☐ Clutch housing/friction plate clearance excessive (Chapter 2).
☐ Wear between the clutch housing splines and input shaft splines (Chapter 2).
☐ Worn release bearing (Chapter 2).

### Transmission noise

☐ Bearings worn. Also includes the possibility that the shafts are worn. Overhaul the transmission (Chapter 2).
☐ Gears worn or chipped (Chapter 2).
☐ Metal chips jammed in gear teeth. Probably pieces from a broken clutch, gear or selector mechanism that were picked up by the gears. This will cause early bearing failure (Chapter 2).

☐ Engine oil level too low, causes a howl from transmission (Pre-ride checks).

### Final drive noise

☐ Drive chain excessively loose/worn or drive sprockets excessively worn. Adjust chain or replace chain and sprockets as a set (Chapter 1 and Chapter 6).
☐ Front or rear sprocket loose. Tighten fasteners (Chapter 6).
☐ Sprockets and/or chain worn. Fit new sprockets and chain (Chapter 6).
☐ Rear sprocket warped. Fit a new sprocket (Chapter 6).
☐ Rubber dampers in rear wheel worn (Chapter 6).

# Abnormal frame and suspension noise

### Front end noise

☐ Low fluid level or improper viscosity oil in forks. This can sound like spurting and is usually accompanied by irregular fork action (Chapter 5).
☐ Spring weak or broken. Makes a clicking or scraping sound. Fork oil, when drained, will have a lot of metal particles in it (Chapter 5).
☐ Steering head bearings loose or damaged. Clicks when braking. Check and adjust or replace with new ones as necessary (Chapter 1 and Chapter 5).
☐ Fork yoke clamp bolts loose – ensure all the bolts are tightened to the specified torque (Chapter 6).
☐ Forks bent. Good possibility if machine has been dropped. Replace the inner tubes with new ones as required (Chapter 5).
☐ Front axle or axle pinch bolt loose. Tighten them to the specified torque (Chapter 6).
☐ Loose or worn wheel bearings. Check and replace with new ones as needed (Chapter 1 and Chapter 6).

### Rear end noise

☐ Shock absorber fluid level incorrect. Indicates a leak caused by defective seal. Shock will be covered with oil. Replace shock with a new one or seek advice on repair from a suspension specialist (Chapter 5).
☐ Defective shock absorber with internal damage. The shock must be replaced with a new one or rebuilt (Chapter 5).
☐ Bent or damaged shock body. Replace the shock with a new one (Chapter 5).
☐ Loose or worn swingarm bearings, and/or suspension linkage

bearings on the Bobber. Check and replace with new ones as necessary (Chapter 5).
☐ Loose or worn wheel bearings/sprocket bearing. Check and replace with new ones as needed (Chapter 1 and Chapter 6).

### Brake noise

☐ Squeal caused by pad shim not installed or positioned correctly (where fitted) (Chapter 6).
☐ Squeal caused by dust on brake pads. Usually found in combination with glazed pads. Clean using brake cleaning solvent (Chapter 6).
☐ Pads glazed. Caused by excessive heat from prolonged hard use or from contamination. DO NOT use sandpaper, emery cloth, carborundum cloth or any other abrasive to roughen the pad surfaces as abrasives will stay in the pad material and damage the disc. A very fine flat file can be used, but new pads is the best remedy (Chapter 6).
☐ Contamination of brake pads. Oil or brake fluid can cause the brake pads to chatter or squeal. Fit new pads. Identify the cause of the contamination, especially check the caliper piston seals for leaking fluid. Clean disc thoroughly with brake system cleaner (Chapter 6).
☐ Disc warped. Can cause a chattering, clicking or intermittent squeal. Usually accompanied by a pulsating lever and uneven braking. Replace the disc and pads (Chapter 6).
☐ Loose or worn wheel bearings. Check and replace with new ones as needed (Chapter 1 and Chapter 6).
☐ Forks incorrectly aligned on front wheel axle causing caliper or mounting to contact disc. Loosen front axle pinch bolt and re-align (Chapter 6).

# Engine lubrication system

## Oil pressure warning light comes on

- [ ] Oil level low. Inspect for leak or other problem causing low oil level and add recommended oil (see Pre-ride checks).
- [ ] Blocked oil strainer gauze, faulty oil pump or pressure relief valve. Check the strainer, change the oil and filter, then carry out an oil pressure check (Chapter 2).
- [ ] Oil viscosity too low. Very old, thin oil or an improper weight of oil used in the engine. Change to correct oil (Chapter 1).
- [ ] Camshaft or crankshaft journals worn. Excessive wear causing drop in oil pressure. Abnormal wear could be caused by oil starvation at high rpm from low oil level or improper weight or type of oil (Chapter 1).
- [ ] Oil pressure switch defective. Check the switch according to the procedure in Chapter 8. Replace it with a new one if it is defective.

# Excessive exhaust smoke

## White smoke

- [ ] Piston rings worn or broken, causing oil from the crankcase to be pulled past the piston into the combustion chamber. Replace the rings with new ones (Chapter 2).
- [ ] Cylinders worn or scored. Caused by overheating or oil starvation. Install a new cylinder block and pistons (Chapter 2).
- [ ] Valve stem oil seal damaged or worn. Replace all valve stem oil seals with new ones (Chapter 2).
- [ ] Valve guide worn. Perform a complete valve job (Chapter 2).
- [ ] Engine oil level too high, which causes the oil to be forced past the rings. Drain oil to the proper level (see Chapter 1 and Pre-ride checks).
- [ ] Head gasket broken between oil return and cylinder. Causes oil to be pulled into the combustion chamber. Replace the head gasket with a new one and check the head for warpage (Chapter 2).
- [ ] Abnormal crankcase pressurisation which forces oil past the rings, usually caused by a clogged breather.

## Black smoke

- [ ] Air filter clogged. Replace it with a new one (Chapter 1).
- [ ] Fuel injection system malfunction (Chapter 4).

## Brown smoke

- [ ] Air filter poorly sealed or not installed (Chapter 1).
- [ ] Fuel injection system malfunction (Chapter 4).

# Poor handling or stability

## Handlebars hard to turn

- [ ] Steering head bearing adjuster nut too tight. Check adjustment as described in Chapter 1.
- [ ] Bearings damaged. Roughness can be felt as the bars are turned from side-to-side. Replace the bearings with new ones (Chapter 5).
- [ ] Races dented or worn. Denting results from wear in only one position (e.g., straight ahead), from a collision or hitting a pothole or from dropping the machine. Replace the bearings with new ones (Chapter 5).
- [ ] Steering stem lubrication inadequate. Causes are grease getting hard from age or being washed out by high pressure car washes. Disassemble steering head and repack bearings (Chapter 5).
- [ ] Steering stem bent. Caused by a collision, hitting a pothole or by dropping the machine. Replace damaged part. Don't try to straighten the steering stem (Chapter 5).
- [ ] Front tyre air pressure too low (Pre-ride checks).

## Handlebar shakes or vibrates excessively

- [ ] Tyres worn or out of balance.
- [ ] Swingarm bearings worn. Replace the bearings with new ones (Chapter 5).
- [ ] Wheel rim(s) warped or damaged. Inspect wheels for runout (Chapter 6).
- [ ] Wheel bearings worn. Worn front or rear wheel bearings can cause poor tracking. Worn front bearings will cause wobble (Chapter 6).
- [ ] Fork yoke clamp bolts or handlebar clamp bolts loose. Tighten them to the specified torque (Chapter 5).
- [ ] Engine mounting bolts loose. Will cause excessive vibration with increased engine rpm – ensure all the bolts are tightened to the specified torque settings (Chapter 2).

## Machine pulls to one side

- [ ] Frame bent. Definitely suspect this if the machine has been dropped. May or may not be accompanied by cracking near the steering head, swingarm mountings or engine mountings. Replace the frame with a new one (Chapter 5).
- [ ] Wheels out of alignment. Caused by improper location of axle spacers or from bent steering stem or frame (Chapter 5).
- [ ] Forks bent. Disassemble the forks and replace the damaged parts (Chapter 5).
- [ ] Swingarm bent or twisted. Replace the swingarm with a new one (Chapter 5).
- [ ] Fork oil level uneven. Check and add or drain as necessary (Chapter 5).

## Poor shock absorbing qualities

- [ ] Too hard – Front fork oil level excessive (Chapter 5).
- [ ] Too hard – Front fork oil viscosity too high. Use the correct oil (see the Specifications in Chapter 5).
- [ ] Too hard – Front fork tube bent. Causes a harsh, sticking feeling (Chapter 5).
- [ ] Too hard – Fork internal damage (Chapter 5).
- [ ] Too hard – Rear shock pre-load too high (Chapter 5).
- [ ] Too hard – Rear shock shaft or body bent or damaged, or shock internal failure (Chapter 5).
- [ ] Too hard – Tyre pressure too high (Pre-ride checks).
- [ ] Too soft – Front fork oil level too low (Chapter 5).
- [ ] Too soft – Front fork oil viscosity too light (Chapter 5).
- [ ] Too soft – Front fork springs weak or broken (Chapter 5).
- [ ] Too soft – Front fork oil leaking. Strip fork and renew seals (Chapter 5).
- [ ] Too soft – Rear shock pre-load too low for weight load (Chapter 5).
- [ ] Too soft – Rear shock oil leaking or internal damage (Chapter 5).

# Braking problems

## Brakes are spongy, don't hold

☐ Low brake fluid level (see Pre-ride checks).
☐ Air in hydraulic system. Caused by inattention to master cylinder fluid level or by leakage. Locate problem and bleed brakes (Chapter 6).
☐ Pads worn. Fit new pads (Chapter 6).
☐ Disc worn. Measure disc thickness and replace with a new one if necessary (Chapter 6).
☐ Contaminated pads. Caused by contamination with oil, grease, brake fluid, etc. Fit new pads. Identify the cause of the contamination, especially check the caliper piston seals for leaking fluid. Clean disc thoroughly with brake system cleaner (Chapter 6).
☐ Brake fluid deteriorated. Fluid is old or contaminated. Drain system, replenish with new fluid and bleed the system (Chapter 6).
☐ Master cylinder internal seals worn or damaged causing fluid to bypass (Chapter 6).
☐ Master cylinder bore scratched by foreign material or broken spring. Fit a new master cylinder (Chapter 6).
☐ Disc warped. Replace disc with new one (Chapter 6)

## Brake lever or pedal pulsates

☐ Disc warped. Replace disc with new one (Chapter 6).
☐ Axle bent. Replace axle with new one (Chapter 6).

☐ Brake caliper bolts loose – tighten the bolts to the specified torque (Chapter 6).
☐ Wheel warped or otherwise damaged (Chapter 6).
☐ Wheel bearings damaged or worn (Chapters 1, 6).

## Brakes drag

☐ Brake caliper piston seized in bore. Caused by corrosion behind dust seals or ingestion of dirt past deteriorated seal (Chapter 6).
☐ Brake caliper slider pins sticking or corroded, preventing full movement of caliper (Chapter 6).
☐ Brake pad damaged. Pad material separated from backing plate. Usually caused by faulty manufacturing process or from contact with chemicals. Fit new pads (Chapter 6).
☐ Pads improperly installed (Chapter 6).
☐ Brake caliper incorrectly installed (Chapter 6).
☐ Master cylinder piston seized. Caused by wear or damage to piston or cylinder bore (Chapter 6).
☐ Lever balky or stuck. Check pivot and lubricate (Chapter 6).
☐ Forks incorrectly aligned on front wheel axle. Loosen front axle pinch bolt and re-align (Chapter 6).

## ABS and TCS systems

☐ System fault indicated by indicator light coming on while the machine is being ridden. Check the fault code to identify the problem (Chapter 6).

# Electrical problems

## Battery dead or weak

☐ Battery faulty. Caused by sulphated plates which are shorted through sedimentation. Confirm by terminal voltage check (Chapter 8).
☐ Battery leads making poor contact. Clean and reconnect leads (Chapter 8).
☐ Load excessive. Caused by addition of high wattage lights or other electrical accessories.
☐ Ignition switch defective. Switch either grounds (earths) internally or fails to shut off system. Renew the switch (Chapter 8).
☐ Regulator/rectifier defective (Chapter 8).
☐ Alternator stator coil open or shorted (Chapter 8).

☐ Electrical system fault. Check for excessive current leakage (Chapter 8).
☐ Wiring faulty. Wiring grounded (earthed) or connections loose in ignition, charging or lighting circuits (Chapter 8).

## Battery overcharged

☐ Regulator/rectifier defective. Overcharging is noticed when battery gets excessively warm (Chapter 8).
☐ Battery faulty. Confirm with battery terminal voltage check (Chapter 8).
☐ Battery amperage too low, wrong type or size of battery. Install manufacturer's specified amp-hour battery to handle charging load (Chapter 8).

# A

**ABS (Anti-lock braking system)** A system, usually electronically controlled, that senses incipient wheel lockup during braking and relieves hydraulic pressure at wheel which is about to skid.

**Aftermarket** Components suitable for the motorcycle, but not produced by the motorcycle manufacturer.

**Allen key** A hexagonal wrench which fits into a recessed hexagonal hole.

**Alternating current (ac)** Current produced by an alternator. Requires converting to direct current by a rectifier for charging purposes.

**Alternator** Converts mechanical energy from the engine into electrical energy to charge the battery and power the electrical system.

**Ampere (amp)** A unit of measurement for the flow of electrical current. Current = Volts ÷ Ohms.

**Ampere-hour (Ah)** Measure of battery capacity.

**Angle-tightening** A torque expressed in degrees. Often follows a conventional tightening torque for cylinder head or main bearing fasteners **(see illustration)**.

**Angle-tightening con-rod bolts**

**Antifreeze** A substance (usually ethylene glycol) mixed with water, and added to the cooling system, to prevent freezing of the coolant in winter. Antifreeze also contains chemicals to inhibit corrosion and the formation of rust and other deposits that would tend to clog the radiator and coolant passages and reduce cooling efficiency.

**Anti-dive** System attached to the fork lower leg (slider) to prevent fork dive when braking hard.

**Anti-seize compound** A coating that reduces the risk of seizing on fasteners that are subjected to high temperatures, such as exhaust clamp bolts and nuts.

**API** American Petroleum Institute. A quality standard for 4-stroke motor oils.

**Asbestos** A natural fibrous mineral with great heat resistance, commonly used in the composition of brake friction materials. Asbestos is a health hazard and the dust created by brake systems should never be inhaled or ingested.

**ATF** Automatic Transmission Fluid. Often used in front forks.

**ATU** Automatic Timing Unit. Mechanical device for advancing the ignition timing on early engines.

**ATV** All Terrain Vehicle. Often called a Quad.

**Axial play** Side-to-side movement.

**Axle** A shaft on which a wheel revolves. Also known as a spindle.

# B

**Backlash** The amount of movement between meshed components when one component is held still. Usually applies to gear teeth.

**Ball bearing** A bearing consisting of a hardened inner and outer race with hardened steel balls between the two races.

**Bearings** Used between two working surfaces to prevent wear of the components and a build-up of heat. Four types of bearing are commonly used on motorcycles: plain shell bearings, ball bearings, tapered roller bearings and needle roller bearings.

**Bevel gears** Used to turn the drive through 90°. Typical applications are shaft final drive and camshaft drive **(see illustration)**.

**Bevel gears are used to turn the drive through 90°**

**BHP** Brake Horsepower. The British measurement for engine power output. Power output is now usually expressed in kilowatts (kW).

**Bias-belted tyre** Similar construction to radial tyre, but with outer belt running at an angle to the wheel rim.

**Big-end bearing** The bearing in the end of the connecting rod that's attached to the crankshaft.

**Bleeding** The process of removing air from an hydraulic system via a bleed nipple or bleed screw.

**Bottom-end** A description of an engine's crankcase components and all components contained there-in.

**BTDC** Before Top Dead Centre in terms of piston position. Ignition timing is often expressed in terms of degrees or millimetres BTDC.

**Bush** A cylindrical metal or rubber component used between two moving parts.

**Burr** Rough edge left on a component after machining or as a result of excessive wear.

# C

**Cam chain** The chain which takes drive from the crankshaft to the camshaft(s).

**Canister** The main component in an evaporative emission control system (California market only); contains activated charcoal granules to trap vapours from the fuel system rather than allowing them to vent to the atmosphere.

**Castellated** Resembling the parapets along the top of a castle wall. For example, a castellated wheel axle or spindle nut.

**Catalytic converter** A device in the exhaust system of some machines which converts certain pollutants in the exhaust gases into less harmful substances.

**Charging system** Description of the components which charge the battery, ie the alternator, rectifer and regulator.

**Circlip** A ring-shaped clip used to prevent endwise movement of cylindrical parts and shafts. An internal circlip is installed in a groove in a housing; an external circlip fits into a groove on the outside of a cylindrical piece such as a shaft. Also known as a snap-ring.

**Clearance** The amount of space between two parts. For example, between a piston and a cylinder, between a bearing and a journal, etc.

**Coil spring** A spiral of elastic steel found in various sizes throughout a vehicle, for example as a springing medium in the suspension and in the valve train.

**Compression** Reduction in volume, and increase in pressure and temperature, of a gas, caused by squeezing it into a smaller space.

**Compression damping** Controls the speed the suspension compresses when hitting a bump.

**Compression ratio** The relationship between cylinder volume when the piston is at top dead centre and cylinder volume when the piston is at bottom dead centre.

**Continuity** The uninterrupted path in the flow of electricity. Little or no measurable resistance.

**Continuity tester** Self-powered bleeper or test light which indicates continuity.

**Cp** Candlepower. Bulb rating commonly found on US motorcycles.

**Crossply tyre** Tyre plies arranged in a criss-cross pattern. Usually four or six plies used, hence 4PR or 6PR in tyre size codes.

**Cush drive** Rubber damper segments fitted between the rear wheel and final drive sprocket to absorb transmission shocks **(see illustration)**.

**Cush drive rubbers dampen out transmission shocks**

# D

**Decarbonisation** The process of removing carbon deposits - typically from the combustion chamber, valves and exhaust port/system.

**Degree disc** Calibrated disc for measuring piston position. Expressed in degrees.

**Detonation** Destructive and damaging explosion of fuel/air mixture in combustion chamber instead of controlled burning.

**Dial gauge** Clock-type gauge with adapters for measuring runout and piston position. Expressed in mm or inches.

**Diaphragm** The rubber membrane in a master cylinder or carburettor which seals the upper chamber.

**Diaphragm spring** A single sprung plate often used in clutches.

**Direct current (dc)** Current produced by a dc generator.

**Diode** An electrical valve which only allows current to flow in one direction. Commonly used in rectifiers and starter interlock systems.

**Disc valve (or rotary valve)** A induction system used on some two-stroke engines.

**Double-overhead camshaft (DOHC)** An engine that uses two overhead camshafts, one for the intake valves and one for the exhaust valves.

**Drivebelt** A toothed belt used to transmit drive to the rear wheel on some motorcycles. A drivebelt has also been used to drive the camshafts. Drivebelts are usually made of Kevlar.

**Driveshaft** Any shaft used to transmit motion. Commonly used when referring to the final driveshaft on shaft drive motorcycles.

# E

**Earth return** The return path of an electrical circuit, utilising the motorcycle's frame.

**ECU (Electronic Control Unit)** A computer which controls (for instance) an ignition system, or an anti-lock braking system.

**EGO** Exhaust Gas Oxygen sensor. Sometimes called a Lambda sensor.

**Electrolyte** The fluid in a lead-acid battery.

**EMS (Engine Management System)** A computer controlled system which manages the fuel injection and the ignition systems in an integrated fashion.

**Endfloat** The amount of lengthways movement between two parts. As applied to a crankshaft, the distance that the crankshaft can move side-to-side in the crankcase.

**Endless chain** A chain having no joining link. Common use for cam chains and final drive chains.

**EP (Extreme Pressure)** Oil type used in locations where high loads are applied, such as between gear teeth.

**Evaporative emission control system** Describes a charcoal filled canister which stores fuel vapours from the tank rather than allowing them to vent to the atmosphere. Usually only fitted to California models and referred to as an EVAP system.

**Expansion chamber** Section of two-stroke engine exhaust system so designed to improve engine efficiency and boost power.

# F

**Feeler blade or gauge** A thin strip or blade of hardened steel, ground to an exact thickness, used to check or measure clearances between parts.

**Final drive** Description of the drive from the transmission to the rear wheel. Usually by chain or shaft, but sometimes by belt.

**Firing order** The order in which the engine cylinders fire, or deliver their power strokes, beginning with the number one cylinder.

**Flooding** Term used to describe a high fuel level in the carburettor float chambers, leading to fuel overflow. Also refers to excess fuel in the combustion chamber due to incorrect starting technique.

**Free length** The no-load state of a component when

measured. Clutch, valve and fork spring lengths are measured at rest, without any preload.

**Freeplay** The amount of travel before any action takes place. The looseness in a linkage, or an assembly of parts, between the initial application of force and actual movement. For example, the distance the rear brake pedal moves before the rear brake is actuated.

**Fuel injection** The fuel/air mixture is metered electronically and directed into the engine intake ports (indirect injection) or into the cylinders (direct injection). Sensors supply information on engine speed and conditions.

**Fuel/air mixture** The charge of fuel and air going into the engine. See Stoichiometric ratio.

**Fuse** An electrical device which protects a circuit against accidental overload. The typical fuse contains a soft piece of metal which is calibrated to melt at a predetermined current flow (expressed as amps) and break the circuit.

# G

**Gap** The distance the spark must travel in jumping from the centre electrode to the side electrode in a spark plug. Also refers to the distance between the ignition rotor and the pickup coil in an electronic ignition system.

**Gasket** Any thin, soft material - usually cork, cardboard, asbestos or soft metal - installed between two metal surfaces to ensure a good seal. For instance, the cylinder head gasket seals the joint between the block and the cylinder head.

**Gauge** An instrument panel display used to monitor engine conditions. A gauge with a movable pointer on a dial or a fixed scale is an analogue gauge. A gauge with a numerical readout is called a digital gauge.

**Gear ratios** The drive ratio of a pair of gears in a gearbox, calculated on their number of teeth.

**Glaze-busting** see **Honing**

**Grinding** Process for renovating the valve face and valve seat contact area in the cylinder head.

**Gudgeon pin** The shaft which connects the connecting rod small-end with the piston. Often called a piston pin or wrist pin.

# H

**Helical gears** Gear teeth are slightly curved and produce less gear noise that straight-cut gears. Often used for primary drives.

**Helicoil** A thread insert repair system. Commonly used as a repair for stripped spark plug threads **(see illustration)**.

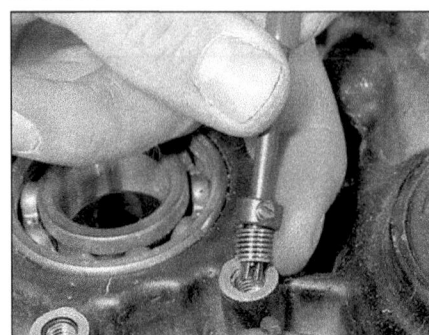

**Installing a Helicoil thread insert**

**Honing** A process used to break down the glaze on a cylinder bore (also called glaze-busting). Can also be carried out to roughen a rebored cylinder to aid ring bedding-in.

**HT (High Tension)** Description of the electrical circuit from the secondary winding of the ignition coil to the spark plug.

**Hydraulic** A liquid filled system used to transmit pressure from one component to another. Common uses on motorcycles are brakes and clutches.

**Hydrometer** An instrument for measuring the specific gravity of a lead-acid battery.

**Hygroscopic** Water absorbing. In motorcycle applications, braking efficiency will be reduced if DOT 3 or 4 hydraulic fluid absorbs water from the air - care must be taken to keep new brake fluid in tightly sealed containers.

# I

**lbf ft** Pounds-force feet. An imperial unit of torque. Sometimes written as ft-lbs.

**lbf in** Pound-force inch. An imperial unit of torque, applied to components where a very low torque is required. Sometimes written as in-lbs.

**IC** Abbreviation for Integrated Circuit.

**Ignition advance** Means of increasing the timing of the spark at higher engine speeds. Done by mechanical means (ATU) on early engines or electronically by the ignition control unit on later engines.

**Ignition timing** The moment at which the spark plug fires, expressed in the number of crankshaft degrees before the piston reaches the top of its stroke, or in the number of millimetres before the piston reaches the top of its stroke.

**Infinity (∞)** Description of an open-circuit electrical state, where no continuity exists.

**Inverted forks** (upside down forks) The sliders or lower legs are held in the yokes and the fork tubes or stanchions are connected to the wheel axle (spindle). Less unsprung weight and stiffer construction than conventional forks.

# J

**JASO** Quality standard for 2-stroke oils.

**Joule** The unit of electrical energy.

**Journal** The bearing surface of a shaft.

# K

**Kickstart** Mechanical means of turning the engine over for starting purposes. Only usually fitted to mopeds, small capacity motorcycles and off-road motorcycles.

**Kill switch** Handlebar-mounted switch for emergency ignition cut-out. Cuts the ignition circuit on all models, and additionally prevent starter motor operation on others.

**km** Symbol for kilometre.

**kmh** Abbreviation for kilometres per hour.

# L

**Lambda (λ) sensor** A sensor fitted in the exhaust system to measure the exhaust gas oxygen content (excess air factor).

**Lapping** see Grinding.

**LCD** Abbreviation for Liquid Crystal Display.

**LED** Abbreviation for Light Emitting Diode.

**Liner** A steel cylinder liner inserted in a aluminium alloy cylinder block.

**Locknut** A nut used to lock an adjustment nut, or other threaded component, in place.

**Lockstops** The lugs on the lower triple clamp (yoke) which abut those on the frame, preventing handlebar-to-fuel tank contact.

**Lockwasher** A form of washer designed to prevent an attaching nut from working loose.

**LT Low Tension** Description of the electrical circuit from the power supply to the primary winding of the ignition coil.

# M

**Main bearings** The bearings between the crankshaft and crankcase.

**Maintenance-free (MF) battery** A sealed battery which cannot be topped up.

**Manometer** Mercury-filled calibrated tubes used to measure intake tract vacuum. Used to synchronise carburettors on multi-cylinder engines.

**Micrometer** A precision measuring instrument that measures component outside diameters **(see illustration)**.

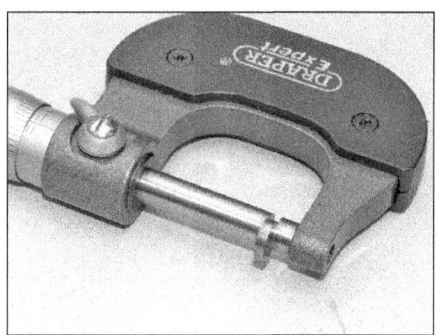

**Tappet shims are measured with a micrometer**

**MON (Motor Octane Number)** A measure of a fuel's resistance to knock.

**Monograde oil** An oil with a single viscosity, eg SAE80W.

**Monoshock** A single suspension unit linking the swingarm or suspension linkage to the frame.

**mph** Abbreviation for miles per hour.

**Multigrade oil** Having a wide viscosity range (eg 10W40). The W stands for Winter, thus the viscosity ranges from SAE10 when cold to SAE40 when hot.

**Multimeter** An electrical test instrument with the capability to measure voltage, current and resistance. Some meters also incorporate a continuity tester and buzzer.

# N

**Needle roller bearing** Inner race of caged needle rollers and hardened outer race. Examples of uncaged needle rollers can be found on some engines. Commonly used in rear suspension applications and in two-stroke engines.

**Nm** Newton metres.

**NOx** Oxides of Nitrogen. A common toxic pollutant emitted by petrol engines at higher temperatures.

# O

**Octane** The measure of a fuel's resistance to knock.

**OE (Original Equipment)** Relates to components fitted to a motorcycle as standard or replacement parts supplied by the motorcycle manufacturer.

**Ohm** The unit of electrical resistance. Ohms = Volts ÷ Current.

**Ohmmeter** An instrument for measuring electrical resistance.

**Oil cooler** System for diverting engine oil outside of the engine to a radiator for cooling purposes.

**Oil injection** A system of two-stroke engine lubrication where oil is pump-fed to the engine in accordance with throttle position.

**Open-circuit** An electrical condition where there is a break in the flow of electricity - no continuity (high resistance).

**O-ring** A type of sealing ring made of a special rubber-like material; in use, the O-ring is compressed into a groove to provide the sealing action.

**Oversize (OS)** Term used for piston and ring size options fitted to a rebored cylinder.

**Overhead cam (sohc) engine** An engine with single camshaft located on top of the cylinder head.

**Overhead valve (ohv) engine** An engine with the valves located in the cylinder head, but with the camshaft located in the engine block or crankcase.

**Oxygen sensor** A device installed in the exhaust system which senses the oxygen content in the exhaust and converts this information into an electric current. Also called a Lambda sensor.

# P

**Plastigauge** A thin strip of plastic thread, available in different sizes, used for measuring clearances. For example, a strip of Plastigauge is laid across a bearing journal. The parts are assembled and dismantled; the width of the crushed strip indicates the clearance between journal and bearing.

**Polarity** Either negative or positive earth (ground), determined by which battery lead is connected to the frame (earth return). Modern motorcycles are usually negative earth.

**Pre-ignition** A situation where the fuel/air mixture ignites before the spark plug fires. Often due to a hot spot in the combustion chamber caused by carbon build-up. Engine has a tendency to 'run-on'.

**Pre-load (suspension)** The amount a spring is compressed when in the unloaded state. Preload can be applied by gas, spacer or mechanical adjuster.

**Premix** The method of engine lubrication on older two-stroke engines. Engine oil is mixed with the petrol in the fuel tank in a specific ratio. The fuel/oil mix is sometimes referred to as "petroil".

**Primary drive** Description of the drive from the crankshaft to the clutch. Usually by gear or chain.

**PS** Pfedestärke - a German interpretation of BHP.

**PSI** Pounds-force per square inch. Imperial measurement of tyre pressure and cylinder pressure measurement.

**PTFE** Polytetrafluroethylene. A low friction substance.

**Pulse secondary air injection system** A process of promoting the burning of excess fuel present in the exhaust gases by routing fresh air into the exhaust ports.

# Q

**Quartz halogen bulb** Tungsten filament surrounded by a halogen gas. Typically used for the headlight **(see illustration)**.

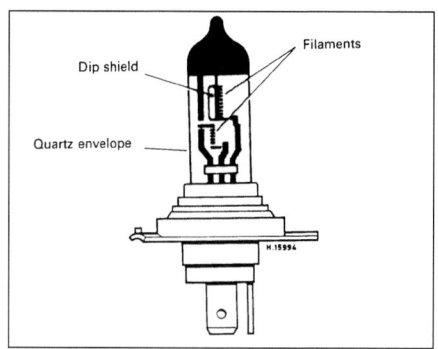

**Quartz halogen headlight bulb construction**

# R

**Rack-and-pinion** A pinion gear on the end of a shaft that mates with a rack (think of a geared wheel opened up and laid flat). Sometimes used in clutch operating systems.

**Radial play** Up and down movement about a shaft.

**Radial ply tyres** Tyre plies run across the tyre (from bead to bead) and around the circumference of the tyre. Less resistant to tread distortion than other tyre types.

**Radiator** A liquid-to-air heat transfer device designed to reduce the temperature of the coolant in a liquid cooled engine.

**Rake** A feature of steering geometry - the angle of the steering head in relation to the vertical **(see illustration)**.

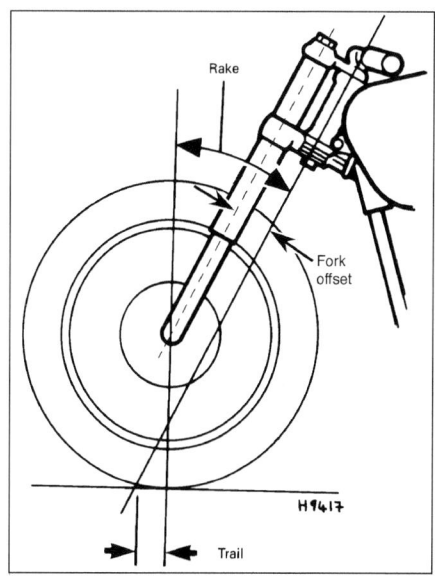

**Steering geometry**

**Rebore** Providing a new working surface to the cylinder bore by boring out the old surface. Necessitates the use of oversize piston and rings.

**Rebound damping** A means of controlling the oscillation of a suspension unit spring after it has been compressed. Resists the spring's natural tendency to bounce back after being compressed.

**Rectifier** Device for converting the ac output of an alternator into dc for battery charging.

**Reed valve** An induction system commonly used on two-stroke engines.

**Regulator** Device for maintaining the charging voltage from the generator or alternator within a specified range.

**Relay** A electrical device used to switch heavy current on and off by using a low current auxiliary circuit.

**Resistance** Measured in ohms. An electrical component's ability to pass electrical current.

**RON (Research Octane Number)** A measure of a fuel's resistance to knock.

**rpm** revolutions per minute.

**Runout** The amount of wobble (in-and-out movement) of a wheel or shaft as it's rotated. The amount a shaft rotates 'out-of-true'. The out-of-round condition of a rotating part.

# S

**SAE (Society of Automotive Engineers)** A standard for the viscosity of a fluid.

**Sealant** A liquid or paste used to prevent leakage at a joint. Sometimes used in conjunction with a gasket.

**Service limit** Term for the point where a component is no longer useable and must be renewed.

**Shaft drive** A method of transmitting drive from the transmission to the rear wheel.

**Shell bearings** Plain bearings consisting of two shell halves. Most often used as big-end and main bearings in a four-stroke engine. Often called bearing inserts.

**Shim** Thin spacer, commonly used to adjust the clearance or relative positions between two parts. For example, shims inserted into or under tappets or followers to control valve clearances. Clearance is adjusted by changing the thickness of the shim.

**Short-circuit** An electrical condition where current shorts to earth (ground) bypassing the circuit components.

**Skimming** Process to correct warpage or repair a damaged surface, eg on brake discs or drums.

**Slide-hammer** A special puller that screws into or hooks onto a component such as a shaft or bearing; a heavy sliding handle on the shaft bottoms against the end of the shaft to knock the component free.

**Small-end bearing** The bearing in the upper end of the connecting rod at its joint with the gudgeon pin.

**Spalling** Damage to camshaft lobes or bearing journals shown as pitting of the working surface.

**Specific gravity (SG)** The state of charge of the electrolyte in a lead-acid battery. A measure of the electrolyte's density compared with water.

**Straight-cut gears** Common type gear used on gearbox shafts and for oil pump and water pump drives.

**Stanchion** The inner sliding part of the front forks, held by the yokes. Often called a fork tube.

**Stoichiometric ratio** The optimum chemical air/fuel ratio for a petrol engine, said to be 14.7 parts of air to 1 part of fuel.

**Sulphuric acid** The liquid (electrolyte) used in a lead-acid battery. Poisonous and extremely corrosive.

**Surface grinding (lapping)** Process to correct a warped gasket face, commonly used on cylinder heads.

# T

**Tapered-roller bearing** Tapered inner race of caged needle rollers and separate tapered outer race. Examples of taper roller bearings can be found on steering heads.

**Tappet** A cylindrical component which transmits motion from the cam to the valve stem, either directly or via a pushrod and rocker arm. Also called a cam follower.

**TCS** Traction Control System. An electronically-controlled system which senses wheel spin and reduces engine speed accordingly.

**TDC** Top Dead Centre denotes that the piston is at its highest point in the cylinder.

**Thread-locking compound** Solution applied to fastener threads to prevent slackening. Select type to suit application.

**Thrust washer** A washer positioned between two moving components on a shaft. For example, between gear pinions on gearshaft.

**Timing chain** See **Cam Chain**.

**Timing light** Stroboscopic lamp for carrying out ignition timing checks with the engine running.

**Top-end** A description of an engine's cylinder block, head and valve gear components.

**Torque** Turning or twisting force about a shaft.

**Torque setting** A prescribed tightness specified by the motorcycle manufacturer to ensure that the bolt or nut is secured correctly. Undertightening can result in the bolt or nut coming loose or a surface not being sealed. Overtightening can result in stripped threads, distortion or damage to the component being retained.

**Torx key** A six-point wrench.

**Tracer** A stripe of a second colour applied to a wire insulator to distinguish that wire from another one with the same colour insulator. For example, Br/W is often used to denote a brown insulator with a white tracer.

**Trail** A feature of steering geometry. Distance from the steering head axis to the tyre's central contact point.

**Triple clamps** The cast components which extend from the steering head and support the fork stanchions or tubes. Often called fork yokes.

**Turbocharger** A centrifugal device, driven by exhaust gases, that pressurises the intake air. Normally used to increase the power output from a given engine displacement.

**TWI** Abbreviation for Tyre Wear Indicator. Indicates the location of the tread depth indicator bars on tyres.

# U

**Universal joint or U-joint (UJ)** A double-pivoted connection for transmitting power from a driving to a driven shaft through an angle. Typically found in shaft drive assemblies.

**Unsprung weight** Anything not supported by the bike's suspension (ie the wheel, tyres, brakes, final drive and bottom (moving) part of the suspension).

# V

**Vacuum gauges** Clock-type gauges for measuring intake tract vacuum. Used for carburettor synchronisation on multi-cylinder engines.

**Valve** A device through which the flow of liquid, gas or vacuum may be stopped, started or regulated by a moveable part that opens, shuts or partially obstructs one or more ports or passageways. The intake and exhaust valves in the cylinder head are of the poppet type.

**Valve clearance** The clearance between the valve tip (the end of the valve stem) and the rocker arm or tappet/follower. The valve clearance is measured when the valve is closed. The correct clearance is important - if too small the valve won't close fully and will burn out, whereas if too large noisy operation will result.

**Valve lift** The amount a valve is lifted off its seat by the camshaft lobe.

**Valve timing** The exact setting for the opening and closing of the valves in relation to piston position.

**Vernier caliper** A precision measuring instrument that measures inside and outside dimensions. Not quite as accurate as a micrometer, but more convenient.

**Wet liner arrangement**

**VIN** Vehicle Identification Number. Term for the bike's engine and frame numbers.

**Viscosity** The thickness of a liquid or its resistance to flow.

**Volt** A unit for expressing electrical "pressure" in a circuit. Volts = current x ohms.

# W

**Water pump** A mechanically-driven device for moving coolant around the engine.

**Watt** A unit for expressing electrical power. Watts = volts x current.

**Wear limit** see **Service limit**

**Wet liner** A liquid-cooled engine design where the pistons run in liners which are directly surrounded by coolant **(see illustration)**.

**Wheelbase** Distance from the centre of the front wheel to the centre of the rear wheel.

**Wiring harness or loom** Describes the electrical wires running the length of the motorcycle and enclosed in tape or plastic sheathing. Wiring coming off the main harness is usually referred to as a sub harness.

**Woodruff key** A key of semi-circular or square section used to locate a gear to a shaft. Often used to locate the alternator rotor on the crankshaft.

**Wrist pin** Another name for gudgeon or piston pin.

**Note:** *References throughout this index are in the form - "Chapter number" • "Page number"*

**Note:** *References throughout this index are in the form - "Chapter number" • "Page number"*

**Note:** *References throughout this index are in the form - "Chapter number" • "Page number"*

# Preserving Our Motoring Heritage

< *The Model J Duesenberg Derham Tourster. Only eight of these magnificent cars were ever built – this is the only example to be found outside the United States of America*

Almost every car you've ever loved, loathed or desired is gathered under one roof at the Haynes Motor Museum. Over 300 immaculately presented cars and motorbikes represent every aspect of our motoring heritage, from elegant reminders of bygone days, such as the superb Model J Duesenberg to curiosities like the bug-eyed BMW Isetta. There are also many old friends and flames. Perhaps you remember the 1959 Ford Popular that you did your courting in? The magnificent 'Red Collection' is a spectacle of classic sports cars including AC, Alfa Romeo, Austin Healey, Ferrari, Lamborghini, Maserati, MG, Riley, Porsche and Triumph.

## A Perfect Day Out

Each and every vehicle at the Haynes Motor Museum has played its part in the history and culture of Motoring. Today, they make a wonderful spectacle and a great day out for all the family. Bring the kids, bring Mum and Dad, but above all bring your camera to capture those golden memories for ever. You will also find an impressive array of motoring memorabilia, a comfortable 70 seat video cinema and one of the most extensive transport book shops in Britain. The Pit Stop Cafe serves everything from a cup of tea to wholesome, home-made meals or, if you prefer, you can enjoy the large picnic area nestled in the beautiful rural surroundings of Somerset.

> *John Haynes O.B.E., Founder and Chairman of the museum at the wheel of a Haynes Light 12.*

< *The 1936 490cc sohc-engined International Norton – well known for its racing success*

The Museum is situated on the A359 Yeovil to Frome road at Sparkford, just off the A303 in Somerset. It is about 40 miles south of Bristol, and 25 minutes drive from the M5 intersection at Taunton.
Open 9.30am - 5.30pm (10.00am - 4.00pm Winter) 7 days a week, *except Christmas Day, Boxing Day and New Years Day*
Special rates available for schools, coach parties and outings  Charitable Trust No. 292048